TREATIES

Their Making and Enforcement

(SECOND EDITION)

By

SAMUEL B. CRANDALL, Ph.D.

**Of the bar of New York
and of the
District of Columbia**

THE LAWBOOK EXCHANGE, LTD.
Clark, New Jersey

ISBN 978-1-58477-492-1

Lawbook Exchange edition 2005, 2022

The quality of this reprint is equivalent to the quality of the original work.

THE LAWBOOK EXCHANGE, LTD.
33 Terminal Avenue
Clark, New Jersey 07066-1321

*Please see our website for a selection of our other publications
and fine facsimile reprints of classic works of legal history:*
www.lawbookexchange.com

Library of Congress Cataloging-in-Publication Data

Crandall, Samuel B. (Samuel Benjamin), b. 1874.
   Treaties, their making and enforcement / by Samuel B. Crandall.—
2nd ed.
     p.cm.
   Originally published: 2nd ed. Washington, D.C. : J. Byrne & Co.,
1916.
   Includes bibliographical references and index.
   ISBN 1-58477-492-4 (cloth: alk. paper)
   1. Treaties. 2. Treaty-making power. 3. United States—Foreign
   relations—Treaties. 4. Treaty-making power—United States. I.
   Title.

KZ1301.C73 2005
341.3'7—dc22   2004048747

Printed in the United States of America on acid-free paper

TREATIES

Their Making and Enforcement

(SECOND EDITION)

By

SAMUEL B. CRANDALL, Ph.D.

**Of the bar of New York
and of the
District of Columbia**

WASHINGTON, D. C.

JOHN BYRNE & COMPANY

1916

PREFACE TO SECOND EDITION.

The first edition appeared in 1904, in the Columbia University Studies in History, Economics and Public Law. It has been possible in the second edition to consider more fully many of the topics touched upon in the first, and to add many new sections. A digest of decisions of American courts construing treaties, arranged by countries and treaties, has been added as an appendix.

S. B. C.

Washington, D. C., January, 1916.

PREFACE TO FIRST EDITION.

Even the frequency with which authorities are cited in the foot-notes can but partially indicate my indebtedness to others. I desire here to acknowledge the most generous assistance. Although the portions of the dissertation relating to treaty making in the United States and in France had been prepared and presented before the seminar at Columbia University prior to the appearance of *The Treaty-Making Power of the United States,* by Charles Henry Butler, and of *Les Traités Internationaux devant les Chambres,* by Louis Michon, both have been of great service in the final revision. To Mr. Andrew H. Allen, of the Department of State, for generous privileges given in the use of the manuscripts and publications deposited in the Bureau of Rolls and Library, and to my co-workers in the Department, for many courtesies extended, my thanks are especially due. To the members of the Faculty of Political Science of Columbia University, and more especially to Professor John Bassett Moore, at whose suggestion the work was undertaken, and whose advice throughout has been unceasing, I feel my chief indebtedness; and I take this occasion to express my high appreciation of the privilege of having enjoyed for a considerable period their counsel on the general principles of public law.

S. B. C.

Washington, D. C., May, 1904.

TABLE OF CONTENTS

CHAPTER I.

Introduction.

Page.

§1. Organs of Government entrusted with Treaty Making 1
§2. The Treaty-making Power of a State 1
§3. Powers of the Negotiators and the Right of Ratification 2
§4. Essentials of the Validity of Treaties 3
§5. Reality of Consent 3
§6. Form 5
§7. Sanction 8

PART I. THE UNITED STATES.

DIVISION I. PRIOR TO THE CONSTITUTION.

CHAPTER II.

Prior to the Articles of Confederation.

§8. Independence and Treaty Making 19
§9. Negotiation and Ratification of the first Treaties with France 19
§19. Amendment of Text of Treaty recommended by the Congress 21
§11. Powers of the Congress 21
§12. Other Negotiations 22
§13. Organs of Communication with Foreign Governments 23

CHAPTER III.

Under the Articles of Confederation.

§14. Treaty-making Power exclusively vested in Congress 24
§15. Control Exercised by Congress over Negotiations 25
§16. Power of Seven States to modify Instructions 27
§17. Treaties Concluded during this Period 28
§18. Ratification.   Amendments 29
§19. Ratification of the Treaty of Peace 30
§20. Stipulations Involving Subjects otherwise under Control of
       the States 32
§21. Legislation by State Legislatures to give Effect to Treaties .. 34
§22. Treaties Operative as Laws 36

CHAPTER IV.

The Federal Convention.

§23. The Treaty-making Power vested in the President and Senate 43
§24. Concurrence of Two-thirds of the Senators Present. Treaties
       of Peace, for Cession of Territory, etc. 44

Page.

§25. Treaties not to be Approved by Congress 46
§26. The States expressly Prohibited from Entering into Treaties 48
§27. Treaties a Part of the Supreme Law of the Land 49
§28. Jurisdiction of Federal Courts 51
§29. Treaty Making and the Formation of the New Union 51

CHAPTER V.

Discussion Preceding the Adoption of the Constitution.

§30. In the Press 53
§31. In the State Conventions 56
§32. Amendments of the Treaty Provisions Proposed by the State
     Conventions 62

DIVISION II. UNDER THE CONSTITUTION.

I. THE MAKING.

CHAPTER VI.

The Advice and Consent of the Senate.

§33. The President in the Senate Chamber 67
§34. Advice Sought by Message 68
§35. Advice by Resolution 72
§36. Consultation with Individual Members 75
§37. Confirmation of Negotiators 75
§38. Special Agents 77
§39. Consular Convention of 1788 with France 78
§40. Qualified Approval of the Jay Treaty 79
§41. Specific Amendments Advised 81
§42. Treaties Rejected by the Senate 82
§43. Reconsideration by the Senate 82
§44. Secret Sessions 84
§45. Explanations of Senate Amendments 85
§46. Consent to Extension of Period for Exchange of Ratifications 89

CHAPTER VII.

Powers of the President.

§47. Negotiation 93
§48. Ratification 94
§49. Reservation in Full Powers of Right of Ratification 94
§50. Proclamation 94
§51. Treaties Withheld from the Senate 95
§52. Submitted to the Senate with Recommendation for Amend-
     ment 95
§53. Refusal of President to Ratify Treaties Approved by the
     Senate 97
§54. Treaties Withdrawn from the Senate 99
§55. Re-submission to the Senate after Delay in Ratification 100

CHAPTER VIII.

Agreements Reached by the Executive without the Advice and Consent of the Senate.

Page.

§56. Agreements Involving the Military Power of the President ... 102
§57. Adjustment and Settlement of Pecuniary Claims of Citizens against Foreign Governments 108
§58. Agreements as Basis of Future Negotiations, or of Foreign Policy 111
§59. Modi Vivendi 112
§60. Miscellaneous Instances 114
§61. Agreements in Execution of Treaty Stipulations 117

CHAPTER IX.

Agreements Reached by the Executive in Virtue of Acts of Congress.

§62. Navigation and Commerce 121
§63. International Copyright 127
§64. Trade-marks 129
§65. International Postal and Money Order Regulations 131
§66. Agreements with Indian Tribes 133
§67. Acquisition of Territory 135

CHAPTER X.

Agreements Entered into by States of the Union.

§68. With Foreign Powers 141
§69. Between States of the Union 145

II. The Execution or Enforcement.

CHAPTER XI.

Operation of Treaties as Municipal Law.

§70. Operation without the Aid of State Legislation 153
§71. Operation without Congressional Action 160
§72. Conflict between Acts of Congress and Treaties 161
§73. Legislation to give Effect to Stipulations 162

CHAPTER XII.

Treaties Involving an Appropriation.

§74. Money Appropriated only by Act of Congress 164
§75. Proposed Treaty with Algiers 164
§76. Debates on the Jay Treaty in 1796 165
§77. Treaties of 1802 and 1803 171
§78. Convention with France of 1831 174
§79. Treaty with Russia of 1867 175
§80. Views of Authorities 177
§81. Conclusion 178

CHAPTER XIII.

Treaties Involving a Modification of the Revenue Laws.

                                                              Page.
§82. Early Precedents 183
§83. Convention with Great Britain of 1815 184
§84. Convention with France of 1822 188
§85. Convention with France of 1831 188
§86. Convention with the States of the German Zollverein of 1844 189
§87. Convention with Great Britain of 1854 190
§88. Subsequent Conventions for Commercial Reciprocity 191
§89. Conclusion 195

CHAPTER XIV.

Treaties for the Acquisition and Cession of Territory.

§90. Power to Acquire Territory by Treaty 200
§91. Effect of Treaty on Status of Territory and its Inhabitants.. 200
§92. Legislation to Give Effect to Stipulations for Incorporation of
      Territory 202
§93. Treaty with France of 1803 202
§94. Treaty with Spain of 1819 205
§95. Treaties with Mexico of 1848 and 1853 207
§96. Organization of Various Western Territories 209
§97. Treaty with Russia of 1867 210
§98. Treaty with Spain of 1898 212
§99. Power to Cede Territory 220

CHAPTER XV.

Legislation to Give Effect to Various Other Treaties.

§100. Extradition of Fugitives from Justice 230
§101. Apprehension of Deserting Seamen 233
§102. Jurisdiction of Foreign Consuls 234
§103. Protection of Industrial Property 236
§104. Miscellaneous Cases 239

CHAPTER XVI.

**Treaties Involving Subjects Otherwise Under the Control of
the Individual States.**

§105. Distribution of Powers 246
§106. Treaties for Removal of Alien Disability 247
§107. Discriminatory Legislation 252
§108. Administration of Estates of Deceased Aliens 260
§109. Miscellaneous Subjects 262
§110. Extent and Limitations of the Treaty-Making Power as
      Vested in the Central Government 265

CHAPTER XVII.

Jurisdiction of Federal Courts.

Page.

§111. Suits of a Civil Nature 269
§112. Criminal Actions 269
§113. Writ of Habeas Corpus 272
§114. Writ of Error 272

PART II. FOREIGN STATES.

CHAPTER XVIII.

Great Britain.

§115. Power to Make Treaties a Prerogative of the Crown 279
§116. Treaties Involving the Finances 280
§117. Commercial Treaties 280
§118. General Legislation to Give Effect to Treaties. Naturalization 282
§119. Extradition 284
§120. Apprehension of Deserting Seamen 286
§121. Patents, Trade-Marks, Copyright and Posts 286
§122. Miscellaneous Subjects 288
§123. Treaties Affecting Private Rights 289
§124. Treaties for Cession of Territory 292
§125. Submission of Treaties to Parliament Before Ratification 298

CHAPTER XIX.

France.

§126. The States-General and Parlement of Paris 301
§127. The Constituent Assembly 302
§128. Constitutional Provisions, 1793-1871 303
§129. National Assembly of 1871-1875 307
§130. Article VIII of the Constitutional Law 308
§131. Treaties of Peace 308
§132. Treaties of Commerce 309
§133. Treaties Involving the Finances 311
§134. Treaties Relating to the Status of Persons and Property
        Rights of French Subjects Abroad 312
§135. Acquisition or Cession of Territory 312
§136. Treaties Not Submitted for Approval of Chambers 314

CHAPTER XX.

Other Foreign States.

§137. Belgium 315
§138. Luxemburg, ... 317
§139. The Netherlands 317
§140. Italy 320
§141. Germany 323
§142. Austria-Hungary 327

Page.

§143. Sweden 329
§144. Norway 330
§145. Denmark 331
§146. Spain 332
§147. Portugal 333
§148. Switzerland 333
§149. Greece 335
§150. Balkan States 335
§151. Russia and Japan 336
§152. Turkey 337
§153. Mexico and the other American Republics 337
§154. Dependencies 339

PART III. THE OPERATION OF TREATIES AS BETWEEN STATES.

CHAPTER XXI.

Date of Taking Effect.

§155. As a Compact between States 343
§156. As Affecting Rights of Individuals 345
§157. Treaties for Transfer of Territory 347
§158. Extradition Conventions 351
§159. Treaties of Peace 352

CHAPTER XXII.

Determination of Disputed Interpretations of Treaties.

§160. Difference between the Enforcement of Treaties and of Private Contracts 358
§161. Obligatory Arbitration. (a) General International Conventions 358
§162. (b) Special Clauses and Treaties for Arbitration 361
§163. Questions for the Courts and for the Political Departments in the United States 364

CHAPTER XXIII.

Aids in the Interpretation of Treaties.

§164. Intention of the Parties 371
§165. General Purpose of the Treaty 371
§166. Contemporaneous Declarations and Prior Negotiations 377
§167. Practical Construction by Parties 383
§168. Casus Omissus 387
§169. Discrepancies between the Two Texts 389
§170. Construed in the Light of Accepted Principles of International Law 394
§171. General Rules 396

CHAPTER XXIV.

The American Construction of the Most-Favored-Nation Clause.

Page.

§172. Concessions in Matters of Commerce 404
§173. Administration on Estates of Deceased Aliens 411
§174. Consular Jurisdiction over Seamen 414
§175. Patents and Trade-marks 416
§176. Right to Hold and Dispose of Real Estate 416
§177. Rights of Residence 417

CHAPTER XXV.

Termination of Treaties.

§178. Effect of Change in Form of Government 423
§179. Effect of Change in State Entity 425
§180. Rebus Sic Stantibus 440
§181. Effect of War 442
§182. Effect of Infractions 456
§183. Termination by Agreement 458
§184. Termination by Notice in the United States 458
§185. Termination in the United States in case of Adverse Breach .. 462
§186. Repeal of Treaty as Municipal Law in the United States 465

APPENDIX I.

A Digest of Decisions of American Courts Construing Treaties, Arranged by Countries and Treaties.

(a) COUNTRIES.

Algiers 466
Argentine Republic 466
Austria-Hungary 467
Belgium, ... 469
Brazil 470
Chile 470
China 470
Colombia 483
Cuba 483
Denmark 484
Dominican Republic 485
France 486
German Empire 501
German States 504
    Baden 504
    Bavaria 504
    Hanover 505
    Hanseatic Republics (Bremen, Hamburg, and Lubeck) 506
    Hesse 506
    Prussia 507
    Saxony 510
    Württemberg 511

TABLE OF CONTENTS.

	Page.
Great Britain	512
Greece	539
Italy,	540
Japan	547
Mexico	548
Netherlands	558
Norway	559
Ottoman Empire	559
Panama	559
Paraguay	559
Persia	560
Peru	560
Portugal	560
Russia	561
Salvador	565
Spain	566
Sweden and Norway	580
Sweden	584
Switzerland	586
Two Sicilies	588
International Conventions	589

(b) GENERAL SUBJECTS.

Alien Disability	591
Discriminatory Legislation	606
Property Rights in Ceded Territory	621

APPENDIX II.

FORMS.

The United States
Full Power to Sign a Treaty	635
Resolution of the Senate Advising and Consenting to the Ratification	636
Ratification by the President	636
Protocol of Exchange of Ratifications	637
Proclamation by the President	638

Great Britain
Ratification by the King	638

France
Ratification by the President	639

Index	641

TABLE OF CASES

Acosta, United States v., 1 How. 24 .... 573, 632, 633
Adams v. Akerlund, 168 Ill. 632 .... 33, 250, 581, 602
Adela, The, 6 Wall. 266 245
Adula, The, 176 U. S. 361 522
Adutt, In re, 55 Fed. 376 468
Advocate-General of Bengal v. Ranee Surnomoye Dossee, 2 Moore
   P. C. 22 292
Ah Chong, In re, 6 Sawy. 451 .... 255, 419, 472, 607
Ah Fawn, United States v., 57 Fed. 591 475
Ah Fook, Ex parte, 49 Cal. 402 .... 472, 607
Ah How v. United States, 193 U. S. 65 482
Ah Kee, In re, 22 Blatchf. 520 474
Ah Lung, In re, 9 Sawy. 306 474
Ah Moy, In re, 21 Fed. 785 478
Ah Ping, In re, 23 Fed. 329 478
Ah Quan, In re, 21 Fed. 182 478
Ahrens v. Ahrens, 144 Iowa 486 .... 251, 505, 599
Ah Sing, In re (Chinese Cabin Waiter), 7 Sawy. 536 474
Ah Tie et al., In re (Chinese Laborers), 7 Sawy. 542 473
Ah Yow, In re, 59 Fed. 561 475
Ainsa v. United States, 161 U. S. 208 .... 551, 628
Ainsworth v. Munoskong Hunting & Fishing Club, 159 Mich. 61 ... 524
Allgeyer v. Louisiana, 165 U. S. 578 422
Alling v. United States, 114 U. S. 562 558
Altman & Co. v. United States, 224 U. S. 583 .... 124, 500
Amalia, The, 3 Fed. 652 .... 235, 583
Amat, Succession of, 18 La. Ann. 403 .... 252, 411, 498, 611
American Express Co. et al. v. United States, 4 Ct. Cust. Appls. 146
   .... 198, 408, 580, 621
American Insurance Co. v. Canter, 1 Pet. 511 .... 200, 201, 206, 570
American Railroad Co. of Porto Rico v. Birch, 224 U. S. 547 216
American Railroad Co. of Porto Rico v. Didricksen, 227 U. S. 145.. 216
American Sugar Refining Co. v. Bidwell, 124 Fed. 677, 683 .... 351, 577
American Sugar Refining Co., United States v., 202 U. S. 563..194, 346, 484
Amiable Isabella, The, 6 Wheat. 1 .... 241, 387, 568
Amistad, The, 15 Pet. 518 .... 241, 394, 400, 567, 568
Anderson, Ex parte, 184 Fed. 114 .... 236, 583
Anderson's Estate, In re, 147 N. W. 1098 .... 251, 253, 485, 602, 610
Angarica v. Bayard, 4 Mackey 310 .... 109, 574
Angarica v. Bayard, 127 U. S. 251 574
Apollon, The, 9 Wheat. 362 566
Arkansas v. Kansas & Texas Coal Co., 183 U. S. 185 275
Armstrong v. Bidwell, 124 Fed. 690 .... 343, 351, 576
Armstrong v. United States, 182 U. S. 243 351
Aroa Mines v. Venezuela, Ralston's Rept. 344 .... 380, 396, 397
Arredondo, United States v., 6 Pet. 691 ....
   .... 343, 344, 345, 346, 365, 391, 397, 491, 569, 571, 572, 630, 632
Arton, In re (1896), 1 Q. B. 108 286
Ashbaugh v. United States, 35 C. Cls. 554 347
Astiazaran v. Santa Rita & Mining Co., 148 U. S. 80 ...... 551, 628
Atocha v. United States, 8 C. Cls. 427; 17 Wall. 439 .... 548, 553
Austro-Hungarian Consul v. Westphal, 120 Minn. 122....262, 413, 468, 585

Baglieri's Estate, In re, 137 N. Y. S. 175 ....262, 413, 546, 559, 585
Bahuaud v. Bize, 105 Fed. 485 ....251, 498, 593
Bain v. Schooner Speedwell, 2 Dall. 40 513
Baiz v. Malo, 58 N. Y. S. 806 ....414, 483, 497
Baker, The, 157 Fed. 485 ....235, 503
Baker v. City of Portland, 5 Sawy. 566 ....253, 417, 472, 606
Baker v. Grice, 169 U. S. 284 272
Baker v. Shy, 9 Heisk. 85 ....250, 499, 593
Baldwin v. Ely, 9 How. 580 549
Baldwin v. Franks, 120 U. S. 678 ....256, 268, 271, 272, 479, 608
Baldwin v. Goldfrank, 9 Tex. Civ. App. 269; 88 Tex. 249 ....552, 629
Baldwin v. Kansas, 129 U. S. 52 274
Balensi, In re, 120 Fed. 864 500
Bank v. Turnbull & Co., 16 Wall. 190 269
Barbier v. Connolly, 113 U. S. 27 ....256, 422, 479, 607
Barney v. Dolph, 97 U. S. 652 ....533, 626
Barrington v. Missouri, 205 U. S. 483 ....524, 611
Bartram v. Robertson, 122 U. S. 116 ....196, 406, 459, 484, 610
Baruch, In re, 41 Fed. 472 467
Basse v. Brownsville, 154 U. S. 610 ....550, 626
Bayard v. United States, 127 U. S. 246 558
Beam v. United States, 43 C. Cls. 61 345
Beck, In re, 11 N. Y. S. 199 ....251, 433, 507, 508, 601
Behrendt, In re, 22 Fed. 699 ....432, 510
Bello Corrunes, The, 6 Wheat. 152 ....241, 242, 401, 567
Benson v. McMahon, 127 U. S. 457 ....399, 528, 554, 556
Bergere v. United States, 168 U. S. 66 ....551, 628
Berrigan, United States v., 2 Alaska 442 ....212, 563
Bertuch & Co. et al. v. United States, 4 Ct. Cust. Appls. 146 ......
.... 198, 408, 580, 621
Best v. Polk, 18 Wall. 112 245
Bethlehem Steel Co., United States v., 205 U. S. 105 377
Betsey, The Brig, 39 C. Cls. 452 400
Billings v. United States, 232 U. S. 261 ....525, 612
Binns v. United States, 194 U. S. 486 ....212, 563
Bishop of Nesqually v. Gibbon, 158 U. S. 155 ....533, 626
Blagge v. Balch, 162 U. S. 439 489
Blandford v. State, 10 Tex. App. 627 ....160, 556
Blight's Lessee v. Rochester, 7 Wheat. 535 ....248, 516, 519, 594, 596
Bluhm, In re (1901), 1 Q. B. 764 286
Blythe v. Hinckley, 127 Cal. 431 251
Blythe v. Hinckley, 173 U. S. 501 160
Blythe v. Hinckley, 180 U. S. 333 247
Bodemüller v. United States, 39 Fed. 437 500
Bolchos v. Darrell, Bee 74 ....241, 487
Bollermann v. Blake, 94 N. Y. 624 ....507, 600
Bondi v. MacKay, 87 Vt. 271 ....260, 543, 617
Bosque v. United States, 209 U. S. 91 ....202, 578, 580, 633
Botiller v. Dominguez, 130 U. S. 238 ....465, 551, 637
Bound Brook, The, 146 Fed. 160 ....235, 502
Boyd v. Thayer, 143 U. S. 135 200
Boynton v. Blaine, 139 U. S. 306 558
Brawley v. United States, 96 U. S. 168 377
Breen, In re, 73 Fed. 458 556
Breward, United States v., 16 Pet. 143 ....573, 632
Brine v. Insurance Co., 96 U. S. 627 247
Bristow, In re, 118 N. Y. S. 686 ....261, 412, 467, 546
British Consul v. Schooner Favourite, Bee 39 ....236, 487
British Consul v. Ship Mermaid, Bee 69 ....236, 487
British Prisoners, The, 1 Woodb. & M. 66 ....232, 233, 528
Brooks, United States v., 10 How. 442 245

Brown v. Sprague, 5 Denio 545 ....517, 594
Brown v. United States, 8 Cranch 110 522
Bryan v. Kennett, 113 U. S. 179 ....492, 623
Bryant v. United States, 167 U. S. 104 527
Burchard, The, 42 Fed. 608 ....235, 502
Burthe v. Denis, 133 U. S. 514 500
Burton v. Williams, 3 Wheat. 529 147
Bush v. United States, 29 C. Cls. 144 345
Butchers' Union Co. v. Crescent City Co., 111 U. S. 746 421
Butschkowski v. Brecks, 94 Neb. 532 ....160, 251, 433, 509, 601
Buttfield v. Stranahan, 192 U. S. 470 123

Caldwell, United States v., 8 Blatchf. 131 527
California Powder Works v. Davis, 151 U. S. 389 274
Callsen v. Hope, 75 Fed. 758 ....563, 629
Cameron Septic Tank Co. v. City of Knoxville, 227 U. S. 39 .....238, 590
Cannon, In re, 14 Can. Cr. Cas. 186 351
Cantini v. Tillman, 54 Fed. 969 ....264, 542, 616
Carneal v. Banks, 10 Wheat. 181 ....33, 249, 487, 591
Carpenter v. Rannels, 19 Wall. 138 ....492, 623
Carpigiani v. Hall, 172 Ala. 287 ....261, 412, 467, 545
Carrier, In re, 57 Fed. 578 532
Carter v. Territory, 1 N. M. 317 ....209, 553
Carter Medicine Company's Trade-Mark, In re (1892), 3 Ch. D. 472 287
Carver v. Jackson, 4 Pet. 1, 100 ....246, 516
Castant, United States v., 12 How. 437 ....571, 631
Castro v. De Uriarte, 16 Fed. 93 ....233, 556, 575
Ceballos & Co. v. United States, 214 U. S. 47 578
Central Transportation Co. v. Pullman's Car Co., 139 U. S. 24 390
Cessna v. United States, 169 U. S. 165 ....554, 629
Chae Chan Ping v. United States (Chinese Exclusion Case), 130 U.
   S. 581 ....161, 268, 465, 473
Champion Lumber Co. v. Fisher, 227 U. S. 445 276
Chapman v. Toy Long, 4 Sawy. 28 ....254, 418, 472, 606
Chappell v. Bradshaw, 128 U. S. 132 274
Charles River Bridge v. Warren Bridge, 11 Pet. 420 390
Charleston, In re, 34 Fed. 531 532
Charlton, Ex parte, 185 Fed. 880 ....368, 464, 540
Charlton v. Kelly, 229 U. S. 447 ....161, 233, 368, 369, 465, 540, 546
Chaves, United States v., 159 U. S. 452 ....551, 628
Chavez v United States, 3 Moore Int. Arb. 2510 209
Cherokee Nation v. State of Georgia, 5 Pet. 1 ....135, 365
Cherokee Tobacco Cases, 11 Wall. 616 465
Chew Heong, In re, 10 Sawy. 361 478
Chew Heong v. United States, 112 U. S. 536 478
Chicago, Rock Island & Pacific R. R. Co. v. McGlinn, 114 U. S. 542 202
Chin Ah On, In re, 9 Sawy. 343 478
Chin Ark Wing, In re, 115 Fed. 412 478
Chin Bak Kan v. United States, 186 U. S. 193 481
Chinese Exclusion Case, 130 U. S. 581 ....161, 268, 465, 473
Chirac v. Chirac, 2 Wheat. 259 ....33, 249, 486, 490, 591, 592
Choctaw Nation v. United States, 119 U. S. 1 399
Chourreau v. United States, Boutwell's Rept. 134 392
Chouteau v. Eckhart, 2 How. 344 ....493, 624
Chu Chee et al., United States v., 93 Fed. 797 476
Chung Ki Foon, United States v., 83 Fed. 143 476
Chung Toy Ho, In re, 42 Fed. 398 478
Chu Poy, In re, 81 Fed. 826 477
Church of St. Francis, &c., v. Martin, 4 Rob. (La.) 62 ....204, 494, 624
Chy Lung v. Freeman et al., 92 U. S. 275 ....472, 607
Circassian, The, 2 Wall. 135 244

Citizens Bank v. Cannon, 164 U. S. 319 269
City of Sault Ste. Marie v. International Transit Co., 234 U. S. 333.264, 538
Clairmont v. United States, 225 U. S. 551 263
Clark v. Graham, 6 Wheat. 577 247
Clarke v. Clarke, 178 U. S. 186 247
Clarke, United States v., 8 Pet. 436 ....569, 571, 572, 630, 631
Clarke, United States v., 9 Pet. 168 ....572, 632
Clarke's Heirs, United States v., 16 Pet. 228 ....573, 632, 633
Coffee v. Groover, 123 U. S. 1 224
Cohn v. Jones, 100 Fed. 639 530
Collins v. Johnston, 237 U. S. 502 527
Collins v. O'Neil, 214 U. S. 113 ....396, 527
Columbia Water Power Co. v. Columbia Electric Street, &c., Co.,
    172 U. S. 475 274
Comegys et al. v. Vasse, 1 Pet. 193 ....494, 574
Commercial Acetylene Co. v. Schroeder, 203 Fed. 276 ....238, 590
Commercial Acetylene Co. v. Searchlight Gas Co., 197 Fed. 908 ..237, 590
Commonwealth v. Hawes, 13 Bush 697 527
Commonwealth v. Patsone, 231 Pa. 46; 232 U. S. 138 ....543, 616
Commonwealth v. Sheafe, 6 Mass. 441 ....248, 521, 598
Compagnie Francaise de Navigation a Vapeur v. Louisiana State
    Board of Health, 186 U. S. 380....260, 265, 409, 524, 539, 543, 612, 613, 616
Compagnie Francaise de Navigation a Vapeur v. Louisiana State
    Board of Health, 51 La. Ann. 645 264
Comparetto, In re, 151 N. Y. S. 961 ....262, 414
Cooper, In re, 143 U. S. 472 ....365, 562
Cooper, United States v., Fed. Cases No. 14865 ....230, 523
Coppage v. Kansas, 236 U. S. 1 422
Corkran Oil Co. v. Arnaudet, 199 U. S. 182 275
Cortes, In re, 42 Fed. 47; 136 U. S. 330 575
Cosgrove v. Winney, 174 U. S. 64 536
Cotzhausen v. Nazro, 107 U. S. 215 ....132, 589
Coy, Ex parte, 32 Fed. 911 556
Craig v. Radford, 3 Wheat. 594 ....248, 518, 595
Crane v. People of New York, 239 U. S. 195 ....422, 544, 617
Crane v. Reeder, 21 Mich. 24 ....248, 517, 522, 599, 625
Crews v. Burchman, 1 Black 356 245
Crosby, United States v., 7 Cranch 115 247
Cross, In re, 43 Fed. 517 530
Cross v. Harrison, 16 How. 164 ....208, 549
Crowell v. Randell, 10 Pet. 368 274
Crusius, Succession of, 19 La. Ann. 369 ....252, 504, 606
Curtis's Admx. v. Fiedler, 2 Black 461 ....561, 620
Cushing, Admr., v. United States, 22 C. Cls. 1 ....403, 489

D'Adamo's Estate, In re, 141 N. Y. S. 1103; 144 N. Y. S. 429; 212
    N. Y. 214 ....262, 414, 468, 546, 560, 585
D'Agostino, In re, 151 N. Y. S. 957 ....262, 414
Dainese v. Hale, 91 U. S. 13 ....415, 559
Dainese v. United States, 15 C. Cls. 64 559
Dallemagne v. Moisan, 197 U. S. 169 ....235, 499
Dashing Wave, The, 5 Wall. 170 245
D'Auterive, United States v., 10 How. 609 ....345, 349, 492, 571, 622, 631
Davenport, In re, 89 N. Y. S. 537 ....261, 412, 467, 545
Davis v. Police Jury of Concordia, 9 How. 280....345, 347, 349, 351, 492, 622
Deacon v. Oliver, 14 How. 610 549
De Baca et al. v. United States, 37 C. Cls. 482; 189 U. S. 505....209, 553
Debitulia v. Lehigh & Wilkes-Barre Coal Co., 174 Fed. 886....259, 542, 615
Debs, In re, 158 U. S. 564 271
De la Croix v. Chamberlain, 12 Wheat. 599 365
Delafield v. Colden, 1 Paige 139 574

Delassus v. United States, 9 Pet. 117 ....492, 623
De Lemos v. Venezuela, Ralston's Rept. 302 397
Delespine, United States v., 15 Pet. 319 ....573, 632
De Lima v. Bidwell, 182 U. S. 1 ....178, 196, 203, 205, 208, 213, 347, 576
Deni v. Pennsylvania R. R. Co., 181 Pa. 525 ....259, 542, 615
Dent v. Emmeger, 14 Wall. 308 ....493, 624
Desbois, 2 Mart. 185 204
De Vaughn v. Hutchinson, 165 U. S. 566 247
Devine v. Los Angeles, 202 U. S. 313 275
Dick v. United States, 208 U. S. 340 263
Diekelman, United States v., 92 U. S. 520 ....108, 432, 507, 508
Dillon, In re, 7 Sawy. 561 ....414, 497
Dinehart, Ex parte, 188 Fed. 858 558
Di Paolo v. Laquin Lumber Co., 178 Fed. 877 ....259, 542, 615
Disconto Gesellschaft v. Umbreit, 208 U. S. 570 ....368, 432, 507, 619
Divina Pastora, The, 4 Wheat. 52 366
Dockstader v. Kershaw, 4 Pennewill 398 ....251, 537, 599
Doe v. Beardsley, 2 McLean 417 245
Doe v. Braden, 16 How. 635 ....88, 349, 367, 569
Doe v. Wilson, 23 How. 457 245
Doehrel v. Hillmer, 102 Iowa 169 ....251, 433, 509, 601
Dooley v. United States, 182 U. S. 222 ....196, 213, 576
Dooley v. United States, 183 U. S. 151 ....215, 351, 576
Dorr v. United States, 195 U. S. 138 ....200, 218, 579
Douglas, United States v., 17 Fed. 634 474
Dowdell v. United States, 221 U. S. 325 219
Downes v. Bidwell, 182 U. S. 244 ....
.... 196, 200, 202, 203, 204, 208, 214, 218, 225, 268, 576
Dubuque & Pacific R. R. Co. v. Litchfield, 23 How. 66 390
Duck Lee v. Boise Development Co., 21 Idaho 461 ....256, 417, 419, 481, 609
Dufour, Succession of, 10 La. Ann. 391 ....252, 498, 611
Dugau, In re, 2 Lowell 367 532
Duncan v. Beard, 2 Nott & McC. 400 ....248, 521, 598
Dunlop & Wilson v. Alexander's Admr., 1 Cranch C. C. 498 .....246, 515
Dutilh's Admr. v. Coursault, 5 Cranch C. C. 349 496

Eastern Extension, Australasia & China Telegraph Co. v. United
  State, 46 C. Cls. 646; 48 C. Cls. 33; 231 U. S. 326 579
Ehrlich v. Weber, 114 Tenn. 711 ....160, 251, 433, 511, 601
Eighteen Packages of Dental Instruments, United States v., 222 Fed.
  121 132
Elias v. Ramirez, 215 U. S. 398 ....528, 556
Eliza Ann, The, 1 Dod. 244 ....352, 353
Elk v. Wilkins, 112 U. S. 94 ....135, 200
Elwine Kreplin, The, 9 Blatchf. 438 ....235, 432, 508
Emperor of Austria v. Day and Kossuth, 3 DeG. & J. 217 366
Endeavor, The Schooner, 44 C. Cls. 242 486
Erickson v. Carlson, 95 Neb. 182 ....33, 251, 582, 603
Erie R. R. Co. v. Purdy, 185 U. S. 148 274
Ester, The, 190 Fed. 216 ....236, 584
Ezeta, In re, 62 Fed. 972 565

Faber v. United States, 221 U. S. 649 ....213, 483, 609
Fairfax's Devisee v. Hunter's Lessee, 7 Cranch 603 ....248, 518, 595
Fama, The, 5 C. Rob. 106 ....347, 368
Fame, The, Fed. Cases No. 4634 514
Farez, In re, 7 Blatchf. 34; 7 Blatchf. 345 ....555, 587, 588
Farney v. Towle, 1 Black 350 274
Fattosini's Estate, In re, 67 N. Y. S. 1119 ....261, 412, 467, 545
Fellows v. Blacksmith, 19 How. 366 368
Fergus, In re, 30 Fed. 607 532

Ferreira, United States v., 13 How. 40 574
Ferrelle, In re, 28 Fed. 878 532
Field v. Clark, 143 U. S. 649 122
Fiott v. Commonwealth, 12 Grat. 564 ....248, 520, 597
Fisher v. Harnden, 1 Paine 55; 1 Wheat. 300 ....246, 516
Fisher's Lessee v. Cockerell, 5 Pet. 248 274
Fitzsimmons v. Newport Insurance Co., 4 Cranch 185 ....241, 522
Fleming v. Page, 9 How. 603 205
Fletcher v. Peck, 6 Cranch 87 425
Fok Yung Yo v. United States, 185 U. S. 296 482
Fong Yue Ting v. United States, 149 U. S. 698....161, 231, 268, 422, 480, 523
Fontana v. Hynes, 146 Pac. 651 ....262, 413, 539, 586
Forbes v. Scannell, 13 Cal. 242 471
Forbes v. State Council of Virginia, 216 U. S. 396 275
Forsyth v. Reynolds, 15 How. 358 ....517, 625
Fort Leavenworth R. R. Co. v. Lowe, 114 U. S. 525 ....224, 225, 268
Forty-three Gallons of Whiskey, United States v., 93 U. S. 188; 108
  U. S. 491 ....263, 465
Fossat, United States v., 20 How. 413 ....551, 627
Foster v. Neilson, 2 Pet. 253 ....160, 162, 365, 366, 491, 570, 571, 630, 631
Fourteen Diamond Rings v. United States, 183 U. S. 176 ....213, 382, 577
Foushee v. Blackwell, 1 Rob. 488 523
Fowler, In re, 4 Fed. 303 532
Fox v. Southack, 12 Mass. 143 ....248, 250, 447, 520, 597
Fox, United States v., 95 U. S. 670 271
Foxwell v. Craddock, 1 Pat. & H. 250 ....248, 521, 598
Frank, In re, 107 Fed. 272 531
Franklin Sugar Refining Co. v. United States, 202 U. S. 580 484
Frederickson v. State of Louisiana, 23 How. 445 ....253, 417, 512, 605
Frelinghuysen v. Key, 110 U. S. 63 ....108, 558
French v. Hopkins, 124 U. S. 524 274
French Republic v. Saratoga Vichy Co., 191 U. S. 427 589
Frevall v. Bache, 14 Pet. 95 494
Fudera, Ex parte, 162 Fed. 591 540
Fulco v. Schuylkill Stone Co., 163 Fed. 124; 169 Fed. 98 .....259, 542, 615
Furman v. Nichol, 8 Wall. 44 274

Gaar, Scott & Co. v. Shannon, 223 U. S. 468 274
Galwey, In re (1896), 1 Q. B. 230 286
Gandolfo v. Hartman, 49 Fed. 181 ....256, 419, 481, 608
Garcia v. Lee, 12 Pet. 511 ....365, 366, 491, 571, 631
Garrison v. United States, 30 C. Cls. 272 403
Geer v. Connecticut, 161 U. S. 519 ....260, 543, 616
Gelston v. Hoyt, 3 Wheat. 246 366
General McPherson, The, 100 Fed. 860 ....261, 501
Geofroy v. Riggs, 133 U. S. 258 ....
  ....224, 249, 250, 251, 267, 376, 399, 401, 490, 498, 592, 593
Georgia, The, 7 Wall. 32 245
Georgia v. Brailsford, 3 Dall. 1 514
Geyer v. Michel, 3 Dall. 285 488
Ghio's Estate, In re (See Rocca v. Thompson).
Giacomo, In re Angelo de, 12 Blatchf. 391 ....351, 540
Gill v. Oliver's Executors, 11 How. 529 549
Glaser, Ex parte, 176 Fed. 702 ....432, 510
Glass v. Sloop Betsey, 3 Dall. 6 ....236, 487
Glucksman v. Henkel, 221 U. S. 508 ....528, 564
Gonzales v. Williams, 192 U. S. 1 ....200, 216, 579
Gordhan v. Kanji, 1 App. Cas. 332 295
Gordon's Lessee v. Kerr et al., 1 Wash. C. C. 322 ....39, 246, 515
Grand Rapids, &c., R. R. Co., United States v., 165 Fed. 297 ......345, 346
Gray, Admr., v. United States, 21 C. Cls. 340..403, 486, 488, 489, 495, 523, 574

Great Western Insurance Co. v. United States, 19 C. Cls. 206; 112 U. S. 193 ....108, 534
Green v. Biddle, 8 Wheat. 1 ....145, 147
Greene v. United States, 154 Fed. 401 535
Grin v. Shine, 187 U. S. 181 ....399, 528, 564
Guastini v. Venezuela, Ralston's Rept. 730 ....391, 397
Gue Lim, United States v., 83 Fed. 136 478

Hall v. Patterson, 45 Fed. 352 532
Hamilton v. Dillin, 21 Wall. 73 103
Hamilton & Co. v. Eaton, 1 Hughes 249 ....41, 156, 158, 246, 514
Hanson, United States v., 16 Pet. 196 ....573, 633
Harcourt v. Gaillard, 12 Wheat. 523 ....293, 444, 513
Harden v. Fisher, 1 Wheat. 300 ....248, 518, 595
Harris v. Dennie, 3 Pet. 292 274
Harrold, In re, 1 Pa. L. J. 119 ....204, 494
Hart v. Executors of Hart, 2 Desaus. Eq. 57 ....507, 600
Hathaway, United States v., 4 Wall. 404 533
Hauenstein v. Lynham, 100 U. S. 483 ....160, 249, 401, 587, 603
Haver v. Yaker, 9 Wall. 32 ....345, 586
Hawaii v. Mankichi, 190 U. S. 197 219
Hawkins v. Barney, 5 Pet. 457 147
Hays v. United States, 175 U. S. 248 ....551, 628
Head Money Cases, 112 U. S. 580 ....161, 409, 484, 609
Heard v. Bradford, 4 Mass. 326 517
Heilbronn, In re, Fed. Cases No. 6323 531
Heim et al. v. McCall et al., 239 U. S. 175 ....254, 422, 544, 617
Henderson v. Poindexter's Lessee, 12 Wheat. 530 ....513, 566
Hennebique Construction Co. v. Myers, 172 Fed. 869 ....238, 590
Henrich, In re, 5 Blatchf. 414 515
Herrera v. United States, 222 U. S. 558 ....354, 578
Herres, In re, 33 Fed. 165 ....528, 532, 556
Herskovitz, In re, 136 Fed. 713 ....531, 532
Hiawatha, The, 2 Black 635 244
Hibbs, Ex parte, 26 Fed. 421 ....527, 532
Hickey's Lessee v. Stewart, 3 How. 750 566
Higginson v. Mein, 4 Cranch 415 ....246, 515
Highland Glass Co. v. Schmertz Wire Glass Co., 178 Fed. 944 237
Hijo v. United States, 194 U. S. 315 ....352, 354, 578
Ho King, In re, 8 Sawy. 438 474
Holden v. Joy, 17 Wall. 211 245
Holmberg's Estate, In re, 193 Fed. 260 ....261, 584
Holmes v. Jennison, 14 Pet. 540 144
Holmes v. Jennison, 12 Vt. 631 144
Home for Incurables v. New York, 187 U. S. 155 275
Hong Wing v. United States, 142 Fed. 128 482
Hooper, Admr., v. United States, 22 C. Cls. 408 ......425, 441, 463, 486, 489
Hopkirk v. Bell, 3 Cranch 454; 4 Cranch 164 ....246, 515
Horner v. United States, 143 U. S. 570 161
Hornsby v. United States, 10 Wall. 224 ....366, 492, 550, 551, 623, 627
Howell v. Bidwell, 124 Fed. 688 ....346, 351, 577
Hoyt v. Shelden, 1 Black 518 274
Hubbell v. United States, 15 C. Cls. 546 471
Huertas, United States v., 9 Pet. 171 ....573, 632
Hughes v. Edwards, 9 Wheat. 489 ....248, 519, 596
Humphrey's Admx. v. United States, Dev. C. Cls. §§678-693 ......163, 574
Hunt v. United States, 166 U. S. 424 269
Hutchinson v. Brock, 11 Mass. 119 ....447, 520, 597
Huus v. New York & Porto Rico S. S. Co., 182 U. S. 392 576
Hylton's Lessee v. Brown, 1 Wash. C. C. 298, 343 ....246, 512, 514

Infelise's Estate, In re, 149 Pac. 365 ....414, 546, 586
Inglis v. Trustees of Sailors' Snug Harbor, 3 Pet. 99   514
Internal Improvement Co. v. Root, 63 Fla. 666   569
International Transit Co. v. City of Sault Ste. Marie, 194 Fed. 522;
    234 U. S. 333 ....
Iowa v. Rood, 187 U. S. 87 ....264, 538
Iowa v. Rowe, 104 Iowa 323 ....494, 624
Isabella Thompson, The, 3 Wall. 155   556
                                                                245

Jackson v. Clarke, 3 Wheat. 1 ....248, 518, 595
Jackson v. Decker, 11 Johns. 418 ....248, 521, 598
Jackson v. Lunn, 3 Johns. Cases 109 ....247, 248, 520, 597
Jackson, ex. dem. Sparkman, v. Porter, 1 Paine 457 ....397, 517, 625
Jackson v. Wright, 4 Johns. 75 ....248, 250, 521, 598
Jacobi v. Alabama, 187 U. S. 133   274
James and William, The Ship, 37 C. Cls. 303 ....463, 486, 488
J. & P. Baltz Brewing Co. v. Kaiserbrauerei, Beck & Co., 74 Fed.
    222 ....469, 503
Jane, The Schooner, 23 C. Cls. 226 ....489, 496
Japanese Immigrant Case, The, 189 U. S. 86 ....258, 548, 618
Jarema's Estate, In re, 137 N. Y. S. 176 ....262, 413, 468
Joe Dick, United States v., 134 Fed. 988   477
John, The, 2 Dod. 336   356
Johnson v. Browne, 205 U. S. 309 ....161, 376, 401, 527, 536
Johnson v. McIntosh, 8 Wheat. 543   245
Johnson v. Olson, 92 Kan. 819 ....582, 603
Jonathan Brown v. United States, 32 C. Cls. 432   134
Jonathan Robbins, The case of, Bee 266 ....230, 523
Jones v. Meehan, 175 U. S. 1 ....135, 245, 399
Jones v. St. Louis Land Co., 232 U. S. 355 ....552, 628
Jones v. United States, 137 U. S. 202 ....93, 140, 366
Jones v. Walker, 2 Paine 688 ....38, 156, 158, 246, 368, 400, 514
Josephs v. United States, 1 C. Cls. 197 ....491, 622
Jost v. Jost, 1 Mackey 487 ....587, 603
Juan Santistevan, United States v., 1 N. M. 583 ....200, 209
Judson v. Corcoran, 17 How. 612   553
Julius Wile Bro. & Co., United States v., 130 Fed. 331 ..124, 501
Jung Ah Lung, United States v., 124 U. S. 621 ....478, 481

Kagama, United States v., 118 U. S. 375   135
Kaine, Ex parte, 3 Blatchf. 1   531
Kaine, In re, 14 How. 103 ....230, 523, 531
Kansas Indians, 5 Wall. 737   399
Kaukauna Co. v. Green Bay &c., Canal, 142 U. S., 254   274
Keene v. McDonough, 8 Pet. 308 ....366, 491, 622
Keene v. Whitaker, 14 Pet. 170   491
Kelley, In re, 2 Lowell 339   529
Kelley, In re, 25 Fed. 268; 26 Fed. 852   532
Kendept v. Korner, Fed. Cases No. 7693 ....235, 506
Kepner v. United States, 195 U. S. 100   218
Ker v. Illinois, 119 U. S. 436   560
Kerry et al. v. Toupin, 60 Fed. 272   589
King, United States v., 7 How. 833 ....491, 621
Kinkead v. United States, 150 U. S. 483 ....378, 563, 629
Knight v. United States Land Assoc., 142 U. S. 161 ......551, 552, 628
Koenigin Luise, The, 184 Fed. 170 ....235, 503
Kopel v. Bingham, 211 U. S. 468   216
Krojanker, In re, 44 Fed. 482 ....432, 510
Kull v. Kull, 37 Hun 476 ....250, 433, 511, 604
Kummerow v. Venezuela, Ralston's Rept. 526   397

La Abra Silver Mining Co. v. Frelinghuysen, 110 U. S. 63 558
La Abra Silver Mining Co. v. United States, 29 C. Cls. 432; 175 U.
S. 423 558
Lai Moy v. United States, 66 Fed. 955 475
La Manna, Azema & Farnam v. United States, 144 Fed. 683 ......124, 501
Lane, Ex parte, 6 Fed. 34 ....532, 556
La Ninfa, 75 Fed. 513 ....227, 537
Lapeyre v. United States, 17 Wall. 191 347
La Republique Francaise v. Schultz, 57 Fed. 37 ....458, 500, 589
La Roche v. Jones, 9 How. 155 566
Lascelles v. United States, 49 C. Cls. 382 ....351, 577
Lattimer v. Poteet, 14 Pet. 4 ....225, 365
Lau Ow Bew v. United States, 144 U. S. 47 480
Laverty, United States v., 3 Mart. 733 ....204, 494
Lawrence, United States v., 3 Dall. 42 489
Lawrence, United States v., 13 Blatchf. 295 527
Layton v. Missouri, 187 U. S. 356 274
Leathe v. Thomas, 207 U. S. 93 274
Leavit v. The Shakespeare, Fed. Cases No. 8167 506
Lee v. Thorndike, 2 Metc. 313 496
Lee Kan v. United States, 62 Fed. 914 475
Lee Lung v. Patterson, 186 U. S. 168 481
Leeper v. Texas, 139 U. S. 462 274
Lee Sing, In re, 43 Fed. 359...........................255, 419, 480, 608
Lee Sing, In re, 85 Fed. 635 478
Lee Yen Tai, United States v., 185 U. S. 213 ....161, 238, 481
Lehman v. State, 45 Ind. App. 330 ....587, 604
Leigh v. Green, 193 U. S. 79 275
Leighton v. United States, 29 C. Cls. 288 368
Leong Mow v. Board of Commissioners, 185 Fed. 223.....255, 419, 481, 609
Leong Yick Dew, In re, 10 Sawy. 38 478
Leo Won Tong, United States v., 132 Fed. 190 478
Lestapies v. Ingraham, 5 Barr 71 495
Le Tigre, Case of, 3 Wash. C. C. 567 567
Leung, In re, 86 Fed. 303 476
Lewis v. Bell, 17 How. 616 470
Lew Jim v. United States, 66 Fed. 953 475
Li Foon, In re, 80 Fed. 881 478
Lincoln v. United States, 197 U. S. 419; 202 U. S. 484 ....213, 351, 577
Linford v. Ellison, 155 U. S. 503 276
Little v. Watson, 32 Me. 214 ....224, 403, 526
Liu Hop Fong v. United States, 209 U. S. 453 483
Lobrasciano's Estate, In re, 77 N. Y. S. 1040 ....261, 412, 467, 545
Loeb v. Trustees, 179 U. S. 472 275
Loeber v. Schroeder, 149 U. S. 580 275
Logiorato's Estate, In re, 69 N. Y. S. 507 ....261, 412, 466, 545
Lombardi, In re, 138 N. Y. S. 1007 ....262, 413, 546, 585
Loney, In re, 134 U. S. 372 272
Louie Juen, United States v., 128 Fed. 522 478
Lownsdale et al. v. Parrish, 21 How. 290 ....533, 626
Lucero, United States v., 1 N. M. 422 ....200, 209, 553
Lum Lin Ying, In re, 59 Fed. 682 478
Luyties, United States v., 130 Fed. 333 ....124, 501
Lynch, United States v. 137 U. S. 280 276
Lynde, United States v., 11 Wall. 632 ....345, 365, 366, 491, 571, 631

McBlair v. Gibbes, 17 How. 232 549
McCabe, Ex parte, 46 Fed. 363 557
McCulloch v. State of Maryland, 4 Wheat. 316 270
Macdonnel, In re, 11 Blatchf. 79, 170 ....532, 556

McDonogh v. Millaudon, 3 How. 693 ....494, 624
McEvoy v. Wyman, 191 Mass. 276 ....261, 412, 467, 561
McFarland v. Alaska Perseverance Mining Co., 3 Alaska 308 ....212, 563
McGoon v. Scales, 9 Wall. 23 247
McGovern v. Philadelphia and Reading Ry. Co., 235 U. S. 389..259, 542, 615
M'Ilvaine v. Coxe's Lessee, 4 Cranch 209 ....293, 444, 513
McKay v. Campbell, 2 Sawy. 118 525
McKeown v. Brown, 149 N. W. 593 ....253, 485, 537, 610, 612
McKinney v. Saviego, 18 How. 235 ....549, 626
McLean v. Railroad Co., 203 U. S. 38 276
MacLeod v. United States, 229 U. S. 416 ....351, 352, 354, 577
McMillen v. Ferrum, 197 U. S. 343 275
McNair v. Ragland et al., 16 N. C. 516 ....246, 248, 447, 515
McNamara v. Henkel, 226 U. S. 520 527
McPhun, In re, 30 Fed. 57 532
Madaloni's Estate, In re, 141 N. Y. S. 323 ....262, 413, 546, 586
Mahoney v. United States, 10 Wall. 62 ....427, 466
Maiden v. Ingersoll, 6 Mich. 373 368
Maiorano v. Baltimore & Ohio R. R. Co., 216 Pa. 402; 213 U. S.
    268 ....259, 541, 542, 614, 615
Maisi Tribe v. Attorney General et al., 8 Am. J. of Int. Law 380 ... 368
Malignani v. Hill-Wright Electric Co., 177 Fed. 430 ....237, 590
Malignani v. Jasper Marsh Consolidated Electric Lamp Co., 180
    Fed. 442 ....237, 590
Mallet v. North Carolina, 181 U. S. 589 275
Maltass v. Maltass, 1 Rob. Ecc. Cases 67 397
Mar Bing Guey v. United States, 97 Fed. 576 477
Marie, The, 49 Fed. 286 ....235, 583
Marlatt v. Silk, 11 Pet. 1 147
Marryat v. Wilson, 1 Bos. & P. 429 401
Marshall v. Conrad, 5 Call 364 ....521, 597
Martinez v. Asociacion de Señoras, 213 U. S. 20 ....216, 580
Maryland v. West Virginia, 217 U. S. 577 142
Massachusetts v. Rhode Island, 12 Pet. 657 147
May v. Specht et al., 1 Manning 187 ....248, 521, 598
Mayer v. White, 24 How. 317 549
Meade v. United States, 2 C. Cls. 224; 9 Wall. 691 574
Megrath v. Administrators of John and Ann Robertson, 1 Desaus.
    Eq., 445 ....248, 520, 597
Meier v. Lee, 106 Iowa 303 ....581, 602
Mena v. Venezuela, Ralston's Rept. 931 397
Mentor, The, 1 C. Rob. 179 357
Metzger, In re, Fed Cases No. 9511 ....232, 345, 496
Metzger, In re, 5 How. 176 ....232, 496
Metzger, In re, 1 Barb. 248 ....232, 285, 389, 497
Meyer v. Basson, 10 Phila. 414 503
M. H. Pulaski Co. et al. v. United States 199
Migliavacca Wine Co. v. United States, 148 Fed. 142 ......124, 501
Mihalovitch, Fletcher & Co. v. United States, 160 Fed. 988....124, 501, 503
Miller, In re, 23 Fed. 32 527
Miller v. Nicholls, 4 Wheat. 411 274
Mills' Heirs, United States v., 12 Pet. 215 ....572, 632
Mineau, In re, 45 Fed. 188 532
Minnesota Canal & Power Co. v. Pratt, 101 Minn. 197 526
Minook, In re, 2 Alaska 200 ....212, 563
Miranda, United States v., 16 Pet. 153 ....573, 632, 633
Missouri, Kansas & Texas R. R. Co. v. United States, 47 C. Cls. 59.. 135
Mitchel v. United States, 9 Pet. 711 ....245, 569, 572, 630, 631
Mitchell, In re, 171 Fed. 289 532
M. J. Dalton Co., United States v., 151 Fed. 144 484
Moncon, In re, 8 Sawy. 350 474

Monongahela Bridge Co. v. United States, 216 U. S. 177 123
Montault v. United States, 12 How. 47 ....345, 349, 571, 631
Moodie v. Ship Amity, Bee 89 ....236, 487
Moodie v. Ship Phœbe Anne, 3 Dall. 319 488
Moore v. United States, 32 C. Cls. 593 89
More v. Steinbach, 127 U. S. 70 ....366, 382, 550, 551, 627
Moreno, United States v., 1 Wall. 400 ....202, 550, 626
Mormon Church v. United States, 136 U. S. 1 200
Morris v. United States, 174 U. S. 196 ....142, 517
Morton v. Nebraska, 21 Wall. 660 ....492, 623
Mountain View Mining & Milling Co. v. McFadden, 180 U. S. 53 ... 275
Moynihan's Estate, In re, 151 N. W. 504 ....253, 538, 613
Moy Yim, United States v., 115 Fed. 652 478
Mrs. Gue Lim, United States v., 176 U. S. 459 478
Muller's Case, Fed. Cases No. 9913 532
Munro v. Merchant, 26 Barb. 383; 28 N. Y. 9 ....248, 250, 521, 598
Muse v. Arlington Hotel Co., 168 U. S. 430 276
Mutual Life Insurance Co. v. McGrew, 188 U. S. 291 275

Narciso Basso v. United States, 40 C. Cls. 202 ....216, 580
Neagle, In re, 135 U. S. 1 272
Neck, The, 138 Fed. 144 ....235, 371, 502
Neely v. Henkel, 180 U. S. 109 ....241, 575
Nereide, The, 9 Cranch 388 ....241, 371, 397, 402, 568
Neustra Señora de la Caridad, The, 4 Wheat. 497 ....241, 566, 567
Newcomb v. Newcomb, 108 Ky. 582 533
Newman, Ex parte, 14 Wall. 152 ....432, 508
Newman, In re, 79 Fed. 622 ....530, 532
New Orleans v. Abbagnato, 62 Fed. 240 ....260, 542, 616
New Orleans v. Armas, 9 Pet. 224 ....204, 493, 624
New Orleans v. United States, 10 Pet. 662 ....491, 493, 621, 624
New York Indians v. United States, 170 U. S. 1 ....89, 245
New York Insurance Co. v. Roulet, 24 Wend. 505 495
Ng Park Tan, United States v., 86 Fed. 605 476
Ng Quong Ming, Ex parte, 135 Fed. 378 477
Nicholas v. United States, 122 Fed. 892 ....124, 501
Ninfa, La, 75 Fed. 513 ....227, 537
Norris v. City of Boston, 7 How. 283 ....524, 611
Norberg v. Hillgreu, 5 N. Y. Leg. Obs. 177................235, 583
North American Commercial Co. v. United States, 171 U. S. 110.... 536
North Carolina v. Tennessee, 235 U. S. 1 146
North German Lloyd S. S. Co. v. Hedden, 43 Fed. 17 .409, 420, 432, 508, 619
Norton, United States v., 97 U. S. 164 347

Ogden v. Blackledge, 2 Cranch 272 ....246, 352, 515
O'Hara v. United States, 15 Pet. 275 ....573, 632
Oldfield v. Marriott, 10 How. 146 ....121, 560, 618
Old Settlers, United States v., 148 U. S. 427 ....275, 368
Olsen v. Smith, 195 U. S. 332 ....265, 409, 524, 612
One Hundred Thirty-Four Thousand, &c., Feet of Pine Lumber,
    4 Blatchf. 182 533
Ong Lung, In re, 125 Fed. 814 482
Opel v. Shoup, 100 Iowa 407 ....251, 433, 504, 591
Open Boat, The, Fed. Cases No. 10548 523
Opinions of the Justices, 68 Me. 589 525
Oregon Railway v. Oregonian Railway, 130 U. S. 1 390
O'Reilly de Camara v. Brooke, 209 U. S. 45 ....202, 269, 578, 633
Ornelas v. Ruiz, 161 U. S. 502 ....272, 528, 555
Orpen, In re, 86 Fed. 760 532
Orr v. Hodgson, 4 Wheat. 453 ....248, 516, 518, 593, 595
Orser v. Hoag, 3 Hill 79 ....521, 598

Ortega v. Lara, 202 U. S. 339 201
Ortiz, Ex parte, 100 Fed. 955 ....345, 352, 577
Oscanyan v. Arms Co., 103 U. S. 261 559
Oteiza y Cortes, In re, 136 U. S. 330 ....528, 575
Owings v. Norwood's Lessee, 5 Cranch 344 ....246, 515, 518, 595
Ow Yang Dean v. United States, 145 Fed. 801 478
Oxley Stave Co. v. Butler County, 166 U. S. 648 ....274, 275

Padron v. Venezuela, Ralston's Rept. 923 397
Page v. Pendleton, 1 Wythe 211 ....368, 514
Palmer, In re, Fed. Cases No. 10679 529
Palmer, United States v., 3 Wheat. 610 366
Parlement Belge, The, L. R., 4 Pro. Div. 129; L. R., 5 Pro. Div. 197   290
Parrott, In re Tiburcio, 6 Sawy. 349 ....254, 417, 472, 607
Passenger Cases, 7 How. 283 ....524, 525, 611, 612
Patsone v. Commonwealth of Pennsylvania, 232 U. S. 138; 231 Pa.
  46 ....260, 543, 544, 616
Pearcy v. Stranahan, 205 U. S. 257 ....366, 575
Pearl, The, 5 Wall. 574 245
Pederson, In re, Fed. Cases No. 10899a 584
Pelican, The, Edw. Adm. Appx. D 366
Pennsylvania v. Wheeling & Bridge Co., 13 How. 518 147
People v. Board of Supervisors, 8 N. Y. S. 752 532
People v. Crane, 214 N. Y. 154; 239 U. S. 195 ....544, 617
People v. Curtis, 50 N. Y. 321 144
People v. De la Guerra, 40 Cal. 311 ....200, 209, 553
People v. Fiske, 45 How. Pr. 294 532
People v. Gerke, 5 Cal. 381 ....250, 251, 268, 508, 600
People v. Gray, 66 Cal. 271 556
People v. I. M. Ludington's Sons, 131 N. Y. S. 550 ....260, 417, 544, 617
People v. Naglee, 1 Cal. 232 ....200, 209, 553
People v. Snyder, 51 Barb. 589 ....248, 521, 598
People v. Tyler, 7 Mich. 161 ....264, 526
People v. Warren, 34 N. Y. S. 942 ....260, 417, 544, 617
Percheman, United States v., 7 Pet. 51 ....162, 389, 394, 569, 571, 630
Peterhoff, The, 5 Wall. 28 245
Peterson's Estate, In re, 151 N. W. 66 ....251, 252, 581, 602, 621
Peterson's Will, In re, 101 N. Y. S. 285 ....411, 467, 485, 497, 544
Pettit v. Walshe, 194 U. S. 205 ....276, 528
Phelps v. McDonald, 99 U. S. 298 534
Philadelphia & New Orleans, United States v., 11 How. 609 ....
  .... 493, 571, 624, 631
Piaza, United States v., 133 Fed. 998 531
Pico, United States v., 23 How. 321 ....366, 550, 627
Pim v. St. Louis, 165 U. S. 273 275
Pinkerton v. Ledoux, 129 U. S. 346 ....551, 627
Pin Kwan, United States v., 100 Fed. 609 475
Pizarro, The, 2 Wheat. 227 ....241, 568
Pollard's Heirs v. Kibbe, 14 Pet. 353 ....162, 365, 571, 573, 631, 632
Pollard's Lessee v. Files, 2 How. 591 ....365, 571, 631
Pollard's Lessee v. Hagan, 3 How. 212 ....491, 566, 569, 621, 630
Ponce v. Roman Catholic Church, 210 U. S. 296 ....202, 578, 633
Poole v. Fleeger, 11 Pet. 185 ....142, 145
Portier v. Le Roy, 1 Yeates 371 489
Powell v. Brunswick County, 150 U. S. 433 275
Powers v. Comly, 101 U. S. 789 ....409, 560, 618
Prevost v. Greneaux, 19 How. 1 ....253, 417, 498, 592
Prize Cases, The, 2 Black 635 392
Puget Sound Agricultural Co. v. Pierce County, 1 Wash. T. 159..
  .... 163, 533, 626

Queen v. Wilson (1877), 3 Q. B. D. 42 286
Quimby, United States v., 4 Wall. 408 533
Quintana v. Tomkins, 1 N. M. 29 ....209, 553
Quong Woo, In re, 13 Fed. 229 ....256, 419, 480, 608

Rabasse, Succession of, 47 La. Ann. 1452 ....260, 411, 470, 499
Rabasse, Succession of, 49 La. Ann. 1405 ....252, 411, 499, 611
Radcliff v. Coster, 1 Hoff. Ch. 99 495
Railroad Co. v. Rock, 4 Wall. 177 274
Rainey v. United States, 232 U. S. 310 ....525, 612
Rassmussen v. United States, 197 U. S. 516 ....212, 563
Rauscher, United States v., 119 U. S. 407 ....144, 233, 376, 467, 527
Read v. Read, 5 Call 160 ....521, 597
Reid v. Ship Vere, Bee 66 ....236, 487
Reiner, In re, 122 Fed. 109 ....432, 510
Reinitz, In re, 39 Fed. 204 ....467, 529
Repentigny, United States v., 5 Wall. 211 ....514, 517, 625
Republic of Peru v. Dreyfus, 38 Ch. D. 348 366
Republic of Peru v. Peruvian Guano Co., 36 Ch. D. 489 366
Respublica v. Gordon, 1 Dall. 233 ....39, 40, 516, 593
Reynes, United States v., 9 How. 127 ....
..................345, 348, 349, 365, 366, 491, 492, 493, 622, 624
Riccardo, In re, 140 N. Y. S. 606 ....262, 413, 546, 585
Rice v. Ames, 180 U. S. 371 ....528, 536
Rice, United States v., 4 Wheat. 246 392
Richter v. Reynolds, 59 Fed. 577 503
Ridgway v. Hays, 5 Cranch C. C. 23 495
Rio Grande Irrigation Co., United States v., 174 U. S. 690; 184 U.
   S. 416 549
Risch, In re, 36 Fed. 546 ....432, 510
Rixner, Succession of, 48 La. Ann. 552 ....251, 252, 417, 499, 544, 611
Robbins, United States v., Fed Cases No. 16175 ....230, 523
Roberts v. United States, Dev. C. Cls. §702 495
Robinson v. Campbell, 3 Wheat. 212 147
Robinson v. Minor, 10 How. 627 566
Rocca v. Thompson, 157 Cal. 552 ....261, 412, 466
Rocca v. Thompson, 223 U. S. 317 ....262, 371, 397, 412, 466, 545
Rodgers, United States v., 150 U. S. 249 ....264, 523, 526
Rodriguez, In re, 81 Fed. 337 ....200, 209, 553
Rogers v. Jones, 214 U. S. 196 274
Ronchi, Ex parte, 164 Fed. 288 541
Ropes v. Clinch, 8 Blatchf. 304 ....198, 407, 561, 620
Rose, United States v., 23 How. 262 ....551, 627
Ross, Ex parte, 2 Bond 252 528
Ross, In re, 140 U. S. 453 ....268, 375, 387, 458, 547
Rossmann v. Garnier, 211 Fed. 401 590
Roth, In re, 15 Fed. 506 ....555, 587, 588
Rousseau v. Brown, 21 App. Cas. (D. C.) 73 ....237, 589
Rowe, In re, 77 Fed. 161 557

Sala, Succession of, 50 La. Ann. 1009 ....567, 601
Salderondo v. Ship Nostra Signora del Camino et al., Bee 43 .....236, 487
Salomoni, The, 29 Fed. 534 ....235, 545
Sambiaggio v. Venezuela, Ralston's Rept. 666 ....396, 397
Sanchez v. United States, 216 U. S. 167 ....202, 579, 633
Sandoval, United States v., 167 U. S. 278 ....551, 628
Santa Fe, United States v., 165 U. S. 675 ....551, 628
Santiago v. Nogueras, 214 U. S. 260 ....214, 351, 577
Santissima Trinidad, The, 7 Wheat. 283 ....241, 567, 568
Satterlee v. Matthewson, 2 Pet. 380 274
Saxlehner v. Eisner & Mendelson Co., 179 U. S. 19 469

Sayward v. Denny, 158 U. S. 180 275
Sayward, United States v., 160 U. S. 493 269
Scharpf v. Schmidt, 172 Ill. 255 ....250, 433, 512, 605
Schlippenbach, In re, 164 Fed. 783 564
Schooner Exchange v. McFaddon, 7 Cranch 116 106
Schooner Peggy, United States v., 1 Cranch 103 ....160, 161, 345, 490
Schultze v. Schultze, 144 Ill. 290 ....250, 433, 506, 600
Schunk v. Moline, &c., Co., 147 U. S. 500 269
Science, The, 5 Wall. 178 244
Scottish Union, &c., v. Herriott, 109 Iowa 606 ....524, 611
Scutella's Estate, In re, 129 N. Y. S. 20 ....261, 412, 467, 545
Sena v. United States, 189 U. S. 233 553
Shanks v. Dupont, 3 Pet. 242 ....401, 514, 519, 596
Shaw & Co. v. United States, 1 Ct. Cust. Appls. 426 ....407, 411
Shepard v. Northwestern Insurance Co., 40 Fed. 341 346
Sheppard v. Taylor, 5 Pet. 710 494
Shively v. Bowlby, 152 U. S. 1 532
Shong Toon, In re, 10 Sawy. 268 478
Sibbald, United States v., 10 Pet. 313 ....343, 345, 569, 572, 632
Siebold, Ex parte, 100 U. S. 371 271
Silvetti's Estate, In re, 122 N. Y. S. 400 ....261, 412, 467, 545
Simpson v. United States, 199 U. S. 397 377
Sims v. Irvine, 3 Dall. 425 147
Sing Lee, United States v., 71 Fed. 680 476
Sir William Peel, The, 5 Wall. 517 244
Slidell v. Grandjean, 111 U. S. 412 ....390, 491, 621
Smith v. Adams, 130 U. S. 167 269
Smith v. State of Maryland, 6 Cranch 286 ....515, 518
Smith v. Turner, 7 How. 283 ....524, 611
Smith v. United States, 10 Pet. 326 ....492, 572, 623, 631
Society for Propagation of the Gospel, &c., v. Town of New Haven
    et al., 8 Wheat. 464 ....248, 447, 516, 519, 594, 596
Society for Propagation of the Gospel, &c., v. Town of Pawlet, 4
    Pet. 480 ....518, 595
Society for Propagation of the Gospel, &c., v. Wheeler, et al., 2
    Gall. 105 ....248, 447, 520, 597
Somerset, The, 2 Dod. 56 356
Soon Hing v. Crowley, 113 U. S. 703 ....256, 479, 607
Soulard v. United States, 4 Pet. 511 ....492, 623
Spears v. State, 8 Tex. App. 467 570
Speedwell, The Schooner, 2 Dall. 40 513
Spies v. Illinois, 123 U. S. 131 ....274, 524, 611
Springbok, The, 5 Wall. 1 244
Stannick v. Ship Friendship, Bee 40 ....236, 487
Stark v. Starr, 94 U. S. 477 ....533, 626
State v. Gallardo, 135 S. W. 664 ....554, 629
State v. Primrose, 3 Ala. 546 ....200, 204, 494
State v. Vanderpool, 39 Ohio 273 527
Stearns v. United States, 6 Wall. 589 ....366, 550, 627
Stephens v. Choctaw Nation, 174 U. S. 445 135
Stephen's Heirs v. Swann, 9 Leigh 404 ....248, 521, 598
Sternaman, Ex parte, 77 Fed. 595; 80 Fed. 883; 83 Fed. 690 .....532, 556
Sternaman v. Peck, 83 Fed. 690 530
Stewart v. Kahn, 11 Wall. 493 200
Stewart's Admx. v. Callaghan, 4 Cranch C. C. 594 588
Stixrud's Estate, In re, 58 Wash. 339 ....33, 251, 252, 582, 602, 621
Storti v. Massachusetts, 183 U. S. 138 ....259, 541, 614
Strobel's Estate, In re, 39 N. Y. S. 169 ....433, 458, 512, 605
Strother v. Lucas, 12 Pet. 410 ....162, 492, 493, 623
Struckmann v. United States, 44 C. Cls. 202; 223 U. S. 712 ......578, 620
Stupp, In re, 11 Blatchf. 124 ....432, 510

Stupp, In re, 12 Blatchf. 501 ....469, 528
Sun, United States v., 76 Fed. 450 477
Sutter, United States v., 21 How. 170 ....551, 627
Sutton v. Sutton, 1 Russ. & M. 663 447
Sweringen v. St. Louis, 185 U. S. 38 275

Talbot v. Janson, 3 Dall. 133 487
Tannis v. St. Cyre, 21 Ala. 449 ....200, 206, 570
Tartar Chemical Co. v. United States, 116 Fed. 726 366
Tartar Chemical Co., United States v., 127 Fed. 944 ....124, 501
Taylor, In re, 118 Fed. 196 531
Taylor v. Barclay, 2 Sim. 213 366
Taylor v. Morton, 2 Curtis 454 ....198, 368, 407, 465, 561, 620
Tellefsen v. Fee, 168 Mass. 188 ....235, 583
Tennessee v. Virginia, 190 U. S. 64 148
Terlinden v. Ames, 184 U. S. 270 ....368, 432, 509, 528
Teti v. Consolidated Coal Co., 217 Fed. 443 ....260, 547, 617
Texas, United States v., 143 U. S. 621 ....365, 434
Texas, United States v., 162 U. S. 1 ....377, 378, 383, 570
Thingvalla Line et al. v. United States, 24 C. Cls. 255 ....409, 484, 610
Thomas, In re Hermann, 12 Blatchf. 370 ....432, 504
Thomas v. United States, Dev. C. Cls. §§694-695 574
Thompson, Succession of, 9 La. Ann. 96 ....260, 584
Tobin v. Walkinshaw et al., 1 McAll. 186 ....209, 552
Tokai Maru, The, 190 Fed. 450 ....258, 548, 618
Tom, The Ship, 29 C. Cls. 68; 39 C. Cls. 290 ....403, 489
Tom Hong v. United States, 193 U. S. 517 477
Tong Ah Chee, In re, 9 Sawy. 346 478
Torres v. United States, 4 Moore Int. Arb. 3798 ....352, 354
Toscano, Ex parte, 208 Fed. 938 ....245, 591
Town v. DeHaven, 5 Sawy. 146 ....397, 533, 626
Townsend v. Greeley, 5 Wall. 326 ....550, 627
Trade Mark Cases, 100 U. S. 82 240
Tripp v. Spring, 5 Sawy. 209 ....397, 552, 628
Truax et al. v. Raich, 239 U. S. 33 ....255, 421
Trumbull, United States v., 48 Fed. 94 ....414, 470
Tsoi Sim v. United States, 116 Fed. 920 479
Tucker v. Alexandroff, 183 U. S. 424 ....105, 234, 400, 401, 561
Tucker v. United States, 157 Fed. 386 562
Tully, In re, 20 Fed. 812 529
Tung Yeong, In re, 9 Sawy. 620 478
Tunno v. Preary, Bee 6.. 488
Turner v. American Baptist Missionary Union, 5 McLean 344 178

Ubeda v. Zialcita, 226 U. S. 452 ....580, 634
Union Typewriter Co. v. L. C. Smith & Bros., 173 Fed. 288 238
United Shoe Machinery Co. v. Duplessis Shoe Machinery Co., 155
   Fed. 842 ....161, 237, 238, 590
United States v. Acosta, 1 How. 24 ....573, 632, 633
United States v. Ah Fawn, 57 Fed. 591 475
United States v. American Sugar Refining Co., 202 U. S. 563..194, 346, 484
United States v. The Amistad, 15 Pet. 518 ....241, 394, 400, 567, 568
United States v. Arredondo, 6 Pet. 691 ....
   ....343, 344, 345, 346, 365, 391, 397, 491, 569, 571, 572, 630, 632
United States v. Berrigan, 2 Alaska 442 ....212, 563
United States v. Bethlehem Steel Co., 205 U. S. 105 377
United States v. Billings, 190 Fed. 359 ....525, 612
United States v. Breward, 16 Pet. 143 ....573, 632
United States v. Brooks, 10 How. 442 245
United States v. Caldwell, 8 Blatchf. 131 527
United States v. Castant, 12 How. 437 ....571, 631

3

United States v. Chaves, 159 U. S. 452 ....551, 628
United States v. Chu Chee et al., 93 Fed. 797 476
United States v. Chung Ki Foon, 83 Fed. 143 476
United States v. Clarke, 8 Pet. 436 ....569, 571, 572, 630, 631
United States v. Clarke, 9 Pet. 168 ....572, 632
United States v. Clark's Heirs, 16 Pet. 228 ....573, 632, 633
United States v. Cooper, Fed. Cases No. 14865 ....230, 523
United States v. Crosby, 7 Cranch 115 247
United States v. D'Auterive, 10 How. 609 ......345, 349, 492, 571, 622, 631
United States v. Delespine, 15 Pet. 319 ....573, 632
United States v. Diekelman, 92 U. S. 520 ....108, 432, 507, 508
United States v. Douglas, 17 Fed. 634 474
United States v. Eighteen Packages of Dental Instruments, 222
    Fed. 121 132
United States v. Ferreira, 13 How. 40 574
United States v. Forty-three Gallons of Whiskey, 93 U. S. 188;
    108 U. S. 491 ....263, 465
United States v. Fossat, 20 How. 413 ....551, 627
United States v. Fox, 95 U. S. 670 271
United States v. Grand Rapids, &c., R. R. Co., 165 Fed. 297 ....345, 346
United States v. Gue Lim, 83 Fed. 136 478
United States v. Hanson, 16 Pet. 196 ....573, 633
United States v. Hathaway, 4 Wall. 404 533
United States v. Huertas, 9 Pet. 171 ....573, 632
United States v. Joe Dick, 134 Fed. 988 477
United States v. Juan Santistevan, 1 N. M. 583 ....200, 209
United States v. Julius Wile Bro. & Co., 130 Fed. 331 ....124, 501
United States v. Jung Ah Lung, 124 U. S. 621 ....478, 481
United States v. Kagama, 118 U. S. 375 135
United States v. King, 7 How. 833 ....491, 621
United States v. La Abra Silver Mining Co., 29 C. Cls. 432; 175
    U. S. 423 558
United States v. Laverty, 3 Mart. 733 ....204, 494
United States v. Lawrence, 3 Dall. 42 489
United States v. Lawrence, 13 Blatchf. 295 527
United States v. Lee Yen Tai, 185 U. S. 213 ....161, 238, 481
United States v. Leo Won Tong, 132 Fed. 190 478
United States v. Louie Juen, 128 Fed. 522 478
United States v. Lucero, 1 N. M. 422 ....200, 209, 553
United States v. Luyties, 130 Fed. 333 ....124, 501
United States v. Lynch, 137 U. S. 280 276
United States v. Lynde, 11 Wall. 632 ....345, 365, 366, 491, 571, 631
United States v. Mills' Heirs, 12 Pet. 215 ....572, 632
United States v. Miranda, 16 Pet. 153 ....573, 632, 633
United States v. M. J. Dalton Co., 151 Fed. 144 484
United States v. Moreno, 1 Wall. 400 ....202, 550, 626
United States v. Moy Yim, 115 Fed. 652 478
United States v. Mrs. Gue Lim, 176 U. S. 459 478
United States v. Ng Park Tan, 86 Fed. 605 476
United States v. Norton, 97 U. S. 164 347
United States v. Old Settlers, 148 U. S. 427 ....275, 368
United States v. Palmer, 3 Wheat. 610 366
United States v. Percheman, 7 Pet. 51 ....162, 389, 394, 569, 571, 630
United States v. Philadelphia & New Orleans, 11 How. 609......
    .... 493, 571, 624, 631
United States v. Piaza, 133 Fed. 998 531
United States v. Pico, 23 How. 321 ....366, 550, 627
United States v. Pin Kwan, 100 Fed. 609 475
United States v. Quimby, 4 Wall. 408 533
United States v. Rauscher, 119 U. S. 407 ....144, 233, 376, 467, 527
United States v. Repentigny, 5 Wall. 211 ....514, 517, 625

United States v. Reynes, 9 How. 127...........................
.... 345, 348, 349, 365, 366, 491, 492, 493, 622, 624
United States v. Rice, 4 Wheat. 246 392
United States v. Rio Grande Irrigation Co., 174 U. S. 690; 184 U.
S. 416 549
United States v. Robbins, Fed. Cases No. 16175 ....230, 523
United States v. Rodgers, 150 U. S. 249 ....264, 523, 526
United States v. Rose, 23 How. 262 ....551, 627
United States v. Sandoval, 167 U. S. 278 ....551, 628
United States v. Santa Fe, 165 U. S. 675 ....551, 628
United States v. Sayward, 160 U. S. 493 269
United States v. Schooner Peggy, 1 Cranch 103 ....160, 161, 345, 490
United States v. Sibbald, 10 Pet. 313 ....343, 345, 569, 572, 632
United States v. Sing Lee, 71 Fed. 680 476
United States v. Sun, 76 Fed. 450 477
United States v. Sutter, 21 How. 170 ....551, 627
United States v. Tartar Chemical Co., 127 Fed. 944 ....124, 501
United States v. Texas, 143 U. S. 621 ....365, 434
United States v. Texas, 162 U. S. 1 ....377, 378, 383, 570
United States v. Trumbull, 48 Fed. 94 ....414, 470
United States v. Watts, 14 Fed. 130 527
United States v. Weld, 127 U. S. 51 534
United States v. Wiggins, 14 Pet. 334 ....493, 572, 623, 632
United States v. Winans, 198 U. S. 371 399
United States v. Wong Ah Gah, 94 Fed. 831 476
United States v. Wong Ah Hung, 62 Fed. 1005 475
United States v. Wong Kim Ark, 169 U. S. 649 200
United States v. Yee Gee You, 152 Fed. 157 477
United States v. Yong Yew, 83 Fed. 832 476
United States v. Yorba, 1 Wall. 412 ....366, 382, 550, 627
United States, ex rel. Buccino, v. Williams, 190 Fed. 897 ....260, 544
United States, ex rel. Falco, v. Williams, 191 Fed. 1001 ....260, 544
University v. Miller, 14 N. C. 188 ....33, 250, 368, 429, 559, 600
Urzua, In re, 188 Fed. 540 556

Valk v. United States, 29 C. Cls. 62; 168 U. S. 703 ....505, 614
Vallejos v. United States, 35 C. Cls. 489 ....209, 552
Van Aernam, Ex parte, 3 Blatchf. 160 531
Vance v. Vandercook Co., 170 U. S. 468 269
Vandervelpen, In re, 14 Blatchf. 137 ....352, 469
Van Dissel & Co. v. Venezuela, Ralston's Rept. 568 380
Van Hoven, Ex parte, 4 Dill. 411, 415 ....469, 556
Van Reynegan v. Bolton, 95 U. S. 33 ....551, 627
Venus, The Brig, 27 C. Cls. 116 488
Vilas v. City of Manila, 220 U. S. 345 ....202, 395, 579, 633
Virginia v. Tennessee, 148 U. S. 503 ....146, 148
Virginia v. West Virginia, 11 Wall. 39 146
Volant, The, 5 Wall. 179 244
Von Thodorovich v. Franz Josef Beneficial Assn., 154 Fed. 911 468

Wadge, In re, 15 Fed. 864; 16 Fed. 332 532
Walker v. Baird (1892), App. Cas. 491 292
Wan Shing v. United States, 140 U. S. 424 473
Ware v. Hylton, 3 Dall. 199 ....21, 41, 154, 156, 246, 368, 514
Washburn, In re, 3 Wheeler's Cr. Cas. 473 ....230, 523
Waters-Pierce Oil Co. v. Texas, 212 U. S. 112 275
Watson v. Donnelly, 28 Barb. 653 ....248, 250, 521, 598
Watts v. United States, 1 Wash. Ter. 288 107
Watts, United States v., 14 Fed. 130 527
Weld, United States v., 127 U. S. 51 534
Welhaven, The, 55 Fed. 80 ....235, 583

West Chicago R. R. Co. v. Chicago, 201 U. S. 506 274
Weston v. Charleston, 2 Pet. 449 269
West Rand Central Gold Mining Co. v. Rex (1905), L. R., 2 K. B.
  391 425
Wharton v. Wise, 153 U. S. 155 142
Whitney v. Robertson, 124 U. S. 190 ....161, 162, 196, 406, 465, 485, 611
Whitten v. Tomlinson, 160 U. S. 231 ....272, 275
Wiegand, In re, 14 Blatchf. 370 432
Wieland v. Renner, 65 How. Pr. Repts. 245 ....251, 433, 511, 604
Wiggins, United States v., 14 Pet. 334 ....493, 572, 623, 632
Wilcke v. Wilcke, 102 Iowa 173 ....433, 509, 601
Wildenhus's Case, 120 U. S. 1 ....236, 272, 470
William, The Brig, 23 C. Cls. 201 ....425, 441, 486
Williams v. Gibbes, 17 How. 239; 20 How. 535 549
Williams v. Heard, 140 U. S. 529 534
Williams v. Suffolk Insurance Co., 13 Pet. 415 366
Williams, United States, ex rel. Buccino v., 190 Fed. 897 ....260, 544
Williams, United States, ex rel. Falco v., 191 Fed. 1001 ....260, 544
Wilson v. Blackbird Creek Marsh Co., 2 Pet. 245 274
Wilson v. Shaw, 204 U. S. 24 ....200, 399, 559
Wilson v. Wall, 6 Wall. 83 ....364, 494, 625
Winans, United States v., 198 U. S. 371 399
Wisconsin v. Pelican Insurance Co., 127 U. S. 265 269
Wolsey v. Chapman, 101 U. S. 755 93
Wong Ah Gah, United States v., 94 Fed. 831 476
Wong Ah Hung, United States v., 62 Fed. 1005 475
Wong Fong v. United States, 77 Fed. 168 476
Wong Kim Ark, United States v., 169 U. S. 649 200
Wong Wai v. Williamson, 103 Fed. 1 ....258, 420
Wong Yung Quy, In re, 6 Sawy. 237, 442 ....264, 471
Worcester v. Georgia, 6 Pet. 515 399
Wo Tai Li, In re, 48 Fed. 668 478
Wright v. Henkel, 190 U. S. 40 ....399, 535
Wunderle v. Wunderle, 144 Ill. 40 ....250, 251, 399, 502, 504, 593

Yard v. Cramond, 5 Rawle 18 574
Yeaker's Heirs v. Yeaker's Heirs, 4 Metc. 33 ....250, 345, 586
Yee Gee You, United States v., 152 Fed. 157 477
Yew Bing Hi, In re, 128 Fed. 319 478
Yick Wo v. Hopkins, 118 U. S. 356 ....256, 265, 421, 422, 479, 607
Yong Yew, United States v., 83 Fed. 832 476
Yorba, United States v., 1 Wall. 412 ....366, 382, 550, 627
Yordi v. Nolte, 215 U. S. 227 ....528, 556

Zadiz v. Baldwin, 166 U. S. 485 275
Zeiger v. Pennsylvania R. R. Co., 158 Fed. 809; 151 Fed. 348..259, 542, 615
Zentner, Ex parte, 188 Fed. 344 ....432, 504

CHAPTER I.

INTRODUCTION.

§1. Organs of Government Entrusted with Treaty Making.—
Napoleon III, of France, and Francis Joseph, of Austria, each
enjoying sovereign powers, met in person at Villafranca, July
11, 1859, and agreed upon preliminary articles of peace. A treaty
so concluded is immediately upon its signature perfect and complete as an international compact. The articles of the Holy
Alliance of September 26, 1815, were likewise signed in person
by the Emperors of Austria and Russia and the King of Prussia.
The treaties concluded at Tilsit, July 7, 1807, although not signed
by the sovereigns themselves, embodied the results of the personal conference on the Niemen between Napoleon I and the
Emperor Alexander. For states, other than those in which
the sovereign power is legally centered in a single person, to meet
in their sovereign capacities is quite inconceivable. The organization and powers of the agencies through which states enter
into treaties are defined by their fundamental laws, or constitutions. This delegation of power by the state, in first instance, is
final, and an obligation constitutionally contracted is binding on
the entire state. The determination of the agencies in the different
states entrusted with this power is the first step in a work on
treaty making.

§2. The Treaty-making Power of a State.—It is a principle
of international law that a sovereign state is restrained only by
self-limitations or by such as result from a recognition of like
powers in others. Accordingly, the full power to enter into
treaties is an attribute of every such state, as likewise a limitation
on its exercise is a first mark of dependence. It does not follow
that the power resides unrestricted in the regularly constituted
treaty-making organ. A subject with which it assumes to deal
may be entrusted by the state to another organ of government,
and the consent of that organ may be necessary to the exercise of
the power. In a federal system of government, the subject may
possibly be reserved to the several States or even to the people,
but the power nevertheless exists, and the presumption always is,
if there is no express limitation to the contrary, that the state

intended that the power vested in the regularly constituted organ should extend to all the usual subjects of international regulation, and should be sufficient to meet any exigency arising from contact with other states.

§3. **Powers of the Negotiators and the Right of Ratification.** —The powers of the special agents—for it is seldom practicable for the treaty-making organs of two states to meet in conference —appointed to conduct and conclude negotiations, are defined by special commissions and instructions. By the early writers on international law, living at a time when the theory of personal sovereignty generally obtained, and the negotiator was the immediate agent of the sovereign, the rule of the Roman law, that the principal is bound by the agent acting within his powers,[1] was applied to treaty negotiations.[2] The advantages of entrusting full and general powers to the negotiators, and the importance of the trust, have led recent writers quite generally to admit the right of ratification, even if no express reservation be made in the treaty or full powers. A reservation of this right is now by the practice of nations to be read into the full powers of the negotiator. A right of ratification implies a right of refusal. Accordingly, the qualification imposed by some writers, that, when the negotiator has acted within his powers and specific instructions, ratification may be refused only for real and substantial reasons, is of good faith only; and it can have no application unless the powers and instructions of the plenipotentiary are given by the full treaty-making organ of the state. In the United States, for instance, a treaty is regularly negotiated on the authority of the President, while it can be ratified only with the authorization of the Senate. The plenipotentiary, commissioned and instructed by the President alone, acts on the authority not of the treaty-making power, but on that of a separate branch of it only.

The maxim of the early Roman law, "qui cum alio contrahit, vel est vel debet esse non ignarus condicionis ejus,"[3] applies in the making of treaties. To know the powers of him with whom negotiations are conducted requires a knowledge not only of his

---

1 See Pothier, Obligations, Pt. I, c. I, Art. V, §4, (Evans' translation, I, 47).

2 See in this relation Gentilis, Bk. III, c. XIV; Grotius, Bk.II, c. XI, §12; Pufendorf, Bk. III, c. IX, §2; Vattel, Bk. II, c. XII, §156.

3 Ulpian, Digest of Justinian, Lib. L, Tit. XVII (De diversis regulis juris antiqui), 19.

special mandate and powers, the exhibition of which may always be demanded before the opening of the negotiations, but also of the fundamental law or constitution of the state which he professes to represent, and of any limitations which may result from an incomplete sovereignty. Many instances are recorded of delays in negotiations as the result of defective powers. The proceedings of the Congress of Westphalia afford an early instance. The powers of the French envoys were considered defective because they gave authority merely to negotiate but not to sign, and were signed by the minor king without any reference to the regency.[4] A recent instance is found in the negotiations for peace between China and Japan in 1895, in which the powers first presented by the plenipotentiaries on the part of China were unsatisfactory to the Japanese government.[5] The protocol of August 12, 1898, between the United States and Spain, was signed by Mr. Cambon, on the part of Spain, in virtue of special powers received by telegraph, with the understanding that documentary full powers in regular and due form would later be communicated to the United States.[6]

§4. **Essentials of the Validity of Treaties.**—Treaties are contracts between states. To their validity it is essential that the contracting parties have power over the subject-matter, that consent be reciprocally and regularly given, and that the object of the treaty be possible and lawful under the accepted principles of international law.

§5. **Reality of Consent.**—Consent is considered as freely given in the case of treaties under conditions that might render contracts between private individuals voidable. In the negotiation of treaties between independent states, the parties are supposed to be on the same footing with equal opportunities of ascertaining the facts.[7] Treaties of peace cannot be avoided by the unsuccess-

---

4　Garden, Traités de Paix, I, 140.

5　For. Rel., 1894, App., I, 97.

6　The documentary full powers, dated August 11, 1898, were communicated by Mr. Cambon to the Secretary of State, August 30, 1898. For. Rel., 1898, pp. 825-827.

7　"If *suppressio veri* abrogated treaties to the extent it abrogates contracts, few treaties would stand." Wharton, Int. Law Digest, II, 36.

During the negotiations leading up to the Webster-Ashburton treaty, a map supposed to be very favorable to the British contention as to the northeastern boundary was unearthed by Jared Sparks in his private re-ful party on the ground that concessions have been extorted by threat of a continuation of hostilities. This rule must prevail so long as it is recognized that rights can be acquired through the use of force.[8] "It was her own free choice to prefer a certain and immediate loss, but of limited extent, to an evil of a more dreadful nature, which, though yet at some distance, she had but too great reason to apprehend."[9] Phillimore draws a possible analogy in this respect to a private contract entered into to avoid, or to stop, litigation, which, although the party was induced to enter into it through the apprehension of delay, expense, and the uncertain event of a lawsuit, is nevertheless binding.[10] But force or intimidation applied to the person of the negotiator, in whom is vested the full and final treaty-making power of the state—and unless the power is thus fully and finally vested, the right of ratification renders the use of force futile—vitiates the act. Such a case is hardly to be contemplated at the present time.[11]

searches in Paris. It was shown by Mr. Webster to the commissioners from Maine, but not to Lord Ashburton. Subsequently, it became public by being sent to the Senate. In the midst of the popular outcry which followed in England, an English diarist records (Greville, February 9, 1843): "At the same time, our successive Governments are much to blame in not having ransacked the archives at Paris, for they could certainly have done for a public object what Jared Sparks did for a private one, and a little trouble would have put them in possession of whatever that repository contained." Lord Ashburton, in a communication of February 7, 1843, said: "The public are very busy with the question whether Webster was bound in honor to damage his own case by telling all. I have put this to the consciences of old diplomatists without getting a satisfactory answer. My own opinion is that in this respect no reproach can fairly be made." Id., II, 177, 180. Not only was the map a doubtful piece of evidence, but there existed at the time in the British foreign office the veritable copy of the Mitchell map, with the red line, used in the negotiations of 1782. Moore, Int. Law Digest, V, 719.

8 See the decision of The Hague Tribunal of Arbitration of 1903, sustaining the claim of the "war" powers to preferential treatment in the payment of their claims against Venezuela, Penfield's Report, 95, 984.

9 Vattel, Bk. IV, c. IV, §37. See also Grotius, Bk. II, c. XVII, §19.

10 Int. Law, (2 ed.), II, 71, 72.

11 Text writers, with great uniformity, cite as an instance the concessions extorted from Ferdinand VII at Bayonne. As to the circumstances under which the treaty was signed by Santa Anna, dictator of Mexico, after his capture at San Jacinto, April 21, 1836, in which he acknowledged the independence of Texas, see annual message of President Polk, December 8, 1846, Richardson, Messages and Papers of the Presidents, IV, 480. As to the treaty of alliance between Japan and

§6. Form.—The importance of the subject-matter, the frequent changes in the personnel of the agencies through which treaties are concluded, the inability to confirm by witness the utterances of a state, render it even more necessary that treaties between nations should be carefully expressed in writing than in case of contracts between private individuals.[12] They often run for long periods of time. In a return of the most-favored-nation clauses in treaties of commerce and navigation (a class of treaties not of the most permanent character) between Great Britain and other powers, in force, January 1, 1907, there are included treaties signed with Sweden, April 11, 1654, July 17, 1656, October 21, 1661, and February 5, 1766, and with various other powers during the seventeenth and eighteenth centuries.[13] Although no particular form is essential to the validity, it is customary in case of formal treaties to make out and sign under seal as many counterparts as there are parties, one counterpart to be retained by each. In case of two parties only, which have no common language, each counterpart is regularly made out in the languages of both. The texts may appear on separate sheets but more often they appear in parallel columns or on opposite pages, the text in the language of the party by which the counterpart is to be retained occupying the left hand column or page. Likewise, with the development of the principle of the equality in law of states, precedence in the enumeration of the negotiators in the preamble and in the signatures is given in the particular counterpart to the state by which it is to be retained.[14] Otherwise the two instru-

Korea, concluded at Seoul, August 26, 1894, see Douglas, Europe and the Far East, 307, 310; For. Rel., 1894, App. I, 41, 56, 93.

12 F. de Martens cites, as an instance of an oral treaty, the alliance of 1697 entered into at Pillau between Peter the Great, of Russia, and Frederick III, Elector of Brandenburg. Droit Int. (Léo's translation), I, §111.

13 Parl. Papers, Com. No. 3, (1907) Cd. 3395. Prof. Nys refers to a treaty between the King of Babylon and the King of Egypt, concluded in the fifteenth century before our era, which was involved in a controversy of recent date in the Near East. Le Droit Int., III, 18.

14 For the development of the custom of the alternat, see G. F. Von Martens, Law of Nations, (Cobbett's translation), 140. "France and Great Britain established it as a rule, in 1456, 1551, 1559, to yield the precedence to each alternately." Id., 140. See, also, Phillimore, Int. Law (2 ed.), II, 59. Article VII of the Regulation signed by the plenipotentiaries of the powers represented at the Vienna Congress, March 19, 1815, and which forms Annex XVII to the general treaty signed June 9, 1815, provides that in acts or treaties between several powers which admit the al-

ments are supposed to be identical. In case of several parties, having various languages, the instrument is often drawn up in only one language, customarily in Europe, the French, formerly the Latin. Precedence is given in the particular counterpart to the party by which it is to be retained, the order of the other contracting parties being alphabetical or determined by lot. If the parties are numerous, not infrequently one original only is signed, which is deposited at a place specified in the treaty, and each of the contracting parties accepts, in lieu of an original, a duly certified copy.[15] The ratification of each party is not only attached to the instrument retained by it, but, for the assurance of the other contracting party or parties, is also attached to an exact copy of the retained instrument, which is exchanged for a similar copy from the other party, or, in case of several parties, is deposited at such place as is designated in the treaty. Accordingly, each state, in case of two parties only, has regularly not only the original counterpart with its own ratification attached, but a copy of the counterpart retained by the other party with the latter's ratification attached. A protocol signed by the plenipotentiaries by whom the exchange is made records the act.[16] Although these formalities are usually observed, a treaty no less perfect may be effected by a mere exchange of notes, or declarations, if authorized by the full treaty-making organs of the two states with power over the subject-matter. The denomination of the instrument is not an essential. The term protocol is regularly applied to a record, or minute, of the proceedings of a conference between plenipotentiaries,[17] or of an agreement between plenipotentiaries as to the result of their negotiations or as to the basis of future negotiations. It is also often used to denominate an ex-

ternity the order to be observed in the signatures of ministers shall be decided by ballot. The general treaty was signed by the plenipotentiaries, alphabetically according to states. Hertslet's Map of Europe by Treaty, I, 63.

15 The various conventions signed at The Hague Conferences of 1899 and 1907, the Geneva Conference of 1906, and the Algeciras Conference of 1906, may be noted as examples.

16 As to the duties of the college of fecials, and the forms observed by the early Romans in the conclusion of treaties of alliance and peace, see Mommsen, Manuel des antiquités romaines, VII, Droit public romain (Traduction de l'allemand par Girard), 209; Larivière, Traités conclus par Rome, 23, 29; Hill, History of European Diplomacy, I, 10; Phillipson, Int. Law and Custom of Ancient Greece and Rome, I, 375-419.

17 The term procès-verbal is equally applicable.

planatory note made and attached to a treaty by the negotiators. A modus vivendi is a temporary regulation of a matter, pending negotiations for a permanent settlement.[18] The words treaty and convention have come to be used without any clear distinction. "The terms are synonymous, and even the usage of calling the more important acts treaties, the less important ones conventions, is far from being uniformly followed."[19] There are certain agree-

[18] See Foster, Practice of Diplomacy, 246, 324.

[19] Westlake, Int. Law (2 ed.), I, 290. It appears from an examination of the treaties and conventions of the United States, formally ratified and proclaimed during the period 1778-1909, that those acts which cover a variety of subjects, as for instance, those of general amity, commerce and navigation, of peace, or of the character of those concluded with Great Britain, August 9, 1842, and May 8, 1871, have been denominated in the text (as distinguished from an editorial caption) of the instruments themselves more often as treaties than as conventions; and that those which relate to a single specific subject, as for instance, that of consuls, extradition, naturalization, pecuniary claims, arbitration of future differences, import duties, tenure and disposition of property, droit d'aubaine and emigration taxes, patents, or trade-marks, have in like manner been denominated more often as conventions than as treaties. The relative numbers may, it is believed, be given approximately as follows:

	Treaty.	Convention.	Terms Used Interchangeably.
Alliance,	1		
Peace,	4		
Amity, commerce and navigation,	64	9	18
Consuls,		12	1
Extradition,	17	29	10
Naturalization,	1	16	1
Pecuniary claims,	1	36	
Abolition of droit d'aubaine and emigration taxes,		5	
General arbitration,		20	
Tenure and disposition of property,		5	
Commercial reciprocity,	1	5	
Acqusition of territory, (not including treaties of peace),	4	1	
Trade-marks,		10	

With respect to various other subjects, the numbers seem to be nearly equal. The term convention has been used almost exclusively in describing those important acts, to which the United States is a party, for the establishment as between a large number of states of uniform rules of conduct as to the particular subject-matter of the agreement, such for instance as those concerning the amelioration of the condition of the wounded in

ments, which are entered into in virtue of an implied delegation of power as incidental to an official station and not in the regular exercise of the treaty-making power of the state. Such are, for instance, truces or armistices for the temporary suspension of military operations, cartels for the regulation of direct intercourse between belligerents, especially for the exchange of prisoners, and capitulations for the surrender of besieged fortresses. Such agreements are necessarily within the discretion of those entrusted with the power to conduct military operations.[20] Concordats are agreements entered into by the Pope, not as a territorial sovereign, but as head of the Catholic Church, and are accordingly not to be classed as international treaties.[21]

§7. **Sanction.**—The usual parties to treaties are sovereign states over which no tribunal, except by their own consent, can exercise jurisdiction. Although the obligation of a treaty is, accordingly, not perfect for want of a tribunal in which it can of right be enforced, it has such sanctions as impel observance of a recognized right under international law, since a violation of a treaty engagement is a violation of such right.[22] "He who violates

time of war signed at Geneva in 1864 and 1906, uniformity in weights and measures signed at Paris in 1875, protection of industrial property signed at Paris in 1883, protection of submarine cables signed at Paris in 1884, exchange of official documents and scientific and literary publications signed at Brussels in 1886, publication of customs tariffs signed at Brussels in 1890, protection of literary and artistic property signed at Mexico in 1902, international sanitary measures signed at Paris in 1903 and at Washington in 1905, the exemption of hospital ships in time of war from payment of duties and taxes signed at The Hague in 1904, the creation of an international institute of agriculture signed at Rome in 1905, and the importation of liquors into Africa signed at Brussels in 1906, and the various agreements signed at the two Peace Conferences at The Hague in 1899 and 1907, except the one on the lauuching of projectiles and explosives, which was denominated a declaration.

20 Wheaton, Elements of Int. Law, §254; Twiss, Law of Nations (Peace 2 ed.), §251.

21 See Hall, Int. Law (6 ed.), 317.

22 Pothier includes under perfect obligations both civil (actionable) and natural (non-actionable). Obligations (Evans' translation), I, 2. Vattel says: "As the engagements of a treaty impose on the one hand a perfect obligation, they produce on the other a perfect right." Bk. II, c. XII, §164. The civil obligation of the Roman law was one which could be enforced judicially, whereas a natural obligation could not be. Pothier, I, 108; Savigny, Obligations in Roman Law (Brown's epitome), §7. This distinction was the result of the difference in the rights under the jus civile

his treaties, violates at the same time the law of nations; for, he disregards the faith of treaties,—that faith which the law of nations declares sacred; and, so far as depends on him, he renders it vain and ineffectual. Doubly guilty, he does an injury to his ally, he does an injury to all nations, and inflicts a wound on the great society of mankind."[23]

To insure execution and observance, it was customary at one time to give to important treaties a special sanction by oath, the pledge of securities, the delivery of hostages, or a guarantee. The oath was but a survival of the religious ceremonies of the ancient peoples with which the conclusion of a peace or an alliance was usually accompanied, such as the pouring of libations, the offering of sacrifices, and the invocation of the deities to witness the transaction, with an imprecation for their vengeance in case of violation of the compact.[24] In the treaty of peace concluded between the Athenians and Lacedæmonians in 421 B. C., it was provided that the Athenians should bind themselves by oath to the Lacedæmonians and their allies, city by city; and that the Lacedæmonians and their allies should bind themselves by a similar oath to the Athenians. The oath was to be renewed annually by both parties; and pillars were to be erected at Olympia, Delphi, and the Isthmus, at Athens in the Acropolis, and at Lacedæmon in the temple of Apollo at Amyclæ.[25] In the treaty of alliance concluded in 420 B. C. between the Athenians and the Argives, Mantineans, and Eleans, and their allies, it was likewise provided that each party should swear to the peace; that the oath should be taken at Athens by the senate and the home magistrates, at Argos by the senate, the council of eighty and the artynæ, at Mantinea

---

and the jus gentium; and the term natural obligation has come to have quite a different meaning in the English. "Where there is a perfect obligation, there is a right coupled with a remedy, i. e., an appropriate process of law by which the authority of a competent court can be set in motion to enforce the right." Pollock, Contracts (8th ed.), 682.

23 Vattel, Bk. II, c. XV, §221.

24 See for early use of the oath in private contracts, Pothier, Obligations Pt. I, c. I, Art. VIII, (Evans' translation, I, 63); Pollock and Maitland, History of English Law (2 ed.), II, 188, et seq.

25 Barbeyrac, Histoire des Anciens Traités, Corps Diplomatique, Supplement, Pt. I, p. 145; Thucydides, Bk. V, 18. (Jowett's translation (1900), II, 117). A treaty of alliance concluded during the same period between the Athenians and the Lacedæmonians contained similar provisions. Id., Bk. V, 23. (Jowett's translation (1900), II, 120).

by the demiurgi, the senate, and the other magistrates, and at Elis
by the demiurgi, the magistrates and the six hundred; and that
the articles of the treaty and the oaths should be inscribed, by the
Athenians on a stone column in the Acropolis, by the Argives on a
similar column in the temple of Apollo, and by the Mantineans
in the temple of Zeus, in the market places. The form of the oath
was prescribed in the treaty. The oaths were to be renewed by
the Athenians going to Elis, Mantinea and Argos thirty days before the Olympic games, and by the Argives, Mantineans and
Eleans going to Athens ten days before the feast of the Pana-
thenæa.[26] In treaties between states with absolute sovereigns,
it was regularly provided that the oath should be taken by the
respective sovereigns in the presence of such persons as the other
might designate. The treaty of peace and alliance between Elizabeth, Queen of England, and Charles IX, King of France, signed
at Troies, April 11, 1564, provided, for instance, that each should,
as soon as requested by the duly authorized ambassadors sent by
the other for that purpose, swear, on the Holy Gospels, and in
the presence of the ambassadors, faithfully to observe the provisions of the treaty.[27] A common form in treaties, to which a
sovereign of the Catholic faith was a party, is found in the treaty
of the Pyrenees between the crowns of France and Spain, signed
November 7, 1659. The treaty provides that, after the exchange
of the ratifications, "the said most Christian king, as soon as it
may be, and in the presence of such person or persons as the said
lord the Catholick king shall be pleased to appoint, shall solemnly
swear upon the Cross, the Holy Evangelists, the Canons of the
Mass, and upon his honour, to observe and perform fully, really
and bona fide, the whole contents of the article of the present
treaty. And the like shall be done also, as soon as possibly may be,
by the said lord the Catholick king, in the presence of such person
or persons as the said lord the most Christian king shall be pleased

---

26 Barbeyrac, 153; Thucydides, Bk. V, 47, (Jowett's translation (1900),
II, 141).

27 Collection of Treatys (2 ed., 1732), II, 63. Similar provisions are
found in the treaties between Queen Elizabeth and Charles IX of France,
signed April 29, 1572, (Id., II, 80), between James I of England, and
Louis XIII of France, signed August 29, 1610, (Id., II, 176), and between
Charles I of England, and Phillip IV of Spain, signed November 15, 1630.
(Id., II, 291). See, for the form of the oath, Id., II, 291. See also Id.,
II, 146; III, 79.

to appoint." Their majesties met in person for this purpose, June 6, 1660, on the Isle of Pheasants in the river Bidassoa.[28] The oath being necessarily personal, its use diminished with the development of the distinction between the state and the individual monarch, and came to an end as between states of Europe with the treaty of alliance between France and Switzerland of May 28, 1777, which was solemnly confirmed by oath in the Cathedral at Solothurn.[29]

An instance of the use of sureties is found in a treaty of amity and commerce between Henry VII, of England, and Philip, Archduke of Austria, signed February 24, 1495, in which it was provided that one archbishop, two bishops, one marquis, five earls, one viscount, one prior, and the mayors and aldermen of seventeen of the principal cities of England, should be joined as sureties on the part of the King of England.[30] Again, in the treaty between Elizabeth, Queen of England, and Henry II, King of France, signed April 2, 1559, for the restitution by the latter of the town of Calais, it was agreed that, for the more safe and certain performance, the King of France should give, as soon as possible, seven or eight foreign merchants, not his subjects nor under his jurisdiction, but living without his kingdom and dominions, sufficiently rich and responsible, who should oblige themselves to pay the sum of five hundred thousand "golden crowns of the sun" to the Queen of England, or her heirs and successors in the kingdom of England, which sum should be in place and instead of a penalty, in case the King of France, his heirs or successors, should refuse to perform or delay beyond due time the restitution.[31] Moreover, the King of France agreed to give certain persons, prominent officers of his kingdom, as hostages, to be held until the sureties had been obtained. The last instance of the exaction of hostages as between the powers of Europe is af-

---

28 Art. CXXIV. Collection of Treatys (2 ed.), I, 98. See for procès-verbal containing the oath of the French King, Id., II, Sup. p. 21. See, for other instances, the treaties of peace between the same parties signed at Aix la Chapelle, May 2, 1668 (Id., I, 161), at Nimeguen, September 17, 1678 (Id., I, 233), and at Ryswick, September 20, 1697, (Id., I, 345).

29 Martens, Recueil de Traités (1 ed.), I, 618. History affords many instances of absolution from the oath by the Pope. See Vattel, Bk. II, c. XV, §223; Phillimore (2 ed.), II, 78.

30 Collection of Treatys (2 ed.), II, 21.

31 Arts. IX and X. Collection of Treatys (2 ed.), II, 52.

forded by the treaty of peace signed at Aix la Chapelle, October 18, 1748, under which Great Britain engaged to deliver two persons of rank and consideration as hostages for the restitution of Cape Breton and other captures that might have been made in the Indies.[32] In more modern times possession of territory has been retained as security for faithful performance. The treaty of peace between France and Germany signed at Frankfort, May 10, 1871, provided for the gradual evacuation by the German troops of certain departments then under military occupation, as the payments of the indemnity stipulated for in the treaty were made. The last installment was paid by France, September 5, 1873, and the last German troops passed the French frontier, September 16, 1873.[33] Likewise, in the treaty of peace between China and Japan signed at Shimonoseki, April 17, 1895, provision was made for the temporary occupation by the military forces of Japan of Wei-hai-wei, as security for faithful performance.[34] In the treaties of peace concluded in 1866 with Württemberg, Baden, Bavaria, Hesse-Darmstadt and Saxony, respectively, Prussia required the deposit of certain State obligations as security for the payment of the war indemnities as stipulated for in the treaties.[35].

An early instance of the use of the guarantee is found in the treaty of peace between the Emperor and States of Germany and the King of France signed at Münster in Westphalia, October 24, 1648. It was agreed that all parties should be obliged to defend and protect all and every article of the peace; that, if any point should be violated, the offended should "before all things exhort the offender not to come to any hostility, submitting the cause to a friendly composition, or the ordinary proceedings of justice"; that, if for the space of three years the difference could not be terminated by any of these means, all and every one should be obliged to join the injured party and assist him with

32 Jenkinson's Treaties, II, 381. Hostages have however since been required in concluding treaties with unorganized peoples. The United States has for instance requested them of Indian tribes on concluding treaties with them.

33 Art. VII. Article III of the preliminary treaty signed at Versailles, February 26, 1871. Hertslet's Map of Europe by Treaty, III, 1915, 1958.

34 Art. VIII.

35 Hertslet's Map of Europe by Treaty, III, 1703, 1708, 1712, 1730, 1773.

counsel and force to repel the injury, "being first advertised by the injured that gentle means and justice prevailed nothing; but without prejudice, nevertheless, to every one's jurisdiction, and the administration of justice conformable to the laws of each prince and state."[36] The obligations of the guarantee of this treaty formed the basis for the intervention of Austria and Prussia in the French Revolution in 1792.[37] Recent history records many instances of the use of the guarantee as a sanction for the observance of treaties. Under the treaty of Vienna of June 9, 1815, Austria, France, Great Britain, and Russia undertook to guarantee to the King of Prussia, his descendants and successors, the possession of the territory ceded under the treaty by Saxony to Prussia.[38] The engagements entered into at Vienna as to the perpetual neutrality of Switzerland were specifically guaranteed in an act signed at Paris, November 20, 1815, by Austria, France, Great Britain, Prussia, and Russia.[39] The obligations of this guarantee have since been recognized by the parties on various occasions. By treaties between Austria, Great Britain, Prussia, and Russia, signed at Paris, November 20, 1815, those powers engaged to maintain, with the whole of their forces if necessary, the conditions of peace, as set forth in the treaty with France of even date, especially those provisions by which Napoleon Bonaparte and his family were forever excluded from supreme power in France. Nevertheless, Prince Louis Napoleon Bonaparte was proclaimed President of the French Republic in 1848, and Emperor of the French in 1852, and was recognized as such by the parties to the treaties of 1815.[40] A treaty between Belgium and the Netherlands, signed at London, April 19, 1839, for the establishment of permanent relations between them, in which Belgium was recognized as an independent and perpetually neutral state, was placed under the guarantee of Austria, France, Great Britain, Prussia and Russia by a treaty entered into on the same day between these five powers on the one part, and Belgium on the other.[41] In view of the obligations as a guarantor under this

36 Arts. CXXIII and CXXIV. Collection of Treatys (2 ed.), I, 36.
37 Wheaton, History of Law of Nations, 346; Phillimore, Int. Law (2 ed.), II, 83.
38 Art. XVII. Hertslet's Map of Europe by Treaty, I, 223.
39 Id., I, 370.
40 Id., I, 342, 372, 373, 375.
41 Id., II, 997.

4

treaty, Great Britain, during the Franco-Prussian war in 1870, entered into separate agreements with France and Prussia by which she engaged, in case either party should violate the neutrality of Belgium as guaranteed under the treaty, to use her naval and military forces to insure its observance.[42] And it was on the basis of her obligations under the treaty of 1839 that Great Britain became a participant in the present war. Again, under a treaty signed at Paris, April 15, 1856, Austria, France and Great Britain undertook to guarantee, jointly and severally, the independence and integrity of the Ottoman Empire as established in the general treaty signed March 30, 1856.[43] Under the usual treaty of guarantee of the past the ultimate determination of the casus foederis has been with the guarantor. As a condition precedent to a satisfactory guarantee of treaty engagements, even a collective general guarantee by all powers not parties to the engagements, it is essential that either party may of right by the same compulsion cause the question of the breach and of the duty of the guarantor to be submitted for determination to an unprejudiced international tribunal. A guarantee of this character has yet to be established. In the meantime, it is in the desire of each nation to maintain its standing with other nations that treaties have their chief sanction. "The sanction of the positive law of nations is found in the isolation of the state which disregards it."[44] "Every state has to execute the obligations incurred by treaty bona fide, and is urged thereto by the ordinary sanctions of international law in regard to observance of treaty obligations. Such sanctions are, for instance, appeal to public opinion, publication of correspondence, censure by parliamentary vote, demand for arbitration with the odium attendant on a refusal to arbitrate, rupture of relations, reprisals, etc."[45] "Contracts between nations, like contracts between individuals, should be faithfully executed, even though the sword in the one case, and the law in the other, did not compel it. Honest nations like

42 Id., III, 1887, 1890.

43 Id., II, 1254, 1281. See for guarantees of similar character, as to Greece, treaties of May 7, 1832 and July 13, 1863, and as to Luxemburg, treaty of May 11, 1867. Id., II, 893, 895, 1545; III, 1803.

44 Twiss, Law of Nations (Peace, 2 ed.), 146.

45 Decision of The Hague Tribunal of Arbitration, in re North Atlantic Coast Fisheries, rendered, September 7, 1910. Sen. Doc. No. 870, 61st Cong., 3d Sess., I, 82.

honest men require no constraint to do justice; and though impunity and the necessity of affairs may sometimes afford temptations to pare down contracts to the measure of convenience, yet is is never done but at the expense of that esteem, and confidence, and credit which are of infinitely more worth than all the momentary advantages which such expedients can extort. But although contracting nations cannot like individuals avail themselves of courts of justice to compel performance of contracts, yet an appeal to Heaven and to arms is always in their power, and often in their inclination."[46] The pains with which nations, as well as all individuals with self-respect, attempt to explain away charges of breach of faith but shows the force of the sanction. No nation can long maintain treaty relations and a standing with other nations, and persistently refuse to abide by its promise. Seldom indeed would the sanction prove ineffectual were the fact of breach to be determined by an independent and impartial tribunal recognized as such by the parties.

46 Federal Letter to the States, prepared by John Jay, Secretary for the Department of Foreign Affairs, and agreed to in the Congress of the Confederation, April 13, 1787. Secret Journals, (1821), IV, 333.

PART I.   THE UNITED STATES.

DIVISION I.   PRIOR TO THE CONSTITUTION.

CHAPER II.

PRIOR TO THE ARTICLES OF CONFEDERATION.

§8. Independence and Treaty Making.—The advisability of entering into treaties was considered in the Continental Congress at an early date; but to many of the delegates there seemed to be an impropriety in seeking acknowledgement from a foreign power before the colonies had publicly declared their independence and taken a stand as an independent nation. During the debate, February 16, 1776, on the question of opening the ports of the colonies to foreign commerce, the conclusion of treaties for this purpose was suggested. To this suggestion, George Wythe, of Virginia, replied that, before inviting foreign powers to enter into treaties with us, we should consider in what character we should treat—"as subjects of Great Britain?—as rebels?" "No," he added, "we must declare ourselves a free people." He then moved that the colonies had a right to enter into alliances with foreign powers. An objector observed that this was independence.[1] To those, who, in the memorable debate on independence of June 8 and 10, 1776, urged the advisability of first fixing terms of treaties to be proposed to foreign powers, reply was made "that a declaration of independence alone could render it consistent with European delicacy for European powers to treat with us."[2] On June 11, 1776, the date on which the committee to draft a declaration of independence was chosen, the Congress resolved that committees to prepare a form of confederation and a plan of treaties to be proposed to foreign powers should be constituted. On the following day the two committees were chosen.[3] Closely associated then in origin are these three features of our national life—independence, union, and treaty making.

§9. Negotiation and Ratification of the First Treaties with France.—The committee to prepare a plan of treaties—John

---

[1] Brancroft, History of the United States (author's last revision), IV, 335; Works of John Adams (C. F. Adams ed.), II, 485. See also letter of December 19, 1775 from Franklin to C. W. F. Dumas; and instructions of March 3, 1776 to Silas Deane. Wharton, Dip. Cor. Am. Rev., II, 65, 76.

[2] Jefferson credits the argument to "J. Adams, Lee, Wythe and others." Writings (Ford ed.), I, 21, 23.

[3] Journals of Congress (1800 ed.), II, 197, 198.

Dickinson, Benjamin Franklin, John Adams, Benjamin Harrison, and Robert Morris—reported, July 18, 1776, articles of a treaty to be proposed to the King of France.[4] They were debated August 22 and August 27, and were finally adopted, with amendments, September 17, 1776.[5] Accompanying instructions were reported, September 10, and after debate were adopted by the Congress, September 24, 1776.[6] By these instructions certain of the articles of the proposed treaty were to be insisted upon, and others might be waived.[7] On September 26, 1776, Benjamin Franklin, Silas Deane and Thomas Jefferson were chosen commissioners to negotiate the treaty. Jefferson, being unable to serve, was, on October 22, replaced by Arthur Lee. The purpose of the mission, as expressed in the letters of credence, which had been prepared by a special committee, and adopted by the Congress September 28, was to secure the beneficial results of a trade upon equal terms between the subjects of the two countries. Full power was given "to communicate, treat, agree and conclude," the delegates of the several States in the Congress assembled promising in good faith to ratify whatsoever the commissioners should transact in the premises.[8] On December 23, 1776, the commissioners, then at Paris, addressed a communication to Count de Vergennes requesting an audience, and advising him that they were fully empowered by the Congress of the United States of America to propose and negotiate a treaty of amity and commerce.[9] More than a year late, February 6, 1778, a treaty of commerce, a treaty of alliance, and a separate and secret article were signed. The treaty of commerce followed closely the projet as adopted by the Congress, with the implied reciprocal concessions. An alliance had from the first been contemplated as a result of the negotiations. The Committee of Secret Correspondence, in notifying Silas Deane, had referred to the plan of a treaty of

4 The draft is in the handwriting of John Adams. MSS. Continental Congress Papers, No. XLVII, p. 129.

5 Journals of Congress, II, 304, 311, 339.

6 Id., II, 361. Secret Journals, II, 6, 27.

7 R. H. Lee and James Wilson had been added to the committee on August 27, 1776; and the main draft of the instructions is in the handwriting of James Wilson. MSS. Cont. Cong. Papers, No. XLVII, p. 157.

8 Secret Journals, II, 31, 32, 35.

9 For. Rel., 1877, p. 155.

commerce and alliance.[10] Subsequent instructions had been more explicit. Those adopted by the Congress, December 30, 1776, had authorized the negotiations of an article, according to which the forces of the two countries should co-operate in reducing British possessions in America.[11] But in the nature and permanent character of the alliance as negotiated, the commissioners without doubt had exceeded their instructions. The treaties were received by the Congress late on Saturday, May 2, 1778, and were unanimously ratified on the following Monday.[12]

§10. **Amendment of Text of Treaty Recommended by the Congress.**—In Article XI of the treaty of commerce, corresponding to Article XIII of the projet, it was stipulated that no export duty should ever be imposed on molasses taken by the subjects of the United States from islands of America which then were or should thereafter be under French jurisdiction. Article XII, which was not specially authorized in the projet, provided in compensation for this concession that no export duties should ever be levied on any kind of merchandise which French subjects might take from the United States and possessions, present and future, for the use of the islands furnishing the molasses. The commissioners at Paris had differed as to the relative values of these concessions. To the Congress they seemed unequal; and, on the day following the ratification, a resolution was adopted directing the commissioners at Paris to notify the French government that, although the treaties had been readily ratified, Congress was desirous that Articles XI and XII should be expunged.[13] The ratifications of the treaty as signed were exchanged, July 17, 1778,[14] but subsequently, in accordance with the directions of the Congress, the two articles were rescinded by counter-declarations.[15]

§11. **Powers of the Congress.**—No written compact of government bound the States or defined the powers of the Congress during this period. The treaties were not submitted to the States for their approval or ratification. "It has been enquired," said Mr. Justice Chase in Ware v. Hylton, "what powers Congress

10 Wharton, Dip. Cor. Am. Rev., II, 162, 181.
11 Secret Journals, II, 39.
12 Journals of Congress, IV, 183, 184.
13 Id., IV, 185.
14 Wharton, Dip. Cor. Am. Rev., II, 650.
15 Id., I, 344.

possessed from the first meeting, in September 1774, until the ratification of the Articles of Confederation on the 1st of March, 1781? It appears to me, that the powers of Congress, during that whole period, were derived from the people they represented, expressly given, through the medium of their State Conventions, or State Legislatures; or that after they were exercised they were impliedly ratified by the acquiescence and obedience of the people. * * * The powers of Congress originated from necessity, and arose out of, and were only limited by, events; or, in other words, they were revolutionary in their very nature. Their extent depended on the exigencies and necessities of public affairs. It was absolutely and indispensably necessary that Congress should possess the power of conducting the war against Great Britain, and therefore if not expressly given by all (as it was by some of the States), I do not hesitate to say, that Congress did rightfully possess such power. The authority to make war, of necessity implies the power to make peace; or the war must be perpetual. I entertain this general idea, that the several States retained all internal sovereignty; and that Congress properly possessed the great rights of external sovereignty: Among others, the right to make treaties of commerce and alliances; as with France on the 6th of February, 1778."[16]

§12. **Other Negotiations.**—During this period other commissioners were appointed to negotiate with various European states: May 7, 1777, Ralph Izard, to negotiate with the Grand Duke of Tuscany;[17] May 9, 1777, William Lee, with the Courts of Vienna and Berlin;[18] September 27, 1779, John Jay, with Spain;[19] September 27, 1779, John Adams, with Great Britain;[20] November 1, 1779, Henry Laurens, with the Netherlands;[21] December 19, 1780, Francis Dana, with Russia;[22] and December 29, 1780, John Adams, with the Netherlands.[23] The commissions, with the exception of those issued to William Lee and Ralph Izard under date of July 1, 1777, and to Francis Dana under date

16 3 Dall. 199, 231.
17 Secret Journals, II, 44.
18 Id., 45.
19 Id., 256.
20 Id., 257.
21 Id., 286.
22 Id., 357.
23 Id., 376.

of December 19, 1780,[24] gave full powers to "confer, treat, agree and conclude," the Congress promising to ratify whatsoever should be transacted in the premises.[25] The commission to Francis Dana contained a clause specifically requiring the transmission of the treaty to the Congress for final ratification.[26] No treaty resulted during this period from these missions. The instructions and the form and authority of the commissions were, before the opening of the formal negotiations, approved by the Congress, and the projet of the French treaty formed the basis of the instructions, so far as they were confined to amity and commerce.

§13. **Organs of Communication with Foreign Governments.** —The committee through which the correspondence with foreign countries was chiefly conducted had originally, November 29, 1775, been formed for the sole purpose of corresponding with friends of the colonies in Great Britain, Ireland and other parts of the world, and was known as the Committee of Secret Correspondence. On April 17, 1777, the name was changed to Committee of Foreign Affairs. On January 10, 1781, a permanent department of foreign affairs, the occupant of which was to be known as Secretary for Foreign Affairs, was created.[27]

24 Id., 49, 358.
25 Id., 258, 264, 276, 290.
26 See Livingston to Dana, May 1, 1783. Wharton, Dip. Cor. Am. Rev., VI, 403; also Secret Journals, III, 353.
27 Secret Journals, II, 5, 479, 581. See as to the defects of the committee, Wharton, Dip. Cor. Am. Rev., III, 288; IV, 105, 107.

CHAPTER III.

UNDER THE ARTICLES OF CONFEDERATION.

1. The Making.

§14. Treaty-making Power Exclusively Vested in Congress. —Of the three committees chosen by the Congress in the early part of June, 1776, the committee to prepare a draft of a declaration of independence reported, June 28, and the declaration was adopted, July 4; the committee to prepare a plan of treaties reported, July 18, and a plan was adopted, September 17; the committee to prepare a form of union reported, July 12;[1] but the plan was not adopted until November 15, 1777, and did not become effective until March 1, 1781, upon its ratification by the Maryland delegates. The provisions directly relating to treaty making in the draft as reported, July 12, 1776, and in the Articles of Confederation as finally adopted, were essentially the same. In both, not only was the sole and exclusive right and power to make treaties vested in Congress,[2] but the States were expressly prohibited from entering, without the consent of Congress, into any "conference, agreement, alliance or treaty" with any king, prince, or state,[3] or any "treaty, confederation or alliance whatever" with another State of the Confederation.[4] Each State had

---

1 The draft is in the handwriting of John Dickinson.

2 "The United States in Congress assembled, shall have the sole and exclusive right and power of determining on peace and war, except in the cases mentioned in the sixth article—of sending and receiving ambassadors —entering into treaties and alliances, provided that no treaty of commerce shall be made whereby the legislative power of the respective States shall be restrained from imposing such imposts and duties on foreigners, as their own people are subjected to, or from prohibiting the exportation or importation of any species of goods or commodities whatsoever. * * * The United States in Congress assembled shall never * * * enter into any treaties or alliances * * * unless nine States assent to the same." Art. IX. See Dickinson's draft, Art. XVIII.

3 In Dickinson's draft the terms used are "treaty, convention, or conference."

4 "No State without the consent of the United States in Congress assembled, shall send any embassy to, or receive any embassy from, or enter into any conference, agreement, alliance or treaty with any king prince or state. * * * No two or more States shall enter into any treaty, confedera-

one vote in Congress. No treaty could be entered into unless nine States assented to the same.[5] Congress was expressly prohibited from entering into any treaty whereby the States should be restrained from imposing such duties and imposts on foreigners as their own people were subjected to, or from prohibiting the exportation or importation of any species of goods whatsoever.[6] On the other hand, the States were expressly prohibited from laying imposts or duties which might interfere with any stipulations in treaties entered into by the United States with any foreign power in pursuance of any treaties theretofore proposed by the Congress to the courts of France and Spain.[7]

§15. **Control Exercised by Congress Over Negotiations.—** In the resolutions for the re-organization of the Department of Foreign Affairs, adopted by Congress February 22, 1782, it was provided that all communications with diplomatic officers and consular agents of the United States in foreign countries, or with ministers of foreign powers, should be conducted through the Secretary of the United States for the Department of Foreign Affairs; that all instructions to ministers of the United States or letters to ministers of foreign powers having direct reference to treaties proposed to be entered into should be submitted to the inspection and receive the approbation of Congress before they were transmitted; and that all instructions, communications, letters of credence, plans of treaties and other acts of Congress relative to foreign affairs should, when the substance of them had been previously agreed to in Congress, "be reduced to form in the office of foreign affairs, and submitted to the opinion of Congress; and when passed, signed and attested, sent to the office

tion or alliance whatever, between them, without the consent of the United States in Congress assembled, specifying accurately the purpose for which the same is to be entered into, and how long it shall continue." Art. VI. In Dickinson's draft the words "previous and free" appear before the word "consent" in the prohibition as against compacts between States of the Confederation.

5 In the margin of Dickinson's draft it is questioned whether so large a majority is necessary in concluding a treaty of peace. A clause was inserted in the draft excepting treaties of peace from the requirement of the assent of nine States, and appeared in subsequent copies, but not in the final Articles as adopted. MSS. Cont. Cong. Papers, XLVII, 17.

6 Art. IX.

7 Art. VI.

of foreign affairs to be countersigned and forwarded."[8] The absolute dependence of the Secretary upon authority from Congress is illustrated in the negotiations at our own seat of government with the Spanish chargé d'affaires, respecting boundaries, the navigation of the Mississippi, and commerce. To enable the Secretary to conduct the negotiations, a special commission was issued, July 21, 1785. In the resolutions adopted by Congress, July 20, 1785, authorizing the negotiations, it was provided that, before making any proposition or agreeing upon any article, compact, or convention, the Secretary should communicate to Congress the proposition to be made or received.[9] The inconvenience, which would necessarily result from this procedure, led the Secretary to observe in a communication to Congress, August 15, 1785, that while it was usual to instruct ministers on great points to be agitated it was very seldom thought necessary to leave nothing at all to their discretion; that while the instruction restraining him from agreeing to any article without the previous approbation of Congress seemed to be prudent and wise, the requirement that he must communicate, for the approval of Congress, every proposition that he might deem expedient to make to the Spanish negotiator in the conferences was exceedingly embarrassing.[10] By instructions adopted August 25, this requirement was modified; but the Secretary was still directed that no treaty should be signed until approved by Congress.[11]

In the negotiations conducted at Paris during this period, Congress came to recognize the necessity of entrusting greater power to the negotiator. The instructions, adopted October 29, 1783, authorizing negotiations with the various commercial powers of Europe, contained the reservation that no treaty should be "finally conclusive" until it had "been transmitted to the United States

---

8 Secret Journals, III, 93, 96. Robert R. Livingston was chosen Secretary August 10, 1781, assumed the duties of the office on October 20, 1781, and resigned in June, 1783. John Jay was chosen May 7, 1784, qualified on December 21, 1784, and continued in office until the adoption of the Constitution. During the interim from June, 1783, to December, 1784, the President of Congress acted as the Secretary. Notes to Treaties and Conventions (1889 ed.), 1230.

9 Secret Journals, III, 570.

10 Dip. Cor. 1783-9 (1833 ed.), VI, 100.

11 Id., 102.

in Congress assembled for their examination and final direction."[12]
This was construed by the commissioners as requiring them to
transmit the proposed treaty to Congress before they signed it.[13]
By the supplementary instructions of May 7, 1784, and the com-
missions issued May 11, this provision was modified so that
Congress reserved only the right of final ratification.[14]

§16. **Power of Seven States to Modify Instructions.**—During
the negotiations with the Spanish chargé, respecting commerce,
boundaries and the navigation of the Mississippi, the question of
the power of the delegates of a majority of the States to repeal
instructions adopted by nine States was raised. In the instructions
of August 25, 1785, nine States concurring, the Secretary was required "particularly" to stipulate for the right of the United
States to its territorial bounds and the free navigation of the
Mississippi from its source to the ocean, as established in the
treaty of peace. On August 29, 1786, Congress voted, seven States
in the affirmative, to repeal this instruction. The views of the
minority as expressed in the resolutions, moved, August 31,
1786, by Charles Pinckney, were: "If a treaty entered into in
pursuance of instructions be not ratified, by the law of nations it
is causa belli. If only seven States repeal the said last-recited
clause of Mr. Jay's instructions, and he thereupon proceeds to
enter into a treaty upon different principles than those under
which he was formerly authorized by nine States, the said treaty
cannot be considered as formed under instructions constitutionally sanctioned by the authority required under the Confederation; nor are the United States, under the laws or usages of nations, bound to ratify and confirm the same."[15] The effect of the
vote of repeal was never tested, since the negotiations were,
September 16, 1788, postponed by Congress for the consideration
of the government about to be organized under the Constitution.
It may be observed, in support of the proposed resolutions, that
the negotiator with the instructions thus amended would not act
as the agent of the treaty-making power. By a vote of seven
States the commission issued to John Adams, empowering him to
negotiate with Great Britain, was revoked;[16] but the termination

12 Secret Journals, III, 413.
13 Works of John Adams, IX, 521; Dip. Cor. 1783-9, II, 134.
14 Secret Journals, III, 489, 499.
15 Secret Journals, IV, 125.
16 Writings of Madison (Hunt ed.), II, 38.

of a mission and the modification of instructions under which a treaty may be negotiated are however quite different acts.

§17. **Treaties Concluded During This Period.**—There were signed, and subsequently ratified by Congress, during this period: July 16, 1782, and February 25, 1783, two agreements, relative to loans, with France; October 8, 1782, a treaty of commerce, and separate articles relative to recaptured vessels, with the Netherlands; April 3, 1783, a treaty of commerce, together with separate articles, with Sweden; November 30, 1782, provisional articles of peace, and September 3, 1783, a definitive treaty of peace, with Great Britain; July 9, July 28, August 5, and September 10, 1785, a treaty of amity and commerce with Prussia;[17] and a treaty with Morocco ratified by Congress July 18, 1787.[18] A consular convention with France was signed November 14, 1788, but was not ratified until after the adoption of the Constitution. The stipulations in these treaties are in general reciprocal in nature. They cover a wide range of subjects, including the following: peace; most-favored-nation treatment in respect of commerce, navigation, duties and imposts;[19] loans; the rights of the subjects of the one in the territories of the other;[20] rules of maritime warfare;[21] the disposition of prizes of the one in the ports of the other;[22] definitions of contraband of war;[23] proofs of nationality of vessels;[24] prohibitions against visitation and search;[25] and declarations for the punishment as pirates of subjects of the one accepting from another country at war with the

17 It was impossible for the commissioners to meet at the same place to sign this treaty. Franklin signed at Passy, July 9, Jefferson, at Paris, July 28, Adams, at London, August 5, and F. G. de Thulemeier, the Prussian negotiator, at The Hague, September 10, 1785. Jay, to whom Congress referred the treaty, advised that the date of the treaty was September 10, 1785. Dip. Cor., II, 329, 330, 335.

18 The treaty with Morocco, negotiated on the part of the commissioners at Paris by Thomas Barclay, was signed and approved by Jefferson, January 1, 1787, and by Adams, January 25, 1787.

19 The Netherlands, Art. II; Sweden, Arts. II and III; Prussia, Arts. II and XXVI.

20 See infra, 33.

21 The Netherlands, Art. XII; Sweden, Arts. VII, XIV; Prussia, Art. XII.

22 Sweden, Art. XIX; Prussia, Art. XIX.

23 The Netherlands, Art. XXIV; Sweden, Art. IX.

24 The Netherlands, Art. XXV; Prussia, Art. XIV.

25 Sweden, separate Article V.

other contracting party letters of marque and reprisal.[26] Various fruitless negotiations were likewise entered into during this period. At our own seat of government, the French chargé d'affaires, on November 28, 1785, transmitted to Jay, for submission to Congress, a plan of a postal convention.[27] Congress in resolutions adopted, May 7, 1784, declared it advantageous to conclude treaties with "Russia, the court of Vienna, Prussia, Denmark, Saxony, Hamburg, Great Britain, Spain, Portugal, Genoa, Tuscany, Rome, Naples, Venice, Sardinia and the Ottoman Porte."[28] Negotiations were opened by the commissioners at Paris with many of these powers, but with Prussia alone does a treaty record their efforts and the advanced principles of international law upon which their instructions were based.[29]

§18. Ratification. Amendments.—Congress, in which were combined the negotiating and ratifying functions, recognized an obligation to ratify what it had previously authorized. A consular convention with France, signed at Paris, July 29, 1784, having met with some opposition in the Congress, was referred to the Secretary for Foreign Affairs, John Jay, for examination. Proceeding on the principle that a refusal to ratify would be justified only on the grounds that the commissioners either had exceeded the powers delegated by their commission or had departed from the instructions given them, the Secretary made a careful comparison of the convention with the projet and instructions, which had been adopted by Congress, nine States concurring, January 25, 1782. He concluded that the convention differed from the projet not merely in wording and arrangement, but in subject-matter, and advised against ratification of the convention in the form in which it was signed. He added, however, that although conventions of the character of the one under consideration were contrary to the true policy of the United States, nevertheless since Congress had proceeded so far, assurance should be given to the King of France of the readiness of Congress to ratify a convention made in conformity with the projet, provided an article were added limiting its duration. Congress, following the recommendation, withheld ratification and at the same time in-

26 The Netherlands, Art. XIX; Sweden, Art. XXIII; Prussia, Art. XX.

27 Dip. Cor. 1783-9, I, 255.

28 Secret Journals, III, 484.

29 Dip. Cor., II, 239, 255, 264, 281, 299, 308, 323, 330, 335, 386.

5

structed Jefferson, the plenipotentiary at Paris, to make the explanations, and to secure the modifications, in accordance with the suggestions of the Secretary.[30]   In case of the treaty concluded with Sweden, April 3, 1783, certain verbal changes seemed to Congress to be essential.   The national title as used in the treaty was the "United States of North America," whereas the title as defined in the Articles of Confederation was the "United States of America."   Likewise, the expression, "the counties of New Castle, Kent and Sussex on the Delaware," was used, although the title of the State was Delaware.   Congress, however, ratified the treaty as signed, but at the same time directed Franklin, the plenipotentiary who negotiated the treaty, to have these verbal corrections made.[31]

§19. **Ratification of the Treaty of Peace.**—The provisional articles of peace, signed November 30, 1782, were, by express terms, to be inserted in, and to constitute, the treaty of peace proposed to be concluded between Great Britain and the United States, which treaty should not be concluded until terms of peace had been agreed upon between Great Britain and France.   They contained no provision for ratification, the only reference to the subject being found in Article VI, in which it was stipulated that those confined at the time of the ratification of the treaty in America for the part taken by them in the war should be immediately set free and the prosecutions so commenced be discontinued.   A letter from Franklin, dated January 21, 1783, notifying Congress that provisional articles of peace had been signed January 20, 1783, by Great Britain on the one hand, and France and Spain, respectively, on the other, was received, April 10.   A report of the Secretary for Foreign Affairs advising the ratification of the provisional articles was referred to a committee of which Madison and Hamilton were members.   The committee reported, April 14, Hamilton dissenting, that Congress was in no wise bound to the ratification, since the act to be ratified was not the provisional articles but the peace proposed by the articles to be concluded—an act "distinct, future, and even contingent"; and that a ratification might oblige Congress immediately to fulfill the stipulations of the treaty without assurance that a corresponding obligation would be assumed by the other party.   Hamilton, on

30 Dip. Cor., I, 305, 312, 322.   Secret Journals, III, 66; IV, 132.
31 Secret Journals, III, 392.

the other hand, urged that Congress was bound by the tenor of the treaty immediately to ratify it and to execute the several stipulations. The ratification was unanimously voted on the following day, and the exchange of ratifications in due form ordered if necessary.[32] The definitive treaty, signed September 3, 1783, differed only in unessential wording from the provisional articles. A question arose in Congress as to the necessity of a new ratification. Only seven States were, at the time of the receipt of the treaty, December 13, 1783, represented in Congress, and the ratifications were by the terms of the treaty to be exchanged within six months from the date of signing. It was suggested, and a motion to that effect debated, that the representatives of seven States were competent to authorize the exchange of ratifications, since the ratification was authorized by the action of nine States on the provisional articles. On the other hand it was contended, among others by Jefferson and Monroe, that there should be a complete ratification, since, as was admitted, the treaty did not agree literally with the one ratified, and that it was for the treaty-making authority to decide whether or not the changes were material. Later, a plan for a provisional ratification by the seven States, with a promise that the question of ratification would be taken up as soon as nine States were assembled, was reported.[33] Letters had in the meantime been addressed to the governors of the delinquent States urging on them the necessity of an immediate representation, and the arrival of new delegates rendered the provisional ratification unnecessary. On January 14, 1784, the treaty received the unanimous ratification of the nine States represented.[34] As a result of the delay of more than a month it was impossible to effect the exchange of ratifications within the time specified in the treaty for that purpose. It was not, however, deemed necessary on the part of the British government that a formal convention for the prolongation of the period should be concluded, since the delay in America appeared to have resulted "merely in consequence of the inclemency of the season"; and the ratifications were duly exchanged at Paris, May 12, 1784.[35]

32 Secret Journals, III, 327; Writings of Madison (Hunt ed.), I, 446, 448, 450; MSS. Cont. Cong. Papers, No. 25, Vol. II, p. 197.

33 Writings of Jefferson (Ford ed.), I, 77-83; III, 372.

34 Secret Journals, III, 433.

35 Wharton, Dip. Cor. Am. Rev., VI, 789, 806. The ratification of the treaty with Sweden was also delayed through the failure of delegates to attend Congress.

In the instrument of ratification as adopted by Congress, there seemed to the British government to be a want of form, wherein the United States was mentioned "before His Majesty, contrary to the established custom in every treaty in which a crowned head and a republic" were parties.[36] To this objection, Franklin, after having noted the difference between a treaty, which was the act of both parties jointly, and the instrument of ratification, which was the act of each party separately, replied: "I am confident there was no intention of affronting His Majesty by their order of nomination, but that it resulted merely from that sort of complaisance which every nation seems to have for itself, and of that respect for its own government, customarily so expressed in its own acts, of which the English among the rest afford an instance, when in the title of the King they always name Great Britain before France."[37] It may be added that it was not until the conclusion of the treaty of commerce with Great Britain of July 3, 1815, that the United States obtained recognition of the right in negotiations with a crowned head of Europe to alternate precedence in the text of the treaty.

2. Enforcement.

§20. **Stipulations Involving Subjects Otherwise Under Control of the States.**—By the Articles of Confederation each State retained its "sovereignty, freedom and independence and every power, jurisdiction and right" which was not expressly delegated to the United States in Congress assembled.[38] The sole and exclusive right and power of determining on peace and war, of communicating with foreign powers, and of entering into treaties were so delegated. Congress could make requisitions on the States to defray expenses incurred for the common defense and general welfare. It could borrow money, but could not levy a tax. All taxes, duties, imposts and excises were levied by the States. No power to regulate commerce with foreign nations was expressly delegated to Congress. That its regulation by treaty was, however, contemplated appears from the express limitation in the grant of the treaty-making power, that no treaty of commerce should be made whereby the legislative power of the respective

---

36 Hartley to Franklin, June 1, 1784, Id., VI, 811.
37 Id., VI, 811, 813.
38 Art. II.

States should be restrained from imposing such imposts and duties on foreigners as their own people were subjected to, or from prohibiting the exportation or importation of any species of goods or commodities whatsoever.[39] Likewise the States were expressly prohibited from laying any impost or duty which might interfere with the stipulations in treaties entered into with any foreign country in pursuance of any treaties proposed by the Congress to France and Spain.[40] In the treaties concluded during this period liberal privileges of residence, trade, and commerce were granted upon terms of reciprocity to foreign subjects. Most-favored-nation treatment in respect of commerce, navigation, imposts and duties was pledged to the subjects of France,[41] the Netherlands[42], Sweden[43], and Prussia.[44] Loans were negotiated with the King of France, and their repayment pledged.[45] It was also stipulated in these treaties that subjects of the other contracting party might reciprocally enjoy in the United States exemption from the droit d'aubaine;[46] that they might by testament, donation, or otherwise, dispose of their goods, moveable and immoveable, in favor of such persons as they might choose, and that their heirs, subjects of the contracting parties, wherever residing, might receive such successions even ab intestato.[47] In the Prussian treaty it was provided that a reasonable time should be allowed a Prussian subject to sell real estate, which, were he not disqualified by alienage, would by the law of the land descend to him, and to remove the proceeds thereof without molestation,

39 Art. IX.
40 Art. VI.
41 Arts. II and III, treaty of 1778.
42 Art. II, treaty of 1782.
43 Arts. II and III, treaty of 1783.
44 Arts. II and XXVI, treaty of 1785.
45 Agreements of July 16, 1782, and February 25, 1783.
46 France, Art. XI.
47 France, Art. XI. "Upon every principle of fair construction, this article gave to the subjects of France a right to purchase and hold lands in the United States." Marshall, C. J., Chirac v. Chirac, 2 Wheat. 259, 271. See also Carneal v. Banks, 10 Wheat. 181. In the treaty with the Netherlands, Art. VI, and with Sweden, Art. VI, the words "goods and effects" are used, which have been construed by some courts to include real property as well as personal. University v. Miller, 14 N. C. 188; Adams v. Akerlund, 168 Ill. 632; In re Stixrud's Estate, 58 Wash. 339; Erickson v. Carlson, 95 Neb. 182.

and exempt from all rights of detraction.[48] Liberty of conscience and freedom of worship, subject in case of public demonstration to the laws of the country, were guaranteed to the subjects of the Netherlands,[49] and Sweden.[50] The stipulation in the Prussian treaty was in broader terms and granted to Prussian subjects "the most perfect freedom of conscience and worship, * * * without being liable to molestation in that respect for any cause other than an insult on the religion of others."[51] In accordance with the frank but far-reaching statement of John Adams it was agreed in the treaty of peace that British creditors should meet with no lawful impediment to the recovery of all bona fide debts theretofore contracted.[52] The consular convention with France, which, although not ratified until after the adoption of the Constitution, was negotiated during this period, stipulated for certain exemptions of consular officers from local jurisdiction, and for the exercise by them of certain powers with respect to French subjects and the property of French subjects within the States.[53] Among these was the right of administration in certain cases on the estate of a French subject dying within this country.[54] French consuls were also given jurisdiction over differences between captains and crews, and disputes in civil matters, arising in the internal administration of French vessels,[55] and the right to cause deserting seamen to be arrested and returned.[56] Most-favored-nation treatment in respect of consular powers and privileges was pledged.[57]

§21. **Legislation by State Legislatures to Give Effect to Treaties.**—These stipulations embraced subjects over which Congress had no legislative power. There was no process within its control by which it could compel observance. It could only recommend to the States the passage of laws to give them effect. In resolutions adopted, January 14, 1780, Congress urged the

48 Art. X.
49 Art. IV.
50 Art. V.
51 Art. XI.
52 Art. IV.
53 Art. II.
54 Art. V.
55 Arts. VIII and XII.
56 Art. IX.
57 Art. XV.

legislatures of the several States to make, where not already made, provision for extending to French subjects privileges in accordance with the spirit of Article XI of the treaty of commerce.[58] This article provided that French subjects should enjoy the privilege of disposing of their goods, movable and immovable, by testament, donation, or otherwise to whomsoever they might please, and that their heirs wherever residing might succeed them, ab intestato, without being obliged to obtain letters of naturalization. In compliance with this recommendation the legislatures of various of the States passed laws by which these privileges were expressly extended to French subjects.[59] A committee composed of Madison, Clymer, and Duane, in a report to Congress July 5, 1782, advised against the incorporation of a similar stipulation in the proposed treaty with the Netherlands, observing, that in the opinion of the committee it was at least questionable whether the extension of this privilege to the subjects of other powers than France and Spain would not encroach on the rights reserved by the articles of union to the individual States.[60] Such a stipulation was, however, incorporated in Article VI of the treaty as finally negotiated.

The proclamation of the treaty of peace with Great Britain was accompanied with a resolution in which Congress earnestly recommended that the legislatures of the respective States make provision for the restitution of confiscated estates, and revise all their acts or laws so as to conform to Articles IV and V of the treaty. The proclamation enjoined all bodies of magistracy, legislative, executive and judicial, and citizens of the States to carry the treaty into effect. In the proclamations of the treaties with France, the Netherlands and Sweden, Congress directly enjoined the citizens and inhabitants, and more especially the military and

58 Secret Journals, II, 568.

59 See for instances, the acts as passed by Connecticut in January, 1780 (Records of the State of Connecticut (Hoadly ed.), II, 481); Massachusetts, May 5, 1780 (Acts and Resolves of Province of Massachusetts Bay (1886 ed.), V, 1197); and Pennsylvania, September 20, 1782. (Stats. at Large of Penna. (1904 ed.), X, 509). The act as passed by Pennsylvania confirmed the titles as of the date of February 6, 1778, the date of the treaty, and in general terms enacted that the subjects of the French king, whether residing within that commonwealth or elsewhere, should be and they thereby were entitled to all the rights, privileges and immunities stipulated for in and by the eleventh article of the treaty.

60 Writings of Madison (Hunt ed.), I, 214.

naval officers, of the United States, to govern themselves strictly in all things according to the provisions of the treaties.[61] Fruitless attempts were made to obtain from the States a delegation of the power to regulate foreign commerce. Jefferson in a letter to Monroe, June 17, 1785, at a time when the commercial independence of the several States had become intolerable, said: "Congress by the Confederation have no original and inherent power over the commerce of the States. But by the 9th article they are authorized to enter into treaties of commerce. The moment these treaties are concluded the jurisdiction of Congress over the commerce of the States springs into existence, and that of the particular States is superseded so far as the articles of the treaty may have taken up the subject. There are two restrictions only on the exercise of the power of treaty by Congress. 1st. That they shall not by such treaty restrain the legislatures of the States from imposing such duties on foreigners as their own people are subject to. 2dly. Nor from prohibiting the exportation or importation of any particular species of goods. Leaving these two points free, Congress may by treaty establish any system of commerce they please. But, as I before observed, it is by treaty alone they can do it." He advised the negotiation of such treaties so as to remove foreign commerce from State interference.[62]

§22. **Treaties Operative as Laws.**—The stipulation in Article IV of the treaty of peace, that British creditors should meet with no lawful impediment to the recovery of bona fide debts theretofore contracted, was unpopular by reason of the natural prejudice then prevailing against the loyal subjects of Great Britain, whose rights it was aimed to protect. There existed at the time of the conclusion of the treaty various State laws for the sequestration or confiscation of debts due British subjects, which were repugnant to the stipulation.[63] Congress could not as a legislative body give the treaty the sanction of a law. Were these acts of the State legislatures to remain as laws binding the courts until expressly repealed by these same legislatures? Such acts of repeal by the States were not forthcoming. Assured by the British government of its willingness to co-operate in the execution of the treaty

61 Journals of Congress, IV, 189; Secret Journals, III, 318, 395, 444, 446.

62 Writings of Jefferson (Ford ed.), IV, 55.

63 See for acts alleged by the British government to be in contravention of the treaty, Am. State Papers, For. Rel., I, 198.

whenever the United States should manifest a "real determination" to fulfill its part, John Jay, the Secretary for Foreign Affairs, made a careful investigation of the subject and came to the conclusion that the failure of the States could not be justified by violations on the part of Great Britain.[64] In his elaborate report to Congress, dated October 13, 1786, the Secretary said: "Your Secretary considers the thirteen independent sovereign States as having, by express delegation of power, formed and vested in Congress a perfect though limited sovereignty for the general and national purposes specified in the Confederation. In this sovereignty they cannot severally participate (except by their delegates) or have concurrent jurisdiction; for the ninth article of the Confederation most expressly conveys to Congress the sole and *exclusive* right and power of determining on war and *peace,* and of entering into treaties and alliances, &c., &c. When therefore a treaty is constitutionally made, ratified and published by Congress, it immediately becomes binding on the whole nation, and superadded to the laws of the land, without the intervention, consent or fiat of State legislatures."[65] He added: "The United States must, however, eventually answer for the conduct of their respective members; and for that, and other reasons suggested by the nature of their sovereignty and of the Articles of Confederation, your Secretary thinks they have good right to insist and require that national faith and national treaties be kept and observed throughout the union; for otherwise it would be in the power of a particular State, by injuries and infractions of treaties, to involve the whole confederacy in difficulties and war."[66] He recommended the adoption of certain resolutions. These were agreed to in Congress, without a dissenting vote, March 21, 1787; and were communicated to the several States in the federal letter, likewise prepared by the Secretary, and adopted by Congress, April 13, 1787. They read: "Resolved, That the legislatures of the several States cannot of right pass any act or acts for interpreting, explaining or construing a national treaty, or any part or clause of it; nor for restraining, limiting or in any manner impeding, retarding or

64 "An investigation of the subject had proved that the violations on our part were not only most numerous and important, but were of earliest date." Madison to Edmund Pendleton, April 22, 1787. Writings of Madison (Hunt ed.), II, 355.

65 Secret Journals, IV, 203.

66 Id., 281.

counteracting the operation and execution of the same; for that on being constitutionally made, ratified and published, they become in virtue of the Confederation, part of the law of the land, and are not only independent of the will and power of such legislatures but also binding and obligatory on them. Resolved, That all such acts or parts of acts as may be now existing in any of the States repugnant to the treaty of peace ought to be forthwith repealed, as well to prevent their continuing to be regarded as violations of that treaty as to avoid the disagreeable necessity there might otherwise be of raising and discussing questions touching their validity and obligation." The third resolution recommended that the repeal be made in the form of a general declaratory act binding the courts of law and equity to decide and adjudge according to the true intent and meaning of the treaty "any thing in the said acts or parts of acts to the contrary thereof in any wise notwithstanding."[67] The requests in the second and third resolutions for acts of repeal by the States seemed to some of the members of Congress to be unnecessary, and even to be inconsistent with the first resolution. To this suggestion, Madison replied that a law of repeal by the States was both expedient and necessary, since the judges were bound by their oaths more strongly to State than to federal authority, and, that even if the treaty had the validity of a law only, while it would repeal all prior inconsistent laws, doubt might exist as to those passed after its conclusion.[68] At a later period in a letter to Edmund Pendleton, January 2, 1791, in direct answer to the question whether Congress did not, in calling on the States to repeal the laws, consider Article IV of the treaty a covenant that a law of repeal should be passed rather than a law of repeal in itself, Madison said: "As well as I recollect, the act of Congress on that occasion supposed the impediments to be repealed by the treaty, and recommended a repeal

---

67 Secret Journals, IV, 185, 282, 295, 329. See also Jones v. Walker, 2 Paine C. C. 688, 712. In a later report to Congress, October 13, 1787, Secretary Jay advised that an act of the legislature of Virginia, which according to his construction was in contravention of the most-favored-nation clause of the treaty with the Netherlands, would doubtless as conditions then existed continue to be recognized as the law until repealed by the State legislature. On the same date Congress requested the Virginia legislature to revise the act at its earliest opportunity. Secret Journals, IV, 410, 413.

68 Madison Papers, II, 595, 596.

by the States, merely as declaratory, and in order to obviate doubts
and discussions."[69]   Acts in compliance with these recommendations of Congress were passed by Massachusetts, April 30, 1787;[70]
Maryland, May, 1787;[71] Connecticut, May, 1787;[72] New Jersey,
June 5, 1787;[73] New Hampshire, June 21, 1787;[74] Rhode Island,
September, 1787;[75] Virginia, December 12, 1787;[76] North Carolina, December 22, 1787;[77] Delaware, February 2, 1788;[78] and
New York, February 22, 1788.[79]   The General Assembly of Pennsylvania, by resolution dated March 3, 1788, declared that no act
of the legislature, then in force, could be found, which was repugnant to the treaty of peace or tended in any manner to impede
its operation and execution.[80]   The Supreme Court of that State
in the January term of 1788 had held that the treaty was a law
of the land binding the court.[81]   In urging the New York legislature to pass a law in accordance with the resolutions of Congress,
Hamilton declared, in reply to the contention that such a law
would place too much power in the judges, that the judges were
bound not less without the law of repeal than with it to enforce
the treaty, regardless of any act of the State legislature to the
contrary.[82]   Jefferson, as Secretary of State, in a communication to
Mr. Hammond, the British minister, May 29, 1792, said, in reference to these declaratory acts of repeal on the part of the several

69 Letters and Writings of Madison, I, 523.

70 Laws of the Commonwealth of Massachusetts 1780-1807 (1807 ed.),
I, 393.

71 Laws of Maryland (1800 ed.), II, c. XXV.

72 Acts and Laws, 351.

73 Laws of New Jersey 1703-1799 (Paterson ed.), I, 82.

74 An act had previously been passed, September 15, 1786, for this
purpose. Perpetual Laws 1766-1788 (1789 ed.), 162-164.

75 Acts and Resolves, 9.

76 Hening's Statutes at Large, XII, 528. The act was not to take effect
until Great Britain had taken measures to fulfill her part of the treaty
with reference to the delivery of the western posts, and the restitution of
slaves.

77 Laws of North Carolina (1787), 1.

78 Laws of General Assembly, 3.

79 Laws of New York (1789 ed.), II, 256. Am. State Papers, For. Rel.,
I, 228-231.

80 Id., 231.

81 Respublica v. Gordon, 1 Dall. 233. See also Washington, J., Lessee
of Gordon v. Kerr, 1 Wash. C. C. (1806) 322, 325.

82 Works (Lodge ed.), III, 508.

States: "Indeed all this was supererogation. It resulted from the instrument of Confederation among the States, that treaties made by Congress, according to the confederation, were superior to the laws of the States. The circular letter of Congress had declared and demonstrated it, and the several States by their acts and explanations before mentioned, had shown it to be their own sense, as we may safely affirm it to have been the general sense of those, at least, who were of the profession of the law."[83]

83 Am. State Papers, For. Rel., I, 209. In summarizing the reports on the subject received from the various States, Jefferson said: "Thus, in Rhode Island, Governor Collins, in his letter * * * says, 'The treaty, in all its absolute parts, has been fully complied with, and to those parts that are merely recommendatory, and depend upon the legislative discretion, the most candid attention hath been paid.' Plainly implying that the absolute parts did not depend upon the legislative discretion. Mr. Channing, the attorney for the United States in that State, * * * speaking of an act passed before the treaty, says, 'This act was considered by our courts as annulled by the treaty of peace, and subsequent to the ratification thereof no proceedings have been had thereon.' The governor of Connecticut in his letter * * * says, 'The sixth article of the treaty was immediately observed on receiving the same with the proclamation of Congress; the courts of justice adopted it as a principle of law. No further prosecutions were instituted against any person who came within that article, and all such prosecutions as were then pending were discontinued.' Thus, prosecutions going on, under the law of the State, were discontinued, by the treaty operating as a repeal of the law. In Pennsylvania, Mr. Lewis, attorney for the United States, says, in his letter * * * 'The judges have, uniformly and without hesitation, declared in favor of the treaty, on the ground of its being the supreme law of the land. On this ground, they have not only discharged attainted traitors from arrest, but have frequently declared that they were entitled by the treaty to protection.' The case of the Commonwealth vs. Gordon, January, 1788, Dallas's Reports, 233, is proof of this. In Maryland, in the case of Mildred vs. Dorsey, * * * a law of the State, made during the war, had compelled those who owed debts to British subjects to pay them into the treasury of that State. This had been done by Dorsey, before the date of the treaty; yet the judges of the State general court decided that the treaty not only repealed the law for the future, but for the past also, and decreed that the defendant should pay the money over again to the British creditor. In Virginia, Mr. Monroe, one of the Senators of that State in Congress, and a lawyer of eminence, tells us, * * * that both court and counsel there avowed the opinion, that the treaty would control any law of the State opposed to it. * * * In New York, Mr. Harrison, attorney for the United States in that district, assures us, * * * that the act of 1782, of that State, relative to debts due to persons within the enemy's lines, was, immediately after the treaty, restrained by the su-

Likewise, in the debates on the adoption of the Constitution it was frequently declared that treaties operated under the Articles of Confederation as laws superior to acts of the State legislatures. Charles Cotesworth Pinckney, in the debate on the proposed Constitution in the South Carolina House of Representatives, said: "I contend that the article in the new Constitution, which says that treaties shall be paramount to the laws of the land, is only declaratory of what treaties were, in fact, under the old compact. They were as much the law of the land under that Confederation, as they are under this Constitution."[84] John Rutledge expressed the same view.[85] William R. Davie, in the North Carolina convention, in referring to the declaratory act of repeal passed by the assembly of that State, said: "But no doubt that treaty was the supreme law of the land without the sanction of the assembly; because, by the Confederation, Congress had power to make treaties. It was one of those original rights of sovereignty which were vested in them; and it was not the deficiency of constitutional authority in Congress to make treaties that produced the necessity of a law to declare their validity; but it was owing to the entire imbecility of the Confederation."[86] At a later date, Mr. Justice Chase, in the case of Ware v. Hylton, said: "It seems to me that treaties made by Congress, according to the Confederation, were superior to the laws of the States; because the Confederation made them obligatory on all the States. They were so declared by Congress on the 13th of April, 1787; were so admitted by the legislatures and executives of most of the States; and were so decided by the judiciary of the general government, and by the judiciaries of some of the State governments."[87] Again, Chief Justice Ellsworth, in Hamilton and Company v. Eaton, said: "The treaty [Article IV of the treaty of peace] now under consideration was made on the part of the United States by a

perior courts of the State from operating on British creditors, and that he did not know a single instance to the contrary—a full proof that they considered the treaty as a law of the land, paramount to the law of their State." Id., 209. See also Rutgers v. Waddington, Works of Hamilton (Lodge ed.), IV, 408.

84 Elliot's Debates, (2 ed.), IV, 278.

85 Id., IV, 267.

86 Id., IV, 120.

87 3 Dall. 236. See also opinions of Iredell and Wilson, JJ., Id. 277, 281.

Congress composed of deputies from each State, to whom were delegated by the Articles of Confederation, expressly, 'the sole and exclusive right and power of entering into treaties and alliances'; and being ratified and made by them, it became a complete national act and law of every State."[88]

As a result of the inability of Congress, and the failure of the States, to give by legislative enactment effect to treaties concluded under the authority of the Confederation, there was developed the doctrine that treaties by their own fiat, without the aid or intervention of acts of legislation, became a part of the law of the land binding the courts, laws theretofore existing to the contrary notwithstanding. This was the view so forcibly set forth in the federal letter, unanimously adopted by Congress, April 13, 1787, just one month prior to the assembling of the delegates in convention at Philadelphia to revise the articles of union.

88 1 Hughes 249, 259.

CHAPTER IV.

THE FEDERAL CONVENTION.

§23. The Treaty-making Power Vested in President and Senate.—In the sketch of government presented to the Convention by Hamilton, June 18, 1787, the "Governor," in whom was to be vested the supreme executive authority, was to have, with the "advice and approbation of the Senate, the power of making all treaties."[1] The Senate was to consist of persons elected to serve during good behavior by electors chosen for that purpose by the people in election districts, into which the States were to be divided. Although the sketch made no provision as to the apportionment of the Senators among the States, in the paper turned over to Madison, about the close of the Convention, in which Hamilton delineated the Constitution which he had wished to see proposed by the Convention, and in which the organization of the treaty-making power was retained in similar form, the States were not to share equally in representation in the Senate, but in general, according to population.[2] In the draft of the Constitution as reported by the Committee of Detail, August 6, power to make treaties and to appoint ambassadors was by Article IX vested in the Senate.[3] The executive power was to be vested in a single person, to be known as President, and to be elected by the legislature. During the discussion, August 15, on the question of restricting the power of the Senate in originating bills for raising and appropriating money, Francis Mercer, who had taken his seat in the Maryland deputation on August 6, suggested that the Senate ought not to have the power of making treaties; that this power belonged to the executive department.[4] On August 23, Article IX of the draft being under consideration, Madison observed "that the Senate represented the States alone,

---

1 Documentary History of the Constitution, I, 327.

2 Id., III, 773. On May 30, Hamilton moved that the rights of suffrage in the national legislature ought to be proportioned according to the number of free inhabitants; and on June 11, he supported a resolution providing that the same ratio of representation should be applied in both houses. Id., III, 24, 108.

3 Id., III, 451.

4 Id., III, 536.

and that for this as well as other obvious reasons it was proper that the President should be an agent in treaties."[5] No amendment, however, was made; but the section was referred to the Committee of Five. In the report of the Committee of Eleven, September 4, to which, on August 31, the undetermined sections had been referred, it was recommended that "The President, by and with the advice and consent of the Senate," should have power to make treaties; but that no treaty should be made "without the consent of two-thirds of the members present." The clause was agreed to as reported.[6]

§24. **Concurrence of Two-thirds of the Senators Present. Treaties of Peace, for Cession of Territory, Etc.**—On September 7 and 8, the clause requiring the concurrence of two-thirds of the Senators present was the subject of a protracted debate. James Wilson thought it objectionable to require the concurrence of two-thirds since a minority might thus control the will of a majority and perpetuate war against the wish of the majority.[7] Rufus King concurred in this view.[8] An amendment proposed by Madison was agreed to, September 7, excepting treaties of peace from the requirement of a two-thirds vote. Different views were expressed as to what proportion should be required in case of such treaties. Madison suggested the consent of two-thirds of the Senate without the concurrence of the President, since the President would derive so much power and influence from a state of war that he might be tempted to impede the conclusion of a treaty of peace. Pierce Butler concurred with Madison. Nathaniel Gorham, of Massachusetts, thought the precaution unnecessary since the means of carrying on war were in the control of the legislature.[9] Gouverneur Morris desired the concurrence of the President and a majority only of the Senate, for, if a majority of the Senate were for peace and were not allowed to make it, they would be apt to effect their purpose in the more disagreeable mode of negativing the supplies for the

5 Id., III, 604.

6 Id., III, 669, 697, 706. The Committee of Eleven was composed of Nicholas Gilman, Rufus King, Roger Sherman, David Brearley, Gouverneur Morris, John Dickinson, Daniel Carroll, James Madison, Hugh Williamson, Pierce Butler, and Abraham Baldwin.

7 Id., III, 700, 704.

8 Id., III, 700.

9 Id., III, 700.

war.[10] Elbridge Gerry thought that a greater proportion should be required in the case of treaties of peace than in case of other treaties, since in treaties of peace the dearest interests would be at stake, such "as the fisheries, territories, &c."; that in treaties of peace there was more danger of the "extremities of the continent" being sacrified, than on any other occasions. He was opposed to putting the "essential rights of the Union" in the hands of so small a number as a majority of the Senate which might represent less than one-fifth of the people.[11] An amendment, reading "but no treaty of peace shall be entered into, whereby the United States shall be deprived of any of their present territory or rights without the concurrence of two-thirds of the members of the Senate present," was proposed.[12] Roger Sherman, of Connecticut, moved to add as a proviso that no rights established by the treaty of peace should be ceded without the sanction of the legislature. Gouverneur Morris supported this amendment.[13] Upon a reconsideration of the clause the exception as to the treaties of peace was stricken out by a vote of 8 to 3.[14] Motions were thereupon made, but voted down, to strike out the clause requiring the consent of two-thirds of the members present,[15] to substitute for the requirement of two-thirds of the members "present," two-thirds of all the members,[16] and to require a majority of the whole number of the Senate.[17] An amendment offered by Madison that two-thirds of all the members should constitute a quorum likewise failed,[18] as did also an amendment

10 Id., III, 700, 703.

11 Id., III, 701, 704.

12 Id., I, 188. Madison gives the amendment as moved by Hugh Williamson and Richard Dobbs Spaight, both of North Carolina, as follows: "That no treaty of peace affecting territorial rights should be made without the concurrence of two-thirds of the members of the Senate present." Rufus King, of Massachusetts, moved to extend the amendment to "all present rights of the United States." Id., III, 703.

13 Id., III, 704.

14 New Jersey, Delaware, and Maryland voted in the negative. Id., III, 704.

15 Delaware voted in the affirmative. Connecticut was divided.

16 North Carolina, South Carolina and Georgia voted in the affirmative.

17 Massachusetts, Connecticut, Delaware, South Carolina, and Georgia voted in the affirmative.

18 New Hampshire, Massachusetts, Connecticut, New Jersey, Pennsylvania and Delaware voted in the negative; Maryland, Virginia, North Carolina, South Carolina, and Georgia, in the affirmative.

6

that no treaty should be made without previous notice to the members and a reasonable time for their attendance.[19] The provision was finally agreed to as reported by the committee, Pennsylvania, New Jersey and Georgia, voting in the negative.[20] The requirement as adopted, of two-thirds of the members "present," would, it was urged, remove the possibility of embarrassment experienced under the Articles of Confederation through the failure of delegates from nine States to attend, and would at the same time serve to insure more regular attendance.

§25. **Treaties Not to be Approved by Congress.**—In supporting a motion that all bills for raising or appropriating money should originate in the House of Representatives, George Mason, on August 15, said that he was extremely anxious to take this power from the Senate, which "could already sell the whole country by means of treaties." Francis Mercer, after observing that the Senate ought not to have the power of making treaties since it belonged to the executive department, added "that treaties would not be final so as to alter the laws of the land, till ratified by legislative authority. This was the case of treaties in Great Britain; particularly the late treaty of commerce with France." To this observation, Mason replied that he "did not say that a treaty would repeal a law; but that the Senate by means of a treaty might alienate territory &c. without legislative sanction. The cessions of the British Islands in the W. Indies by treaty alone were an example. If Spain should possess herself of Georgia therefore the Senate might by treaty dismember the Union."[21] On August 17, during the debate on the clause vesting the power to declare war in Congress, a motion to add "and to make peace" was unanimously rejected. Elbridge Gerry in supporting the amendment urged that even eight Senators might possibly exercise the power and might consequently give up part of the United States.[22] On August 23, while the treaty-making power was still vested solely in the Senate, Gouverneur Morris, after expressing doubt as to whether he would agree to confer the power to make treaties on the Senate at all, moved to amend the section by adding "but no treaty shall be binding on the United

19 North Carolina, South Carolina and Georgia voted in the affirmative.
20 Id., III, 700, 701, 703, 705, 706.
21 Id., III, 535-536.
22 Id., I, 129; III, 554.

States which is not ratified by a law." Madison suggested the inconvenience of requiring a "legal" ratification of treaties of alliance for purposes of war. Nathaniel Gorham pointed out the disadvantages which must be experienced if treaties of peace and all negotiations were previously to be ratified by Congress. If they were not previously so ratified, the ministers, he observed, would be at a loss to know how to proceed, for they must go abroad without instructions from the authority by which their proceedings were ultimately to be ratified. To Madison's suggestion as to the inconvenience of requiring a legal ratification of treaties of alliance, Gouverneur Morris replied that in general he was not "solicitous to multiply and facilitate treaties," and that as to treaties of alliance his amendment would necessitate their negotiation at our own seat of government, which he considered desirable. James Wilson in supporting the amendment observed that in the case of the most important treaties the king of Great Britain was obliged to resort to Parliament for their execution and was therefore under the same fetters as the proposed amendment would impose on the Senate; that under the clause, without the amendment, the Senate could make a treaty requiring all the rice of South Carolina to be sent to some particular port, although the legislature was not permitted to lay any duties on exports. John Dickinson, of Delaware, favored the amendment although the smaller States would otherwise share equally in the making of treaties. William Samuel Johnson, of Connecticut, thought that there was something of a "solecism in saying that the acts of a minister with plenipotentiary powers from one body, should depend for ratification on another body." The example of the king of Great Britain was not, he said, parallel, since the full and complete power was in the king, and if Parliament should fail to provide the necessary means for the execution of a treaty, the treaty would be violated. In the vote on the proposed amendment, Pennsylvania was alone in the affirmative with North Carolina divided.[23] Subsequently to the vote, Madison raised the question whether a distinction might not be made between different kinds of treaties, allowing the President and Senate the power to make "treaties eventual and of alliance for limited terms," but requiring the concurrence in other treaties of the whole legisla-

23 New York and New Hampshire were not represented.

ture. The section was then referred to the Committee of Five.[24]
On September 6, James Wilson, in opposing the organization
and powers of the Senate as tending toward aristocracy, observed
that treaties were to be "laws of the land" and that the power to
make treaties involved "the case of subsidies." On the following
day he moved to add after the word "Senate" in the section as
reported by the Committee of Eleven, vesting the treaty power
in the President and Senate, the clause "and the House of Representatives." "As treaties," he said, "are to have the operation
of laws, they ought to have the sanction of laws also." Roger
Sherman, of Connecticut, replied that it was solely a question as
to whether the power could be safely entrusted to the Senate.
He added: "The necessity of secrecy in the case of treaties forbade a reference of them to the whole legislature." In the vote,
Pennsylvania alone supported the amendment. Later, September
8, Roger Sherman suggested that no rights acquired by the treaty
of peace should be ceded without the sanction of the legislature.
The proposition was supported by Gouverneur Morris but was
not brought to a vote.[25] From these debates it appears that the
House was excluded from participation in the making of treaties
by the framers of the Constitution with the understanding that
treaties were to have the force of laws.[26]

§26. **States Expressly Prohibited From Entering into Treaties.**—By the Articles of Confederation the States were expressly
prohibited, without the consent of Congress, from entering into any
"conference, agreement, alliance or treaty" with a foreign power,
or any "treaty, confederation or alliance" with another State of

24 Id., III, 604-606. See also Notes of McHenry, Am. Hist. Rev.,
XI, 611.

25 Doc. Hist. of Const., III, 686, 697, 704. McHenry gives the argument of Wilson on September 6, as follows: "The Senate may exercise the powers of legislation, and executive and judicial powers. To make
treaties legislative, to appoint officers executive for the executive has only
the nomination. To try impeachments judicial." Notes, Am. Hist. Rev.
XI, 615.

26 It may be noted that in the draft of the Constitution reported September 12 by the Committee on Style and Arrangement, the treasurer of the
United States was to be appointed by joint ballot of Congress. Art. I,
sec. 8. On September 14, by a vote of 8 to 3, on motion of John Rutledge, this provision was stricken out in order that the treasurer might be
appointed in the same manner as other officers. Doc. Hist. of Const., I,
369; III, 724, 743.

the Confederation. Nevertheless, said Madison, in the debates in the Convention on June 19, Virginia and Maryland in one instance, and Pennsylvania and New Jersey in another, had entered into "compacts without previous application or subsequent apology."[27] The draft of the Constitution as reported August 6, by the Committee of Detail, provided that no State should enter into any "treaty, alliance, or confederation,"[28] or, without the consent of the national legislature, enter into any "agreement or compact" with another State or a foreign power.[29] These inhibitions were agreed to August 28, and incorporated without change or debate into the Constitution.[30]

§27. Treaties a Part of the Supreme Law of the Land.—In respect of one provision there seemed to be a unity of sentiment throughout the Convention. In Randolph's enumeration on May 29 of the defects of the Articles of Confederation, under the first group, was placed the inability of Congress to prevent the infraction of treaties.[31] In the resolutions submitted by him, it was recommended that the national legislature be invested with the power to negative all State laws which in its opinion contravened "the articles of Union," as also with the power to coerce a disobedient State. On May 31, on motion made by Franklin, the clause "or any treaties subsisting under the authority of the Union" was inserted after the word "Union."[32] As thus amended the section was agreed to in the committee of the whole without debate or objection. William Paterson, of the conservative element, recommended in his resolutions, introduced June 15, that all treaties made and ratified under the authority of the United States should "be the supreme law of the respective States," and that the judiciaries of the several States should be bound thereby in their decisions "anything in the respective laws of the individual States to the contrary notwithstanding." The executive was to be authorized to use the power of the confederated States to enforce and compel obedience.[33] In the debate, June 19, on

27 Doc. Hist. of Const., III, 155.
28 Art. XII.
29 Art. XIII.
30 Id., III, 632, 633, 748, 752.
31 Id., III, 16.
32 Id., 33. See also Notes by McHenry, Am. Hist. Rev., XI, 602.
33 Doc. Hist. of Const., I, 325; III, 127. As there seems to be unmistakable evidence that the copy of a plan of a Constitution, submitted

the Paterson plan of revision, Madison questioned its effectiveness
to prevent those violations of the law of nations and of treaties
which might involve the country in the calamities of foreign wars,
and added that "it ought to be effectually provided that no part
of a nation should have it in its power to bring them on the
whole."[34]   On July 17, Paterson's resolution with a few verbal
changes was, on the motion of Luther Martin, substituted for the
direct negative by the national legislature; and, with this substitution, the power to negative was transferred from the legislative
to the judiciary branch.[35]   On August 23, 1787, the provision,
as reported by the Committee of Detail, was slightly modified on
motion of John Rutledge so as to read: "This Constitution and
the laws of the United States made in pursuance thereof, and all
treaties made under the authority of the United States, shall be
the supreme law of the several States, and of their citizens and
inhabitants; and the judges in the several States shall be found
thereby in their decisions; any thing in the constitutions or laws
of the several States to the contrary notwithstanding."[36]   Two
days later, on the motion of Madison, seconded by Gouverneur
Morris, the article was reconsidered and the clause "or which
shall be made" was inserted after the words "treaties made," in
order to remove any possible doubt as to the force of pre-existing
treaties.   With these words inserted, referring to future treaties,
the words "all treaties made" would, it was observed, refer to those
already concluded.[37]   In the Committee on Style and Arrangement, composed of William Samuel Johnson, Alexander Hamil-

---

by Charles Pinckney to the Secretary of State, December 30, 1818, and to
which so much credit has been given, was a copy made subsequently to the
Convention from one of the several drafts in his possession, and that it
differs from the one originally presented to the Convention on May 29,
1787, it has been entirely passed over in this discussion. It may, however,
be noted that in his letter of December 30, 1818, to the Secretary of State,
communicating the plan, he said: "I can assure you as a fact that for
more than four months and a half out of five, the power of exclusively
making treaties, appointing public ministers and judges of the Supreme
Court was given to the Senate after numerous debates and considerations of the subject both in committee of the whole and in the house."
Id., I, 310.

   34   Id., III, 154.
   35   Id., III, 353.
   36   Id., I, 148; III, 600.
   37   Id., III, 619.

ton, Gouverneur Morris, James Madison and Rufus King, the article was moulded into the form in which it appears in the Constitution, the committee having modified the expression "supreme law of the several States and of their citizens and inhabitants" so as to read "the supreme law of the land."[38] In the draft of the Constitution as reported by the Committee of Detail, it was expressly provided that the national legislature should have the power to call forth the aid of the militia "to execute the laws of the Union, enforce treaties, suppress insurrections and repel invasions." On August 23, the words "enforce treaties" were stricken out on the suggestion of Gouverneur Morris that they were superfluous, since treaties were to be laws.[39]

§28. Jurisdiction of Federal Courts.—In the New Jersey resolutions, submitted by William Paterson, June 15, the establishment of a Federal judiciary was recommended, which should have on appeal final jurisdiction in certain cases. Included in these were "all cases in which foreigners may be interested in the construction of any treaty or treaties."[40] In Article XI of the draft of the Constitution, as reported by the Committee of Detail, August 6, in which the jurisdiction of the Federal courts was defined, no reference was made to treaties. By an amendment adopted August 27, the judicial power of the United States was expressly extended to all cases in law and equity arising under "treaties made or which shall be made under their authority."[41]

§29. Treaty Making and the Formation of the New Union. —The recognition of the necessity of a more effective control by the central government over the enforcement of treaties is closely associated with the formation of the new Union as established by the Constitution. In resolutions prepared by Hamilton, and which, according to his indorsement, were intended for presentation to Congress in 1783, providing for the assembling of a convention to revise the Articles of Confederation, the defect in the power to give effect to treaties was mentioned as one of the reasons for the need of a revision.[42] Attempts were made in March, 1785, to secure amendments to the Articles of Confederation, by

38 Id., III, 733.
39 Id., III, 601.
40 Id., I, 324; III, 127.
41 Id., III, 626.
42 MSS. Hamilton Papers, V.

which exclusive power to regulate trade should be given to Congress; and in the letter prepared to be addressed to the States for this purpose, the necessity of an exclusive control by Congress over the execution and interpretation of treaties was urged.[43] The Federal Convention in commending the new Constitution to the consideration of the United States in Congress assembled, said: "The friends of our country have long seen and desired, that the power of making war, peace, and treaties, that of levying money and regulating commerce, and the correspondent executive and judicial authorities should be fully and effectually vested in the general government of the Union."[44]

43 MSS. Cont. Cong. Papers, XXIV, 125.
44 The President's letter of September 17, 1787, transmitting the proposed Constitution to Congress. Doc. Hist. of Const., II, 1.

CHAPTER V.

DISCUSSION PRECEDING THE ADOPTION OF THE CONSTITUTION.

§30. In the Press.—During the discussion that preceded the adoption of the Constitution, the provisions relating to treaties received full consideration.[1] In the Letter of a Federal Farmer, dated October 12, 1787, within one month after the adjournment of the Convention, R. H. Lee, in referring to Article VI of the proposed Constitution, said: "By the article before recited, treaties also made under the authority of the United States shall be the supreme law. It is not said that these treaties shall be made in pursuance of the Constitution—nor are there any constitutional bounds set to those who shall make them. The President and two-thirds of the Senate will be empowered to make treaties indefinitely, and when these treaties shall be made, they will also abolish all laws and State constitutions incompatible with them. This power in the President and Senate is absolute, and the judges will be bound to allow full force to whatever rule, article or thing the President and Senate shall establish by treaty. Whether it be practicable to set any bounds to those who make treaties, I am not able to say; if not, it proves that this power ought to be more safely lodged."[2] George Mason, who was a member of the Federal Convention and refused to sign the Constitution, in his printed objections to the Constitution, said: "By declaring all treaties supreme laws of the land the executive and the Senate have, in many cases, an exclusive power of legislation, which might have been avoided by proper distinctions with respect to treaties and requiring the assent of the House of Representatives where it could be done with safety."[3] To this objection, James Iredell, in the State Gazette of North Carolina, replied: "It seems to result unavoidably from the nature of the thing, that when the constitutional right to make treaties is exercised

---

1 "The articles relating to treaties, to paper money, and to contracts, created more enemies than all the errors in the system, positive and negative put together." Madison to Jefferson, October 17, 1788. Writings of Madison, I, 423.

2 Ford's Pamphlets on the Constitution, 312.

3 Id., 331.

the treaty so made should be binding upon those who delegated authority for that purpose. * * * Mr. Mason wishes the House of Representatives to have some share in this business, but he is immediately sensible of the impropriety of it and adds 'where it can be done with safety.' "[4] In the Federalist, No. 22, of December 14, 1787, Hamilton, in urging the necessity of Federal control over the making and enforcement of treaties, wrote: "No nation acquainted with the nature of our political association would be unwise enough to enter into stipulations with the United States, by which they conceded privileges of any importance to them, while they were apprised that the engagements on the part of the Union might at any moment be violated by its members. * * * The treaties of the United States, to have any force at all, must be considered as part of the law of the land. Their true import, as far as respects individuals, must, like all other laws, be ascertained by judicial determinations. To produce uniformity in these determinations, they ought to be submitted, in the last resort, to one SUPREME TRIBUNAL. * * * If there is in each State a court of final jurisdiction, there may be as many different final determinations on the same point as there are courts. * * * The treaties of the United States, under the present Constitution, are liable to the infractions of thirteen different legislatures, and as many different courts of final jurisdiction, acting under the authority of those legislatures. The faith, the reputation, the peace of the whole Union, are thus continually at the mercy of the prejudices, the passions, and the interests of every member of which it is composed."[5] The Federalist, No. 64, of March 7, 1788, written by Jay, was entirely devoted to a consideration of the treaty-making power. After discussing the importance of the power to make treaties, relating as they might to war, peace, and commerce, and the peculiar fitness of the Senate, by reason of the tenure, manner of election and qualification of its members, to co-operate with the President in the exercise of this power, Jay said: "It seldom happens in the negotiation of treaties, of whatever nature, but that perfect *secrecy* and immediate *dispatch* are sometimes requisite. * * * The Convention have done

---

4 Id., 355. See also address of David Ramsay to his fellow countrymen as to the impracticability of admitting the House of Representatives to an agency in the making of treaties, Id., 375.

5 Ford ed., 131, 140, 141.

well, therefore, in so disposing of the power of making treaties that although the President must, in forming them, act by the advice and consent of the Senate, yet he will be able to manage the business of intelligence in such a manner as prudence may suggest." He added, however, that the President might proceed independently in those preparatory and auxiliary measures important only "to facilitate the attainment of the objects of the negotiation." "The Constitution provides that our negotiations for treaties shall have every advantage which can be derived from talents, information, integrity, and deliberate investigations, on the one hand, and from secrecy and dispatch on the other." To those who were averse to treaties being the supreme law of the land and who professed to believe that "treaties like acts of assembly, should be repealable at pleasure," he replied: "This idea seems to be new and peculiar to this country, but new errors, as well as new truths, often appear. These gentlemen would do well to reflect that a treaty is only another name for a bargain, and that it would be impossible to find a nation who would make any bargain with us which should be binding on them *absolutely,* but on us only so long and so far as we may think proper to be bound by it. They who make laws may, without doubt, amend or repeal them; and it will not be disputed that they who make treaties may alter or cancel them; but still let us not forget that treaties are made, not by only one of the contracting parties, but by both; and, consequently, that as the consent of both was essential to their formation at first, so must it ever afterward be to alter or cancel them. The proposed Constitution, therefore, has not in the least extended the obligation of treaties. They are just as binding, and just as far beyond the lawful reach of legislative acts now, as they will be at any future period or under any form of government."[6] In the Federalist, No. 75, of March 26, 1788, Hamilton discussed the peculiar nature of the treaty-making power as distinguished from the executive and legislative powers. "It relates," he said, "neither to the execution of the subsisting laws nor to the enaction of new ones, and still less to an exertion of the common strength. Its objects are CONTRACTS with foreign nations, which have the force of law, but derive it from the obligations of good faith. They are not rules prescribed by the sovereign to the subject, but agreements between sovereign and

6 Lodge ed., 400; Ford ed., 426.

sovereign. The power in question seems, therefore, to form a distinct department, and to belong, properly, neither to the legislative nor to the executive. The qualities elsewhere detailed as indispensable in the management of foreign negotiations point out the Executive as the most fit agent in those transactions; while the vast importance of the trust, and the operation of treaties as laws, plead strongly for the participation of the whole or a portion of the legislative body in the office of making them." As to the co-operation of the House, he observed: "The fluctuating and, taking its future increase into the account, the multitudinous composition of that body, forbid us to expect in it those qualities which are essential to the proper execution of such a trust. Accurate and comprehensive knowledge of foreign politics; a steady and systematic adherence to the same views; a nice and uniform sensibility to national character; decision, *secrecy,* and dispatch, are incompatible with the genius of a body so variable and so numerous. * * * The greater frequency of the calls upon the House of Representatives and the greater length of time which it would often be necessary to keep them together when convened, to obtain their sanction in the progressive stages of a treaty, would be a source of so great inconvenience and expense as alone ought to condemn the project."[7]

§31. **In the State Conventions.**—In the various State conventions that adopted the Constitution, the provisions relating to treaties were frequently the topic of debate. The discussion in the South Carolina House of Representatives on the proposed Constitution, January 16, 1788, was in large measure devoted to the subject of treaties.[8] Pierce Butler, who had been a member of the Federal Convention, explained that it had first been proposed in the Convention to vest the sole power of making peace or war in the Senate; that later it had been proposed to add the House of Representatives, but that an "insurmountable objection was made to this proposition—which was, that negotiations always required the greatest secrecy, which could not be expected in a large body."[9] Charles Cotesworth Pinckney, who had likewise been a

7 Lodge ed., 465; Ford ed., 499. For other references to the treaty-making power in the Federalist, see No. 3 by Jay; No. 42 by Madison; No. 66 by Hamilton; and No. 69 by Hamilton. Ford ed., 13-15, 271, 445, 461.

8 Elliot's Debates (2 ed.), IV, 263-278.

9 Id., IV, 263.

member, in referring to the proceedings in the Federal Convention, said: "Some members were for vesting the power for making treaties in the legislature; but the secrecy and despatch which are so frequently necessary in negotiations evinced the impropriety of vesting it there."[10]   He observed that the treaty provision had evoked much debate in the Convention, but that "at last it was agreed to give the President a power of proposing treaties, as he was the ostensible head of the Union, and to vest the Senate (where each State had an equal voice) with the power of agreeing or disagreeing to the terms proposed. * * * On the whole, a large majority of the Convention thought this power would be more safely lodged where they had finally vested it, than anywhere else. It was a power that must necessarily be lodged somewhere; political caution and republican jealousy rendered it improper for us to vest it in the President alone; the nature of negotiation, and the frequent recess of the House of Representatives, rendered that body an improper depository of this prerogative. The President and Senate joined were, therefore, after much deliberation, deemed the most eligible corps in whom we could with safety vest the diplomatic authority of the Union." John Rutledge, also a member of the Federal Convention, likewise defended the provisions.[11]

In the debates in the Pennsylvania convention, December 11, 1787, James Wilson, who in the Federal Convention had proposed an amendment to require the approval of treaties by Congress, said: "Much has been said on the subject of treaties; and this power is denominated a blending of the legislative and executive powers in the Senate. * * * There is no doubt, sir, but, under this Constitution, treaties will become the supreme law of the land; nor is there any doubt but the Senate and President possess the power of making them. But though the treaties are to have the force of laws, they are in some important respects very different from other acts of legislation. In making laws, our own consent alone is necessary. In forming treaties, the concurrence of another power becomes necessary. Treaties, sir, are truly contracts, or compacts, between the different states, nations, or princes, who find it convenient or necessary to enter into them. Some gentlemen are of opinion that the power of making

10 Id., IV, 264.
11 Id., IV, 265, 267. See also speech of David Ramsay, Id., IV, 270.

treaties should have been placed in the legislature at large; there are, however, reasons that operate with great force on the other side. Treaties are frequently (especially in time of war) of such a nature, that it would be extremely improper to publish them, or even commit the secret of their negotiation to any great number of persons. For my part, I am not an advocate for secrecy in transactions relating to the public; not generally even in forming treaties, because I think that the history of the diplomatic corps will evince, even in that great department of politics, the truth of an old adage, that 'honesty is the best policy', and this is the conduct of the most able negotiators; yet sometimes secrecy may be necessary, and therefore it becomes an argument against committing the knowledge of these transactions to too many persons. But in their nature treaties originate differently from laws. They are made by equal parties, and each side has half of the bargain to make; they will be made between us and powers at the distance of three thousand miles. A long series of negotiation will frequently precede them; and can it be the opinion of these gentlemen that the legislature should be in session during the whole time? It well deserves to be remarked, that, though the House of Representatives possess no active part in making treaties, yet their legislative authority will be found to have strong restraining influences upon both President and Senate. In England, if the king and his ministers find themselves, during their negotiation, to be embarrassed because an existing law is not repealed, or a new law is not enacted, they give notice to the legislature of their situation, and inform them that it will be necessary, before the treaty can operate, that some law be repealed, or some be made. And will not the same thing take place here? Shall less prudence, less caution, less moderation, take place among those who negotiate treaties for the United States, than among those who negotiate them for the other nations of the earth? And let it be attended to, that, even in the making of treaties, the States are immediately represented, and the people mediately represented; two of the constituent parts of government must concur in making them. Neither the President nor the Senate, solely, can complete a treaty; they are checks upon each other, and are so balanced as to produce security to the people."[12]

In the Virginia convention, Patrick Henry objected particularly

12 Id., II, 505-507.

to the treaty-making provisions of the proposed Constitution. He urged that the President and two-thirds of a quorum of the Senate "might relinquish and alienate territorial rights, and our most valuable commercial advantages. In short, if any thing should be left us, it would be because the President and Senators were pleased to admit it. The power of making treaties, by this Constitution, ill-guarded as it is, extended farther than it did in any country in the world." To say that treaties were to operate as municipal laws was to him a doctrine totally novel; and to make them paramount to the constitution and laws of the States was without precedent.[13] George Mason likewise declared "that there is nothing in that Constitution to hinder a dismemberment of the empire. Will any gentleman say that they may not make a treaty, whereby the subjects of France, England, and other powers, may buy what lands they please in this country? * * * The President and Senate can make any treaty whatsoever. We wish not to refuse, but to guard, this power, as it is done in England. The empire there cannot be dismembered without the consent of the national Parliament. We wish an explicit declaration, in that paper, that the power which can make other treaties cannot, without the consent of the national Parliament—the national legislature—dismember the empire. The Senate alone ought not to have this power; much less ought a few States to have it. No treaty to dismember the empire ought to be made without the consent of three-fourths of the legislature in all its branches. Nor ought such a treaty to be made but in case of the most urgent and unavoidable necessity."[14] George Nicholas, in defending the provisions, said: "The worthy member [Grayson] says, that they can make a treaty relinquishing our rights, and inflicting punishments; because all treaties are declared paramount to the constitutions and laws of the States. An attentive consideration of this will show the committee that they can do no such thing. The provision of the 6th article is, that this Constitution, and the laws of the United States which shall be made in pursuance thereof, and all the treaties made, or which shall be made, under the authority of the United States, shall be the supreme law of the land. They can, by this, make no treaty which shall be repugnant to the spirit of the Constitution, or inconsistent with the dele-

13 Id., III, 500.
14 Id., III, 508.

gated powers. The treaties they make must be under the authority of the United States, to be within their province. It is sufficiently secured, because it only declares that, in pursuance of the powers given, they shall be the supreme law of the land, notwithstanding any thing in the constitution or laws of particular States."[15] Madison, in his concluding argument on the subject, said: "I am persuaded that, when this power comes to be thoroughly and candidly viewed, it will be found right and proper. As to its extent, perhaps it will be satisfactory to the committee that the power is, precisely, in the new Constitution as it is in the Confederation. In the existing Confederacy, Congress are authorized indefinitely to make treaties. Many of the States have recognized the treaties of Congress to be the supreme law of the land. Acts have passed, within a year, declaring this to be the case. I have seen many of them. Does it follow, because this power is given to Congress, that it is absolute and unlimited? I do not conceive that power is given to the President and Senate to dismember the empire, or to alienate any great, essential right. I do not think the whole legislative authority have this power. The exercise of the power must be consistent with the object of the delegation. One objection against the amendment proposed is this, that, by implication, it would give power to the legislative authority to dismember the empire—a power that ought not to be given, but by the necessity that would force assent from every man. I think it rests on the safest foundation as it is. The object of treaties is the regulation of intercourse with foreign nations, and is external. I do not think it possible to enumerate all the cases in which such external regulations would be necessary. Would it be right to define all the cases in which Congress could exercise this authority? The definition might, and probably would, be defective. They might be restrained, by such a definition, from exercising the authority where it would be essential to the interest and safety of the community. It is most safe, therefore, to leave it to be exercised as contingencies may arise. It is to be presumed that, in transactions with foreign countries, those who regulate them will feel the whole force of national attachment to their country. The contrast being between their own nation and a foreign nation, is it not presumable they will, as far as possible, advance the interest of their own country? * * * I think the argument of the

15 Id., III, 507.

gentleman [Corbin] who restrained the supremacy of these to the laws of particular States, and not to Congress, is rational. Here the supremacy of a treaty is contrasted with the supremacy of the laws of the States. It cannot be otherwise supreme. If it does not supersede their existing laws, as far as they contravene its operation, it cannot be of any effect. To counteract it by the supremacy of the State laws, would bring on the Union the just charge of national perfidy, and involve us in war."[16] Later in the debates, in discussing the jurisdiction of the Federal courts, Madison added: "With respect to treaties, there is a peculiar propriety in the judiciary's expounding them. These may involve us in controversies with foreign nations. It is necessary, therefore, that they should be determined in the courts of the general government. There are strong reasons why there should be a Supreme Court to decide such disputes. If, in any case, uniformity be necessary, it must be in the exposition of treaties."[17] William Grayson contended that "it ought to be expressly provided that no dismemberment should take place without the consent of the legislature. * * * There is an absolute necessity for the existence of the power. It may prevent the annihilation of society by procuring a peace. It must be lodged somewhere. The opposition wish it to be put in the hands of three-fourths of the members of both houses of Congress. It would be then secure. It is not so now."[18]

In the North Carolina convention, it was urged that, since treaties were to be the supreme law of the land, the House of Representatives ought to have a voice in making them.[19] The objection also was made that the President and ten Senators might make treaties of alliance and dispose of the country in such manner as they might please.[20] To these objections, William R. Davie, who had been a member of the Federal Convention, replied: "Although treaties are mere conventional acts between the contracting parties, yet, by the law of nations, they are the supreme law of the land to their respective citizens or subjects. All civilized nations

16 Id., III, 514.
17 Id., III, 532.
18 Id., III, 613. For debates in the Virginia convention on the treaty-making provisions, see, generally, Id., III, 419-517, 227, 332, 347, 349, 357, 402, 610.
19 Id., IV, 119.
20 Id., IV, 119.

7

have concurred in considering them as paramount to an ordinary act of legislation. This concurrence is founded on the reciprocal convenience and solid advantages arising from it. * * * The power of making treaties has, in all countries and governments, been placed in the executive departments. This has not only been grounded on the necessity and reason arising from that degree of secrecy, design, and despatch, which is always necessary in negotiations between nations, but to prevent their being impeded, or carried into effect, by the violence, animosity, and heat of parties, which too often infect numerous bodies. Both of these reasons preponderated in the foundation of this part of the system."[21] "It was necessary that treaties should operate as laws upon individuals. They ought to be binding upon us the moment they are made. They involve in their nature not only our own rights, but those of foreigners. If the rights of foreigners were left to be decided ultimately by thirteen distinct judiciaries, there would necessarily be unjust and contradictory decisions. If our courts of justice did not decide in favor of foreign citizens and subjects when they ought, it might involve the whole Union in a war: there ought, therefore, to be a paramount tribunal, which should have ample power to carry them into effect. * * * It is certainly clear that where the peace of the Union is affected, the general judiciary ought to decide."[22]

These fragments from the debates in the State conventions will serve to show the consideration given to these provisions by those who adopted the Constitution.

§32. **Amendments of the Treaty Provisions Proposed by the State Conventions.**—In the committee, appointed by the Maryland convention to consider amendments to the Constitution, an amendment that no treaty should "be effectual to repeal or abrogate the constitutions or bills of rights of the States, or any part of them" was proposed but expressly rejected.[23] John Lansing, who had been a member of the Federal Convention but had withdrawn before the Constitution was agreed to, proposed in the New York convention on July 7, 1788, as an amendment, that "no treaty ought to operate so as to alter the constitution of any

---

21 Id., IV, 119-120.
22 Id., IV, 158. See also speech of James Iredell. Id., IV, 125.
23 MSS. Jefferson Papers, series 2, Vol. XIV, No. 87, p. 6; Elliot's Debates, II, 553.

State; nor ought any commercial treaty to operate so as to abrogate any law of the United States."[24] In the "explanations" of the Constitution adopted by the New York convention as a part of its act of ratification, it was declared that no treaty was to be "construed so to operate as to alter the constitution of any State."[25] The seventh of the amendments to the body of the Constitution, proposed by the Virginia convention, provided that no commercial treaty should be ratified without the concurrence of two-thirds of the whole number of Senators, and that no treaty for the cession, or the compromise in any manner, of the rights or claims of the United States to territory, fisheries in the American seas, or the navigation of American rivers, should be concluded, except in the most urgent and extreme necessity, and then only with the concurrence of three-fourths of all the members of both houses respectively.[26] The first convention in North Carolina, which proceeded on the principle that the proposed modifications should be obtained before ratification, and adjourned in August, 1788, without having definitively acted on the Constitution, recommended the same amendment, as also another which should provide that no treaty which might be directly opposed to existing laws of Congress should be valid until such laws had been repealed or made conformable to the treaty, and that no treaty should be valid which was contradictory to the Constitution of the United States.[27] The conference that met at Harrisburg in September, 1788, subsequently to the ratification of the Constitution by Pennsylvania, petitioned the State legislature to obtain certain modifications of the Constitution, one of which should provide that no treaty thereafter concluded should be "deemed or construed to alter or affect any law of the United States, or of any particular State," until assented to by the House of Representatives.[28]

None of these proposed amendments as to the treaty-making power were, however, submitted by Congress to the States for ratification.

24 Elliot's Debates, II, 409. MSS. Hamilton Papers, VI, 83a.
25 Doc. Hist. of the Const., II, 194.
26 Id., II, 382. See as to comment on the proposed amendment, **Madi**son to Monroe, Feb. 26, 1796. MSS. Writings of Madison, V, 108.
27 Doc. Hist. of the Const., II, 271, 274.
28 Elliot's Debates, II, 546.

DIVISION II. UNDER THE CONSTITUTION.

I. THE MAKING.

"He [the President] shall have Power, by and with the Advice and Consent of the Senate, to make Treaties, provided two thirds of the Senators present concur."—Constitution, Article II, section 2.

CHAPTER VI.

THE ADVICE AND CONSENT OF THE SENATE.

(1) Prior to the Negotiation.

§33. The President in the Senate Chamber.—In the conference with the committee appointed by the Senate, August 6, 1789, to confer with the President as to the manner in which communications between the Executive and the Senate respecting treaties and nominations should be conducted, President Washington suggested that, in case of treaties, oral communications seemed to be indispensably necessary because of the variety of subjects embraced in them, which not only would require consideration but might undergo much discussion. To do this by written communications would be tedious without being satisfactory.[1] The report of the committee based upon this suggestion resulted in the adoption by the Senate, August 21, 1789, of a rule as to the procedure to be followed whenever the President should meet the Senate either in the Senate chamber or in such other place as that body might be convened by him. The rule had just been adopted when a message was received in which the President gave notice of his intention to meet with the Senate on the following day to consider the terms of a treaty to be negotiated with the Southern Indians. In accordance with the notification, the President, accompanied by General Knox, who although not a cabinet officer at the time was familiar with Indian affairs and prepared to answer questions, appeared in the Senate chamber. After taking the chair, the President briefly stated the purpose of his meeting the Senate.[2] A short paper containing a few explanations was read, after which the Senate was called upon to give its

---

1 Writings (Ford ed.), XI, 417. On July 21, 1789, the Senate requested the attendance of John Jay, who had continued in charge of foreign affairs, to give information respecting the consular convention negotiated with France. Jay complied with the request. Ex. Journal, I, 7.

2 Maclay says: "The President was introduced, and took our President's chair. He rose and told us bluntly that he had called on us for our advice and consent to some propositions respecting the treaty to be held with the Southern Indians." Sketches of Debate in the First Senate of the United States (G. W. Harris ed.), 122.

advice and consent by an affirmative or negative vote on seven specific questions as to the proposed negotiations.[3] The Senate seemed unwilling to do this without having first fully considered the articles. Robert Morris moved to refer the matter to a special committee. To this it was objected that a council never referred anything to a committee. The President stated that, while he had no objection to a postponement, the reference to a committee would defeat the very purpose of his meeting the Senate. The questions were accordingly postponed until Monday, at which time a vote was taken on each of them separately. The Senate maintained its right to exercise an independent judgment by voting in favor of a part only of the propositions submitted.[4]

§34. **Advice Sought by Message.**—Although President Washington did not again visit the Senate chamber to consult that body on proposed treaty negotiations, he continued to seek its advice by message before opening negotiations.[5] By special messages of August 4, 1790, August 11, 1790, January 18, 1792, and March 23, 1792, he sought the advice of the Senate as to the conclusion of treaties with certain Indian tribes;[6] and the advice and consent of the Senate was in each case given to the conclusion of the treaty in conformity with the articles submitted.[7] In a communication to the Senate, February 9, 1790, concerning the differences that had arisen between the United States and Great Britain as to the northeastern boundary, the President stated that he considered it advisable to postpone any negotiations on the

3 Ex. Journal, I, 19, 20-23.

4 Maclay, Sketches of Debate in the First Senate of the United States (G. W. Harris ed.), 122-126. In speaking of the withdrawal of the President on August 22, with a "discontented air," Maclay says: "Had it been any other than the man who I wish to regard as the first character in the world, I would have said, with sullen dignity." Id., 125.

5 Rule XXXVI of the Standing Rules of the Senate still provides the manner in which the President is to meet the Senate in executive session. Henry Cabot Lodge, in referring to the recognition in this rule of the right of the President to meet with the Senate in the consideration of treaties, said, in the U. S. Senate, January 24, 1906: "Yet I think we should be disposed to resent it if a request of that sort was made to us by the President." Cong. Record, 59th Cong., 1st Sess., 1470.

6 Ex. Journal, I, 55, 60, 98, 116.

7 At a meeting of the heads of the departments, February 25, 1793, the President was unanimously advised not to consult the Senate prior to opening proposed negotiations with the Indians north of the Ohio. MSS. Letters to Washington, CXVI, 252.

subject until he had received the advice of the Senate as to the propositions to be offered on the part of the United States.[8] By a message of May 8, 1792, the President enquired of the Senate whether it would approve a treaty, if one were concluded, with Algiers for the payment of ransom and peace money not to exceed certain amounts.[9] Jefferson, the Secretary of State, in an oral opinion on March 11, and in a written communication on April 1, 1792, had advised the President that it was advisable whenever possible to consult the Senate before the opening of negotiations, since its subsequent approbation was necessary to valdidate a treaty.[10] In communicating, January 11, 1792, to the Senate the nominations of William Carmichael, chargé d'affaires at Madrid, and William Short, chargé d'affaires at Paris, as commissioners plenipotentiary to negotiate a convention with Spain, respecting the navigation of the Mississippi, explanations were made by the President as to the nature of the mission and the reasons for opening the negotiations at Madrid.[11] Subsequently to the Senate's confirmation of the nominations, the Executive decided to extend the negotiations to commercial matters.[12] Jefferson, in submitting to the President instructions for this purpose, observed that they ought to be laid before the Senate to determine whether that body would advise and consent that a treaty be entered into in conformity with them.[13] The instructions with observations were communicated to the Senate, March 7, for its advice and consent to the extension of the powers, and to the ratification of a treaty which should conform to these instructions.[14] On March 16, the Senate (two-thirds of the members present concurring) approved of the extension of the powers, and promised that it would advise and consent to the ratification of a treaty negotiated in conformity with these additional instructions.[15] Formal instructions elaborating upon these general principles were, under date of March 18, prepared by Jefferson.[16]

8 Ex. Journal, I, 36-7.
9 Id., 122-3.
10 MSS. Washington Papers, XXI, 91; Jefferson Papers, series 4, Vol. II, No. 18.
11 Ex. Journal, I, 95, 96.
12 Id., 99.
13 Writings of Jefferson (Ford ed.), V, 442.
14 Ex. Journal, I, 106.
15 Id., 115.
16 Am. State Papers, For. Rel., I, 252.

The negotiations as continued and consummated by Thomas Pinckney, whose nomination had been confirmed by the Senate with knowledge of the nature of his mission, were conducted on the basis of these instructions, together with those subsequently given relative to spoliation claims.[17] In the negotiations leading up to the treaty with Great Britain of November 19, 1794, a different policy was pursued by the Executive. The message of April 16, 1794, communicating to the Senate the nomination of John Jay as envoy extraordinary to Great Britain, contained only a general statement as to the serious aspect of our relations with that country, and was not accompanied with his instructions, nor does it appear that they were subsequently submitted.[18] This fact was not overlooked by the Senate. A resolution was introduced on April 17, prior to Jay's confirmation on April 19, requesting the President to inform the Senate of the "whole business" with which the proposed envoy was to be charged; but the resolution was defeated.[19] Gouverneur Morris had in October, 1789, been commissioned by the President, without confirmation by the Senate, in a private and unofficial character, to enter informally into conferences with the British government. His instructions, with explanations as to the nature and results of the mission, were subsequently, February 14, 1791, laid before the Senate.[20] Although John Paul Jones and David Humphreys had been commissioned without confirmation by the Senate to negotiate with Algiers, the Senate had in other ways approved of the negotiations.[21]

These first attempts of the Executive to follow out the clear intention of the framers of the Constitution, in consulting the Senate prior to the opening of negotiations, have been followed only in exceptional instances. President Jackson, in a message of May 6, 1830, sought the advice of the Senate as to the conclusion of a treaty with the Choctaw Indians in accordance with certain propositions therewith submitted.[22] President Polk submitted, June 10, 1846, the proposed Oregon treaty for the Senate's advice as to its conclusion. The conclusion of the treaty having been

17 Id., 533; Ex. Journal, I, 163-4.
18 Ex. Journal, I, 150.
19 Id., I, 151.
20 Id., I, 73; Am. State Papers, For. Rel., I, 122.
21 Id., 290, 294.
22 Ex. Journal, IV, 97.

advised (two-thirds concurring) the treaty was signed June 15, and thereupon submitted to the Senate for its advice and consent to the ratification.[23] In a message of August 4, 1846, President Polk advised the Senate of his intention to propose terms of peace to Mexico, and suggested for the consideration of the Senate in executive session the expediency of a contingent appropriation to be available in case Mexico should agree to a cession of territory for a fair equivalent.[24] President Buchanan communicated with the Senate, February 21, 1861, in relation to the differences that had arisen as to the meaning to be given to the clause of the Oregon treaty defining the northwestern water boundary, and enquired whether the Senate would approve a treaty by which the controversy should be referred to arbitration.[25] President Lincoln adopted this procedure of his predecessor and sought in a message of March 16, 1861, further advice of the Senate.[26] Again, on December 17, 1861, President Lincoln transmitted to the Senate for its advice a draft of a convention, which the American minister in Mexico had proposed to that government, to guarantee the payment of claims urged by certain European powers

23 Id., VII, 84, 89, 90, 95. Mr. Buchanan, Secretary of State, in instructions to Mr. McLane, minister to Great Britain, under date of February 26, 1846, said: "The Federal Constitution has made the Senate, to a certain extent, a co-ordinate branch of the treaty-making power. Without their advice and consent, no treaty can be concluded. This power could not be entrusted to wiser or better hands. Besides, in their legislative character, they constitute a portion of the war making, as in their executive capacity they compose a part of the treaty-making power. * * * A rejection of the British ultimatum might probably lead to war, and as a branch of the legislative power, it would be incumbent upon them to authorize the necessary preparations to render this war successful. Under these considerations, the President, in deference to the Senate, and to the true theory of the constitutional responsibilities of the different branches of the Government, will forego his own opinions so far as to submit to that body any proposition which may be made by the British Government, not, in his judgment, wholly inconsistent with the rights and honor of the country. Neither is the fact to be disguised that from the speeches and proceedings in the Senate, it is probable that a proposition to adjust the Oregon question on the parallel of 49° would receive their favorable consideration." MSS. Instructions to Great Britain, XV, 303; Works of Buchanan (Moore ed.), VI, 379.

24 Ex. Journal, VII, 132.

25 Id., XI, 279.

26 Id., XI, 308.

against Mexico.[27] In a message of February 10, 1868, President Johnson sought the advice of the Senate as to the transfer to the United States by the Dominican Republic of the peninsula and bay of Samana upon the terms proposed in a draft of a convention which accompanied the message.[28] Again, in a message of January 15, 1869, President Johnson consulted the Senate as to the expediency of concluding with Great Britain a naturalization convention on the basis of a protocol signed at London, October 9, 1868. The Senate by resolution, dated April 15, 1869, advised the negotiation of a convention in accordance with the terms of the protocol.[29] President Grant, upon receiving a dispatch from our minister resident at Honolulu, relative to the annexation of the Hawaiian Islands to the United States, transmitted it to the Senate, observing at the same time that the views of the Senate with reference to any future course which there might be a disposition to adopt would be acceptable.[30] In a message of May 13, 1872, the President submitted an article proposed by the British government for the adjustment of the differences that had arisen in the proceedings of the Geneva tribunal, and asked the advice of the Senate as to its formal adoption. The Senate recommended, May 25, the negotiation of an article, which did not conform to the one proposed.[31] On June 18, 1874, the President submitted a draft of a proposed agreement with Great Britain for commercial reciprocity with Canada. The Senate by a resolution of February 3, 1875, declared it inexpedient to negotiate such a convention.[32] A proposal from the King of the Hawaiian Islands, for the extension for a period of seven years of the reciprocity convention then in force, was, on June 9, 1884, before negotiations for that purpose were opened, communicated by President Arthur to the Senate for consideration.[33] These are, however, as stated above, exceptional instances.[34]

§35. **Advice by Resolution.**—The Senate may by means of

27 Id., XII, 24.
28 Id., XVI, 163.
29 Id., XVI, 441; XVII, 174.
30 Id., XVIII, 59.
31 Id., XVIII, 264.
32 Id., XIX, 355, 502.
33 Id., XXIV, 280.
34 See for a comprehensive article on this topic by Henry Cabot Lodge, Scribner's Magazine, XXXI, 33.

resolutions advise the negotiation of treaties by the Executive. But such resolutions are merely advisory not mandatory, and the right of the Senate to adopt them is not dependent upon its treaty-making power. Such resolutions may be joint or concurrent, and originate as well in the House of Representatives as in the Senate.[85] For instance, a joint resolution was passed by Congress and approved March 2, 1883, by which the President was requested to open negotiations with Venezuela with a view to the renewal of the convention of April 25, 1866, for the adjudication of claims of American citizens.[86] The convention of December 5, 1885, resulted. By a concurrent resolution adopted by the Senate February 14, and by the House, April 3, 1890, the President was requested to invite negotiations with other powers to the end that differences, which might arise and which could not be settled through diplomatic channels, should be referred to arbitration for adjustment. Negotiations were eventually instituted which resulted in the signature on January 11, 1897, of a convention of arbitration with Great Britain. The convention, however, failed to receive the required approval of the Senate.[37] An act of Congress, approved June 28, 1902, authorized the President to acquire of Colombia, or, in the event of the failure to acquire of Colombia, of Costa Rica and Nicaragua, perpetual control of territory deemed necessary for the construction and operation of an interoceanic canal.[38] A convention for this purpose was negotiated and signed with the Colombian Government, January 22, 1903, but failed to receive the approval of the Colombian Congress. A convention for the same purpose was thereafter concluded,

---

35 See for examples of House resolutions of this character, 17th Cong., 2d Sess., Journal, 280; 44th Cong., 1st Sess., Record, 2158; 46th Cong., 1st Sess., Journal, 190, 584; 60th Cong., 2d Sess., Record, 1070, 3505, 3741, 3811, 3822, 3831. In May, 1826, John Forsyth, then a member of the House of Representatives, later Secretary of State, objected to a resolution of this nature on the ground that it was irregular for the House of Representatives to request the President to exercise any of his constitutional powers. Journal, 19th Cong., 1st Sess., 567, 576; Register of Debates, 19th Cong., 1st Sess., 2636.

36 28 Stats. at L. 1053.

37 Moore, Int. Arb., I, 962.

38 32 Stats. at L. 481. A joint resolution, approved March 2, 1867, directed the Secretary of State to negotiate with Colombia as to the terms upon which a right of way to construct an interoceanic canal might be obtained. 14 Stats. at L. 572.

November 18, 1903, with the new republic of Panama. A joint resolution, approved April 8, 1904, requested the President to open negotiations with Great Britain, Russia and Japan for the revision of the rules regulating the taking of fur seals in the North Pacific Ocean and the Bering Sea.[39] By a joint resolution, approved April 28, 1904, Congress declared that it was desirable for the President to bring about an understanding between the principal maritime powers for the exemption from capture of un-offending private property at sea.[40] A joint resolution, approved March 4, 1909, requested the President to renew negotiations with Russia to secure by treaty, or otherwise, uniformity of treatment and protection to American citizens holding passports.[41] In each of the instances above noted, the desired negotiations either were pending at the time of the adoption of the resolution or were eventually instituted. Although it is not to be doubted that the President will always give careful consideration to the views of Congress, deliberately expressed, as to instituting negotiations, he cannot be compelled by a resolution of either house or of both houses of Congress to exercise a power entrusted to him under the Constitution.[42]

The disadvantages of attempting to prescribe in advance the conditions under which negotiations are to be conducted by the Executive, were fairly set forth by Mr. Bibb in a report from the Senate Committee on Foreign Relations, February 15, 1816. After the adoption of the resolution advising the ratification of the treaty of commerce with Great Britain of July 3, 1815, reso-lutions were introduced in the Senate requesting the President to continue the negotiations on certain specific matters outlined in the resolutions. Mr. Bibb, in his report, observed that an exam-ination of the correspondence furnished satisfactory evidence that no effort which belonged to the negotiators had been neglected, and that the failure to arrange for the subjects embraced in the resolutions resulted from the manifest indisposition of the British plenipotentiaries to concur in any satisfactory stipulations con-

39 33 Stats. at L. 586.
40 33 Id. 592.
41 35 Id. 1170.
42 See for other examples, joint resolutions approved February 14, 1859 (11 Stats. at L. 441), and May 14, 1880 (21 Id. 306); and acts ap-proved August 3, 1883 (22 Id. 217), July 9, 1888 (25 Id. 243), and March 3, 1897 (29 Id. 624).

cerning them; that if the proper moment had arrived to renew the negotiations the President would doubtless take advantage of it, for he had, in common with the Senate, the interests of the country at heart, and, since he conducted correspondence with foreign nations, would be more competent to determine when, how, and upon what subjects negotiations could be urged with the greatest prospect of success; and that, moreover, the differences of opinion between members of the Senate on propositions about which to advise the President would prevent that unity of design, secrecy and dispatch so requisite for successful negotiations.[43]

§36. **Consultation with Individual Members.**—As a matter of expediency individual members, and especially those on the Committee on Foreign Relations, to which all treaties are referred in the Senate, are not infrequently consulted on important negotiations. For instance, in 1871, after the unqualified rejection (44 to 1) by the Senate of the Johnson-Clarendon convention, Mr. Fish, Secretary of State, did not feel warranted in reopening negotiations without some understanding with members of that body. He accordingly conferred with prominent Senators on both sides of the chamber, and sought the advice of Mr. Sumner, who was then chairman of the Committee on Foreign Relations, concerning the basis of the proposed negotiations, although he did not afterwards follow the particular course that Mr. Sumner recommended.[44]

§37. **Confirmation of Negotiators.**—Prior to 1815, the President, in the greater number of instances, submitted to the Senate for confirmation the names of the commissioners designated to negotiate treaties, and at the same time advised that body of the general purpose of the negotiations about to be instituted. In the message to the Senate of January 11, 1792, nominating William Carmichael and William Short as commissioners to negotiate a treaty with the Spanish government for the navigation of the Mississippi River, there was included a report of the Secretary of State on the proposed negotiations.[45] In communicating, May

43 Compilation of Reports of the Sen. Com. on For. Rel., S. Doc. No. 231, 56th Cong., 2d Sess., VIII, 22. See also to the same effect, a report on February 19, 1862, by Mr. Sumner, Id., 132.

44 Moore, Int. Arb., I, 525.

45 Ex. Journal, I, 95. With reference to the nomination of Jay to negotiate with Great Britain, see supra, 70.

31, 1797, to the Senate for confirmation the nominations of C. C. Pinckney, Francis Dana and John Marshall as envoys extraordinary and ministers plenipotentiary to the French Republic, President Adams explained in general terms that they were appointed "to negotiate with the French Republic, to dissipate umbrages, to remove prejudices, to rectify errors, and adjust all differences by a treaty between the two powers."[46] The Senate on June 5, confirmed the nominations, and on June 22, the substitution of Elbridge Gerry for Francis Dana.[47] When negotiations were re-opened in 1799, the Senate was called upon to confirm the new nominations.[48] President Jefferson submitted to the Senate, January 11, 1803, for confirmation the nominations of James Monroe and Robert R. Livingston as commissioners with full powers to enter into a treaty with the First Consul of France, for the purpose of enlarging, and more effectually securing, our rights and interests in the river Mississippi, and in the territories eastward thereof.[49] The nominations of J. Q. Adams, James A. Bayard, Henry Clay and Jonathan Russell, were advised and consented to by the Senate on January 18, 1814, and that of Albert Gallatin, who had previously been rejected on the grounds that the duties of an envoy were incompatible with those of the Secretary of the Treasury,[50] on February 9, as ministers plenipotentiary and extraordinary to negotiate and sign a treaty of peace and a treaty of commerce with Great Britain.[51]

Since 1815, this course has been exceptional. Treaties have with few exceptions been negotiated through the Secretary of State, the regular diplomatic representatives and consular officers, or special agents, empowered and commissioned to negotiate the treaty by the President without special confirmation for this purpose by the Senate.[52]

46 Id., I, 241.

47 Id., I, 243, 245.

48 Id., I, 317, 326.

49 Id., I, 431.

50 His successor in the office of Secretary of the Treasury was confirmed February 9, immediately preceding his own confirmation as minister to negotiate with Great Britain. Id., II, 355, 389.

51 Id., II, 454, 471. For other confirmations during this period of special commissioners appointed to negotiate treaties, see Id., I, 265, 310, 311, 432, 440; II, 25, 29.

52 In a minority report of the Senate committee on Foreign Relations, signed by John T. Morgan, Eli Saulsbury, Joseph E. Brown and

§38. **Special Agents.**—The practice of negotiating treaties through special agents, appointed by the President, with countries with which at the time diplomatic relations do not exist, has evoked some criticism in the Senate. Treaties with the King of Siam and the Sultan of Muscat were signed, March 20, 1833, and September 21, 1833, respectively, on the part of the United States by Edmund Roberts, a special and secret agent commissioned for this purpose by the President. Immediately after the adoption by the Senate of the resolutions advising the ratifications, to which there appears to have been no opposition, a resolution was introduced declaring that, while the Senate deemed the ratification expedient, it felt itself constrained by a high sense of its constitutional duty to express its decided disapprobation of the practice of appointing diplomatic agents to foreign countries by the President alone, without the advice and consent of the Senate. On the motion of Mr. Webster the resolution was tabled.[53] In the resolutions of January 9, 1883, advising and consenting to the ratification of the treaty with the kingdom of Korea, signed May 22, 1882, on the part of the United States by Commodore R. W. Shufeldt, specially commissioned by the President, the Senate declared that it did not by this act admit or acquiesce in any right or constitutional power in the President to authorize any person to negotiate treaties with a foreign power unless such person had been appointed for such purpose or clothed with such power by and with the advice and consent of the Senate, except in the case

H. B. Payne, in reference to the unratified fisheries treaty with Great Britain, signed February 15, 1888, this question is examined in detail. It is stated in this report that the "whole number of persons appointed or recognized by the President, without the concurrence or advice of the Senate, or the express authority of Congress, as agents to conduct negotiations and conclude treaties [prior to June 25, 1887] is four hundred and thirty-eight. Three have been appointed by the Secretary of State and thirty-two have been appointed by the President with the advice and consent of the Senate." According to the list attached to the report, only the commissioners to the Panama Congress, and those of 1880 to negotiate with China, have, since 1815, been specially commissioned by and with the advice and consent of the Senate to negotiate treaties. S. Doc. No. 231, 56th Cong., 2d Sess., VIII, 332, et seq. It should, however, be noted that the five commissioners on the part of the United States who negotiated and signed the treaty of May 8, 1871, with Great Britain, were confirmed by the Senate. Ex. Journal, XVII, 644, 651.

53 Ex. Journal, IV, 413, 445.

8

of a Secretary of State or a diplomatic officer appointed by the President to fill a vacancy during the recess of the Senate.[54] A resolution of similar import was introduced in the Senate, July 20, 1888, relative to the negotiation of the unratified fisheries treaty with Great Britain.[55] The Executive has, however, recognized no limitation in this respect.[56] Numerous treaties have been concluded by special agents employed by the President.[57]

Of the five commissioners appointed by the President, September 13, 1898, to negotiate a treaty of peace with Spain, three were members of the Senate and of the Committee on Foreign Relations. Two of the five American members of the Joint High Commission of 1898, for the adjustment of questions then pending between the United States and Great Britain, were likewise members of the Senate.[58]

(2) Subsequently to the Negotiation.

§39. Consular Convention of 1788 with France.—The consular convention with France, signed November 14, 1788, on the authority of instructions approved by the Congress of the Confederation, in which was vested the treaty-making power, was communicated to the Senate, June 11, 1789, and was the first treaty to come before the government under the Constitution for ratification.[59] John Jay, who continued in charge of foreign af-

54 Id., XXIII, 585.

55 Id., XXVI, 314.

56 See, however, message of President Van Buren to the Senate, June 7, 1838, in reference to proposed negotiations with Ecuador. Richardson, Messages and Papers of the Presidents, III, 477.

57 Besides the three treaties mentioned above, note may be made of those signed in 1815 and 1816 with Algiers; May 7, 1830, with the Ottoman Porte; in 1846, and 1847, (negotiated by A. Dudley Mann), with certain of the German States; February 2, 1848, with Mexico; November 25, 1850, with Switzerland; and March 31, 1854, with Japan. See for lists of special missions authorized by the President, Moore, Int. Law Digest, IV, 452-457; Foster, Practice of Diplomacy, 199-203. "The President of the United States has the power to propose treaties, subject to ratification by the Senate, and he may use such agencies as he chooses to employ, except that he cannot take any money from the treasury to pay those agents without an appropriation by law. He can use such instruments as he pleases." Mr. Sherman, chairman of the Committee on Foreign Relations, in the Senate, August 7, 1888. Record, 7285.

58 See for criticism of this practice, Cong. Record, 57th Cong., 2d Sess., 2695, et seq. See also Secret Journals, II, 551; and Ex. Journal, I, 152.

59 Certain Indian treaties were submitted, May 25, 1789, but were not considered by the Senate until after its action on the French convention.

fairs, was, on July 22, requested by the Senate to give his opinion as to the extent to which he considered the faith of the United States pledged to the ratification of the convention in the form in which it was signed. In his report to the Senate, July 25, Jay observed that the original scheme, however exceptionable, had been framed and agreed to by Congress; that the refusal to ratify the convention of 1784, because of its deviation from that scheme, had been accompanied with a promise to ratify one in conformity with it, provided the new convention should be limited in its duration; that in the commission to Jefferson, Congress had likewise promised ratification in case these conditions were complied with; that, while he apprehended that the new convention would prove more inconvenient than beneficial to the United States, the circumstances under which it had been negotiated made, in his opinion, its ratification by the Senate indispensable.[60] On July 29, it was unanimously resolved that "the Senate do consent to the said convention, and advise the President of the United States to ratify the same."[61] So also in its action on Indian treaties, negotiated with its advice and consent, the Senate recognized an obligation to confirm what it had already authorized. The committee, to which the treaty of July 2, 1791, with the Cherokees, had been referred, observed, in its report to the Senate, that the treaty strictly conformed to the instructions of the President based upon the advice and consent of the Senate as given August 11, 1790.[62]

§40. Qualified Approval of the Jay Treaty.—In the ratification of the treaty with Great Britain, signed November 19, 1794, the position of the Senate was essentially different. Although Jay's nomination as commissioner to negotiate with Great Britain had been confirmed by the Senate, his instructions were not submitted to that body, and in the negotiations he acted upon the authority of but one branch of the treaty-making power. No doubt could therefore exist as to the constitutional right of the Senate, as a co-ordinate branch of the treaty-making power, to give an independent approval or disapproval of the treaty thus negotiated. If the treaty was in the main acceptable, but contained objectionable provisions, two courses were at this stage open to the Senate. It could withhold action altogether until the

60 Ex. Journal, I, 7; Dip. Cor. 1783-9, I, 304-322.
61 Ex. Journal, I, 9.
62 Id., I, 88.

desired changes had been effected, or it could advise the ratification of the treaty subject to these desired changes. On June 22, 1795, a motion, providing that further consideration of the treaty be postponed and that the President be advised to proceed to effect certain specific modifications, was offered.[63] The ratification was, however, on June 24, advised and consented to "on condition" that an article be added to the treaty whereby it should be agreed to suspend the operation of so much of the twelfth article as related to the trade between the United States and the British West Indies. The Senate moreover advised the President to proceed without delay to further friendly negotiations with Great Britain on the subject of the said trade and of the terms and conditions in question.[64] The Secretary of State, Edmund Randolph, seemed at first to be somewhat in doubt whether the resolution was to be considered as the final act of the Senate, or whether the proposed new article must be submitted to that body before the treaty could take effect. On June 29, the President requested the written opinions of the heads of the departments on the question. They were agreed that it would be unnecessary again to submit the treaty to the Senate. Hamilton, who, although not an officer of the government at the time, was consulted, expressed a different view.[65] The Secretary of State, in his written opinion dated July 12, argued that, since the final ratification was given by the President and not by the Senate, the action of the Senate even in case it advised and consented unconditionally was taken on a treaty the completion of which was reserved to the President; that the Senate consequently might give its advice and consent without having the very treaty which was to be ratified before it; that if the President should ratify the treaty without again consulting that body he would be responsible for the accuracy with which its advice was followed; that if he should ratify what had not been advised the treaty would not be the supreme law of the land, and that the rights of the Senate would for this very reason be safeguarded.[66] The suspension of the operation of the twelfth article was agreed to by the British

63 Id., I, 183.

64 Id., I, 186.

65 See Washington to Hamilton, July 14, 1795. MSS. Hamilton Papers.

66 MSS. Washington Papers, XXII, 148, 184, 200. See also MSS. Letters to Washington, CXVII, 271.

government and the ratifications of the treaty were exchanged at London October 28, 1795, without the treaty being again submitted to the Senate.[67]

In consenting, March 6, 1798, to the ratification of a treaty with Tunis, signed in August, 1797, the Senate likewise attached a condition that Article XIV should be suspended, and advised the President to enter into further negotiations on the subject of the article. As the result of the subsequent negotiations certain changes were made in other articles. Accordingly, the articles were re-submitted by President Adams to the Senate, and their ratification was advised December 24, 1799.[68]

§41. Specific Amendments Advised.—Not usually consulted as to the conduct of negotiations, the Senate has freely exercised its co-ordinate power in treaty making by means of amendments. In case a treaty as negotiated is not acceptable in some of its provisions to the Senate, it is the practice of that body, if it gives its advice and consent to the ratification, to do so with specific amendments, which renders unnecessary the re-submission of the instrument after the consent of the other party to the designated changes has been obtained. But the approval, whether qualified or unqualified, of the treaty by the Senate is not to be confused with the act of ratification. The latter is performed by the President, and is unconditional, even where it relates to a treaty which, because of amendments by the Senate, differs from the one first signed.[69] There can be no doubt of the constitutional right of the Senate to reject in toto a treaty, the negotiation of which it has not advised, or to withhold action thereon until the changes which it may indicate by resolution or otherwise have been negotiated, or to advise and consent to the ratification with certain specific amendments. Against this last procedure the objection usually

67 Certain Senators in the opposition had expressed the opinion that the resolution advising ratification was so worded as to require the re-submission of the treaty to the Senate. See Tazewell to Monroe, June 27, 1795. MSS. Monroe Papers, VIII, 951.

68 Ex. Journal, I, 263, 264, 328, 330.

69 In advising the ratifications of the extradition conventions with the Netherlands signed May 29, 1856, and November 24, 1903, the Senate attached amendments. In both instances upon the representation of the Netherlands government that procedure in that country made no provision for an amendment to a treaty, new treaties were signed embodying the amendments, and submitted to the Senate.

urged is that the amendments are in the nature of an ultimatum and are made by those not familiar with the prior negotiations. The proposed treaty is not infrequently so amended as to be unacceptable to the other power, and no treaty results.

§42. **Treaties Rejected by the Senate.**—Of treaties rejected by the Senate either expressly by a resolution to that effect, or impliedly through a failure to act on them, note may be made of those signed as follows: March 25, 1844, with the States of the German Zollverein, for commercial reciprocity; July 20, 1855, and May 21, 1867, with Hawaii, for commercial reciprocity; October 24, 1867, with Denmark, for the cession to the United States of the islands of St. Thomas and St. John; November 29, 1869, for the annexation of the Dominican Republic; December 10, 1824, with Colombia, for the suppression of the African slave trade; March 6, 1835, with the Swiss Confederation; April 12, 1844, for the annexation of Texas; December 14, 1859, with Mexico, relative to transits and commerce; July 13, 1882, with Mexico, for re-opening the Weil and La Abra Mining Company claims; March 5, 1860, with Spain, for the settlement of claims; January 14, 1869, with Great Britain, for the adjustment of outstanding claims; June 25, 1886, with Great Britain, for the extradition of fugitives; February 15, 1888, with Great Britain, for the regulation of the fisheries; January 11, 1897, with Great Britain, for the settlement of disputes by arbitration; and the various so-called Kasson conventions, for commercial reciprocity, negotiated in 1899 and 1900.

§43. **Reconsideration by Senate.**—All motions in the Senate in the consideration of a treaty, except to postpone indefinitely and to give its final advice and consent to the ratification, both of which require a two-thirds vote, are decided by a majority.[70] A resolution advising the ratification of a treaty with amendments may fail to receive the required two-thirds vote, be reconsidered, and, with different amendments, be agreed to.[71] The action of the Senate being advisory, an adverse vote on the resolution advising and consenting to the ratification does not constitute in itself a rejection by the United States of the treaty. The

70 Standing Rule XXXVII, clause 1.
71 See for instances, Ex. Journal, IX, 306, 312; X, 139, 144; XIII, 416, 423; XIX, 281, 289, 291; XXIV, 141, 205; XXVII, 469, 470; XXX, 358, 359, 377, 378.

President as the sole organ of communication with foreign powers alone can communicate the acceptance or rejection of the United States. On March 16, 1860, the Senate voted adversely on the ratification of a treaty with Nicaragua, signed March 16, 1859, and ordered the resolution to that effect laid before the President. Four days later the Senate requested the return of the resolution. The request being complied with, the Senate reconsidered its action, and on June 26 advised ratification of the treaty with amendments.[72] The ratification of an agreement with Venezuela, signed January 14, 1859, for the settlement of the Aves Island claims, was advised, with amendment, June 26, 1860, and the resolution to that effect laid before the President. On January 24, 1861, the Senate requested the return of the agreement for further consideration. In complying with the request, President Buchanan recommended the withdrawal of the amendment. On February 21, 1861, the ratification was advised without amendment.[73] On March 27, 1874, the Senate unanimously advised the ratification of an extradition convention with Belgium, signed March 19, 1874, and ordered the resolution laid before the President. On April 8, after the ratification by the President on March 31, but prior to the exchange of the ratifications on April 30, the Senate passed a resolution rescinding its resolution of March 27, and requesting the President to return the convention and resolution. Two days later, however, the resolution of April 8 was rescinded.[74] On June 12, 1884, the Senate unanimously voted against the accession of the United States to the international convention for the protection of industrial property, signed at Paris, March 20, 1883. The convention was returned to the Senate, February 2, 1885, by President Arthur, with a message recommending a reconsideration; and on March 2, 1887, the Senate consented to the accession.[75] On January 17, 1900, the Senate requested the President to return the Samoan convention, concluded at Washington, December 2, 1899, between the United States, Great Britain and Germany, together with its resolution advising ratification dated January 16. This request was complied with, but a motion to reconsider the resolution of ratifica-

72 Id., XI, 165, 218.
73 Id., XI, 222, 254, 276.
74 Id., XIX, 281, 291. See also, Id., XI, 147, 153.
75 Id., XXIV, 287, 455; XXV, 763.

tion was defeated, and the original resolution was again laid before the President.[76]

§44. **Secret Sessions.**—The Senate sat with closed doors during its legislative as well as its executive sessions down to the end of the first session of the third Congress. A resolution adopted February 20, 1794, provided that the legislative proceedings, except in such cases as might in the opinion of the Senate require secrecy, should, after the end of that session, be with open doors.[77] On December 22, 1800, a rule was adopted, which provided that all treaties laid before the Senate should be kept secret until the injunction of secrecy had been removed by a resolution.[78] This rule obviated the necessity of voting a special injunction of secrecy. According to clause 3 of Rule XXXVI of the Standing Rules of the Senate, "all treaties which may be laid before the Senate, and all remarks, votes, and proceedings thereon shall also be kept secret, until the Senate shall, by their resolution, take off the injunction of secrecy, or unless the same shall be considered in open executive session." This has been interpreted by the Committee on Rules as extending to each step in the consideration of treaties, including the fact of ratification. The injunction of secrecy is not infrequently removed from the text of the treaty before final action on the resolution advising ratification has been taken. The proposed fisheries treaty with Great Britain, signed February 15, 1888, and the proposed arbitration conventions with Great Britain and France, signed, respectively, on August 3, 1911, were formally debated in open executive session, and appear to be the only treaties so debated, pursuant to a vote of the Senate. Motions were likewise made, but failed of passage, to consider in open executive session the treaty for the annexation of San Domingo, signed November 29, 1869, the proposed commercial convention with Mexico, signed January 20, 1883, the proposed arbitration convention with Great Britain, signed January 11, 1897, and the Hawaiian annexation treaty, signed June 16, 1897.[79]

76 Id., XXXII, 345, 348, 362.
77 Annals 3d Congress, 9, 47.
78 Ex. Journal, I, 361.
79 Ex. Journal, XVII, 390; XXIV, 205, 206; XXX, 394; XXXI, 470. During the proceedings on the Jay treaty, a copy of the treaty was given out for publication by Senator Mason, of Virginia, contrary to the special resolution of the Senate imposing an injunction of secrecy.

§45. **Explanations of Senate Amendments.**—Since the proposed amendments are formulated by the Senate in secret session, and the other contracting party has no part in the formation and wording of them, the Executive is often met, before proceeding to the exchange of ratifications, with requests for explanations as to their meaning and the reasons for their insertion. A protracted discussion as to the value of such explanations resulted from the signing by the American commissioners of the protocol of May 26, 1848, explanatory of the amendments made by the Senate to the treaty of peace with Mexico. The American commissioners, Ambrose H. Sevier and Nathan Clifford, were commissioned on March 18, 1848, to exchange the ratifications of the treaty in the form in which it had been amended by the Senate. An additional power was given them to obtain a modification in the method of payment, as provided for in Article XII as amended, specifically reserving to the President, with the advice and consent of the Senate, the right of ratification of such modification. In the accompanying instructions the commissioners were carefully reminded that they were not sent to Mexico for the purpose of negotiating a new treaty; that the amendments adopted by the Senate could not be rejected or modified except by authority of that body; that, if it should become necessary, as it most probably would, to explain the reasons which had influenced the Senate in adopting the several amendments, such explanations should be given so far as possible informally and verbally; that the authority of their mission did not extend to the making of the slightest modification of the provisions of the treaty. Subsequently to the approval of the treaty by the Mexican Congress, but prior to its ratification by the President, *ad interim,* of Mexico, the American commissioners were induced to sign in the name of their government, the protocol making "suitable explanations in regard to the amendments." President Polk, considering the explanations to be in accordance with the treaty, did not deem it necessary to take any action on the subject, but treated them in the same manner as if they had been "verbally given." In February, 1849, the Mexican minister at Washington requested a definite assurance that the United States would never give to the amended articles any other sense or interpretation than that expressed in the protocol. To this, Mr. Clayton, Secretary of State, on April 11, replied at length and in conclusion said:

"It is clear, therefore, that the protocol must be regarded merely as an instrument stating the opinions of the commissioners of the United States upon the amendments of the Senate, and utterly void if not approved by that body."[80] A resolution was introduced in the Senate by Mr. Benton, March 22, declaring that the explanations of the commissioners, duly commissioned to give them, ought to be held binding on the United States. On the following day, Mr. Seward offered a resolution reciting that the attached protocol was no part of the treaty, not having been passed upon by the Senate.[81] Neither resolution was brought to a vote.[82]

While the foreign government, which refuses to exchange the ratifications of a treaty until explanations are made, cannot plead ignorance of the constitutional provisions under which all treaty obligations of the United States must be contracted, such explanations, even if only tacitly approved by the Executive, and although they cannot without the approval of the Senate modify or form part of the treaty and of the law of the land, are not without weight in a diplomatic controversy thereafter arising as to the meaning of the provisions in question. Safe precedents have been established in this respect. The Senate in advising the ratification of the convention with France of September 30, 1800, struck out Article II. The ratification of the First Consul, received in exchange at Paris, July 31, 1801, was given subject to the condition "that by this retrenchment [elimination of Article II] the two states renounce the respective pretensions which are the object of the said article." The ratification "not being pure and simple in the ordinary form," President Jefferson thought it his duty before proclaiming the convention as the law of the land to re-submit it to the Senate. The Senate resolved, two-thirds of the members present concurring, that it considered the convention as duly ratified, and directed that it be returned to the President for the usual promulgation. The "retrenchment" proved to be far-reaching.[83] In advising the ratification of a naturalization

80 S. Doc. No. 1, 31st Cong., 1st Sess., 69, 84, 85; Ex. Doc. No. 50, 30th Cong., 2d Sess., 9, 47, 48.

81 Ex. Journal, VIII, 94, 96.

82 See for other instances of explanations of Senate amendments, Mr. Evarts, Secretary of State, to Mr. Neyt, Belgian chargé d'affaires, August 13, 1880, For. Rel., 1880, p. 73; Mr. Bayard, Secretary of State, to Mr. Mc-Lane, minister to France, November 24, 1886, For. Rel., 1887, p. 274; Moore, Int. Law Digest, V, 206, 207.

convention with Turkey signed August 11, 1874, the Senate attached amendments. According to the convention as signed, a naturalized person who went back to the country of his origin without an intention to return to the country of his adoption, was to be considered as having renounced his naturalization; and the absence of an intention to return was conclusively to be presumed from a residence of more than two years. By the convention as amended this presumption was to be merely prima facie. In the ratification exchanged at Constantinople, a proviso was introduced by the Sublime Porte to the effect that the Ottoman government should have the right to consider native Ottoman subjects who had resided in the Empire more than two years as having renounced their naturalization in the United States, the latter country to have the same right as to its citizens naturalized in the Empire. Although the proviso rendered the Senate amendment practically nugatory, the American minister proceeded to the exchange of ratifications. On being informed of the proviso, Mr. Fish, Secretary of State, immediately declared the exchange of ratifications to be invalid; and the convention was not proclaimed.[84] Again, Mr. Bayard, Secretary of State, on being asked by the Hawaiian minister at Washington to confirm the view, that an amendment made by the Senate to the convention of December 6, 1884, for the purpose of giving to the United States the exclusive use of Pearl Harbor for a naval station, did not diminish the autonomous jurisdiction of Hawaii or convey a privilege that would survive the convention, replied in the sense desired, but added: "The limitation of my official powers does not make it competent for me in this connection to qualify, expand, or explain the amendments ingrafted on that convention by the Senate."[85] During the negotiations at London in 1861, with a view to the incorporation of the principles of the Declaration of Paris into a convention between the United States and Great Britain, the British government proposed to make, upon the signing of such convention, a declaration that Her Majesty did not intend thereby to undertake any engagement which should have any bearing direct or indirect on the internal differences then prevailing in the United States. To this proposition, Charles Francis Adams, American minister, replied that if

83 Ex. Journal, I, 397-9.
84 For. Rel., 1896, pp. 930, 934.

the declaration were to be considered as a part of the convention, it must be submitted to the Senate for its advice and consent; and that if it were not so to be considered, the party making it could obtain no advantage from it.[86]

It need hardly be added that such a declaration or explanation when agreed to by the Senate and duly ratified by both parties forms a part of the treaty and is as binding and obligatory as if it were inserted in the body of the treaty.[87]   Of this character is the declaration of the Japanese ambassador to the United States, made upon the conclusion of the treaty of commerce and navigation of February 21, 1911, that his government was fully prepared to maintain with equal effectiveness the limitation and control which it had for the past three years exercised in the regulation of the emigration of laborers to the United States.   The explanatory protocol, signed April 29, 1872, upon the exchange of ratifications of the consular convention of December 11, 1871, with the German Empire, construing terms in that convention, was expressly authorized by a resolution of the Senate dated April 24, 1872, and is in effect a part of the treaty.[88]   In advising, March 26, 1868, the ratification of the naturalization convention, signed February 22, 1868, with the North German Confederation, the Senate attached an amendment declaring that Article I of the convention should apply as well to those theretofore, as to those thereafter, naturalized.   This amendment was duly communicated to the government of the North German Confederation, and was accepted as the true interpretation of the article.   It was, however, omitted in the exchange copy given by that government, May 9, 1868.   Later, this omission was noticed, and on June 12, 1871, a protocol was signed in which the amendment was recognized by the two governments as a part of the convention.   In consenting, June 11, 1838, to the ratification of a treaty with certain Indian tribes, the Senate in executive session attached a proviso.   The President in his proclamation made no allusion to this proviso and it was never communicated to the Indian tribes.   There being no evidence that the President approved the proviso, and the other contracting party never having been advised of its existence,

85 For. Rel., 1887, p. 591.
86 Dip. Cor., 1861, p. 138.
87 Doe v. Braden, 16 How. 635, 636.
88 Ex. Journal, XVIII, 240.

the Supreme Court held that it formed no part of the treaty. Mr. Justice Brewer, speaking for the court, said: "There is something, too, which shocks the conscience in the idea that a treaty can be put forth as embodying the terms of an arrangement with a foreign power or an Indian tribe, a material provision of which is unknown to one of the contracting parties, and is kept in the background to be used by the other only when the exigencies of a particular case may demand it."[89] Upon signing the arbitration convention with Great Britain, April 4, 1908, Mr. Bryce, British ambassador, addressed a note to Mr. Root, Secretary of State, in which it was stated that the final sentence of Article II had been inserted in order to reserve to both governments the freedom of action secured to the government of the United States under the Constitution, and further that it was understood that the convention would not apply to existing pecuniary claims or to the conclusion of the special treaty recently recomended by the International Waterways Commission or any other such treaty for the settlement of questions connected with boundary waters. On the same date Mr. Root replied concurring in these views. These notes were communicated with the convention to the Senate for its information but not as forming part of the convention.

§46. **Consent to Extension of Period for Exchange of Ratifications.**—The manner in which the consent of the Senate has been given to the extension of the period fixed in the treaty, within which the exchange of ratifications is to take place, has not been uniform. The ratifications of the treaty of September 30, 1800, with France, were by the terms of the treaty to be ex-

---

89 New York Indians v. United States, 170 U. S. 1, 23. The Senate in advising the ratification of a treaty negotiated with the Sioux and other tribes of Indians introduced an amendment. The modification was consented to by some tribes but not by others, and the treaty was never proclaimed. Both Congress and the President nevertheless recognized the validity and binding force of the treaty as to the United States—Congress in making appropriations to carry the treaty into effect from 1853 to 1865, and the President in extending the time for the payment of the annuities for five additional years. The Court of Claims held "that the action of the Congress and the Executive in respect of the treaty aforesaid and the acceptance by the Indians of the fruits thereunder were sufficient to constitute the contract a treaty within the intent of Congress as expressed in the act of 1885." The peculiar nature of a treaty with an Indian tribe, as distinguished from one with a foreign nation, was, however, pointed out by the court. Moore v. United States, 32 C. Cls. 593, 598.

changed within six months, but they were not exchanged until July 31, 1801. The treaty was, however, subsequently re-submitted by the President to the Senate because of the proviso attached to the ratification by the First Consul. The exchange of ratifications of the treaty of September 4, 1816, with Sweden and Norway, did not take place until September 25, 1818, more than a year and four months after the expiration of the time limit, and it does not appear that the Senate was asked to consent to the exchange. In the treaty with Spain of February 22, 1819, the period for the exchange was limited to six months. The King of Spain failed to ratify the treaty until October 24, 1820. The time having expired, President Monroe in a message of February 13, 1821, asked for the advice and consent of the Senate to receive the Spanish ratification in exchange for the ratification of the United States theretofore executed. The Senate considered both the Spanish ratification and the treaty itself, and, on February 19, 1821, again advised the ratification of the treaty, not, however, unanimously, as on the first occasion. It was on the authority of this second resolution that the treaty was finally ratified by President Monroe, February 22, 1821.[90] The time for the exchange of the ratifications of the treaty with Prussia of May 1, 1828, having elapsed, President Jackson, "to avoid all future questions," asked in a message of March 6, 1829, the advice and consent of the Senate as to the proposed exchange. The Senate re-examined the treaty, and advised, on March 9, 1829, the President to proceed to the exchange of ratifications, notwithstanding the expiration of the time limit.[91] Four other cases arose during Jackson's administration, namely, with the treaties signed: January 12, 1828, with Mexico; August 27, 1829, with Austria-Hungary; May 7, 1830, with the Ottoman Porte; and May 16, 1832, with Chile. In each instance the Senate was called upon to consent to the exchange of ratifications. In case of the treaties with Mexico and Chile, additional articles for the extension of the time were concluded and submitted to the Senate. This procedure has since been regularly, but not uniformly, followed.[92] The exchange of ratifications of the treaty of March 26, 1844, with the Grand Duchy of Hesse, was effected twenty days after the expiration of

90 Ex. Journal, III, 242-4.
91 Id., IV, 7, 9.
92 Id., IV, 146, 150, 151, 213, 237, 391.

the period fixed by the treaty. President Tyler submitted the matter to the Senate. By a resolution dated January 13, 1845, the Senate agreed to an extension of time, and declared that an exchange made prior thereto should be deemed and taken to have been regularly made.[93] In advising and consenting, February 13, 1850, to the ratification of the treaty with Austria-Hungary of May 8, 1848,—the time for the exchange of ratifications having expired—the Senate advised and consented to the exchange at any time prior to July 4, 1850. Similar authorization is found in the resolution of June 23, 1852, advising ratification of the treaty with Borneo of June 23, 1850. The Senate on March 12, 1861, having previously advised ratification, advised and consented to the extension of the period for the exchange of ratifications of a claims convention with Costa Rico, signed July 2, 1860, to such time as might be convenient.[94] On the exchange of ratifications, June 2, 1852, of a treaty with Salvador concluded January 2, 1850, which exchange did not take place within the time specified, a proviso was signed declaring that the convention should not be binding until the Senate had sanctioned the exchange.[95] The Senate by a resolution of April 4, 1853, advised and consented to the exchange. A similar proviso was inserted in the certificate of exchange of ratifications, on May 13, 1852, of the treaty with Guatemala of March 3, 1849. The exchange was duly sanctioned by the Senate, June 7, 1852. A proviso of the same nature was likewise inserted in the certificate of exchange of ratifications, on May 22, 1865, of the treaty with Haiti of November 3, 1864. On January 24, 1860, the Senate advised and consented to the exchange of ratifications of the treaty with China, signed June 18, 1858, which was effected on August 16, 1859, the limitations contained in the treaty to the contrary notwithstanding. On March 2, 1870, the Senate advised and consented to the exchange of ratifications of the treaty with Württemburg of July 27, 1868, and of the treaty with Belgium of December

93 Id., VI, 363, 379.

94 See also resolutions of the Senate of May 12, 1871, May 8, 1879, and January 5, 1881, advising and consenting to extensions of the periods for exchange of ratifications of the treaties of July 11, 1870, with Austria-Hungary, May 23, 1878, with the Netherlands, and March 9, 1880, with Belgium, respectively.

95 Id., VIII, 437; IX, 144.

5, 1868, although the exchange in each case had taken place subsequently to the time stipulated for that purpose.[96]

In order to effect the exchange of the ratifications of the commercial convention with Cuba of December 11, 1902, within the stipulated time, a constructive exchange was resorted to. On notification that the Cuban exchange copy had in good form been placed in transmission, the exchange copy of the United States was delivered to the Cuban minister in Washington, and a protocol was signed reciting the fact of the exchange. So also in the case of the treaty of commerce and navigation with China of October 8, 1903, upon the delivery of the American exchange copy to the Chinese minister in Washington, and upon the receipt by the American minister at Peking, for transmission, of the Chinese exchange copy, the protocol reciting the fact of the exchange was signed.[97] The exchanges of the ratifications of the treaty with Mexico of January 20, 1883, and with Chile of August 7, 1892, were effected under similar conditions, and recorded in protocols signed, May 20, 1884, and January 26, 1893, respectively.[98]

96 See also treaty with Bolivia of May 13, 1858; with Peru of March 17, 1841; and with Sweden-Norway of May 26, 1869.

97 Mr. Conger, minister to China, to Mr. Hay, Secretary of State, January 13, 1904.

98 "Inasmuch as in this country the pleasure of the Senate must be known before a treaty can be ratified, and as delays may accordingly supervene, it is the preference of this Government that it be provided that the ratification and the exchange of ratifications shall be effected 'as soon as possible,' rather than within a specified time." Instructions to Diplomatic Officers, §246.

CHAPTER VII.

POWERS OF THE PRESIDENT.

§47. Negotiation.—To the President is entrusted the exclusive power of communication with foreign states. "The President is the sole organ of the nation in its external relations, and its sole representative with foreign nations."[1] Accordingly, with him resides the right of determining finally on all negotiations to be conducted with foreign powers. Although such negotiations are regularly conducted through the Secretary of State, they originate in legal contemplation with the President.[2] Treaties are signed by the Secretary of State, as also by all other agents, and the ratifications are exchanged, by virtue of special powers conferred by the President.[3]

---

1 John Marshall, in the House of Representatives, March 7, 1800. Annals, 6th Cong., 613.

2 Jones v. United States, 137 U. S. 202, 217; Wolsey v. Chapman, 101 U. S. 755, 770. The Department of Foreign Affairs was established by the act of Congress approved July 27, 1789. By an act approved September 15, 1789, the name was changed to Department of State. 1 Stats. at L. 28, 68. Gouverneur Morris submitted to the Federal Convention, August 20, 1787, propositions providing for a Council of State, in which there was to be a Secretary of Foreign Affairs, to be appointed at the pleasure of the President, to whom was to be entrusted, among other duties, the preparation of plans of treaties and the examination of such as might be transmitted from abroad. Doc. Hist. of the Const., III, 566. "The act creating the Department of State, in 1789, was an exception to the acts creating the other Departments of the Government. * * * It is a Department which from the beginning the Senate has never assumed the right to direct or control, except as to clearly defined matters relating to duty imposed by statute and not connected with the conduct of our foreign relations. We *direct* all the other heads of Departments to transmit to the Senate designated papers or information. We do not address directions to the Secretary of State. We direct requests to the real head of that Department, the President of the United States, and, as a matter of courtesy, we add the qualifying words, 'if in his judgment not incompatible with the public interest.'" John C. Spooner, in the U. S. Senate, January 23, 1906, Cong. Record, 59th Cong., 1st Sess., 1420.

3 Section 243 of the standing Instructions to Diplomatic Officers of the United States (1897) reads: "In case of urgent need a written international compact between a diplomatic representative of the United States and a foreign government may be made in the absence of specific instruc-

§48. Ratification.—The final act of ratification of a treaty is not delegated, but is performed by the President by and with the advice and consent of the Senate, two-thirds of the Senators present concurring. The authorization of the Senate is a condition precedent to the validity of the treaty, and is regularly given after its negotiation in the form of a resolution advising and consenting to the ratification.

§49. Reservation in Full Powers of Right of Ratification.—From the first there has been inserted in the full powers of the negotiators, as likewise in the text of the treaty, a reservation of the right of ratification, which regularly, although not uniformly, explicitly provides that the ratification shall be by the President, by and with the advice and consent of the Senate.[4] In commenting on Jefferson's rough draft of the instructions to the commissioners appointed in the early part of 1792 to negotiate with the court of Spain, Hamilton suggested that the clause in which the right of ratification was to be reserved should be so worded as to indicate the participation of the Senate. Jefferson, on the other hand, considered a stipulation, that the treaty should be ratified, without the particular body of individuals by which it was to be ratified being designated, to be sufficient.[5] The instruction was not modified, and the treaty of October 27, 1795 was drawn up accordingly. In the treaty with Great Britain of November 19, 1794, as has since been the more regular practice, the clause reserving the right of ratification specifically provided that the treaty should be ratified by the President by and with the advice and consent of the Senate. However, even if the reservation is not so expressed, the constitutional requirement of the consent of the Senate to the conclusion of treaties, of which requirement all nations have notice, is to be read into the full powers conferred by the President, and into all treaties negotiated under his authority.

§50. Proclamation.—After the final ratification and the exchange or deposit of ratifications, the treaty is proclaimed by the President. This serves as a public announcement as well of the

---

tions or powers. In such cases it is preferable to give to the instrument the form of a simple protocol, and it should be expressly stated in the instrument that it is signed subject to the approval of the signer's Government."

4 See Am. State Papers, For. Rel., I, 471, 533.

5 Writings of Jefferson (Ford ed.), V, 445.

terms of the treaty as of the fact of its due ratification. Proclamation is made only by the President.[6]

§51. **Treaties Withheld from the Senate.**—Since all treaties must receive the final ratification of the President, he may at will as a constitutional right withhold from the Senate a treaty already negotiated. Of proposed treaties thus withheld, note may be made of a treaty of commerce and navigation with Great Britain, negotiated on the part of the United States by James Monroe and William Pinkney, and signed December 31, 1806; a convention with Mexico, signed March 21, 1853, relative to a transit way across the Isthmus of Tehuantepec; a convention with the Netherlands, signed December 15, 1863, for the regulation of emigration of freedmen from the United States to Dutch Guiana; conventions with Colombia, signed March 30, 1872 and November 1, 1879, for the extradition of fugitives from justice; a convention with Switzerland, signed February 14, 1885, for the protection of trade-marks; the general act of the Berlin Conference, signed February 26, 1885, with reference to the Kongo;[7] a treaty of commerce with Japan, signed February 20, 1889; a convention for the establishment of a tribunal of arbitration, adopted in April, 1890, by the First International American Conference; a convention of arbitration with Japan, signed February 11, 1905; and two conventions with Roumania, one of extradition, the other for most-favored-nation treatment in commerce, signed, respectively, at Bucharest, April 16, 1908.

§52, **Submitted to the Senate with Recommendation for Amendment.**—Or the treaty may be submitted by the President to the Senate accompanied with recommendations for amendments. President Washington in a message of February 13, 1793, and President Adams in a message of December 6, 1797, in submitting certain Indian treaties, suggested qualified ratifications.[8] In submitting for the approval of the Senate the treaty of peace

6 Mr. Blaine, Secretary of State, to Mr. Angell, October 10, 1881, MSS. Inst. to China, III, 266; Moore, Int. Law Digest, V, 210. The treaty with China of July 28, 1868 was proclaimed under the seal of the American legation in China, November 23, 1869, immediately upon the exchange of ratifications at Peking. Subsequently, February 5, 1870, the treaty was duly proclaimed by the President.

7 See message of President Cleveland, December 8, 1885. Richardson, Messages and Papers of the Presidents, VIII, 330.

8 Id., I, 135, 259.

with Mexico, signed February 2, 1848, by N. P. Trist, whose powers had previously been revoked, President Polk, after noting that the treaty substantially conformed in respect of boundaries and indemnity with the terms which the commissioner had originally been empowered to offer, recommended the rejection by the Senate of the tenth article respecting grants of land within the limits of Texas. He also suggested the rejection of the additional and secret article.[9] The Senate followed these recommendations. President Taylor, in submitting, April 22, 1850, the Clayton-Bulwer treaty, signed April 19, 1850, suggested an amendment either of the treaty submitted or of the treaty with Nicaragua, signed September 3, 1849, then pending before the Senate, in order that the provisions of the two treaties might not be inconsistent with each other in their spirit and intent.[10] In submitting, February 13, 1851, the treaty of commerce with the Swiss Confederation, signed November 25, 1850, President Fillmore directed the attention of the Senate to objectionable provisions and recommended amendments.[11] President Pierce, in submitting, February 10, 1854, the Gadsden treaty of December 30, 1853, recommended certain specific amendments.[12] In submitting, February 5, 1863, the claims convention with Peru, signed January 12, 1863, President Lincoln recommended a material amendment.[13] President Grant, by message dated May 31, 1870, suggested the amendment by the Senate in certain particulars of the treaty for the annexation of San Domingo, signed November 29, 1870, and then pending in the Senate, to obviate objections which might be urged against the treaty as signed.[14] On May 22, 1872, President Grant submitted an agreement signed February 17, 1872, with the Chief of the Island of Tutuila, and recommended it to the favorable consideration of the Senate, subject to certain modifications.[15] President Cleveland, in submitting, July 5, 1888, an extradition convention with Colombia, signed May 7, 1888, directed the attention of the Senate to certain amendments sug-

9 Id., IV, 573.
10 Id., V, 42.
11 Id., V, 98.
12 Id., V, 229.
13 Id., VI, 152.
14 Id., VII, 61.
15 Id., VII, 169.

gested by the Secretary of State.[16] President Harrison, in submitting, February 20, 1891, the treaty of commerce and navigation with the Independent State of the Kongo, signed January 24, 1891, recommended the rejection by the Senate of the ninth article, which related to extradition. The Senate in advising ratification complied with the recommendation.[17] President Roosevelt, in submitting, February 27, 1908, the conventions and declaration signed at the Second International Peace Conference at The Hague, directed the attention of the Senate to an accompanying report by the Secretary of State, in which it was recommended that the ratification of the convention for the peaceful adjustment of international differences should be given, and the convention concerning the rights and duties of neutral powers in naval warfare, not signed by the delegates of the United States, should be adhered to, subject in each case to certain reservations.[18] These recommendations were embodied in the resolutions of the Senate advising and consenting to the ratification.[19]

§53. **Refusal of President to Ratify Treaties Approved by the Senate.**—The resolution of the Senate advising and consenting to the ratification of a treaty, while a condition precedent to its validity, is not mandatory; and the President may of right refuse to ratify a treaty although the Senate has advised its ratification.[20] President Polk, in submitting to the Senate, December 16, 1845, an extradition convention with Prussia and certain other German States, signed January 29, 1845, recommended a

16 Id., VIII, 615.

17 Ex. Journal, XXVII, 883.

18 Sen. Doc. No. 444, 60th Cong., 1st Sess., 61.

19 Id., 87, 153.

20 "The President is so supreme under the Constitution in the matter of treaties, excluding only the Senate's ratification, that he may negotiate a treaty, he may send it to the Senate, it may receive by way of 'advice and consent' the unanimous judgment of the Senate that it is in the highest degree for the public interest, and yet the President is as free when it is sent back to the White House with resolution of ratification attached, to put it in his desk never again to see the light of day as he was free to determine in the first instance whether he would or would not negotiate it. That power is not expressly given to the President by the Constitution, but it inheres in the executive power conferred upon him to conduct our foreign relations, and it is a power which inheres in him as the sole organ under the Constitution through whom our foreign relations and diplomatic intercourse are conducted." John C. Spooner, in the U. S. Senate, January 23, 1906. Cong. Record, 59th Cong., 1st Sess., 1419.

modification of Article III, in which it was stipulated, contrary to the rule then consistently maintained by the United States, that the contracting parties should not be bound to deliver up their own citizens. The Senate failed, in advising the ratification, to make the amendment, and the President for this as well as for other reasons did not ratify the convention.[21] On March 10, 1857, the Senate advised the ratification with amendment of a treaty of amity, commerce and extradition with Venezuela, signed July 10, 1856. The President decided not to ratify the treaty, but to negotiate a new treaty in order to effect other changes. Such a treaty was signed August 27, 1860, and submitted to the Senate, January 2, 1861.[22] On March 1, 1905, the Senate advised and consented to the adhesion of the United States to the project of a convention for the suppression of the white slave traffic, adopted July 25, 1902 by the delegates of various powers represented at the Paris conference. The Executive did not at the time ratify the convention because of doubts entertained as to the ability of the government of the United States to carry it into effect for want of a national system of police. Subsequently, however, on June 6, 1908, the President pursuant to the advice of the Senate of March 1, 1905, declared the adherence of the United States to the arrangement as incorporated literally in the formal agreement signed at Paris, May 18, 1904. The ratification of the general arbitration conventions negotiated by Mr. Hay, Secretary of State, and signed November 1, 1904, with France; November 1, 1904, with Switzerland; November 22, 1904, with Germany; November 23, 1904, with Portugal; December 12, 1904, with Great Britain; December 14, 1904, with Italy; December 31, 1904, with Spain; January 6, 1905, with Austria-Hungary; January 18, 1905, with Mexico; and January 20, 1905, with Sweden and Norway, was advised and consented to by the Senate in each instance subject to an amendment substituting the word "treaty" for the word "agreement," with the understanding that

21 Ex. Journal, VII, 7, 433. In his message to the Senate, July 28, 1848, giving the reasons for his refusal to ratify, the President laid special stress on the failure of the Senate to remedy Article III, but added also as a sufficient justification the reorganization which had taken place in the German States since the negotiation of the convention. Id., 462. See also, Mr. Buchanan, Secretary of State, to Mr. Donelson, minister to Prussia, August 3, 1848, MSS. Inst. to Prussia, XIV, 126.

22 Richardson, Messages and Papers of the Presidents, V, 654.

every such special "treaty" should be referred to the Senate for its advice and consent. The amendment was not acceptable to the Executive, and the conventions were not ratified. At a later date, new conventions, embodying in principle the amendment of the Senate, were, however, negotiated by Mr. Root, Secretary of State, submitted to the Senate and duly ratified.

§54. **Treaties Withdrawn from the Senate.**—Many instances may be cited of the withdrawal of treaties by the President from the consideration of the Senate, either to effect changes by negotiation or to terminate proceedings thereon. President Pierce in a message of August 9, 1856, requested the return of an extradition convention with the Netherlands, signed May 29, 1856. The convention was re-submitted to the Senate on January 12, 1857.[23] A convention with Belgium, signed November 4, 1884, for the regulation of the right of succession to and the acquisition of property, was returned by the Senate to President Arthur in compliance with his request of February 17, 1885, and was not re-submitted.[24] President Cleveland, in messages of March 13, 1885, April 2, 1885, and March 9, 1893, requested the return of treaties concluded by his predecessors: November 18, 1884, with Spain, for commercial reciprocity; December 1, 1884, with Nicaragua, relative to the construction of an interoceanic canal; December 4, 1884, with the Dominican Republic, for commercial reciprocity; June 22, 1884, with the Argentine Republic, supplementary to the treaty of commerce of July 27, 1853; and February 14, 1893, for the annexation of the Hawaiian Islands.[25] President Roosevelt, in a message of December 8, 1902, requested the return of a commercial convention with the Dominican Republic, signed June 25, 1900, together with an additional article thereto, and a convention with Great Britain, signed January 30, 1897, relative to the demarcation of the Alaskan boundary. Instances of withdrawals for the purpose of making verbal corrections are quite numerous. The convention with Spain, signed August 7, 1882, supplementary to the extradition convention of January 5, 1877, was returned for verbal changes at the request of the Secretary of State made to the chairman of the Committee

23 Id., V, 383, 419.
24 Ex. Journal, XXIV, 474.
25 Richardson, Messages and Papers of the Presidents, VIII, 303; IX, 393.

on Foreign Relations.[26] The Senate by resolutions, dated December 6, 1899, December 16, 1901, and January 31, 1903, respectively, in compliance with requests of the President of even dates, returned the conventions signed March 2, 1899, with Great Britain, concerning the tenure and disposition of property, October 26, 1901, with Belgium, for the extradition of criminals, and January 24, 1903, with Great Britain, relative to the boundary between Alaska and British possessions. They were later re-submitted and ratified.

§55. Re-submission to the Senate After Delay in Ratification.—On January 22, 1875, the Senate advised the ratification with certain amendments of a naturalization convention concluded at Constantinople, August 11, 1874. These amendments were not fully accepted by the Turkish government, and the convention was not proclaimed by the President.[27] After the lapse of fourteen years, that government decided to accept the amendments. In view of the long period which had elapsed since the Senate advised ratification, President Cleveland, in a message of February 27, 1889, before proclaiming the convention, gave the Senate an opportunity again to act on the matter. The Senate by resolution, dated February 28, 1889, advised the President to exchange the ratifications, but with the distinct understanding that the provisions of Article II of the convention, as amended, should not be construed as applying to persons already naturalized in either country.[28] The condition imposed by the Senate was the source of further delay. To the suggestion made by the Sublime Porte in 1896, that measures be taken to give effect to the convention, Mr. Olney, Secretary of State, replied that in view of the peculiar circumstances, of the various conflicting constructions of the Senate resolution, and especially of the length of time that had elapsed since the convention was last before the Senate, the first step in the direction desired must obviously be to bring the convention again before that body for its reconsideration.[29] The two governments have, however, never been able to reach an agreement in accordance with the requirements of the Senate resolu-

26 Ex. Journal, XXIII, 565.
27 See supra, §45.
28 Ex. Journal, XXVI, 467, 469.
29 Mr. Olney to Mavroyeni Bey, October 15, 1896. For. Rel., 1896, pp. 932, 933.

tion. So also, Mr. Root, on reopening negotiations in 1908 for the conclusion of arbitration conventions, did not proceed to the ratification of those negotiated by his predecessor and consented to by the Senate with amendments in 1905, but signed new conventions substantially incorporating the Senate amendments and submitted them to the Senate. The Senate may at any time prior to the ratification by the President rescind its resolution of advice and consent, but in the absence of such act of revocation it may be doubted that the President is under any constitutional obligation to re-submit a treaty the ratification of which has once been advised.

CHAPTER VIII.

AGREEMENTS REACHED BY THE EXECUTIVE WITHOUT THE ADVICE AND CONSENT OF THE SENATE.

§56. Agreements Involving the Military Power of the President.—The executive power is by the Constitution vested in the President. He is also the commander-in-chief of the army and navy of the United States. As incident and necessary to the exercise of these powers as also of the power of negotiation temporary arrangements and administrative agreements are frequently made by the President with foreign governments, which are not submitted to the Senate for its approval.[1]

An agreement, terminable on six months' notice, was reached with Great Britain and recorded in notes exchanged at Washington, April 28-29, 1817, between Mr. Bagot, British minister, and Mr. Rush, Acting Secretary of State, for the limitation of the naval forces to be maintained by the two governments on the Great Lakes. Nearly one year later, April 6, 1818, President Monroe submitted the correspondence to the Senate for its consideration whether it was such an arrangement as the Executive was competent to enter into by the powers vested in him by the Constitution, or was such as required the advice and consent of the Senate. The Senate by a resolution of April 16 (two-thirds of the Senators present concurring), approved of and consented to the arrangement, and recommended that it be carried into effect by the President.[2] There was no formal exchange of ratifications, but the arrangement was proclaimed by the President, April 28, 1818. An act of Congress approved February 27, 1815, had authorized the President to cause all armed vessels on the Lakes, except such as in his opinion were necessary for the execu-

---

1 "It [the conduct of foreign relations] involves intercourse, oral and written, conferences, administrative agreements and understandings, not included in the generic word 'treaty,' as used in the Constitution. All treaties are agreements, but all international agreements and understandings are not 'treaties.'" John C. Spooner, in the U. S. Senate, January 23, 1906, Cong. Record, 59th Cong., 1st Sess., 1420.

2 Ex. Journal, III, 132, 134.

tion of the revenue laws, to be dismantled and sold or laid up.[3] Immediately upon the exchange of notes and prior to any action thereon by the Senate, the President had proceeded to give effect to the arrangement;[4] and in his annual message to Congress, December 2, 1817, he had referred to the arrangement as having been concluded. Its submission to the Senate appears to have been an afterthought and as an act of prudence.[5] This wise and beneficial arrangement has in its general principle now continued in force for nearly a century.

Note may also be made of the agreements recorded in the protocols signed November 23, 1863, and December 24, 1863, by the Secretary of State and the diplomatic representatives in Washington of France and Austria-Hungary, respectively, permitting the exportation from the United States of certain quantities of tobacco from places within the limits of the blockaded section.[6] At the outbreak of the war with Spain, the Swiss government proposed the adoption by the United States and Spain, as a modus vivendi during the continuance of hostilities, of the additional articles proposed by the Geneva Conference of 1868, extending to naval warfare, so far as practicable, the provisions of the Red Cross Convention of 1864. This proposal was simultaneously accepted by both governments. The Senate had, however, on March 16, 1882, in advising and consenting to the accession of the United States to the convention of 1864, also advised and consented to the accession of the United States to the additional articles of 1868; but the ratifications of the additional articles had never been exchanged.[7] The most important agreement of this character entered into by the Executive, without the advice and consent of the Senate, is the protocol of August 12, 1898, which

3 3 Stats. at L. 217.

4 H. Doc. No. 471, 56th Cong., 1st Sess., 14.

5 Id., 14. See also Memoirs of J. Q. Adams, IV, 41, 84; Richardson, Messages and Papers of the Presidents, II, 12.

6 Hamilton v. Dillin (1874), 21 Wall. 73. See as to legislative authority, section 5 of the act approved July 13, 1861. 12 Stats. at L. 257.

7 For. Rel., 1898, pp. LXXXII, 1148. During the progress of the European War, a protocol of an agreement was signed October 10, 1914, by Mr. Lansing, Acting Secretary of State, and Mr. Morales, minister of Panama, in which it was agreed that hospitality extended in the waters of Panama to a vessel in the military or naval service of a belligerent should serve to deprive for a period of three months such vessel of like hospitality in the Panama Canal Zone, and vice versa.

constituted preliminary articles of peace with Spain. By the terms of the protocol Spain, as a basis for the establishment of peace, agreed to relinquish all claim of sovereignty over and title to Cuba, and to cede to the United States Porto Rico and other islands under Spanish sovereignty in the West Indies, and also an island in the Ladrones to be selected by the United States. The disposition of the Philippines was to be determined by the treaty of peace. It further provided for the suspension of hostilities and for the immediate evacuation by Spain of Cuba and Porto Rico. The evacuation of Porto Rico was completed by October 18, 1898, and of Cuba by January 1, 1899, although the treaty of peace was not signed until December 10, 1898, and did not become finally effective until the exchange of ratifications, April 11, 1899.[8] The final protocol signed at Peking, September 7, 1901, by the foreign powers on the one hand, and by China on the other, at the conclusion of the Boxer uprising, likewise was not submitted to the Senate.[9] By this protocol the powers, on their part, agreed to evacuate, with certain exceptions and within a certain period, the city of Peking and the province of Chihli. Among other things China, on her part, agreed to punish certain of the authors of the crimes committed against the foreign governments and their citizens, to pay an indemnity of four hundred and fifty millions of taels as representing the total amount of state and private indemnities, to assign as security for the payment of the indemnity certain revenues, to raze certain forts which might impede communication between Peking and the sea, and to co-operate in the improvement of certain water-courses.

On July 29, 1882, a memorandum of an agreement was signed by Mr. Frelinghuysen, Secretary of State, and Mr. Romero, Mexican minister, providing reciprocally for the crossing of the international boundary line in unpopulated places by the troops of the respective countries in close pursuit of savage bands of Indians. It was recited in the memorandum that since the Mexican Senate had authorized the President of that republic to allow the passing of Mexican troops into the United States and of the troops of the United States into Mexico, and that since the Constitution of the United States empowered the President to allow the passage

8 For. Rel., 1898, p. LXV; For. Rel., 1899, p. XXVIII; Moore, Int. Law Digest, I, 285.
9 For. Rel., 1901, Appendix, 312.

without the consent of the Senate, the agreement did not require the sanction of the Senate of either country, and would take effect on August 18, 1882. Subsequently, on September 21, 1882, a protocol was signed limiting the duration of the agreement to one year. By protocols of agreement signed June 28, 1883, October 31, 1884, and October 16, 1885, the provisions of the agreement of July 29, 1882 were renewed and the period of its duration extended. A provisional and temporary agreement of similar nature was signed by Mr. Blaine, Secretary of State, and Mr. Romero, June 25, 1890. This agreement was renewed November 25, 1892. On June 4, 1896, Mr. Olney, Secretary of State, and Mr. Romero reached a similar agreement which was to remain in force until Kid's band of hostile Indians had been entirely exterminated or rendered obedient to one of the two governments. In 1883, an arrangement with Great Britain as to the crossing of the Canadian boundary, similar to that with Mexico, was proposed by Mr. Frelinghuysen, but the proposal was not acceptable to Canada.[10] Mr. Justice Brown in writing the opinion of the court in the case of Tucker v. Alexandroff,[11] after noting instances in which permission had been granted by the Executive for the entry into the United States of troops of foreign nations—in 1862, to the British government to land troops at Portland and transport them to Canada; in 1876, to the Mexican government to land troops in Texas supposed to be intended to aid in the defense of Matamoras; and in 1893, and 1901, to various nations to participate in the celebrations at Chicago and Buffalo of those years—said: "While no act of Congress authorizes the executive department to permit the introduction of foreign troops, the power to give such permission without legislative assent was probably assumed to exist from the authority of the President as commander-in-chief of the military and naval forces of the United States." In a dissenting opinion, Mr. Justice Gray observed: "The jurisdiction of every nation within its own territory is absolute and exclusive; by its own consent only can any exception to that jurisdiction exist in favor of a foreign nation; and

10 For. Rel., 1883, pp. 496, 527. As to the deportation and delivery to Canadian authorities of refugee Cree Indians, see S. Rept. No. 821, 54th Cong., 1st Sess.; 29 Stats. at L. 117. As to the removal of remnants of Sitting Bull's band, see For. Rel., 1884, pp. 234, 236, 239.

11 183 U. S. 424, 435.

any authority in its own courts to give effect to such an exception by affirmative action must rest upon express treaty or statute. * * * It is not necessary in this case to consider the full extent of the power of the President in such matters."[12] The grant of free passage to foreign armed troops implies a waiver of all jurisdiction over them during their passage.[13]

In 1892 with a view to uphold the judicature established in the Samoan Islands by the General Act of Berlin of 1889, the Governments of the three powers,—Great Britain, Germany and the United States—signatories of that act, agreed to support the authority of the Supreme Court therein established in the execution of warrants of arrest, on condition that the ships should be used for that purpose only in case the resident consuls of the three powers were unanimously of opinion that such support was necessary. This agreement was taken into consideration by the arbitrator under the Samoan claims convention of November 7, 1899, in determining the necessity of the co-operation of all three of the powers in enforcing a decision of the court.[14] In August, 1904, an agreement was reached between the governments of the United States and Great Britain as to the patrol for the protection of seals in the region of Commander Islands in the Northern Pacific during the Russo-Japanese War.[15] By an exchange of notes in 1859, an agreement was reached between the governments of the United States and Great Britain for the joint military occupation of the island San Juan, which agreement continued in force until the final evacuation of the island in 1873 by the British forces in consequence of the arbitral decision of the German Emperor under the treaty of May 8, 1871.[16] The Supreme Court of the Territory of Washington, in giving effect to this agreement, by Greene, J., said: "The power to make and enforce such a temporary convention respecting its own territory is a necessary incident to every national govern-

---

12 Id., 456, 459. See for other instances in which permission for entry of foreign troops has been granted by the President, Moore, Int. Law Digest, II, 389. See also For. Rel., 1898, p. 358.

13 Schooner Exchange v. McFaddon, 7 Cranch 116, 139.

14 Translation of memorandum presented by the German government, 10, Annex No. 90; Counter Case of the British government, 7.

15 For. Rel., 1904, pp. 339-342.

16 Moore, Int. Arb., I, 223; Sen. Ex. Doc. No. 29, 40th Cong., 2d Sess., 263.

ment, and adheres where the executive power is vested. Such conventions are not treaties within the meaning of the Constitution, and, as treaties, supreme law of the land, conclusive on the courts, but they are provisional arrangements, rendered necessary by national differences involving the faith of the nation and entitled to the respect of the courts. They are not a casting of the national will into the firm and permanent condition of law, and yet in some sort they are for the occasion an expression of the will of the people through their political organ, touching the matters affected; and to avoid unhappy collision between the political and judicial branches of the government, both which are in theory inseparably all one, such an expression to a reasonable limit should be followed by the courts and not opposed, though extending to the temporary restraint or modification of the operation of existing statutes. Just as here, we think, this particular convention respecting San Juan should be allowed to modify for the time being the operation of the organic act of this Territory, so far forth as to exclude to the extent demanded by the political branch of the government of the United States, in the interest of peace, all territorial interference for the government of that island."[17] On November 29, 1873, Mr. Fish, Secretary of State, and Rear Admiral Polo, Spanish minister, signed a protocol of an agreement in which the Spanish government agreed forthwith to restore the steamer Virginius and the survivors of her passengers and crew, which had been seized on the high seas by a Spanish man-of-war, and to salute the flag of the United States, or, in case the United States should become satisfied that the vessel was not entitled at the time of capture to carry the flag of the United States, to make a disclaimer of intent of indignity to the flag of the United States. A subsequent protocol, signed December 8, 1873, prescribed the manner in which the protocol of November 29 should be carried out.[18] By an agreement

17 Watts v. United States (1870), 1 Wash. Ter. 288, 294. It was held that a murder committed on San Juan, in 1869, while that island was under the joint military occupancy of the United States and Great Britain, pursuant to the agreement, pending the final adjustment of the boundary, was not an offense committed at a place within the sole and exclusive jurisdiction of the United States within the meaning of section 3 of the act of Congress of April 30, 1790.

18 Report of Secretary of State, March 15, 1875, For. Rel., 1874, p. 987; H. Ex. Doc. No. 30, 43d Cong., 1st Sess. It was subsequently established to the satisfaction of the government of the United States, that the Vir-

signed at Madrid, February 27, 1875, by Mr. Cushing, American minister, and the Spanish minister of state, the government of Spain agreed to pay, and the government of the United States agreed to accept, in full satisfaction of claims for personal indemnification, the sum of eighty thousand dollars.

§57. **Adjustment and Settlement of Pecuniary Claims of Citizens Against Foreign Governments.**—The President, being entrusted with the right of conducting all negotiations with foreign governments, is the sole judge of the expediency of instituting, conducting or terminating them in respect of reclamations for injuries sustained by citizens abroad. Agreements for the adjustment or settlement of pecuniary claims of citizens against foreign governments, which meet with the approval of the claimants, and by which no obligation, except to relinquish the claim, is assumed on the part of the United States, are not usually submitted to the Senate.[19] President Buchanan, in submitting to the Senate, February 9, 1860, an agreement with Venezuela, signed January 14, 1859, for the settlement of claims of citizens of the United States as the result of their expulsion by the Venezuelan authorities from the Aves Island, said: "Usually it is not deemed necessary to consult the Senate in regard to similar instruments relating to private claims of small amount when the aggrieved parties are satisfied with their terms." In the particular instance, it was thought advisable on account of the unstable condition of the Venezuelan government to give the agreement a formal ratification with the advice and consent of the Senate.[20]

ginius was not entitled under the laws of the United States to fly the American flag, and the salute was dispensed with. The Spanish minister duly expressed on behalf of his government "a disclaimer of an intent of indignity to the flag of the United States." Richardson, Messages, VII, 256.

19 See in this relation, veto message of President Jackson, March 3, 1835 (Richardson, Messages and Papers of the Presidents, III, 146); opinion of Drake, C. J., in Great Western Insurance Co. v. United States, (19 C. Cls. 206, 217, s. c. 112 U. S. 193); decision of William R. Day, arbitrator, in the claim of Metzger & Co. against Haiti under the protocol signed October 18, 1899 (For. Rel., 1901, pp. 270-271); report of Mr. Bayard, Secretary of State, to the President, January 30, 1887, on the claims of Antonio Pelletier and A. H. Lazare against Haiti (S. Ex. Doc. No. 64, 49th Cong., 2d Sess., 2-3, 19-20); United States v. Diekelman, 92 U. S. 520, 524; Frelinghuysen v. Key, 110 U. S. 63.

20 Ex. Journal, XI, 142. See Mr. Cass to Mr. Sanford, October 22, 1859, S. Ex. Doc. No. 10, 36th Cong., 2d Sess., 472.

The agreement may be recorded by an exchange of notes, or it may be embodied in a protocol or memorandum. Instances of adjustment and direct settlement are numerous. A notable instance is that of the Mora claim against Spain, finally settled by the agreement of August 10, 1895, for the payment by Spain of the sum of 1,500,000 gold pesos. An agreement for the settlement and payment of the claim had originally been reached by exchange of notes in 1886, but the Spanish Cortes failed to vote the necessary appropriation. The Congress of the United States by a joint resolution, approved March 2, 1895, requested the President to insist upon the payment of the sum so agreed upon, with interest from the date when payment should have been made under the agreement.[21] Another notable instance of agreement for direct settlement is recorded in notes exchanged, May 28, 1881, between Sir Edward Thornton, British minister, and Mr. Blaine, Secretary of State, in which the government of Great Britain agreed to pay, and the government of the United States agreed to receive, the sum of £15,000 in full satisfaction of claims of American fishermen for injuries sustained in their fishing operations on the coasts of Newfoundland, with particular reference to the Fortune Bay episode of January 6, 1878. These claims grew out of mob enforcement of local regulations alleged by the government of the United States to have been in violation of the fishery liberties secured to inhabitants of the United States under the treaty with Great Britain of 1818.[22]

Of important agreements for the submission to arbitration of such claims, made and carried into effect without the advice and consent of the Senate, mention may be made of those recorded in notes exchanged, or protocols of agreement signed, as follows: February 11-12, 1871, claims of citizens of the United States against Spain for injuries committed by Spanish authorities in Cuba;[23] August 17, 1874, claims of citizens against Colombia for the seizure of the "Montijo"; June 13, 1891, claims of Amer-

21 28 Stats. at L. 975; For. Rel., 1894, Appendix I, 364-450; For. Rel., 1895, II, 1162-1176.

22 Proceedings in the North Atlanic Coast Fisheries Arbitration, III, 736. Many references to the adjustment and direct settlement of claims of citizens may be found in the annual messages of the Presidents. See for instances, Richardson, Messages and Papers of the Presidents, IV, 263; For. Rel., 1899, p. XV; Id., 1900, p. XXII. See also For. Rel., 1881, pp. 589-591; Id., 1885, pp. 323, 493; Id., 1894, p. 287.

23 In the case of Angarica v. Bayard, it was declared by the Supreme

ican citizens and British subjects against Portugal on account of
the recision by the Portuguese government of the concession to
the Lourenco Marques Railroad Company; July 6, 1897, claim of
the Cheek estate against Siam;[24] May 28, 1884, May 24, 1888, and
October 18, 1899, claims of Pelletier and Lazare, Van Bokkelen,
and Metzger & Company, respectively, against Haiti; March 14,
1870, claims against Brazil resulting from the wreck of the "Canada"; September 6, 1902, claim of Brenner, et al., against Brazil;
April 28, 1902, claim of Sala & Company against the Dominican
Republic; January 31, 1903, certain questions as to the time and
manner of payments to be made by the Dominican Republic to the
San Domingo Improvement Company; February 23, 1900, claim
of Robert H. May against Guatemala and the counter-claim of
Guatemala against May; March 2, 1897, claims of Charles Obe-
lander and Barbara Messenger against Mexico; March 22, 1900,
amounts to be awarded by Nicaragua to Orr and Laubenheimer
and the Post-Glover Electric Company; May 17, 1898, amount of
damages to be awarded by Peru to Victor H. MacCord; December 19, 1901, claim of the Salvador Commercial Company against
Salvador; September 8, (August 26) 1900, claims against Russia
for the detention of certain American schooners by Russian
cruisers; May 22, 1902, (ratified by the Mexican Senate, May 30,
1902), the Pious Fund claim against Mexico; February 17, 1903,
the unsettled claims of American citizens against Venezuela;
May 7, 1903, the question of the preferential treatment of the
claims of certain powers against Venezuela; February 13, 1909,
the claims of the Orinoco Steamship Company, the Orinoco Corporation, and the United States and Venezuela Company against
Venezuela;[25] May 25, 1909, claim of the George D. Emery Com-

Court of the District of Columbia that this agreement was not a treaty
and that it could not modify the operation of a statute even if such had
been the intention. 4 Mackey (1885) 310.

24 The case of E. V. Kellett, U. S. vice-consul general in Siam, likewise
submitted to a board of arbitration, involved the question of an affront
to an American consular officer. Moore, Int. Arb., II, 1862.

25 Only the claim of the first named company was finally submitted.
The claims of the others were settled and the settlements recorded in protocols signed September 9, 1909, and August 21, 1909, respectively. The
claim of A. F. Jaurett was settled and a memorandum of settlement was
signed at Caracas by Mr. Buchanan and the Venezuelan minister for foreign affairs, February 13, 1909. A settlement of the case of the New
York and Bermudez Company was reached on the same date by the claimant acting directly with the Venezuelan government. Sen. Doc. No. 13,
61st Cong., 1st Sess., 10.

pany against Nicaragua;[26] and December 1, 1909, the Alsop claim against Chile.[27]

§58. Agreements as Basis of Future Negotiations, or of Foreign Policy.—Protocols of agreement as to the basis of future negotiations are clearly within the authority of the President. Such are for instance the protocols signed with Costa Rica and

26 The claim was subsequently settled by direct agreement and a protocol of settlement signed September 18, 1909.

27 Note may also be made of the claims of the owners of the steamer "Colonel Lloyd Aspinwall" against Spain, submitted in 1870 (Moore, Int. Arb., II, 1013; Richardson, Messages, VII, 98); the claim of the owner of the bark "Masonic" against Spain, submitted in 1885 (Moore, Int. Arb., II, 1055, 1060); the claim for the seizure of the "Good Return" against Chile, submitted in 1873, which was subsequently settled by direct agreement, (Id., 1466-1468); the claim of Henry Savage against Guatemala, submitted by agreement signed May 4, 1864 (Id., 1855, 1857); the claim of Dr. Ashmore against China, submitted in 1884 (Id., 1857); and the claims of various citizens against Haiti resulting from riots in Port au Prince in 1883. (Id., 1859). See also For. Rel., 1904, p. 368; Moore, Int. Law Digest, I, 50-51. Of claims against the government of the United States of nominal amounts adjusted by the Executive, note may be made of the claim of Zambrano, formally presented by the Mexican ambassador, and settled by the Secretary of State by the payment of $500, (For. Rel., 1904, pp. 481, 482), and the claim of Luciano Arestuche, settled by the payment to the Cuban government of $500. For. Rel., 1905, pp. 276, 277, 279). By an arrangement effected by exchange of notes between the United States, Great Britain, and Germany, in 1900, (For. Rel., 1900, pp. 476, 627, 899, 902), the arbitrator under the treaty between those powers of November 7, 1899, was requested to include in his awards claims of foreigners not under the jurisdiction of the treaty powers, to which by the treaty he was limited. As the result of this arrangement the United States was found liable for claims of Danish subjects in the sum of $760 (Sen. Doc. No. 160, 59th Cong., 1st Sess.), and of French subjects in the sum of $3,391.13. (H. Doc. No. 612, 59th Cong., 1st Sess.) An act of Congress, approved June 30, 1906, made provision for the payment of these amounts. See for agreement between Great Britain and the United States that each should pay one-half of the amount found due German subjects, Sen. Doc. No. 85, 59th Cong., 1st Sess. The question of the fault of the U. S. S. "San Jacinto" for the collision with the French brig "Jules et Marie" on November 3, 1861, was referred by the Executive to a commission composed of American and French naval officers with a naval officer of Italy as arbiter. It was found that the collision resulted through the fault of the "San Jacinto," and that the sum of $9,500 would be an equitable allowance to the injured party. (Richardson, Messages, VI, 142). By an act approved December 15, 1862, Congress made provision for the payment to the French government of the amount so found due. (12 Stats. at L. 912).

Nicaragua, December 1, 1900, in reference to possible future negotiations for the construction of an interoceanic canal by way of Lake Nicaragua. Of like character was the memorandum signed December 18, 1891, by Mr. Blaine, Secretary of State, and Sir Julian Pauncefote, British minister, as to the articles agreed upon in prior correspondence between them to be included in a treaty for the Bering Sea arbitration. These articles were subsequently incorporated into the treaty signed February 29, 1892, as Articles VI to IX.[28]

Notable examples of agreements as to a foreign policy may be found in the notes exchanged with Great Britain, France, Germany, Russia, Italy and Japan in 1899 and 1900, as to the Open-Door Policy in China,[29] and in the notes exchanged by Mr. Root, Secretary of State, and Baron Takahira, Japanese ambassador, November 30, 1908, as to the policy of the United States and Japan in the Far East.[30]

§59. **Modi Vivendi.**—By exchange of memoranda in April-June, 1885, by Mr. Bayard, Secretary of State, and Sir Lionel West, British minister, a temporary extension was obtained of the privileges enjoyed by American fishermen under the fisheries articles of the treaty of Washington, on the termination of those articles on July 1, 1885. As a part of the agreement the President agreed to bring the whole question of the fisheries before Congress, and to recommend the appointment of a joint commission.[31] Upon the signing of the proposed fisheries treaty of February 15, 1888, the British negotiators executed a protocol to afford a modus vivendi pending the ratification of the treaty. The protocol set forth the terms on which American fishing vessels might enter the bays and harbors of the Atlantic coasts of Canada and Newfoundland for the purchase of bait and other supplies. In a protocol of even date the American negotiators on their part expressed satisfaction with the terms of the protocol as signed by the British negotiators. The treaty was never ratified and the modus vivendi was continued in practical effect indefinitely.[32]

28 See also Moore, Int. Law Digest, I, 873; For. Rel., 1899, p. XXI.
29 Treaties and Conventions, etc. (1910 ed.), 244-260; President McKinley, annual message, December 3, 1900, For. Rel., 1900, pp. VIII-X.
30 For. Rel., 1908, p. 510.
31 For. Rel., 1885, pp. 460-466.
32 S. Ex. Doc. No. 113, 50th Cong., 1st Sess., 125. "So far as Canada is concerned this modus vivendi has been continued in practical effect

Agreements as to a modus vivendi, pending negotiations, in respect of the Newfoundland fisheries, were effected by exchange of notes, October 6-8, 1906, September 4-6, 1907, July 15-23, 1908, and July 22-September 8, 1909. An agreement for a modus vivendi in relation to the fur seal fisheries in Bering Sea was signed by Mr. Wharton, Acting Secretary of State, and Sir Julian Pauncefote, British minister, June 15, 1891, and proclaimed by the President on the same date.[33] By this agreement the two powers undertook temporarily to prohibit seal killing in certain designated areas in Bering Sea. The convention signed, April 18, 1892, for the renewal of this modus vivendi, contemplated, in Article V, the possibility of an award of damages against the United States, and was submitted to the Senate.

On February 27, 1839, Mr. Forsyth, Secretary of State, and Mr. Fox, British minister, signed a memorandum in which they agreed to recommend, the one to the Province of New Brunswick and the other to the State of Maine, the regulation of future proceedings in the disputed territory according to the terms therein set forth, pending the final settlement of the boundary controversy.[34] A modus vivendi was effected October 20, 1899, by exchange of notes between Mr. Hay, Secretary of State, and Mr. Tower, British chargé d'affaires, as to a provisional boundary line between Alaska and the Dominion of Canada in the vicinity of Lynn Canal, which remained in force until the boundary was settled by the decision of the Alaskan boundary tribunal constituted under the treaty of January 24, 1903.[35] A temporary arrangement as to the boundary line on the Stickine River, which was effected by exchange of notes, January 19, and February 20, 1878, by Mr. Evarts, Secretary of State, and Sir Edward Thornton, British minister, likewise continued in force until the award of the tribunal in 1903.[36] By an exchange of notes in July,

down to the present time by action of the Canadian government without formal extension." Case of the United States, North Atlantic Coast Fisheries Arbitration (1910), S. Doc. No. 870, 61st Cong., 3d Sess., I, 206. See to same effect, case of Great Britain, Id., IV, 15.

33 For. Rel., 1891, p. 570.

34 MSS. Northeastern Boundary Papers; Moore, Int. Arb., I, 145; Richardson, Messages and Papers of the Presidents, III, 521, 526.

35 For. Rel., 1899, pp. 328-330. See as to the status of the Alaskan Indians under the modus vivendi, Mr. Adee, Acting Secretary of State, to Mr. French, August 27, 1900, 247 Dom. Letters 355.

36 For. Rel., 1878, pp. 339, 346; Foster, Practice of Diplomacy, 325.

1907, between the Secretary of State and the British ambassador, a temporary arrangement was made for the administration and lease of certain small islands near the coast of Borneo by the British North Borneo Company. The arrangement was to continue in force until the two governments should by treaty determine the boundary between their respective domains, or until the expiration of one year from notice of denunciation.[37]

The American commissioners to the Kongo Conference of 1890 at Brussels, having found it impossible to accede to the Kongo general tariff act as agreed to by the signatories of the Berlin Act of 1885, signed on July 2, 1890, under instructions from Mr. Blaine, Secretary of State, with the commissioners on the part of the Independent State of the Kongo, a provisional declaration to have effect until a commercial treaty should be concluded. By this provisional declaration it was agreed that import duties might be levied on merchandise imported into the Kongo, the United States to enjoy in this respect most-favored-nation treatment. The imposition of such duties was contrary to the Sanford-Frelinghuysen Declaration of April 22, 1884, which had been sanctioned by the Senate. By the provisional declaration it was further agreed that the two governments would substitute therefor a treaty of commerce and navigation to be concluded upon the basis of the declaration. Such a treaty was signed, January 24, 1891, and duly ratified.[38] By exchange of notes March 31-April 1, 1905, a modus vivendi was arranged with the Dominican Republic to take effect on April 1, and to remain in force pending action by the Senate on the convention, signed February 7, 1905 for the administration of the customs revenues of the Dominican Republic. By this modus vivendi the revenues of certain ports were to be collected by persons designated by the President of the United States, but appointed by the Dominican government, and the proportion thereof, which by the convention would be applied to the payment of the creditors, was to be held in trust pending the action of the Senate on the convention.[39]

§60. **Miscellaneous Instances.**—A protocol was signed at London, December 9, 1850, by Abbott Lawrence, American minister, and Viscount Palmerston, by which such portion of Horse Shoe

---

37 For. Rel., 1907, pp. 542-549.
38 See Moore, Int. Law Digest, V, 566.
39 For. Rel., 1905, pp. 365-366.

Reef in the Niagara River as might be requisite for a lighthouse was ceded to the United States, on condition that no fortifications should be maintained on the reef and that the United States would erect and maintain a lighthouse thereon.[40] In an instruction of January 17, 1851, Mr. Webster, Secretary of State, advised Mr. Lawrence that the President, to whom the protocol had been submitted, approved the proceedings. An appropriation for the erection of the lighthouse was subsequently made by Congress, and the lighthouse was duly erected.[41] On January 12, 1877, Caleb Cushing, American minister, and Señor Don Fernando Calderon, Spanish minister of state, signed a protocol of a conference concerning judicial procedure in their respective countries. The declaration on the part of Mr. Cushing was in the nature of a recital of the rights of trial guaranteed in the United States by the Constitution and acts of Congress. This protocol, says Wharton, is "to be regarded as simply an opinion by the parties as to the state of the law in this relation in the United States and Spain. As to the United States it has not the force of a law."[42] The Spanish minister on his part declared that citizens of the United States residing in Spain, her adjacent islands, or her ultramarine possessions, charged with sedition, treason or conspiracy, should enjoy trial by the ordinary jurisdiction, except in case of being captured with arms in hand, in which case they should be tried by ordinary council of war in conformity with the law of April 17, 1821. During the insurrection in Cuba of 1895-98, the American government insisted on the right of American citizens to trial as set forth in the protocol; and it was held by the Spanish Treaty Claims Commission that the protocol was in full force and effect during the insurrection and applied in determining the liability of Spain.[43] The protocol as to the rights of citizens of the United States to hold real estate in the Ottoman dominions, signed at Constantinople, August 11, 1874, was accepted and proclaimed by the President under the express authorization of section 2 of the act of Congress approved March 23, 1874.[44] A protocol was

40 Treaties and Conventions (1889 ed.), 444, 445.

41 H. Doc. No. 471, 56th Cong., 1st Sess., 17; 9 Stats. at L. 380, 627; 10 Stats. at L. 343.

42 Int. Law Digest, II, 623.

43 Am. Journal of Int. Law, IV, 809, 816.

44 18 Stats. at L. 23; Richardson, Messages and Papers of the Presidents, VII, 277. See also proclamation of March 27, 1876, by virtue of

signed at Athens, February 10, 1890, (January 30) by Mr. Snowden, minister resident of the United States, and the minister for foreign affairs of Greece, in which the minister of the United States declared, in return for a similar declaration on the part of the minister for foreign affairs, that joint stock companies and other associations, commercial, industrial and financial, constituted in conformity with the laws in force in Greece, might, under Article I of the treaty of 1837 between the two countries, exercise in the United States the rights and privileges of subjects of Greece, including the right to appear before tribunals for the purpose of bringing an action or for defense, with the sole condition that in exercising these rights they should always conform to the laws and customs existing in the United States and the several States. The declaration on the part of the American minister was authorized by instructions, dated September 19, 1889. The Attorney General had previously advised that such associations and corporations were entitled under Article I of the treaty (the word "subjects" being construed to include corporations), to lawful rights and remedies in the United States, it being understood that these rights and remedies were to be enjoyed subject to the appropriate laws of the United States and of the several States. In the course of the instructions of September 19, 1889, authorizing the signing of the protocol, Mr. Adee, Acting Secretary of State, said: "Since the exercise of those rights and remedies may be enjoyed by corporations and associations of Greece under the Constitution and laws of the United States, taken in connection with the treaty above referred to, it is not thought to be necessary that a specific agreement to continue for a certain time and to be terminable upon a certain notice should be entered into with the Hellenic minister of foreign affairs. It is thought that a proper precedent for the present case may be found in the protocol of conferences and declarations concerning judicial procedure, signed at Madrid on the 12th of January, 1877, by the minister of the United States and the minister of state of His Majesty the King of Spain."[45] The protocol was approved by Mr. Blaine, Secretary of State, in his in-

section 1 of the same act, suspending the act of June 22, 1860, and accepting jurisdiction of certain tribunals organized in the Ottoman dominions. Id., VII, 390, 403.

45 For. Rel., 1889, p. 481.

structions to Mr. Snowden, March 21, 1890.[46] An agreement, signed at St. Petersburg, June (12) 25, 1904, by Mr. McCormick, American ambassador, and Count Lamsdorff, minister for foreign affairs, as to the status of duly organized corporations and other commercial associations in the United States and Russia, which by its terms was to go into effect on the same date, was submitted to the Senate, and ratified by the President June 7, 1909, with the advice and consent of the Senate. As illustrative of recent administrative agreements, which have not been submitted to the Senate, the following may be noted: the declaration of November 7, 1901, with the Spanish government, for the exemption from the necessity of authentication of signatures attached to letters rogatory exchanged between Porto Rico and the Philippines and Spain; the agreement recorded by notes exchanged, December 3 and December 8, 1910, with the British government, for the exemption from customs inspection of commercial travellers' samples so far as compatible with the laws of the respective countries;[47] the agreement in notes exchanged, April 17, 1913, with the government of Panama, reciprocally permitting consuls to take note of declarations of values of exports made by shippers before customs officers; and the arrangement effected by exchange of notes with the British government, September 1 and September 23, 1913, for extradition, between the Philippine Islands or Guam and British North Borneo, of fugitive offenders for offenses specified in the extradition conventions existing between the two countries. The agreement concluded at Brussels, November 29, 1906, between various governments, for the unification of the pharmacopœial formulas for potent drugs, and not submitted to the Senate, was signed by the delegate on the part of the United States subject to the reservation that his government assumed no other obligation than that of exercising its influence to bring the American Pharmacopœia into harmony with the agreement.

§61. **Agreements in Execution of Treaty Stipulations.**—On February 24, 1870, a declaration was signed by Mr. Fish, Secretary of State, and Sir Edward Thornton, British minister, to approve and adopt for their governments the maps prepared by the joint commission for the survey and marking of the boundaries between the United States and the British possessions along the

46 For. Rel., 1890, p. 511.
47 See also earlier agreement for same purpose of November 19, 1907.

49th parallel under Article I of the treaty of June 15, 1846. A similar protocol was signed March 10, 1873, in which it was recited that the boundary line described in Article I of the treaty of June 15, 1846, had been traced and marked on charts prepared for that purpose in accordance with the award of the German Emperor rendered under Article XXXIV of the treaty of 1871, and that the charts had been severally signed to serve as a perpetual record of agreement between the governments in the matter of the boundary.[48] By exchange of notes, March 25, 1905, between Mr. Adee, Acting Secretary of State, and Mr. Durand, British ambassador, the two governments accepted the report of the commissioners appointed to carry out the delimitation of certain sections of the Alaskan boundary left undefined in the award of the tribunal constituted under the convention of January 24, 1903.[49] Attorney General Cushing advised in 1855 that, under Article I of the treaty with Mexico of December 30, 1853, the establishment of the line consisted of the official agreement of the two commissioners appointed, one by each government, to survey, mark, and establish the line, and that the agreement when duly made was conclusive against both governments.[50]

By Article II of the extradition convention concluded June 16, 1852, between the United States and Prussia and other States of the Germanic Confederation, it is provided that the stipulations of the convention shall be applied to any other State of the Germanic Confederation which may declare its accession thereto. The Secretary of State by direction of the President accepted the accession of the Free City of Bremen, October 14, 1853; of Mecklenburg-Schwerin, January 5, 1854; of Mechlenburg-Strelitz, January 26, 1854; of Oldenburg, March 21, 1854; of Schaumburg-Lippe, July 26, 1854; and of Württemberg, December 24, 1853.[51] On February 22, 1879, Mr. Arosemena, minister for foreign affairs of Colombia, and Mr. Dichman, American minister, signed a protocol as to the exercise by the United States of the right of transit across the Isthmus under Article XXXV of

48 As to statutory authority to sign these protocols, see the acts approved August 11, 1856, and February 14, 1873. 11 Stats. at L. 42; 17 Stats. at L. 437.

49 For. Rel., 1904, pp. 325, 326; For. Rel., 1905, pp. 478, 479.

50 7 Op. Atty. Gen., 582.

51 See also declaration signed March 10, 1847 with Oldenburg, under Article XII of the treaty of June 10, 1846 with Hanover.

the treaty of December 12, 1846.[52] Examples of administrative agreements, which might be noted under this heading, are numerous.[53]

Much has appeared in print of late, especially during the consideration by the Senate of the proposed arbitration conventions negotiated in 1904-5 by Mr. Hay, and in 1911 by Mr. Knox, on the question of the power of the President and Senate under the Constitution to conclude a treaty for the arbitration of future differences of a defined character, by the terms of which the Senate would not have a voice in the submission of the particular case thereafter arising.[54] That the Senate cannot delegate to an-

[52] For. Rel., 1879, p. 275; Moore, Extradition, I, 713-718; Moore, Int. Law Digest, §348.

[53] By Article II of the convention concluded with Spain, February 17, 1834, it was provided that the interest on the perpetual indebtedness therein recognized should be paid by Spain in Paris, semi-annually. By an executive arrangement reached in April, 1841, the payments were made at Havana, yearly. Mr. Vail, in his dispatch from Madrid, April 6, 1841, to Mr. Webster, Secretary of State, in adverting to this deviation from the treaty, said: "The clause in the treaty touching this head imposes an obligation on Spain and confers an advantage on the United States. When my instructions were made out it was thought, I presume, that, if the United States were willing to waive their right under that clause and accept another in its stead, Spain would be free to assume an additional or larger obligation in a matter merely of form in the execution of the treaty, without a formal amendment of the treaty itself." H. Ex. Doc. No. 129, 48th Cong., 1st Sess., 34, 38, 49.   Subsequently, by agreement, the payments were regularly made in Washington. See as to the agreement negotiated with the Sultan and other chiefs of the Sulu Archipelago by Brig. Gen. J. C. Bates, August 10, 1899, by which the sovereignty of the United States over these islands was recognized, and by which the United States was to assume certain obligations, Moore, Int. Law Digest, I, 531; V, 212. In the fifth annual report of the Philippine Commission (p. 23), it is said: "Acting under the direction of the President of the United States the civil governor on March 21, 1904, notified the Sultan of Sulu, through Major-General Wood, that the so-called Bates treaty was abrogated. Whilst it had never been formally recognized as valid and binding, and indeed as to the provision relating to slavery had been repudiated by the President, still it had been lived up to by the Americans in every particular, including the payment of annual subsidies to the Sultan and his principal datos, but it had been systematically and persistently violated by them."

[54] See especially reports from the Senate Committee on Foreign Relations presented by Mr. Morgan, S. Doc. No. 155, 58th Cong., 3d Sess.; by Mr. Lodge, Mr. Root, Mr. Cullom, Mr. Burton, and Mr. Rayner, S.

other body a power conferred on it by the Constitution is clear.[55]
It seems equally clear that, if the United States by a treaty entered
into through the constitutional treaty-making organs—the President and the Senate—agrees to submit to arbitration, in a prescribed manner, an exactly and definitely described class of cases,
or all cases or controversies, which may arise in the future between this nation and other nations, and which cannot be settled
by negotiation, the mere submission of an individual case so
arising is not an exercise of the treaty-making power. The consent of the nation to the submission has already been given, and
the faith of the nation pledged. It is immaterial whether the instrument by which the particular case is to be submitted, defining
the issue and the terms of submission for the guidance of the
arbitrators, is termed an agreement, a protocol, or a declaration.
It is essentially an administrative act in the execution of an existing international treaty and a municipal law, provided the terms
of the treaty are such as to leave no discretion in the matter and
are not open to construction. The President in whom is exclusively vested the power to conduct negotiations with foreign powers alone can determine the fact that the controversy cannot be
settled by negotiation. But it is the undoubted right of the Senate
as a co-ordinate branch of the treaty-making power to refuse to
give its consent to the conclusion of a treaty by which the faith
of the nation is thus pledged.

Doc. No. 98, 62d Cong., 1st Sess. See also speech by Mr. Lodge in the
U. S. Senate, printed as S. Doc. No. 353, 62d Cong., 2d Sess., and an
article in the *North American Review* by Mr. Bacon, printed as S. Doc.
No. 654, 62d Cong., 2d Sess. For excerpts from articles and opinions on
the subject, see Advocate of Peace (December, 1911), LXXIII, No. 12.

55 "By the custom of our forefathers it has been brought to pass that
an officer who can delegate his jurisdicto can only be one who possesses it
in his own right and not by the gift of another." Digest of Justinian, Bk.
II, Tit. I, 5.

CHAPTER IX.

AGREEMENTS REACHED BY THE EXECUTIVE IN VIRTUE OF ACTS OF CONGRESS.

§62. **Navigation and Commerce.**—The act of March 3, 1815, declared a repeal of so much of any act as imposed discriminating duties against the vessels, and the products of the country to which the vessel belonged imported therein, of any country in which discriminating duties against the United States did not exist, the President to determine in each instance the application of the repeal.[1] The acts of January 7, 1824, and May 24, 1828, likewise directed the President to suspend by proclamation discriminating duties so far as they affected the vessels of a foreign nation, when possessed of satisfactory evidence that no such discriminating duties were imposed by that nation on the vessels of the United States.[2] Section 11 of the act of June 19, 1886, as amended by the act of April 4, 1888, entrusted duties of similar character to the President.[3] A partial suspension is allowed by the act of July 24, 1897.[4] On the authority of these statutes numerous arrangements have been reached with foreign countries and made operative by proclamation. The evidence accepted by the President as sufficient may be recorded in a note or dispatch, or a memorandum of an agreement. The proclamations for the removal of discriminating duties on trade with Cuba and Porto Rico of February 14, 1884, October 27, 1886, and September 21, 1887, were based on memoranda of agreements with the Spanish government signed, respectively, February 13, 1884, October 27, 1886, and September 21, 1887.[5]

1 3 Stats. at L. 224.

2 4 Stats. at L. 3, 308; brought forward in Rev. Stats., §4228. See also acts of May 31, 1830, and July 13, 1832, 4 Id. 425, 579.

3 24 Stats. at L. 82; For. Rel., 1888, p. 1859. See for repeal of this section, act of August 5, 1909, section 36, 36 Stats. at L. 112.

4 30 Stats. at L. 214. See Rev. Stats., §4228.

5 See as to arrangement with Spain of December, 1831, Richardson, Messages and Papers of the Presidents, II, 575; IV, 399. See as to the removal of discriminating duties on vessels of Great Britain, the most important commercial nation, instructions of the Secretary of the Treasury, October 15, 1849. H. Ex. Doc. No. 76, 41st Cong., 3d Sess., 46; Oldfield v.

Section 3 of the tariff act of October 1, 1890, authorized and directed the President, whenever the government of any country, producing and exporting certain enumerated articles, imposed duties or made other exactions on the products of the United States, which, in view of the free introduction of the enumerated articles into the United States, were in his opinion reciprocally unreasonable and unequal, to suspend by proclamation as to that country the privilege of free importation, and to subject the articles in question to certain prescribed discriminating duties.[6] Ten commercial arrangements were concluded and made effective in virtue of this section—January 31, 1891, with Brazil; June 4, 1891, with the Dominican Republic; June 16, 1891, with Spain; December 30, 1891, with Guatemala; January 30, 1892, with Germany; February 1, 1892, with Great Britain; March 11, 1892, with Nicaragua; April 29, 1892, with Honduras; May 25, 1892, with Austria-Hungary; and November 29, 1892, with Salvador. These were all terminated by section 71 of the tariff act of August 27, 1894.[7] Section 3 of the act of 1890, having been assailed as an attempt to delegate legislative and treaty-making powers, was upheld by the Supreme Court in the case of Field v. Clark. Speaking for the court, Mr. Justice Harlan said: "As the suspension was absolutely required when the President ascer-

Marriott, 10 How. 146. See also Moore, Int. Law Digest, I, 811. See for suspensions of discriminating duties, proclamations dated, as regards Austria, May 11, 1829, June 3, 1829 (Richardson, Messages and Papers of the Presidents, II, 440, 441); Brazil, November 4, 1847 (Id., IV, 522); Bremen, July 24, 1818 (Id., II, 37); Chile, November 1, 1850 (Id., V, 76); China, November 23, 1880 (Id., VII, 600); France, June 24, 1822, April 20, 1847, June 12, 1869, November 20, 1869, September 22, 1873 (Id., II, 183; IV, 521; VII, 15, 19, 228); Great Britain, October 5, 1830 (Id. II, 497); Greece, June 14, 1837 (Id., III, 322); Hamburg, August 1, 1818 (Id., II, 38); Hanover, July 1, 1828 (Id., II, 404); Hawaiian Islands, January 29, 1867 (Id., VI, 515); Italy, June 7, 1827, February 25, 1858 (Id., II, 376; V, 491); Japan, September 4, 1872 (Id., VII, 177); Lubeck, May 4, 1820 (Id., II, 73); Mecklenburg-Schwerin, April 28, 1835 (Id., III, 146); Nicaragua, December 16, 1863 (Id. VI, 215); Norway, August 20, 1821 (Id., II, 96); Oldenburg, November 22, 1821, September 18, 1830 (Id., II, 97, 496); Portugal, February 25, 1871 (Id., VII, 126); Spain, December 19, 1871, February 14, 1884, October 27, 1886, September 21, 1887 (Id., VII, 174; VIII, 223, 490, 570); and Tuscany, September 1, 1836 (Id., III, 233).

6 26 Stats. at L. 612.

7 Sen. Doc. No. 52, 55th Cong., 1st Sess., 2. The provision for free introduction was suspended by proclamation as to various countries.

tained the existence of a particular fact, it cannot be said that in ascertaining that fact and in issuing his proclamation, in obedience to the legislative will, he exercised the function of making laws. Legislative power was exercised when Congress declared that the suspension should take effect upon a named contingency. What the President was required to do was simply in execution of the act of Congress. It was not the making of law. He was the mere agent of the law-making department to ascertain and declare the event upon which its expressed will was to take effect. * * * The court is of opinion that the third section of the act of October 1, 1890, is not liable to the objection that it transfers legislative and treaty-making power to the President."[8] Section 3 of the act of July 24, 1897, provided not only, as did section 3 of the act of 1890, for the imposition by proclamation of certain differential rates, but also for the conclusion by the President of commercial agreements with countries producing certain enumerated articles, in which concessions should be secured in favor of the products of the United States; and it further authorized the President, when such concessions were in his judgment reciprocal and equivalent, to suspend by proclamation the collection on these articles of the regular duties imposed by the act, and to subject them to special rates as provided for in the section.[9] On the authority of this section the President concluded and made effective the commercial agreements of May 28, 1898, August 20, 1902, and January 28, 1908, with France; of May 22, 1899 (protocol making corrections of January 11, 1900), and November 19, 1902, with Portugal; of July 10, 1900, February 27, 1906, and April 22-May 2, 1907, with Germany;[10] of February 8, 1900, and March 2, 1909, with Italy; of January 1, 1906, with Switzerland; of August 1, 1906, and February 20, 1909, with Spain; of September 15, 1906, with Bulgaria; of May 16, 1907, with the Netherlands; and of November 19, 1907, with Great Britain. Full force and effect has been given to these agreements by the

8 143 U. S. 649, 693. See also Buttfield v. Stranahan, 192 U. S. 470, 496, and Monongahela Bridge Co. v. United States, 216 U. S. 177.

9 30 Stats. at L. 203.

10 In this last named agreement, the government of the United States besides extending the benefits of section 3 of the act of 1897, agreed to effect certain changes in the customs and consular administrative regulations. See H. Rep't. No. 1833, 59th Cong., 1st Sess.

courts;[11] and it has been held by the Supreme Court that such agreements come within the meaning and intent of the word "treaty" as used in the Circut Court of Appeals Act giving the right of review by direct appeal when the validity or construction of any treaty made under the authority of the United States is drawn in question. Mr. Justice Day, speaking for the court, said: "While it may be true that this commercial agreement, made under authority of the tariff act of 1897, §3, was not a treaty possessing the dignity of one requiring ratification by the Senate of the United States, it was an international compact, negotiated between the representatives of two sovereign nations and made in the name and on behalf of the contracting countries, and dealing with important commercial relations between the two countries, and was proclaimed by the President. If not technically a treaty requiring ratification, nevertheless it was a compact authorized by the Congress of the United States, negotiated and proclaimed under the authority of its President. We think such a compact is a treaty under the Circuit Court of Appeals Act, and, where its construction is directly involved, as it is here, there is a right of review by direct appeal to this court."[12] In section 2 of the tariff act of August 5, 1909, it was provided that whenever and so long thereafter as the President should be satisfied, in view of the concessions granted by the minimum tariff of the United States, that the government of any foreign country imposed no restrictions or exactions of any character upon the importation or sale of products of the United States, which unduly discriminated against the United States or its products, and that such foreign country paid no export bounty or imposed no export duty or prohibition upon exportations to the United States which unduly discriminated against the United States or its products, and that such country accorded to the products of the United States treatment which was reciprocal and equivalent, upon proclamation to this effect by the President, articles from such country imported

11 Nicholas v. United States, 122 Fed. 892; United States v. Tartar Chemical Co., 127 Fed. 944; United States v. Luyties, 130 Fed. 333; United States v. Julius Wile Bro. & Co., 130 Fed. 331; La Manna, Azema, &c., v. United States, 144 Fed. 683; Migliavacca Wine Co. v. United States, 148 Fed. 142; Mihalovitch, Fletcher & Co. v. United States, 160 Fed. 988.

12 Altman & Co. v. United States (1912), 224 U. S. 583, 601. Provision for the termination of these agreements was made in section 4 of the tariff act of August 5, 1909, 36 Stats. at L. 83.

into the United States or any of its possessions (except the Philippine Islands and the islands of Guam and Tutuila) should be admitted under the minimum tariff.[13] The maximum tariff imposed by the act became effective on April 1, 1910, but prior to that date, one hundred and thirty-four proclamations, which practically included the entire commercial world, had been issued by the President applying the minimum tariff.[14] By an exchange of notes, January 21, 1911, between the Secretary of State of the United States and representatives of the Dominion of Canada, an arrangement was reached in which it was agreed that the Governments of the two countries would use their utmost efforts to bring about by concurrent legislation certain tariff changes. Such legislation was duly passed by the Congress of the United States, but failed of passage in the Canadian Parliament.[15]

The special acts of August 5, 1854, March 1, 1873, August 15, 1876, and December 17, 1903, to carry into effect, respectively, the conventions for commercial reciprocity with Great Britain of June 5, 1854, and May 8, 1871 (Arts. XVIII to XXV and XXX), with the Hawaiian Islands of January 30, 1875, and with Cuba of December 11, 1902, were to be effective only when the President had received satisfactory evidence that the other contracting parties had passed the necessary laws to carry the conventions into effect.[16] Formal protocols were signed June 7, 1873, and May 28, 1874, by Mr. Fish, Secretary of State, and Sir Edward Thornton, British minister, reciting the fact that the laws required to carry into effect the articles of the treaty of May 8, 1871, had been passed, and fixing the date on which the articles should take effect in respect of Prince Edward's Island and Newfoundland. A protocol, containing similar recitals in respect of the operation of the Hawaiian treaty of January 30, 1875, was signed September 9, 1876.

Acts of Congress authorizing and directing the President to apply by proclamation provisions thereof, when possessed of satisfactory evidence that certain conditions have been complied with by a foreign power, are numerous. Section 1 of the act approved June 11, 1864, to give effect to treaties between the United States

13   36 Stats. at L. 82.

14   Annual message, December 6, 1910, For. Rel., 1910, p. XVI.

15   Special message of January 26, 1911. Act approved July 26, 1911, 37 Stats. at L. 4.

16   10 Stats. at L. 587, 1179; 17 Id. 482; 19 Id. 200, 666; 33 Id. 3.

11

and foreign nations respecting consular jurisdiction over crews of the vessels of such foreign nations in the waters and ports of the United States, provided that, before the act should take effect as to the vessels of any particular nation having such treaty with the United States, the President should be satisfied that similar provisions had been made by that nation to give effect to the treaty, whereupon proclamation to that effect should be made.[17] The provisions of the act were extended by proclamation, February 10, 1870, to France, Italy, Prussia and the other States of the North German Union,[18] and May 11, 1872, to Norway and Sweden.[19] Section 2 of the act approved August 5, 1882, as amended by section 10 of the act of February 14, 1903, provides that, whenever it is made to appear to the Secretary of Commerce that the rules concerning the measurements for tonnage of vessels of the United States have been substantially adopted by any foreign country, he may direct that the vessels of such foreign country be deemed to be of the tonnage denoted in their certificates of register, and that thereupon it shall be unnecessary for such vessels to be re-measured at ports of the United States.[20] Formal instruments of agreement for the mutual exemption from re-measurement of vessels of the one country in the ports of the other were executed by the Secretary of State with the Russian minister, June 6, 1884, and with the Danish minister, February 26, 1886. An agreement was reached with Sweden and Norway as to Norwegian vessels by exchange of notes in 1894.[21] Section 4400 of the Revised Statutes, as amended by the act approved March 17, 1906, provides for the reciprocal exemption of

17 13 Stats. at L. 121.

18 Richardson, Messages and Papers of the Presidents, VII, 84.

19 Id., 175.

20 22 Stats. at L. 300; Rev. Stats., §4154, Supp. I, 379.

21 For. Rel., 1894, pp. 636-645. "A similar mode of admeasurement having been adopted by Great Britain, Belgium, Denmark, Austria-Hungary, the German Empire, Italy, Sweden, Norway, Spain, the Netherlands, Russia, Finland, Portugal, and Japan, and the like courtesy having been extended to vessels of the United States, it is directed that vessels of those countries whose registers indicate their gross and net tonnage under their present law shall be taken in the ports of the United States to be of the tonnage so expressed in their documents, with the addition of the amount of the deductions and omissions made under such law not authorized by the admeasurement law of the United States." Customs Regulations (1908), 55.

steamboats from inspection in case the laws of a foreign country for this purpose are similar to those of the United States.[22] An arrangement for such reciprocal exemption was effected with the Japanese government by exchange of notes, April 3-November 30, 1906.[23] The act of Congress approved June 19, 1878, as amended by the acts approved May 24, 1890, and March 3, 1893, extended, on conditions of reciprocity to be determined by the President, to Canadian vessels privileges of access to our inland waters in aid of wrecked and disabled vessels. A proclamation of the President to give effect to the provisions of the act was made July 17, 1893.[24] The act of Congress of August 19, 1890, as amended by the acts of May 28, 1894, August 13, 1894, and June 10, 1896, to adopt the international regulations for the prevention of collisions at sea, contained the reservation that the act should take effect at a time to be fixed by proclamation of the President. Such proclamations were made July 13, 1894, and December 31, 1896.[25]

§63. **International Copyright.**—Section 13 of the copyright act of March 3, 1891, provided that the act should apply to a citizen or subject of a foreign state only when such state permitted to citizens of the United States the benefit of copyright on substantially the same basis as its own citizens, or was a party to an international agreement which provided for reciprocity in the granting of copyright by the terms of which the United States might at its pleasure become a party. The existence of either of these conditions was to be determined by the President.[26] Under

22   34 Stats. at L. 68.

23   For. Rel., 1906, pp. 990-994.

24   28 Stats. at L. 1220. See annual message of the President, December 3, 1888, For. Rel., 1888, p. XII. See also the act approved February 21, 1893, for the protection of fur seals by international agreement, 27 Stats. at L. 472, Moore, Int. Law Digest, I, 920; the act approved March 3, 1887, for retaliation against Canada, 24 Stats. at L. 475; the act approved August 30, 1890, for the inspection of meats, 26 Id. 414, 415; the act approved July 26, 1892, for the enforcement of reciprocal commercial relations between the United States and Canada, and proclamation of August 18, 1892, 27 Id. 267, 1032, For. Rel., 1892, p. 339; and the joint resolution approved March 14, 1912, to prohibit the exportation of munitions of war, and proclamation of even date, 37 Stats. at L. 630, 1733.

25   Richardson, Messages and Papers of the Presidents, IX, 501, 761; 26 Stats. at L. 320; 28 Id. 82; 29 Id. 885. See for agreements in this respect with Great Britain and France, For. Rel., 1894, pp. 218-219, 260-274; For. Rel., 1895, pp. 683-686.

26   26 Stats. at L. 1110.

the first alternative, the President extended the benefits of the act by proclamation to subjects of Belgium, France, Great Britain and possessions, and Switzerland, July 1, 1891; Germany, April 15, 1892;[27] Italy, October 31, 1892; Denmark, May 8, 1893; Portugal, July 20, 1893; Spain, July 10, 1895;[28] Mexico, February 27, 1896; Chile, May 25, 1896; Costa Rica, October 19, 1899; the Netherlands and possessions, November 20, 1899; Cuba, November 17, 1903; Norway, July 1, 1905; and Austria, September 20, 1907. Section 8 of the act approved March 4, 1909, to amend and consolidate the acts respecting copyright, provides that the benefits of the act shall extend to a citizen or subject of a foreign state, only (a) when an alien author or proprietor is domiciled within the United States at the time of the first publication of his work; or (b) when the foreign state of which the author or proprietor is a citizen or subject grants, either by treaty, agreement, or law, to citizens of the United States the benefit of copyright on substantially the same basis as to its own citizens, or copyright protection substantially equal to the protection secured to such foreign author under this act or by treaty; or when such foreign state is a party to an international agreement which provides for reciprocity in the granting of copyright, by the terms of which agreement the United States may, at its pleasure, become a party. The existence of these reciprocal conditions is to be determined by the President by proclamation.[29] By proclamation dated April 9, 1910, it was declared that the subjects and citizens of Austria, Belgium, Chile, Costa Rica, Cuba, Denmark, France, Germany, Great Britain and possessions, Italy, Mexico, the Netherlands and possessions, Norway, Portugal, Spain, and Switzerland were entitled, and had been entitled since July 1, 1909 (the date on which the act became effective), to all the benefits of the act, other than those under section I (e), in reference to the reproduction of musical compositions.[30] The benefits of the act, subject to the same ex-

27 The proclamation as regards Germany was based upon an agreement signed at Washington by the Secretary of State and the German chargé d'affaires, January 15, 1892.

28 For restoration of agreement after the war of 1898, see notes exchanged January 29, 1902, November 18 and November 26, 1902.

29 35 Stats. at L. 1077.

30 The exception was removed as to the citizens and subjects of Germany, Belgium, Norway, Cuba, Great Britain and the British dominions, colonies and possessions (except Canada, Australia, New Zealand, South

ception, were extended to the subjects of the Grand Duchy of Luxemburg by proclamation dated June 29, 1910,[31] of Sweden by proclamation dated May 26, 1911, and of Tunis by proclamation dated October 4, 1912.[32]

§64. Trade-marks.—The United States has entered into various formal treaty stipulations for the protection of trade-marks.[33] Section 1 of the act of February 20, 1905, provides that the owner of a trade-mark, used in interstate or foreign commerce, who is domiciled in the United States or who resides or is located in any foreign country which by treaty, convention, or law, affords similar privileges to citizens of the United States, may obtain registration for such trade-mark by complying with certain designated requirements.[34] Under similar provisions in section 1 of the act approved March 3, 1881,[35] agreements for the reciprocal registration and protection of trade-marks were effected by exchange of notes, February 10 and 16, 1893, with the Netherlands, and April 27 and May 14, 1883, with Switzerland.[36] A declaration for the reciprocal protection of trade-marks was signed July 9, 1894, with the Greek government by Mr. Alexander, minister at Athens. The American negotiator considered the declaration as merely explanatory of rights already secured under the treaty of 1837 between the two countries. Mr. Gresham, Secretary of State,

Africa, and Newfoundland), and Italy by proclamations dated respectively, December 8, 1910, June 14, 1911, June 14, 1911, November 27, 1911, January 1, 1915, and May 1, 1915.

31 Exception was removed by proclamation dated June 14, 1911.

32 The United States is a party to the convention on the protection of literary and artistic copyright, signed August 11, 1910, at the Fourth International American Conference. Stipulations for the protection of copyrights are found in various treaties, as for instance, in the treaty with China of October 8, 1903 (Art. XI), in the convention with Japan of November 10, 1905, in two conventions with Japan concluded May 19, 1908, for protection of trade-marks and copyrights in Korea and China, respectively, and in the convention with Hungary concluded January 30, 1912. The United States did not accede to the international copyright convention concluded at Berne, September 9, 1886. See for report of the delegate to the Berlin conference of 1908, for the revision of the Berne convention, H. Doc. No. 1208, 60th Cong., 2d Sess.

33 See Sen. Doc. No. 20, 56th Cong., 2d Sess., 47-54.

34 33 Stats. at L. 724. See as to patents, act of March 3, 1903, 32 Stats. at L. 1225; Rev. Stats., §4887.

35 21 Stats. at L. 502.

36 Sen. Doc. No. 20, 56th Cong., 2d Sess., 334, 337.

did not entertain the same view, but considered the declaration as practically a new treaty which could be ratified only with the consent of the Senate.[37]   Agreements for the reciprocal protection in consular courts of trade-marks in China were effected by exchange of notes with Belgium, November 27, 1905 (explanatory note of January 22, 1906); with Denmark, March 19, 1907-June 12, 1907; with France, October 3, 1905 (explanatory note of January 22, 1906); with Germany, December 6, 1905 (explanatory note of January 22, 1906); with Great Britain, June 28, 1905; with Italy, December 18, 1905 (explanatory note of January 22, 1906); with the Netherlands, October 23, 1905 (explanatory note of January 27, 1906); and with Russia, June 28, 1906. Notes as to protection in consular courts of trade-marks in Morocco were exchanged with Germany, September 28-October 28, 1901; with Great Britain, December 1-6, 1899; and with Italy,

37 For. Rel., 1895, pp. 759, 763, 765; Moore, Int. Law Digest, V, 196. Mr. Hay, in a letter to the Secretary of the Interior, dated November 4, 1898, said: "My predecessors, Mr. Gresham and Mr. Olney, in instructions to our minister at Athens (Foreign Relations, 1894, pp. 293-295; and Foreign Relations, 1895, pp. 759-765), took the position that a declaration signed by the minister and the Greek minister for foreign affairs, to the effect that the treaty of 1837 between the United States and Greece conferred upon the citizens of either country in the dominions of the other the same rights as respects trade-marks as such citizens may enjoy in their own, would not accomplish the end desired, but that a formal treaty was necessary. I think it is plain that a simple declaration would not bind this government to grant trade-mark privileges to Mexican citizens, but in view of the Mexican law, which (the Commissioner of Patents states) allows citizens of the United States to register their trade-marks in Mexico, it would appear that Mexicans can *now* obtain registration of their trade-marks here, under the provisions of our law of March 3, 1881. * * * It will be observed that the provision of section 3 [of the act of March 3, 1881] is in the alternative; that in order to entitle a trade-mark to registration, it must appear: 1. That it is lawfully used as such by the applicant in foreign commerce, the owner being domiciled in the United States *or located in a foreign country* which, by treaty, convention or by law, affords similar privileges to citizens of the United States; *or 2.* That such trade-mark is within the provision of a treaty, convention or declaration with a foreign power. While registration could not be claimed by a Mexican under the second alternative, it seems to me that it could properly be claimed under the first. I think an exchange of notes with the Mexican government would be entirely proper to establish the fact that under the Mexican law, citizens of the United States may obtain registration of their trade-marks. This was done with the Netherlands in 1883." Moore, Int. Law Digest, II, 36.

June 13, 1903-March 12, 1904.[38]   By notes exchanged June 22 and June 26, 1906, an agreement was reached with Denmark as to the protection afforded by the laws of the respective countries to industrial designs or models, in case the articles which they represent are not manufactured in the country where protection is sought.

§65. **International Postal and Money Order Regulations.**— By section 26 of the general act of February 20, 1792, to establish the post office and post roads, and to prescribe the rates of postage, the Postmaster General was authorized to make "arrangements with the postmasters in any foreign country for the reciprocal receipt and delivery of letters and packets, through the post-offices."[39]   This provision was textually re-enacted in the successive general post-office acts of May 8, 1794,[40] March 2, 1799,[41] April 30, 1810,[42] and March 3, 1825.[43]   In section 2 of the act of March 3, 1851, to reduce and modify the rates of postage, the Postmaster General was authorized by and with the advice and consent of the President "to reduce or enlarge, from time to time, the rates of postage upon all letters and other mailable matter conveyed between the United States and any foreign country, for the purpose of making better postal arrangements with other governments, or counteracting any adverse measures affecting our postal intercourse with foreign countries."[44]   This provision as modified and incorporated as section 167 of the general act of June 8, 1872, to consolidate and revise the laws

38 The international convention for the protection of industrial property, signed at Paris, March 30, 1883, was ratified by the President with the advice and consent of the Senate, March 29, 1887, and the ratification was communicated to the Swiss government on May 30, 1887. The ratification of the additional act, signed at Brussels, December 14, 1900, was deposited at Brussels, May 3, 1901. These two conventions have been superseded by the convention signed at Washington, June 2, 1911, which has been duly ratified and proclaimed on the part of the United States. The United States is also a party to the general convention for the protection of inventions, patents, designs and industrial models, signed August 20, 1911, at the Fourth International American Conference.

39 1 Stats. at L. 239.

40 Sec. 26. 1 Id. 366.

41 Sec. 25. 1 Id. 740.

42 Sec. 32. 2 Id. 603.

43 Sec. 34. 4 Id. 112.

44 9 Id. 589.

relating to the Post Office Department,[45] and brought forward as section 398 of the Revised Statutes reads: "For the purpose of making better postal arrangements with foreign countries, or to counteract their adverse measures affecting our postal intercourse with them, the Postmaster General, by and with the advice and consent of the President, may negotiate and conclude postal treaties or conventions, and may reduce or increase the rates of postage on mail-matter conveyed between the United States and foreign countries."[46] Section 103 of the act of June 8, 1872,[47] brought forward as section 4028 of the Revised Statutes, likewise authorizes the Postmaster General to conclude arrangements with the post departments of foreign governments, with which postal conventions have been concluded, for the exchange by means of postal orders, of sums of money not exceeding in amount one hundred dollars,[48] at such rates of exchange and under such regulations as may be deemed expedient. In virtue of these provisions, postal and money order conventions have been concluded by the Postmaster General with the approval of the President without submission to the Senate. Among these are the general postal union convention signed at Berne, October 9, 1874, and the universal postal union conventions signed at Vienna, July 4, 1891, at Washington, June 15, 1897, and at Rome, May 26, 1906.[49] It has been held that the provision in Article XXV of the Regulations attached to the Berne convention, in which it was declared that no article liable to customs duties should be admitted for con-

---

45 17 Id. 304.

46 See for careful examination of these various legislative enactments, opinion of William H. Taft, Solicitor General, March 20, 1890, 19 Op. Atty. Gen. 513, and speech of Henry Cabot Lodge in the U. S. Senate, February 29, 1912, on the proposed arbitration conventions with Great Britain and France, S. Doc. No. 353, 62d Cong., 2d Sess., 15. The conclusion by the Postmaster General, by and with the advice and consent of the President, of arrangements with adjoining countries, for the transportation of mails, is authorized by §4012, Rev. Stats.

47 17 Stats. at L. 297. Section 15 of the act of July 27, 1868. 15 Id. 196.

48 As amended by the act of January 30, 1889. 25 Id. 654.

49 19 Stats. at L. 577; 28 Id. 1078; 30 Id. 1629; 35 Id. 1639.

50 Cotzhausen v. Nazro (1882), 107 U. S. 215. In United States v. Eighteen Packages of Dental Instruments (1914), 222 Fed. 121, it is stated that the authority to enter into post conventions with other countries is to be found in the treaty-making power.

veyance by the post, was the law of the land, and that goods so imported were liable to seizure.[50] Of postal conventions submitted by the President to the Senate for its advice and consent as to the ratification, prior to the passage of the act of 1872, note may be made of those signed as follows: March 6, 1844, with New Granada; December 15, 1848, with Great Britain; July 31, 1861, and December 11, 1861, with Mexico; and June 9, 1862, with Costa Rica. The ratification was in each instance advised by the Senate.[51]

§66. **Agreements with Indian Tribes.**—On July 12, 1775, three departments of Indian affairs—the northern, southern and middle—were organized and the superintendence of each placed under commissioners.[52] By the general ordinance for the regulation of Indian affairs of August 7, 1786, two district were organized, the superintendents of which were placed under the immediate control of the Secretary at War.[53] Treaties concluded through these agencies do not appear to have been formally ratified. [54] In the act of August 7, 1789, for the organization of the War Department under the Constitution, the conduct of Indian affairs was recognized as belonging to the Secretary of War. Later, it was transferred to the Department of the Interior.[55] The Senate, in approving an Indian treaty submitted for its "consideration and advice" by President Washington, May 25, 1789—the first to be submitted under the Constitution—simply advised the President "to execute and enjoin an observance." The President, in a message of September 17, requested information as to the meaning of the action of the Senate, and suggested a ratification as in case of other treaties. The committee appointed by the Senate to examine the question reported against a formal ratification; but the Senate complied with the suggestion of the President by voting, September 22, to advise and consent to the ratification.[56]

51 Ex. Journal, VI, 275, 321; VIII, 16, 17; XI, 497, 563; XII, 102, 116, 398, 406. See for collection of postal conventions, 16 Stats. at L. 783-1123; 17 Id. 879.

52 Journals of Congress (1800 ed.), I, 151.

53 Id., XI, 127.

54 See Id., X, 137; XI, 39, 40, 42, 44.

55 1 Stats. at L. 50.

56 Ex. Journal, I, 25, 27, 28. The following entry appears in the Journal under date of May 25, 1789: "General Knox brought the following message from the President, which he delivered into the hands of the Vice-President, and withdrew." Id., 3.

This procedure was followed until 1871, during which period treaties with Indian tribes were far more numerous than those with foreign powers. In the Indian appropriations act of March 3, 1871, it was enacted that thereafter no Indian nation or tribe within the territory of the United States should be acknowledged or recognized as an independent nation, tribe, or power with which the United States might contract by treaty; but that the obligation of existing treaties was in no way to be impaired or invalidated by the act.[57] No formal treaties with the Indian tribes have since been made, but agreements with them have been laid before Congress for its approval.[58] "Since the act 3d March, 1871, the Indian tribes have ceased to be treaty-making powers and have become simply the wards of the nation. As such, Congress speaks for them and has become the legislative exponent of both guardian and ward."[59]

The peculiar status of the Indian tribes within the United States was defined in 1831 by Chief Justice Marshall, with his usual felicity of expression, as follows: "It may well be doubted whether those tribes which reside within the acknowledged boundaries of the United States can, with strict accuracy, be denominated foreign nations. They may, more correctly, perhaps, be denominated domestic dependent nations. They occupy a territory

[57] 16 Stats. at L. 566; Rev. Stats., §2079. See section 6 of the act of March 29, 1867, and the act of July 20, 1867. 15 Stats. at L. 9, 18.

[58] See, for instances, acts of Congress approved as follows: April 29, 1874, to ratify an agreement with the Ute tribe of Indians (18 Stats. at L. 36); December 15, 1874, to ratify an agreement with the Shoshone Indians (18 Id. 291); February 28, 1877, to ratify an agreement with certain bands of the Sioux Indians and certain other tribes (19 Id. 254); June 15, 1880, to ratify an agreement with the Ute Indians (21 Id. 199); April 11, 1882, to ratify an agreement with the Crow Indians (22 Id. 42); July 3, 1882, to ratify an agreement with the Shoshone and Bannock Indians (22 Id. 148); July 10, 1882, to ratify an agreement with the Crow Indians (22 Id. 157); March 1, 1889, to ratify an agreement with the Creek Indians (25 Id. 757); February 13, 1891, to ratify an agreement with the Sac and Fox Indians (26 Id. 749); March 1, 1901, to ratify an agreement with the Cherokees (31 Id. 848); March 1, 1901, to ratify an agreement with the Creek Indians (31 Id. 861); June 30, 1902, to ratify a sunpplemental agreement with the Creek Indians (32 Id. 500, 2021); and July 1, 1902, to ratify an agreement with the Choctaw and Chickasaw tribes of Indians (32 Id. 641).

[59] Nott, C. J., Jonathan Brown v. United States (1897), 32 C. Cls. 432, 439.

to which we assert a title independent of their will, which must take effect in point of possession when their right of possession ceases. Meanwhile they are in a state of pupilage. Their relation to the United States resembles that of a ward to his guardian."[60] Mr. Justice Gray, at a later date, said: "The Indian tribes within the limits of the United States are not foreign nations; though distinct political communities, they are in a dependent condition; and Chief Justice Marshall's description, that 'they are in a state of pupilage,' and 'their relation to the United States resembles that of a ward to his guardian,' has become more and more appropriate as they have grown less powerful and more dependent."[61]

§67. **Acquisition of Territory.**—Although the important acquisitions of 1803, 1819, 1848, 1853, 1867 and 1898 were made by formal treaty, territory has under special circumstances been acquired by virtue of an act of Congress. A treaty was signed at Washington, April 12, 1844, with the republic of Texas, by which that republic agreed to convey and transfer to the United States all its rights of separate and independent sovereignty and jurisdiction. On June 8, 1844, the treaty was rejected by the Senate by a vote of 35 to 16.[62] In resolutions, submitted by Mr. Benton, May 13, 1844, it was declared that the ratification of the treaty would be the adoption of the Texan War; that the treaty-making power of the President and Senate did not include the power of making war, either by declaration or by adoption; and that the territory disencumbered from the United States by the treaty of 1819 ought to be united to the American Union as soon as this could be accomplished with the consent of a majority of the people of the United States and of Texas, and when Mexico should either consent to the transfer or acknowledge the independence of Texas, or cease to wage war against her on a scale commensurate with the conquest of the country.[63] The opinion was frequently expressed that the ratification of the treaty would be the adoption of a war

60 Cherokee Nation v. State of Georgia, 5 Pet. I, 17.

61 Jones v. Meehan (1899), 175 U. S. 1, 10, citing Cherokee Nation v. Georgia, 5 Pet. I, 17; Elk v. Wilkins, 112 U. S. 94, 99; United States v. Kagama, 118 U. S. 375, 382, 384; Stephens v. Choctaw Nation, 174 U. S. 445, 484. See also Missouri, Kansas and Texas R. R. Co. v. United States, 47 C. Cls. 59, for resumé of legislation affecting the Indian tribes.

62 Ex. Journal, VI, 312.

63 Id., VI, 277.

with Mexico, and accordingly not within the province of the treaty-making power. To an enquiry made by the Senate whether any military preparations had been made in anticipation of war, and, if so, for what cause and with whom was war apprehended, President Tyler, in a message of May 15, 1844, replied that, in consequence of an announcement of Mexico of its determination to regard as a declaration of war the definitive ratification of the treaty of annexation, a portion of the naval and military forces of the United States had as a precautionary measure been assembled in the region of Texas. He observed further that the United States having by the treaty of annexation acquired a title to Texas, which required only the action of the Senate to perfect it, no other power could invade and by force of arms possess itself of any portion of the territory of Texas, pending the deliberations of the Senate on the treaty, without placing itself in a hostile attitude to the United States.[64] Immediately preceding the rejection of the treaty, a resolution was introduced by Mr. Henderson declaring that the annexation would be properly achieved on the part of the United States by an act of Congress admitting the people of Texas with defined boundaries as a new State into the Union on an equal footing with the other States.[65] This course was followed, and on March 1, 1845, a joint resolution was approved consenting to the erection of the territory rightfully belonging to the republic of Texas into a new State. A proviso, attached in the Senate through the efforts of Mr. Benton, gave the President an opportunity, before communicating the resolution to Texas, to resort to negotiations upon terms of admission and cession either by treaty to be submitted to the Senate or by articles to be submitted to both houses.[66] The purpose of the proviso was to effect if possible the acquisition, and at the same time maintain peaceful relations with Mexico.[67] Negotiations were not resorted to;[68] and Texas, having accepted and complied with the

64 Id., VI, 274, 277, 279.

65 Id., VI, 311.

66 5 Stats. at L. 797.

67 Benton, Thirty Years in the United States Senate, II, 602, 619, et seq.

68 Mr. Calhoun, Secretary of State, in communicating a copy of the joint resolution to Mr. Donelson, chargé d'affaires to Texas, March 3, 1845, said: "The President has deliberately considered the subject, and is of opinion that it would not be desirable to enter into the negotiations

conditions of the resolution,[69] was admitted by a joint resolution approved December 29, 1845, as a State into the Union.[70]

A treaty for the incorporation of the Dominican Republic, signed November 29, 1869, was rejected by the Senate on June 30, 1870. President Grant in his annual message of December 5, 1870, urged upon Congress early action expressive of its views as to the best means of making the acquisition, and suggested that this might be accomplished either by the action of the Senate on a treaty, or by the joint action of the two houses of Congress on a resolution of annexation as in the case of the acquisition of Texas.[71]

authorized by the amendment of the Senate; and you are accordingly instructed to present to the government of Texas, as the basis of its admission, the proposals contained in the resolution as it came from the House of Representatives. * * * But the decisive objection to the amendment of the Senate is, that it would endanger the ultimate success of the measure. It proposes to fix, by negotiation between the governments of the United States and Texas, the terms and conditions on which the State shall be admitted into our Union, and the cession of the remaining territory to the United States. Now, by whatever name the agents conducting the negotiation may be known * * * the compact agreed on by them in behalf of their respective governments would be a treaty; whether so called or designated by some other name. * * * And if a treaty (as it clearly would be) it must be submitted to the Senate for its approval and run the hazard of receiving the votes of two-thirds of the members present, which could hardly be expected, if we are to judge from recent experience. This, of itself, is considered by the President as a conclusive reason for proposing the resolution of the House, instead of the amendment of the Senate, as the basis of annexation." MSS. Inst. to Texas, I, 107. Mr. Buchanan, Secretary of State, in instructions to Mr. Donelson, dated March 10, 1845, stated that, while the new President did not concur in the opinion of his predecessor that terms of admission agreed upon under the proviso would necessarily be a treaty which must be submitted to the Senate for its advice and consent, he had decided not to reverse the decision of his predecessor. Works of James Buchanan (Moore ed.), VI, 120.

69 "The executive government, the Congress, and the people of Texas in convention have successively complied with all the terms and conditions of the joint resolution * * * the people of Texas at the polls have accepted the terms of annexation and ratified the Constitution." President Polk, annual message, December 2, 1845, Richardson, Messages and Papers of the Presidents, IV, 386.

70 9 Stats. at L. 108. Mr. Archer, of the Committee on Foreign Relations, submitted a report to the Senate, February 4, 1845, in which he objected on constitutional grounds to this method of acquisition. Compilation of Reports of Sen. Com. on For. Rel., VI, 78.

71 Richardson, Messages and Papers of the Presidents, VII, 100.

A treaty was signed at Washington, June 16, 1897, with the republic of Hawaii for the annexation of that republic to the United States. The treaty was ratified by the Hawaiian legislature, but the cession was accepted and confirmed on the part of the United States by a joint resolution approved July 7, 1898.[72] Although, as a matter of fact, the resolution was agreed to in the Senate, July 6, by a two-thirds vote,[73] the annexation was effected by an act of the legislative, not the treaty-making, power. In 1845, a foreign state was by an act of Congress incorporated and admitted as a State into the Union; in 1898, a foreign state was by an act of Congress brought within the territorial jurisdiction of the United States. In each case, however, the other contracting party by the very agreement lost its identity as a separate nation with which international relations could thereafter exist, and the agreement by which the incorporation was effected ceased thereupon to be an international compact.[74]

72 30 Stats. at L. 750.

73 42 to 21. Cong. Globe, 55th Cong., 2d Sess., 6712.

74 See Westlake, Int. Law, I, 64. On April 24, 1802, an agreement was entered into with the State of Georgia for the cession to the United States of western lands. The commissioners on the part of the United States, James Madison, Albert Gallatin, and Levi Lincoln, were appointed by President Adams under an act of Congress, approved April 7, 1798. An act of May 10, 1800, vested final powers in the commissioners. On the part of Georgia the agreement was ratified and confirmed by the legislature, June 16, 1802. H. Mis. Doc. No. 45, 47th Cong., 2d Sess., pt. 4, pp. 78-81. For an agreement between the Federal government and the government of the State of Texas as to boundaries, effected by an act of Congress of September 9, 1850, and an act of the legislature of Texas of November 25, 1850, see Richardson, Messages, V, 95. Such agreements are at all stages, during their negotiation, as well as after their conclusion, entirely an internal affair. During the northeastern boundary negotiations in 1832, an agreement with the State of Maine for the cession to the government of the United States of the territory under dispute, and claimed by that State, east of the St. Francis River and north of the St. John, was signed. The agreement was never consummated; but in the fifth article of the Webster-Ashburton treaty a clause was inserted, by which the government of the United States agreed "with the States of Maine and Massachusetts to pay them the further sum of three hundred thousand dollars, in equal moieties, on account of their assent to the line of boundary described in this treaty, and in consideration of the conditions and equivalents received therefor from the government of Her Britannic Majesty." The irregularity of incorporating into an international treaty a stipulation of this character was not overlooked by the British negotiator.

In defining the relations which should exist between the United States and Cuba, Article VII of the act of Congress, approved March 2, 1901, provided that, to enable the United States to maintain the independence of Cuba and to protect the people thereof, as well as for its own defense, the Cuban government would sell or lease to the United States lands necessary for coaling and naval stations at points to be agreed upon with the President of the United States. This same provision was adopted by Cuba as Article VII of the Appendix to its Constitution. By virtue thereof an agreement was signed, by the President of Cuba, February 16, 1903, and by the President of the United States, February 23, 1903, for the lease to the United States, subject to terms to be agreed upon by the two governments, of lands at Guantanamo and Bahia Honda for coaling and naval stations. Neither this agreement nor the protocol of July 2, 1903, prescribing the conditions of the lease, and in which the United States agreed to pay to Cuba annually, as long as it should occupy the designated areas, the sum of $2,000 in gold, was submitted to the Senate, although the latter agreement was formally approved by the President and the ratifications exchanged.[74a]

The act of Congress of August 18, 1856, brought forward as sections 5570-5578 of the Revised Statutes, provides that, whenever any citizen of the United States discovers a deposit of guano on any island, rock or key, not within the lawful jurisdiction of any other government and not occupied by the citizens of any other government, and takes peaceable possession thereof and occupies the same, such island or key may at the discretion of the President

On signing the treaty, Lord Ashburton addressed a note to Mr. Webster, in which he stated that the introduction of an agreement between the central and State governments would have been "irregular and inadmissible, if it had not been deemed expedient to bring the whole of these transactions within the purview of the treaty." He requested an assurance that his government should incur no responsibility for these engagements. To this Mr. Webster replied on the same date: "It purports to contain no stipulation on the part of Great Britain, nor is any responsibility supposed to be incurred by it on the part of your government." Moore, Int. Arb., I, 138; Webster's Works, VI, 289-290.

74a The agreement for the relinquishment of the lease-hold rights at Bahia Honda in exchange for an enlargement of the naval station at Guantanamo Bay, referred to in the President's message on foreign relations of December 3, 1912, is now awaiting the approval of the Cuban government.

be considered as appertaining to the United States. Under the provisions of this act numerous guano islands have been announced as appertaining to the United States.[75]

75　11 Stats. at L. 119. Jones v. United States, 137 U. S. 202. See for list of these islands, Moore, Int. Law Digest, I, 567.

CHAPTER X.

AGREEMENTS ENTERED INTO BY STATES OF THE UNION.

§68. With Foreign Powers.—By Article I, section 10, of the Constitution, the States are forbidden, absolutely, to enter into "any treaty, alliance or confederation," and, without the consent of Congress, to enter into "any agreement or compact with another State, or with a foreign power." The exact distinction between the expressions "treaty, alliance or confederation" and "agreement or compact," has not been determined. Under the Articles of Confederation, the States were forbidden to enter, without the consent of Congress, into any "conference, agreement, alliance or treaty" with any king, prince or state, or into any "treaty, confederation or alliance" with another State. The latter clause is incorporated as the absolute prohibition in the Constitution. In the Federalist of January 25, 1788, Madison said: "The prohibition against treaties, alliances, and confederations makes a part of the existing articles of Union; and for reasons which need no explanation, is copied into the new Constitution."[1] The proceedings of the Federal Convention shed little light as to the intention of the framers. Madison, on June 19, 1787, observed that although the States had by the Articles of Confederation been forbidden to enter into treaties, without the consent of Congress, Virginia and Maryland, in one instance, and Pennsylvania and New Jersey, in another, had entered into "compacts without previous application or subsequent apology."[2] The clauses, as incorporated in the Constitution, are found in the draft reported August 6, by the Committee of Detail.[3] A natural inference is that the expression "agreement or compact" was intended to comprehend such agreements as had been considered by the States, under the Articles of Confederation, as not included under the terms "treaty, confederation or alliance." Several boundary agreements had been entered into by the States during the period. A compact between Virginia and Maryland, dated March 28, 1785,

---

1 No. 44, (Ford ed.), 294.
2 Doc. Hist. of the Const., III, 155.
3 Id., 455.

included stipulations in reference to the entry of vessels of commerce and of war of the one State into the ports of the other, and as to the jurisdictional rights of each in boundary waters. This agreement has been recognized by the Supreme Court as continuing in force after the adoption of the Constitution, so far as not inconsistent therewith.[4] Mr. Justice Field, in Wharton v. Wise, said, in respect of the inhibitions of the Articles of Confederation: "The articles inhibiting any treaty, confederation, or alliance between the States without the consent of Congress were intended to prevent any union of two or more States, having a tendency to break up or weaken the league between the whole; they were not designed to prevent arrangements between adjoining States to facilitate the free intercourse of their citizens, or remove barriers to their peace and prosperity. * * * So, in the present case, looking at the object evidently intended by the prohibition of the Articles of Confederation, we are clear they were not directed against agreements of the character expressed by the compact under consideration [between Virginia and Maryland of 1785]. Its execution could in no respect encroach upon or weaken the general authority of Congress under those articles. Various compacts were entered into between Pennsylvania and New Jersey and between Pennsylvania and Virginia, during the Confederation, in reference to boundaries between them, and to rights of fishery in their waters, and to titles to land in their respective States, without the consent of Congress, which indicated that such consent was not deemed essential to their validity. * * * In our judgment the compact of 1785 was not prohibited by the Articles of Confederation. It was not a treaty, confederation, or alliance within the meaning of those terms as there used."[5]

The prohibition in the Constitution as to agreements between a State and a foreign power was the subject of an elaborate opinion by Chief Justice Taney in 1840. The governor of Vermont had issued a warrant ordering a sheriff of that State to arrest one Holmes, a fugitive from Canada, to convey him to some convenient place on the boundary between the State and the Province

4 Wharton v. Wise, 153 U. S. 155; Morris v. United States, 174 U. S. 196; Maryland v. West Virginia, 217 U. S. 577. See for examples of State agreements entered into during the period of the Confederation, Poole v. Fleeger, 11 Pet., 185; Wharton v. Wise, 153 U. S. 155, 163, 171.

5 153 U. S. 155, 167.

of Lower Canada, and there to deliver him up to such person as might be empowered by the Canadian authorities to receive him. In the course of the opinion the Chief Justice observed that all would admit that an agreement between Vermont and Canada formally made to deliver up offenders would be unconstitutional; that, since the surrender of the fugitive to the Canadian authorities was not the exercise of a power which operated only upon the internal concerns of the State, it was a part of the foreign intercourse of the country; that the warrant of the governor authorized by State law was a State act; that, although no application by the governor of Canada for the arrest appeared in the record, and it could not be assumed to have been made, nevertheless the warrant itself imported an agreement with the Canadian authorities; that from the nature of the transaction the act of delivery necessarily implied a mutual agreement. How, asked the Chief Justice, was the fugitive to be delivered unless they accepted him; and if the authorities of Vermont agreed to deliver him up, and the authorities of Canada agreed to accept him, was not that an agreement between them? It was mutually understood in some way that the fugitive should be seized, in order to be delivered up pursuant to this understanding. The terms "treaty," "agreement," and "compact," were not used superfluously, but indicated that the framers of the Constitution had intended to use the broadest and most comprehensive terms in order to cut off all communication between a State and a foreign power. Accordingly, the term "agreement" must be so construed as "to prohibit every agreement, written or verbal, formal or informal, positive or implied, by the mutual understanding of the parties." The Chief Justice added that the States might, with the consent of Congress, and under its direct and specific supervision, enter into such an agreement as that under consideration. The court being equally divided on the question of jurisdiction to entertain the writ of error, the case was dismissed. Justices Story, McLean, and Wayne, concurred in the opinion delivered by the Chief Justice. The other four justices did not express any clear opinion upon the power of the State of Vermont to deliver a fugitive to the government of Canada. Upon a reconsideration of the case by the Supreme Court of Vermont, Holmes was discharged. The record before that tribunal contained an application from the governor of

Canada for the fugitive's surrender.[6] In 1886, Mr. Justice Miller, in the case of United States v. Rauscher,[7] said: "There can be little doubt of the soundness of the opinion of Chief Justice Taney, that the power exercised by the governor of Vermont is a part of the foreign intercourse of this country, which has undoubtedly been conferred upon the Federal government; and that it is clearly included in the treaty-making power and the corresponding power of appointing and receiving ambassadors and other public ministers."[8]

On February 27, 1839, Mr. Forsyth, Secretary of State, and Mr. Fox, British minister, signed a memorandum in which it was agreed that certain recommendations would be made to the authorities of the State of Maine and the Province of New Brunswick as to a modus vivendi in the disputed territory pending a settlement of the boundary controversy. In March, following, an arrangement for this purpose was reached by the concurrence of the governor of the State of Maine and the lieutenant governor of New Brunswick in propositions submitted by General Winfield Scott, acting under the directions of the Secretary of War. The

6 Holmes v. Jennison, 14 Pet. 540, 561, 572, 573, 578. 12 Vt. 631. Moore, Extradition, I, 57. "I think, from the whole argument of the bench in the case of Holmes v. Jennison, 14 Pet. 540, we may consider it as law: 1st. That no State can, without the consent of Congress, enter into any agreement or compact, express or implied, to deliver up fugitives from justice from a foreign state who may be found within its limits." Legare, Atty. Gen. (1841), 3 Op. 661.

7 119 U. S. 407, 414.

8 Cases of extradition by State authorities can nevertheless be found, most notably by New York under a statute of that State passed in 1822. See for instances of State action, Moore, Extradition, I, 53-78. In 1872, the New York Court of Appeals declared the statute of 1822 to be in conflict with the Constitution of the United States. People v. Curtis, 50 N. Y. 321. Article IX of the extradition convention with Mexico signed February 22, 1899, permits requisitions for fugitives, which have committed crimes in the frontier States or Territories, to be made either through the regular diplomatic officers, or through the chief civil authorities of the State or Territory or such other authority as may be designated by the chief executive of the State or Territory. Article II of the convention of December 11, 1861 contained a similar provision. In the extradition convention with the Netherlands of January 18, 1904, and in the supplementary extradition convention with Denmark of November 6, 1905, provisions are made for direct application to and by the governor or chief magistrate of the island possession or colony of the contracting parties.

arrangement so reached was not in strict accord with the recommendations of the memorandum of February 27.[9]

§69. **Between States of the Union.**—It was urged by Mr. Clay, in his argument before the Supreme Court in Green v. Biddle, that the consent of Congress to agreements between the States being required, it must be evidenced by some positive act, and could not be implied from silence; that it was not necessary for Congress to interpose in order to prevent that which without its consent would be a mere nullity.[10] The case before the court involved a compact between the State of Virginia and the people of Kentucky. Virginia, by an act of its legislature of December 18, 1789, agreed to the separation of the Kentucky district under certain conditions, one of which was that the central government should, prior to a certain day, agree to the separation. The people of Kentucky in convention accepted the offer and incorporated the compact into their constitution. By an act approved February 4, 1791, Congress consented to the erection of the district into a new State and its admission into the Union.[11] The Supreme Court held that the consent of Congress to the agreement was found in the act admitting Kentucky into the Union under a constitution in which the compact was incorporated. An agreement of nine articles between Kentucky and Tennessee, signed February 2, 1820, relative to boundaries, subsequently consented to by Congress, was upheld by the Supreme Court in 1837 in Poole v. Fleeger.[12]

In 1870 a case came before the Supreme Court in which the consent of Congress was not so clearly expressed. The State of Virginia through the so-called Pierpont government, which was recognized by Congress as the lawful government of Virginia, agreed to the erection into a new State of certain western counties. The consent of Congress was given by an act approved December 31, 1862, for the admission of the State of West Virginia into the Union. Subsequently, in 1863, two counties of Virginia, Jefferson and Berkeley, with the concurrence of the two States, were joined to West Virginia; but before the passage by Congress of the joint resolution of March 10, 1866, specifically consenting to the transfer, the legislature of Virginia repealed the several acts by

9 H. Doc. No. 169, 26th Cong., 1st Sess. See also Barnett, International Agreements (reprinted from the Yale Law Journal), 9.

10 8 Wheat. 1, 40, 41.

11 1 Stats. at L. 189.

12 11 Pet. 185, 209.

which her assent had been given to the erection of the new State and to the separation of the two counties. In the acts of August 20, 1861, and May 13, 1862, of the Virginia legislature, consenting to the erection of certain designated counties into a separate State, consent was, however, given to the incorporation into the new State of Jefferson, Berkeley and other counties, whenever the inhabitants thereof should express a wish for it. The constitution adopted by West Virginia, after reciting the counties composing the State, provided that additional counties might form a part of it, if by a majority vote their inhabitants should adopt the constitution. No vote on this proposition had been taken in the counties of Jefferson and Berkeley in 1862, at the time of the admission of West Virginia, but Congress had before it at that time the statutes of Virginia of 1861 and 1862, and the constitution of West Virginia. The Supreme Court held that, although the act of Congress did not expressly recite every proposition embraced in the agreement, the inference was clear that Congress intended to consent to the admission of the new State with the contingent boundaries provided for in the constitution and the statutes, and that in so doing it necessarily consented to the agreement of the States on that subject.[18]

In the case of Virginia v. Tennessee, decided in 1893, the Supreme Court, Mr. Justice Field delivering the opinion, held that the consent of Congress might be implied from its subsequent legislation. A boundary line as run by commissioners appointed by the States of Virginia and Kentucky was, by acts of the legislatures of the respective States in 1803, ratified, established and confirmed. The line was recognized by Congress as the boundary in establishing judicial and revenue districts, and in federal elections and appointments. Such recognition in a single instance, said the court, "would not perhaps be considered as absolute proof of the assent or approval of Congress to the boundary line; but the exercise of jurisdiction by Congress over the country as a part of Tennessee, on one side, and as a part of Virginia on the other, for a long succession of years without question or dispute from any quarter furnishes as conclusive proof of assent to it by that body as can usually be obtained from its most formal proceedings."[14]

---

13 Virginia v. West Virginia, 11 Wall. 39, 60.
14 148 U. S. 503, 522. See also North Carolina v. Tennessee (1914), 235 U. S. 1.

Numerous compacts as to boundaries have been entered into by the States with the express consent of Congress. The State of New York has, for instance, entered into the following agreements: with New Jersey, respecting territorial limits and jurisdiction, consented to by Congress in an act approved June 28, 1834;[15] with Connecticut, respecting boundaries, consented to by Congress in an act approved February 26, 1881;[16] with Massachusetts, by which New York acquired from that State a small tract of land known as "Boston Corner," consented to by Congress in an act approved January 3, 1855;[17] with Vermont, by which New York acquired a small tract of land, consented to by Congress in an act approved April 7, 1880;[18] and with Pennsylvania, respecting the boundary line, consented to by Congress in an act approved August 19, 1890.[19] In 1874, Virginia and Maryland referred their controversies as to territorial limits and boundary to arbitration. The consent of Congress to the award of the arbitrators was given in an act approved March 3, 1879.[20]

A compact, signed June 3, 1897, by the governors of Nebraska and South Dakota in virtue of acts of the legislatures of the respective States, concerning the boundary line between these States in the Missouri River, was by express provision made subject to the consent of Congress. Such consent was given in an act approved July 24, 1897.[21] Congress, by a joint resolution approved March 3, 1901, gave its consent to a compact between Virginia and Tennessee, embodied in concurrent laws passed by the legislatures of these States in 1901, in which Tennessee ceded,

15 4 Stats. at L. 708.

16 21 Id. 351.

17 10 Id. 602.

18 21 Id. 72.

19 26 Id. 329. For other boundary agreements, see Gannett, Boundaries of the United States. See also the following cases: Sims v. Irvine, 3 Dall. 425; Marlatt v. Silk, 11 Pet. 1; Robinson v. Campbell, and Burton v. Williams, 3 Wheat. 212, 218, 529, 533; Green v. Biddle, 8 Wheat. 1, 16, 89, 90, 92; Hawkins v. Barney, 5 Pet. 457, 464, 465; Massachusetts v. Rhode Island, 12 Pet. 657, 725; Pennsylvania v. Wheeling, &c., Bridge Co., 13 How. 518, 561, 562. By an act approved October 3, 1914, Congress consented to the boundary line between Connecticut and Massachusetts as determined in accordance with an act of the legislature of Connecticut approved June 6, 1913, and of the legislature of Massachusetts approved March 19, 1908. 38 Stats. at L. 727.

20 20 Stats. at L. 481.

21 30 Id. 214.

and Virginia accepted, a small strip of land.[22]   Other recent instances are found in the acts of Congress approved March 1, 1905, consenting to a compact between South Dakota and Nebraska as to the boundary in the Missouri,[23] and January 24, 1907, consenting to a compact between New Jersey and Delaware as to territorial limits and jurisdiction.[24]   Congress by joint resolutions approved June 7, June 10, and June 22, 1910, authorized the conclusion of compacts, respectively, by Missouri and Kansas, as to boundary and jurisdiction in the Missouri, by Oregon and Washington, as to boundaries in the Columbia, and by Wisconsin, Illinois, Indiana, and Michigan, or any two or more of them, as to their respective jurisdictions over offenses against their laws on waters of Lake Michigan.[25]

Mr. Justice Field, in writing the opinion of the court in Virginia v. Tennessee, suggested as possible instances of arrangements between States, not in his opinion prohibited by the terms "agreement" and "compact" in the Constitution, a concerted plan for draining a common malarial or disease-producing district, or for preventing a sudden invasion of a plague or other causes of sickness, or a contract between Massachusetts and New York for the transportation over the Erie Canal of exhibits for the World's Fair at Chicago.   He added: "The mere selection of parties to run and designate the boundary line between two States, or to designate what line should be run, of itself imports no agreement to accept the line run by them, and such action of itself does not come within the prohibition.   Nor does a legislative declaration, following such line, that it is correct, and shall thereafter be deemed the true and established line, import by itself a contract or agreement with the adjoining State.   It is a legislative declaration which the State and individuals, affected by the recognized boundary line, may invoke against the State as an admission, but not as a compact or agreement.   The legislative declaration will take the form of an agreement or compact when it recites some consideration for it from the other party affected by it, for example, as made upon a similar declaration of the border or contracting State.   The mutual declarations may then be reasonably

22 31 Id. 1465. See Tennessee v. Virginia, 190 U. S. 64, 66.
23 33 Stats. at L. 820.
24 34 Id. 858.
25 36 Id. 881, 882.

treated as made upon mutual considerations. The compact or agreement will then be within the prohibition of the Constitution, or without it, according as the establishment of the boundary line may lead or not to the increase of the political power or influence of the States affected, and thus encroach or not upon the full and free exercise of Federal authority. If the boundary established is so run as to cut off an important and valuable portion of a State, the political power of the State enlarged would be affected by the settlement of the boundary; and to an agreement for the running of such a boundary, or rather for its adoption afterwards, the consent of Congress may well be required. But the running of a boundary may have no effect upon the political influence of either State; it may simply serve to mark and define that which actually existed before, but was undefined and unmarked. In that case the agreement for the running of the line, or its actual survey, would in no respect displace the relation of either of the States to the general government. There was, therefore, no compact or agreement between the States in this case which required, for its validity, the consent of Congress, within the meaning of the Constitution, until they had passed upon the report of the commissioners, ratified their action, and mutually declared the boundary established by them to be the true and real boundary between the States. Such ratification was mutually made by each State in consideration of the ratification of the other."[26]

26 148 U. S. 503, 518, 520. See for instances of the appointment by two States of joint commissioners to run and mark boundary lines, Gannett, Boundaries of the United States (3d ed.), 42, 45, 47, 49, 50, 53, 65, 68, 72, 80, 81, 87, 103, 107, 116.

II. THE EXECUTION OR ENFORCEMENT.

"This Constitution, and the Laws of the United States which shall be made in Pursuance thereof; and all Treaties made, or which shall be made, under the Authority of the United States, shall be the supreme Law of the Land; and the Judges in every State shall be bound thereby, any Thing in the Constitution or Laws of any State to the Contrary notwithstanding."—Article VI of the Constitution.

CHAPTER XI.

OPERATION OF TREATIES AS MUNICIPAL LAW.

§70. Operation Without the Aid of State Legislation.—The primary purpose of the clause in the Constitution, declaring treaties to be the supreme law of the land, was to ensure their faithful observance without the aid or intervention of legislation on the part of the States, anything in the constitution or laws of the States to the contrary notwithstanding. Under the Articles of Confederation, although the power to make treaties was entrusted to the Congress, the fulfillment of the promise was ultimately dependent upon the action of the State legislatures. On various occasions the Congress was obliged to resort to recommendations to the legislatures for this purpose. Although, in the Federal letter to the States prepared by Jay and adopted unanimously by the Congress, April 13, 1787, shortly before the assembling of the Federal Convention, it was declared that treaties constitutionally made, ratified and published became in virtue of the Confederation part of the law of the land and were not only independent of the will and power of the legislatures of the States but obligatory on them, the States were nevertheless requested to repeal all acts then existing which might be repugnant to the treaty of peace, "as well to prevent their continuing to be regarded as violations of that treaty, as to avoid the disagreeable necessity there might otherwise be of raising and discussing questions touching their validity and obligation." Early in the Federal Convention, May 31, 1787, on motion of Franklin, it was unanimously agreed that the national legislature should have the power to negative all laws of the States which might contravene any treaties subsisting under the authority of the Union. On July 17, 1787, a provision was agreed to declaring that all treaties made and ratified under the authority of the United States should be the "supreme law of the respective States," and that the judiciaries of the several States should be bound thereby anything in the respective laws of the individual States to the contrary notwithstanding. The clause, "supreme law of the respective States," was changed to "supreme law of the land" in the Committee on Style and Arrangement near the close of the Convention. On August 23, 1787, a provision expressly giving to the central government power to use the militia in the enforcement of treaties was stricken out on the suggestion of Gouverneur Morris that the provision was superfluous since treaties were to be laws.

That treaties, made under the authority of the United States, operate by virtue of Article VI of the Constitution, *proprio vigore*, as laws, and, without the aid of State legislation, supersede conflicting State acts, was fully established in Ware v. Hylton, decided by the Supreme Court, March 7, 1796. Opinions were read seriatim by the several justices who sat in the case, but upon this proposition there was no disagreement. Mr. Justice Chase, in the leading opinion, said: "A treaty cannot be the supreme law of the land, that is of all the United States, if any act of a State legislature can stand in its way. If the constitution of a State (which is the fundamental law the State, and paramount to its legislature) must give way to a treaty, and fall before it; can it be questioned, whether the less power, an act of the State legislature, must not be prostrate? It is the declared will of the people of the United States that every treaty made, by the authority of the United States, shall be superior to the constitution and laws of any individual State; and their will alone is to decide. If a law of a State, contrary to a treaty, is not void, but voidable only by a repeal, or nullification by a State legislature, this certain consequence follows, that the will of a small part of the United States may control or defeat the will of the whole."[1] Mr. Justice Paterson, in referring to the fourth article of the treaty of peace with Great Britain, said: "All lawful impediments of whatever kind they might be, whether they related to personal disabilities, or confiscations, sequestrations, or payments into loan offices or treasuries, are removed. No act of any State legislature, and no payment made under such act into the public coffers, shall obstruct the creditor in his course of recovery against the debtor. The act itself is a lawful impediment, and therefore is repealed; the payment under the act is also a lawful impediment, and is made void. * * * The fourth article embraces all creditors, extends to all pre-existing debts, removes all lawful impediments, repeals the legislative act of Virginia, which has been pleaded in bar, and with regard to the creditor annuls every thing done under it."[2] In the

1 3 Dall. 199, 236.
2 Id., 250, 256.

opinion read by Mr. Justice Iredell, who did not concur in the decision on the ground that the treaty did not have the effect of reviving as against the original debtor a debt then extinguished, it is declared in equally clear language that under the Constitution, "so far as a treaty constitutionally is binding, upon principles of moral obligation, it is also by the vigor of its own authority to be executed in fact. It would not otherwise be the supreme law in the new sense provided for, and it was so before in a moral sense. The provision extends to subsisting as well as to future treaties. I consider, therefore, that when this Constitution was ratified, the case as to the treaty in question stood upon the same footing, as if every act constituting an impediment to a creditor's recovery had been expressly repealed, and any further act passed, which the public obligation had before required, if a repeal alone would not have been sufficient."[3] The concise statement of Mr. Justice Wilson was: "But even if Virginia had the power to confiscate, the treaty annuls the confiscation. The fourth article is well expressed to meet the very case. * * * It is impossible by any glossary, or argument, to make the words more perspicuous, more conclusive, than by a bare recital. Independent, therefore, of the Constitution of the United States (which authoritatively inculcates the obligation of contracts) the treaty is sufficient to remove every impediment founded on the law of Virginia."[4] And Mr. Justice Cushing said: "Was there a power, by the treaty, supposing it contained proper words, entirely to remove this law, and this bar, out of the creditor's way? This power seems not to have been contended against, by the defendant's counsel. And, indeed, it cannot be denied; the treaty having been sanctioned, in all its parts, by the Constitution of the United States, as the supreme law of the land."[5] It was held that, under the provision in the fourth article of the treaty of peace that creditors on either side should meet with no lawful impediment to the recovery of all bona fide debts theretofore contracted, a British creditor could recover against the original debtor, although the debt had been paid to the State of Virginia under an act of the legislature of that State of 1777, which declared such payment to be a lawful discharge. A like conclusion was reached in circuit by

3 Id., 277.
4 Id., 281.
5 Id., 282.

Chief Justice Jay (who had retired prior to the date of the decision of the Supreme Court in Ware v. Hylton) in respect of payment under the act of Virginia,[6] and by Chief Justice Ellsworth
(whose commission bearing date of March 4 was read in court
March 8, 1796, the day following the date of the decision in Ware
v. Hylton) in respect of payment under a similar act of North
Carolina. With reference to the repeal of the act of the legislature by the treaty, Chief Justice Ellsworth said: "As to the
opinion that a treaty does not annul a statute, so far as there is an
interference, it is unsound. * * * A treaty, when it is in fact
made, is, with regard to each nation that is a party to it, a national
act, an expression of the national will as much so as a statute can
be. And it does, therefore, of necessity annul any prior statute
so far as there is an interference."[6a]

6　Jones v. Walker, 2 Paine 688.

6a　Hamilton & Co. v. Eaton (argued at the June term, 1796), 1 Hughes
249, 259; s. c. 2 Martin's Repts. 1. See infra, 514, for other cases in
which the provisions of Articles IV and V of the treaty of peace with
Great Britain were enforced and held to have superseded conflicting State
legislation.

An eminent author has, after an extensive examination of the record,
reached the conclusion that the decision of the issue raised by the plead-
ings in Ware v. Hylton did not cover the question of the effect of a treaty
on an inconsistent statute of a State. It is his view that a majority of
the court were of the opinion that the act of Virginia of October, 1777,
was "invalid or inoperative," and that, accordingly, the decision of the
court could not reach the question of the effect of the treaty on this act.
The case was argued February 6, 8, 9, 10, 11 and 12, 1796, before Justices
Chase, Paterson, Iredell, Wilson, and Cushing. It is admitted that each of
the justices, who sat in the case and concurred in the decision, took occasion to declare in unequivocal language the supremacy of the treaty over the
State statute. It was provided in the treaty that "creditors" on either side
should meet with "no lawful impediment" to the recovery of all "bona
fide debts" thertofore contracted. The Virginia statute of 1777 provided
that it should be lawful for any citizen of the State, owing money to a
subject of Great Britain, to pay the same or any part thereof into the
loan office of the State, receiving therefor a receipt, which receipt should
"discharge him from so much of the debt" as had been so paid. This was
a suit against the original debtor who had made such payment. The
argument of Marshall for the defendant in error (i. e., the original debtor)
before the Supreme Court was, as reported, in effect that the debt having
been extinguished by payment to the State under the statute prior to the
date of the treaty, no "debt" existed on the date of the treaty, which by
its terms was protected; that there could be no "creditor" where there
was no debt; and that the provision in the treaty "must be construed

with reference to those creditors, who had bona fide debts, subsisting, in legal force, at the time of making the treaty." (3 Dall. 210-213). This argument was based on two distinct propositions: 1st. That the payment under the Virginia statute was a complete extinguishment of the debt; and 2d. That the provision in the treaty applied only to debts subsisting in legal force on the date of the treaty. It is to these two questions that the justices in their several opinions addressed themselves. Five opinions were read—by Justices Chase, Paterson, Iredell, Wilson, and Cushing—and are reported in this order. Of these, all concurred in the final decision, sustaining the right of action against the original debtor, except Mr. Justice Iredell. The opinion read by him was prepared in support of the decision of the circuit court, now reversed. Mr. Justice Chase in the leading opinion held, with respect to the first proposition advanced by Marshall, that under the law of nations Virginia had at the time of the passage of the act a right to confiscate a debt due a British subject, and that the act of 1777, and payment in virtue thereof, amounted either to a "confiscation or extinguishment" of the debt. It is admitted that after having reached this conclusion it was necessary for Mr. Justice Chase to pass on the question of the supremacy of the treaty provision over the State statute. Mr. Justice Paterson did "not deem it necessary to enter on the question, whether the legislature of Virginia had authority to make an act, confiscating the debts due from its citizens to the subjects of the king of Great Britain, or whether the authority in such case was exclusively in Congress." After examining the provisions of the act in question, he says: "The act does not confiscate debts due to British subjects. The preamble reprobates the doctrine as being inconsistent with public faith, and the law and usages of nations. The payments made into the loan office were voluntary and not compulsive; for it was in the option of the debtor to pay or not. * * * It is, however, said, that the payment being made under the act, the faith of Virginia is plighted. True— but to whom is it plighted—to the creditor or debtor—to the alien enemy, or to its own citizen, who made the voluntary payment? * * * On the part of the defendants, it has been also urged, that it is immaterial whether the payment be voluntary or compulsive, because the payor, on complying with the directions of the act, shall be discharged from so much of the debt. Be it so. If the legislature had authority to make the act, the Congress could, by treaty, repeal the act, and annul everything done under it. This leads us to consider the treaty and its operation." He then proceeds to an examination of the treaty and concludes: "The fourth article embraces all creditors, extends to all pre-existing debts, removes all lawful impediments, repeals the legislative act of Virginia, which has been pleaded in bar, and with regard to the creditor annuls every thing done under it. This article reinstates the parties; the creditor and debtor before the war, are creditor and debtor since; as they stood then, they stand now." (Id., 246, 247, 249, 256). In declaring that the act of Virginia by its terms did not confiscate the debt, it is not held that the act did not contain a bar to the recovery in a suit by the creditor against the original debtor. Mr. Justice Paterson seems to have accepted the argument of

13

counsel for plaintiffs, that to have constituted a confiscation and final extinguishment of the debt the payment must have been made compulsory, and of the entire debt, without any implied promise of indemnification. (Id., 208). Entertaining this view of the effect of the act, it was unnecessary to meet Marshall's argument that the treaty covered only debts existing on the date of its signature and did not have the effect of reviving one already extinguished. Although the debt existed, the act interposed a bar to an action for its recovery against the original debtor. This distinction between the confiscation of the debt and the interposition of a bar to the recovery against the original debtor is considered more fully in the opinion of Chief Justice Jay in Jones v. Walker, 2 Paine 688, and of Chief Justice Ellsworth in Hamilton & Co. v. Eaton, 1 Hughes 249, 258. The language of Chief Justice Ellsworth is: "It is also pertinent to the inquiry whether the debt in question be within the before recited article, to notice an objection which has been stated by the defendant, viz., that at the date of the treaty, what is now sued for as a debt, was not a debt but a non-entity; payment having been made, and a discharge effected under the act of confiscation, and therefore that the stipulation concerning debts did not reach it. In the first place it is not true that in this case there was no debt at the date of the treaty. A debt is created by contract, and exists until the contract is performed. Legislative interference to exonerate a debtor from performance of his contract, whether upon or without conditions, or to take from the creditor the protection of law, does not in strictness destroy the debt, though it may, locally, the remedy for it. The debt remains, and in a foreign country payment is frequently enforced." In concurring in the decision, holding the original debtor liable, it seems that it was necessary for Mr. Justice Paterson to pass upon the question of the effect of the treaty on so much at least of the act as provided for a discharge on payment to the State. Evidently, Mr. Justice Paterson entertained the same view, for the concluding and greater portion of his opinion is devoted to this question. In the opinion read by Mr. Justice Iredell, it was maintained that even admitting that the legislature of the State did not have "strictly a right, agreeably to the law of nations, to confiscate the debt in question; yet, if they in fact did so, it would, while it remained unimpeached by any subsequent sufficient authority, have been valid and obligatory within the limits of the State, so as to bar any suit for the recovery of the debt." Accordingly, he was "clearly of opinion that under the act of sequestration, and of payment and discharge, the discharge will be a complete bar in the present case, unless there be something in the treaty of peace to *revive* the right of the creditor against the defendant." (Id., 265, 270). He held, however, that the treaty did not have this effect. The opinion of Mr. Justice Wilson fills less than a printed page, and is reported immediately after that of Mr. Justice Iredell. He states the case as follows: "There are two points involved in the discussion of this power of confiscation: The first arising from the rule prescribed by the law of nations; and the second arising from the construction of the treaty of peace." His answer to the first question may be considered a denial of the right of the State to confiscate private debts. As to the second question

The principle is now well established that a treaty duly made under the authority of the United States is as much a part of the law of every State, of which its courts must take notice and en-

he said: "But even if Virginia had the power to confiscate, the treaty annuls the confiscation * * * the treaty is sufficient to remove every impediment founded on the law of Virginia." (Id., 281). It seems reasonable to conclude that Mr. Justice Wilson intended to place his decision on the second of these propositions. Otherwise, there would have been some attempt to answer the argument of counsel, as also the clear statement in the opinion of Mr. Justice Chase as also in that of Mr. Justice Iredell, that, even if under the modern law of nations the State did not have the right to confiscate the debt, the law of the State could be pleaded within the limits of the State as a bar until repealed by competent authority. Mr. Justice Cushing opens his brief opinion with the statement: "I shall not question the right of a State to confiscate debts," and closes with the sentence quoted above in the text declaring the supremacy of the clear words of the treaty over any law of the State aimed against the recovery. In the course of the opinion in reply to the objection that the construction placed upon the terms of the treaty would work a hardship on the original debtor who had made payment to the State under the invitation of the act, Mr. Justice Cushing uses the following language: "But it can hardly be considered as an odious thing, to enforce the payment of an honest debt according to the true intent and meaning of the parties contracting; especially if, as in this case, the State having received the money, is bound in justice and honor, to indemnify the debtor, for what it in fact received. In whatever other light this act of assembly may be reviewed, I consider it in one, as containing a strong implied engagement, on the part of the State, to indemnify every one who should pay money under it, pursuant to the invitation it held out. Having never confiscated the debt, the State must, in the nature and reason of things, consider itself answerable to the value. And this seems to be the full sense of the legislators upon this subject, in a subsequent act of assembly; but the treaty holds the original debtor answerable to his creditor, as I understand the matter. The State, therefore, must be responsible to the debtor." The remainder of the opinion is devoted to a consideration of the effect of the treaty. Mr. Justice Cushing evidently entertained the views of Mr. Justice Paterson, that to constitute a confiscation there must be an appropriation with no implied agreement of indemnification. But in holding that the original debtor was answerable to his creditor, it was necessary, so it seems, to pass on the question of the effect of the treaty on the provision in the Virginia statute declaring the payment to the State to be a discharge of the debt.

If the views here given are correct, it was necessary for each of the justices concurring in the decision to pass upon the question of the supremacy of the treaty over inconsistent State legislation. The fact that each justice took occasion to express a clear opinion on this question, and to devote the main and concluding portion of his opinion to its consideration, supports this conclusion.

force, as its own local laws and constitution, and in case of conflict the treaty must prevail.[7]

§71. Operation Without Congressional Action.—During the debate in the House of Representatives on the Jay treaty, Chief Justice Ellsworth, in a written opinion communicated to Jonathan Trumbull, March 13, 1796, said: "The instant the President and Senate have made a treaty, the Constitution makes it a law of the land; and of course, all persons and bodies in whatever station or department within the jurisdiction of the United States are bound to conform their actions and proceedings to it. Such a treaty ipso facto repeals all existing laws so far as they interfere with it."[8] Chief Justice Marshall, in 1801, in the case of the United States v. Schooner Peggy, declared that a treaty under the Constitution of the United States became upon its conclusion the law of the land, as much to be regarded by the courts as an act of Congress, and as such affected the rights of parties litigating.[9] In 1829, just forty years after the Constitution went into operation, the same great judge, after noting the contractual nature of a treaty and its usual dependence for infra-territorial operation upon subsequent acts of the respective parties, said: "In the United States a different principle is established. Our Constitution declares a treaty to be the law of the land. It is, consequently, to be regarded in courts of justice as equivalent to an act of the legislature, whenever it operates of itself without the aid of any legislative provision."[10] Although a treaty is primarily a contract between nations it operates by virtue of Article VI of the Constitution as a municipal law and so far as it prescribes a rule by which rights of individuals under it may be determined the

7 Blythe v. Hinckley, 173 U. S. 501, 508; Hauenstein v. Lynham, 100 U. S. 483; Blandford v. State, 10 Tex. App. 627; Ehrlich v. Weber, 114 Tenn. 711; Butschkowski v. Brecks, 94 Neb. 532.

8 MSS. Letters to Washington, CXVII, 287.

9 1 Cranch 103, 109.

10 Foster v. Neilson, 2 Pet. 253, 314, 315. "If treaties, made in those circumstances, be obligatory between the respective states or sovereigns, they are also binding, with regard to the subjects of each prince in particular. They oblige, as compacts between the contracting powers; but they have the force of laws, with respect to the subjects considered as such; for it is evident that two sovereigns, who conclude a treaty, lay their subjects thereby under an obligation of doing nothing contrary to it." Burlamaqui, Principles of Natural and Politic Law, (translation by Nugent, 2 ed.), II, 316.

courts look to the treaty as they would to a statute for a rule of decision.[11]

§72. **Conflict Between Acts of Congress and Treaties.**—Treaties and laws of the United States are both declared by the Constitution to be the supreme law of the land. No superiority is here given to the one over the other. Accordingly, it has been held by the Supreme Court that an act of Congress supersedes a prior inconsistent treaty as a law binding the courts. Conversely, it has frequently been declared that so far as a treaty operates of its own force as municipal law, it supersedes prior inconsistent acts of Congress.[12] "When the two relate to the same subject, the courts will always endeavor to construe them so as to give effect to both, if that can be done without violating the language of either; but if the two are inconsistent, the one last in date will control the other, provided always the stipulation of the treaty on the subject is self-executing."[13] Mr. Justice Harlan, in reading the opinion of the court in United States v. Lee Yen Tai, although no conflict between the treaty and statute in question was found to exist, added: "That it was competent for the two countries by treaty to have superseded a prior act of Congress on the same subject is not to be doubted; for otherwise the declaration in the Constitution that a treaty, concluded in the mode prescribed by that instrument, shall be the supreme law of the land, would not have due effect. As Congress may by statute abrogate, so far at least as this country is concerned, a treaty previously made by the United States with another nation, so the United States may by treaty supersede a prior act of Congress on the same subject."[14] Again, in the recent case of Charlton v. Kelly, Mr. Justice Lurton, speaking for the court, said: "Of course, the effect of the supplementary treaty of 1884, being later than the statutory require-

11 Head Money Cases, 112 U. S. 580, 598; Whitney v. Robertson, 124 U. S. 190, 194.

12 United States v. Schooner Peggy, 1 Cranch 103; Head Money Cases, 112 U. S. 580, 599; the Chinese Exclusion Case, 130 U. S. 581, 600; Horner v. United States, 143 U. S. 570; Fong Yue Ting, 149 U. S. 698; Johnson v. Browne, 205 U. S. 309, 321; Charlton v. Kelly, 229 U. S. 447, 463; United Shoe Machinery Co. v. Duplessis Shoe Machinery Co., 155 Fed. 842, 845. See, as to acts of Congress over-riding treaties, views expressed by Mr. Cushing in a dispatch from Madrid to Mr. Fish, Secretary of State, January 13, 1877, For. Rel., 1877, p. 492.

13 Field, J., Whitney v. Robertson, 124 U. S. 190, 194.

14 185 U. S. 213, 220.

ments above referred to, is to supersede the statute in so far as there is a necessary conflict in the carrying out of the extradition obligation between this country and Italy."[15]

§73. Legislation to Give Effect to Stipulations.—But, as was observed by Chief Justice Marshall in Foster v. Neilson, not all treaty stipulations are self-executing. They may either by their terms or from their nature require legislative action to give them full effect. In such cases Congress must execute them before they can be enforced in the courts. In the eighth article of the treaty of February 22, 1819, which was before the court in Foster v. Neilson, it was stipulated, according to the English text, alone considered by the court, that all grants of land made by His Catholic Majesty in the ceded territory prior to January 24, 1818, "shall be ratified and confirmed to the persons in possession of the lands." The language, said Chief Justice Marshall, indicated merely a contract in which the United States engaged to do a particular act, and, until Congress had confirmed the grants, the courts were not at liberty to disregard the existing laws on the subject; that, as such a stipulation addressed itself to the political not the judicial department, the legislature must execute the contract before it could become a law for the courts. He added, had the words "are hereby confirmed" been used, the article would have been self-executing and have repealed acts of Congress repugnant to it.[16] Mr. Justice Field, in Whitney v. Robertson, likewise ob-

15   229 U. S. 447, 463.

16   Only one other justice considered this point essential to the decision (2 Pet. 313) ; and in the later case of United States v. Percheman, (7 Pet. 51, 89) the court, construing the English and the Spanish texts together, held that the article was self-executing. See also Strother v. Lucas, 12 Pet. 410, 439, and the numerous cases thereafter arising, infra, 492, Mr. Justice Baldwin, in 1840, in Lessee of Pollard's Heirs v. Kibbe, said: "All treaties, compacts, and articles of agreement in the nature of treaties to which the United States are parties, have ever been held to be the supreme law of the land, executing themselves by their own fiat, having the same effect as an act of Congress, and of equal force with the Constitution; and if any act is required on the part of the United States, it is to be performed by the executive, and not the legislative power, as declared in the case of the Peggy in 1801; and since affirmed with the exception of only Foster and Elam." (14 Pet. 353, 415). It has been held that the provision in the treaty of June 15, 1846, with Great Britain, that the property on the north side of the Columbia River belonging to the Puget's Sound Agricultural Company "shall be confirmed to the said company," vested title in the property at once upon the ratification of the treaty, and was to be

served: "When the stipulations are not self-executing they can only be enforced pursuant to legislation to carry them into effect, and such legislation is as much subject to modification and repeal by Congress as legislation upon any other subject. If the treaty contains stipulations which are self-executing, that is, require no legislation to make them operative, to that extent they have the force and effect of a legislative enactment."[17]

In order to determine what treaty provisions have been considered as requiring legislation to give them effect, it is necessary to examine legislative precedents, since the promptness with which Congress has usually met these obligations has in large measure removed the question from judicial determination.

considered by the courts as equivalent to a legislative act to that effect. Puget Sound Agricultural Co. v. Pierce County (1861), 1 Wash. Ter. 159. The Court of Claims has held that the stipulation in Article IX of the treaty of 1819 with Spain, that the "United States will cause satisfaction to be made" for injuries in certain cases, imported a contract to be executed by Congress. Humphrey's Admx. v. United States, Devereux's Court of Claims Reports, 164.

17 124 U. S. 194.

CHAPTER XII.

TREATIES INVOLVING AN APPROPRIATION.

§74. Money Appropriated Only by Act of Congress.—The Constitution, in Article I, section 9, provides that "no money shall be drawn from the treasury, but in consequence of appropriations made by law." Treaties stipulating for the payment of money are caried into effect only pursuant to legislation of Congress for this purpose. Although a treaty is declared to be a part of the supreme law of the land, it has never been considered a sufficient warrant for the payment of money out of the treasury. Such payments are made only on the authority of a law enacted by Congress. Even a judgment of a court upon which Congress has conferred jurisdiction to entertain suits against the United States can be satisfied only by an appropriation for that purpose made by Congress. The question to what extent a treaty duly made by the President and Senate obligates Congress to make the appropriation necessary to carry it into effect has been much mooted.

§75. Proposed Treaty with Algiers.—Jefferson records a meeting with President Washington, under date of April 9, 1792, in which questions for consultation with the Senate on the proposed treaty with Algiers were considered. It having been suggested by Jefferson that the seal should not be put to the treaty until the two houses had voted the money, which was to be paid to Algiers, the President asked whether if such a treaty were ratified by him with the consent of the Senate it would not be valid under the Constitution and obligatory on the representatives to furnish the money. Jefferson replied that "it certainly would, and that it would be the duty of the representatives to raise the money, but that they might decline to do what was their duty * * * it might be incautious to commit himself by a ratification with a foreign nation, where he might be left in the lurch in the execution; it was possible, too, to conceive a treaty which it would not be their duty to provide for." The President did not favor the precaution, and declared that if the representatives "would not do what the Constitution called on them to do, the government would be at an end, and must then assume another form."[1]

§76. Debates on the Jay Treaty in 1796.—The Jay treaty, after due ratification, was proclaimed by the President on February 29, 1796; and on the following day a copy of it was communicated to Congress for its information. It contained no express stipulation for the payment of money, but an expenditure was necessarily involved in the organization of the mixed commissions provided for in various articles. The treaty met with disfavor in the House; and on March 24, a resolution, introduced by Edward Livingston, was passed by a vote of 62 to 37, by which the President was requested to communicate to that body copies of the instructions to the negotiator, and other documents relative to the treaty, excepting such as pending negotiations might render it improper to disclose.[2] Fully appreciating the importance as a precedent of his reply to the request, President Washington notified the committee, Livingston and Gallatin, appointed to present the resolution, that he would consider the matter. Before replying, the President called for the written opinions of the heads of the departments. He also wrote to Hamilton for his views. The heads of the departments were unanimous in denying the right of the House to insist on the request, and in asserting that the exclusive power to make treaties on all the usual subjects of negotiation with foreign states belonged to the President and Senate, and that treaties thus concluded were legally binding on all bodies of men within the jurisdiction of the United States. Chief Justice Ellsworth, who had been a member of the Federal Convention, and whose appointment to the Supreme Court bears the date of March 4, 1796, in a carefully prepared letter on the subject, under date of March 13, 1796, expressed similar views. The treaty-making power as vested by the Constitution in the President and Senate went, he said, to all kinds of treaties, for no exception was expressed and no treaty-making power was elsewhere granted to others, and it was not to be supposed that the Constitution had omitted to vest sufficient power to make all kinds of treaties which had been usually made, or which the existence or interests of the

1 Writings of Jefferson (Ford ed.), I, 191; MSS. Jefferson Papers, series 4, Vol. II, No. 36. See message to the Senate of May 8, 1792, Richardson, Messages and Papers of the Presidents, I, 123.

2 Annals, 4th Cong., 1st Sess., 759, 760.

nation might require. That an appropriation was necessary to carry the treaty into effect was an accidental circumstance, and did not give the House any more right to examine into the expediency of the treaty or control its operation than it would have without that circumstance. "Their obligation to appropriate the requisite sums," so he concluded, "does not result from any opinion they may have of the expediency of the treaty, but from their knowledge of its being a treaty, an authorized and perfect compact which binds the nation and its representatives. The obligation is indispensable, as it is to appropriate for the President's salary, or that of the judges, or in any other cases where fidelity to the Constitution does not leave an option to refuse."[3] Hamilton, in a letter dated March 26, advised against compliance with the request, and three days later submitted a draft of a message in reply. President Washington had, however, already reached his decision, and his message was in final form before the receipt of Hamilton's draft.[4] The reply, as communicated March 30, concluded with an unqualified refusal in the following words: "As, therefore, it is perfectly clear to my understanding that the assent of the House of Representatives is not necessary to the validity of a treaty; as the treaty with Great Britain exhibits in itself all the objects requiring legislative provision, and on these the papers called for can throw no light, and as it is essential to the due administration of the government that the boundaries fixed by the Constitution between the different departments should be preserved, a just regard to the Constitution and to the duty of my office, under all the circumstances of this case, forbids a compliance with your request."[5] In reaching this conclusion, President Washington made several observations as to the mode of making treaties under the Constitution. He spoke with some confidence of the purpose of the treaty-making provision, since

---

3 MSS. Letters to Washington, CXVII, 287.

4 Writings of Washington (Ford ed.), XIII, 181; Works of Hamilton (Lodge ed.), VIII, 386, 389.

5 Richardson, Messages and Papers of the Presidents, I, 194, 196. See in this relation message of President Polk, January 12, 1848, in which he declined to comply with the request of the House for copies of instructions to Mr. Slidell, as a commissioner to negotiate with Mexico, and debates thereon, Cong. Globe, 30th Cong., 1st Sess., 166-170. See also message of President Jackson, December 28, 1832, Richardson, Messages and Papers of the Presidents, II, 608.

he had been a member of the Convention, which had framed it, and an observer of the proceedings of the State conventions, which had adopted it. He recalled that a proposition, that no treaty should be binding which was not ratified by a law, had been proposed and had received explicit rejection in the Convention. He had ever entertained but one opinion on this subject, which from the establishment of the government until that time had been acquiesced in by the House, namely, that the power of making treaties was exclusively vested in the President and Senate, and that every treaty so made and promulgated thenceforward became the law of the land.[6] In reply to this message, the House passed a resolution on April 7, by a vote of 57 to 35, in which it disclaimed any agency in the making of treaties, but asserted that in case a treaty contained stipulations on any of the subjects entrusted by the Constitution to Congress, it must depend for its execution as to such stipulations on a law to be passed by Congress; and that it was "the constitutional right and duty of the House of Representatives, in all such cases, to deliberate on the expediency or inexpediency of carrying such treaty into effect."[7] Much was said and written on the question at the time in and out of Congress. As expositions of the views entertained by those who defended the action of the House, a letter from Jefferson to Monroe, dated March 21, 1796, and the speech of Albert Gallatin in the House of Representatives, March 9, 1796, may be taken. In his letter to Monroe, Jefferson observed that

6 It appears from the manuscript Washington Papers that the reply was made after careful investigation. Extracts from the proceedings of the Federal Convention, relating to the making of treaties, are found. Mr. Pickering, Secretary of State, made an investigation of the previous practice of the administration and was convinced that the instances of the treaties with certain Indian tribes and the Barbary States, in which appropriations had been made before their conclusion, were not applicable, since the money had been a necessary antecedent to the negotiation of these treaties. A draft of the message in Pickering's handwriting, which appears, however, to have been prepared after consultation with the President, contains the concise expressions of the final message. MSS. Letters to Washington, CXVII, 312, 314. The same views as entertained in 1796 were expressed by Mr. Pickering in the House of Representatives in 1816 in the debate on the bill to carry into effect the treaty of July 3, 1815, with Great Britain. Annals, 14th Cong., 1st Sess., 612.

7 Annals, 4th Cong., 1st Sess., 771, 782. A resolution in similar language was adopted without debate by the House, April 20, 1871. Cong. Globe, 42d Cong., 1st Sess., 835.

the President and Senate had the general power of making treaties, but that whenever treaties included matters confided by the Constitution to the three branches of the legislature, a legislative act was necessary to "confirm" those articles, and the House of Representatives as one branch was perfectly free to refuse its assent, when in its judgment the good of the people would not be served by letting the treaty go into effect.[8] Gallatin, in his speech in the House of Representatives, argued that if any specific power was given by the Constitution to a branch of the government it limited a general power, and so far as the powers clashed the branch holding the specific power must concur in order to give validity to the act; that the power to make treaties was a general power, while the power to make appropriations was specifically given to Congress; that if the power of making treaties as vested in the President and Senate were unlimited, the Executive with the Senate might, under color of a treaty, entirely eliminate the House of Representatives from legislation by substituting a foreign nation or some petty Indian tribe. If treaties, whatever their provisions might be, were laws, why not, he enquired, have inserted another article in the treaty itself appropriating the necessary sums, and thus have dispensed altogether with any action on it by the House? Unless, he contended, it were conceded either that the power of the House over the purse-strings was a check, or that existing laws could not be repealed by a treaty, or that the special powers granted to Congress limited the general power to make treaties granted to the President and Senate, there were no bounds to it.[9]

As illustrative of the views of the administration, the opinions of Oliver Walcott, Secretary of the Treasury, and Alexander Hamilton may be taken. The written opinion of the former bears date of March 26. After a careful historical research, he reached the conclusion that the people of this country at the time of the adoption of the Constitution entertained the opinion, as expressed in the Federal letter of April, 1787, that the power of making treaties as vested in the Congress under the Articles of Confederation was capable of controlling the legislative powers, which then resided in the several State legislatures. Embar-

---

8 Writings (Ford ed.), VII, 67. See also Id., 38, 40, 41. See for views of Marshall at this time, Id., VII, 37.

9 Annals, 4th Cong., 1st Sess., 464, 467.

rassment having been experienced in consequence of the non-execution of the treaty of peace, the Convention which framed the Constitution must have intended such an organization and deposit of the power of making treaties as would render its exercise at once safe and efficacious. The great object of that part of the Constitution which defined the legislative power was to fix the limits between the central and State governments, rather than to distribute power between the departments of the central government. In the specification of the executive powers, found in Article II of the Constitution, that of making treaties, subject to the control or negative voice of the Senate, was expressly mentioned. Treaties were compacts between sovereign states, originating in free consent and deriving their obligations from the plighted faith. The Constitution expressly committed to the President and Senate the power to pledge the faith of the nation; and "the obligations arising from public faith when pledged by the representative organ of our nation in all foreign concerns, agreeably to the mode prescribed by the Constitution, are justly and properly declared to be laws—the legislative power is bound not to contravene them, on the contrary, it is bound to regard and give them effect." If to omit the exercise of the power committed to any branch of the government would be to annul a treaty, such an omission would be a violation of the Constitution by that branch which refused to act. With reference to the question whether a treaty could repeal an act of Congress, he observed that since the power to make peace could not be exercised by treaty without repealing the act declaring war, the power to make treaties of this most common form implied of necessity the power to repeal a pre-existing law. To the question, what, if treaties might repeal existing laws, were the limits which restrained the President and Senate from absorbing all the powers of the legislature, he replied that the power to make treaties must necessarily be indefinite. "It must be allowed to be competent to the adjustment of every dispute with a foreign nation under any circumstances." That the power was indefinite was no proof that it was not fully vested solely in the President and Senate. That it was capable of abuse was no argument that the House possessed a controlling authority. Many of the powers vested in Congress were likewise indefinite with no restraints except in the virtue and discretion of Congress. That Congress might raise and equip armies and navies for purposes of ambition, or tax unwisely, was not proof that the powers were not vested in it. Statutes and treaties of the United States were alike supreme laws of the land, and the last act, of whichever description, would control. He added, however, as a qualification: "It is not intended to assert that treaties can extend to every object of legislation, there is no doubt that the forms of the Constitution and the powers of the different departments and organs of government are superior to the influence of a treaty; the limitation of the power of making treaties may in some respects be difficult, as the exigencies of society cannot be foreseen, but in respect to matters of mere internal concern, there appears to be nothing upon which the power of making treaties can operate, in derogation or extension of the power of legislation."[10]

The argument of Hamilton, as expressed in various letters written at the time and in his draft of a message, was that the Constitution empowered the President and Senate to make treaties; that to make a treaty as between nations meant to conclude a contract obligatory on their good faith; that a contract could not be obligatory to the validity of which the assent of another body was constitutionally necessary; that the Constitution declared a treaty made under the authority of the United States to be a supreme law, but that that could not be a supreme law to the validity of which the assent of another body in the state was constitutionally necessary; that a right of discretionary assent to a contract, under whatever color it might be claimed, was a right to participate in the making of it; and hence that a discretionary right in the House to assent to a treaty, or what was equivalent, to execute it, would negative two important provisions of the Constitution, namely, that the President and Senate have the power to make treaties, and that the treaties so made were laws. It was, he contended, one thing, that a treaty pledging the faith of the nation should by force of moral duty oblige the legislative will to carry it into effect, quite another that it should be itself a law. The latter was the case under the Constitution. There were no express limits to the treaty-making power, and it was a reasonable presumption that it was intended to extend to all treaties usual among nations and so to be commensurate with the variety of exigencies which might arise from intercourse with

10 MSS. Letters to Washington, CXVII, 293.

other nations. Treaties of peace, alliance and commerce were usual among nations. Treaties of peace frequently included indemnification, pecuniary or otherwise. Treaties of alliance necessarily stipulated for the union of forces, and the furnishing of pecuniary or other aid. Treaties of commerce regulated the external commerce of the nation. Unless the treaty power could embrace objects upon which the legislative power might also act, it would often be inadequate for mere treaties of peace, and always so for treaties of alliance and of commerce. The action of the House was not always deliberative in making appropriations—as, for instance, in making an appropriation to defray the expense of an office created by the Constitution or a prior act of Congress. It was discretionary only when the Constitution and laws placed it under no obligation or prohibition. There was, however, this difference between the obligation of the Constitution and the obligation of laws, the former enjoined obedience always, the latter, until annulled by the proper authority. While it was true that the Constitution provided no method of compelling the legislative body to act, it was, nevertheless, under a constitutional, legal, and moral obligation to act where action was prescribed. If the legislative power was competent to repeal this law by a subsequent law, it must be by the whole legislative power, not by the mere refusal of one branch to give effect to it. A legal discretion to refuse the execution of a pre-existing law was virtually a power to repeal it. "Hence," he said, "it follows that the House of Representatives have no moral power to refuse the execution of a treaty which is not contrary to the Constitution, because it pledges the public faith; and have no legal power to refuse its execution because it is a law—until at least it ceases to be a law by a regular act of revocation of the competent authority."[11]

On April 30, by the close vote of 51 to 48 the House resolved that provision ought to be made for carrying the treaty into effect; and on May 6, three acts were approved making appropriations for carrying into effect the treaties with Great Britain, Spain and Algiers, respectively.[12]

§77. **Treaties of 1802 and 1803.**—The question has since been

---

11 MSS. Letters to Washington, CXVII, 323; Works of Hamilton, (Lodge ed.), VII, 118; Works of Hamilton, (J. C. Hamilton ed.), VI, 92, 94; Id., VII, 556-570.

12 Annals, 4th Cong., 1st Sess., 1291; 1 Stats. at L. 459, 460.

frequently raised, but little has been added to the arguments advanced in 1796. Jefferson had in Washington's administration advised consulting the House in the matter of an appropriation before entering into the negotiations with the Dey of Algiers, on the ground that, whenever the agency of either or both houses would be requisite to carry a treaty into effect, it would be prudent to consult them previously, if the occasion permitted.[13] By the convention signed at London, January 8, 1802, the United States agreed to pay Great Britain in discharge of certain claims the sum of six hundred thousand pounds in three annual installments. On April 27, 1802, after the ratification by the President with the advice and consent of the Senate had taken place, but prior to the exchange of ratifications at London, July 15, 1802, President Jefferson communicated copies of the convention to both houses of Congress, trusting that in the free exercise of the authority which the Constitution had given them on the subject of public expenditures they would deem it for the public interest to appropriate the sum necessary for carrying the convention into effect.[14] An appropriation for this purpose was duly made by an act approved May 3, 1802.[15] During the negotiations with France in 1803, for the purchase of lands at the mouth of the Mississippi, Congress made a provisional appropriation of two million dollars to be applied under the direction of the President. Jefferson considered the act making the appropriation as conveying the sanction of Congress to the acquisition proposed.[16] Quite unexpectedly and without instructions the commissioners at Paris signed a treaty for the purchase of the entire Louisiana territory for which the provisional appropriation was entirely inadequate. The President drafted a message with a view of submitting the treaty to both houses of Congress, but Madison, the Secretary of State, and Gallatin, the Secretary of the Treasury, who in 1796 had been leaders in the House, advised against this procedure. Madison doubted that the theory of our Constitution admitted "the influence of deliberations and anticipations of the House of Representatives on a treaty depending in the Senate." Gallatin observed that the House of Representatives neither could

13 MSS. Jefferson Papers, Series 4, Vol. II, Nos. 18, 36.
14 Richardson, Messages and Papers of the Presidents, I, 341.
15 2 Stats. at L. 192.
16 Act approved February 26, 1803. 2 Stats. at L. 202. Annals, 8th Cong., 1st Sess., 12.

nor "ought to act on the treaty until after it is a treaty"; that, although at times it might be necessary to obtain a grant of money before opening negotiations, in the case under consideration, since the negotiations had been closed, there was no necessity of consulting or communicating with the House until the instrument had been completed by the President's ratification, and that there was no apparent object, unless it was supposed that the House might act, or in other words express its opinion and give its advice, on the inchoate instrument which would, at the same time, be constitutionally before the Senate.[17] In accordance with these suggestions the treaty was communicated October 17, to the Senate only; but the House was advised by the annual message of even date that a treaty had been signed which would, as soon as the sanction of the Senate had been received, be communicated to it for the exercise of its function as to those conditions which were within the powers vested by the Constitution in Congress.[18] On October 21, the ratifications having been exchanged, the President communicated the treaty to Congress for consideration in its legislative capacity, observing at the same time that some important conditions could be carried into effect only with the aid of the Congress.[19] The Federalists were now in the opposition. By those, who in 1796 had opposed the call for the papers, a resolution was now supported, requesting the President to communicate certain papers which might tend to prove the validity of the French title to the ceded territory. When charged with inconsistency, Roger Griswold, of Connecticut, replied that the papers were needed to aid Congress in proceeding intelligently with the legislation, and that he still entertained the opinion that when a treaty was once duly ratified it was the duty of every department of the government to carry it into effect. The Republicans, who opposed the motion, found a less plausible defense to a similar charge. By a vote of 59 to 57 the resolution was defeated.[20] The appropriations necessary to give effect to the treaty were duly made.

17 MSS. Jefferson Papers, Series 3, Vol. VIII, No. 83; and Vol. IV, No. 128. See also Writings of Jefferson (Ford ed.), VIII, 266; Writings of Gallatin (Adams ed.), I, 156.

18 Annals, 8th Cong., 1st Sess., 11.

19 Id., 17, 18.

20 Id., 385, 403, 419.

§78. **Convention with France of 1831.**—By the convention concluded July 4, 1831, the French government engaged to pay to the United States in six annual installments the sum of 25,000,-000 francs in full discharge of certain claims of American citizens against France. Upon the failure of the French Chamber of Deputies to vote the appropriation for the payment of these installments, the House of Representatives, on March 2, 1835, after debate, unanimously adopted a resolution declaring that in the opinion of the House the convention should be maintained and its execution insisted on, and that preparation ought to be made to meet any emergency growing out of our relations with France.[21] The convention had been concluded on the part of the French government under the authority of the King, although appropriations could be made only by a vote of the Chamber of Deputies. In the course of the debate in the House of Representatives, John Quincy Adams said: "The indemnity was stipulated by that department of the French government, which was authorized to pledge the faith of the nation to its payment. The question is no longer whether indemnity is due, or to what amount; but the question is, whether we will suffer a nation to violate its engagements to us, entered into under a solemn treaty."[22] The argument of Samuel McDowell Moore, of Virginia, is reported as follows: "It had been contended here as well as in the French Chamber of Deputies that the treaty of the 4th of July, 1831, was not to be regarded as complete, until sanctioned by the French Chambers, inasmuch as the Chambers have an undoubted right to make or withhold the appropriations necessary to carry the treaty into effect. He admitted the right of the Chambers to grant or refuse the appropriations in its fullest extent; but denied that the treaty was, for that reason, to be regarded as incomplete, until the appropriations were made. The Chambers might refuse the appropriations, but they must do so on the responsibility of the nation. * * * If the treaty was not complete until the appropriations were made, would its validity be considered as determined by the passage of an act by the Chambers appropriating a sufficient sum to pay the amount due to us, at the time when the several installments should become due? Gentlemen would say, yes. But suppose before the second installment becomes due, a new election

21 Debates, 23d Cong., 2d Sess., 1531-1634.
22 Id., 1533.

takes place; the Chambers convene, and repeal the law making the appropriations (as they have clearly a right to do), what then becomes of the treaty? Is the treaty, which was valid and binding on all parties, to be thus annulled and destroyed by one party, after it is partly executed? Suppose a treaty to stipulate that a certain sum shall be paid in ten annual installments, and the legislative branch of the government, which is to pay, passes a law appropriating the money and at the end of nine years, the law is repealed; is the treaty, which has been in full force for nine years, to cease to be binding the moment the law is repealed? Or suppose what may possibly be regarded as an extreme case, that the people should refuse to pay the taxes necessary to enable the government to meet its engagements with another power, and should dismiss all their agents in the legislative and executive branch of their government, and continue the government itself, as they have a right to do, will they be thereby released from obligations binding on them as a nation? Surely not; and yet such is the legitimate conclusion to which this principle leads us. * * * When the treaty was ratified by the executive branch of the French government, it was ratified by, and binding on, the French nation; and they could no longer fail or refuse to comply with its engagements without a breach of national faith."[23]

§79. **Treaty with Russia of 1867.**—The treaty with Russia for the acquisition of Alaska, after being duly ratified, was proclaimed by President Johnson, June 20, 1867. On July 6, 1867, the President communicated a copy of it to Congress, and invited attention to the subject of an appropriation for the payment of the $7,200,-000 stipulated for in the treaty, as also to the subject of proper legislation for the occupation and government of the new territory.[24] In reporting a bill making the appropriation, the majority of the House Committee on Foreign Affairs took the view, as expressed in the report submitted by the chairman, Nathaniel P. Banks, that "it is now conceded that the House is entitled to consider the merits of a treaty; that it may determine whether its object is within the scope of the treaty power; but, if it be not inconsistent with the spirit and purpose of the government, Congress

23 Id., 1590. Diplomatic relations between the two countries were broken off, but were restored through the mediation of the British government. The several installments due under the convention were subsequently paid in full. Moore, Int. Arb., V, 4463-4468.

24 Richardson, Messages and Papers of the Presidents, VI, 524.

is bound to give it effect, by necessary legislation, as a contract between the government and a foreign nation."[25]　In considering
the bill as reported, the House, on July 14, 1868, inserted, by a vote
of 98 to 49 (53 not voting), an amendment in part, as follows:
"Whereas the subjects thus embraced in the stipulations [for the
payment to Russia of $7,200,000, and for the admission of cer-
tain of the inhabitants of the ceded territory to the enjoyment of
the privileges and immunities of citizens of the United States] of
said treaty are among the subjects which by the Constitution of
the United States are submitted to the power of Congress, and
over which Congress has jurisdiction; and it being for such reason necessary that the consent of Congress should be given to
said stipulation before the same can have full force and effect;
having taken into consideration the said treaty, and approving of
the stipulations therein, to the end that the same may be carried
into effect.　*　*　*　Be it enacted, That the assent of Congress
is hereby given to the stipulations of said treaty."[26]　Another
amendment was proposed in which it was declared that thereafter no territory should be purchased until provision for its payment had been made by law, and that the powers vested by the
Constitution in the President and Senate to enter into treaties
with foreign governments did not include the power to complete
the purchase of foreign territory before the necessary appropriation had been made by an act of Congress; but this amendment
was defeated by a vote of 80 to 78 (42 not voting).　On the refusal of the Senate to agree to the bill as passed by the House,
a committee of conference was appointed.　As agreed to in
conference, and finally passed by the two houses,[27] the bill, after
reciting that the treaty had been entered into by the President
and its ratification advised and consented to by the Senate, and
that the stipulations for the payment of the money and the admission of certain of the inhabitants could not be "carried into
full force and effect except by legislation to which the consent"
of both houses of Congress was necessary, simply appropriated the
sum of $7,200,000 "to fulfill stipulations" in the sixth article of

25　H. Rept. No. 37, 40th Cong., 2d Sess., 5.　A minority report was sub-
submitted by C. C. Washburn.

26　H. Journal, 40th Cong., 2d Sess., 1064.　See for the debate on the
resolution, Cong. Globe, 3621, 3658, 3661, 3804, 3809, 3883, 4052, 4392; Appendix, 305, 377, 382, 385, 400, 406, 421, 429, 452, 466, 473, 485.

27　The vote in the House was 91 to 48 (77 not voting).

the treaty.[28] The formal transfer of the territory had already taken place.

§80. Views of Authorities.—It is conceded, and it has never been questioned, that the stipulations of a treaty which involve the payment of money can be carried into effect only by an act of Congress. That Congress is under no obligation to make the appropriation has not been seriously advanced by the House since 1868,[29] although individual advocates of this view have not been wanting. Such a view was expressed by John Randolph Tucker in his able and elaborate report from the House Committee on the Judiciary, March 3, 1887.[30] On the other hand, in a report from the House Committee on Foreign Affairs, submitted by George A. Bicknell, February 14, 1881, a resolution, which asserted that the treaty-making power did not extend to treaties affecting the revenues or requiring an appropriation but that in such cases the consent of the law making power was required, was declared to affirm a proposition which could not be sustained.[31] The United States circuit court, McLean, C. J., in passing on an Indian treaty in 1852, said: "A treaty under the Federal Constitution is declared to be the supreme law of the land. This, unquestionably, applies to all treaties, where the treaty-making power, without the aid of Congress, can carry it into effect. It is not, however, and cannot be the supreme law of the land, where the concurrence of Congress is necessary to give it effect. Until this power is exercised, as where the appropriation of money is required, the treaty is not perfect. It is not operative, in the sense of the Constitution, as money cannot be appropriated by the treaty-making power. This results from the limitations of our government. The action of no department of the government, can be regarded as a law, until it shall have all the sanctions required by the Constitution to make it such. As well might it be contended, that an ordinary act of Congress, without the signature of the President, was a law, as that a treaty which engages to pay a sum of money, is in itself a law. And in such a case, the representatives of the people and the States, exercise their own judgments in granting or withholding

28 Cong. Globe, 40th Cong., 2d Sess., 4392-4394, 4404; 15 Stats. at L. 198.

29 The resolution of April 20, 1871 was adopted under suspension of rules and without debate.

30 H. Rept. No. 4177, 49th Cong., 2d Sess.

31 H. Rept. No. 225, 46th Cong., 3d Sess.

the money. They act upon their own responsibility, and not upon the responsibility of the treaty-making power. It cannot bind or control the legislative action in this respect, and, every foreign government may be presumed to know, that so far as the treaty stipulates to pay money, the legislative sanction is required."[32] Other eminent jurists, of these, Kent and Duer, have expressed a different opinion.[33] The Supreme Court has yet to pass on the question. Mr. Justice Brown in De Lima v. Bidwell, in referring to the treaty of peace with Spain, observed: "We express no opinion as to whether Congress is bound to appropriate the money * * * it is not necessary to consider it in this case, as Congress made prompt appropriation of the money stipulated in the treaty."[34]

§81. **Conclusion.**—Under the Articles of Confederation the power over the purse-strings remained with the States, while that of making treaties was vested in the Congress. In March, 1787, immediately prior to the assembling of the delegates in the Federal Convention, the Congress unanimously resolved that treaties made in virtue of the Confederation were obligatory on the legislatures of the several States. The subjects embraced in the treaty stipulations referred to in these resolutions were otherwise within the legislative power of the States. The intention of those who framed the Constitution as disclosed in the records of the Convention was to vest the treaty-making power efficaciously in the President and Senate. That the treaty-making power under the Constitution extends to all the usual subjects of negotiation between nations, has often been declared by the Supreme Court. Stipulations that require, expressly or tacitly, immediately or ultimately, an expenditure, although the sums involved may not form a material item in the total expenditures of the government, enter into a large proportion of the treaties concluded.[35] With reference to stipulations that have directly

---

32 Turner v. American Baptist Missionary Union, 5 McLean 344, 347.

33 See Wharton, Int. Law Digest, II, 23, et seq.

34 182 U. S. 1, 198.

35 For instance, the Jay treaty with reference to which the question was first raised in the House, although it did not expressly stipulate for a payment of money, required numerous appropriations to carry it into effect. Appropriations for this purpose were made in the acts approved May 6, 1796, June 30, 1797, January 15, 1798, March 19, 1798, March 2, 1799, May 7, 1800, March 3, 1801, May 1, 1802, March 2, 1803, November 16, 1803,

involved appropriations, note may be made of the acts of Congress approved as follows: May 3, 1802, appropriating $2,664,-000, for carrying into effect the convention with Great Britain of January 8, 1802;[36] November 10, 1803, authorizing the creation of stock to the amount of $11,250,000 in favor of the French Republic, for carrying into effect the convention of April 30, 1803;[37] November 10, 1803, appropriating the sum of $3,750,000, to discharge the claims of citizens of the United States against France assumed by the convention of April 30, 1803;[38] February 26, 1849, appropriating $7,260,000, September 26, 1850, appropriating $3,360,000, and February 10, 1852, appropriating $3,180,-000, to fulfill the stipulations of Article XII of the treaty with Mexico of February 2, 1848;[39] June 29, 1854, appropriating $10,-000,000, to fulfill the stipulations of the treaty with Mexico of December 30, 1853;[40] March 3, 1855, appropriating $277,102.88, in payment of awards against the United States under the convention with Great Britain of February 8, 1853;[41] March 4, 1858, appropriating $393,011, to carry into effect Article III, and $15,720.44, to carry into effect Article VI, of the treaty with Denmark of April 11, 1857, for the discontinuance of the Sound dues;[42] June 1, 1864, appropriating $42,952.38, for the payment of claims of Peruvian citizens under the convention of January 12, 1863;[43] July 27, 1868, appropriating $7,200,000, to fulfill the stip-

November 24, 1804, April 18, 1806, and February 20, 1811. (1 Stats. at L. 459, 523, 536, 545, 723; 2 Id. 66, 120, 188, 214, 248, 307, 389, 647). Appropriations to carry into effect the treaty concluded October 27, 1795, with Spain, were made by acts approved May 6, 1796, March 19, 1798, July 16, 1798, March 2, 1799, May 7, 1800, and March 3, 1801. (1 Stats. at L. 459, 545, 609, 723; 2 Id. 66, 120). Again to defray the expenses that arose in carrying into effect Articles IV, VI, and VII of the treaty of Ghent, appropriations were made in acts approved April 16, 1816, March 3, 1817, April 9, 1818, April 11, 1820, April 30, 1822, March 3, 1823, April 2, 1824, February 25, 1825, March 14, 1826, and March 2, 1827. (3 Id. 283, 358, 422, 561, 673, 762; 4 Id. 16, 91, 148, 214. See Am. St. Pap., For. Rel., V, 50. Stipulations incidentally involving an appropriation are very numerous.

36   2 Stats. at L. 192.
37   2 Id. 245.
38   2 Id. 247.
39   9 Id. 348, 473; 10 Id. 2.
40   10 Id. 301.
41   10 Id. 703.
42   11 Id. 261.
43   13 Id. 95, 141.

ulations of Article VI of the treaty with Russia of March 30, 1867;[44] July 11, 1870, and February 21, 1871, appropriating $650,-000, in payment of the awards against the United States in favor of Hudson's Bay and Puget's Sound Agricultural Companies, under the convention with Great Britain of July 1, 1863;[44a] June 11, 1874, appropriating $1,929,819, for the payment of awards in favor of British subjects under Article XII of the treaty with Great Britain of May 8, 1871;[45] June 18, 1878, for the payment of awards against the United States under the convention with Mexico of July 4, 1868;[46] June 20, 1878, appropriating $5,500,000, for the payment of the award of the Halifax Commission under the treaty with Great Britain of May 8, 1871;[47] March 3, 1885, appropriating $594,288.04, and August 4, 1886, appropriating $15,639.16, in payment of awards against the United States under the convention with France of January 15, 1880;[48] June 15, 1898, appropriating $473,151.26, in payment of awards against the United States under the convention with Great Britain of February 8, 1896;[49] March 2, 1899, appropriating $20,000,000, to carry out the obligations of the treaty with Spain of December 10, 1898;[50] March 3, 1901, appropriating $100,000, to carry out the obligations of the treaty with Spain of November 7, 1900;[51] and April 28, 1904, appropriating $10,000,000, in partial fulfillment of Article XIV of the treaty with Panama of November 18, 1903.[52]

If the assent of the House is essential to the validity of treaty stipulations of this character, it has an agency in the making of many of the treaties concluded. In the first case of a treaty that expressly provided for the payment of a large amount, a precedent was intentionally established by those, who in 1796 had led in asserting the rights of the House, of withholding the treaty from the House until it had been ratified. If the concurrence

44 15 Id. 198.
44a 16 Id. 386, 419.
45 18 Id. 71.
46 20 Id. 144.
47 20 Id. 240.
48 23 Id. 478; 24 Id. 256.
49 30 Id. 470.
50 30 Id. 993.
51 31 Id. 1010.
52 33 Id. 429.

of the House is necessary to the validity of the stipulation, its action should precede the final ratification; since the execution of a treaty cannot with safety be commenced on our part, or be requested of the other contracting party, if its validity is still dependent upon the action of an independent legislative body. The inter-relation of stipulations in a treaty often renders them inseverable, so that the failure to confirm one of them would operate as the rejection of the entire instrument. The House early declared, however, that it had no claim to an agency in the making of the treaty, but only to a free action in giving it effect. But if the House has no agency in the making of the treaty, its action is not essential to its validity. For the House to disclaim any agency in the making of the international compact, but at the same time to deny any obligation to give it effect, is to recognize another organ of the government as competent to bind the nation, but at the same time to except itself from the obligation. Important in this relation is the practice of more than a century. A preliminary appropriation by Congress has never been considered necessary to give validity to the proceedings under a convention by which disputed claims have been submitted to a tribunal of arbitration.[53] During the negotiations of 1803, for the purchase of lands at the mouth of the Mississippi, and of 1806, for the purchase of Florida, provisional appropriations were made.

53 In a note to Sir Julian Pauncefote, August 21, 1894, Mr. Gresham, Secretary of State, proposed the payment by the United States of the sum of $425,000, in full satisfaction and direct settlement of the claims presented by the British government for the seizure of British vessels in the Bering Sea. The liability of the United States for the seizures had been determined by the award of the Paris Tribunal of August 15, 1893. This proposition was made "subject to the action of Congress on the question of appropriating the money." "The President," said Mr. Gresham, "can only undertake to submit the matter to Congress at the beginning of its session in December next, with a recommendation that the money be appropriated and made immediately available for the purpose." The British minister in a note of even date accepted the proposition. Such a recommendation was made in the annual mesage of December 3, 1894, but Congres failed to make the necessary appropriation during the ensuing session. Negotiations were reopened, and on February 8, 1896, a convention was signed providing for the submission of the claims to a mixed commission. This commission on December 17, 1897, rendered an award of $473,151.26 against the United States. By an act approved June 15, 1898, Congress made the appropriation to satisfy the award. For. Rel., 1894, p. X, Appendix I, 224, 225; For. Rel., 1898, p. 372; Moore, Int. Law Digest, I, 921.

President Polk, before opening the Mexican negotiations, asked for a provisional appropriation.[54] President Buchanan, in his annual message of December 6, 1858, suggested a provisional appropriation for the purchase of Cuba.[55] By an act approved June 28, 1902, Congress made a provisional appropriation for the acquisition by treaty of certain territorial rights of Colombia to facilitate the construction of an interoceanic canal.[56] In the convention with Denmark of April 11, 1857, for the abolition of the Sound dues, it was provided that the convention should take effect as soon as the stipulated sum had been tendered by the United States, or received by Denmark.[57] The unratified treaty of November 29, 1869, for the annexation of the Dominican Republic, likewise contained the reservation that the payment by the United States of the $1,500,000, as provided therein, should not be made until an appropriation for the purpose had been voted by Congress.[58] These instances are however exceptions. Stipulations involving the payment of money have regularly been made without qualification or reservation as to any action thereon by Congress, and have been ratified by the President upon the advice and consent of the Senate only. When so ratified they have been considered by this government as also by the other contracting parties as valid and definitively concluded, and Congress has never failed to vote the necessary appropriation.

54 Richardson, Messages and Papers of the Presidents, IV, 456, 459, 538.

55 Id., V, 511.

56 32 Stats. at L. 481.

57 See also Article V of the convention of November 6, 1861, with Hanover, for the abolition of the Stade and Brunshausen dues, and Article IV of the convention of May 20, 1863, with Belgium, for the capitalization of the Scheldt dues.

58 The Senate, in its resolution of March 2, 1892, advising ratification of the supplementary industrial property convention signed at Madrid, April 15, 1891, incorporated the reservation made by the United States plenipotentiary to the conference, to the effect that the share to be contributed by the United States should not be augmented until Congress had approved the augmentation.

CHAPTER XIII.

TREATIES INVOLVING A MODIFICATION OF THE REVENUE LAWS.

§82. Early Precedents.—The Constitution expressly provides that all bills for raising revenue shall originate in the House of Representatives, but that the Senate may propose or concur with amendments as on other bills.[1]

Article III of the treaty with Great Britain, proclaimed February 29, 1796, provided reciprocally on the part of the United States that British subjects might freely pass and repass by land or inland navigation the boundary line between the territories of the two nations; that all goods and merchandise, the importation of which should not be wholly prohibited, might be brought in this manner by British subjects into the United States; and that articles so imported should be subject to no higher or other duties than were payable on the same articles when imported in American vessels into the Atlantic ports. The tonnage and revenue laws then in force imposed a discriminating duty of ten per cent. on goods imported in other than American vessels, and appear to have contained no such exemptions as stipulated for in the treaty.[2] Section 104 of the revenue act of March 2, 1799, "for the purpose of conforming this act to certain stipulations contained in treaties made and ratified under the authority of the United States," incorporated the provisions of Article III of the treaty with Great Britain, as a part of the law.[3] It does not appear whether the article was considered as self-operative prior to this act, and that the section was inserted to exempt the article from repeal, or whether the section was designed to give it effect.[4]

---

1 Art. I, Sec. 7. For precedents as to the prerogatives of the House in revenue legislation, see Hinds, Precedents, II, §§1480-1501. See as to the nature of a revenue law, United States v. Norton, 91 U. S. 566.

2 See 1 Stats. at L. 411.

3 1 Stats. at L. 701.

4 See 1 Op. Atty. Gen. 155. Jefferson, at a meeting of the heads of the departments, July 29, 1790, expressed the view, with respect to a proposed Indian treaty, that a treaty made by the President with the concurrence of two-thirds of the Senate would repeal past laws and legally control the duty acts, but could not itself be repealed by future laws. This was, how-

Article X of the treaty with Spain of October 27, 1795 provided that cargoes of Spanish vessels arriving in distress in ports of the United States might be re-shipped to the port of destination without the payment of any duties or charges. Provision for giving effect to this article was made in section 60 of the general act of March 2, 1799, to regulate the collection of duties, and in the special act for this purpose of February 14, 1805.[5] In Article VII of the treaty with France of April 30, 1803, it was stipulated that, for a period of twelve years, French ships coming directly from France or her colonies, and Spanish ships coming directly from Spain or her colonies, loaded with native products and manufactures, should be admitted into all the legal ports of entry in the ceded territory of Louisiana on the same terms of duty and tonnage as American ships coming from the same ports. The act of February 24, 1804, extending certain of the revenue laws of the United States to the new territory, specifically enacted, in section 8, this provision of the treaty.[6]

§83. **Convention with Great Britain of 1815.**—In the convention with Great Britain, signed July 3, and proclaimed December 22, 1815, it is stipulated reciprocally on the part of the United States, that no higher charges or duties shall be imposed in the ports of the United States on British vessels than payable by American vessels, and that the duties on articles, the growth, produce or manufacture of His Britannic Majesty's territories in Europe, shall be the same whether imported in British or in American vessels. President Madison, in a message of December 23, 1815, notified Congress of the due ratification and proclamation of the convention, and recommended such legislative provisions as the convention might call for on the part of the United States.[7] Although the stipulations of the convention were in di-

---

ever, he later wrote, a first impression which subsequent investigation proved to be erroneous. Writings (Ford ed.), V, 215, 216, 237. Edmund Randolph, at a meeting of the heads of the departments, November 21, 1793, asserted that an act of the legislature would be necessary to confirm treaties affecting the tariff duties. Id., I, 268.

5 1 Stats. at L. 672; 2 Id. 314. See also Repts. of Senate Com. on For. Rel., VIII, 17.

6 2 Stats. at L. 253. See similar provision in the act of March 3, 1821, extending, "subject to the modification stipulated" by Article XV of the treaty of February 22, 1819, the revenue laws to Florida. 3 Id. 639.

7 Annals, 14th Cong., 1st Sess., 29.

rect conflict with the general revenue and tonnage laws, a special act approved March 3, 1815,[8] had repealed discriminating duties on tonnage so far as they affected any foreign nation which, to the satisfaction of the President, had abolished its laws which operated to discriminate against the United States. Mr. Calhoun, in the debates on the convention in the House of Representatives, observed that whatever might be the ipso facto effect of the convention on existing legislation, the act of March 3, 1815 made quite unnecessary any further legislation to give it effect, since no better evidence could be furnished the Executive of the removal of the discriminating duties by Great Britain than the treaty stipulation.[9] Bills were, however, introduced in each house, agreeably to the President's recommendation. As adopted by the Senate, January 10, 1816, the bill simply declared that so much of any acts as might be contrary to the provisions of the convention should be deemed and taken to be of no effect. It was assumed that the convention of itself effected the repeal of any inconsistent laws, and that the only purpose of any action by Congress was, by a declaratory act, to remove any doubts in this respect should any arise.[10] On the other hand, in the bill as passed by the House, January 13, by a vote of 86 to 71, entitled "an act to regulate the commerce between the United States and the territories of His Britannic Majesty according to the convention," it was assumed that the prior acts of Congress with which the convention conflicted were in full force, and that a specific legislative enactment was necessary to effect the modifications.[11] The two houses being unable to agree, a conference committee was appointed.[12] The conferees on the part of the Senate (Rufus King, James Barbour and W. W. Bibb), in their report to the Senate admitted the doctrine that some treaties made in pursuance of the Constitution might call for legislative provisions to secure their execution, which provision Congress, in all such cases, was bound to make. They contended, however, that in the case before them no such legislation was necessary, because the convention did no more than to suspend the alien disability of British subjects in com-

8   3 Stats. at L. 224.
9   Annals, 14th Cong., 1st Sess., 526.
10 Id., 36, 40, 46.
11 Id., 419, 674.
12 Id., 130, 134, 136, 960, 1018.

mercial matters in return for a like suspension in favor of American citizens, a subject within the peculiar province of the treaty power to adjust, and which could be adjusted in no other way; that a treaty duly made to adjust the matter was conclusive and by its own force suspended antecedent laws in conflict with it, and that even a declaratory act added nothing to the efficacy of the treaty but served merely to remove any possible doubt that might arise. The report does not indicate what class of treaties the Senate conferees considered as requiring Congressional legislation to secure their execution.[13] Mr. Forsyth, however, in his report for the House conferees, observed that it was believed that the Senate acknowledged that legislative enactments were necessary to carry into execution all treaties which contained "stipulations requiring appropriations, or which might bind the nation to lay taxes, to raise armies, to support navies, to grant subsidies, to create States, or to cede territory; if indeed this power exists in the government at all."[14] The bill as finally agreed to in conference and passed by both branches reads: "Be it enacted and declared by the Senate and House of Representatives of the United States of America, in Congress, assembled, That so much of any act as imposes a higher duty of tonnage, or of impost on vessels and articles imported in vessels of Great Britain, than on vessels and articles imported in vessels of the United States, contrary" to the convention, "be, from and after the date of the ratification of the said convention, and during the continuance thereof, deemed and taken to be of no force or effect."[15] The act was clearly a compromise. The insertion of the words "and declared" after the word "enacted" seemed to the Senate conferees most essential as indicating the effective force of the treaty itself in the repeal. To this the conferees of the House yielded, in the belief that these words were "mere surplusage not changing the character, or impairing the force of the legislative act." The House conferees insisted on a law enacting a repeal of any law not in accord with the treaty. To this the Senate conferees agreed, provided no precedent should be established which should bind them thereafter to assist in passing laws in cases in which "such doubts might not exist."[16] The House conferees observed

13 Id., 160.
14 Id., 1019.
15 3 Stats. at L. 255.
16 Annals, 14th Cong., 1st Sess., 1022.

that it was safer in all doubtful cases to provide by legislation for the execution of treaties than to "endanger the public faith by a failure to perform the provisions of a treaty" which had received a constitutional ratification.[17] The convention seems to have met with general approval in Congress; and the debates were confined in large measure to the constitutional question involved. The Senate was composed of 24 Republicans and 12 Federalists, and the House, of 117 Republicans, and 65 Federalists. Of those who urged the necessity of legislative enactment were John Forsyth,[18] Philip P. Barbour,[19] John Randolph,[20] Cyrus King,[21] and Henry St. George Tucker.[22] Of those who held the opposite view were John C. Calhoun,[23] Benjamin Hardin,[24] William Pinkney,[25] Alexander C. Hanson,[26] Timothy Pickering,[27] Asa Lyon,[28] William Gaston,[29] and Thomas R. Gold,[30] It may be observed that John Forsyth, later Secretary of State, who led in the contention as to the rights of the House, said in his reply speech of January 13: "The basis of the bill is not the principle stated, that legislative aid is necessary to the validity of treaties. Gentlemen have exhausted their ingenuity, their time, and their eloquence, in the discussion of a doctrine utterly denied by the bill and those who advocate it. The doctrine contended for is, that in certain cases specified by the Constitution, legislative aid is necessary to the execution of treaties. Is there no difference between the two propositions? * * * The distinction between the validity of an instrument and the execution of its provisions, between the obligation of contract and the performance of that obligation? * * * We insist not that it is the figment or shadow of a treaty, but that it shall be neither more nor less than a

17 Id., 1020.
18 Id., 474, 652.
19 Id., 478.
20 Id., 533.
21 Id., 538.
22 Id., 557.
23 Id., 526.
24 Id., 543.
25 Id., 564.
26 Id., 605.
27 Id., 612.
28 Id., 884.
29 Id., 466, 489.
30 Id., 482.

treaty, valid and obligatory as such as a contract, but not having the force of law in its operation upon the municipal concerns of this people, without legislative enactment." He added: "Every treaty ratified imposes upon the government, in all its departments, the obligation to fulfill it. The extent of that obligation is a question not now necessary to be examined or discussed. So far as relates to the late convention with Great Britain, no disposition is felt in any part of the House to avoid the discharge of all the duties which are imposed by its ratification."[31]

§84. **Convention with France of 1822.**—The act of May 15, 1820 imposed a duty of eighteen dollars per ton on French vessels entering the United States.[32] By the convention with France signed June 24, 1822, and proclaimed February 12, 1823, it was stipulated on the part of the United States that the products of France imported in French vessels should pay a duty not exceeding three dollars and seventy-five cents per ton, in excess of the duty collected on the same products when imported in American vessels. Copies of the convention were, on February 18, 1823, communicated to both houses of Congress to the end that "the necessary measures for carrying it into execution" might be adopted.[33] In his annual message of December 3, 1822, President Monroe had said: "Should the constitutional sanction of the Senate be given to the ratification of the convention with France, legislative provisions will be necessary to carry it fully into effect."[34] The act of March 3, 1823, for this purpose, repealed all acts incompatible with the execution of the convention, specifically mentioning the act of May 15, 1820; and enacted that French vessels should pay the additional duty of three dollars and seventy-five cents according to the tenor of the convention.[35]

§85. **Convention with France of 1831.**—Article VII of the convention with France, signed July 4, 1831, provided that the United States should, on and after the exchange of ratifications, impose duties on French wines not to exceed certain enumerated rates, which were less than those then imposed.[36] On February 7, 1832, after the ratification of the convention, President Jackson

31 Id., 653, 654.
32 3 Stats. at L. 605.
33 Richardson, Messages and Papers of the Presidents, II, 203.
34 Id., 186.
35 3 Stats. at L. 747.
36 See act of May 24, 1828, 4 Stats. at L. 309.

communicated a copy of it to Congress in its legislative capacity, observing that some important conditions could be carried into execution only with the aid of Congress.[37] The convention contained, besides the stipulation for the reduction of import duties, a provision for the payment of indemnities due the citizens of the respective parties, in which each party engaged to provide for the distribution to those entitled to share in the indemnity. Section 10 of the act approved July 13, 1832, expressly provided that French wines should, after February 2, 1832, be admitted into the United States upon the payment of duties not to exceed certain rates, which rates corresponded with those stipulated for in the convention. The ratifications had been exchanged February 2, 1832, but the convention was not proclaimed by the President until July 13, 1832, the date of the approval of this act.[38] Attorney General Cushing in an opinion, dated February 16, 1854, declared that the wines became chargeable with the lower duty upon the exchange of ratifications of the convention on February 2, 1832, as provided for in the convention, regardless of the pre-existing statutes.[39] The article in question had met with opposition in the Senate. Mr. Clay, on February 8, 1832, after the ratification of the convention had been advised, offered a resolution in which it was declared that the Senate did not intend that the article should "be taken and held as a precedent in the future exercise of the treaty-making power." The resolution was tabled.[40]

§86. Convention of 1844 with the States of the German Zollverein.—In submitting to the Senate, April 29, 1844, a convention for commercial reciprocity concluded with the States of the German Zollverein, March 25, 1844, President Tyler observed that, inasmuch as the convention conflicted to some extent with existing laws, it was his intention, should the Senate consent to its ratification, to communicate a copy of it to the House of Representatives in order that such action might be taken as deemed necessary to

37 Richardson, Messages and Papers of the Presidents, II, 564.

38 4 Stats. at L. 576.

39 6 Op. 295. See the view expressed by Attorney General Miller, April 5, 1889, as to the Hawaiian reciprocity convention, 19 Op. 277.

40 Ex. Journal, IV, 209. See acts of March 16, 1866, and June 1, 1866, to secure to American citizens certain privileges under Article III of the treaty with Great Britain of August 9, 1842, for the admission, free of duty, of certain forest products. 14 Stats. at L. 9, 56.

15

give effect to the provisions.[41] On June 14, 1844, Rufus Choate, from the Senate Committee on Foreign Relations, reported against the ratification. Without reference to the particular merits of the convention, the committee was not prepared, he said, "to sanction so large an innovation upon ancient and uniform practice in respect of the department of government by which duties on imports shall be imposed. The convention which has been submitted to the Senate changes duties which have been laid by law. It changes them either ex directo and by its own vigor, or it engages the faith of the nation and the faith of the legislature through which the nation acts to make the change. * * * In the judgment of the committee, the legislature is the department of government by which commerce should be regulated and laws of revenue be passed."[42] This view was reaffirmed in a later report from the same committee, February 26, 1845, submitted by William S. Archer, formerly chairman of the House Committee on Foreign Affairs, occasioned by a message from the President urging action on the convention. In the course of the report, Mr. Archer said: "The question has been debated, how far Congress would be bound to give effect, in cases requiring its co-operation, to regulations by treaty on subjects put within its express province by the Constitution. Whichever may be the better opinion, the doubt supplies reason enough against putting the question to trial in other circumstances than those in which the concurrence of Congress may be safely assumed. And the reason is the stronger for this forbearance from the fact that, in the contingency of conflict, it would be not the interests only, but the faith, too, of the nation which might be compromised, as this would have been committed by the adoption of the treaty regulations."[43] The Senate failed to advise ratification.

§87. **Convention with Great Britain of 1854.**—President Fillmore, in his annual message of December 6, 1852, in referring to

41 Richardson, Messages and Papers of the Presidents, IV, 314. A treaty of amity and commerce with Texas, signed at Washington, July 30, 1842, in which it was stipulated that for a period of five years raw cotton might be imported free of duty, was submitted to the Senate by President Tyler, August 18, 1842. In advising ratification, March 3, 1843, the Senate as one of the amendments struck out the article which contained this stipulation. Ex. Journal, VI, 189.

42 Reports of Sen. Com. on For. Rel., VIII, 36.

43 Id., 38.

proposed negotiations with Great Britain in respect of the fisheries and commercial intercourse between the United States and the British Provinces, said: "The control of Congress over all the provisions of such an arrangement affecting the revenue will of course be reserved."[44] The convention as finally signed, under direction of his successor, June 5, 1854, in which the free introduction into the United States of certain products of the British possessions in North America was stipulated for, contained, in Article V, an express reservation that it should take effect as soon as the "laws required to carry it into operation" should have been passed by the Imperial Parliament of Great Britain and the local parliaments of the British colonies affected, on the one hand, and by the Congress of the United States on the other. The act of Congress of August 5, 1854, to give effect to the convention, specifically enumerated the products, corresponding with those named in the convention, to be exempted from duties.[45] To a proposal of the British government to extend the period of the convention, Mr. Seward, Secretary of State, in a note to Sir Frederick W. A. Bruce, British minister, February 17, 1866, replied that the subjects embraced in the convention were expressly confided by the Constitution to Congress, and that any proposal to extend the system of reciprocal trade with the British Provinces would await the decision of the proper committees of Congress.[46]

§88. **Subsequent Conventions for Commercial Reciprocity.**— In the conventions for commercial reciprocity involving special concessions in tariff duties, concluded and ratified since the convention of 1854, a clause has been inserted, either by the Executive, or as an amendment by the Senate, expressly making their operation contingent upon action by Congress. The reservation in Article XXXIII of the treaty of May 8, 1871, with Great Britain, as to the operation of Articles XVIII to XXV, and Article XXX, which stipulated for certain concessions in tariff rates, was in terms similar to those found in Article V of the convention of 1854. An act was approved March 1, 1873, to carry these articles into effect.[47] Section 3 of this act likewise made provi-

---

44 Richardson, Messages and Papers of the Presidents, V, 164. See also annual message of December 2, 1851, Id., V, 119.

45 10 Stats. at L. 587.

46 Dip. Cor., 1866, I, 226.

47 17 Stats. at L. 482.

sion for carrying into effect the stipulation in Article XXIX, for the transportation in bond through the territory of the United States of merchandise destined for British possessions in North America.[48] To a proposal that American fishermen would be accorded certain rights in the Newfoundland fisheries in return for the free admission of the products of the Newfoundland sea fishery, Mr. Fish, Secretary of State, in a note to Sir Edward Thornton, British minister, June 25, 1873, replied that such a measure would require the sanction of Congress, and that it was not considered probable that the assent of Congress would be given.[49] The convention with the Hawaiian Islands for commercial reciprocity, as signed January 30, 1875, contained the reservation in language similar to that used in Article V of the convention of 1854. The Senate in advising ratification struck out the words "the laws required," and amended the clause so as to read "but not until a law to carry it into operation shall have been passed by the Congress of the United States."[50] An act was approved August 15, 1876, to carry the convention into operation.[51] The reservation in the reciprocity convention with Mexico, as signed January 20, 1883, provided that the convention should not take effect "until the laws and regulations that each" should "deem necessary to carry it into operation" had been passed by the respective governments. In advising ratification, March 11, 1884, the Senate amended this reservation so as to read "but not until laws necessary to carry it into operation" had been passed by the Congress of the United States and the government of Mexico, and regulations provided accordingly.[52] The language of this amendment has since been cited as containing an admission by the Senate, in the nature of a precedent, of the necessity of legislative ac-

48 In a special message to Congress with reference to this article, February 2, 1893, President Harrison said: "It will be noticed that the treaty does not expressly call for legislation to put article 29 into operation. Senator Edmunds, in the discussion in the Senate of the joint resolution terminating the fisheries article, took the view that no legislation was necessary. It seems to me, however, that such legislation was necessary, and Congress acted upon this view in the law of 1873." S. Ex. Doc. No. 40, 52d Cong., 2d Sess., 4. As to the question of the termination of this article, see also Moore, Int. Law Digest, V, 327-335.

49 Moore, Int. Law Digest, I, 802.

50 Ex. Journal, XX, 42.

51 19 Stats. at L. 200.

52 Ex. Journal, XXIV, 211.

tion to give effect to treaty stipulations of this character.[53] The convention further stipulated that the laws should be passed within twelve months from the date of the exchange of ratifications. This period was extended by subsequent conventions; but Congress failed to take any action, and the convention remained ineffective, although the ratifications were exchanged May 20, 1884. In the unratified conventions for commercial reciprocity, signed July 20, 1855,[54] and May 21, 1867, with the Hawaiian Islands;[55] November 18, 1884, with Spain, relative to Cuba and Porto Rica;[56] and December 4, 1884, with the Dominican Republic,[57] provisions were incorporated by which their operation was expressly made contingent upon action by Congress.[58] Although no such reservation was made in the various unratified conventions for commercial reciprocity as negotiated by Mr. Kasson in 1899 and 1900, an amendment to each, that it should not take effect until approved by Congress, was proposed by the Senate Committee on Foreign Relations.[59] The convention with Cuba as negotiated and signed December 11, 1902, likewise

53 See for instance, reports from the House Committee on Ways and Means, June 17, 1884, H. Rept. No. 1848, 48th Cong., 1st Sess., and May 25, 1886, H. Rept. No. 2615, 49th Cong., 1st Sess. See also speech of Justin S. Morrill, of Vermont, in the Senate, January 7, 1885, in which it was urged that a treaty made by the President and Senate was ineffectual to modify the revenue laws. Record, 48th Cong., 2d Sess., 506. For a reply to this argument, see speech of Elbridge G. Lapham in the Senate, January 8, 1885. Id., 548.

54 Art. IV.

55 Art. IV.

56 Art. XXVI. The reservation in this article—"until after the Congress of the United States shall have passed the laws necessary to carry it into effect"—is in conformity with the amendment of the Senate to the Mexican convention.

57 Art. XVI. In Article XV of the unratified convention of February 15, 1888, with Great Britain, the provision reads: "Whenever the United States shall remove the duty," &c.

58 The draft of a convention for commercial reciprocity with Canada, submitted by President Grant to the Senate June 18, 1874 (Article XIII), and the proposed convention for the improvement of commercial relations between the United States and Newfoundland, as agreed upon in December, 1890, by Mr. Blaine, Secretary of State, and Sir Robert Bond (Article VI), likewise contained express provisions that they should take effect "as soon as the laws required" to carry them into effect had been passed, on the part of the United States, by Congress.

59 S. Doc. No. 47, 57th Cong., 2d Sess.

contained no such specific clause; but the Senate in its resolution of March 19, 1903, advising ratification, attached an amendment in which it was expressly provided that the convention should not take effect until it had been "approved" by Congress. In order to make the legislative approval as broad as the convention, it was provided in the act, approved December 17, 1903, to carry the convention into effect, that during the continuance of the convention no sugar the product of any other foreign country should "be admitted by treaty or convention into the United States" at a lower rate of duty than that specified in the tariff act of July 24, 1897. To prevent the implication from this language, that the duties might be modified by treaty or convention, a saving clause was inserted, declaring that nothing in the act should be construed as an admission on the part of the House that customs duties could be changed otherwise than by an act of Congress originating in the House.[60]

Section 4 of the tariff act of July 24, 1897, to which the Senate as a branch of the legislature agreed, provided that whenever

60 33 Stats. at L. 3. That the act of Congress governs as to the date on which the convention went into effect, a provision in the treaty as originally negotiated to the contrary, see United States v. American Sugar Refining Co., 202 U. S. 563. In the debate in the Senate on the bill to give effect to the convention, Mr. Bailey declared that the President and Senate could not by treaty change the tariff rates. (Record, 58th Cong., 2d Sess., 178, 277). Mr. Spooner said: "It is claimed unanimously in the House of Representatives, and has been many times, I think almost continuously, that the President and Senate have no power by treaty alone to change tariff rates. I do not intend to controvert that proposition. It is a grave controversy. Much is to be said on each side of it. All I care to say about my own opinion now is that I am strongly inclined to agree with the Senator from Texas and the attitude of the House of Representatives that the President and the Senate by treaty alone cannot change tariff rates. * * * I confess, Mr. President, it has not seemed to me that the framers of the Constitution industriously inserted in that instrument a provision that all bills for raising revenues shall originate in the House of Representatives, obviously intending to place in the hands of that body primarily the scope of taxation and the selection of objects of taxation, could have intended by the clause conferring treaty-making power to turn over the *whole subject,* without limitation, to the President and Senate." (Id., Appendix, 68). Mr. Hoar expressed a different view. (Id., 277). See also the carefully prepared speech of Mr. Cullom, chairman of the Senate Committee on Foreign Relations, January 29, 1902, in which the rights of the Senate and President in this respect are maintained. (Record, 57th Cong., 1st Sess., 1077.)

within a period of two years treaties for the modification within defined limits of the rates fixed by the act should be negotiated, and duly "ratified by the Senate and approved by Congress, and public proclamation made accordingly," duties should thereafter be collected as provided for and specified in the treaty.[61] Likewise in the act approved July 26, 1911, to establish by concurrent legislation a reciprocal trade arrangement between the United States and the Dominion of Canada, the President was authorized and requested to negotiate trade agreements with Canada for freer trade relations, provided, however, that such trade agreements before becoming operative should be submitted to Congress "for ratification or rejection."[62]

By the terms of the tariff act of October 3, 1913, the President is "authorized and empowered to negotiate trade agreements with foreign nations wherein mutual concessions are made looking toward freer trade relations and further reciprocal expansion of trade and commerce: *Provided, however,* That said trade agreements before becoming operative shall be submitted to the Congress of the United States for ratification or rejection."[62a]

§89. Conclusion.—It appears that whatever may be the ipso facto effect of treaty stipulations, entered into on the authority of the President and Senate, on prior inconsistent revenue laws, not only has the House uniformly insisted upon, but the Senate has acquiesced in, legislation by Congress to give effect to such stipulations; that in case of proposed extensive modifications a clause has been inserted in the treaty by which its operation has expressly been made dependent upon such action by Congress; and that in the recent Cuban treaty such a clause was inserted on the initiative of the Senate. The contention, that, because a treaty may repeal prior acts of Congress, this legislative action by Congress is mere surplusage, rests upon the hypothesis that the President and Senate would not in such cases be acting ultra vires. On January 26, 1880, the House by a vote of 175 to 62 (54 not voting), adopted a resolution in which it declared that the negotiation by the executive department of the government of commercial treaties whereby the rates of duty to be imposed on foreign goods entering the United States for consumption should be

61 30 Stats. at L. 204.
62 Sec. 3. 37 Stats. at L. 12.
62a 38 Stats. at L. 192.

fixed, "would, in view of the provision of section 7 of Article I of the Constitution of the United States, be an infraction of the Constitution and an invasion of one of the highest prerogatives of the House of Representatives."[63] It cannot be overlooked that the exclusive power of originating bills for raising revenue was given to the House by the framers of the Constitution in lieu of an exclusive power of originating all bills for raising or appropriating money, as first voted in Committee of the Whole, July 6, and reported in the draft of the Constitution by the Committee of Detail on August 6.[64] In a dissenting opinion in Dooley v. United States,[65] as also in a concurring opinion in Downes v. Bidwell,[66] Mr. Justice, now Chief Justice, White took occasion to object to the principle of the decision of the court in De Lima v. Bidwell—that upon the exchange of the ratifications of the treaty with Spain, independently of any legislative action, goods arriving from Porto Rico were not subject to the payment of duties under the revenue laws then existing—on the ground that, if it were carried to its logical result, the President and Senate might by treaty materially affect the revenues, as, for instance, by the acquisition and incorporation of a country producing in large quantities articles from the importation of which, under the existing tariff, the revenues of the government were chiefly derived. Likewise, in a dissenting opinion in Downes v. Bidwell, Chief Justice Fuller said: "And it certainly cannot be admitted that the power of Congress to lay and collect taxes and duties can be curtailed by an arrangement made with a foreign nation by the President and two-thirds of a quorum of the Senate."[67] Mr. Justice Field, in Bartram v. Robertson, in construing the most-favored-nation stipulations in Articles I and IV of the treaty of April 26, 1826, with Denmark, in relation to the special concessions in the Hawaiian convention of January 30, 1875, observed: "Those stipulations, even if conceded to be self-executing by the way of a proviso or exception to the general law imposing the duties, do not cover concessions like those made to the Hawaiian Islands for a valuable consideration."[68] In the later case of Whitney v. Rob-

63 H. Journal, 46th Cong., 2d Sess., 323.
64 Doc. Hist. of Const., I, 81; III, 445.
65 182 U. S. 241.
66 182 U. S. 313.
67 Id., 370. See also in this relation Magoon's Reports, 151.
68 122 U. S. 116.

ertson, the most-favored-nation clause in Article IX of the treaty of February 8, 1867, with the Dominican Republic, came before the court. While it was held that the rule of construction applied by the court in Bartram v. Robertson to the most-favored-nation provisions in the treaty with Denmark was entirely applicable to the clause in Article IX of the Dominican treaty (the case before the court therefore being covered by the decision in Bartram v. Robertson), "another and complete answer" was to be found, said Mr. Justice Field, in the fact that the act of Congress under which the duties were collected was of general application and made no exception in favor of goods coming from any particular country, and, being of later date than the treaty, if there was any conflict between the two, the act must control. He added that, if a treaty and a law of Congress were inconsistent, the one last in date would control the other, "provided always the stipulation of the treaty on the subject is self-executing." In conclusion he said: "It follows, therefore, that when a law is clear in its provisions, its validity cannot be assailed before the courts for want of conformity to stipulations of a previous treaty not already executed."[69] It is true that the law under which the duties were collected was approved July 14, 1870 (amended December 22, 1870),[70] while the treaty with the Dominican Republic was concluded February 8, 1867. But the convention with the Hawaiian Islands, the concessions of which were claimed, was not signed until January 30, 1875, and did not become operative until September 9, 1876, in virtue of an act of Congress. Prior to this last date no obligation to extend to the Dominican Republic the tariff modifications stipulated for in the Hawaiian convention could under any construction arise; nor before that date could the stipulations of the Dominican treaty, so far as regards those modifications, operate as municipal law and consequently be subject to legislative repeal. Assuming that the construction of Article IX admitted such an obligation (and this may be assumed if this second answer is to be taken as "complete"), it would be difficult to reconcile the contention that treaty stipulations are so far self-executing as to effect a repeal of prior inconsistent revenue laws, with the statement of the learned justice in this case, that he

69 124 U. S. 190.
70 16 Stats. at L. 262, 397.

found no exception in the revenue laws in favor of the Dominican Republic.[71]

The same concessions in the tariff schedule as made to France under section 3 of the tariff act of July 24, 1897, in consideration for equivalent concessions, were, in view of the exceptional construction placed by the Secretary of State on the most-favored-nation clause in the treaty with Switzerland of November 25, 1850, extended by the Secretary of the Treasury to products of Switzerland.[72] Likewise the Court of Customs Appeals has held that the right of free entry into the United States of untaxed pulp made from untaxed wood, provided for in section 2 of the act of July 26, 1911, "to promote reciprocal trade relations with the Dominion of Canada and for other purposes," having been granted to Canada gratuitously and without consideration, passed automatically to other powers enjoying most-favored-nation treatment.[73] Attorney General Williams advised that the provisions of Article IV of the treaty with Belgium of July 17, 1858, which exempted steam vessels of the United States and of Belgium, engaged in regular navigation between the two countries, from the payment of tonnage, anchorage, and light house dues, became immediately applicable, mutatis mutandis, to Sweden and Norway, by virtue of Article II of the treaty of April 3, 1783, and Articles VIII and XVII of the treaty of July 4, 1827, with those countries, and to Bremen by virtue of Article IX of the treaty of December 20, 1827, with the Hanseatic Republics.[74] This view was accepted by the Secretary of State and resulted in the denunciation of the treaty with Belgium. It has likewise been held by the Court of Customs Appeals in a recent decision that, under the provision in section IV, J, subsection 7, of the tariff act of October 3, 1913,—that a discount of 5 per cent. on all duties imposed by the act shall be allowed on importations in vessels of American registry, provided that "nothing in this subsection shall be so construed as to abrogate or in any manner impair or affect the provisions of any treaty concluded between the United States and any foreign power,"—merchandise imported in the registered vessels

71 See also Taylor v. Morton, 2 Curtis 454, and Ropes v. Clinch, 8 Blatchf. 304.

72 T. D. No. 20386.

73 American Express Co. et al. v. United States; Bertuch & Co. et al. v. United States, (1913), 4 Ct. Cust. Appls. 146.

74 14 Op. 468, 530. See also 16 Op. 276, 626.

of a foreign power having a treaty with the United States stipulating for the payment of no higher or other duties on merchandise when imported in vessels of that power than are payable when imported in American vessels, is subject to the same discount of 5 per cent. as allowed on importations in vessels of American registry.[75] To reach this decision, so far as regards the operation of treaties, it was necessary only to find that the intent of Congress as expressed in the proviso was that the pledge to foreign powers against discriminatory duties should be fulfilled.

75 M. H. Pulaski Co. et al. v. United States; R. B. Henry Co. et al. v. United States; and various other cases, decided May 25, 1915. These cases are now before the Supreme Court for review.

CHAPTER XIV.

TREATIES FOR THE ACQUISITION AND CESSION OF TERRITORY.

§90. **Power to Acquire Territory by Treaty.**—"The Constitution confers absolutely on the government of the Union, the powers of making war, and of making treaties; consequently, that government possesses the power of acquiring territory, either by conquest or by treaty."[1] It is now too late to question the power of the United States to acquire territory by treaty either in time of peace,[2] or as the result of war in making effective terms of peace.[3] This power has been recognized by the Supreme Court from an early date.

§91. **Effect of Treaty on Status of Territory and its Inhabitants.**—The treaty with possession is effectual to change as between the two nations the sovereignty over the territory, and, in the absence of provision to the contrary, the allegiance of the native inhabitants from that of the former sovereign to that of the United States.[4] Upon this change of allegiance, the native in-

---

1 Marshall, C. J., American Insurance Co. v. Canter, 1 Pet. 511, 542.

2 Brewer, J., Wilson v. Shaw, 204 U. S. 24, 32; Swayne, J., Stewart v. Kahn, 11 Wall. 493, 507; Bradley, J., Mormon Church v. United States, 136 U. S. 1, 42.

3 Day, J., Dorr v. United States, 195 U. S. 138, 140; White, J., concurring, Downes v. Bidwell, 182 U. S. 244, 302.

4 American Insurance Co. v. Canter, 1 Pet. 511, 542; Boyd v. Thayer, 143 U. S. 135, 162; Gonzales v. Williams, 192 U. S. 1, 9; People v. Naglee, 1 Cal. 232; People v. de la Guerra, 40 Cal. 311; State v. Primrose, 3 Ala. 546; Tannis v. St. Cyre, 21 Ala. 449, 455; United States v. Lucero, 1 N. M. 422, 434; United States v. Juan Santistevan, 1 Id., 583; In re Rodriguez, 81 Fed. 337, 351. In Boyd v. Thayer, 143 U. S. 135, 162, Fuller, C. J., said: "Congress in the exercise of the power to establish an uniform rule of naturalization has enacted general laws under which individuals may be naturalized, but the instances of collective naturalization by treaty or by statute are numerous." For instances of collective naturalization of Indians by treaty, see Elk v. Wilkins, 112 U. S. 94. In Wong Kim Ark, 169 U. S. 649, 702, Gray, J., said: "A person born out of the jurisdiction of the United States can only become a citizen by being naturalized, either by treaty, as in the case of annexation of foreign territory; or by authority of Congress, exercised either by declaring certain classes of persons to be citizens, as in the enactments conferring citizenship upon foreign-born children of citizens, or by enabling foreigners individually to become citizens by proceedings in the judicial tribunals, as in the ordinary provisions of the naturalization acts."

habitants of the ceded territory are so far impressed with the nationality of the United States as to be entitled as against all other nations to its protection.

Under international law "the ceded territory becomes a part of the nation to which it is annexed; either on the terms stipulated in the treaty of cession, or on such as its new master shall impose," and the law in force in the new territory at the time of the transfer, "which may be denominated political, is necessarily changed, although that which regulates the intercourse and general conduct of individuals remains in force until altered by the newly created power of the state."[5] "In case of cession to the United States, laws of the ceded country inconsistent with the Constitution and laws of the United States so far as applicable would cease to be of obligatory force; but otherwise the municipal laws of the acquired country continue."[6] "It is a general rule of public law, recognized and acted upon by the United States, that whenever political jurisdiction and legislative power over any territory are transferred from one nation or sovereign to another, the municipal laws of the country, that is, laws which are intended for the protection of private rights, continue in force until abrogated or changed by the new government or sovereign. By the cession public property passes from one government to the other, but private property remains as before, and with it those municipal laws which are designed to secure its peaceful use and enjoyment. As a matter of course, all laws, ordinances, and regulations in conflict with the political character, institutions, and constitution of the new government are at once displaced. Thus, upon a cession of political jurisdiction and legislative power—and the latter is involved in the former—to the United States, the laws of the country in support of an established religion, or abridging the freedom of the press, or authorizing cruel and unusual punishments, and the like, would at once cease to be of obligatory force without any declaration to that effect; and the laws of the country on other subjects would necessarily be superseded by existing laws of the new government upon the same matters. But with respect to other laws affecting the possession, use and transfer of property, and designed to secure good order

5 Marshall, C. J., American Insurance Co. v. Canter, 1 Pet. 511, 542.
6 Fuller, C. J., Ortega v. Lara, 202 U. S. 339, 342.

and peace in the community, and promote its health and prosperity, which are strictly of a municipal character, the rule is general, that a change of government leaves them in force until, by direct action of the new government, they are altered or repealed."[7]

§92. **Legislation to give Effect to Stipulations for Incorporation of Territory.**—To what extent legislation by Congress is necessary to bring the territory acquired by treaty within the full and complete operation of all the provisions of the Constitution as applicable to the States and organized Territories has not been fully determined. The Constitution expressly provides that "new States may be admitted by the Congress into this Union," and that "the Congress shall have power to dispose of and make all needful rules and regulations respecting the territory or other property belonging to the United States."[8] Congress is likewise given the power to establish a uniform rule of naturalization.[9] It would not be contended that the treaty-making power could admit territory directly as an organized State into the Union, since the power to admit new States is expressly given to Congress.[10] In the treaties of purchase of 1803, 1819, and 1867, and the treaty of peace of 1848, it was expressly stipulated that the inhabitants of the acquired territory should be incorporated into the Union and admitted to the enjoyment of the rights of citizens of the United States.

§93. **Treaty with France of 1803.**—The provision in the treaty with France of April 30, 1803, reads: "The inhabitants of the ceded territory shall be incorporated in the Union of the United States and admitted as soon as possible according to the principles of the Federal Constitution to the enjoyment of all the rights, advantages and immunities of citizens of the United States; and in the meantime they shall be maintained and protected in the free enjoyment of their liberty, property and the religion which they

7 Field, J., Chicago, Rock Island & Pacific Railway Co. v. McGlinn, 114 U. S. 542, 546. See also United States v. Moreno, 1 Wall. 400; Downes v. Bidwell, 182 U. S. 244, 298; Vilas v. Manila, 220 U. S. 345, 357; Ponce v. Roman Catholic Church, 210 U. S. 296, 324; Bosque v. United States, 209 U. S. 91; O'Reilly de Camara v. Brooke, 209 U. S. 45; Sanchez v. United States, 216 U. S. 167.

8 Art. IV, sec. 3.

9 Art. I, sec. 8.

10 Harlan, J., dissenting, Downes v. Bidwell, 182 U. S. 389.

profess." The President and Congress considered this a stipulation looking to future action and requiring legislation to carry it into effect. The ratifications of the treaty were exchanged, October 21, 1803, and the treaty was proclaimed on the same date. By an act approved October 31, 1803, the President was authorized to take possession of the territory and temporarily to administer its government, until further action by Congress.[11] Possession of the territory was delivered in December, 1803. On February 24, 1804, an act was approved in which express provision was made for the extension of certain revenue and other laws over the new territory.[12] Prior to March 25, 1804, the date on which this act went into effect, Louisiana was considered by the Secretary of the Treasury, Mr. Gallatin, in the administration of the revenues, as not within the customs union of the United States.[13] By the act approved March 26, 1804,[14] the territory was divided into two parts; the southern part was designated the Territory of Orleans, and the northern part, the District of Louisiana. Many general laws were by the terms of this act expressly extended to the Territory of Orleans, and specific provision for its government made. The District of Louisiana was placed under the government of the Territory of Indiana. It was specifically provided that no law should be valid in the District which was inconsistent with the Constitution and laws of the United States, and that in all criminal prosecutions the trial should be by a jury of twelve men. In the act approved March 2, 1805,[15] provision was made for the government of the Territory of Orleans, subject to certain exceptions, in conformity with the Ordinance of 1787. It was expressly provided that, upon the establishment of the government, the inhabitants of the Territory should "be entitled to and enjoy all the rights, privileges and advantages secured by the said Ordinance" and then enjoyed by the people of the Mississippi Territory. Speaking of this act, Mr. Justice White, in a concurring opinion in Downes v. Bidwell,[16] said: "Thus, strictly in accord with the thought embodied in the amendment contemplated by Mr. Jefferson, citizenship was conferred, and the Territory of

11 2 Stats. at L. 245.
12 2 Stats. at L. 251.
13 Brown, J., De Lima v. Bidwell, 182 U. S. 188.
14 2 Stats. at L. 283.
15 2 Stats. at L. 322.
16 182 U. S. 332.

Orleans was incorporated into the United States to fulfill the requirements of the treaty, by placing it exactly in the position which it would have occupied had it been within the boundaries of the United States as a territory at the time the Constitution was framed." By an act approved April 8, 1812, the Territory was admitted as the State of Louisiana into the Union.[17] The Superior Court of Louisiana in the case of Desbois,[18] and the U. S. district court in the case of United States v. Laverty,[19] held that, by the several acts of Congress and the admission of the State of Louisiana into the Union, all the bona fide inhabitants, at the time of the cession, became citizens of the State and of the United States.[20] In respect of the upper part of the Louisiana territory, designated by the act of March 26, 1804, as the District of Louisiana, by the act of March 3, 1805, as the Territory of Louisiana, and by the act of June 4, 1812, as the Territory of Missouri, many acts were passed for its government and to secure rights to its inhabitants. Important of these is the act approved June 4, 1812.[21] By this act, said Mr. Justice White, "though the Ordinance of 1787 was not in express terms extended over the territory—probably owing to the slavery agitation—the inhabitants of the territory were accorded substantially all the rights of the inhabitants of the Northwest Territory. Citizenship was in effect recognized in the ninth section, whilst the fourteenth section contained an elaborate declaration of the rights secured to the people of the territory."[22] By subsequent acts the territory has been divided and admitted as States into the Union on an equality with the original States. In the act of April 20, 1836, for the or-

---

17 2 Stats. at L. 701.

18 (1812) 2 Mart. 185.

19 3 Mart. 733, 739.

20 See also State v. Primrose, (1842) 3 Ala. 546, 549, in which the Supreme Court of Alabama, by Ormond, J., said that the bona fide inhabitants of the territory at the time of the cession "were by the operation of the treaty itself created citizens of the United States." It was held by the French-American Claims Commission of 1880, in the case of Aubry (No. 25), that a French subject, who resided in the territory at the time of the cession, ceased upon its transfer to be a citizen of France. Final Report of Agent, 54. See also New Orleans v. Armas, (1835) 9 Pet. 224; In re Harrold, (1840) 1 Pa. L. J. 119; Church of St. Francis v. Martin, (1843) 4 Rob. (La.) 62.

21 2 Stats. at L. 743.

22 Downes v. Bidwell, 182 U. S. 332.

ganization of the Territory of Wisconsin,[23] and of August 14, 1848, for the organization of the Territory of Oregon,[24] it was expressly enacted that the inhabitants should be entitled to all the rights, privileges and advantages granted to the people of the Northwest Territory by the Ordinance of 1787. The Oregon act likewise expressly provided for the extension of the revenue laws over the Territory.[25]

§94. **Treaty with Spain of 1819.**—The treaty with Spain of February 22, 1819, contained the provision that the inhabitants of the ceded territory should "be incorporated in the Union of the United States, as soon as may be consistent with the principles of the Federal Constitution, and admitted to the enjoyment of all the privileges, rights, and immunities of the citizens of the United States."[26] The ratifications of the treaty were exchanged February 22, 1821, and the treaty was proclaimed on the same date. By an act approved March 3, 1821, the President was authorized to take possession of and temporarily to govern the territory. By the same act the revenue laws, subject to the exception stipulated for in Article XV of the treaty in favor of Spanish vessels, were in terms expressly extended to the territory.[27] By the act approved March 30, 1822,[28] full provision for the organization and local

---

23 Sec. 12. 5 Stats. at L. 10.

24 Sec. 14. 9 Stats. at L. 323.

25 Sec. 26.

26 Art. VI.

27 3 Stats. at L. 637. An act of like import had been approved March 3, 1819. 3 Id., 523. Taney, C. J., in Fleming v. Page, 9 How. 603, 617, said: "After Florida had been ceded to the United States, and the forces of the United States had taken possession of Pensacola, it was decided by the Treasury Department, that goods imported from Pensacola before an act of Congress was passed erecting it into a collection district, and authorizing the appointment of a collector, were liable to duty. That is, although Florida had, by cession, actually become a part of the United States, and was in our possession, yet, under our revenue laws, its ports must be regarded as foreign until they were established as domestic, by act of Congress; and it appears that this decision was sanctioned at the time by the Attorney General of the United States." Brown, J., in De Lima v. Bidwell, however, said: "As the act extending the revenue laws to the Floridas was passed before the surrender of the province to the United States, there was no interval of time upon which the Treasury Department could act, the provinces, immediately upon the surrender, becoming subject to the act of March 3, 1821." 182 U. S. 1, 190.

28 3 Stats. at L. 654.

16

government of the territory was made. It provided that certain laws, expressly enumerated, and all other public laws of the United States not repugnant to the provisions of the act, should extend to and have full force and effect in the territory. It was likewise expressly enacted that no law should be passed in restraint of the freedom of religious opinions, professions or worship; that the inhabitants should be entitled to the benefit of the writ of habeas corpus; that they should be bailable, except for capital offences where the proof was evident or the presumption great; that excessive bail should not be required, nor cruel or unusual punishment inflicted; that no ex post facto law or law impairing the obligation of contracts should be passed; and that private property should not be taken for public use without just compensation.[29] The provisions of this act indicate that the legislative branch of the government entertained doubts that the provisions of the Constitution were completely and fully applicable in the government of the new territory. In the case of American Insurance Co. v. Canter, decided in 1828, the Supreme Court held that the provision in the Constitution that the judicial power of the United States shall be vested in one Supreme Court and in such inferior courts as Congress shall establish, and that the judges both of the Supreme Court and of the inferior courts shall hold office during good behavior, did not apply as a limitation in constituting courts in the territory of Florida. In the course of the opinion, Chief Justice Marshall, in adverting to Article VI of the treaty, said: "This treaty is the law of the land, and admits the inhabitants of Florida to the enjoyment of the privileges, rights, and immunities, of the citizens of the United States. It is unnecessary to enquire, whether this is not their condition, independent of stipulation. They do not, however, participate in political power; they do not share in the government, till Florida shall become a State. In the meantime, Florida continues to be a territory of the United States; governed by virtue of that clause in the Constitution, which empowers Congress 'to make all needful rules and regulations, respecting the territory, or other property belonging to the United States.'"[30] Florida was admitted as a State into

29 Sec. 10.

30 1 Pet. 511, 542. The Supreme Court of Alabama held in 1852 in the case of Tannis v. St. Cyre, (21 Ala. 449), that a free negro who was an inhabitant of Florida at the date of the treaty lost by operation of the treaty the status of an alien as regards alien disability to take lands by descent.

the Union, March 3, 1845, upon an equal footing with the original States.[31]

§95. **Treaties with Mexico of 1848 and 1853.**—Article VIII of the treaty with Mexico of February 2, 1848, provided that the Mexicans then established in the territories previously belonging to Mexico, might, if they continued to reside in the territories, either retain the title and rights of Mexican citizens, or acquire those of citizens of the United States; but that those who remained in the territories after the expiration of one year from the date of the exchange of ratifications without having declared their intention to retain the character of Mexicans should be considered to have elected to become citizens of the United States. Article IX reads: "The Mexicans who, in the territories aforesaid, shall not preserve the character of citizens of the Mexican Republic, conformably with what is stipulated in the preceding article, shall be incorporated into the Union of the United States, and be admitted at the proper time (to be judged of by the Congress of the United States) to the enjoyment of all the rights of citizens of the United States, according to the principles of the Constitution; and in the meantime, shall be maintained and protected in the free enjoyment of their liberty and property, and secured in the free exercise of their religion without restriction." The ratifications of the treaty were exchanged May 30, 1848, and the treaty was proclaimed July 4, 1848. The treaty did not in express terms provide for a cession of territory by Mexico to the United States, but for a change in the boundaries between the two countries. "In consideration of the extension acquired by the boundaries of the United States, as defined in the fifth article" of the treaty, Mexico was to receive $15,000,000. The territory was at the time of the conclusion of the treaty in the military occupation of the United States. The Secretary of State, Mr. Buchanan, in a letter to Wm. V. Vorhies, October 7, 1848, and the Secretary of the Treasury, Mr. Walker, in a circular letter of even date to collectors, took the view that California had, upon the exchange of ratifications of the treaty, become domestic territory in the administration of the revenue laws, and that products shipped from California after May 30, 1848, were entitled to free entry in all ports of the United States, and, conversely, that products of the States were entitled to free admission in the ports of California.[32]

---

31   5 Stats. at L. 742. See also act of March 3, 1823, 3 Stats. at L. 750.
32   Ex. Doc. No. 1, 30th Cong., 2d Sess., 45, 47.

Congress failed to make any provision for the collection of duties in the new territory until March 3, 1849. This act in words expressly extended the revenue laws of the United States to that portion of the ceded territory known as Upper California, and provided for its erection into a collection district.[33] The collector appointed under this act did not assume charge of his office until November 13, 1849. Import duties were collected prior to the receipt of notice of the exchange of ratifications of the treaty at rates fixed by the President as commander-in-chief, and, after the receipt of this notice and until the arrival of the collector, November 13, 1849, in conformity with the rates fixed in the revenue laws then in force in the United States. In the case of Cross v. Harrison, the Supreme Court upheld the right to impose and collect these rates of duty. The goods involved in the case before the court came from ports other than those of the United States.[34] In the course of the opinion for the court, Mr. Justice Wayne observed that "after the ratification of the treaty California became a part of the United States, or a ceded, conquered territory";[35] that by the ratifications of the treaty California became a part of the United States, and as there was "nothing differently stipulated in the treaty with respect to commerce, it became instantly bound and privileged by the laws which Congress had passed to raise a revenue from duties on imports and tonnage."[36] By an act approved September 9, 1850, prior to any legislation as to its territorial organization, California was admitted as a State into the Union;[37] and by an act approved September 28, 1850, it was expressly enacted that all the laws of the United States not locally inapplicable should have the same force and effect in the State of California as elsewhere in the United States.[38] An act approved

33 9 Stats. at L. 400.

34 16 How. 164, 183, 184, 193.

35 Id., 191.

36 Id., 197. This statement would seem to be inconsistent with a decision sustaining the right to collect the duties according to the war tariff from May 30, 1848, the date of the exchange of ratifications, until August 7, 1848, the date notice of this fact was received at San Francisco. See for analysis of this decision, Brown, J., De Lima v. Bidwell, 182 U. S. 185; White, J., concurring, Downes v. Bidwell, 182 U. S. 309. Mr. Justice White in his opinion says: "It was stated, in so many words, that a different rule would have been applied had the stipulations in the treaty been of a different character."

37 9 Stats. at L. 452.

38 9 Stats. at L. 521.

September 9, 1850 provided for the organization and government of the remaining territory lying between the States of Texas and California, and designated the Territory of New Mexico. By section 17 of this act it was expressly enacted that the Constitution and all laws of the United States which were not locally inapplicable should have the same force and effect within the Territory as elsewhere within the United States. Section 19 provided that no citizen of the United States should be deprived of his life, liberty, or property in the Territory except by the judgment of his peers and the laws of the land.[39] By an act approved August 4, 1854, the additional territory acquired from Mexico by the Gadsden treaty, concluded December 30, 1853, and proclaimed June 30, 1854, was incorporated with, and made subject to all the laws of, the Territory of New Mexico.[40]

As regards the Mexicans, who were established in the territory at the time of the conclusion of the treaty, and who continued to reside in the territory without making the declaration of intention to retain Mexican citizenship as provided for in the treaty, it has been held in various cases coming before State and Territorial courts that they ceased by operation of the treaty to be aliens, and acquired the nationality of the United States.[41]

§96. Organization of Various Western Territories.—In the acts for the organization and establishment of territorial government, in Utah, of September 9, 1850; in Kansas and Nebraska, of May 30, 1854, (subject to certain specific exceptions); in Colorado, of February 28, 1861; in Dakota, of March 2, 1861; in Nevada, of March 2, 1861; in Arizona, of February 24, 1863, (by reference to New Mexico); in Idaho, of March 3, 1863; in Montana, of May 26, 1864; and in Wyoming, of July 25, 1868, it was in each instance expressly enacted that the Consti-

39 9 Stats. at L. 446, 452.
40 10 Stats. at L. 575.
41 People v. Naglee, (1850) 1 Cal. 232; People v. de la Guerra, (1870) 40 Cal. 311; United States v. Lucero (1869), 1 N. Mex. 422, 434; United States v. Juan Santistevan, (1874) 1 Id. 583; In re Rodriguez, (1897) 81 Fed. 337, 351; Chavez v. United States, United States and Mexican Claims Commission of 1868, Moore, Int. Arb., III, 2510; Vallejos v. United States, (1900) 35 C. Cls. 489; De Baca v. United States, (1901) 37 C. Cls. 482; 189 U. S. 505. See as to the exercise of election to retain Mexican citizenship, Quintana v. Tomkins, (1853) 1 N. Mex. 29; Carter v. Territory, (1859) 1 Id. 317; Tobin v. Walkinshaw et al., (1856) 1 McAllister 186. See, generally, Van Dyne, Citizenship of the United States, 151.

tution and laws of the United States, which were not locally inapplicable, should have the same force and effect in the Territory so organized as elsewhere within the United States.[42] Section 1891 of the Revised Statutes reads: "The Constitution and all laws of the United States which are not locally inapplicable shall have the same force and effect within all the organized Territories, and in every Territory hereafter organized as elsewhere within the United States." In the act approved May 2, 1890, for the erection of the Territory of Oklahoma, and for its organization and government, it was likewise expressly provided that the Constitution and all laws of the United States not locally inapplicable should, except so far as modified by the act, have the same force and effect as elsewhere within the United States.[43]

§97. **Treaty with Russia of 1867.**—By the treaty signed March 30, 1867, Russia agreed to cede to the United States, immediately upon the exchange of ratifications, all her territory and dominion on the continent of North America and adjacent islands.[44] Specific provision was made for the formal delivery, but the cession, with the right of immediate possession, was to be deemed complete and absolute upon the exchange of ratifications, without waiting for formal delivery.[45] With respect to the inhabitants of the ceded territory it was stipulated that, reserving their natural allegiance, they might return to Russia, but that if they should prefer to remain in the ceded territory, they, with the exception of uncivilized native tribes, should "be admitted to the enjoyment of all the rights, advantages, and immunities of citizens of the United States," and should be maintained and protected in the free enjoyment of their liberty, property, and religion; that the uncivilized tribes should be subject to such laws and regulations as the United States might from time to time adopt in regard to aboriginal tribes of that country.[46] The ratifications of the treaty were exchanged, June 20, 1867, and the treaty was proclaimed on the same date. The formal transfer took place on October 18,

---

42 9 Stats. at L. 458; 10 Id. 282, 289; 12 Id. 176, 214, 244, 665, 813; 13 Id. 91; 15 Id. 183.

43 Section 1850 of the Revised Statutes was expressly excepted. As regards the Indian Territory as defined in the act, see especially the last paragraph of section 31. 26 Stats. at L. 93, 96.

44 Art. I.

45 Art. IV.

46 Art. III.

1867.[47]   In transmitting a copy of the treaty to Congress, July 6, 1867, the President directed attention not only to the subject of an appropriation but also to the subject of proper legislation for the occupation and government of the territory as a part of the dominion of the United States.[48]   Congress however adjourned without making any provision in this regard.   The President in his annual message of December 3, 1867 again brought the subject to the attention of Congress, observing that, possession having been formally delivered, the territory remained in care of a military force, awaiting such civil organization as should be directed by Congress.[49]   On July 27, 1868, two acts were approved, one making the required appropriation, the other expressly extending over the territory the laws of the United States relating to customs, commerce and navigation, and constituting it a collection district.[50] In the annual messages of 1879, 1880, 1881, 1882, and 1883, the President recommended legislation for the organization and establishment of a civil government in Alaska.   In his message of December 4, 1883, President Arthur said: "I trust that Congress will not fail at its present session to put Alaska under the protection of law.   Its people have repeatedly remonstrated against our neglect to afford them the maintenance and protection expressly guaranteed by the terms of the treaty whereby that territory was ceded to the United States.   For sixteen years they have pleaded in vain for that which they should have received without the asking."[51]   By an act approved May 17, 1884, Alaska was constituted a civil and judicial district, and provision was made for a civil government.   The general laws of the State of Oregon then in force were declared to be the law in the district so far as applicable and not in conflict with the provisions of the act or the laws of the United States.[52]   In view of section 1891 of the Revised Statutes, the incorporation of Alaska as an integral part of the United States may be considered as having been accom-

47 H. Ex. Doc. No. 125, 40th Cong., 2d Sess., 8.

48 Richardson, Messages and Papers of the Presidents, VI, 524.

49 Id., 580.

50 15 Stats. at L. 198, 240.   Sections 20 and 21 of the act of June 30, 1834, to regulate trade and intercourse with Indian tribes, were extended to Alaska by the act of March 3, 1873.   17 Stats. at L. 530.

51 Richardson, Messages and Papers of the Presidents, VII, 570, 621; VIII, 64, 144, 184.

52 Sec. 7.   23 Stats. at L. 24.

plished with the approval of this act.[53] In the case of Rassmussen v. the United States, it was held that, under the treaty
and the subsequent legislation of Congress, Alaska had been incorporated into the United States; that in legislating therefor
Congress was under the prohibitions of Articles V and VI of the
Amendments to the Constitution giving to one accused of a misdemeanor the right of a trial by a common law jury; and that a
provision in the Alaskan Code,[54] constituting six persons a legal
jury in the trial of misdemeanors, was unconstitutional and
void.[55]

§98. Treaty with Spain of 1898.—By the treaty of peace,
signed December 10, 1898, Spain ceded to the United States Porto
Rico and other islands then under Spanish sovereignty in the
West Indies, the island of Guam, and the Philippine Islands.[56]
No date was expressly fixed, as in the Alaskan treaty, on which
the change of sovereignty should take effect. Spain had already
under the protocol of August 12, 1898 evacuated Porto Rico. It
was expressly provided in the treaty that Spain would upon the
exchange of the ratifications proceed to evacuate the Philippines.
Article IX provided that Spanish subjects, natives of the Peninsula, then residing in the ceded territory, might remain in the territory or might remove therefrom, retaining in either event all their
rights of property; that in case they should remain in the territory
they might preserve their allegiance to the crown of Spain by
making, within one year from the date of the exchange of ratifications, a declaration to that effect, but in default of such declaration they should be held to have renounced it and have adopted
the nationality of the territory in which they might reside. Specific provision was made that the inhabitants of the ceded territory should be secured in the free exercise of their religion. In
contrast with prior treaties by which territory had been acquired,
the treaty contained no provision for the incorporation and the

---

53 See Binns v. United States, 194 U. S. 486, 490-491; In re Minook,
2 Alaska 200; McFarland v. Alaska Perseverance Mining Co., 3 Alaska 308.

54 31 Stats. at L. 358.

55 197 U. S. 516. In the case of In re Minook, decided in 1904, it was
held that Russian subjects, who remained in Alaska, became by virtue of
the treaty and the subsequent laws passed by Congress citizens of the
United States. 2 Alaska 200. As to the status of uncivilized tribes, see
United States v. Berrigan, 2 Alaska 442.

56 Arts. II and III.

admission of the inhabitants to the enjoyment of all the rights, advantages, and immunities of citizens of the United States. On the contrary it was expressly provided that the "civil rights and political status" of the native inhabitants of the ceded territories should be determined by the Congress of the United States.

Various cases have come before the Supreme Court involving the status of the territory so acquired. In De Lima v. Bidwell,[57] recovery was sought of duties paid under protest on goods brought into New York from the island of Porto Rico in 1899, after the exchange of ratifications of the treaty, but prior to any legislation by Congress as to the duties to be imposed on goods coming from Porto Rico. The court held that upon the exchange of ratifications of the treaty, April 11, 1899, Porto Rico ceased to be a foreign country within the meaning of the tariff laws then existing, and that the duties were not legally exacted.[58] In the case of the Fourteen Diamond Rings[59] the same decision was reached as to the Philippine Islands.[60] In Dooley v. United States,[61] an attempt was made to recover duties paid under protest in Porto Rico on goods arriving from New York, between July 26, 1898 and May 1, 1900. From July 26, 1898 to August 19, 1898, the duties were collected under orders of the United States military authorities in occupation, under which the former Spanish rates of duties were continued. From August 19, 1898 to May 1, 1900, the date on which the act of April 12, 1900 took effect, the duties were collected under a tariff for Porto Rico promulgated by authority of the President. It was held—first, that the duties collected on goods arriving from New York during the period from the time military possession of the island was taken until the exchange of ratifications of the treaty of peace were legally exacted under the war power of the President;[62]

---

57 182 U. S. 1.

58 Brown, J., wrote the opinion of the court. Fuller, C. J., Harlan, Brewer, and Peckham, JJ., concurred. McKenna, Shiras, White and Gray, JJ., dissented.

59 183 U. S. 176.

60 See also Lincoln v. United States, 197 U. S. 419; s. c. 202 U. S. 484. In Faber v. United States, 221 U. S. 649, 658, it was held that Porto Rico and the Philippines were not "another country" within the meaning of the treaty with Cuba, proclaimed December 17, 1903.

61 182 U. S. 222.

62 All the justices concurred in this part of the decision.

and second, as a corollary to the decision in De Lima v. Bidwell, that this right of the Executive to collect duties on goods brought into Porto Rico from New York ceased upon the final ratification of the treaty of peace, Porto Rico having ceased to be a foreign country.[63] In other words, it has been held that, in the absence of any legislation, Porto Rico upon the final ratification of the treaty became so far appurtenant to the United States that the laws then existing for the imposition of duties upon goods coming from a foreign country were inapplicable to goods arriving at New York from Porto Rico, and that the right of the Executive to exact duties upon goods arriving in Porto Rico from New York ceased. In Santiago v. Nogueras,[64] it was held that, upon the ratification of the treaty, Porto Rico ceased to be subject to Spain, and became subject to the legislative power of Congress; but that, pending action by Congress to establish civil government, the authority to govern the territory was, by the law applicable to conquest and cession, under the military control of the President as commander-in-chief.

On April 12, 1900, an act was approved to provide for the civil government of Porto Rico. It was enacted that, subject to certain provisos, the same tariffs, customs, and duties should be paid upon articles imported into Porto Rico from ports other than those of the United States, as paid upon articles imported into the United States from foreign countries. As regards merchandise coming into the United States from Porto Rico and into Porto Rico from the United States, a temporary duty equal to fifteen per centum of that paid upon imports from foreign countries was imposed.[65] In the distribution of powers under the Constitution the power to lay and collect duties, imposts and excises is given to Congress, but with the qualification that "all duties, imposts and excises shall be uniform throughout the United States."[66] The case of Downes v. Bidwell[67] involved the right to impose the duty prescribed in the above act on merchandise coming from Porto Rico. The court held the act in this respect to be constitutional, and sustained the right to impose the duty. In other words,

63　White, Gray, Shiras, and McKenna, JJ., dissented.
64　214 U. S. 260.
65　Sec. 3.　31 Stats. at L. 77.
66　Art. I, sec. 8.
67　182 U. S. 244.

it was held that the uniformity clause of the Constitution was not applicable in legislating in respect of Porto Rico; that Porto Rico while "appurtenant and belonging" to the United States was not a part of the United States within the meaning of the revenue clauses of the Constitution.[68]   In the second case of Dooley v. United States, decided in the following term,[69] the court upheld the correlative right of Congress to impose duties on merchandise entering Porto Rico from the United States.   In the act of April 12, 1900, it is provided that the statutory laws of the United States not locally applicable shall, except as otherwise provided therein, have the same force and effect in "Porto Rico as in the United States."[70]   No reference is made to the Constitution, as has been customary in the acts heretofore noted in providing for the organization and government of a Territory.   The inhabitants (excepting those who elected to retain Spanish nationality), who were residing in Porto Rico on April 11, 1899, and their children born thereafter, are declared to be citizens of Porto Rico and as such entitled to the protection of the United States.[71] Subject to certain exceptions, the laws and ordinances then in force in Porto Rico, not in conflict with the act or the statutory laws of the United States not locally inapplicable, are continued in full force and effect.[72]   As regards the status of the native inhabitants of Porto Rico, Mr. Hay, Secretary of State, in circular instructions of May 2, 1899 to the diplomatic and consular officers of the United States, declared that, pending legislation by Congress on the subject, they were entitled to the protection of the United States as against every foreign government; and he directed that when duly registered they should be given official protection in all matters where a citizen of the United States

68 Brown, J., announced the decision of the court. White, Gray, Shiras, and McKenna, JJ., concurred in the decision. Fuller, C. J., Harlan, Brewer and Peckham, JJ., dissented. The concurring justices, consistent with their dissenting views in De Lima v. Bidwell, based their decision upon the principle that legislation by Congress was necessary to incorporate territory, acquired by treaty, as an integral part of the United States and bring it within the customs union; that the treaty, especially in view of a manifest intent to the contrary, did not of itself effect such an incorporation.

69 183 U. S. 151.

70 Sec. 14.

71 Sec. 7.

72 Sec. 8.

similarly situated would be entitled thereto.[73] The same view was taken in reference to natives of the Philippines temporarily in a foreign land.[74] In Gonzales v. Williams[75] it was held by the Supreme Court that citizens of Porto Rico entering the port of New York were not alien immigrants within the intent and meaning of the immigration act of March 3, 1891.[76] In a recent case, it was said by Mr. Justice Lurton, speaking for the court: "Though for all purposes the Island of Porto Rico has not been fully incorporated into the United States, it obviously is not foreign territory, nor its citizens aliens. Gonzales v. Williams, 192 U. S. 1, 15. Its organization is in most essentials that of those political entities known as Territories. It has a territorial legislature and a territorial system of courts. By the fourteenth section of the Foraker Act of April 12, 1900, 31 Stat. 77, 80, c. 191, 'the statute laws of the United States not locally inapplicable * * * have the same force and effect in Porto Rico as in the United States, except the revenue law.' In Kopel v. Bingham, 211 U. S. 468, Porto Rico was held to be a Territory within the meaning of §5278, Revised Statutes, providing for the surrender of fugitive criminals by governors of Territories." It was held that the Safety Appliance Act of March 2, 1903 was in force in Porto Rico.[77] It has also been held that the Employers' Liability Act of April 22, 1908, extended to Porto Rico.[78]

An amendment to the army appropriation act, approved March 2, 1901, provided that all military, civil, and judicial powers necessary to govern the Philippine Islands should, until otherwise provided by Congress, be vested in such persons, and should be exercised in such manner, as the President of the United States should direct, for the establishment of civil government and for

73 For. Rel., 1900, p. 894.

74 Mr. Hay, Secretary of State, to Mr. Leishman, minister to Switzerland, December 28, 1900. For. Rel., 1900, p. 905.

75 192 U. S. 1.

76 See also Narciso Basso v. United States, 40 C. Cls. 202, holding that a citizen of Porto Rico is not an alien and is not prohibited by §1068, Rev. Stats. from maintaining an action in the Court of Claims. See also Bosque v. United States, 209 U. S. 91; Martinez v. Asociacion de Señoras, 213 U. S. 20.

77 American Railroad Co. of Porto Rico v. Didricksen, 227 U. S. 145, 148. 32 Stats. at L. 943.

78 American Railroad Co. of Porto Rico v. Birch, 224 U. S. 547. 35 Stats. at L. 65.

maintaining and protecting the inhabitants of the Islands in the free enjoyment of their liberty, property, and religion.[79] By an act approved March 8, 1902, to provide a revenue for the Philippine Islands, duties were imposed on articles entering the Philippines from the United States as also on those coming into the United States from the Philippines.[80] This act, besides regulating the revenues, contained, in section 9, provision that no person in the Philippine Islands should, under the authority of the United States, be convicted of treason by any tribunal, civil or military, unless on the testimony of two witnesses to the same overt act, or on confession in open court. This was in effect an enactment by Congress that the first clause in section 3, Article III of the Constitution should apply in the government of the Philippines. By the act of July 1, 1902, passed after the decision of the Supreme Court in Downes v. Bidwell, for the administration of civil government in the Philippine Islands, it is expressly enacted that section 1891 of the Revised Statutes—that the Constitution and laws of the United States not locally inapplicable shall have the same force and effect in Territories thereafter organized as elsewhere within the United States—shall not apply to the Philippines.[81] The inhabitants of the Islands, who were residing there on April 11, 1899, and who have not elected to retain their Spanish nationality in accordance with the stipulations of the treaty, and their children born subsequently thereto, are declared to be citizens of the Philippine Islands and as such entitled to the protection of the United States.[82] The act also embodies many of the guarantees as to private rights found in the Constitution, but not all of them.[83] It is expressly declared that no ex post facto law, bill of attainder, law imparing the obligation of contracts, granting titles of nobility, depriving any person of life, liberty or property without due process of law, or denying any person therein the equal protection of the law, shall be enacted. Provisions against imprisonment for debt, against slavery, and the suspension of the privilege of the writ of habeas corpus are made. The rights and immunities as to religious freedom, bail, cruel and

79 31 Stats. at L. 910.
80 32 Stats. at L. 54.
81 Sec. 1. 32 Stats. at L. 691, 692.
82 Sec. 4.
83 Sec. 5.

unusual punishment, searches and seizures, public trial, witnesses, and jeopardy, which are guaranteed in the first nine Articles of the Amendments to the Constitution, are substantially incorporated in this act.[84] The rights and immunities found in Articles II, III, V, and VI of the Amendments, as to keeping and bearing arms, quartering of soldiers in time of peace, guaranteeing the right of trial by jury, and of presentment and indictment by a grand jury are not expressly included.   Mr. Justice Day, Secretary of State during the war with Spain, negotiator of the protocol of August 12, 1898, and one of the American Commissioners, who negotiated and signed the treaty at Paris, in the opinion of the court in Dorr v. United States, said: "Until Congress shall see fit to incorporate territory ceded by treaty into the United States, we regard it as settled by that decision [Downes v. Bidwell] that the territory is to be governed under the power existing in Congress to make laws for such territories and subject to such constitutional restrictions upon the powers of that body as are applicable to the situation * * *. If the treaty-making power could incorporate territory into the United States without Congressional action, it is apparent that the treaty with Spain, ceding the Philippines to the United States, carefully refrained from so doing; for it is expressly provided that (Article IX) 'the civil rights and political status of the native inhabitants of the territories hereby ceded to the United States shall be determined by the Congress.' In this language it is clear that it was the intention of the framers of the treaty to reserve to Congress, so far as it could be constitutionally done,[85] a free hand in dealing with these newly acquired possessions.   The legislation upon the subject shows that not only has

84 See Day, J., Kepner v. United States, 195 U. S. 100, 123.

85 "We are also of opinion that the power to acquire territory by treaty implies not only the power to govern such territory, but to prescribe upon what terms the United States will receive its inhabitants, and what their status shall be in what Chief Justice Marshall termed the 'American Empire.' There seems to be no middle ground between this position and the doctrine that if their inhabitants do not become, immediately upon annexation, citizens of the United States, their children thereafter born, whether savages or civilized, are such, and entitled to all the rights, privileges and immunities of citizens." Brown, J., Downes v. Bidwell, 182 U. S. 279. "It is then, as I think, indubitably settled by the principles of the law of nations, by the nature of the government created under the Constitution, by the express and implied powers conferred upon that government by the Constitution, by the mode in which those powers have been executed, from the beginning, and by an unbroken line of decisions of this court, first an-

Congress hitherto refrained from incorporating the Philippines into the United States, but in the act of 1902, providing for temporary civil government, 32 Stat. 691, there is express provision that section eighteen hundred and ninety-one of the Revised Statutes of 1878 shall not apply to the Philippine Islands. This is the section giving force and effect to the Constitution and laws of the United States, not locally inapplicable, within all the organized Territories, and every Territory thereafter organized, as elsewhere within the United States." And it was held in this case "that the power to govern territory, implied in the right to acquire it, and given to Congress in Article IV, §3 [of the Constitution] to whatever other limitations it may be subject, the extent of which must be decided as questions arise, does not require that body to enact for ceded territory, not made a part of the United States by Congressional action, a system of laws which shall include the right of trial by jury, and that the Constitution does not, without legislation and of its own force, carry such right to territory so situated."[86] In the later case of Dowdell v. United States,[87] it was held that in the absence of legislation by Congress there was no right in the Philippine Islands to a trial by jury, or to an indictment by a grand jury as required in Article V of the Amendments to the Constitution.[88]

nounced by Marshall and followed and lucidly expounded by Taney, that the treaty-making power cannot incorporate territory into the United States without the express or implied assent of Congress, that it may insert in a treaty conditions against immediate incorporation, and that on the other hand when it has expressed in the treaty the conditions favorable to incorporation, they will, if the treaty be not repudiated by Congress, have the force of the law of the land, and therefore by the fulfillment of such conditions cause incorporation to result." White, J., Id., 338. "The office of a treaty of cession ordinarily is to put an end to all authority of the foreign government over the territory; and to subject the territory to the disposition of the Government of the United States. The government and disposition of territory so acquired belong to the Government of the United States, consisting of the President, the Senate, elected by the States, and the House of Representatives, chosen by and immediately representing the people of the United States. Treaties by which territory is acquired from a foreign state usually recognize this. It is clearly recognized in the recent treaty with Spain, especially in the ninth article." Gray, J., Id., 346.

86 195 U. S. 138, 143, 149.

87 221 U. S. 325.

88 See as to the Territory of Hawaii, section 5 of the act of April 30, 1900, 31 Stats. at L. 141, and the case of Hawaii v. Mankichi, 190 U. S. 197.

§99. **Power to Cede Territory.**—In the Federal Convention, August 15, 1787, while the treaty power was still vested in the Senate alone, George Mason, in urging that all bills for raising or appropriating money should originate in the House of Representatives, said that he was extremely anxious to take this power from the Senate, which "could already sell the whole country by means of treaties." "The Senate might," he added, "by means of treaty alienate territory, etc., without legislative sanction. The cessions of the British Islands in the W. Indies by treaty alone were an example. If Spain should possess herself of Georgia therefore the Senate might by treaty dismember the Union."[89] Elbridge Gerry on August 17, in supporting a motion to give Congress the power to make peace, said: "Eight Senators may possibly exercise the power if vested in that body, and fourteen if all should be present; and may consequently give up part of the United States."[90] On September 7, during the debate on the question of the proportion of the Senate to be required for concurrence in treaties of peace (it having been voted to except them from the requirement of a two-thirds vote), Gerry urged that a greater proportion should be required than in case of other treaties, since in treaties of peace the dearest interests would be at stake, such as the fisheries and territories. He objected to putting the "essential rights of the Union" in the hands of a majority of the Senate which might represent less than a fifth of the people.[91] An amendment was offered by the terms of which no treaty of peace should be entered into whereby the United States should be deprived of any of their present territory or rights without the concurrence of two-thirds of the members of the Senate present. Another amendment was offered which provided that no rights established by the treaty of peace should be ceded without the sanction of the legislature. Upon a reconsideration of the clause, the exception as to treaties of peace was stricken out.[92]

In the Virginia convention that ratified the Constitution, Patrick Henry, in a bitter attack on the treaty-making provision, said that the President and two-thirds of a quorum of the Senate "might relinquish and alienate territorial rights, and our most

89 Doc. Hist. of the Const., III, 535, 536.
90 Id., III, 554.
91 Id., III, 701, 704.
92 Id., III, 703, 704.

valuable commercial advantages. In short, if anything should be left us, it would be because the President and Senators were pleased to admit it."[93] George Mason, in the same convention, declared that there was "nothing in the Constitution to hinder a dismemberment of the empire"; and he urged the adoption of an amendment by which it should be expressly provided that no treaty to dismember the empire should be made except in case of the most urgent and unavoidable necessity, and then only with the consent of three-fourths of both branches of Congress.[94] Madison, in replying to these objections, said: "I do not conceive that power is given to the President and Senate to dismember the empire, or to alienate any great, essential right. I do not think the whole legislative authority have this power."[95] Grayson contended that express provision ought to be made that no dismemberment should take place without the consent of the legislature. He added: "There is an absolute necessity for the existence of the power. It may prevent the annihilation of society by procuring a peace. It must be lodged somewhere. The opposition wish it to be put in the hands of three-fourths of the members of both houses of Congress. It would be then secure. It is not so now."[96] Similar objections were raised in the first North Carolina convention.[97] An amendment to the Constitution, that no treaty ceding or compromising in any manner the rights or claims of the United States to territory, fisheries in the American seas, or navigation of American rivers should be concluded except in case of the most urgent and extreme necessity, and then only with the concurrence of three-fourths of all the members of both houses of Congress, was proposed both by the Virginia convention and by the first North Carolina convention.[98]

The question as to the power of the central government to cede by treaty territory lying within a State came under consideration in President Washington's administration during the negotiations with Spain relative to the boundary between Georgia and the Floridas. In the draft of the instructions of March 18, 1792, to Carmichael and Short, the American commissioners, Jefferson,

---

93 Elliot's Debates (2 ed.), III, 500.
94 Id., III, 508.
95 Id., III, 514.
96 Id., III, 613.
97 Id., IV, 119.
98 Doc. Hist. of the Const., II, 271, 382.

17

Secretary of State, stated that the right to alienate even an inch of territory belonging to a member of the Union did not exist in the central government. In another part of the instructions, he admitted that, as the result of a disastrous war, necessity might compel an abandonment of a part of a State.[99] Hamilton, in commenting on these instructions, expressed doubt that there was such a limitation on the power of the central government to accommodate itself to exigencies that might arise, especially as to unpeopled territory. The instructions remained unchanged.[100]

During the northeastern boundary controversy, the legislature of Massachusetts in 1838 passed a resolution in which it was asserted that no power delegated to the central government by the Constitution authorized it to cede territory within the limits of the States of the Union. To a request of Edward Everett, governor of Massachusetts, for an opinion on the resolution, Mr. Justice Story, in a private communication dated April 17, 1838, replied that he could not admit it to be universally true that the government of the United States was not authorized to make such cessions. He recalled that Chief Justice Marshall, when the question was under discussion some years before, was "unequivocally of opinion, that the treaty-making power did extend to cases of cession of territory, though he would not undertake to say that it could extend to all cases; yet he did not doubt it must be construed to extend to some."[101] Mr. Webster, in the final negotiations for the settlement of the boundary, for reasons which were not necessarily constitutional ones, sought to a certain extent the co-operation of the States of Maine and Massachusetts. Shortly after the arrival of Lord Ashburton, letters were addressed to the two States inviting the appointment of commissioners to confer with the central government as to terms, conditions, considerations and equivalents, with an understanding that no line would be agreed upon without the assent of such commissioners.[102] Commissioners were duly appointed, and the final settlement was communicated to them for approval before the treaty was

99 Am. State Papers, For. Rel., I, 252, 255.

100 Writings of Jefferson (Ford ed.), V, 443, 476. See opinions expressed at a meeting of the heads of the departments in February, 1793, on the proposition to transfer rights in territory to Indian tribes, Id., I, 219.

101 Life and Letters of Joseph Story (Wm. Story ed.), II, 286, 288.

102 Webster's Works, VI, 272-4.

signed.[103]   The treaty was not strictly a determination of the actual line but a friendly adjustment of it, in which it was admitted that concessions had been made on the northeastern boundary in consideration of equivalents elsewhere received.   By the same instrument the United States agreed to pay to the two States in equal moities the sum of $300,000 "on account of their assent to the line of boundary described in this treaty, and in consideration of the conditions and equivalents received therefor from the Government of Her Britannic Majesty."[104]   The stipulation in Article IV of the treaty, that all grants of land theretofore made by either party, which by the treaty fell within the dominion of the other, should be held valid, ratified and confirmed to the person in possession under such grant to the same extent as if such territory had by the treaty fallen within the dominion of the party by whom such grants were made, was held by the Supreme Judicial Court of Maine for the county of Washington to be so far self-operative as to confirm the grant without the aid of legislation; and that one, who at the time of the ratification of the treaty was, and for several years prior thereto had been, in possession of land under a grant from the Province of New Brunswick, had, by virtue of this article of the treaty, a title good as against one claiming under a grant from the State of Massachusetts, although the land in question lay within the limits of the United States as conventionally established by the treaty.   In the course of the opinion, Shepley, C. J., said: "It is the duty of this court to consider that treaty to be a law operating upon the grant made under the authority of the British government, and declaring, that it shall be held valid, ratified and confirmed.   It is further insisted that it cannot be permitted so to operate and thereby defeat the title of the demandant to the land without a violation of that provision of the Constitution of the United Sates which declares that private property shall not be taken for public use without just compensation.   It is not in the argument denied that public or private property may be sacrificed by treaty; but it is said that such a provision of a treaty as would take private property without compensation must remain inoperative or suspended, until compensation has been made.   Such a construction would infringe upon the treaty-making power, and make its acts depend

103   Moore, Int. Arb., I, 147.
104   Art. V.

for their validity upon the will of the legislative department, while the Constitution provides that treaties shall be the supreme law. The clause of the Constitution referred to, is a restriction imposed upon the legislative department, in its exercise of the right of eminent domain. It must of necessity have reference to that department, which has the power to make compensation, and not to the treaty-making power, which cannot do it. This provision of the Constitution will not prevent the operation of the treaty upon the grant of the tenant. * * * The demandant must seek compensation for the loss of his land, from the justice of his country."[105] As a result of this decision numerous claims were presented to, and paid by, Congress for compensation for land, title to which was lost by operation of Article IV of the treaty.[106]

In Fort Leavenworth Railroad Co. v. Lowe, Mr. Justice Field, in delivering the opinion of the court, observed that, before the cession to a foreign country "of sovereignty or political jurisdiction" over territory within a State could be made, the consent of the State was necessary; and that, conversely, a State could not make such cession without the concurrence of the central government. The case decided in this relation only that lands acquired by the central government in a State, without the consent of the latter, were exempt from the legislative power of the State only when such lands were used as instrumentalities of the central government; and that lands acquired with the consent of the State for purposes specified in Article I, section 8, of the Constitution were entirely exempt from State legislation.[107] The same learned justice in the case of Geofroy v. Riggs said: "The treaty power, as expressed in the Constitution, is in terms unlimited except by those restraints which are found in that instrument against the action of the government or of its departments,

105 Little v. Watson, (1850) 32 Me. 214, 224.

106 A summary of reports on these claims and of appropriations to satisfy them is found in S. Rept. No. 2132, 58th Cong., 2d Sess., 5-9. See also act approved March 3, 1877, for compensating owners of certain lands ceded by the United States to Great Britain by this treaty. 19 Stats. at L. 343. That grants by the government de facto in disputed territory, which by subsequent treaty is admitted to belong to the other nation, are, in the absence of confirmation by the treaty, invalid as against grants of that other nation, see Coffee v. Groover, 123 U. S. 1.

107 114 U. S. 525, 537, 539, 540.

and those arising from the nature of the government itself and of that of the States. It would not be contended that it extends so far as to authorize what the Constitution forbids, or a change in the character of the government or in that of one of the States, or a cession of any portion of the territory of the latter, without its consent. Fort Leavenworth Railroad Co. v. Lowe, 114 U. S. 525, 541. But with these exceptions, it is not perceived that there is any limit to the questions which can be adjusted touching any matter which is properly the subject of negotiation with a foreign country."[108]   Likewise, Mr. Justice White, in his concurring opinion in the case of Downes v. Bidwell, observed: "True, from the exigency of a calamitous war or the necessity of a settlement of boundaries, it may be that citizens of the United States may be expatriated by the action of the treaty-making power, impliedly or expressly ratified by Congress. But the arising of these particular conditions cannot justify the general proposition that territory which is an integral part of the United States may, as a mere act of sale, be disposed of."[109]

In the consideration of this question a distinction is to be made between territory organized into States and that still in territorial form. In respect of territory within the boundaries of a State, it is not to be considered that the President and Senate will ever attempt by treaty to transfer title and sovereignty to a foreign power, except in case of extreme necessity in making terms of peace or in establishing boundaries. That the President and Senate, exclusively entrusted by the Constitution with the power of making treaties and without express limitation, and charged with the duty of conducting all negotiations with foreign powers, have the power to meet such an exigency, should it arise, is not to be doubted. Treaties for the submission to arbitration of disputed boundaries, which have involved territory over which States claimed jurisdiction, have from the first been concluded and their validity has never been successfully assailed. Mr. Justice McLean, in the case of Lattimer v. Poteet, observed: "It is a sound principle of national law, and applies to the treaty-making power of this government, whether exercised with a foreign nation or an Indian tribe, that all questions of disputed boundaries may be settled by the parties to the treaty. And to the exercise of these

108   133 U. S. 258, 267.
109   182 U. S. 317.

high functions by the government, within its constitutional powers, neither the rights of a State nor those of an individual can be interposed."[110] A treaty for the determination of a disputed line operates not as a treaty of cession, but of recognition.

In respect of territory not within the boundaries of a State, the central government exercises, subject to the express prohibitions of the Constitution applicable thereto, all the powers of government enjoyed by both the central and State governments over territory within the limits of a State. Accordingly, the power to cede such territory, if it exists as a power of government, resides in the organs of the central government. That the consent of the inhabitants of the territory to be ceded is essential to give validity to the transfer cannot be maintained.[111] The power to cede out-

110 14 Pet. 4, 14.

111 Hall, Int. Law (6th ed.), 46. It has nevertheless happened that as a matter of expediency, or through deference to the inhabitants of the territory to be ceded, the transfer has been made dependent upon such consent. A plebiscite of Savoy and Nice, under the treaty of Turin of March 24, 1860, for their transfer to France, and of the Danish Islands of St. Thomas and St. John, under the unratified treaty signed October 24, 1867, for their cession to the United States, was in each case taken. In the latter case, the government of the United States at first objected to the insertion of such a condition, but yielded in the end rather than to break off the negotiations. The Danish government was at the time very much interested in the subject of a vote of the people of North Schleswig. By Article V of the treaty of Prague of August 23, 1866, Austria transferred all her rights over Holstein and Schleswig to Prussia "with the condition" that Northern Schleswig should be ceded to Denmark, if by a free vote the population expressed a wish to be united to that country. Much to the disappointment of Denmark such a vote was not taken. Hertslet's Map of Europe by Treaty, III, 1722. Reports of the Sen. Com. on For. Rel., VIII, 169, 176, 198. In the unratified treaty signed November 29, 1869, for the annexation of the Dominican Republic to the United States, provision was likewise made for the expression of the will of the people as to the cession. Arts. I and IV. The retrocession under the treaty of August 10, 1877, by Sweden to France, of the Island of St. Bartholomew was made dependent upon a vote of the inhabitants. In 1860, the plebiscite in various Italian states was taken upon the proposition to consolidate with the Kingdom of Sardinia; but it was in each instance a question not of the cession of a portion of the state's territory, but of state extinguishment. Article III of the treaty of October 20, 1883, between Peru and Chile, provided for a plebiscite in the provinces of Tacna and Arica to determine to which of the two countries these provinces should ultimately belong. In the same treaty Peru, however, ceded unconditionally to Chile the territory of the coast province of Tarapacá.

lying territory is no less essential to the full exercise of the treaty-making power of the United States, which "extends to all the proper subjects of negotiation between our government and the governments of other nations," than is the power to acquire. Various treaties have been concluded by which the United States has relinquished extraterritorial rights theretofore enjoyed in other countries.[112] By the convention between the United States, Great Britain and Germany, signed December 2, 1899, the United States renounced in favor of Germany all its rights and claims in respect of certain islands of the Samoan group, in consideration of like renunciations by Great Britain and Germany in favor of the United States of all rights and claims to the Island of Tutuila and all other islands of the Samoan group east of longitude 171° west. As the result of decisions of tribunals of arbitration, to which the determinations of disputed boundary lines have been referred, territory over which the United States had theretofore exercised jurisdiction has fallen within the jurisdiction of foreign powers. Thus, to take a recent case, by the decision of the Alaskan boundary tribunal, constituted under the treaty with Great Britain of January 24, 1903, to determine the boundaries of Alaska as described in the treaty between Russia and Great Britain of 1825, Wales Island fell to Great Britain, although Russia, and her successor, the United States, had continuously exercised jurisdiction over the island since 1825, in which Great Britain had acquiesced. It also appears that the government of the United States had erected a public building on the island.[113] In treaties for the adjustment and direct settlement of disputed boundaries, notably in case of the Oregon treaty of 1846, and of the Florida treaty of 1819, the United States has accepted, in compromise, boundary limits much more restricted than those to which claim had been made. In the Oregon treaty, the United States accepted the 49th parallel, although the parallel of 54° 40′

112 See for recent instance, the treaty with Great Britain, signed February 25, 1905, in which the United States relinquished extraterritorial rights in the British protectorate of Zanzibar. The award of the arbitrators under the treaty with Great Britain of February 29, 1892, that the United States had no exclusive jurisdiction in the waters of the Bering Sea outside the ordinary three mile limit, was by virtue of the treaty the supreme law of the land and as binding on the courts as an act of Congress. La Ninfa (1896), 75 Fed. 513.

113 S. Rept. No. 2132, 58th Cong., 2d Sess.

had been claimed. In the reciprocal renunciations of the Florida treaty, the United States, in the language of the treaty, agreed to "cede to His Catholic Majesty, and renounce forever, all their rights, claims, and pretensions, to the territories lying west and south" of a line beginning at the mouth of the Sabine.[114] The United States had claimed the Rio Grande as the boundary. In referring to the Florida treaty, President Monroe, in his annual message of December 7, 1819, said: "On the part of the United States this treaty was evidently acceded to in a spirit of conciliation and concession. * * * For territory ceded by Spain other territory of great value, to which our claim was believed to be well founded, was ceded by the United States, and in a quarter more interesting to her [Spain]."[115] Resolutions were introduced in the House of Representatives by Mr. Clay, in which it was asserted that no treaty purporting to alienate any portion of the territory belonging to the United States was valid without the concurrence of Congress; and that the equivalent proposed to be given by Spain to the United States in the treaty for that part of Louisiana lying west of the Sabine, was inadequate. The resolutions were debated at length in the Committee of the Whole, April 3 and 4, 1820; but no vote appears to have been taken on them.[116] Mr. Clay in his argument admitted that a treaty could, without the co-operation of Congress, fix the limits of the territories of the United States in dispute "when the fixation of the limits simply was the object, as in the case of the river St. Croix, or the more recent stipulation in the treaty of Ghent, or in that of the treaty with Spain in 1795. In all these cases, the treaty-making power merely reduces to certainty that which was before unascertained. It announces the fact; it proclaims in a tangible form the existence of the boundary; it does not make a new boundary; it asserts only where the new boundary was. But it cannot under color of fixing a boundary previously existing, though not in fact marked, undertake to cede away, without the concurrence of Congress, whole provinces." He contended that if the subject were one of a mixed character, being partly of cession and partly for the "fixation" of prior limits, the consent of Congress was necessary; but that in the Florida treaty it was not pretended

---

114 Art. III.
115 Richardson, Messages and Papers of the Presidents, II, 55.
116 Annals, 16th Cong., 1st Sess., 1719-1738, 1743-1781.

that the object was simply a declaration of where the western limit was; that it was, on the contrary, the case of an avowed cession of territory from the United States to Spain.[117] Mr. Lowndes, of South Carolina, in replying to Mr. Clay, said: "In relation to questions of boundary, it was admitted on all hands that the treaty-making authority was competent to their adjustment; its competency must be equally admitted in relation to all unadjusted claims. He submitted then to the Committee, whether there could be any case of an adjustment of a claim to boundary, which did not include a cession of supposed right to territory by one or the other party. You may establish points; you may say there a colony was planted—here a man was shipwrecked; you may assert that these points include the territory to which you have a right; but the lines of your boundary must, after all, be adjusted by negotiation—by reciprocal agreement."[118] Mr. Anderson, of Kentucky, likewise observed: "There is nothing which can, under the distribution of powers in our Constitution, be more certainly assigned to the President and Senate, than the settlement of disputed boundaries. Probably, there is no single subject on which so many treaties have been made. None which is more peculiarly the attribute of the department to which belongs the peace-making power. From the very great extent of our territory, and the undefined state of its limits, on several sides, this power must be frequently called into exercise. Its frequent operation on the settlement of differences of this kind, must have been contemplated by the Convention; and it could never have been intended, that, in a general grant of the power, it should be construed not to apply to cases, which had been invariably, in all countries, the subjects of its operation."[119]

117 Id., 1726.
118 Id., 1734.
119 Id., 1774. See, for resolution in reference to the Oregon treaty, Globe, 29th Cong., 1st Sess., 979.

CHAPTER XV.

LEGISLATION TO GIVE EFFECT TO VARIOUS OTHER TREATIES.

§100. **Extradition of Fugitives from Justice.**—The only treaty stipulation for the extradition of fugitives from justice, antedating the treaty with Great Britain of August 9, 1842, is found in Article XXVII of the treaty with Great Britain of November 19, 1794. A requisition for the delivery of a fugitive, pursuant to this article, made by the British government in 1799, was complied with, although there was no statute of Congress which authorized the surrender or prescribed the manner in which the treaty stipulation should be given effect.[1] John Marshall, in his speech before the House of Representatives, March 7, 1800, in vindication of the action of the President in causing the fugitive to be delivered up, said: "The treaty, stipulating that a murderer shall be delivered up to justice, is as obligatory as an act of Congress making the same declaration."[2] Mr. Justice Catron, in In re Kaine (1852), expressed doubt as to the propriety of the surrender.[3]

---

1 Bee's Admir. Repts. 266. See also Fed. Cases, No. 16175; United States v. Cooper (1800), Fed. Cases No. 14865; In re Washburn (1819), 3 Wheeler's Crim. Cases 473.

2 Annals, 6th Cong., 614. Resolutions censuring the President were introduced in the House of Representatives by Edward Livingston, and supported by Albert Gallatin, but failed to pass by a vote of 61 to 35. Id., 533, 619.

3 14 How. 103, 111. Mr. Justice Catron describes the proceedings as follows: "The people of this country could hardly be brought to allow an interference of the President with the judges in any degree. The experiment was made during Mr. Adams's administration in 1799, and signally failed. Jonathan (or Nathan) Robbins had been arrested as a fugitive, under the 27th article of Jay's treaty, for murder in the British fleet. He was imprisoned at Charleston under a warrant of the district judge of South Carolina, and had been confined six months, when the Secretary of State addressed a letter to the judge, mentioning that application had been made by the British minister to the President, for the delivery of Robbins, according to the treaty. The letter said: 'The President *advises and requests* you to deliver him up.' On this authority the prisoner was brought before the district court on *habeas corpus*, and his case fairly enough heard, to all appearance, from the accounts we now have of it; and the judge ordered the surrender in the following terms: "I do therefore order

On the other hand, Mr. Justice Gray, in Fong Yue Ting v. United States (1893), said: "The surrender, pursuant to treaty stipulations, of persons residing or found in this country, and charged with crime in another, may be made by the executive authority of the President alone, when no provision has been made by treaty or by statute for an examination of the case by a judge or magistrate. Such was the case of Jonathan Robbins, under article 27 of the treaty with Great Britain of 1794, in which the President's power in this regard was demonstrated in the masterly and conclusive argument of John Marshall in the House of Representatives."[4]

Stipulations for the extradition of fugitive criminals were made in Article X of the treaty of August 9, 1842 with Great Britain, and in the special convention of November 9, 1843 with France. It was held in the first circuit that, under the treaty with Great Britain, fugitives could be apprehended and surrendered without any legislation to carry it into effect. The court expressly found

---

and command the marshal, in whose custody the prisoner now is, to deliver the body of said Nathan Robbins, *alias* Thomas Nash, to the British consul, or such person or persons as he shall appoint to receive him.' The prisoner was accordingly delivered to a detachment of Federal troops stationed there, to aid in the surrender; and they delivered him to an officer of the British navy, who was ready to receive him on board of a vessel of war, in which he was carried away. That the judge acted by order of the President, and in aid of the executive department, was never disputed; and the then administration was defended on the ground that the treaty was a compact between nations, and might be executed by the President throughout; and must be thus executed by him, until Congress vested the courts or judges with power to act in the matter; which had not been done in that instance. 5 Pet. Ap. 19; 7 Am. Law Jour. 13. The subject was brought to the notice of the House of Representatives in Congress, by resolutions impeaching the President's conduct in Robbins's case, and where Mr. Marshall (afterwards Chief Justice of this court) made a speech in defense of the President's course, having much celebrity then and since, for its ability and astuteness. But a great majority of the people of this country were opposed to the doctrine that the President could arrest, imprison, and surrender, a fugitive, and thereby execute the treaty himself; and they were still more opposed to an assumption that he could order the courts of justice to execute his mandate, as this would destroy the independence of the judiciary, in cases of extradition, and which example might be made a precedent for similar invasions in other cases; and from that day to this, the judicial power has acted in cases of extradition, and all others, independent of executive control." Id., 111-112.

4 149 U. S. 698, 714.

that the act to be done was "chiefly ministerial and the details full in the treaty."[5] Woodbury, J., said: "The treaty makes express provision that the certificate be made to the proper executive authority, in order that a warrant may issue by him for the surrender of the fugitives. Now, if a treaty stipulated for some act to be done, entirely judicial, and not provided for by a general act of Congress, like that before cited, as to examinations such as here before magistrates, it could hardly be done without the aid or preliminary direction of some act of Congress prescribing the court to do it, and the form. But where the aid of no such act of Congress seems necessary in respect to a ministerial duty, devolved on the executive, by the supreme law of a treaty, the executive need not wait and does not wait for acts of Congress to direct such duties to be done and how."[6] It was likewise held by the district court for the southern district of New York, Betts, J., that the provisions in the extradition convention with France for the investigation of charges of crime, and the arrest and imprisonment of the accused as for trial, were binding on the courts, and were to be given effect by the courts without other direction or authority.[7] A petition in this case for a writ of habeas corpus was dismissed by the Supreme Court for want of jurisdiction to review the proceedings of the district judge at his chambers. Mr. Justice McLean, in reading the opinion of the court, however observed: "Under the provisions of the Constitution the treaty is the supreme law of the land, and in regard to rights and responsibilities growing out of it, it may become a subject of judicial cognizance."[8] The Supreme Court of New York, Edmonds, J., held, however, that the convention with France was a contract between the two countries to be executed in the future, and that without such legislation the courts had no power to act in the matter; that although the convention might be regarded as executing itself so far as to establish the right of the government of France to the surrender of the criminal, legislation was required to enforce the delivery, and secure the subsequent possession, of the fugitive.[9]

5 The British Prisoners (1845), 1 Woodb. & M. 66.
6 Id., 73.
7 In re Metzger (1847), Fed. Cases No. 9511.
8 5 How. 176, 188.
9 In re Metzger (1847), 1 Barb. 248. See, for other instances, Moore, Extradition, I, 100.

The treaty is the supreme law of the land and so far as it prescribes a rule of action is to be enforced by the executive and the courts in the same manner as an act of Congress.[10] Whether auxiliary legislation is necessary to the effective enforcement is now largely a speculative question, since by the act approved August 12, 1848,[11] brought forward in sections 5270-5279, Revised Statutes, provision is made for carrying into effect not only past treaties but also those thereafter concluded.[12] The act designates the tribunals before which complaint shall be made, and prescribes the manner in which the fugitive shall be apprehended, heard, committed and surrendered upon the requisition of the foreign government, according to the stipulations of the treaty.

§101. **Apprehension of Deserting Seamen.**—The act approved March 2, 1829, as amended by the act of February 24, 1855, brought forward as section 5280, Revised Statutes (repealed by section 17 of the American seaman act of March 4, 1915), provided for the apprehension, examination, and surrender of deserting seamen, upon the application of a consular officer of any country with which the United States had treaty stipulations for the restoration of deserting seamen.[13] Stipulations of this character are found in many of the conventions concluded prior to March

---

10 "The treaty of 1842 being, therefore, the supreme law of the land, which the courts are bound to take judicial notice of, and to enforce in any appropriate proceeding the rights of persons growing out of that treaty, we proceed to inquire, in the first place, so far as pertinent to the questions certified by the circuit judges, into the true construction of the treaty." Miller, J., United States v. Rauscher, 119 U. S. 407, 419. "I concede that the treaty is as much a part of the law of the United States as is a statute." Waite, C. J., dissenting, Id., 434. "Had there been no law of Congress upon the subject, the method of procedure prescribed by the supplementary treaty of 1884 [with Italy] would necessarily have been the proper one, and the committing magistrate could have proceeded only according to the treaty, for that would have been the only law of the land applicable to the case and the only source of his authority." Lurton, J., Charlton v. Kelly, 229 U. S. 447, 464.

11 9 Stats. at L. 302.

12 Castro v. De Uriarte, 16 Fed. 93.

13 4 Stats. at L. 359; 10 Id. 614. "A case, where an act of Congress has been deemed necessary to aid the executive in enforcing treaties, is one passed 2 March, 1829, ch. 41, (4 Stats. at L. 359), for imprisoning deserters from foreign vessels, drawn up by myself." Woodbury, J., The British Prisoners (1845), 1 Woodb. & M. 66, 73.

2, 1829, the date of this act,[14] but, with the exception of the two conventions with France[15] no special acts to carry them into effect appear to have been passed.

§102. **Jurisdiction of Foreign Consuls.**—The act of April 14, 1792, passed at the suggestion of President Washington, to carry into effect the consular convention with France of November 14, 1788, the first consular convention to be ratified under the Constitution, did little more than designate the judges and marshals, whose duty it should be to render assistance to French subjects and French consuls according to the tenor of the treaty. The act related, principally, to the duties of American consular officers abroad.[16] It was the view of Mr. Justice Story that, without previous legislation by Congress, the judiciary could not carry into execution an award of a consular officer of Prussia in a dispute between the captain and crew of a Prussian vessel made pursuant to Article X of the treaty with Prussia of 1828.[17] By an act approved August 8, 1846, embodied in section 728 of the Revised Statutes, provision is made for the enforcement of awards of foreign consuls as stipulated for in Article X of the treaty with Prussia, as also in various other treaties.[18] The act approved June 11, 1864, embodied in Revised Statutes, sections 4079-4081,[19]

14 These include the conventions concluded: November 14, 1788, with France; February 22, 1819, with Spain; June 24, 1822, with France; October 3, 1824, with Colombia; December 5, 1825, with Central America; July 4, 1827, with Sweden and Norway; May 1, 1828, with Prussia; June 4, 1828, with the Hanseatic Republics; and December 12, 1828, with Brazil. See Tucker v. Alexandroff, 183, U. S. 424, 461.

15 See acts of April 14, 1792, 1 Stats. at L. 254, and May 4, 1826, 4 Stats. at L. 160.

16 1 Stats. at L. 254. For statutes to carry into effect stipulations in treaties giving certain judicial powers to American ministers and consuls in foreign countries, see especially acts approved August 11, 1848 (9 Stats. at L. 276), June 22, 1860 (12 Id. 72), July 28, 1866 (14 Id. 322), July 1, 1870 (16 Id. 183), and March 23, 1874 (18 Id. 23).

17 It appears that Mr. Justice Story prepared a bill for this purpose. See Mr. Buchanan, Secretary of State, to Baron Von Gerolt, Prussian minister, November 4, 1845, MSS. Notes to German States, VI, 121; Mr. Buchanan to Samuel K. Betts, D. J., October 27, 1845, MSS. Dom. Letters, XXXV, 302; annual message of President Polk, December 2, 1845, Richardson, Messages, IV, 399.

18 9 Stats. at L. 78.

19 So much of section 4081 as relates to the arrest or imprisonment of deserting officers and seamen was repealed by section 17 of the American seamen act of March 4, 1915. 38 Stats. at L. 1184.

further prescribes the manner in which stipulations in treaties giving consuls of a foreign nation jurisdiction of controversies between officers and crews of vessels of that nation, shall be enforced within the jurisdiction of the United States. It is specifically provided that the act shall take effect as to the vessels of any particular country having such a treaty with the United States only when similar provisions for the execution of the treaty is made by that country, and upon proclamation to that effect by the President.[20] It has been held that this statute, having been passed for the purpose of executing treaty stipulations for the arrest of seamen upon the requisition of foreign consuls, was to be regarded as prescribing the only means proper to be adopted for that purpose; and accordingly that the arrest of a seaman by a chief of police was unauthorized since the statute prescribed that the application of the consul should be made to a court of record of the United States, a judge thereof, or a United States commissioner, and that the arrest should be made by the marshal; but that, if after a seaman so arrested had been produced before the district court on habeas corpus and the court had found that the case came under the treaty and that he should be held, the mere fact that he was arrested by a person not authorized to do so, did not entitle him to a discharge.[21]

So far as the provisions in such treaties stipulate that the consuls of a foreign nation shall have the right without interference by the local authorities to decide differences arising between the captain and crews of vessels of that nation in respect of ship management, of such a character as not to disturb the public order of the port, they operate as the law of the land and are effective to deprive the courts of this country of jurisdiction of such controversies.[22] Article XVII of the treaty of commerce of February

20 13 Stats. at L. 121.

21 Dallemagne v. Moisan, 197 U. S. 169, 175.

22 The Burchard, 42 Fed. 608, The Bound Brook, 146 Fed. 160, and The Koenigin Luise, 184 Fed. 170, under Art. XIII of the treaty of December 11, 1871, with the German Empire (see, for different construction of this article, The Neck, 138 Fed. 144, and The Baker, 157 Fed. 485); Kendept v. Korner, Fed. Cases No. 7693, under Art. I of the treaty of April 30, 1852, with the Hanseatic Republics; The Elwine Kreplin, 9 Blatchf. 438, under Art. X of the treaty of May 1, 1828, with Prussia; The Salomoni, 29 Fed. 534, under Art. XI of the treaty of May 8, 1878, with Italy; The Amalia, 3 Fed. 652, The Marie, 49 Fed. 286, The Welhaven, 55 Fed. 80, Norberg v. Hillgreu, 5 N. Y. Leg. Obs. 177, Tellefsen v. Fee, 168 Mass.

6, 1778 with France was pleaded in bar to the jurisdiction of the district court of the United States in cases of captures by French privateers on the high seas and brought into our ports, and the plea sustained in British Consul v. Schooner Favourite (1794); Stannick v. Ship Friendship (1794); Salderondo v. Ship Nostra Signora del Camino et al. (1794); Reid v. Ship Vere (1795); British Consul v. Ship Mermaid (1795); and Moodie v. Ship Amity (1796).[23]

§103. **Protection of Industrial Property.**—Article II of the international convention for the protection of industrial property, signed at Paris, March 20, 1883, and proclaimed by the President, June 11, 1887, provided that the citizens of each contracting state should enjoy in the other states of the union the advantages in protection of patents, trade-marks and commercial names, which were accorded, or might thereafter be accorded, by law to citizens or subjects. By section 4902 of the Revised Statutes, the privilege of filing caveats in the Patent Office, preliminary to applications for patents, was limited to citizens of the United States and resident aliens who had declared their intention to become citizens. In a communication to the Secretary of the Interior, dated April 5, 1889, Attorney General Miller advised that the above stipulation of Article II of the convention was a covenant to grant in the future; that it was not self-executing, but required legislation to make it effective for the modification of existing laws; and that, Congress having passed no law for its execution, it could not be deemed to have extended the privilege, conferred by section 4902 of the Revised Statutes, to all the subjects and citizens of the countries, parties to the convention.[24] This view that the convention was not self-executing, but required legislation

188, Ex parte Anderson, 184 Fed. 114, and The Ester, 190 Fed. 216, under Art. XIII of the treaty of July 4, 1827, with Sweden and Norway. See also Waite, C. J., in Wildenhus's Case, 120 U. S. 1, 17.

23 Bee's Admir. Repts. 39, 40, 43, 66, 69, 89. See, however, Glass v. Sloop Betsey (1794), 3 Dall. 6, 16.

24 19 Op. 273. See for proposed legislation to give effect to treaty stipulations for the reciprocal protection of trade-marks and commercial names, S. Doc. No. 20, 56th Cong., 2d Sess., 95 et seq. See also acts of March 3, 1881 (21 Stats. at L. 502), and February 20, 1905 (33 Stats. at L. 724). See as to the necessity of legislation to give effect to various provisions of the convention of 1883, Mr. Bayard, Secretary of State, to Mr. Herbert, British chargé d'affaires, January 18, 1889. Moore, Int. Law Digest, II, 42.

to give it effect, was adhered to by the Patent Office, and affirmed in 1903 in a decision of the Court of Appeals of the District of Columbia.[25] By section 4 of the act approved March 3, 1903, section 4902 of the Revised Statutes was amended and the privilege extended to any person.[26]

Article 4 *bis,* of the additional convention for the protection of industrial property, signed at Brussels, December 14, 1900, and proclaimed by the President, August 25, 1902, provides that a patent applied for in the different contracting states, by a person admitted to the benefit of the convention under the terms of Articles 2 and 3, shall be independent of the patent obtained for the same invention in other states, adherents, or non-adherents to the union. It further provides that this provision shall apply to patents existing at the time of its going into effect; and that the same rule shall apply, in the case of the adhesion of new states, to patents already existing on both sides at the time of the adhesion. The statutory law of the United States in force on the date of the proclamation of this additional convention, as judicially construed, limited the American patent granted for an invention, previously patented in another country, to the term of the foreign patent, but in no event should the patent be in force for more than seventeen years.[27] An act of Congress to effectuate the provisions of the additional convention was approved March 3, 1903.[28] In reenacting section 4887 of the Revised Statutes, no reference was made to patents existing at the time the convention went into effect; and it has been held that, as to patents then existing, article 4 *bis* did not enlarge the term of an American patent beyond the term of a foreign patent for the same invention, i. e., did not have the effect of removing the limitation prescribed by the statutes of the United States in force on the date of the issuance of the patent whereby the lifetime of a later domestic patent was limited to that of the foreign patent.[29] The

25   Rousseau v. Brown, 21 App. Cases 73.
26   32 Stats. at L. 1225, 1227.
27   §§4884, 4887, Rev. Stats.
28   32 Stats. at L. 1225.
29   United Shoe Machinery Co. v. Duplessis Shoe Machinery Co., 155 Fed. 842; Malignani v. Hill-Wright Electric Co., 177 Fed. 430; Malignani v. Jasper Marsh Consolidated Electric Lamp Co., 180 Fed. 442; Commercial Acet. Co. v. Searchlight Gas Co., 197 Fed. 908; Highland Glass Co. v. Schmertz Wire Glass Co., 178 Fed. 944; Cameron Septic Tank Co. v.

18

Supreme Court, by McKenna, J., in Cameron Septic Tank Company v. City of Knoxville, said: "If the treaty be construed, as we think it must be construed, in accordance with the declaration of the Conference at the instance of the American delegates, it has no application to the Cameron patent. If it be not self-executing, as it is certainly the sense of Congress that it was not and seems also to be the sense of some of the other contracting nations, and as the act of 1903 did not make effective Article 4 *bis,* the provisions of §4887 apply to the Cameron patent, and caused it to expire with the British patent for the same invention." Although it was held in the United Shoe Machinery Co. v. Duplessis Shoe Machinery Co. that Article 4 *bis* of the additional convention of 1900 was by implication controlled by the passage of the act of March 3, 1903, to give it effect, Putnam, J., in the course of the opinion, said: "Consequently, so far as judicial action is concerned, a later treaty has the same effect on a prior statute as a later statute has; and, so far as the conventions pertinent here are concerned, the fact that the Constitution commits to Congress the power 'to promote the progress of science and useful arts, by securing for limited times to authors and inventors the exclusive right to their respective writings and discoveries,' is of no consequence, because all the powers of Congress are especially vested, either directly or indirectly, by the Constitution in similar manner; and to hold that a treaty could not abrogate a prior statute regarding patents because this particular legislative power is committed to Congress could not be permitted so long as the general rule as to statutes superseding treaties, and, vice versa, declared by the Supreme Court in the way we have pointed out exists. The rules which we have explained with reference to the relation of treaties to statutes, and as to treaties becoming immediately effective, are the necessary sequence of the decisions explained in United States v. Lee Yen Tai, 185 U. S. 213, 220, 221, 222, 22 Sup. Ct. 629, 46 L. Ed. 878. But the respondent, now the appellee, maintains that Article 4 *bis* of the convention of 1900 was not effectual until enacted into a statute by Congress. An examination of the de-

City of Knoxville, 227 U. S. 39; Commercial Acetylene Co. v. Schroeder, 203 Fed. 276. See, however, opinion of Archbald, J., in Hennebique Construction Co. v. Myers, 172 Fed. 869, 885; Union Typewriter Co. v. L. C. Smith & Bros., 173 Fed. 288, 299.

cisions of the Supreme Court on this topic will show there is no practical distinction whatever as between a statute and a treaty with regard to its becoming presently effective, without awaiting further legislation. A statute may be so framed as to make it apparent that it does not become practically effective until something further is done, either by Congress itself or some officer or commission entrusted with certain powers with reference thereto. The same may be said with regard to a treaty. Both statutes and treaties become presently effective when their purposes are expressed as presently effective; and on its face Article 4 *bis* of the convention in question is so expressed."[30]

§104. **Miscellaneous Cases.**—Not infrequently a treaty, although forming a part of the supreme law, may, in order to be fully effective, require legislation to supplement it and impose sanctions for its enforcement.[31] Illustrative legislation of this character may be found in the acts approved: May 19, 1828, for the punishment of contraventions of Article V of the treaty with Russia of April 17, 1824, against the selling of spirituous liquors and fire arms to the natives of the northwestern coast of North America;[32] March 3, 1843, for the appointment of commissioners to run and trace the boundary line, for the payment of the sums pledged to the States of Maine and Massachusetts, and for the maintenance of a naval force to be employed on the coast of Africa in accordance with the stipulations of the treaty with Great Britain of August 9, 1842;[33] March 3, 1847, for the punishment of offenses declared to be piracy in treaties between the United States and other powers;[34] July 11, 1862, to carry into effect the treaty with Great Britain of April 7, 1862, for the suppression of the African slave trade;[35] February 29, 1888, to carry into effect the international convention for the protection of submarine cables, signed at Paris May 14, 1884, prescribing the fines and penalties for its violation and the manner in which they shall be imposed;[36] August 1, 1912, to carry into effect the convention signed at Brussels, September 23, 1910, for the unifica-

30 155 Fed. 842, 845.
31 Cushing, 6 Op. Atty. Gen. 293, 295.
32 4 Stats. at L. 276
33 5 Id. 623.
34 9 Id. 175; §5374, Rev. Stats.; §305, Penal Code.
35 12 Stats. at L. 531.
36 25 Id. 41.

tion of certain rules of law with respect to assistance and salvage at sea;[37] and August 24, 1912, to give effect to the convention between the United States, Great Britain, Russia and Japan, of July 7, 1911, for the preservation and protection of fur seals and sea otter of the north Pacific Ocean.[38] Acts of Congress to carry into effect treaty stipulations for the establishment of commissions to adjudicate and settle claims, or to determine and mark boundaries, are very numerous.[39]

In the Trade-Mark Cases, the Supreme Court, while holding that the acts of Congress of July 8, 1870, and August 14, 1876,[40] encroached on the powers of the States, by Mr. Justice Miller,

37 37 Id. 242.

38 37 Id. 499. Note may also be made of the acts of April 6, 1894, April 24, 1894, and June 5, 1894, to give effect to the award rendered by the Paris Tribunal under the treaty with Great Britain of February 29, 1892, concerning the preservation of the fur seals. 28 Id. 52, 64, 85. See also the act of January 5, 1905, to incorporate the American National Red Cross. 33 Id. 599.

39 See, generally, Moore, Int. Arb. See for acts of Congress to carry into effect stipulations in conventions for the adjudication or settlement of claims, those approved: June 30, 1797, Art. VI of the treaty with Great Britain of November 19, 1794 (1 Stats. at L. 523); March 3, 1823, Art. IX of the treaty with Spain of February 22, 1819 (3 Id., 768); March 2, 1833, convention with the Two Sicilies of October 14, 1832 (4 Id., 666); July 13, 1832, convention with France of July 4, 1831 (4 Id., 574); March 2, 1827, convention with Great Britain of November 13, 1826 (4 Id., 219); February 25, 1831, convention with Denmark of March 28, 1830 (4 Id., 446); June 7, 1836, convention with Spain of February 17, 1834 (5 Id., 34); June 12, 1840, convention with Mexico of April 11, 1839 (5 Id., 383); August 8, 1846, convention with Peru of March 17, 1841 (9 Id., 80); March 3, 1849, convention with Mexico of February 2, 1848 (9 Id., 393); March 29, 1850, convention with Brazil of January 27, 1849 (9 Id., 422); March 3, 1859, convention with China of November 8, 1858 (11 Id., 408); March 3, 1863, convention with Peru of January 12, 1863 (12 Id., 795); February 20, 1861, convention with Costa Rica of July 2, 1860, and with New Granada of September 10, 1857 (12 Id., 145); June 30, 1864, convention with Colombia of February 10, 1864 (13 Id., 323); May 16, 1860, convention with Paraguay of February 4, 1859 (12 Id., 15); June 27, 1864, convention with Great Britain of July 1, 1863 (13 Id., 195); March 28, 1864, convention with Ecuador of November 25, 1862 (13 Id., 37); July 20, 1867, convention with Venezuela of April 25, 1866 (15 Id., 18); April 7, 1869, convention with Mexico of July 4, 1868 (16 Id., 7); June 16, 1880, convention with France of January 15, 1880 (21 Id., 296); and March 2, 1901, Art. VII of the treaty with Spain of December 10, 1898 (31 Id., 877).

40 16 Stats. at L. 198; 19 Id. 141.

said: "In what we have here said we wish to be understood as leaving untouched the whole question of the treaty-making power over trade-marks, and of the duty of Congress to pass any laws necessary to carry treaties into effect."[41] Congress has the power to enact such legislation "as is appropriate to give efficacy to any stipulations which it is competent for the President by and with the advice and consent of the Senate to insert in a treaty with a foreign power."[42] At a meeting of the heads of the departments, November 21, 1793, during Washington's administration, Hamilton expressed the view that the President and Senate could make a treaty of neutrality which might prevent Congress from declaring war in that particular case. Jefferson and Randolph were of a different opinion.[43] Numerous treaties have but recently been entered into by which the United States has reciprocally undertaken "not to declare war nor to open hostilities" pending the investigation of the matter in dispute. Although Congress is given the right to make rules concerning captures, many stipulations to govern captures on the high seas have been entered into, and their validity does not appear to have been questioned by the Supreme Court in construing and applying them.[44] Mr. Marcy,

41 100 U. S. 82, 99.

42 Harlan, J., Neely v. Henkel, 180 U. S. 109, 121. The Congress shall have power to make all "laws which shall be necessary and proper for carrying into Execution the foregoing Powers, and all other Powers vested by this Constitution in the Government of the United States, or in any Department or Officer thereof." Art. I, sec. 8 of the Constitution.

43 Jefferson, Writings (Ford ed.), I, 268.

44 See The Pizarro, 2 Wheat. 227; The Nereide, 9 Cranch 388; The Bello Corrunes, 6 Wheat. 152, 171; The Santissima Trinidad, 7 Wheat. 283; The Neustra Señora de la Caridad, 4 Wheat. 497; The Amistad, 15 Pet. 518; The Amiable Isabella, 6 Wheat. 1; Fitzsimmons v. Newport Insurance Co., 4 Cranch 185, 199. In the early case of Bolchos v. Darrel (1795), in applying the provision in Article XIV of the treaty with France of 1778, for the confiscation of neutral goods found in enemy ships, it was held "that the law of nations would adjudge neutral property, thus circumstanced, to be restored to its neutral owner; but the 14th article of the treaty with France alters that law, by stipulating that the property of friends found on board the vessels of an enemy shall be forfeited." Bee's Admr. Repts. 74, 75. In advising Mr. Wheaton, minister to Prussia, June 28, 1844, of the adverse report of the Senate Committee on Foreign Relations on the proposed convention for commercial reciprocity with Prussia and other German States, Mr. Calhoun, Secretary of State, said: "If this be the true view of the treaty-making power, it may be truly said that its exercise has been one continual series of habitual and uninterrupted

Secretary of State, in an instruction to the American minister to Venezuela, December 9, 1854, declared that an article in a proposed treaty with Venezuela, signed September 20, 1854, which provided that in case one of the parties should be engaged in war with another state no citizen of the other contracting party should accept a commission or letter of marque against the former under pain of being considered a pirate, would encroach on the constitutional power of Congress to define and punish piracies and felonies committed on the high seas.[45] Provisions of this character are, however, found in many of our earliest treaties.[46] Mr. Justice Johnson, in The Bello Corrunes, (1821)

infringements of the Constitution. * * * So far, indeed, is it from being true, as the report supposes, that the mere fact of a power being delegated to Congress excludes it from being the subject of treaty stipulations, that even its exclusive delegation, if we may judge from the habitual practice of the government, does not." Moore, Int. Law Digest, V, 164.

45 Moore, Int. Law Digest, II, 978. President Cleveland, in his annual message to Congress, December 6, 1886, said: "The drift of sentiment in civilized communities toward full recognition of the rights of property in the creations of the human intellect has brought about the adoption by many important nations of an international copyright convention, which was signed at Berne on the 18th of September, 1885. Inasmuch as the Constitution gives to the Congress the power 'to promote the progress of science and useful arts by securing for limited times to authors and inventors the exclusive right to their respective writings and discoveries,' this Government did not feel warranted in becoming a signatory pending the action of Congress upon measures of international copyright now before it; but the right of adhesion to the Berne convention hereafter has been reserved. I trust the subject will receive at your hands the attention it deserves, and that the just claims of authors, so urgently pressed, will be duly heeded." Richardson, Messages and Papers of the Presidents, VIII, 505.

46 Art. XXI of the treaty with France of February 6, 1778; Art. XIX of the treaty with the Netherlands of October 8, 1782; Art. XXIII of the treaty with Sweden of April 3, 1783; Art. XX of the treaty with Prussia of September 10, 1785; Art. XIV of the treaty with Spain of October 27, 1795; Art. XX of the treaty with Prussia of July 11, 1799; Art. XXII of the treaty with Colombia of October 3, 1824; Art. XXIV of the treaty with Central America of December 5, 1825; Art. XXIV of the treaty with Brazil of December 12, 1828; Art. XXII of the treaty with Chile of May 16, 1832; Art. XXV of the treaty with Ecuador of June 13, 1839; Art. XXVI of the treaty with New Granada of December 12, 1846; Art. XXIV of the treaty with Guatemala of March 3, 1849; Art. XXVI of the treaty with Salvador of January 2, 1850; Art. XXVIII of the treaty with Peru of September 6, 1870; Art. XXVI of the treaty with Salvador of December 6, 1870; Art. XXVI of the treaty with Peru of August 31, 1887.

said: "Whatever difficulties there may exist under the free institutions of this country, in giving full efficacy to the provisions of this treaty [Article XIV of the treaty with Spain of 1795], by punishing such aggressions as acts of piracy, it is not to be questioned that they are prohibited acts, and intended to be stamped with the character of piracy; and to permit the persons engaged in the open prosecution of such a course of conduct, to appear, and claim of this court, the prizes they have seized, would be to countenance a palpable infraction of a rule of conduct, declared to be the supreme law of the land."[47] And the captors, American citizens, were denied a standing in the court. A very different question was involved in the proposed convention of October 18, 1907, for the establishment of an international court of prize, under which there was to be an appeal to the proposed court from the decision of national courts. Under the Constitution, the Supreme Court is as to the judicial power of the United States a court of last resort. To obviate the objection that might be raised in an attempt to provide for a direct appeal to an international court, the

47 6 Wheat. 152, 171. The act of March 3, 1847, (9 Stats. at L. 175), as brought forward in §5374, Rev. Stats., §305, Penal Code, provides as follows: "Whoever, being a citizen or subject of any foreign state, is found and taken on the sea making war upon the United States, or cruising against the vessels and property thereof, or of the citizens of the same, contrary to the provisions of any treaty existing between the United States and the state of which the offender is a citizen or subject, when by such treaty such acts are declared to be piracy, is guilty of piracy, and shall be imprisoned for life." The neutrality act of June 5, 1794, in section 9, and the supplementary act of June 14, 1797, in section 2, contained the qualification that nothing therein should be construed to prevent the prosecution or punishment of treason, "or any piracy defined by a treaty or other law of the United States." (1 Stats. at L. 381, 520). This language might be considered as an admission by implication of the efficacy of a treaty provision for the definition and punishment of piracy. In the neutrality act of April 20, 1818, section 13, amending and consolidating the laws relating to neutrality, the clause above quoted was so modified as to read "or any piracy defined by the laws of the United States." (3 Stats. at L. 447, 450). It may also be noted that the provision in the act of June 14, 1797, prohibiting with penal sanction the fitting out, in foreign parts by citizens of the United States, of any private ship or vessel of war to cruise or commit hostilities against the subjects or property of any prince or state with which the United States was at peace, was not brought forward in the act of 1818. The commission of such act within the territory of the United States has been prohibited since the first neutrality act of 1794. See §11, Penal Code.

United States proposed an amendment to the convention, by way
of a supplementary protocol of procedure, under which the action
in the proposed international court would be one de novo in the
form of a direct claim for compensation, the judgment to be in
the form of an award in compensation for the illegal capture irrespective of the decision of the national court involved.[48]   It

48 President Taft, annual message, December 6, 1910, For. Rel., 1910,
p. VIII; identic circular note, Id., 597.   In the identic note it is stated:
"The court contemplated by the prize convention of October 18, 1907, is
pre-eminently a court of appeal, with full power to review the decision of
a national court of justice, both as to facts and as to the law applied, and,
in the exercise of its judicial discretion, not only to affirm or reverse,
in whole or in part, the national decision from which the appeal is lodged,
but also to certify its judgment to the national court for proceedings in
accordance therewith.   The international prize court, therefore, is an ultimate court of appeal of which, by the convention, national courts are intermediate instances.   The purpose of the convention and of the conference
which adopted it undoubtedly was and is to secure determination by an
international tribunal of a controversy affecting neutral rights and property arising from capture and confiscation in war and by a series of well-
considered judgments to establish by international decisions the principles
of international prize law.   The Government of the United States is in
hearty accord with this purpose and desires to co-operate in its realization,
but is, however, of the opinion that the end in view may be effectuated
without violating the spirit of the convention and, indeed, without amending it, so that, for those countries unable or unwilling to submit the judgments of their national courts to international review, a simple expedient
may be devised by virtue of which the question in controversy, instead of
the actual judgment of the national court, may be submitted to the international court at The Hague for final determination without sacrificing substance to form, and without interfering with the practice of the United
States in such matters.   To illustrate this position by concrete examples
taken from controversies with Great Britain arising out of the Civil War:
Questions involved in the following cases upon which decisions had been
rendered by the Supreme Court of the United States were afterwards submitted to arbitration by the United States under the British-American
Claims Convention, sitting under Article 12 of the treaty of Washington,
dated May 8, 1871, for decision 'according to justice and equity': 1. Questions which the international tribunal decided adversely to the decision of
the Supreme Court of the United States, which international decisions
were obeyed by the United States: The Hiawatha, 2 Black 635, 4 Moore's
International Arbitrations, 3902; The Circassian, 2 Wallace 135, 4 Moore
3911; The Springbok, 5 Wallace 1, 4 Moore 3928; The Sir William
Peel, 5 Wallace 517, 4 Moore 3935; The Volant, 5 Wallace 179, 4 Moore
3950; The Science, 5 Wallace 178, 4 Moore 3950.   2. Questions in which
the decision of the international tribunal upheld the decision of the Su-

has been held that the provision in Chapter 2, Article XI, of The Hague convention of October 18, 1907, respecting the rights and duties of neutrals,—that a "neutral power which receives on its territory troops belonging to the belligerent armies shall intern them, as far as possible, at a distance from the theatre of war," which act of internment consists in disarming such troops and keeping them in honorable confinement,—does not violate any provision of the Constitution of the United States, or require legislation to render it effective, and is therefore a part of the law of the land which the President has full power to execute.[49]

"It is well settled that a good title to parts of the lands of an Indian tribe may be granted to individuals by a treaty between the United States and the tribe, without any act of Congress, or any patent from the Executive authority of the United States. * * * The question in every case is whether the terms of the treaty are such as to manifest the intention of the parties to make a present grant to the persons named."[50]

preme Court of the United States: The Peterhoff, 5 Wallace 28, 4 Moore's International Arbitrations 3838; The Dashing Wave, 5 Wallace 170, 4 Moore 3948; The Georgia, 7 Wallace 32, 4 Moore 3957; The Isabella Thompson, 3 Wallace 155, 3 Moore 3159; The Pearl, 5 Wallace 574, 3 Moore 3159; The Adela, 6 Wallace 266, 3 Moore 3159." Id., 599. It should be noted that the award in the case of the Springbok was solely for the damages sustained as the result of the detention of the vessel from the date of the erroneous decree of condemnation of the district court to the date of discharge under the decree of the Supreme Court.

49   Ex parte Toscano et al., (1913) 208 Fed. 938.

50   Gray, J., Jones v. Meehan, 175 U. S. 1, 10, citing, Johnson v. McIntosh, 8 Wheat. 543; Mitchel v. United States, 9 Pet. 711, 748; Doe v. Beardsley, 2 McLean 417, 418; United States v. Brooks, 10 How. 442, 460; Doe v. Wilson, 23 How. 457, 463; Crews v. Burcham, 1 Black 356; Holden v. Joy, 17 Wall. 211, 247; Best v. Polk, 18 Wall. 112, 116; New York Indians v. United States, 170 U. S. 1.

CHAPTER XVI.

TREATIES INVOLVING SUBJECTS OTHERWISE UNDER THE CONTROL OF THE INDIVIDUAL STATES.

§105. Distribution of Powers.—The supremacy of treaties over State legislation has, since the early decision in Ware v. Hylton,[1] been drawn in question only when they relate to subjects otherwise under the control of the States. Mr. Calhoun, in the debate in the House of Representatives, January 9, 1816, on the bill to give effect to the treaty of commerce with Great Britain of July 3, 1815, said: "The limits of the former [legislative power] are exactly marked; it was necessary to prevent collision with similar co-existing State powers. This country is divided into many distinct sovereignties. Exact enumeration here is necessary to prevent the most dangerous consequences. The enumeration of legislative powers in the Constitution has relation then, not to the treaty power, but to the powers of the State. In our relation to the rest of the world the case is reversed. Here the States disappear. Divided within, we present the exterior of undivided sovereignty. The wisdom of the Constitution appears conspicuous. When enumeration was needed, there we find the powers enumerated and exactly defined; when not, we do not find what would be vain and pernicious. Whatever, then, concerns our foreign relations; whatever requires the consent of another nation, belongs to the treaty power; can only be regulated by it; and it is competent to regulate all such subjects; provided, and here are its true limits, such regulations are not inconsistent with the Constitution. If so they are void. No treaty can alter the fabric

---

1 See supra, §70. For other cases in which Arts. IV and V of the treaty of peace of September 3, 1783, were enforced as the law of the land over inconsistent State legislation, see Jones v. Walker, 2 Paine 688; Hamilton & Co. v. Eaton, 1 Hughes 249; Lessee of Hylton v. Brown, 1 Wash. C. C. 298; Hopkirk v. Bell, 3 Cranch 454, 4 Cranch 164; Dunlop & Wilson v. Alexander's Admr., 1 Cranch C. C. 498; Ogden v. Blackledge, 2 Cranch 272; Lessee of Gordon v. Kerr, et al., 1 Wash. C. C. 322; Higginson v. Mein, 4 Cranch 415; Owings v. Norwood's Lessee, 5 Cranch 344; Carver v. Jackson, 4 Pet. 1, 100; Fisher v. Harnden, 1 Paine 55; McNair v. Ragland et al., 16 N. C. 516, 526. See Appendix, 514-516.

of our government, nor can it do that which the Constitution has expressly forbade to be done; nor can it do that differently which is directed to be done in a given mode, and all other modes prohibited."[2] At a later date, June 28, 1844, Mr. Calhoun, Secretary of State, in advising Mr. Wheaton, American minister, of the unfavorable report of the Senate Committee on Foreign Relations on the proposed convention for commercial reciprocity with the States of the German Zollverein, said: "The treaty-making power has, indeed, been regarded to be so comprehensive as to embrace, with few exceptions, all questions that can possibly arise between us and other nations, and which can only be adjusted by their mutual consent, whether the subject matter be comprised among the delegated or the reserved powers."[3]

§106. Treaties for Removal of Alien Disability.—The rule of law in this relation is disclosed in the decisions of the Supreme Court involving treaty stipulations for the removal of alien disability to inherit and dispose of real property,[3a] a matter, in the absence of a treaty, governed by the local law of the State in which the property is located, and not within the province of the central government,[4] but nevertheless a natural and usual subject of treaty stipulation. By Article IX of the treaty of November 19, 1794, with Great Britain, it was agreed, reciprocally, that British subjects who then held lands in the United States should continue to hold them, and might grant, sell, or devise the lands so held to whomsoever they pleased in like manner as if

2 Annals, 14th Cong., 1st Sess., 531.

3 Moore, Int. Law Digest, V, 164. See also Calhoun, Discourse on the Constitution and Government of the United States, Works (Cralle ed.) I, 202 et seq.

3a "There is an essential distinction between the cases of an alien acquiring by purchase, and by operation of law. * * * In the one case, he can take and hold the lands, and maintain an action for them. He continues seised until the inquest of office. In the other case, he cannot take at all, for the law, quæ nihil frustra, will not give the freehold and inheritance, since the alien cannot keep it, and it, therefore, takes no notice of an alien heir, who, as he cannot take by descent, shall not impede the descent to another. For the same reason, an alien cannot take by curtesy, dower, &c., because they are estates created by act of law." Kent, J., Jackson v. Lunn (1802), 3 Johns. Cases 109, 120.

4 United States v. Crosby, 7 Cranch 115; Clark v. Graham, 6 Wheat. 577; McGoon v. Scales, 9 Wall. 23; Brine v. Ins. Co., 96 U. S. 627; De Vaughn v. Hutchinson, 165 U. S. 566, 570; Clarke v. Clarke, 178 U. S. 186, 190; Blythe v. Hinckley, 180 U. S. 333, 341; 12 Op. Atty.-Gen. 6.

they were natives; and that neither they nor their heirs or assigns should, as regards these lands, and the legal remedies incident thereto, be regarded as aliens. In numerous cases it has
been held that the provisions of this article completely removed
alien disability of British subjects as to titles to lands in them at
the time of the conclusion of the treaty, and placed them and their
heirs or devisees, in respect of such lands, on the same footing as
citizens; that a title defeasible on the date of the treaty was by
this article completely protected and confirmed.[5] In the leading
case of Fairfax's Devisee v. Hunter's Lessee, decided in 1813,
the Supreme Court, by Mr. Justice Story, said: "Now, we cannot yield to the argument that Denny Fairfax [a British subject]
had no title, but a mere naked possession or trust estate. In our
judgment, by virtue of the devise to him, he held a fee simple in
his own right. At the time of the commencement of this suit (in
1791) he was in complete possession and seizin of the land. That
possession and seizin continued up to and after the treaty of 1794,
which being the supreme law of the land, confirmed the title to
him, his heirs and assigns, and protected him from any forfeiture
by reason of alienage. It was once in the power of the commonwealth of Virginia, by an inquest of office or its equivalent, to
have vested the estate completely in itself or its grantee. But it
has not so done, and its own inchoate title (and of course the
derivative title, if any, of its grantee) has by operation of the
treaty become ineffectual and void. It becomes unnecessary to

---

5 Fairfax's Devisee v. Hunter's Lessee (1813), 7 Cranch 603; Harden
v. Fisher (1816), 1 Wheat. 300; Jackson v. Clarke (1818), 3 Wheat. 1;
Craig v. Radford (1818), 3 Wheat. 594; Orr v. Hodgson (1819), 4 Wheat.
453; Blight's Lessee v. Rochester (1822), 7 Wheat. 535; Society for Propaga-
tion of Gosepl &c. v. Town of New Haven (1823), 8 Wheat. 464; Hughes
v. Edwards (1824), 9 Wheat. 489; Society for Propagation of Gospel &c.
v. Wheeler (1814), 2 Gall. 105; Megrath v. Admrs. of John and Ann
Robertson (1795), 1 Desaus. Eq. 445; Jackson v. Lunn (1802), 3 Johns.
Cases 109; Jackson v. Wright (1809), 4 Johns. 75; Commonwealth v.
Sheafe (1810), 6 Mass. 441; Jackson v. Decker (1814), 11 Johns. 418;
Fox v. Southack (1815), 12 Mass. 143; Duncan v. Beard (1820), 2 Nott
& McC. 400; McNair v. Ragland (1830), 16 N. C. 516; Stephen's Heirs
v. Swann (1838), 9 Leigh 404; May v. Specht (1849), 1 Manning 187;
Foxwell v. Craddock (1855), 1 Pat. & H. 250; Fiott v. Commonwealth
(1855), 12 Grat. 564; Munro v. Merchant (1858), 26 Barb. 383; Watson
v. Donnelly (1859), 28 Barb. 653; People v. Snyder (1868), 51 Barb. 589;
Crane v. Reeder (1870), 21 Mich. 24. See Appendix, 517, 522.

consider the argument as to the effect of the death of Denny Fairfax, pending the suit, because admitting it to be correctly applied in general, the treaty of 1794 completely avoids it. The heirs of Denny Fairfax were made capable in law to take from him by descent, and the freehold was not, therefore, on his death, cast upon the commonwealth."[6] Of Article XI of the treaty of commerce with France of February 6, 1778, Chief Justice Marshall, in 1817, in the case of Chirac v. Chirac, said: "Upon every principle of fair construction, this article gave to the subjects of France a right to purchase and hold lands in the United States." It was further held in this case that the provision in Article VII of the treaty of September 30, 1800, with France,—that the citizens or subjects of one country might dispose of, by testament, donation, or otherwise, lands holden in the territory of the other, in favor of such persons as they should think proper, and might inherit the same without being obliged to take out letters of naturalization—applied to those who took by descent as well as to those who acquired by purchase; that under the qualifying provision,—that in case the laws of either of the two countries should restrain strangers from the exercise of the rights of property with respect to real estate, such real estate might be sold or otherwise disposed of to the citizens or inhabitants of the country where it might be—a French subject had the right during life to sell or otherwise dispose of lands acquired by descent or devise, if located in a State where, except for the treaty, they would be immediately escheatable; and that the instant the descent was cast on a French subject his rights became complete and could not be affected by the subsequent expiration of the treaty.[7] Again in the later case of Geofroy v. Riggs, decided in 1890, it was held that this article in the treaty of 1800 with France by its terms suspended, during the existence of the treaty, the provisions of the common law of Maryland and of the statutes of that State of 1780 and 1791, so far as by their terms they prevented citizens of France from taking by inheritance from citizens of the United States real or personal property situated therein.[8] In Hauenstein v. Lynham, decided in 1879, it was held that the provision in Article V of the treaty of November 25, 1850, with Switzerland,

6 7 Cranch 603, 627.
7 2 Wheat. 259, 271. See also Carneal v. Banks (1825), 10 Wheat. 181.
8 133 U. S. 258.

—that in case real estate situated within the territories of one of the contracting parties should fall to a citizen of the other party, who on account of his being an alien could not hold such property in the State or canton in which it was situated, such term as the laws of the State or canton permitted should be accorded to the said heir or successor to sell the same,—was the supreme law of the land and so far removed the incapacity of a subject of Switzerland, next of kin of the intestate, as to entitle him to recover and sell the lands of which his intestate died seized in fee; and that his rights thus secured by the treaty were not barred by lapse of time, inasmuch as no statute of the State, in which the lands were situated, prescribed the term within which they were to be asserted. In delivering the opinion of the court, Mr. Justice Swayne said: "If the national government has not the power to do what is done by such treaties, it cannot be done at all, for the States are expressly forbidden to 'enter into any treaty, alliance, or confederation.'"[9] In Geofroy v. Riggs, Mr. Justice Field, speaking for the court, said: "That the treaty power of the United States extends to all proper subjects of negotiation between our government and the governments of other nations, is clear. It is also clear that the protection which should be afforded to the citizens of one country owning property in another, and the manner in which that property may be transferred, devised or inherited, are fitting subjects for such negotiation and of regulation by mutual stipulations between the two countries."[10]

It is not now an open question that the removal of alien disability to inherit and dispose of real property is a proper subject of treaty regulation and within the treaty-making power, and that treaty stipulations to this effect override any inconsistent State legislation. This principle has been asserted not less clearly by the State than by the Federal courts.[11]

---

9   100 U. S. 483, 486, 490.

10   133 U. S. 258, 266.

11   People v. Gerke (1855), 5 Cal. 381; Yeaker's Heirs v. Yeaker's Heirs (1862), 4 Metc. (Ky.) 33, 39; Baker v. Shy (1871), 9 Heisk. 85; Wunderle v. Wunderle (1893), 144 Ill. 40, 53; Schultze v. Schultze (1893), 144 Ill. 290; Scharpf v. Schmidt (1898), 172 Ill. 255, 261; Adams v. Akerlund (1897), 168 Ill. 632; Fox v. Southack (1815), 12 Mass. 143; University v. Miller (1831), 14 N. C. 188; Watson v. Donnelly (1859), 28 Barb. (N. Y.) 653, 657, 660; Munro v. Merchant (1858), 28 N. Y. 9, 39; Jackson v. Wright (1809), 4 Johns. 75; Kull v. Kull (1885), 37 Hun 476;

In re Beck (1890), 11 N. Y. S. 199; Wieland v. Renner (1883), 65 How. Pr. Repts. 245; Opel v. Shoup (1896), 100 Io. 407; Doehrel v. Hillmer (1897), 102 Io. 169; Ahrens v. Ahrens (1909), 144 Io. 486; Succession of Rixner (1896), 48 La. Ann. 552, 565; Dockstader v. Kershaw (1903), 4 Pennewill (Del.) 398; Blythe v. Hinckley, 127 Cal. 431; Ehrlich v. Weber (1905), 114 Tenn. 711; In re Stixrud's estate (1910), 58 Wash. 339; Butschkowski v. Brecks (1913), 94 Neb. 532; Erickson v. Carlson (1914), 95 Neb. 182; In re Anderson's estate (1914), 147 N. W. 1098; In re Peterson's estate (1915), 151 N. W. 66; 8 Op. Atty. Gen. 411; Bahuaud v. Bize, 105 Fed. 485, 487. See note 5, supra, and Appendix, 591-605. "If the treaty-making power which resides in the Federal Government is not sufficient to permit it to arrange with a foreign nation the distribution of an alien's property, then that power resides nowhere, (since it is denied to the States), and we must confess our system of government so weak and faulty, as to be incapable of extending to its citizens in foreign lands that protection which is most common amongst a majority of modern civilized nations." Bryan, J., concurring, People v. Gerke (1855), 5 Cal. 381, 386. "But while it is true that 'the right of foreigners to hold title to real estate is entirely dependent on the laws of the State in which the land is situate' * * * it is also true that the State law must give way if it conflicts with any existing treaty between the government of the United States and the government of the country of which such foreigner is a subject or citizen. * * * In construing this article [Article VI of Constitution] it has been held, that provisions in regard to the transfer, devise or inheritance of property are fitting subjects of negotiation and regulation by the treaty-making power of the United States, and that a treaty will control or suspend the statutes of the individual States whenever it differs from them." Magruder, J., Wunderle v. Wunderle (1893), 144 Ill. 40, 53. Mr. Henry St. George Tucker in his recent very excellent work on Limitations on the Treaty-Making Power, 143-172, has quite clearly shown that in each of the examined cases it was in effect held that the treaty had changed the alien status of the subjects of the treaty power, as regards inheritance laws, rather than suspended the operation of the prohibitions of the State law against inheritance by aliens. This distinction is found in the language of the opinions in the early cases but does not seem to have been carefully observed in later ones. For instance, in the case of Geofroy v. Riggs, the language of the court in the opinion written by Mr. Justice Field is: "This article [Article VII of the convention with France of September 30, 1800], by its terms, suspended, during the existence of the treaty, the provisions of the common law of Maryland and of the statutes of that State of 1780 and of 1791, so far as they prevented citizens of France from taking by inheritance from citizens of the United States, property, real or personal, situated therein." (133 U. S. 258, 266). The power to remove by treaty the badge of alienage, i. e., to change the status of the alien to that of a native as to the particular right of inheritance, seems to carry with it the power to supersede a conflicting State statute. Such would, for instance, be the case if a treaty were concluded with a country conferring the right to inherit on the subjects of that country, which by the laws of a State were particularly prohibited from owning or inheriting real estate.

§107. Discriminatory Legislation.—It has been held by the Supreme Court of Louisiana that, under Article VII of the treaty of 1853 with France, French subjects are exempted from any tax on inheritances not imposed on citizens of the United States, and that a statute of that State inconsistent therewith is pro tanto inoperative during the continuance of the treaty;[12] that citizens of Bavaria are by virtue of the treaty of 1845 with that country likewise exempt from the payment of such tax;[13] and that, under Article XXII of the treaty with Italy of 1871, granting most favored nation treatment in the disposition and inheritance of real property, an heir, a subject and resident of Italy, is entitled to the same exemption from the payment of the tax imposed by the code of Louisiana on real estate inherited by a non-resident alien, as enjoyed by subjects of France, and that the provisions of the code must yield to the "treaty stipulations invoked as part of the supreme law of the land."[14] The Supreme Court of Washington has held that a statute of that State imposing an inheritance tax of 25 per cent. on all property passing to collateral relatives or strangers of the blood, who are aliens not residing in the United States, and of only 3 per cent. on property passing to citizens, is in conflict with Article VI of the treaty with Sweden and Norway of 1783, and must yield to it.[14a] And the Supreme Court of Iowa has likewise held that a provision in the code of that State which, while imposing an inheritance tax of 5 per cent. of the value of property passing to collateral relatives, subjects property passing to persons who are alien non-residents of the United States to a tax of 20 per cent. of its value, is in conflict with and must give way to Article I of the convention with Great Britain of March 2, 1899. This article provides that a citizen or subject of that country shall have the right to sell real property, which

---

12 Succession of Dufour (1855), 10 La. Ann. 391; Succession of Amat, 18 La. Ann. 403; Succession of Rabasse, 49 La. Ann. 1405, 1416.

13 Succession of Crusius (1867), 19 La. Ann. 369.

14 Succession of Rixner, 48 La. Ann. 552, 565.

14a In re Stixrud's estate (1910), 58 Wash. 339. The Supreme Court of Iowa has given a different meaning to the terms of this article, and has found no conflict between them and a State statute which places a tax of 20 per cent. on property passing to alien non-residents and a tax of only 5 per cent. on that passing to citizens. In re Peterson's estate (1915), 151 N. W. 66.

would pass to him were he not disqualified by alienage, and to remove the proceeds therefrom without restraint or interference and "exempt from any succession, probate or administrative duties or charges" other than those which may be imposed in like case upon citizens of the United States. The court said: "It is elementary that treaty provisions between the United States and a foreign nation have force and effect paramount to acts of State legislation."[14b] The Supreme Court held, in Prevost v. Greneaux[15] (1856), that Article VII of the treaty with France, concluded February 23, 1853, had no effect upon the succession of a person who had died in 1848; and, in Frederickson v. State of Louisiana[16] (1859), that Article III of the treaty with Württemberg of April 10, 1844, did not include the case of a subject of one of the respective countries, who resided in his native country and there disposed of property in favor of a citizen or subject of the other, and that, consequently, a statute of the State of Louisiana which imposed a tax of 10 per cent. of the amount of certain legacies left by a citizen of that State to subjects of the King of Württemberg was not in conflict with the treaty.

Article VI of the treaty with China of July 28, 1868 provided that, reciprocally, the citizens or subjects of the one visiting or residing in the territory of the other should enjoy the same privileges, immunities and exemptions in respect of travel or residence as enjoyed by the citizens or subjects of the most favored nation. Several cases involving this article came before the Federal courts of the ninth circuit, in which the supremacy of the treaty stipulation over inconsistent State legislation was asserted in unequivocal language. In Baker v. City of Portland (1879), although the decision was based on other grounds, Deady, D. J., declared the treaty provision to be the supreme law of the land to which an act of the legislature of Oregon designed solely to prohibit the employment of Chinese laborers on public works must yield. He added: "The State cannot legislate so as to interfere with the operation of this treaty or limit or deny the privileges or

---

14b McKeown v. Brown (1914), 149 N. W. 593, 595. The same conclusion was reached as to personal property in In re Moynihan's estate (1915), 151 N. W. (Io.) 504. See for a different construction placed by the same court on the terms of Article VII of the treaty with Denmark of April 26, 1826, In re Anderson's estate (1914), 147 N. W. 1098.

15 19 How. 1.

16 23 How. 445.

19

immunities granted by it to the Chinese residents of this country. * * * So far as this court and the case before it is concerned, the treaty furnishes the law, and with that treaty no State or municipal corporation thereof can interfere. Admit the wedge of State interference ever so little, and there is nothing to prevent its being driven home and destroying the treaty and overriding the treaty-making power altogether."[17] In Chapman v. Toy Long (1876), the same judge said that the provisions in mining regulations which in effect prohibited Chinamen from working in a mining claim for themselves or for others, as well as the clause of the State constitution to the same effect, seemed to be in direct conflict with this article of the treaty with China, and, if so, that they were void.[18] In the case of Tiburcio Parrott (1880), a provision in the constitution of the State of California, and an act of the legislature to give it effect, which prohibited any corporation formed under the laws of the State from employing Chinese or Mongolians, were declared to be void and of no effect because in violation of the provisions of the treaty with China and of the Fourteenth Amendment to the Constitution. Hoffman, D. J., said: "The demand therefore that the treaty shall be rescinded or modified is reasonable and legitimate. But while that treaty exists, the Chinese have the same right of immigration and residence as are possessed by any other foreigners. Those rights it is the duty of the courts to maintain, and of the government to enforce."[19] Upon this question, Sawyer, C. J., in the leading opinion, although he found the inhibitions of the Fourteenth Amendment sufficient to cover the case, said: "There can be no mistaking the significance, or effect of these plain, concise, emphatic provisions [Art. I, Sec. 10, Art. II, Sec. 2, and Art. VI of the Constitution]. The States have surrendered the treaty-making power to the general government, and vested it in the President and Senate; and when duly exercised by the President and Senate, the treaty resulting is the supreme law of the land, to which not only State laws, but State constitutions, are in express terms subordinated. * * * Any legislation or constitutional provision of the State of California which limits or restricts that right to labor to any extent, or in any manner not applicable to

17 5 Sawy. 566, 569, 570. See Heim v. McCall, infra, 422.
18 4 Sawy. 28, 36.
19 6 Sawy. 349, 366.

citizens of other foreign nations visiting or residing in California, is in conflict with this provision of the treaty; and such are the express provisions of the constitution and statute in question. * * * As to the point whether the provision in question is within the treaty-making power, I have as little doubt as upon the point already discussed. Among all civilized nations, in modern times at least, the treaty-making power has been accustomed to determine the terms and conditions upon which the subjects of the parties to the treaty shall reside in the respective countries, and the treaty-making power is conferred by the Constitution in unlimited terms. * * * If it has authority to stipulate that aliens residing in a State may acquire and hold property, and on their death transmit it to alien heirs who do not reside in the State, against the provisions of the laws of the State, otherwise valid—and so the authorities already cited hold—then it, certainly, must be competent for the treaty-making power to stipulate that aliens residing in a State in pursuance of the treaty may labor in order that they may live and acquire property that may be so held, enjoyed, and thus transmitted to alien heirs."[20] Again, in In re Ah Chong, a statute of California which prohibited all aliens incapable of becoming electors of the State from fishing in the waters of the State (taken in connection with various contemporaneous statutes expressly aimed against the Chinese) was declared by the same learned justice to violate the Fourteenth Amendment to the Constitution and Articles V and VI of the treaty with China, and therefore to be void.[21] In the case of Lee Sing[22] it was held that an ordinance of the city of San Francisco, which declared it to be unlawful for any Chinese to locate, reside, or carry on business within the limits of the city and county of San Francisco, except in a certain prescribed district, and required all Chinese inhabitants theretofore located outside

---

20 Id., 369, 375-376. In the recent case of Truax et al. v. Raich (decided November 1, 1915), the Supreme Court held that a statute of the State of Arizona, which prohibited the employment by any corporation, partnership or individual, of less than eighty per cent. qualified electors or native-born citizens in case more than five workers were employed at any one time, was discriminatory and invalid under the Fourteenth Amendment. The court found it unnecessary to pass upon any question of treaty rights.

21 6 Sawy. 451, 455. See, however, Leong Mow v. Board of Commissioners (1911), 185 Fed. 223.

22 43 Fed. (1890), 359.

the prescribed district to remove within a specified time, was in violation of our treaty pledge with China. And in Gandolfo v. Hartman,[23] the circuit court, southern district of California, Ross, D. J., held that a covenant in a deed not to convey or to lease to a Chinaman was in contravention of our treaty with China and not enforceable in a court of equity of the United States.[24] In Quong Woo,[25] Mr. Justice Field, in circuit, declared an ordinance of the city of San Francisco, which arbitrarily prohibited the conduct of the laundry business within certain sections of the city, to be in contravention of the treaty provisions with China. Although in each of the above cases it seems that the inhibitions of the Fourteenth Amendment to the Constitution were sufficient to cover the case, the court took occasion to assert the supremacy of the treaty over the inconsistent State acts. In Yick Wo v. Hopkins, the Supreme Court held that the subjects of the Emperor of China, who had the right temporarily or permanently to reside within the United States, were entitled to enjoy the protection guaranteed by the Constitution and afforded by the laws, and that an administration of a municipal ordinance for the carrying on of a lawful business within the corporate limits violated the provisions of the Constitution if it made arbitrary and unjust discriminations, founded on differences of race, between persons otherwise in similar circumstances.[26]   Chief Justice Waite, in delivering the opinion of the court in Baldwin v. Franks, said: "That the treaty-making power has been surrendered by the States and given to the United States, is unquestionable. It is true, also, that the treaties made by the United States and in force are part of the supreme law of the land, and that they are as binding within the territorial limits of the States as they are elsewhere throughout the dominion of the United States * * * That the United States have power under the Constitu-

---

23 49 Fed. (1892), 181.

24 See also Duck Lee v. Boise Development Co. (1912), 21 Idaho 461, holding that citizens of the Chinese Empire residing permanently or temporarily in the United States, being granted the same rights, privileges, immunities and exemptions as enjoyed by citizens and subjects of the most-favored-nation, are entitled to hold a lease interest in real estate in Idaho.

25 13 Fed. (1882), 229, 233.

26 118 U. S. 356. See also Barbier v. Connolly, 113 U. S. 27; Soon Hing v. Crowley, 113 U. S. 703.

tion to provide for the punishment of those who are guilty of depriving Chinese subjects of any of the rights, privileges, immunities, or exemptions guaranteed to them by this treaty [Articles II and III of the treaty of 1880], we do not doubt." It was however held that such provision had not been made either in §5519, §5508, or in §5336 of the Revised Statutes.[27]

In October, 1906, the board of education of San Francisco adopted a resolution by which the principals of schools were directed to send all Chinese, Japanese, or Korean children to a certain school called the Oriental Public School. Japanese children were thereafter denied admission to the regular public schools of the city. The Japanese government immediately entered a protest against the enforcement of the resolution as in violation of treaty rights secured to Japanese subjects by Article I of the treaty of 1894. Proceedings were instituted in the Federal courts as also in the State courts to determine the issues, but, upon the diplomatic adjustment of the controversy, were terminated before decisions were reached. Much discussion was evoked at the time upon the questions; first, whether the enforcement of the regulation would be in contravention of the provisions of the treaty; and, second, whether, admitting the construction of the treaty as claimed by the Japanese government to be correct, it was competent for the treaty-making power to deprive the local State authorities of the right to adopt the school regulation in question.[28] Of this second question, Mr. Root, then Secretary of State, in an address at the annual meeting of the American Society of International Law, April 19, 1907, said: "The treaty did assert the right of the United States, by treaty, to assure to the citizens of a foreign nation residing in American territory equality of treatment with the citizens of other foreign nations, so that if any State chooses to extend privileges to alien residents as well as to citizen residents, the State will be forbidden by the obligation of the treaty to discriminate against the resident citizens of the particular country with which the treaty is made, and will be forbidden to deny to them the privileges which it grants to the cit-

27 120 U. S. 678, 682, 683.
28 See Cong. Record, 59th Cong., 2d Sess., 297, 301, 303, 674, 1231, 1234, 1235, 1236, 1237, 1515, 1522, 1523, 1579, 3132; Proceedings of the American Society of International Law, April 19-20, 1907, 44, 150, 173, 194, 201, 211, 213.

izens of other foreign countries. The effect of such a treaty, in respect of education, is not positive and compulsory; it is negative and prohibitory. It is not a requirement that the State shall furnish education; it is a prohibition against discrimination when the State does choose to furnish education. * * * Reciprocal agreements between nations regarding the treatment which the citizens of each nation shall receive in the territory of the other nation are among the most familiar, ordinary, and unquestioned exercises of the treaty-making power. To secure the citizens of one's country against discriminatory laws and discriminatory administration in the foreign countries where they may travel or trade or reside is, and always has been, one of the chief objects of treaty making, and such provisions always have been reciprocal. * * * Since the rights, privileges, and immunities, both of person and property, to be accorded to foreigners in our country and to our citizens in foreign countries are a proper subject of treaty provision and within the limits of the treaty-making power, and since such rights, privileges, and immunities may be given by treaty in contravention of the laws of any State it follows of necessity that the treaty-making power alone has authority to determine what those rights, privileges, and immunities shall be. No State can set up its laws as against the grant of any particular right, privilege, or immunity any more than against the grant of any other right, privilege, or immunity. No State can say a treaty may grant to alien residents equality of treatment as to property but not as to education, or as to the exercise of religion and as to burial but not as to education, or as to education but not as to property or religion. That would be substituting the mere will of the State for the judgment of the President and Senate in exercising a power committed to them and prohibited to the States by the Constitution."[29]

It has been held that Articles II, III, and XXIII of the treaty with Italy of 1871, stipulating that citizens of each contracting party shall receive in the States and Territories of the other the most constant protection and security for their persons and property and shall enjoy in this respect the same rights and privileges

29 Proceedings, 48, 50, 54. See The Japanese Immigrant Case, 189 U. S. 86; Wong Wai v. Williamson, 103 Fed. 1; and The Tokai Maru, 190 Fed. 450, involving the rights of Japan under Arts. I and II of the treaty of November 22, 1894, Appendix, 547.

as granted to natives on their submitting to the conditions imposed
upon natives, are fully complied with "if an Italian subject, sojourning in this country, is himself given all the direct protection
and security afforded by the laws to our own citizens, including
all rights of action for himself or his personal representatives to
safeguard the protection, and security, * * * without going
further and giving to his non-resident alien relatives a right of
action for death, although such action is afforded to native resident relatives, and although the existence of such action may indirectly promote his safety." Mr. Justice Moody, in writing the
opinion of the court, observed: "We do not deem it necessary to
consider the constitutional limits of the treaty-making power. A
treaty, within those limits, by the express words of the Constitution, is the supreme law of the land, binding alike national and
State courts, and is capable of enforcement, and must be enforced
by them in the litigation of private rights."[30] The treaty only requires equality of treatment, and that the same rights and privileges be accorded to a subject of Italy as are accorded to a citizen
of the United States under like circumstances.[31] It has been held
that a statute of the State of Pennsylvania, which prohibits the

30 Maiorano v. Baltimore & Ohio R. R. Co., 213 U. S. 268, 272. See
also Fulco v. Schuylkill Stone Co., 163 Fed. 124; 169 Fed. 98; Deni v.
Penna. R. R. Co., 181 Pa. 525; Zeiger v. Penna. R. R. Co., 151 Fed. 348;
158 Fed. 809; Debitulia v. Lehigh & Coal Co., 174 Fed. 886; Di Paolo v.
Laquin Lumber Co., 178 Fed. 877. See also For. Rel., 1910, pp. 657-673,
for correspondence between the two governments as to the alleged discrimination. In the later case of McGovern v. Philadelphia & Reading Ry.
Co. (1914), holding that residence and citizenship do not qualify the right
of recovery under the railroad employers' liability act of Congress of April
22, 1908, as amended April 5, 1910, the Supreme Court by McKenna, J.,
said: "In ruling upon the statute the district court considered that the
reasoning in Deni v. Penna. R. R., 181 Pa. St. 525, and in Maiorano v.
Baltimore & Ohio R. R., 213 U. S. 268, applied. In the Deni case the
Supreme Court of Pennsylvania, passing upon a statute of the State which
permitted certain named relatives to recover damages for death occurring
through negligence, held that the statute had no extra-territorial force and
that plaintiff in the action was not within its purview, though its language
possibly admitted of the inclusion of non-resident aliens. The Maiorano
case came to this court on writ of error to the Supreme Court of Pennsylvania, where the doctrine of the Deni case was repeated and applied.
This ruling was simply accepted by this court as the construction of the
State statute by the highest court of the State." 235 U. S. 389, 398, reversing 209 Fed. 975.
    31 Storti v. Massachusetts, 183 U. S. 138.

hunting and killing of wild game, and, "to that end," the ownership or possession of a shotgun or rifle, by an unnaturalized foreign born resident within the State, is not in contravention of the treaty. Mr. Justice Holmes, speaking for the court, said: "As to Article 2 it will be time enough to consider whether the statute can be construed or upheld as precluding Italians from possessing a stock of guns for purposes of trade when such a case is presented. The act was passed for an object with which possession in the way of trade has nothing to do and well might be interpreted as not extending to it. There remains then only Article 3. With regard to that it was pointed out below that the equality of rights that it assures is equality only in respect of protection and security for persons and property. The prohibition of a particular kind of destruction and of acquiring property in instruments intended for that purpose establishes no inequality in either respect. It is to be remembered that the subject of this whole discussion is wild game, which the State may preserve for its own citizens if it pleases. Geer v. Connecticut, 161 U. S. 519, 529. We see nothing in the treaty that purports or attempts to cut off the exercise of their powers over the matter by the States to the full extent. Compagnie Francaise de Navigation a Vapeur v. State Board of Health, 186 U. S. 380, 394, 395."[32]

§108. **Administration of Estates of Deceased Aliens.**—In Succession of Thompson, the Supreme Court of Louisiana in 1854 held that a Swedish consul was not entitled under any law or treaty to take from an administrator, duly appointed under the laws of the State, the succession opened in the State as of a foreigner, a Swede by birth, not domiciled in the State but leaving property therein; and the court declared that such a right would be incompatible with the sovereignty of the State whose jurisdiction extended over the property of foreigners as well as of citizens found within its limits.[33] The same court, however, in the later case of Rabasse (1895) held that the reciprocal provision in

32 Patsone v. Commonwealth of Pennsylvania (1914), 232 U. S. 138, affirming 231 Pa. 46. See also Teti v. Consolidated Coal Co. (1914), 217 Fed. 443; Bondi v. MacKay (1913), 87 Vt. 271; People v. Warren (1895), 34 N. Y. S. 942; I. M. Ludington's Sons (1911), 131 N. Y. S. 550; City of New Orleans v. Abbagnato (1894), 62 Fed. 240; United States ex rel. Buccino v. Williams (1911), 190 Fed. 897; United States ex rel. Falco v. Williams (1911), 191 Fed. 1001.

33 9 La. Ann. 96.

the treaty between the United States and France of 1853 (adopting by virtue of the most-favored-nation clause the provision in Article XV of the treaty with Belgium of 1880), giving French non-resident heirs the right to be represented here by their consul, or his delegate, related to a subject within the treaty-making power. "It is idle," said the court, by Miller, J., "to call in question the competency of the treaty-making power, nor do we think any question can be raised that the subject of this treaty under discussion here is properly within the scope of the power. That subject is the rights of French subjects to be represented here by the consul of their country. On that subject the treaty provision is plain. The treaty by the organic law is the supreme law of the land, binding all courts, State and Federal."[34]

Article IX of the treaty of July 27, 1853 with the Argentine Republic provides that, if a citizen of either of the contracting parties shall die intestate in the territory of the other, the consular representative of the nation to which the deceased belonged "shall have the right to intervene in the possession, administration and judicial liquidation of the estate of the deceased, conformably with the laws of the country, for the benefit of the creditors and legal heirs." This provision was construed by different Surrogate Courts of New York,[35] the Appellate Division of the Supreme Court of New York,[36] the Supreme Judicial Court of Massachusetts,[37] and the Supreme Court of Alabama,[38] as giving to the foreign consul the right to original administration on the estate of a deceased countryman in preference to one entitled under the local statutes of the States, and was enforced as the law of the land. The Surrogate of New York county,[39] and the Supreme Court of California,[40] placed a different construction on

34   47 La. Ann. 1452, 1455. See also as to the right of a consul under a treaty to represent alien heirs in the settlement of estates, The General McPherson (1900), 100 Fed. 860; In re Holmberg's estate (1912), 193 Fed. 260; In re Peterson's Will (1906), 101 N. Y. S. 285; In re Davenport (1904), 89 N. Y. S. 537; In re Bristow (1909), 118 N. Y. S. 686. See Appendix.

35   In re Fattosini's estate (1900), 67 N. Y. S. 1119; In re Lobrasciano's estate (1902), 77 N. Y. S. 1040; In re Silvetti's estate (1907), 122 N. Y. S. 400.

36   In re Scutella's estate (1911), 129 N. Y. S. 20.

37   McEvoy v. Wyman (1906), 191 Mass. 276.

38   Carpigiani v. Hall (1911), 172 Ala. 287.

39   In re Logiorato's estate (1901), 69 N. Y. S. 507.

40   Rocca v. Thompson (1910), 157 Cal. 552.

the terms of the treaty, and found no conflict between them and the local law. The Supreme Court of the United States affirmed the decision of the Supreme Court of California in its construction of the treaty, namely, that "there was no purpose in the Argentine treaty to take away from the States the right of local administration provided by their laws, upon the estates of deceased citizens of a foreign country, and to commit the same to the consuls of such foreign nation, to the exclusion of those entitled to administer as provided by the local laws of the State within which such foreigner resides and leaves property at the time of decease." In view of this construction of the terms of the treaty, the Supreme Court did not pass upon the question of the power of the President and Senate by treaty to confer upon a foreign consul the right claimed.[41]

§109. **Miscellaneous Subjects.**—It was held by the Supreme

---

41 Rocca v. Thompson (1912), 223 U. S. 317. The Surrogate of New York county ruled that Article XIV of the treaty with Sweden of June 1, 1910, gave to consuls of that country a prior right to administer the estate of countrymen dying intestate in the United States; and that under the most-favored-nation clause the consuls of Italy (In re Baglieri's estate (1912), 137 N. Y. S. 175), and Austria-Hungary (In re Jarema's estate (1912), 137 N. Y. S. 176) enjoyed the same right. The Surrogate Courts of Schenectady (In re Lombardi (1912), 138 N. Y. S. 1007), Herkimer (In re Riccardo (1913), 140 N. Y. S. 606), and Erie (In re Madaloni's estate (1913), 141 N. Y. S. 323) counties made similar rulings. In each of these cases the provisions of the treaty were enforced as the law of the land regardless of local statutes. The Court of Appeals has, however, recently construed the provisions of the article as merely adding such foreign consuls to the list of those eligible as administrators so as to enable them to administer upon the estates of their fellow citizens when no one having a prior right under the local law is competent or willing to act, and as not intended to supersede the local law and confer a right of administration upon the foreign consul that is exclusive and permanent to all others. In view of this construction, the court held that, under the code of New York, in case a subject of the King of Italy died, intestate, in the State, leaving a wife, a child, a father and a mother residing in Italy, and a brother residing in the State, the latter, although he had no interest in decedent's estate, was entitled to letters of adminisration thereon in preference to the Italian consul. In re estate of D'Adamo (1914), 212 N. Y. 214, reversing 144 N. Y. S. 429. The ruling in D'Adamo has been followed in In re D'Agostino (1914), 151 N. Y. S. 957, and In re Comparetto (1914), 151 N. Y. S. 961. The same construction has been placed upon the provisions of the treaty by the Supreme Court of Minnesota in Austro-Hungarian Consul v. Westphal (1912), 120 Minn. 122, and by the Supreme Court of California in Fontana v. Hynes (1915), 146 Pac. 651.

Court, in United States v. Forty-three Gallons of Whiskey, that Congress, under its constitutional power to regulate commerce with the Indian tribes, not only might prohibit the introduction and sale of spirituous liquors in the Indian country, but might extend such prohibition to territory in proximity to that occupied by Indians; that it was competent for the United States, in the exercise of the treaty-making power, to stipulate in a treaty with an Indian tribe that, within the territory thereby ceded, the laws of the United States then and thereafter enacted to prohibit the introduction and sale of spirituous liquors in Indian country should be in full force and effect until otherwise directed by Congress or the President of the United States; and that a stipulation to this effect would operate proprio vigore and be binding on the courts, although the ceded territory was situated within an organized county of a State. The territory in question was part of an organized county of Minnesota; and it was contended that the treaty, so far as it aimed to exclude the jurisdiction of the State over the ceded territory and to interfere with the internal commerce of the State, was an invasion of the rights of the State and to that extent without validity. The court held otherwise. In writing the opinion of the court, Mr. Justice Davis said: "The power to make treaties with the Indian tribes is, as we have seen, co-extensive with that to make treaties with foreign nations. In regard to the latter, it is, beyond doubt, ample to cover all the usual subjects of diplomacy."[42]

In an opinion dated September 20, 1898, Attorney General Griggs advised that the United States had the power to enter into treaty stipulations with Great Britain for the regulation and protection of the fisheries in waters along the international boundary line between the United States and Canada, although the boundary waters were, on the American side, within the territorial jurisdiction of the several riparian States, and although Congress had no authority in the absence of a treaty to pass laws to regulate or protect fisheries within the territorial jurisdiction of the States. The regulation of fisheries had, he observed, frequently been recognized as a proper subject for international agreement, and in the instance before him such an agreement

42 93 U. S. 188, 197; reaffirmed in 108 U. S. 491, 494. See to like effect, Dick v. United States, 208 U. S. 340; Clairmont v. United States, 225 U. S. 551.

seemed necessary for adequate regulation.[43]   A treaty for this
purpose was signed April 11, 1908, and duly ratified.

In holding that a statute of California, which made it an offense
to disinter or remove from the place of burial the remains of a
deceased person without first having obtained a permit, for which
a fee of ten dollars was charged, did not violate the provision in
Article IV of the treaty with China, that Chinese subjects in the
United States should enjoy entire liberty of conscience and should
be exempt from all disability or persecution on account of their
religious faith, Mr. Justice Sawyer said: "Besides, it may well
be questioned whether the treaty-making power would extend to
the protection of practices under the guise of religious sentiment,
deleterious to the public health or morals, or to a subject-matter
within the acknowledged police power of the State."[44]   In a case,
which arose under the South Carolina Dispensary Law of 1892,
the United States circuit court, district of South Carolina, held
that the right to sell intoxicating liquors was not a right inherent
in a citizen or one of the privileges of citizenship within the protection of the Fourteenth Amendment, but a subject within the
police power of the States, and that an Italian subject, under Articles II and III of the treaty of 1871, had no greater rights in this
respect than a citizen of the United States. Simonton, D. J., however, added: "The police power is a right reserved by the States,
and has not been delegated to the general government.   In its lawful exercise, the States are absolutely sovereign.   Such exercise
cannot be affected by any treaty stipulations."[45]   The Supreme
Court of Louisiana[46] has held that a quarantine law enacted
by the State in the exercise of the police power, for the protection and preservation of public health, which empowered the
State Board of Health to prohibit the introduction of persons into
any infected portion of the State when in its judgment the introduction of such persons would increase the prevalence of the
disease, was not unconstitutional as infringing upon the power of

43 22 Op. Atty. Gen. 215. See also United States v. Rodgers (1893),
150 U. S. 249, 265; People v. Tyler (1859), 7 Mich. 161; International
Transit Co. v. City of Sault Ste. Marie (1912), 194 Fed. 522, affirmed in
234 U. S. 333.
44 In re Wong Yung Quy (1880), 6 Sawy. 442, 451.
45 Cantini v. Tillman, 54 Fed. 969, 976.
46 Compagnie Francaise, &c. v. State Board of Health, 51 La. Ann. 645,
662.

Congress to regulate commerce, or in contravention of treaties of the United States. The court, by Nicholls, C. J., said: "The treaties and laws of the United States must be held to have been passed with reference to and subsidiary to the rightful exercise of the police power by the different States, in aid of the protection and preservation of the public health within their respective borders." The decision of the court was affirmed by the Supreme Court of the United States, but on the ground that there was no conflict between the statute in question and the treaties, since the treaties were not intended to, and did not, deprive the United States of those powers (in this instance exercised by one of the States) necessarily inherent in it and essential to the health and safety of its people.[47] Mr. Justice Brown, in a dissenting opinion, in which Mr. Justice Harlan joined, found, however, a conflict between the State law and treaty provisions, and upheld the latter. "Necessary as efficient quarantine laws are, I know of no authority in the States to enact such as are in conflict with our treaties with foreign nations."[48]

§110. **Extent and Limitations of the Treaty-Making Power as Vested in the Central Government.**[49]—In a federal system of government, the sovereign body distributes the powers to be exercised respectively by the central and the local organs of government. The Constitution defines and limits those powers.[50] That a particular power may be exercised, it must be deposited in the one or the other, or in both of these organs of government. If not so deposited it remains dormant with the sovereign body, the

47   186 U. S. 380, 393. See also Olsen v. Smith, 195 U. S. 332.

48   186 U. S. 401.

49   See, generally, Moore, Int. Law Digest, V, §736; Anderson, Extent and Limitations of the Treaty-Making Power under the Constitution, Am. Journal of Int. Law, I, 636; Butler, Treaty-Making Power of the United States, I, 5, et seq.; Devlin, Treaty Power, 128 et seq.; Willoughby on the Constitution, I, 493, et seq.; Burr, Treaty-Making Power of the United States; Corwin, National Supremacy; Tucker, Limitations on the Treaty-Making Power under the Constitution.

50   "Sovereignty itself is, of course, not subject to law, for it is the author and source of law; but in our system, while sovereign powers are delegated to the agencies of government, sovereignty itself remains with the people, by whom and for whom all government exists and acts. And the law is the definition and limitation of power." Matthews, J., Yick Wo v. Hopkins, 118 U. S. 356, 370.

people, whose powers are in law unlimited. As by the Constitution of the United States, the entering into treaty engagements is expressly forbidden the States, the power to enter into any treaty, if it exists as a power of government, is vested in the organs of the central government, either finally, or subject to the co-operation of the States in its enforcement. Because of the failure of the States to co-operate with the Congress of the Confederation in fulfilling treaty engagements there was inserted in the Constitution the clear and concise language of Article VI declaring that all treaties made under the authority of the United States are the supreme law of the land, anything in the constitution or laws of any State to the contrary notwithstanding. There can be no doubt that the framers of the Constitution intended to provide for the full and efficacious exercise of the treaty-making power. By the word "made" in the clause, "treaties made, or which shall be made," in the definition of the judicial power of the United States under the Constitution, they intended expressly to include the treaties then existing. In these treaties are found stipulations prohibiting the exaction by any State of the droit d'aubaine or similar duties;[51] granting to aliens the right to dispose of goods, movable or immovable, by testament, donation or otherwise, and to receive or to inherit the same,[52] and various other rights of residence within the States;[53] conferring on foreign consuls certain rights in the administration of the estates of deceased countrymen and in the adjustment of differences between their countrymen;[54] and dealing with many other of the usual subjects of treaty regulation, which, except for the treaty stipulations, had, under the Articles of Confederation, been entirely within the control of the States.[55] With these treaty provisions the framers of the Consti-

51 Art. XI, treaty of commerce of 1778 with France.
52 Art. XI, treaty of commerce of 1778 with France; Art. VI, treaty of 1782 with the Netherlands; Art. VI, treaty of 1783 with Sweden; Art. X, treaty of 1785 with Prussia.
53 Art. IV, treaty of 1782 with the Netherlands; Art. V, treaty of 1783 with Sweden; Art. II, treaty of 1785 with Prussia.
54 Arts. V, VIII, IX, XII, of the convention with France signed November 14, 1788, but not ratified until after the adoption of the Constitution. Its terms had, however, been fully considered and authorized by the Congress of the Confederation.
55 See supra, §20. Notes to Treaties and Conventions (1889 ed.), 1221.

tution and the people who adopted it were familiar. By Article VII of the treaty of February 23, 1853 with France, the President of the United States engaged to recommend to the States of the Union, by whose laws aliens were not permitted to hold real estate, the passage of such laws as might be necessary to confer that right on French subjects. In fulfillment of this engagement a circular letter was addressed, October 19, 1853, to the governors of the States. Such recommendations have been exceptional.[56] What would be the ultimate result if this government were obliged to resort to this procedure? Few nations would enter into treaty stipulations with us granting such privilege to American citizens in exchange for a promise on our part merely to recommend to the various separate and independently constituted State legislatures the extension of a similar privilege to the subjects of those nations. No assurance that the States would comply with the recommendation could be given. It follows that this government as established under the Constitution would practically be incapable of entering into such agreements, and the clear purpose of those who framed the Constitution be defeated. This unfortunate consequence has been avoided through the tendency of the courts to recognize as within the treaty-making power as organized under the Constitution all those usual and customary subjects of negotiation between sovereign states, restricted in the exercise thereof by such limitations as are imposed on all powers of government under the Constitution. In Geofroy v. Riggs, Mr. Justice Field said: "The treaty power, as expressed in the Constitution, is in terms unlimited except by those restraints which are found in that instrument against the action of the government or of its departments, and those arising from the nature of the government itself and of that of the States. It would not be contended that it extends so far as to authorize what the Constitution forbids, or a change in the character of the government or in that of one of the States, or a cession of any portion of the

56 In Article XXVII of the treaty of May 8, 1871, the government of the United States engaged to urge upon the State governments to secure to British subjects the use of the several State canals connected with the navigation of the lakes or rivers traversed by or contiguous to the boundary line between the United States and British possessions, on terms of equality with the inhabitants of the United States. Letters were accordingly addressed by President Grant under date of November 29, 1871, to the governors of various States. For. Rel., 1871, p. 531.

territory of the latter, without its consent. Fort Leavenworth Railroad Co. v. Lowe, 114 U. S. 525, 541. But with these exceptions, it is not perceived that there is any limit to the questions which can be adjusted touching any matter which is properly the subject of negotiation with a foreign country."[57] That there are limitations on the treaty-making power as vested by the Constitution in the President and Senate, cannot admit of doubt; but an attempt to enumerate these limitations in more specific terms than here used by Mr. Justice Field would be idle. No case has arisen in which a treaty has been declared unconstitutional by the Supreme Court. "That the treaty-making power has been surrendered by the States and given to the United States, is unquestionable."[58] The government of the United States is invested with the entire control of international relations, and with all the powers necessary to maintain that control and to make it effective.[59] "While under our Constitution and form of government the great mass of local matters is controlled by local authorities, the United States, in their relation to foreign countries and their subjects or citizens are one nation, invested with powers which belong to independent nations, the exercise of which can be invoked for the maintenance of its absolute independence and security throughout its entire territory. The powers to declare war, make treaties, suppress insurrection, repel invasion, regulate foreign commerce, secure republican governments to the States, and admit subjects of other nations to citizenship, are all sovereign powers, restricted in their exercise only by the Constitution itself and considerations of public policy and justice which control, more or less, the conduct of all civilized nations."[60]

---

57 133 U. S. 258, 267. Again in the case of In re Ross, the same learned justice said: "The treaty-making power vested in our government extends to all proper subjects of negotiation with foreign governments. It can, equally with any of the former or present governments of Europe, make treaties providing for the exercise of judicial authority in other countries by its officers appointed to reside therein." 140 U. S. 453, 463. See also opinion of Heydenfeldt, J., in People v. Gerke (1855), 5 Cal. 381, 383.

58 Waite, C. J., Baldwin v. Franks, 120 U. S. 678, 682.

59 Gray, J., Fong Yue Ting v. United States, 149 U. S. 698, 711.

60 Field, J., The Chinese Exclusion Case (1889), 130 U. S. 581, 604, 605. See also Fuller, C. J., dissenting, Downes v. Bidwell, 182 U. S. 369; White, J., concurring, Id., 290, 294.

CHAPTER XVII.

JURISDICTION OF FEDERAL COURTS.

"The judicial Power shall extend to all Cases, in Law and Equity, arising under this Constitution, the Laws of the United States, and Treaties made, or which shall be made, under their Authority." Article III, section 2, of the Constitution.

§111. **Suits of a Civil Nature.**—By section 24, paragraphs 1,[1] and 17,[2] of the Judicial Code, approved March 3, 1911, the United States district courts have original jurisdiction of all suits of a civil nature,[3] at common law or in equity, arising under treaties made under the authority of the United States, where the matter in controversy exceeds, exclusive of interest and costs, the sum or value of three thousand dollars;[4] and of all suits brought by an alien for a tort only, in violation of the laws of nations or of a treaty of the United States, without limitation as to the value of the matter in controversy.[4a] Provision is made for the removal of such suits from a State court to a United States district court.

§112. **Criminal Actions.**—The President has on various occasions recommended to Congress the enactment of such legislation as deemed necessary to make offenses against the treaty rights of aliens, domiciled in the United States, cognizable in the Federal courts.[5] It is not to be doubted that Congress has the constitu-

---

1 See act of August 13, 1888, 25 Stats. at L. 433.

2 Rev. Stats., §563, par. 16.

3 For definition of "suits of a civil nature," see Weston v. Charleston, 2 Pet. 449, 464; Bank v. Turnbull & Co., 16 Wall. 190; Wisconsin v. Pelican Insurance Co., 127 U. S. 265; Hunt v. United States, 166 U. S. 424.

4 As to the determination of the amount involved, see Smith v. Adams, 130 U. S. 167; Schunk v. Moline &c. Co., 147 U. S. 500; United States v. Sayward, 160 U. S. 493; Citizens Bank v. Cannon, 164 U. S. 319; Vance v. Vandercook Co., 170 U. S. 468.

4a See for suit by an alien for tort only, O'Reilly de Camara v. Brooke, 209 U. S. 45.

5 "It would, I believe, be entirely competent for Congress to make offenses against the treaty rights of foreigners domiciled in the United States cognizable in the Federal courts." President Harrison, annual message, December 9, 1891. Richardson, Messages, IX, 183. "The necessity for some such provision abundantly appears. Precedent for constituting a Federal jurisdiction in criminal cases where aliens are sufferers is rationally deducible from the existing statute, which gives to the district and

tional power to enact the necessary measures for this purpose. Chief Justice Marshall, in the early case of McCulloch v. State of Maryland, said: "All admit that the government may, legitimately, punish any violation of its laws. * * * No trace is to be found in the Constitution of an intention to create a dependence of the government of the Union on those of the States, for the execution of the great powers assigned to it. Its means are adequate to its ends; and on those means alone was it expected to rely for the accomplishment of its ends. To impose on it the necessity of resorting to means which it cannot control, which another government may furnish or withhold, would render its course precarious, the result of its measures uncertain, and create a dependence on other governments, which might disappoint its most important designs, and is incompatible with the language of the Constitution."[6] Language equally unequivocal has frequently been used in the opinions of the Supreme Court. "There is no doubt of the competency of Congress to provide, by suitable penalties, for the enforcement of all legislation necessary or proper to the execution of powers with which it is intrusted. * * * But an act committed within a State, whether for a good or a bad purpose, or whether with an honest or a criminal intent, cannot

circuit courts of the United States jurisdiction of civil suits brought by aliens where the amount involved exceeds a certain sum." President McKinley, annual message, December 5, 1899, For. Rel., 1899, p. XXIV. "That Congress has the constitutional power so to legislate is not open to argument." Mr. Foraker, in a report from the Senate Committee on Foreign Relations, February 14, 1900, on a bill for this purpose. Sen. Rept. No. 392, 56th Cong., 1st Sess. See also President Roosevelt, annual message, December 3, 1906. For. Rel., 1906, p. XLIII. "I do not think that anyone, however—I will not say extreme, but however strong his view of the necessity of the preservation of State rights under the Federal Constitution—will deny the power of the government to defend, and protect, and provide procedure for enforcing the rights that are given to aliens under treaties made by the Government of the United States. * * * I cannot suppose that the Federal Constitution was drawn by men who proposed to put in the hands of one set of authorities the power to promise and then withhold from them the means of fulfilling them." President Taft, in receiving the members of the American Society of International Law, in April, 1910. Am. Journal of Int. Law, IV, 666. In his annual message of December 6, 1910, President Taft renewed the recommendation made in his inaugural address, and by his predecessors, for legislation in this respect. For. Rel., 1910, p. XIX.

6 4 Wheat. 316, 416, 424.

be made an offense against the United States, unless it has some relation to the execution of a power of Congress, or to some matter within the jurisdiction of the United States."[7] "We hold it to be an incontrovertible principle, that the government of the United States may, by means of physical force, exercised through its official agents, execute on every foot of American soil the powers and functions that belong to it."[8] "As, under the Constitution, power over interstate commerce and the transportation of the mails is vested in the national government, and Congress by virtue of such grant has assumed actual and direct control, it follows that the national government may prevent any unlawful and forcible interference therewith. But how shall this be accomplished? Doubtless, it is within the competency of Congress to prescribe by legislation that any interference with these matters shall be offenses against the United States, and prosecuted and punished by indictment in the proper courts. * * * We hold that the government of the United States is one having jurisdiction over every foot of soil within its territory, and acting directly upon each citizen; that while it is a government of enumerated powers, it has within the limits of those powers all the attributes of sovereignty."[9] In Baldwin v. Franks, although it was held that such provision had not been made either in §5519, §5508 (brought forward as §19 of the Penal Code), or in §5336 (brought forward as §6 of the Penal Code) of the Revised Statutes, Chief Justice Waite, in delivering the opinion of the court, said: "That the United States have power under the Constitution to provide for the punishment of those who are guilty of depriving Chinese subjects of any of the rights, privileges, immunities, or exemptions guaranteed to them by this treaty [of November 17, 1880], we do not doubt."[10] In the dissenting opinions of Mr. Justice Harlan and Mr. Justice Field, this power of the United States to enforce its treaty obligations was asserted in terms not less doubtful.[11] Congress is by the Constitution expressly given the power

---

7 Field, J., United States v. Fox, 95 U. S. 670, 672.

8 Bradley, J., Ex parte Siebold, 100 U. S. 371, 395.

9 Brewer, J., In re Debs, 158 U. S. 564, 581, 599.

10 120 U. S. 678, 683.

11 In a report of a committee, which consisted of Elihu Root, Simeon E. Baldwin and George W. Kirchwey, presented by the last-named member, to the Lake Mohonk Conference, May 26, 1911, it is stated that: "After careful deliberation we have come unanimously to the conclusion

to define and punish "offenses against the law of nations."[12]

§113. **Writ of Habeas Corpus.**—The Federal courts have power to issue writs of habeas corpus which shall extend to a prisoner in jail when "in custody in violation of the Constitution or of a law or treaty of the United States;"[13] but except in cases of peculiar urgency the courts will not discharge the prisoner in advance of a final determination of his case in the courts of the State, and even after such final determination will generally leave the prisoner to his remedy by writ of error.[14] "The reason for this course is apparent. It is an exceedingly delicate jurisdiction given to the Federal courts by which a person under an indictment in a State court and subject to its laws may, by the decision of a single judge of the Federal court, upon a writ of habeas corpus, be taken out of the custody of the officers of the State and finally discharged therefrom, and thus a trial by the State courts of an indictment found under the laws of a State be finally prevented."[15]

§114. **Writ of Error.**—Section 237 of the Judicial Code (embodying section 25 of the Judiciary Act of September 24, 1789),[16] as approved March 3, 1911, reads: "A final judgment or decree in

that the power to make good its treaty obligations is now vested in the government under the Constitution; that what is requisite and all that is requisite is adequate legislation by Congress, vesting specific or general authority in the Federal tribunals to enable them to apply penal and other provisions of the law to the end of protecting the aliens within our borders." The committee suggested for this purpose an amendment of §5508 of the Revised Statutes, by the substitution of the word "person" for the word "citizen." Report of 1911, p. 192. This section (now Penal Code §19) provides for the punishment of a conspiracy to injure, oppress, threaten, or intimidate any "citizen" in the free exercise or enjoyment of any right or privilege secured to him by the Constitution or laws of the United States, or because of his having so exercised the same. In Baldwin v. Franks, supra, it was held that the word "citizen" was used in this section in its political sense as in the Fourteenth Amendment to the Constitution, and not as being synonymous with "resident," "inhabitant," or "person."

12 Art. I, sec. 8.

13 Rev. Stats., §§751, 753. See Wildenhus's Case, 120 U. S. 1, 11; Ornelas v. Ruiz, 161 U. S. 502.

14 Whitten v. Tomlinson, 160 U. S. 231, 242.

15 Peckham, J., Baker v. Grice, 169 U. S. 284, 291. Such exceptional cases were presented in Wildenhus's Case, 120 U. S. 1; In re Loney, 134 U. S. 372; and In re Neagle, 135 U. S. 1.

16 1 Stats. at L. 85; Rev. Stats., §709.

any suit in the highest court of a State in which a decision in the suit could be had, [1] where is drawn in question the validity of a treaty or statute of, or an authority exercised under, the United States, and the decision is against their validity; or [2] where is drawn in question the validity of a statute of, or an authority exercised under any State, on the ground of their being repugnant to the Constitution, treaties, or laws of the United States, and the decision is in favor of their validity; or [3] where any title, right, privilege, or immunity is claimed under the Constitution, or any treaty or statute of, or commission held or authority exercised under, the United States, and the decision is against the title, right, privilege, or immunity especially set up or claimed, by either party, under such Constitution, treaty, statute, commission, or authority, may be re-examined and reversed or affirmed in the Supreme Court upon a writ of error." By an act approved December 23, 1914, there was added to this section the following provision: "It shall be competent for the Supreme Court to require, by certiorari or otherwise, any such case to be certified to the Supreme Court for its review and determination, with the same power and authority in the case as if it had been carried by appeal or writ of error to the Supreme Court, although the decision in such case may have been in favor of the validity of the treaty or statute or authority exercised under the United States or may have been against the validity of the State statute or authority claimed to be repugnant to the Constitution, treaties, or laws of the United States, or in favor of the title, right, privilege, or immunity claimed under the Constitution, treaty, statute, commission, or authority of the United States."[16a] Provision is also made for taking out appeals or writs of error, in cases involving the validity or construction of treaties, to the Supreme Court from the United States district courts, the supreme courts of Porto Rico, Hawaii, and the Philippine Islands, and the Court of Appeals of the District of Columbia.[17]

Under the third class of cases specified in section 237, in which the final decree or judgment of a State court can be re-examined

16a   38 Stats. at L. 790.

17   Judicial Code, §§238, 244, 246, 248, 250, par. 3. By an act approved August 22, 1914, provision is made for the review by the Supreme Court, by certiorari or otherwise, of the final judgments or decrees of the Court of Customs Appeals in any case in which there is drawn in question the construction of a treaty. 38 Stats. at L. 703.

in the Supreme Court on writ of error, the Federal right, title, privilege or immunity must be specially set up or claimed to give the Supreme Court jurisdiction;[18] but under the first and second classes, if the Federal question appears in the record and was decided, or such decision was necessarily involved in the case, and the case could not have been determined without deciding the question, the fact that it was not specially set up and claimed is not conclusive against a review of such question in the Supreme Court.[19] Where the decision complained of rests on an independent ground not involving a Federal question and broad enough to sustain the judgment, the writ of error will be dismissed without considering any Federal question that may also have been presented.[20] But, if the Federal question was properly presented and necessarily controlled the determination of the case, the appellate jurisdiction of the Supreme Court is not defeated because the decision was put upon some matter of local law.[21] Under the third class of cases, in order to maintain the writ of error, the right, title, privilege, or immunity relied on must not only be specially set up or claimed, but at the proper time and in the proper way. "The proper time is in the trial court whenever that is required by the State practice, in accordance with which the highest court of a State will not revise the judgment of the court below on questions not therein raised.[22] The proper way is by pleading, motion, exception, or other action, part, or being

18 Spies v. Illinois, 123 U. S. 131, 181; French v. Hopkins, 124, U. S. 524; Chappell v. Bradshaw, 128 U. S. 132; Baldwin v. Kansas, 129 U. S. 52; Leeper v. Texas, 139 U. S. 462; Oxley Stave Co. v. Butler County, 166 U. S. 648; Columbia Water Power Co. v. Columbia Electric Street &c. Co., 172 U. S. 475, 488.

19 Brown, J., Columbia Water Power Co. v. Columbia Electric Street &c. Co., 172 U. S. 475, 488, citing Miller v. Nicholls, 4 Wheat. 311; Willson v. Blackbird Creek Marsh Co., 2 Pet. 245; Satterlee v. Matthewson, 2 Pet. 380, 410; Fisher's Lessee v. Cockerell, 5 Pet. 248; Crowell v. Randell, 10 Pet. 368; Harris v. Dennie, 3 Pet. 292; Farney v. Towle, 1 Black 350; Hoyt v. Shelden, 1 Black 518; Railroad Co. v. Rock, 4 Wall. 177; Furman v. Nichol, 8 Wall. 44; Kaukauna Co. v. Green Bay &c. Canal, 142 U. S. 254.

20 California Powder Works v. Davis, 151 U. S. 389, 393; Leathe v. Thomas, 207 U. S. 93, 98; Rogers v. Jones, 214 U. S. 196, 204; Gaar, Scott & Co. v. Shannon, 223 U. S. 468, 470.

21 West Chicago R. R. Co. v. Chicago, 201 U. S. 506, 520; Garr, Scott & Co. v. Shannon, 223 U. S. 468, 471.

22 Spies v. Illinois, 123 U. S. 131; Jacobi v. Alabama, 187 U. S. 133; Layton v. Missouri, 187 U. S. 356; Erie R. R. Co. v. Purdy, 185 U. S. 148.

made part, of the record, showing that the claim was presented to the court.[23] It is not properly made when made for the first time in a petition for rehearing after judgment;[24] or in the petition for writ of error; or in briefs of counsel not made part of the record.[25] The assertion of the right must be made unmistakably and not left to mere inference.[26] If the highest court of a State entertains a petition for rehearing, which raises Federal questions, and decides them, that will be sufficient;[27] or if the court decided a Federal question which it assumes is distinctly presented to it in some way.[28] Jurisdiction may be maintained where a definite issue as to the possession of the right is distinctly deducible from the record and necessarily disposed of, but this cannot be made out by resort to judicial knowledge."[29] The final judgment of the highest court of a State in civil or criminal cases may be re-examined.[30] A case arising from or growing out of a treaty is one involving rights given or protected by a treaty.[31] A suit does not arise under a treaty unless it really and substantially involves a dispute or controversy as to the effect or construction of the treaty upon the determination of which the result depends.[32] In order to involve the validity or construction of a treaty, to give appellate jurisdiction, some right, title, privi-

23 Loeb v. Trustees, 179 U. S. 472, 481.

24 "There is an exception to this rule when it appears that the court below entertained the motion for rehearing, and passed upon the Federal question. But it must appear that such Federal question was in fact passed upon in considering the motion for rehearing; if not, the general rule applies. Mallett v. North Carolina, 181 U. S. 589; Leigh v. Green, 193 U. S. 79; Corkran Oil Co. v. Arnaudet, 199 U. S. 182; McMillen v. Ferrum, 197 U. S. 343; Waters-Pierce Oil Co. v. Texas, 212 U. S. 112, 118." Day, J., Forbes v. State Council of Virginia, 216 U. S. 396, 399.

25 Loeber v. Schroeder, 149 U. S. 580, 585; Pim v. St. Louis, 165 U. S. 273; Sayward v. Denny, 158 U. S. 180; Zadig v. Baldwin, 166 U. S. 485, 488; Forbes v. State Council of Virginia, 216 U. S. 396, 399.

26 Oxley Stave Co. v. Butler County, 166 U. S. 648.

27 Mallett v. North Carolina, 181 U. S. 589.

28 Home for Incurables v. New York, 187 U. S. 155; Sweringen v. St. Louis, 185 U. S. 38, 46.

29 Fuller, C. J., Mutual Life Insurance Co. v. McGrew, 188 U. S. 291, 308, citing, Powell v. Brunswick County, 150 U. S. 433; Mountain View Mining & Milling Co. v. McFadden, 180 U. S. 53; Arkansas v. Kansas & Texas Coal Co., 183 U. S. 185.

30 Whitten v. Tomlinson, 160 U. S. 231, 238.

31 United States v. Old Settlers, 148 U. S. 427, 468.

32 Devine v. Los Angeles, 202 U. S. 313, 332.

lege or immunity dependent on the treaty must be so set up or claimed as to require the lower court to pass on the question of validity or construction in disposing of the right asserted.[33] The validity of a statute of the United States or authority exercised thereunder is drawn in question when the existence or constitutionality or legality of such law is denied, and the denial forms the subject of direct inquiry in the case.[34]

33 Muse v. Arlington Hotel Co., 168 U. S. 430, 435; Pettit v. Walshe, 194 U. S. 205, 216; Champion Lumber Co. v. Fisher, 227 U. S. 445, 450.

34 United States v. Lynch, 137 U. S. 280; Linford v. Ellison, 155 U. S. 503; McLean v. R. R. Co., 203 U. S. 38; Champion Lumber Co. v. Fisher, 227 U. S. 445, 451.

PART II. FOREIGN STATES.

CHAPTER XVIII.

GREAT BRITAIN.

§115. Power to Make Treaties a Prerogative of the Crown.
—The power to conclude treaties is in Great Britain a prerogative
of the Crown, exercised on the advice of a responsible ministry.
Before the full development of the present system of parliamentary government, the liability to impeachment of those associated with the King in the negotiations served as the principal
check.[1] At present, while the means of redress are no greater,
the fact that the ministry, through which the treaty must be concluded, possesses the confidence of the Commons, renders the exercise of the power more secure. "The prerogative of the Crown
in this respect is exercised, subject always to the collective responsibility of the Cabinet, through one of His Majesty's Principal
Secretaries of State, to whom is entrusted the business of communicating with the representatives of foreign states in this country, and with our own representatives in other communities."[2]

---

1 The House of Commons brought charges of inpeachment in April,
1701, against the Earls of Portland and Orford, and Lords Somers and
Halifax, for their part in negotiating and advising the conclusion of the
Treaty of Partition (1698). State Trials, XIV, 332, 338. The eleventh
article of the impeachment of Lord Clarendon charged him with having
advised and effected the sale of Dunkirk to the French King. State Trials,
VI, 396; Hallam, Constitutional History of England (2 ed.), II, 498. So
also a principal charge in the impeachment of Lord Danby was his agency
in the conclusion of the secret treaty of May 27, 1678, between Charles II
and Louis of France, by which the former agreed, for a pecuniary compensation, to remain neutral in the contest with the Dutch. State Trials,
XI, 599; Hallam, II, 553. "A Whig House now (1715) directed the impeachment of Oxford, Bolingbroke and Ormond, for high treason, and other
crimes and misdemeanors mainly relating to the Peace of Utrecht.
* * * The proceedings against Oxford and Bolingbroke are the last
instance in our history of a political impeachment. * * * A refine-
ment in men's sense of equity gradually disclosed the hardship of punishing ministers for acts that Parliament and the sovereign had approved;
and second, the remarkable growth of the Cabinet system * * * tended
slowly but decisively to substitute the joint responsibility of the whole body
of ministers for the personal responsibility of an individual minister."
Morley's Walpole, 43-44.

2 Anson, Law and Custom of the Constitution, (3 ed.) pt. II, 97. "For
the purpose of making a treaty, the first stage in the proceedings is the grant

Treaties involving a charge on the people, or a change in the law of the land, can be carried into effect only by an act of Parliament.[3]

§116. Treaties Involving the Finances.—In treaties for the guarantee of loans, and thus potentially involving the finances, it is the practice for the Crown to engage only to recommend to Parliament, or to ask Parliament for authority to guarantee, the payment of the loan. Thus in the convention concluded March 29, 1898, to facilitate a Greek loan, it was stipulated that the Governments of France, Great Britain and Russia undertook to "guarantee jointly and severally, or to apply to their parliaments for authority to guarantee" the payments on the loan.[4] Such authority was on due application given by the British Parliament in an act of April 1, 1898, prior to the deposit of the ratification at Paris on May 18. The act not only provided in detail for the eventual execution of the convention, but authorized Her Majesty to join in the guarantee in accordance with the terms of the convention.[5] Similar provisions are found in the conventions concluded: November 16, 1831, May 7, 1832, June 27, 1855, June 3, 1856, and March 18, 1885, relative to the Russian-Dutch, Greek, Turkish, Sardinian and Egyptian loans, respectively.[6]

§117. Commercial Treaties.—The treaty of commerce concluded with France, at Utrecht in 1713, provided that there should be, as between the two countries, most-favored-nation treatment;

---

of powers to representatives of the Crown to negotiate and conclude the treaty. For this purpose an instrument is prepared containing full powers to the minister representing the Crown to negotiate or conclude a treaty, or convention, with the minister who is invested with similar powers to act for the state, which is the other party to the transaction. To this instrument the great seal is affixed on the authority of a sign manual warrant countersigned by the Secretary of State for Foreign Affairs. * * * And so a warrant is again issued under the sign manual countersigned by the Secretary of State, for affixing the great seal to an instrument ratifying the treaty. The instrument of ratification, which is in fact the treaty with the great seal affixed to it, is then exchanged by the minister empowered to do so, for a ratification with corresponding forms from the other side." Id., II, pt. I, 53, 54. For the organization of the Foreign Office, see Foreign Office List, 1914, 1.

3 Anson, II, pt. I, 54; pt. II, 103.

4 Art. IX. British and Foreign State Papers, XC, 28.

5 61 Vict. c. 4.

6 Arts. I, XII, I, VII, and I, respectively. British and Foreign State Papers, XVIII, 928; XIX, 37; XLV, 18; XLVI, 238; LXXVI, 349; LVIII, 9.

that all laws of Great Britain passed since 1664 for prohibiting the importation of any goods coming from France should be repealed; and that within two months thereafter a law should be passed to provide that no higher duties should be paid on goods imported from France than on those brought from any other country.[7] A bill to make effectual these articles, introduced in the Commons in June, 1713, was after an extended debate rejected.[8] In the important commercial treaty with France concluded January 23, 1860, which stipulated for special reductions in duties, it was expressly provided that the treaty should not be valid unless Her Britannic Majesty should be authorized by the assent of Parliament to carry out the engagements.[9] In stipulations of this character, which involve a modification of the existing revenue laws, it is customary for the Crown merely to engage to recommend to Parliament that the reductions be made. Thus by the protocol attached to the commercial treaty with Austria concluded December 16, 1865, Her Majesty's Government engaged to recommend to Parliament the abolition or reduction of duties payable on certain imports.[10] By the commercial convention with Spain concluded April 26, 1886, the British Crown agreed to apply to Parliament for authority to make certain alterations in the scale of duties then imposed on imported Spanish wines. The convention, which otherwise only granted most-favored-nation treatment, was "drawn up subject to the sanction of the legislatures" of the two countries.[11] In a commercial agreement of three articles with Greece concluded March 28, 1890, Her Majesty's Government engaged to recommend to Parliament a reduction of 5s. per cwt. in the duty on imported currants.[12] By Article VI of the treaty of commerce and navigation with Portugal concluded August 12, 1914, the Crown engaged to recommend to Parliament the prohibition of the importation into, and sale for consumption within, the United Kingdom of any wine or other

7 Arts. VIII and IX. Collection of Treatys (2 ed., 1732), III, 446.

8 Parliamentary History, VI, 1223.

9 Art. XX. Brit. and For. State Papers, L, 26. See act of August 28, 1860, 23 & 24 Vict. c. 110.

10 Art. IV. Brit. and For. State Papers, LV, 5, 15.

11 Arts. II and III. Id., LXXVII, 49. See also declaration concluded with Spain December 1, 1883; also treaty with Portugal of December 26, 1878, with reference to Indian possessions.

12 Art. I. Id., LXXXII, 11. See 53 & 54 Vict. c. 8 sec. 3.

liquor, to which the description "port" or "madeira" should be applied, other than wine the produce of Portugal and of the island of Madeira, respectively. The treaty by express terms was not to come into force until the sanction of Parliament as to the provisions of this article had been obtained.[12a] The articles in the treaties of 1854 and 1871, as to fisheries and commercial reciprocity between the United States and British dominions in North America, were, by express reservations, to take effect only after the laws required to carry them into operation had been passed by the Imperial Parliament and the local parliaments concerned. Similar reservation was made in the treaty with France of January 14, 1857, concerning fishery rights on the coast of Newfoundland.[13] In the usual treaty of general amity, commerce, and navigation, which stipulates on the part of Great Britain for most-favored-nation treatment and not for special concessions, and which requires no modification of existing legislation, no such reservation is made.[14] With respect to the convention signed at Brussels March 5, 1902, for the abolition of bounties and the limitation of the surtax on sugar, the House of Commons, by a resolution adopted November 24, 1902, approved the policy embodied in the convention, and declared that, in the event of its receiving the ratifications required to make it binding, the House was prepared to adopt the necessary measures to enable His Majesty to carry out its provisions.[15] The House thus pledged itself to give effect to the convention. The act of August 11, 1903 was passed for this purpose.[16]

§118. General Legislation to Give Effect to Treaties. Naturalization.—In matters usually subject to uniform international regulation, provision is often made by a general law for giving effect to treaties thereafter to be concluded. More than a century and a half ago, Blackstone wrote: "Natural allegiance is therefore a debt of gratitude, which cannot be forfeited, cancelled, or altered by any change of time, place, or circumstance,

---

12a   The act of November 27, 1914 was passed for this purpose. 5 Geo. 5 c. 1.

13   Art. XX. Brit. and For. State Papers, XLVII, 23.

14   For a return of most-favored-nation clauses in treaties of commerce between Great Britain and foreign powers in force on January 1, 1907, see Parl. Pap. Cd. 3395.

15   Parliamentary Debates (4th series), CXV, 271, 371.

16   3 Edw. 7 c. 21.

nor by anything but the united concurrence of the legislature."[17] In the negotiations with the United States, which ultimately resulted in the naturalization convention of May 13, 1870, the British government maintained that either legislation by Parliament should precede the signing of any convention by which the loss of British nationality by naturalization in the United States should be recognized, or the validity of the convention should by express provision be made dependent upon such legislation. No act for this purpose having been passed by Parliament when the protocol of October 9, 1868, which substantially contained the provisions afterwards incorporated in the convention, was signed, a clause was inserted in which it was expressly declared that, since it would not be practicable for Her Majesty's Government to carry into operation the principles laid down in the protocol until provision had been made by Parliament for a revision of the laws, the protocol should not take effect until such legislation had been accomplished.[18] The convention, as signed May 13, 1870, contained no such reservation, since an act of Parliament of May 12, recognized the principles of the convention and enacted them into law.[19] A supplemental convention was signed February 23, 1871; and to remove all doubts as to whether its stipulations fell within the terms of the act of 1870, the additional act of July 25, 1872, was passed.[20] By the British nationality and status of aliens act of 1914, a "British subject who, when in any foreign state and not under disability, by obtaining a certificate of naturalization, or by any other voluntary and formal act, becomes naturalized therein, shall thenceforth be deemed to have ceased to be a British subject."[20a] The act further provides that where "His Majesty has entered into a convention with any foreign state to the effect that the subjects or citizens of that state to whom certificates of naturalization have been granted may divest themselves of their status as such subjects, it shall be lawful for His Majesty, by order in council, to declare that the convention has been entered into by His Majesty; and from and after the date of the order any person having been originally a subject or citizen of the state therein referred to, who has been naturalized as a British subject,

17 Commentaries (Sharswood ed.), I, 369.
18 Brit. and For. State Papers, LIX, 29, 30, 32.
19 33 & 34 Vict. c. 14.
20 35 & 36 Vict. c. 39.
20a Sec. 13. 4 & 5 Geo. 5 c. 17.

may, within the limit of time provided in the convention, make a declaration of alienage, and on his making the declaration he shall be regarded as an alien and as a subject of the state to which he originally belonged as aforesaid."[20b] Real and personal property of every description may be "taken, acquired, held and disposed of by an alien in the same manner in all respects as by a natural-born British subject; and a title to real and personal property of every description may be derived through, from or in succession to an alien in the same manner in all respects as through, from or in succession to a natural-born British subject." The act is not to be construed, however, as conferring any right on an alien to hold real property situate out of the United Kingdom, or as qualifying an alien to be the owner of a British ship.[20c]

§119. **Extradition.**—A person, not a violator of the law of the land, has at common law a personal right to liberty, which cannot be abridged by act of the Crown. Accordingly, legislation by Parliament is necessary to authorize the apprehension and surrender of fugitive criminals under extradition conventions. The general extradition act of August 9, 1870, provides that "where an arrangement has been made with any foreign state with respect to the surrender to such state of any fugitive criminals, Her Majesty may, by order in council, direct that this act shall apply in the case of such foreign state," subject to such conditions, exceptions and qualifications as may be deemed expedient; and that an order in council for applying the act in the case of any foreign state cannot be made unless the agreement may be terminated on a notice not exceeding one year and is in conformity with the provisions of the act.[21] Prior to the passage of this act special legislation was required to give effect to extradition conventions. Article X of the treaty with the United States of August 9, 1842 was not effective as a law of the land until the passage, August 22, 1843, of an act for that purpose.[22] Another act of the same date, for carrying into effect the convention of extradition with France, concluded February 13, 1843, failed to give full effect to that convention. During the period between 1843 and 1852, of fourteen fugitives requested by France only one was returned under the

---

20b Sec. 15.

20c Sec. 17.

21 33 & 34 Vict. c. 52, secs. 2, 4, 5, 21. This act, with the exception of section 19, relates to the surrender of the fugitive by Great Britain.

22 6 & 7 Vict. c. 76.

convention.[23] In each of the extradition conventions concluded
May 28, 1852 with France, April 15, 1862 with Denmark, and
March 5, 1864 with Prussia, a clause was inserted,[24] by which the
operation of the convention was expressly made dependent upon
the passage by Parliament of the legislation necessary to carry it
into effect. In the first named of these conventions the Crown engaged only to recommend to Parliament the passage of an appropriate act; and, Parliament having failed to make such provision,
the convention remained inoperative, although the ratifications
were exchanged.[25] Since the passage of the act of 1870, extradition
conventions are given effect by orders in council for applying the
extradition acts in favor of the country with which the convention
has been concluded.[26] In case the convention provides for the
surrender of a fugitive for an offense not included in the extradition acts as an extraditable offense, a special act of Parliament is
necessary. Thus the act of August 4, 1906, including bribery as
an extraditable crime, was passed to enable His Majesty to carry
into effect the supplementary extradition convention concluded
with the United States, April 12, 1905, the ratifications of which
were not exchanged until December 31, 1906.[27]

23 6 & 7 Vict. c. 75. Clarke, Extradition (3d ed.), 131; Edmonds, J.,
In re Metzger, 1 Barb. 253.

24 Art. XV, Art. IV and Art. III, respectively. Brit. and For. State
Papers, XLI, 20; LII, 30; LIV, 20.

25 Hansard's Debates, CXXI, 1370; CXXII, 192, 561, 1278.

26 See for instances, orders in council of February 22, 1896, November
27, 1896, August 9, 1898, October 20, 1898, June 15, 1901, June 26, 1901,
March 6, 1902, September 15, 1902, May 10, 1905, May 29, 1905, May 11,
1906, February 11, 1907, May 7, 1907, July 6, 1907, July 6, 1907, August 12,
1907, August 12, 1907, July 5, 1911, August 8, 1911, November 10, 1911, and
February 13, 1912, to make effective, respectively, the extradition conventions concluded February 13, 1896 with France, August 27, 1896 with Belgium, January 26, 1897 with Chile, February 22, 1892 with Bolivia, December 6, 1900 with Servia, December 13, 1900 with the United States, October
29, 1901 with Belgium, June 26, 1901 with Austria-Hungary, October 3,
1904 with Cuba, June 29, 1904 with Switzerland, April 19, 1905 with
Nicaragua, April 12, 1905 with the United States, January 26, 1904 with
Peru, February 18, 1907 with Norway, March 5, 1907 with Belgium, August
25, 1906 with Panama, July 2, 1907 with Sweden, September 12, 1908 with
Paraguay, March 3, 1911 with Belgium, March 4, 1911 with Siam, and
September 24, 1910 with Greece. Brit. and For. State Papers, LXXXVIII,
179, 180; XC, 231, 235; XCIV, 138, 139; XCV, 129, 665; XCVIII, 183,
189; XCIX, 457; C, 57, 88, 91, 92, 109, 113; Hertslet's Commercial Treaties, XXVI, 810, 32, 939, 688.

27 6 Edw. 7 c. 15.

21

By section 6 of the extradition act of 1870, it is provided that, where the act applies in the case of any foreign state, "every" fugitive criminal of that state, who is in Her Majesty's dominions, shall be liable to be apprehended and surrendered in the manner as prescribed in the act. A convention was concluded with Switzerland, which provided that "subjects" should not be surrendered; and an order in council was made, which directed that the act should apply in the case of the convention. It was held in Queen v. Wilson (1877) that the convention must be taken to have been incorporated with, and to limit the operation of the act, and that, accordingly, a British subject could not be surrendered to Switzerland.[28]

§120. Apprehension of Deserting Seamen.—Section 238 of the general merchant shipping act of August 25, 1894 authorizes the Crown to apply by order in council the provisions thereof for the surrender of deserting seamen to any foreign country that guarantees similar facilities for the recovery of deserters from British merchant vessels.[29] These provisions were, for instance, made applicable to Japan by orders in council of February 3, 1898, and October 3, 1911;[30] to Honduras by an order in council of September 26, 1901;[31] to Nicaragua by an order in council of March 1, 1907;[32] and to Roumania by an order in council of November 2, 1907.[33]

§121. Patents, Trade-Marks, Copyright and Posts.—Section 91 of the patents and designs act of August 28, 1907,[34] substan-

---

28 3 Q. B. D. 42. Sir Francis Piggott says, of this case, that "it settles, if there were any doubt on the matter, that treaties made by the Sovereign are part of the law of the land, and, being duly notified [by order in council], will be enforced by the courts so long as they do not interfere with, or infringe the common law." Extradition, 44. See also In re Bluhm (1901), 1 Q. B. 764. Lord Russell of Killowen, in In re Arton (1896), 1 Q. B. 108, 112, however, said: "It is to the expression of the legislature in acts of Parliament, and to that alone, that judicial tribunals can refer." See also In re Galwey (1896), 1 Q. B. 230.

29 57 & 58 Vict. c. 60, sec. 238.

30 Hertslet's Commercial Treaties, XXVI, 751; Brit. and For. State Papers, XC, 201.

31 Id., XCIV, 1046.

32 Id., C, 58.

33 Id., C, 123. See similar provision in the foreign deserters act of 1852, Id., XLI, 680.

34 7 Edw. 7 c. 29. By the act of August 7, 1914, this section was amended for the purpose of giving effect to the convention concluded at Washington in 1911. 4 & 5 Geo. 5 c. 18.

tially re-enacting in this respect section 103 of the general patents, designs and trade-marks act of 1883,[35] gives similar power to the Crown as to patent, design and trade-mark agreements. For instance, under section 103 of the act of 1883, by orders in council dated October 15, 1894, November 20, 1894, October 7, 1899, September 26, 1901, October 9, 1903, and January 12, 1905, the privileges of the act were extended to Greece, Denmark, Japan, Honduras, Germany, and Cuba, respectively.[36] If the stipulations of a copyright convention do not transcend the provisions of the existing law relating to international copyright they may be made effective by an order in council.[37] By section 29 of the general copyright act of 1911, amending and consolidating the law relating to copyright, it is specifically provided that His Majesty may by order in council extend the benefits of the act to works first published in a foreign country and to works of citizens or subjects of a foreign country, provided that His Majesty shall be satisfied that such foreign country (other than one with which a treaty relating to copyright has been concluded) has made or has undertaken to make suitable provision for the protection of works entitled to protection under the act.[38] In virtue of this act, an

35 46 & 47 Vict. c. 57.

36 Brit. and For. State Papers, LXXXVI, 118, 122; XCI, 1130; XCIV, 1047; XCVI, 239; XCVIII, 166. Provisions were made applicable to Austria-Hungary by order in council, May 17, 1909. Hertslet's Commercial Treaties, XXVI, 13. See also trade-marks act of August 11, 1905, 5 Edw. 7 c. 15, sec. 65. Under section 103, a trade-mark although capable of being registered in the country of origin will not be registered unless it is a mark otherwise capable of registration under the law. In re Carter Medicine Company's Trade-Mark (1892), L. R. 3 Ch. D. 472.

37 See for instance order in council of April 30, 1894, to give effect to the special convention with Austria-Hungary of April 24, 1893, Brit. and For. State Papers, LXXXVI, 97. See for list of various orders in council made under authority of the international copyright acts 1844-1886 to give effect to certain conventions, Brit. and For. State Papers, XCVII, 233. The preamble of the international copyright act of 1886 contains the following recital with respect to the draft of a convention agreed to at the Berne conference of 1885: "And whereas, without the authority of Parliament, such convention cannot be carried into effect in Her Majesty's dominions and consequently Her Majesty cannot become a party thereto, and it is expedient to enable Her Majesty to accede to the convention: Be it therefore enacted" &c. 49 & 50 Vict. c. 33.

38 1 & 2 Geo. 5 c. 46. The benefits of the act were for instance made applicable to Austria- Hungary by order in council of June 24, 1912. Hertslet's Commercial Treaties, XXVI, 16.

order in council was made June 24, 1912, to give effect to the international copyright convention concluded at Berlin November 13, 1908.[39] By section 2 of the act of June 14, 1875,[40] re-enacted as section 4 of the act of December 21, 1908, consolidating the enactments relating to the Post Office,[41] the Treasury is authorized to make such regulations as may be deemed necessary to carry into effect arrangements made by His Majesty with any foreign country with respect to the conveyance by post of any postal packets between the British Islands and places outside, and to make provisions as to the charges for the transit of postal packets; and by section 14 of the act of August 18, 1882, the Treasury is authorized to modify or except, on the recommendation of the Commissioners of Customs and the Postmaster-General, for the purpose of carrying into effect any treaty or agreement with a foreign state, the application of any of the customs enactments to foreign parcels.[42]

§122. **Miscellaneous Subjects.**—The act of August 2, 1883, to carry into effect the North Sea fisheries convention of May 6, 1882, and to amend the laws relating to British sea fisheries, authorized Her Majesty to apply the act in whole or in part to carry into effect conventions which might be made with foreign powers respecting sea fisheries.[43] Section 84 of the merchant shipping act of 1894 provides that, whenever it appears that the tonnage regulations of the act have been adopted by any foreign country, Her Majesty in Council may order that the ships of that country shall, without being remeasured, be deemed of the tonnage denoted in their certificates of registry.[44] As examples of

39 Id., 436.

40 38 & 39 Vict. c. 22.

41 8 Edw. 7 c. 48.

42 45 & 46 Vict. c. 74. As to money order arrangements with foreign states, see 8 Edw. 7 c. 48, sec. 87. See also act of July 21, 1891, to enable Her Majesty in Council to carry into effect conventions which may be made with foreign countries respecting ships engaged in postal service. 54 & 55 Vict. c. 31.

43 46 & 47 Vict. c. 22, sec. 23. See, for instance, order in council of March 12, 1903, applying the provisions of the act to the convention concluded with Denmark, June 24, 1901. Brit. and For. State Papers, XCVI, 171.

44 57 & 58 Vict. c. 60, sec. 84; 6 Edw. 7 c. 48, sec. 55. See for orders in council applying the act, Brit. and For. State Papers, XCVII, 105, 108, 147, 149; XCIX, 458; Hertslet's Commercial Treaties, XXVI, 944.

recent acts of Parliament to give effect to particular treaties, note may be made of the following: Act of October 20, 1909, to enable His Majesty by orders in council to make such modifications in the workman's compensation act of 1906 as deemed necessary to give effect to the convention concluded with France, July 3, 1909;[45] act of August 18, 1911, to make such amendments in the law as to enable provisions of the Second Geneva Convention, for the amelioration of the sick and wounded of armies in the field, to be carried into effect;[46] act of December 16, 1911, to amend the law relating to merchant shipping, with a view to carrying into effect the two conventions signed at the Brussels conference of 1910, dealing, respectively, with collisions between vessels and with salvage;[47] act of August 7, 1912, to make such provisions with respect to the prohibition of catching seals and sea otters in certain parts of the Pacific Ocean as necessary to carry out the convention between Great Britain, Japan, Russia and the United States of July 7, 1911;[47a] and the act of August 10, 1914, to make such amendments of the law relating to merchant shipping as necessary or expedient to give effect to the convention for the safety of life at sea concluded at London, January 20, 1914.[47b]

§123. **Treaties Affecting Private Rights.**—By a convention with Belgium, concluded February 17, 1876, packet-boats employed in the conveyance of postal matter between certain ports were to be considered as having the immunities and privileges of ships of war.[48] A collision occurred in British waters between a vessel owned by British subjects and a packet-boat, the Parlement

---

45 9 Edw. 7 c. 16. Article V of the convention expressly provided that ratification should not take place until the legislation in Great Britain in regard to workmen's compensation had been supplemented.

46 1 & 2 Geo. 5 c. 20.

47 1 & 2 Geo. 5 c. 57. See also 4 Edw. 7 c. 16; and 9 Edw. 7 c. 37. See also 37 Geo. 3 c. 97, to give effect to Art. IX of the treaty with the United States of 1794, granting to citizens of the United States the right to grant, sell or devise lands, then held by them, in like manner as British subjects. As to the rejection by the House of Lords of the naval prize bill to give effect to the Prize Court Convention and the Declaration of London, see address of Elihu Root, Proceedings of the American Society of International Law (Sixth Annual Meeting), 12; Hans. Deb. (1911), Lords, X, 817.

47a 2 & 3 Geo. 5 c. 10.

47b 4 & 5 Geo. 5 c. 50.

48 Art. VI.

Belge, running in accordance with the treaty between Dover and Ostend. The Parlement Belge was moreover the property of the King of the Belgians and carried the royal pennon. Acts of Parliament[49] conferred on owners of vessels damaged at sea by collision a statutory right of redress in the Admiralty Court by proceedings in rem. Such proceedings were instituted against the Parlement Belge, and the case came before Sir Robert Phillimore in the Admiralty division, in March, 1879. It was admitted that the convention had never been confirmed by statute. On the part of the Crown it was contended, "both that it was competent to Her Majesty to make this convention, and also to put its provisions into operation without the confirmation of them by Parliament." The libellant admitted the former proposition but denied the latter. The only question before the court, in the opinion of Sir Robert Phillimore, was, whether the convention of itself exempted the vessel from the proceedings, i. e., could a right of a British subject recognized by Parliament be ceded or extinguished by the Crown without the sanction of the legislature? This he decided in the negative, observing: "If the Crown had power without the authority of Parliament by this treaty to order that the Parlement Belge should be entitled to all the privileges of a ship of war, then the warrant, which is prayed for against her as a wrongdoer on account of the collision, cannot issue, and the right of the subject, but for this order unquestionable, to recover damages for the injuries done to him by her is extinguished. This is a use of the treaty making prerogative of the Crown which I believe to be without precedent, and in principle contrary to the laws of the constitution."[50] On appeal the decision was reversed, but on the ground that the Parlement Belge, as a public ship belonging to the King of the Belgians, was, under international law (which was thus recognized as a part of the law of the land), independently of any immunity that might result from the treaty, exempt from the proceedings.[51] The principle on which the decision of the lower court was based has frequently been asserted in debates in Parliament and in diplomatic correspondence. Mr. Gladstone in opposing the course of the Conservatives in 1890, of asking the assent of Parliament to the cession of the

---

49 3 & 4 Vict. c. 65, sec. 6; 24 Vict. c. 10, sec. 7.
50 The Parlement Belge, L. R., 4 Pro. Div. 129, 149, 154.
51 L. R., 5 Pro. Div. 197.

island of Helgoland, observed: "I believe it to be also a principle
—and I speak subject to correction—that where personal rights
and liberties are involved, they cannot be, at any rate, directly
affected by the prerogative of the Crown, but the assent of Parliament, the popularly elected body to a representative chamber, is
necessary to constitute a valid treaty in regard to them."[52] The
same principle was involved in the declaration made by the
Marquess of Salisbury in the Bering Sea correspondence with the
United States in 1890, that Her Majesty's Government could not,
without legislative sanction, exclude for an hour British or Canadian vessels from any portion of the high seas.[53] By a provisional modus vivendi entered into with France in March, 1890,
it was agreed that no lobster factory, not in operation on a certain date, should be permitted, except by joint consent, on the
coasts of Newfoundland where the French enjoyed fishery rights
granted by treaty. A lobster factory owned by a British subject
and operated in contravention of the terms of the modus vivendi
was taken possession of by an officer of the government charged
with the duty of giving effect to the agreement. In a suit
brought by the owner, the government, in defending this act
in derogation of the private rights of a British subject, contended that, as an act and matter of state arising out of political
relations between Her Majesty and the French government, involving the construction of a treaty, it was a matter which could
not be enquired into by the court. The Judicial Committee of the
Privy Council held, on appeal, that this was not a sufficient answer. The Attorney General, who argued the case for the government, conceded that he could not maintain the proposition that
the Crown could sanction an invasion by its officers of the rights
of private individuals whenever it was necessary in order to compel obedience to the provisions of a treaty. He contended for
this right only in case of treaties putting an end to a state of war
or those akin to treaties of peace arrived at to avert war and
having for their object the preservation of peace. With reference to this contention, Lord Herschell, delivering the judgment

52 Hansard's Debates, CCCXLVII, 761.
53 For. Rel. of the United States, 1890, p. 433. "In the United Kingdom, possibly subject to exceptions * * *, a treaty has no effect on
private rights; if the Crown concludes a treaty which is intended to divest
or modify private rights, it must obtain an act of Parliament to give it
that operation." Westlake, Law Quarterly Review, January, 1906, p. 15.

of their Lordships, observed: "Whether the power contended for does exist in the case of treaties of peace, and whether if so it exists equally in the case of treaties akin to a treaty of peace, or whether in both or either of these cases interference with private rights can be authorized otherwise than by the legislature, are grave questions upon which their Lordships do not find it necessary to express an opinion."[54]

§124. **Treaties for Cession of Territory.**—In view of the principle that the Crown cannot by treaty annul a law or abridge private rights of British subjects, the question has often been raised by British statesmen whether territory for which special laws have been passed by Parliament, or territory acquired by settlement, to which according to English jurisprudence a British subject is considered to have carried in some degree the rights and privileges of British subjects and the laws of his country,[55] can be ceded by the Crown without the sanction of Parliament. Territory acquired by conquest or cession falls immediately under the legislative powers of the Crown in Council, while that acquired by settlement does not so fall unless by virtue of an act of Parliament.[56]

The right of the Crown to establish by treaty a boundary, whatever may have been the manner in which the territory affected was acquired or has been governed, seems to be well established and supported by precedents. While a treaty simply to determine a boundary line operates as an acknowledgment of title rather than as a treaty of cession,[57] precedents are to be found in which territory has by express stipulation been exchanged.[58]

54 Walker v. Baird, App. Cas. (1892), 491, 497. The act of June 14, 1819 was passed to carry into effect the fisheries article of the convention with the United States of October 20, 1818. 59 Geo. 3 c. 38. See for acts of the Imperial and local parliaments to give effect to treaty stipulations relating to the fisheries, Hertslet's Commercial Treaties, General Index volume under the heading of "Fisheries."

55 Advocate-General of Bengal v. Ranee Surnomoye Dossee (1863), 2 Moore P. C. 22.

56 Anson, Law and Custom of the Constitution, II, pt. II, 76. The British settlements act of 1887 places under the legislative power of the Crown in Council all possessions acquired by settlement, in contradistinction to those acquired by conquest or cession, not for the time being within the jurisdiction of the legislature of any British possession. 50 & 51 Vict. c. 54, sec. 6.

57 Hall, Int. Law (6 ed.), 97.

58 A notable case is the exchange of territory on the Gold Coast expressly stipulated for in Article I of the treaty with the Netherlands of

The question as to the power of the Crown to cede territory was considered in concluding the first peace with the United States. Special acts had been passed applying to the American colonies. Among these were the act of 16 George 3 c. 5, which prohibited trade, and the act of 17 George 3 c. 7, which authorized hostilities. In arranging terms of peace, it seemed to some to be necessary, in order to annul these and other laws applying to the colonies, that Parliament should give its assent to the recognition of the independence of the colonies, and to the conclusion of a treaty of peace with them. Accordingly, an act was passed to authorize the King to conclude a peace and to annul and make void any inconsistent act.[59] There appears from the debates in Parliament to have been some uncertainty as to the necessity of this measure. Earl Shelburne, on December 13, 1782, in reply to a question respecting the provisional articles of peace said: "That agreement with the Americans had been made in consequence of an act of the last session, empowering His Majesty to conclude the differences between this country and America, so anxious had Parliament been that there should be no obscurity in the matter."[60] The peace as signed was in the nature of a treaty of recognition and partition, and may in this respect be distinguished from a treaty of cession.[61]

Various opinions as to the power of the Crown in this respect have been expressed in Parliament. On May 9, 1854, Sir Alexander Cockburn, Attorney General, stated his views relative to the relinquishment by order in council of British sovereignty over the Orange River territory. When the Cape of Good Hope was acquired, the Boers, in order to avoid the jurisdiction of the English, left the country and established themselves in the territory of the Orange River. They were pursued by the British troops,

March 5, 1867. The act of Parliament of April 11, 1843, placing British settlements on or adjacent to the coast of Africa, under the legislative power of the Crown in Council, was, it would seem, applicable to this territory. 6 & 7 Vict. c. 13.

59 22 George 3 c. 46. The act, as to the exercise of these powers, was to continue in force until July 1, 1783. The definitive treaty of peace was not concluded until September 3, 1783, although the provisional articles were signed November 30, 1782.

60 Parl. Hist., XXIII, 307.

61 McIlvaine v. Coxe's Lessee, 4 Cranch 209, 212; Harcourt v. Gaillard, 12 Wheat. 523, 527.

overcome and compelled to acknowledge British sovereignty over this territory. Accordingly, the territory was, said Sir Alexander Cockburn, acquired by conquest, and the Crown acting under the advice of the Privy Council had a perfect right to give it up. In the course of his argument he observed that colonies might be divided into two classes, such as were acquired by occupancy, and such as were acquired by conquest and by cession. While there was no question as to the right of the Crown to cede those acquired by conquest and cession, he was aware that there existed considerable difference of opinion as to whether those acquired by occupancy could be alienated otherwise than by an act of the legislature.[62] On February 10, 1863, Lord Palmerston, in the debate on the relinquishment of the protectorate influence over the Ionian Islands, after pointing out the radical difference between such a relinquishment and an actual cession of territory, added: "But with regard to cases of territory acquired by conquest during war, and not ceded by treaty, and which are not therefore British freehold, and all possessions that have been ceded by treaty and held as possessions of the British Crown, there is no question that the Crown by its prerogative may make a treaty alienating such possessions without the consent of the House of Commons."[63] In direct answer to a question on the prerogative of the Crown in this respect, Sir Roundell Palmer, Solicitor General, on March 24, 1863, said: "When British subjects have settled in newly-discovered territories—not countries acquired by conquest or cession—they carry with them the laws of this country. In that case cession could not take place without the consent of Parliament. In the case of conquered or ceded countries, if Parliament had legislated concerning those countries, then I apprehend the concurrence of Parliament might be necessary."[63a] In 1870 it was reported that negotiations were taking place for the cession to France of the Gambia Settlement, a region explored and occupied in the early part of the seventeenth century by English, French and Portuguese traders, and expressly apportioned to Great Britain by Article X of the treaty with France of September 3, 1783.[64] Mr. Gladstone, on being asked in the House of Commons

62 Hansard's Debates, CXXXIII, 81, 82.
63 Id., CLXIX, 230.
63a Id., CLXIX, 1808.
64 Chalmers, Collection of Treaties, I, 500.

whether it was possible for the Crown to transfer the Settlement and the great arterial communication of Africa to France without the consent of Parliament, replied, June 10, 1870, that it was his impression that such an agreement could not be carried out without the consent of Parliament. He added that there never had been the slightest intention of taking any proceedings of the kind without such consent.[65] To the observation made by the Duke of Manchester in the House of Lords, that the transaction appeared to involve an undue exercise of the prerogative of the Crown, Earl Granville replied that it had been distinctly stated at the beginning of the negotiations, that "nothing could be completed without the consent of Parliament."[66]

The question was fully argued before the Judicial Committee of the Privy Council in 1876, on an appeal from India. The lower court had based its decision on the principle that it was beyond the power of the British Crown, in time of peace, to cede to a foreign power, without the concurrence of the Imperial Parliament, territory within the jurisdiction of any of the British courts in India. Their Lordships dismissed the appeal, but for reasons not involving the principle on which the decision of the lower court was based. They found as a matter of fact that there had been no cession of territory, but merely an attempted rearrangement of jurisdictional limits within British territory. As to the ground on which the High Court of Bombay rested its decision, Lord Selborne (Sir Roundell Palmer), for their Lordships, said: "But having arrived at the conclusion that the present appeal ought to fail without reference to that question, they think it sufficient to state that they entertain such grave doubts (to say no more) of the soundness of the general and abstract doctrine laid down by the High Court of Bombay, as to be unable to advise Her Majesty to rest her decision on that ground."[67] It may be noted that the eminent jurist, Mr. Forsyth, who has contended for a limitation on the Crown in this respect, and who appeared for the respondents in this case, was unable to cite to the satisfaction of the court an in-

65 Hansard's Debates, CCI, 1843.

66 Id., CCIII, 339, 341.

67 Gordhan v. Kanji, 1 App. Cas. 332, 373, 382. Mr. Fitzjames Stephen, who appeared for the appellant, cited many instances of cessions in India which appear to have been made without legislative sanction. Id., 357.

stance in which the assent of Parliament had been given to a cession of territory.[68]

In the treaty concluded with Germany July 1, 1890, it was expressly stipulated that the cession of the sovereignty over the island of Helgoland and its dependencies was made by Her Britannic Majesty "subject to the assent of the British Parliament."[69] The island had been seized from Denmark in 1807; and the conquest had been formally recognized by that country in the treaty concluded at Kiel, January 14, 1814.[70] It remained under the legislative powers of the Crown in Council, and was peopled chiefly by the native Germanic stock.[71] The course of the Conservatives, in inserting in the treaty a clause requiring the assent of Parliament to the cession, was opposed by the Liberals, especially by Mr. Gladstone and Sir W. Vernon Harcourt. The former declared with some emphasis that in the whole course of its existence the House of Commons had never before been asked to vote a cession of territory, whatever its nature; and that such a procedure had for its support at most only the dicta of legal authorities, as against the uniform practice of the government.[72] The Conservatives defended the procedure as being expedient and desirable, rather than as being compulsory. Mr. Goshen, Chancellor of the Exchequer, in the course of the debate, observed: "We do not for a moment base our argument on the assumption that the assent of Parliament was indispensable to the cession."[73] Mr. Balfour observed that the constitutional law and practice in question was in a nebulous and very uncertain condition. It seemed to him to be an absurd doctrine of constitutional law that any treaty which involved even a sixpence of expenditure should require the assent of Parliament, but that one which might involve the cession of places of vital interest to the safety of the British Empire could be consummated by a ministry, which might be called to account but could not be prevented from carrying out its policy. In reply to Sir W. Vernon Harcourt's objection, that it would establish a binding precedent, Mr. Balfour said: "I do

68 Id., 367.

69 Art. XII. Brit. and For. State Papers, LXXXII, 46.

70 Art. III. Hertslet's Map of Europe by Treaty, I, 27.

71 Attorney General Sir R. Webster, Hansard's Debates, CCCXLVII. 830.

72 Id., CCCXLVII, 760, 764, 773.

73 Id., 771.

not object to its being a binding precedent if you do not exceed the precedent. The precedent is this—that in a time of profound peace, when no great public emergency threatens the state, when no other and ulterior considerations were involved, when no difficulties of negotiation would be produced, then, and then only, a cession of British territory, and the transfer of British subjects to a foreign dominion, should not be undertaken until the assent of both Houses of Parliament had been declared. That is the precedent we have set. * * * It is a precedent which we think ought to be followed."[74] Parliament gave its assent to the cession in the act of August 4, 1890.[75] From subsequent practice it may be concluded that the precedent does not apply to the adjustment, by mutual exchanges of territory, of boundaries of colonial possessions, or to the relinquishment of such rights of sovereignty as were yielded to Germany and the United States in the Samoan treaties of November 14, and December 2, 1899. Even by those who seek to place a limitation on the prerogative of the Crown, it is usually conceded that in concluding peace, and especially in the event of a calamitous war, an unusual power may be exercised.

The agreement concluded with France, April 8, 1904, concerning fisheries and territories, was signed "subject to the approval" of the parliaments of the respective countries. The agreement provided on the part of Great Britain not only for a cession of territory, but also for the eventual payment of a pecuniary indemnity to be awarded to French citizens who might suffer by the relinquishment by France of fishery privileges in Newfoundland. In return for the cancellation of these fishery privileges, and in addition to the pecuniary indemnity, Great Britain agreed to a change in the frontier between Senegambia and the English Colony of the Gambia, by which France acquired Yarbutenda with its landing places; to a readjustment of the boundaries between British and French Nigeria, by which France gained some 14,000 square miles; and to a cession to France of the group of islands known as Iles de Los, which had originally been ceded to Great Britain by the king of the Bago country in 1818.[76] In reply

---

74 Id., 787, 788.

75 53 & 54 Vict. c. 32.

76 See speech of Earl Percy, Under Secretary of State for Foreign Affairs, June 1, 1904, Parl. Debates, CXXXV, 499.

to a question in the House of Commons, April 14, 1904, Mr. Balfour, Prime Minister, said: "I understand that, according to the French constitutional usage, the agreement between Great Britain and France must be submitted to their Chamber before final ratification. As the honorable gentleman is aware, that is not the constitutional practice in this country. But I think it is most desirable that there should be a discussion in this House on the subject. In any case a bill will have to be brought in dealing with portions of the agreement, because, as no doubt honorable members are aware, there can be no cession of any territory of His Majesty without the consent of Parliament."[77] He added: "There are portions of the treaty relating to the cession of territory which require the assent of Parliament, and there are also provisions in the treaty which require the voting of money by Parliament. Parliament must be consulted on both those points. But on other parts of the treaty Parliament need not be consulted, though I think it is desirable that the House should have an opportunity of discussing so great an international instrument."[78] By the act of August 15, 1904, the approval of Parliament was given to the convention. The act further provided that it should be lawful for His Majesty to do everything necessary or proper for carrying the convention into effect, and that any sums payable by way of indemnity under the convention, and any expense incurred in carrying it into effect, should be defrayed out of moneys provided by Parliament.[79]

§125. **Submission of Treaties to Parliament Before Ratification.**—Efforts have been made to require the submission of treaties to Parliament before their final ratification. Three resolutions to this effect were proposed in Parliament in 1873—February 14, declaring that all treaties with foreign powers ought to be laid before both Houses before being ratified; March 3, embodying an address to the Crown praying that all treaties, by which disputed questions with a foreign power were to be referred to arbitration, might be laid before both Houses of Parliament six weeks before they were definitely ratified; and on March

---

77 Parl. Debates, CXXXIII, 207.

78 Id., 210. See also answer of the Marquess of Lansdowne, Secretary of State for Foreign Affairs, in the House of Lords, April 19, 1904. Id., 488.

79 4 Edw. 7 c. 33.

4, declaring that all treaties ought to be made subject to the approval of Parliament, as in the case of the commercial treaty with France of 1860.[80] A resolution declaring that, in the opinion of the House of Commons, it was neither just nor expedient to embark in war, contract engagements involving grave responsibilities, or to add territories to the Empire, without the knowledge and consent of Parliament, was rejected, March 19, 1886, by a vote of 112 to 108.[81] The policy of obtaining the approval of treaties by Parliament in advance of their definitive ratification has on the other hand been opposed on the ground that the efficacy of parliamentary responsibility would thereby be impaired. Lord Palmerston on being asked, April 11, 1864, in reference to the proposed conference on affairs in Denmark, whether the engagements which might be formed would be submitted for the consent of Parliament before the ratification by the Crown was advised, replied: "It is not the practice, nor is it in accordance with the principles of the Constitution, that the Crown should ask the advice of its Parliament with respect to engagements which it may be advised are proper to be contracted."[82] Again, Earl Grey, in the House of Lords, May 22, 1871, in reference to the treaty concluded with the United States, May 8, 1871, said: "Ever since I have been in Parliament I have invariably heard the rule of our Constitution and of Parliament stated by the highest authorities to be this—that treaties were never to be laid before Parliament until they had been ratified; that the responsibility of ratifying or refusing ratification rested with the ministers; that when a treaty had been ratified it was quite competent for Parliament to censure the conduct of ministers, and that the Crown had never been in the habit of abdicating responsibility and presenting treaties before they were signed."[83] Mr. Asquith, Prime Minister, on November 26, 1908, in reply to the question in the House of Commons, whether he would consider the advisability of making provision in some form by which the assent of Parliament to treaties before their final ratification should be required, said: "I am not prepared to give any positive assurance that no treaty concluded by His Majesty's Government will be ratified until

80 Hansard's Debates, CCXIV, 448, 1166, 1178, 1309, 1319.
81 Id., CCCIII, 1386, 1421.
82 Id., CLXXIV, 788.
83 Id., CCVI, 1106. See also, Id., CCIII, 1776, 1790.

Parliament has been consulted and its approval obtained. Such a course would involve a material change in the constitutional usage hitherto followed in this country, and could obviously only be adopted in pursuance of a formal debate and after mature consideration. Nor does it appear to me that any such alteration of procedure is really required, as it will usually happen that an opportunity for debate will be found in the considerable interval that generally takes place between the signature of a treaty and its ratification, and no diplomatic document would be ratified against the declared wishes of this House."[84] Later, December 1, 1908, to the question, whether there was any rule governing the cases in which the assent of the House should be given to treaties before final ratification, especially with reference to treaties dealing with the acquisition or cession of territory, those affecting the personal privileges, status, or property of British subjects, or those involving a change of statute law, Mr. Asquith replied that, if a treaty involved any alteration of statute law, the assent of Parliament was needed, and that, if a treaty required funds to carry it into effect, it would be proper to have the required sum submitted to the House before the treaty was ratified. He added that there was no rule which required that the other matters referred to in the question should be brought before the House, nor had it been the practice to do so.[85] Sir Edward Grey, Secretary of State for Foreign Affairs, in the House of Commons, March 13, 1911, in adverting to a suggestion made by the President of the United States as to the negotiation of a convention by which the parties would be bound to submit to arbitration all questions that might arise between them, without reservation as to national honor and vital interests, said: "We should be delighted to have such a proposal, but I should feel it was something so momentous and so far-reaching in its possible consequences that it would require not only the signature of both Governments, but the deliberate and deciding sanction of Parliament."[86] A convention of the character suggested was signed, but failed of final ratification because of amendments engrafted by the Senate of the United States.[87]

84 197 Parl. Debates 701.
85 197 Parl. Debates 1238.
86 Parl. Debates, (1911), XXII, 1990.
87 In reply to a question, August 8, 1911, after the convention had been signed, Sir Edward Grey stated that it would be laid before Parliament as soon as possible, but that the time at which it should be debated was a matter for the Prime Minister to decide. Id., XXIX, 943.

CHAPTER XIX.

FRANCE.

I. Prior to 1875.

§126. **The States-General and Parlement of Paris.**—Early instances of the repudiation of treaties by the parlement of Paris and the states-general are to be found. The terms of peace agreed to by King John after his defeat and capture at the battle of Poitiers in 1356 were, regardless of the captive king's wish, declared not to be binding by the states-general assembled for that purpose by the Dauphin, and the war continued until the peace of Bretigny in 1360. So also the treaty signed under protest by the captive King, Francis I, at Madrid, in January, 1526, after the defeat of Pavia, was repudiated by the parlement of Paris in accordance with the request of the released King, although hostages had been pledged.[1] The important treaty of Troyes, signed May 21, 1420, by which France and England were ultimately to be joined under one king, was, after important stipulations had been executed, submitted to the states-general for confirmation. To Henry V of England, such a confirmation seemed to afford additional security for the faithful performance of the treaty.[2] At an early date, the states-general protested against the alienation of the royal domain.[3] The parlement of Paris, as also the provincial parlements, besides judicial functions, exercised at times certain duties in the registration and promulgation of laws. They were also called upon at various times to register treaties. For instance, Louis XI caused a treaty concluded with Spain in October, 1478, and a treaty concluded with Maximilian in December, 1482, to be registered in the parlement of Paris.[4] Several treaties were so registered during the reigns of Charles VIII and Louis XII.[5] In the treaty of the Pyrenees, of November 7, 1659, it was ex-

1 Saint Girons, Manuel de Droit Constitutionnel, 465; Martin, Histoire de France, VIII, 104; Kitchin, History of France (3 ed.), I, 460; II, 209, 210.

2 Stubbs, Constitutional History of England, III, 89; Picot, Histoire des Etats-Généraux, I, 298-300.

3 See Picot, I, 210, 283; Martin, IX, 460; Kitchin, II, 373-4.

4 Aubert, Histoire du Parlement de Paris, I, 352.

5 Id., 353.

22

pressly stipulated that, for greater security, it should be published, verified and registered in the court of the parlement of Paris, and in all other parlements of France, as also in the chamber of accounts of Paris.[6] Similar provisions are found in the treaties concluded at Aix la Chapelle, May 2, 1668, with Spain;[7] at Nimeguen, September 17, 1678, with Spain;[8] and at Ryswick, September 20, 1697, with the United Provinces and with Spain.[9]

§127. **The Constituent Assembly.**—The principal discussion as to treaty making in the Constituent Assembly, which framed the constitution of 1791, took place May 16-23, 1790 on the question whether the nation ought to delegate to the King the exercise of the power of peace and war.[10] The lamentable treaties of Louis XV, by which France had been stripped of her colonial possessions, were attributed by some to the unrestrained power of the King in treaty making.[11] Numerous propositions, differing much in their nature, were introduced. On May 16 a project was submitted which provided that the King should not enter into negotiations for peace or alliance without the consent of the assembly.[12] A project submitted the following day gave to the King the power of proposing conditions of peace and projects of treaties, but always subject to the modification and approval of the legislative body.[13] It was contended in the course of debate that the King should be given the power to conclude treaties of peace—by le comte Sérent, without restriction;[14] by le comte Galissonnière, on the authority of a responsible minister;[15] by various others, with the qualification that treaties providing for furnishing subsidies or for the cession of territory or property of the nation should require legislative sanction. With the treaty clause as with many other sections of the constitution of 1791, it was Mirabeau's project that was finally adopted as the basis of the constitutional

6 Art. CXXIV.

7 Art. IX.

8 Art. XXXI.

9 Arts. XXII and XLV of the treaties with the United Provinces, and Art. XXXVII of the treaty with Spain. Collection of Treatys, (2 ed.), I, 97, 160, 232, 316, 331, 345.

10 Le Moniteur, 554, et seq.

11 Id., 557, col. 2.

12 Id., 555, col. 2.

13 Id., 558, col. 1.

14 Id., 554, col. 2.

15 Id., 570, col. 1.

provision. According to his project, as introduced May 20, and later adopted by the Assembly, it appertained to the King to arrange and sign with foreign powers all conventions which he should deem necessary for the welfare of the state, but treaties of peace, of alliance, and of commerce were to be ratified by the legislative body.[16] On May 24, subsequently to the adoption of this project, the wording was, at the suggestion of Mirabeau and with the unanimous consent of the Assembly, so changed as to require legislative approval for all treaties.[17]

§128. **Constitutional Provisions, 1793-1871.**—By the constitution of 1793, treaties were to be negotiated by the Executive Council, and ratified by the national legislature. The Executive Council was composed of twenty-four members chosen by the national legislature from the candidates nominated by department electoral assemblies.[18] The constitution of 1795 committed to the Directory the negotiating and signing of treaties, but all treaties before they could become valid were to be examined and ratified by the legislative body. Secret articles might be arranged, and might receive a provisional execution independently of the legislature, but such articles could not be destructive of the open stipulations, or provide for an alienation of territory.[19] In the constitution of 1799, it was provided that the Government, i. e., the three Consuls, should conduct negotiations, make the preliminary stipulations, sign, have signed, and conclude all treaties of peace, alliance, neutrality and commerce, and other treaties. Treaties of peace, alliance and commerce should be proposed, discussed, decreed, and promulgated as laws. The Government could, however, demand secrecy.[20] The natural inference from the specific enumeration in the two articles, the one immediately following the other, is that treaties other than those of peace, alliance and commerce, were to be consummated on executive authority. The constitution in the form of a sénatus-consulte of August 4, 1802, gave to the First Consul the power to ratify treaties of peace and alliance, after having taken the advice of the

16 Id., 572, col. 3.
17 Id., 589, col. 2. Title III, ch. 4, sec. 3, Art. III, and title III, ch. 3, sec. 1, Arts. II and III of the Constitution. See for text, Dalloz's Répertoire de Jurisprudence, XVIII, 291, 293.
18 Arts. LXX and LV. Id., 299.
19 Arts. CCCXXX, CCCXXXI, CCCXXXIII. Id., 310.
20 Arts. XLIX and L. Id., 313.

privy council. Before promulgation he was to inform the Senate.[21] No reference was made to treaties other than those of peace and alliance. From the organic law of May 18, 1804, accompanying the declaration of the Empire,[22] until the constitution of 1848, the power to make treaties was vested solely in the Executive, or King.[23] The charters of 1814 and 1830 both provided, however, for a responsible ministry.

During this period the question as to the duty of the legislature to give effect to treaties that stipulated for changes in the revenue laws or for the payment of money was the subject of discussion. The charters specifically provided that no impost should be levied or collected unless consented to by the two chambers and sanctioned by the King,[24] and that all propositions for imposts were first to be considered in the Chamber of Deputies.[25] On February 8, 1826, an ordinance was issued to give full effect to a convention with Great Britain, for the abolition of discriminating duties, concluded January 26, 1826.[26] In April, following, while the general tariff law was undergoing revision in the Chamber of Deputies, an amendment was introduced giving to the ordinance of February 8 the sanction of a law.[27] It seemed to have been conceded that the treaty was advantageous to France; indeed, M. Casimir Périer, who proposed the amendment, expressly stated that he entirely approved of its stipulations. The discussion was confined to the constitutional question, whether the King could by means of a treaty modify the revenue laws. The Deputies, by a vote of 183 to 145, insisted upon legislative action.[28]

The convention with the United States of July 4, 1831 provided for the payment by France of 25,000,000 francs, in six annual installments, in settlement of claims of American citizens. The first installment fell due February 2, 1833, but no provision had on that date been made for its payment, nor had the administration requested of the chambers an appropriation for this purpose.

21　Art. LVIII. Id., 318.
22　Id., 318.
23　Art. XIV of the constitutional charter of 1814; Art. XIII of the constitutional charter of 1830. Id., 326, 333.
24　Arts. XLVIII and XL.
25　Arts. XVII and XV.
26　Hertslet's Commercial Treaties, III, 123, 134.
27　Le Moniteur, 548, col. 3.
28　Id., p. 558, col. 3.

In April, following, a bill was introduced in the Chamber of Deputies to authorize the Minister of Finance to take measures for the execution of the convention, but it was not pressed to a vote until a year later, and was then rejected by a vote of 176 to 168.[29] In defense of the action of the Chamber of Deputies, the argument was diplomatically urged by the French government that the financial responsibility of the nation could be pledged only by a vote of the legislature; but in the discussion before the Deputies, the administration, the Duc de Broglie being Minister of Foreign Affairs, gave fair support to the bill, and in the course of the debate the contention was made that the honor of the nation had been pledged by the convention.[30] Moreover, the action of the chambers in ultimately providing for the fulfillment of the terms of the convention may be considered as a further recognition of its obligatory force. In considering the attitude of the American government, the fact is not to be overlooked that the action of the Deputies appeared to be a repudiation of a debt of long standing of which the convention was merely an acknowledgment.[31] It was this circumstance, as well as the fact that Congress had already passed the legislation required on the part of the United States to give effect to the stipulations in respect of concessions in customs duties made to France, which prompted President Jackson to recommend reprisals, and the House of Representatives unanimously to resolve that the execution of the convention on the part of France should be insisted upon.[32]

Under the constitution of 1848, the President of the republic negotiated and ratified treaties; but no treaty was to be definitive until approved by the National Assembly.[33] While the project of a law to authorize the ratification of a treaty with Sardinia, signed November 5, 1850, was being considered in the Assembly, objections were raised to particular articles of the treaty; and a proposal was made to amend them. This was opposed by the presi-

29 Le Moniteur, 770, col. 1; Moore, Int. Arb., V, 4463.

30 H. Ex. Doc. No. 40, 23d Cong., 2d Sess., 80. See Le Moniteur, 764, col. 2.

31 See messages of President Jackson, December 1, 1834, (Richardson, Messages and Papers of the Presidents, III, 100); December 7, 1835, (Id., 152); January 15, 1836, (Id., 188); February 22, 1836, (Id., 215).

32 Resolution adopted March 2, 1835. Cong. Debates, XI, pt. II, 1633, 1634.

33 Art. LIII. Brit. and For. State Papers, XXXVI, 1078.

dent of the Assembly, who maintained that the function of that body was to accept or reject the treaty as signed[34]; that it could not modify a treaty with a party who was not present and with whom it could not negotiate. A member observed that the amendment was made, not to the treaty, but to the law approving it, for the purpose of indicating to the Executive the basis on which the treaty must be concluded in order to meet the approval of the Assembly. To this, the president replied that the wishes of the Assembly would be indicated by the debates, and that action on the question of approval might be postponed until the Executive had negotiated for the desired changes. He made the objection that the vote of the Assembly in advance would be in effect an ultimatum. The motion to authorize the ratification of the treaty with modifications was rejected by the Assembly,[35] and, on March 20, 1851, resolutions were adopted to regulate the procedure of the Assembly in considering treaties. These provided among other things that the Assembly might not present amendments to the text of a treaty; that its function was confined to the adoption or rejection of, or to the suspension of action on, the project of law authorizing the ratification; and that, in case of such suspension, it might call the attention of the Government to the objectionable clauses.[36]

Article VI of the constitution, proclaimed by Louis Napoleon January 14, 1852, gave to the President of the Republic power to make treaties.[37] Article III of the sénatus-consulte of December 25, 1852, modifying the constitution, specifically provided that treaties of commerce made in virtue of Article VI of the constitution should have the force of laws in the modification of tariff rates.[38] Although the treaty-making power was thus vested absolutely in the Executive, the treaty of Turin of March 24, 1860, by which Savoy and the arrondissement of Nice were to be united as an integral part of France, was confirmed by a sénatus-consulte —an act of the sovereign or amending power under the constitution—of June 12, 1860, subsequently to the exchange of the ratifications.[39] The sénatus-consulte of September 8, 1869, amend-

34 Le Moniteur, 3769, col. 2.
35 Le Moniteur, 3771, col. 1.
36 Le Moniteur, 820, col. 3.
37 Brit. and For. State Papers, XLI, 1086.
38 Id., XLI, 1338.
39 De Clercq's Recueil des Traités de la France, VIII, 32, 48.

ing the constitution of 1852 and the sénatus-consulte of December 25, 1852, provided that thereafter treaties that might stipulate for a modification of tariffs or postal rates should be binding only by virtue of a law.[40]

§129. **National Assembly of 1871-1875.**—Upon the defeat at Sedan, a provisional Government of National Defense was formed, September 4, 1870, by whose authority military conventions were concluded and preliminary negotiations of peace conducted. Bismarck requested that the treaty of peace should have the sanction of a national assembly; and in the preliminary articles signed February 26, 1871, there was inserted an express provision for ratification by the National Assembly.[41] From the meeting of the National Assembly in February, 1871, until the adoption of the Constitutional Laws in 1875, treaties were ratified on the authority of a law of the National Assembly. As the law authorized the ratification, it preceded that act.[42]

On March 13, 1873, the National Assembly voted to establish a second chamber and to determine upon the distribution of public powers. Accordingly, M. Dufaure, for the Thiers Government, on May 19 laid before the Assembly a plan, in which it was provided that the President should negotiate and ratify treaties, but that no treaty should be definitive until approved by the two chambers.[43] M. Thiers was compelled to resign soon afterwards, and the project was not adopted. During the period of reaction, a project was, on May 15, 1874, presented by the Duc de Broglie. To the upper house, called the Grand Council, nearly one-half of whose members were to be appointed by the President for life, while most of the remainder were to be elected by the departments to serve for at least seven years, was given the ratification of all treaties negotiated by the President.[44] An amendment made by the Assembly, which provided that the upper house should be entirely elective, rendered the plan unacceptable to

40 Art. X. Dalloz, (1869), pt. IV, 74.

41 Art. X. De Clercq's Recueil des Traités de la France, X, 435.

42 In the case of the two treaties with Germany, concluded October 12, 1871, the one concerning the evacuation of certain departments by that power, and the other concerning commercial relations with Alsace-Lorraine, the law appears to have preceded the negotiations. Id., X, 495, 496, 498.

43 Art. XIV. Journal Officiel, 3209, col. 2.

44 Art. XIX. Id., 3271, col. 3.

its authors, and it was not adopted. On May 18, 1875, M. Dufaure introduced a bill on the distribution of the public powers, Article VII of which, with the addition of clauses requiring the approval of the chambers for treaties of peace and those affecting the person and property of French citizens in foreign countries, was adopted as Article VIII of the Constitutional Law of July 16, 1875, which defines the treaty-making power in France at the present time.[45]

2. The Constitutional Law of July 16, 1875.

§130. **Article VIII of the Constitutional Law.**—Article VIII of the Constitutional Law of July 16, 1875 provides that the President of the Republic shall negotiate and ratify treaties. He is to give information in regard to them to the chambers as soon as the interest and safety of the state permit. Treaties of peace, of commerce, treaties that engage the finances of the state, those that relate to the status of persons and to the right of property of French subjects abroad, are not definitive until they have been voted by the two chambers. No cession, exchange, or annexation of territory can take place except by virtue of a law.[46] The French law thus attempts to classify under five general heads the treaties that are to receive the approval of the legislature. Owing to the complex nature of the subject-matter of treaties, it is, however, necessary, in order to determine specifically what treaties are considered as so included, to examine the practice of the government. The legislative approval, in case it is required, is given in the form of a law authorizing the President to ratify the treaty and to cause it to be executed. It accordingly regularly precedes the exchange of ratifications and follows the signing of the treaty.

§131. **Treaties of Peace.**—The preliminary articles of peace with China, signed at Tien Tsin, May 11, 1884, were on May

45 Id., 3520, col. 1.

46 "Le Président de la République négocie et ratifie les traités. Il en donne connaissance aux Chambres aussitôt que l'intérêt et la sûreté de l'Etat le permettent. Les traités de paix, de commerce, les traités qui engagent les finances de l'Etat, ceux qui sont relatifs à l'état des personnes et au droit de propriété des Francais à l'étranger, ne sont définitifs qu'après avoir été votés par les deux Chambres. Nulle cession, nul échange, nulle adjonction de territoire ne peut avoir lieu qu'en vertu d'une loi." Bulletin des Lois, 12th series, No. 260. See for English translations, Annals of American Academy of Political and Social Science, III, sup. 166; Dodd, Modern Constitutions, I, 292. See also for French text, Brit. and For. State Papers, LXVII, 499.

20 communicated, together with explanations, to the chambers for their consideration.[47] The definitive treaty of peace and commerce, signed June 9, 1885, was also submitted for legislative approval, which was given in the form of a law authorizing the President to ratify and carry it into effect. A similar law was passed by the Deputies, February 27, and by the Senate, March 6, 1886, approving the treaty of peace concluded with Madagascar, December 17, 1885.[48] Treaties often fall within more than one class. The treaty with China, for instance, could also be classed as a treaty of commerce.

§132. **Treaties of Commerce.**—Under treaties of commerce are included not only those that directly affect the existing tariff rates, but also those for the general regulation of trade and intercourse. For instance, the general treaty of amity and commerce with Japan, signed August 4, 1896, was approved by the special law of January 13, 1898, prior to the exchange of ratifications on March 19, and the decree of promulgation of July 30.[49] In the case of commercial treaties about to expire the approval of the chambers to their prolongation may be given in the form of a general law authorizing the President to secure an extension of the time for a period specified in the law; and agreements concluded accordingly are not submitted to the chambers for approval. On the authority of the law of August 4, 1879, agreements of this nature were reached with Great Britain, October 10; Belgium, October 18; Austria-Hungary, November 20; Sweden and Norway, November 25; Portugal, November 25; Italy, November 26; and Switzerland, November 29, 1879.[50] By the law of December 29, 1891, the Government was authorized not only to extend provisionally the whole or parts of treaties of commerce about to expire, but also to apply in whole or in part the minimum tariff rates to products of countries maintaining a conventional tariff, provided that such countries should consent to apply to French products most-favored-nation treatment.[51]

47 De Clercq's Recueil des Traités de la France, XIV, 298, 300.

48 Id., XV, 922.

49 Id., XX, 550. Bulletin des Lois, LVII, 1197, No. 1987.

50 De Clercq's Recueil des Traités, XII, 476, 488, 490, 507, 509-511. See similar laws of July 20, 1881 and February 2, 1882, and the prolongation of treaties, Id., XIII, 59, 80-88, 235, 238, et seq.

51 Art. II, Id., XIX, 304. See also Art. IV of the law of April 5, 1898, Bulletin des Lois, No. 1969.

By virtue of this law a limited reciprocity in commerce was established by exchange of notes with Belgium, the Netherlands, Switzerland, Sweden and Norway, Greece, and Spain.[52] To secure the advantages of the American tariff, so far as it was subject to executive regulation by section 3 of the general tariff act of 1890, the special law of January 27, 1893 was passed, authorizing the Government to apply certain minimum tariff rates to articles produced in the United States.[53] The agreement concluded May 28, 1898, in which reciprocal tariff advantages were secured, was made effective by the President of France, without submission to the chambers, in virtue of existing laws,[54] and by the President of the United States, without submission to the Senate, in virtue of section 3 of the act of July 24, 1897. Treaties securing commercial privileges with African tribes are frequently ratified and promulgated on executive authority. Commercial treaties entered into by the French government, acting in its suzerain capacity under the treaty of May 12, 1881, for Tunis, have not been submitted to the chambers for approval. The President of France, acting in his own name as well as in the name of his Highness the Bey, concluded a treaty of commerce, applying to Tunis, with the Italian government, September 28, 1896. The treaty having been approved by the President, was promulgated and put in force by a decree of the Bey, February 1, 1897, contersigned by the French minister resident in Tunis.[55] Treaty relations were established between Tunis and various other countries in similar manner.[56]

Telegraphic, postal-union, and monetary conventions, and those for the regulation of international railway traffic relate to trade and intercourse with foreign nations, although they may likewise involve the finances of the state. The ratification of the general convention for the regulation of international railway traffic, signed at Berne, October 14, 1890, was authorized by the law of

---

52 De Clercq's Recueil des Traités, XIX, 400, 403, 409, 457; XX, 94.

53 Id., XIX, 547.

54 Id., XXI, 379.

55 Id., XX, 596, 597.

56 Switzerland, October 14, 1896; Austria-Hungary, July 20, 1896; Russia, October 14, 1896; Germany, November 18, 1896; Belgium, January 2, 1897; Spain, January 12, 1897; Denmark, January 21, 1897; the Netherlands, April 3, 1897; Sweden and Norway, May 5, 1897; and Great Britain, September 18, 1897. Id., XX, 626, et seq.

December 29, 1891.[57] An agreement with Italy signed January
20, 1879, relative to the establishment of international railroad
stations; and three agreements signed with Belgium May 9, 1877,
September 23, 1877, and February 20, 1878, relative to the construction and regulation of frontier railroads, were approved by
laws.[58] The approval of the telegraphic conventions signed at
Paris, June 21, 1890, and at Budapest, July 22, 1896, was given
in the laws of June 19, 1891, and June 28, 1897, respectively.[59]
The universal postal conventions signed at Paris, June 1, 1878, at
Vienna, July 4, 1891, and at Washington, June 15, 1897, were approved, respectively, by the laws of December 20, 1878, April 13,
1892, and April 8, 1898.[60] The monetary convention between
France, Belgium, Greece, Italy and Switzerland, signed at Paris,
November 5, 1878, as likewise the amendatory and supplementary
conventions of November 6, 1885 and November 15, 1893, were
approved by special laws.[61] Conventions for the extradition of
fugitives from justice, and those defining the duties and privileges
of consuls are ratified on legislative authority.

§133. **Treaties Involving the Finances.**—Treaties for the
guarantee of loans potentially involve the finances, and accordingly are submitted to the chambers for approval.[62] The convention
with the United States signed at Washington, January 15, 1880,
for the examination and settlement by a mixed commission of
claims of American citizens against France, arising out of the
French operations against Mexico, the Franco-Prussian war, and
the internal disturbances known as the "Insurrection of the Commune," and, on the other hand, of claims of citizens of France

57 Id., XVIII, 601.

58 Id., XII, 20, 41, 67, 376.

59 Id., XVIII, 392; XX, 433. See for special telegraphic and telephone
conventions, and the dates of the laws approving them, Id., XVIII, 471, et
seq.; XIX, 268, 283, 513.

60 Id., XII, 95; XIX, 114; XXI, 82. Examples may be found of special agreements to facilitate postal exchanges of an administrative character, which have been concluded and made effective without submission to
the chambers. See the conventions signed January 17, 1894, with the
Netherlands, and July 9, 1895, with Great Britain, (Id., XX, 109, 110, 259,
263), and arrangements with Great Britain of November 6 and 9, 1894, and
December 2 and 9, 1895, (Id., XX, 181, 262).

61 Id., XII, 356; XV, 892; XX, 71.

62 For instance, the convention of March 29, 1898, to facilitate a Greek
loan, was approved by the law of April 8, 1898. Id., XXI, 350.

against the United States arising out of acts committed against their "persons and property" in the United States during the period between April 13, 1861, and August 20, 1866, engaged the finances of the state, and required the approval of the chambers.[63]

§134. **Treaties Relating to the Status of Persons and Property Rights of French Subjects Abroad.**—The following conventions of a special character have been submitted to the chambers for approval:—the convention with Switzerland of July 23, 1879, concerning the naturalization of children of former French citizens who have become by naturalization Swiss citizens;[64] the convention with Austria-Hungary of May 14, 1879, concerning judicial assistance to be rendered to citizens of the one in the territory of the other;[65] the convention with Russia of July 27, 1896, for the exemption of French citizens bringing action in Russia from any hindrance to which Russians may not be subject;[66] the international convention, and additional protocol, signed at The Hague, November 14, 1896, designed to establish common rules concerning many matters of private international law and civil procedure;[67] the convention for the protection of industrial property, signed at Paris, March 20, 1883;[68] and the international copyright convention signed at Berne, September 9, 1886, together with the additional act of May 4, 1896.[69] Agreements for the reciprocal protection of trade-marks are regularly, it seems, submitted for legislative approval.[70]

§135. **Acquisition or Cession of Territory.**—Of treaties involving an acquisition, cession or exchange of territory, and accordingly subject to legislative approval, note may be made of the following: the treaty with Sweden of August 10, 1877, for the retrocession to France of the island of St. Bartholomew;[71] the agreement with the king of the Society Islands of June 29, 1880, by which the complete sovereignty over these islands was to pass

---

63 De Clercq's Recueil des Traités, XII, 519. Law of June 16, 1880.

64 Id., XII, 407.

65 Id., XII, 400, 527.

66 Id., XX, 547.

67 Id., XX, 642.

68 Id., XIV, 203.

69 Id., XVII, 253; XX, 398.

70 See, for instances, Id., XX, 335, 430; XXI, 632, 774. For agreements of this character, which appear not to have been submitted, see Id., XII, 541, 545. See also Sen. Doc. No. 20, 56th Cong., 2d Sess., 364.

71 De Clercq's Recueil des Traités, XII, 35, 40.

to France;[72] the convention with Tunis of May 12, 1881, by which that country placed itself under the protectorate influence of France;[73] and the convention with Great Britain of April 8, 1904, by which territory was acquired on the West coast of Africa in exchange for the relinquishment of certain fishery privileges on the coast of Newfoundland.[74] Madagascar was made a French colony by a law of August 6, 1896, in which the act of the queen of that island making the cession was accepted. Likewise, by a law of March 19, 1898, the islands to the leeward of Tahiti were declared to be an integral part of the colonial domain of France.[75] Numerous agreements made with the less important African tribes, in which French sovereignty has been recognized, have not been submitted to the chambers for approval. A decree of August 1, 1895, issued on the advice of the ministers of the colonies and foreign affairs, ratified fourteen different agreements of this character negotiated by army officers and other agents between December 21, 1894 and March 12, 1895.[76] Such agreements, however, can hardly be classed as treaties by which territory is acquired, since they cannot be exhibited alone as international titles.[77] Agreements for the adjustment of boundaries, such as were concluded March 15, 1893, and April 4, 1900, with Belgium, each of which provided for an actual exchange of small portions of territory, require legislative approval.[78] Of agreements concerning boundaries of colonial possessions, ratified on the authority of a law, note may be made of those for the determination and settlement of boundaries between possessions in Africa concluded with Germany, December 24, 1885, March 15, 1894, and July 23, 1897;[79] with the Kongo, August 14, 1894;[80] with Spain, June 27, 1900;[81] and with Great Britain, June 14, 1898.[82] Likewise, the conventions of No-

---

72 Id., XII, 571, 624.

73 Id., XIII, 25.

74 Id., XXII, 517.

75 Id., XX, 585; XXI, 349.

76 Id., XX, 297. See similar decree of March 1, 1895, Id., 217.

77 See Art. XXXV of the treaty of Berlin, signed February 26, 1885, as regards coasts of Africa. Brit. and For. State Papers, LXXVI, 19.

78 De Clercq's Recueil des Traités, XX, 16, 21; XXI, 646.

79 Id., XV, 927; XX, 117; XXI, 281.

80 Id., XX, 165.

81 Id., XXI, 660.

82 Id., XXI, 386.

vember 29, 1888 and April 10, 1897, with the Netherlands and
Brazil, respectively, by which the determination of the boundaries
of French Guiana was referred to arbitration, were submitted for
approval.[83] The agreement with Great Britain, signed August
10, 1889, relative to boundaries between French and British possessions on the west coast of Africa, appears to have been ratified
on executive authority, and to be an exception.[84]

§136. **Treaties Not Submitted for Approval of Chambers.**—A
classification of treaties not included under one of the heads
enumerated in Article VIII of the Constitutional Law, and which
accordingly do not require legislative approbation, is quite impossible. The following may serve to illustrate their varied character:—the general treaty signed at Berlin, July 13, 1878, for the
settlement of affairs in the Near East; the treaties of May 24,
1881, and March 10, 1883, with the same powers, concerning the
Turko-Grecian frontiers, and the navigation of the Danube;[85]
the treaty signed at Constantinople, October 29, 1888, for the neutralization of the Suez Canal;[86] the international sanitary convention signed at Dresden, April 15, 1893;[87] the agreement reached
with Great Britain by exchange of declarations at London, August 5, 1890, by which the French government engaged to recognize a British protectorate over the islands of Zanzibar and
Pemba, and the British government engaged to recognize a
French protectorate over the island of Madagascar and a French
influence over certain portions of Africa;[88] the declarations
signed with Great Britain, January 15, 1896, and April 8, 1904,
concerning their respective spheres of influence in portions of
Siam, and in Madagascar and the New Hebrides;[89] and the general convention of arbitration concluded with Great Britain, October 14, 1903.[90]

83 Id., XVIII, 155; XXI, 51.
84 Id., XVIII, 289.
85 Id., XIII, 32; XIV, 178.
86 Id., XVIII, 144.
87 Id., XX, 27.
88 Id., XVIII, 578.
89 Id., XX, 361; XXII, 524.
90 Id., XXII, 439. See also similar conventions of arbitration concluded with Spain, February 26, 1904, Id., 466; with the Netherlands,
April 6, 1904, Id., 499; with Sweden and Norway, July 9, 1904, Id., 600;
with Switzerland, December 14, 1904, Id., 632.

CHAPTER XX.

OTHER FOREIGN STATES.

§137. Belgium.—By Article LXVIII of the Belgian constitution (1831), the King makes treaties of peace, alliance and commerce. He is to give information in regard to them to the chambers as soon as the interest and safety of the state permit, adding suitable explanations. Treaties of commerce and those that may burden the state or bind Belgians individually have effect only after having received the assent of the chambers. No cession, exchange, or addition of territory may take place except by virtue of a law. In no case may secret articles be destructive of the open ones.[1] No decree of the King can take effect until countersigned by a responsible minister.[2]

The action of the chambers is primarily to give effect to the treaty, but it regularly precedes the exchange of ratifications. The law for this purpose does not expressly authorize ratification but provides that the treaty shall be given full effect ("sortira son plein et entier effet"). It appears to have been the earlier practice for the King to withhold his sanction to the law until the exchange of ratifications of the treaty had taken place.[3] With re-

[1] "Le Roi commande les forces de terre et de mer, déclare la guerre, fait les traités de paix, d'alliance et de commerce. Il en donne connaissance aux Chambres aussitôt que l'intérêt et la sûreté de l'Etat le permettent, en y joignant les communications convenables. Les traités de commerce et ceux qui pourraient grever l'Etat ou lier individuellement des Belges, n'ont d'effet qu'après avoir recu l'assentiment des Chambres. Nulle cession, nul échange, nulle adjonction de territoire ne peut avoir lieu qu'en vertu d'une loi. Dans aucun cas, les articles secrets d'un traité ne peuvent être destructifs des articles patents."

[2] Art. LXIV.

[3] The exchange of ratifications of the treaty of commerce with China, signed November 2, 1865, took place at Shanghai, October 27, 1866, while the law by which the chambers expressed approval is dated January 3, 1867. The law, however, was adopted by the Chamber of Representatives, February 25, 1866, and by the Senate, March 6, 1866. Lanckman, Traités de Commerce et de Navigation entre la Belgique et les Pays étrangers, 63. The ratifications of the treaty of commerce with Great Britain, signed July 23, 1862, were exchanged, August 30, 1862. The approbatory law is dated August 31, but it was passed by the Chamber of Representatives, August 13, and by the Senate, August 21, 1862. Id., 189. The ratifications

spect to the more recent treaties of commerce, as for instance, those concluded May 25, 1895, with Greece; June 7, 1895, with Mexico; June 22, 1896, with Japan; June 22, 1904, with Germany; February 12, 1906, with Austria-Hungary, and April (11) 24, 1907, with Servia, the laws were sanctioned by the King prior to the exchange of ratifications.[4]

General laws for the regulation of matters usually subject to uniform international treatment often contain provisions authorizing the King to enter into treaties with foreign states on condition of reciprocity, and to apply the law in execution of them. Treaties concluded in conformity with these laws, though otherwise subject to legislative action, are not submitted to the chambers. Such provisions are, for instance, found in the laws of January 5, 1855, for the restitution of deserting seamen;[5] March 15, 1874, for the extradition of fugitives from justice;[6] April 1, 1879, for the protection of trade-marks;[7] November 27, 1891, for the return of indigents;[8] and January 30, 1892, for the extension, on condition of reciprocity, of the most-favored-nation treatment in matters of commerce, navigation and duties.[9]

Of treaties that may burden the state, i. e., may impose financial obligations, the treaty of July 3, 1890, with the Kongo, relative to a loan to be made by Belgium, may be noted.[10] The restriction as to treaties affecting territorial limits covers such boundary agreements as provide for an exchange of territory of

---

of the treaty of commerce with the United States, signed March 8, 1875, were exchanged, June 11, 1875. The approbatory law of June 14, had been adopted by the Chamber of Representatives June 1, and by the Senate June 3, 1875. Id., 131. The ratifications of the treaty of commerce with Spain, signed May 4, 1878, were exchanged July 23. The approbatory law of July 25 had been adopted by the Chamber of Representatives May 16, and by the Senate May 19, 1878. Id., 111. See also, Id., 9, 21, 51, 267, 295, 318.

4 Busschere, Code de Traités et Arrangements internationaux intéressant la Belgique, II, 241, 289, 270, 581; Recueil des Traités et Conventions concernant le Royaume de Belgique, XX, 48, 187, 628. See for other important treaties of commerce concluded since 1890, in which this procedure has been followed, Busschere, II, 146, 191, 206, 302, 415.

5 Art. II. Busschere, II, 464.

6 Arts. I and VI. Id., I, 575, 578. Moore, Extradition, I, 705, 708.

7 Art. XIX. Busschere, II, 481.

8 Art. XXVIII. Id., II, 440.

9 Id., II, 456.

10 Id., I, 290, 291.

the state, such for instance as the conventions signed with France, March 15, 1893, and April 12, 1905, and with the Netherlands, January 11, 1892.[11] The treaty for the annexation of the Kongo, signed November 28, 1907, was approved by the law of October 18, 1908.[12] The general arbitration conventions concluded with Denmark, April 26, 1905; with Spain, January 23, 1905; with Greece, May 2, 1905; with Sweden and Norway, November 30, 1904; with Russia, October 30, 1904; and with Switzerland, November 15, 1904, were all approved by the law of July 7, 1905.[13] As a permanently neutralized state under Article VII of the convention concluded at London, April 19, 1839, Belgium is not at liberty to enter into treaties that may lead to hostilities, except in defense of her own frontiers, or that may otherwise compromise her neutrality. Thus in the treaty of May 11, 1867, for the neutralization of Luxemburg, to which Belgium is a signatory party, it is expressly provided that as a neutral state Belgium is excepted from the obligation assumed by the other powers of guaranteeing this neutrality.[14]

§138. Luxemburg.—Article XXXVII of the constitution of Luxemburg (1868) gives to the Grand Duke the right to make treaties. He is to give notice thereof to the Chamber as soon as the interest and safety of the state permit. Treaties of commerce and those that may burden the state or bind individually citizens of Luxemburg, and in general all treaties bearing upon a matter that can be regulated only by law, have effect only after having received the assent of the Chamber. No session, exchange, or acquisition of territory can take place without the sanction of a law. Secret articles cannot be in contravention of open ones.[15]

§139. The Netherlands.—Article LIX of the constitution of the Netherlands, as revised in 1887, provides that the King shall make and ratify all treaties with foreign powers. He shall communicate the purport of them to the two chambers of the States-

---

11 Id., I, 174, 264; Recueil des Traités et Conventions, XX, 324.

12 Id., XX, 267.

13 Id., XX, 283. The approval of the various conventions, except the one for the limitation on the employment of force in the recovery of contract debts, signed October 18, 1907, at the Second Peace Conference, was given in a single law, dated May 25, 1910. Id., XXI, 65.

14 Busschere, I, 63.

15 Brit. and For. State Papers, LVIII, 253.

23

General as soon as he thinks that the interest of the state permits. Treaties that contain provisions for changes of the territory of the state, that impose on the kingdom pecuniary obligations, or that contain any other provision concerning rights established by law (legal rights) shall not be ratified by the King until after their approval by the States-General. This approval is not required if the power has been reserved to the King by law to conclude such a treaty.[16]

The limitation as to treaties providing for a change of the territory of the state appears to have been considered as applying to those affecting colonial possessions. This construction is in conformity with the express provision of Article LVIII of the original constitution of 1815. In the conventions concluded November 29, 1888, with France, for the submission to arbitration of the disputed boundary between Dutch and French Guiana; June 20, 1891, with Great Britain, for the determinination of boundaries in the island of Borneo; May 16, 1895, with Great Britain, for the settlement of boundaries between possessions on the island of New Guinea; and October 1, 1904, with Portugal, as to boundaries in the island of Timor, clauses were inserted by which the ratification was expressly made dependent upon the approval of the States-General.[17]

Under treaties imposing a pecuniary obligation, are to be classed not only those that expressly stipulate for a payment of money, but also those in which an expenditure is a necessary or implied consequence. Such, for instance, are the conventions with Bel-

16 "De Koning sluit en bekrachtigt alle verdragen met vreemde Mogendheden. Hij deelt den inhoud dier verdragen mede aan de beide Kamers der Staten-Generaal, zoodra Hij oordeelt dat het belang van den Staat dit toelaat. Verdragen, die wijziging van het grondgebied van den Staat inhouden, die aan het Rijk geldelijke verpligtingen opleggen of die eenige andere bepaling, wettelijke regten betreffende, inhouden, worden door den Koning niet bekrachtigd dan na door de Staten-Generaal te zijn goedgekeurd. Deze goedkeuring wordt niet vereischt, indien de Koning zich de bevoegdheid tot het sluiten van het verdrag bij de wet heeft voorbehouden." Staatsblad (1887), No. 212. See, for French version, Brit. and For. State Papers, LXXVIII, 273; for English translation, Dodd, Modern Constitutions, II, 91.

17 Arts. III, VIII, VI, and XV, respectively. Lagemans, Recueil des Traités et Conventions conclus par le Royaume des Pays-Bas, X, 95, 356; XII, 186; XV, 345.

gium, for the improvement of international canals,[18] and the convention with Great Britain of May 16, 1895, for the submission to arbitration of the question of damages for the arrest by the Dutch authorities of the master of the Costa Rica Packet.[19] Under treaties that contain any other provision concerning rights established by law (wettelijke regten) there seem to be included all those that touch upon such subjects as can be regulated only by means of legislation.[20] It is specifically provided in the constitution that foreigners can be naturalized only by law;[21] that the admission and expulsion of foreigners, and the conditions on which conventions of extradition with foreign powers may be concluded are to be regulated by law;[22] and that no impost or revenue can be established except by law.[23] Conventions concluded in conformity with the general extradition law of April 6, 1875, as modified by the law of April 15, 1886,[24] (and it specifically provides that no convention shall otherwise be entered into) require no action on the part of the legislature to carry them into effect and accordingly do not require submission for approval.[25] The convention of March 20, 1883, for the protection of industrial property, was approved by the law of April 23, 1884.[26] As illustrative of commercial treaties receiving legislative approval, note may be made of the treaty with Spain signed July 12, 1892;[27] the treaty

18 Id., VIII, 204.

19 Id., XIII, 518.

20 Marquardsen, Handbuch des öffentlichen Rechts, IV, pt. I, Div. 4, p. 83.

21 Art. VI.

22 Art. IV.

23 Art. CLXXIV.

24 Moore, Extradition, I, 791; Tripels, Code Politique, 194. See, for naturalization law of December 12, 1892, Brit. and For. State Papers, LXXXIV, 663.

25 Of recent extradition conventions concluded and made effective without submission to the States-General are those signed May 31, 1889, with Belgium; November 4, 1893, with Russia; October 29, 1894, with Spain; December 31, 1896, with Germony; May 28, 1897, with Italy; May 19, 1894, with Portugal; August 26, 1905, with Greece. Lagemans, Recueil des Traités, X, 113; XII, 64, 154; XIII, 230, 294; XII, 107; XIII, 512; XVI, 29.

26 Tripels, Code Politique, 238.

27 Approved by the law of July 24, 1893; and ratifications exchanged December 11, 1893.

with the Orange Free State signed April 9, 1895 ;[28] and the treaty with Japan signed September 8, 1896.[29]

§140. **Italy.**—Article V of the Fundamental Statute, promulgated for Sardinia March 4, 1848, and subsequently extended to the various parts of the present kingdom of Italy, provides that to the King alone belongs the executive power; that he declares war; makes treaties of peace, alliance, commerce, and other treaties, giving notice to the chambers as soon as the interest and safety of the state will permit, with opportune explanations. Treaties that involve financial obligations, or a change of territory of the state, shall not have effect until they have received the assent of the chambers.[30] Laws and government acts can take effect only after they have been signed by a responsible minister.[31]

28 Approved by the law of April 9, 1897; and ratifications exchanged June 26, 1897.

29 Approved by the law of May 2, 1897; and ratifications exchanged August 20, 1897. Lagemans, Recueil des Traités, XII, 346; XIII, 214, 517.

30 "Al Re solo appartiene il potere esecutivo. Egli è il Capo Supremo dello Stato: comanda tutte le forze di terra e di mare: dichiara la guerra: fa i trattati di pace, d'alleanza, di commercio ed altri, dandone notizia alle Camere tosto che l'interesse e la sicurezza dello Stato il permettano, ed unendovi le comunicazioni opportune. I trattati che importassero un onere alle finanze, o variazione di territorio dello Stato, non avranno effetto se non dopo ottenuto l'assenso delle Camere." Raccolta di Constituzioni Italiane (Torino 1852), I, 42. For English translation, see Annals of the American Academy of Political and Social Science, V, sup. 27; Dodd, Modern Constitutions, II, 5. See also for Italian text, Lowell, Governments and Parties in Continental Europe, II, 347.

31 Article LXVII. "There exists in the Italian Parliament no committee of foreign affairs and, in general, the Government may be said to enjoy a wide independence in dealing with international questions. The general rule is such that the Government is empowered to negotiate and ratify without the cognizance of Parliament such treaties as impose no direct financial burden on the country and do not affect its credit; but if any clause necessitates a vote of supplies, the entire treaty must be submitted to the approval of Parliament. This interpretation was insisted upon in respect of the treaty of peace with Austria in 1849, when the Government endeavored to establish the doctrine that only the financial articles required the approval of Parliament; whereupon the Chamber passed an order of the day to the effect that the vote of the required funds did not validate the treaty which required the approval of Parliament before it could have force of law. Apart from this control the Chamber exercises a general supervision over the foreign policy of the Government by means of questions, interpellations, and requests for papers, and the right of unlimited discussion on the Foreign Office vote in much the same way as the British

According to a strict construction of this article, the two speci-fied classes of treaties alone would seem to require the assent of the chambers to make them effective. Treaties of commerce, since they are specified among those within the competency of the King to make, and are omitted in the clause which closely fol-lows specifying those for which the assent of the chambers is nec-essary, would logically be excluded from this category unless con-sidered to involve the finances of the state. In practice, however, treaties of commerce, as well as all treaties touching upon mat-ters, the regulation of which belongs to Parliament, are, it ap-pears, regularly submitted to that body prior to their ratification.[32] The legislative approval is given in the form of a law authorizing that the treaty be carried into effect, and is frequently sanctioned by the King on even date with the exchange of ratifications of the treaty. Such was the case with the treaties of commerce con-cluded March 22, 1883, with Switzerland; May 4, 1883, with Ger-many; June 15, 1883, with Great Britain; December 6, 1891, with Austria-Hungary; December 6, 1891, with Germany; April 19, 1892, with Switzerland, and December 1, 1894, with Japan.[33] A provisional agreement with Spain, reached by exchange of notes,

Parliament. As regards interpellations, the responsible Minister may, with the consent of the House, defer his reply, or even refuse to reply at all; in the latter case, however, the interpellator has the right, before the House takes its decision, to state the reasons for his interpellation, and the Min-ister must then show his grounds for refusing to reply. After the Minister has replied to an interpellation it is open to the interpellator if he is dis-satisfied to move an order of the day hostile to the Government, where-upon the Chamber decides when it shall be discussed. Questions are usually submitted in writing and, as in the case of interpellations, the Minister may, with the consent of the House, refuse to reply; on the other hand, the custom of the Italian Parliament appears to allow members considerable latitude with regard to supplementary questions. As regards the publica-tion of papers dealing with international questions, the Italian Parliament appears always to have recognized that the Minister for Foreign Affairs must be the sole judge as to the opportuneness of publishing correspondence dealing with current questions." Enclosure in despatch from Sir R. Rodd to Sir Edward Grey, December 31, 1911. Parl. Pap. Cd. 6102, p. 13.

32 Marquardsen, Handbuch des öffentlichen Rechts, IV, pt. I, Div. 7, p. 490. On the question whether the courts should enforce a treaty pro-mulgated by a decree and not by a law, and in conflict with a law, see Rivista di diritto internazionale (1909), IV, 452.

33 Trattati e Convenzioni fra il Regno d'Italia e gli altri Stati, IX, 200, 231, 273. Raccolta Ufficiale delle Leggi e dei Decreti del Regno d'Italia, 1892, pp. 46, 1639; 1895, p. 3030.

June 29, 1892, extending on the part of the Italian government to Spanish products the advantages of the conventional tariff contained in the treaties with Austria-Hungary, Germany and Switzerland, and on the part of the Spanish government to Italian products the minimum tariff, was authorized by the special law of June 28, 1892, the day preceding the exchange of notes.[34] The reciprocity agreement with the United States, signed February 8, 1900, expressly provided that it should be approved by the Italian Parliament. Approval was given by the law of July 12; and the agreement became effective July 18, 1900. In the United States it was made effective by executive proclamation in virtue of section 3 of the tariff act of July 24, 1897.[35]

The class of commercial treaties regularly submitted to the chambers does not seem to include general consular conventions. Thus, on September 28, 1896, two treaties were concluded with Tunis, through the government of France, one concerning commercial intercourse, and the other concerning the duties and privileges of consuls. The former was approved by the law of January 28, 1897, while the latter was ratified and put into force by a royal decree.[36] Extradition conventions, not involving a change in the law for their enforcement, are not, it appears, submitted to Parliament.

The important modification of territorial limits stipulated for in the treaty of Turin of March 24, 1860—the cession to France of Nice and Savoy—was concluded subject to the approval of the Italian Parliament.[37] The convention with the King of Ethiopia, concluded May 16, 1908, for the settlement of the boundary between the Italian possessions of Somalia and Ethiopia, likewise expressly provided that it should be submitted to Parliament for approval.[38] A similar reservation was made in the convention for the settlement of the frontier boundary between the Italian colony of Eritrea and Ethiopia.[39] An additional act to the second named convention provided for the payment to Ethiopia of the sum of 3,000,000 lire. The sanction of the King of Italy was given with approval of Parliament, July 17, 1908.[40]

34 Brit. and For. State Papers, LXXXIV, 1318.
35 Trattati e Convenzioni, XVI, 162.
36 Id., XIV, 314, 337.
37 See Art. VII.
38 Art. VIII.
39 Art. VII. Brit. and For. State Papers, CI, 1000, 1002.
40 Id., 1001.

Laws were passed to make effective the postal-union conventions signed at Vienna July 4, 1891, and at Washington June 15, 1897.[41] The act additional to the Paris convention of March 20, 1883, for the protection of industrial property, signed at Brussels December 14, 1900, and the act additional to the Madrid agreement of April 14, 1891, signed at Brussels December 14, 1900, received sanction in laws dated December 12, 1901, prior to the deposit of ratifications, June 14, 1902.[42] Special conventions concerning these subjects that do not involve a modification of the existing laws require no action on the part of Parliament.[43] The telegraphic convention signed at Budapest, July 22, 1896, appears to have been ratified and promulgated by decree without special legislative action.[44] The convention signed March 18, 1885, with the leading powers of Europe, for the guarantee of an Egyptian loan, involved a possible pecuniary obligation. The consent of Parliament was given in a law of November 25, 1886, which authorized the Government to give effect to the convention in conjunction with the other contracting powers in so far as there might arise eventually any charges upon the treasury.[45]

There remain within the competency of the King all of the so-called political conventions. Of these, particularly to be noted, are the treaties of alliance entered into, in 1855 against Russia, in 1858 with France against Austria, in 1866 with Prussia against Austria, and in 1882 with Germany and Austria. It would be impossible to find in the list of treaties concluded by Italy four others that have entailed greater financial burden. The expense of a war was an immediate consequence of each of the first three, and a burden hardly less onerous has resulted from the fourth.

§141. **Germany.**—Article XI of the constitution of Germany (1871) provides that the Emperor has the power to represent the Empire internationally, to conclude peace in the name of the Empire, to enter into alliances and other treaties with foreign states;

41 Leggi, etc., 1892, p. 1805; Trattati e Convenzioni, XV, 128.

42 Id., XVI, 204.

43 See, for instances, the special postal agreements signed July 11, 1896, with Great Britain; March 23, 1898, with Tunis; April 26, 1898, with Costa Rica; and October 18, 1898, with Montenegro. Id., XIV, 172; XV, 386, 390, 430.

44 Id., XIV, 269.

45 Brit. and For. State Papers, LXXVII, 817.

but that in so far as treaties with foreign states relate to matters that, according to Article IV, belong in the field of imperial legislation, the consent of the Bundesrath is necessary for their conclusion, and the approval of the Reichstag for their validity.[46] The Bundesrath, or Federal Council, as organized in the constitution, consists of 58 members apportioned among the States somewhat arbitrarily, and appointed by the several State Governments.[47] The members of the Reichstag are apportioned according to population, and are elected by direct vote of the people.

In a study of the formation of the constitution of the North German Union, which, with the alterations made necessary by the establishment of the German Empire in 1871, serves as the present constitution, the proceedings of two separate bodies are to be considered—the convention of delegates from the several State Governments, and the convention of representatives of the people—which assembled at Berlin in 1866-7. The former proposed a plan of a constitution which, after having been amended in numerous particulars by the convention of the people, was adopted and submitted to the several States for ratification.[48] By the original article of the Prussian project, the President of the Union was to conclude alliances and other treaties with foreign states. The representatives of the States in their deliberations attached the clause that, in so far as treaties related to matters within the field of imperial legislation as defined in Article IV, the consent of the Bundesrath should be necessary for their conclusion. To this, the representatives of the people added the fur-

---

46 "Der Kaiser hat das Reich völkerrechtlich zu vertreten, im Namen des Reichs Krieg zu erklären und Frieden zu schliessen, Bündnisse und andere Verträge mit fremden Staaten einzugehen, Gesandte zu beglaubigen und zu empfangen. * * * Insoweit die Verträge mit fremden Staaten sich auf solche Gegenstände beziehen, welche nach Article 4 in den Bereich der Reichsgesetzgebung gehören, ist zu ihrem Abschluss die Zustimmung des Bundesrathes und zu ihrer Gültigkeit die Genehmigung des Reichstages erforderlich." Reichsverfassung, Art. XI. Gesetzblatt des Deutschen Reichs (1871), No. 16, pp. 63, 69. For English translation, see Larned, History for Ready Reference, I, 549; Dodd, Modern Constitutions, I, 330.

47 Of the 58, Prussia has 17, Bavaria 6, Saxony 4, Württemberg 4, Baden 3, Hesse 3, Mecklenburg-Schwerin 2, Brunswick 2, and the others 1 each. Art. VI. In 1911, Alsace-Lorraine was granted 3 votes, making the total now 61.

48 Burgess, Political Science and Constitutional Law, I, 116.

ther condition that for their validity the approbation of the Reichstag should be necessary.[49]

The question has been much mooted whether the action of the Reichstag is essential to the validity of the treaty as an international compact, or is requisite only to give effect to the treaty so far as it relates to matters that can be regulated only by legislation. Of the advocates of the latter view is the eminent jurist Laband.[50] Of the subjects enumerated in Article IV as under the imperial superintendence and legislation are commerce, customs duties, citizenship, posts, telegraphs, railways,[52] and the protection of literary and industrial property. Amendments to the constitution can be made by acts of legislation, subject to rejection by fourteen votes in the Bundesrath. In 1911 an amendment to the colonial law of July 25, 1900 was adopted, which provides that an imperial law is required for the acquisition or cession of a protectorate, or part thereof, but that this restriction shall not apply in the adjustment of frontiers.[53] The Imperial Chancellor solely is responsible for the government departments, including the foreign office.[54] Article VIII of the constitution provides for the

49 Laband, Das Staatsrecht des deutschen Reichs (1901 ed.), II, 125; Meier, Abschluss von Staatsverträgen, 268. See also for text of drafts, Hahn, Zwei Jahre preussichdeutcher Politik, 1866-7 (Berlin 1868), 121, 483; Binding, Staatsgrundgesetze, Heft I, grössere Ausgabe, 75.

50 Das Staatsrecht des deutschen Reichs, II, 136. See Meier, 275; Von Mohl, Das deutsche Reichsstaatsrecht, 303; Von Rönne, Das Staatsrecht des deutschen Reichs, 298.

52 Subject in Bavaria to Art. XLVI.

53 Enclosure in despatch from Earl Granville to Sir Edward Grey, December 29, 1911. Parl. Pap. Cd. 6102, p. 10.

54 "The only way in which questions can be addressed in the Reichstag to the Imperial Chancellor—for since the subordinate Ministers, including the Foreign Secretary, appear solely as the Chancellor's representatives, questions cannot be addressed to them though they are often deputed to answer them—is by the tabling of an interpellation, signed by not less than thirty deputies. On the day when the interpellation is placed on the order paper the president asks the Imperial Chancellor 'whether and when' he will answer the interpellation. If the Chancellor consents to answer, the interpellator delivers a speech, the Chancellor or his representative replies, and a debate may follow if it is desired by not less than fifty members. Motions on the subject of the interpellation are not permissible. * * * Motions of any kind can be tabled if signed by not less than fifteen deputies, and if they are not withdrawn after debate, votes are taken upon them. The presentation of critical motions is, however, almost invariably checked by the knowledge that the Imperial Chancellor or his 'representatives' will

formation of a committee for foreign affairs in the Bundesrath, or Federal Council, to be composed of the representatives of the kingdoms of Bavaria, Saxony, and Württemberg, and of two other representatives of other Federal States to be elected by the Federal Council yearly, in which committee Bavaria is to occupy the chair. "As the foreign affairs committee of the Federal Council exists solely for the purpose of receiving information about foreign affairs, which is usually conveyed by the Imperial Chancellor himself, and of providing means for an exchange of views, Prussia, in whom the actual conduct of foreign affairs is vested, is not a member of the committee. The proceedings are confidential, and State Ministers, when questioned in their respective Diets, usually say nothing more than that the information conveyed to the committee has been satisfactory, and that unanimity has prevailed. In reality, the committee has met on very few occasions since the foundation of the Empire, but since the domestic crisis of November, 1908, it has become the practice for Bavaria to call meetings in connection with any foreign question of great magnitude and lasting public interest. From 1871 to 1908 only two meetings of the committee appear to have been held. Since 1908 there have been several meetings, including one before the meeting of the Reichstag in October of the present year."[55]

The separate States of the Empire retain the right of separate representation abroad. They may conclude with each other conventions of an administrative character in reference to postal and telegraphic affairs,[56] the collection of customs and excises, the determination of contested jurisdiction, and similar matters when not regulated by imperial legislation.[57] On June 20, 1903, the

neither take part in nor even attend the debate, and by the fact that a motion which is carried remains an academic expression of opinion. The small number of interpellations and motions on foreign questions during the last session of the Reichstag shows to what extent that body makes use of its powers apart from the annual discussion on the estimates." Enclosure in despatch from Earl Granville to Sir Edward Grey, December 29, 1911. Parl. Pap. Cd. 6102, p. 8.

55 Enclosure in despatch from Earl Granville to Sir Edward Grey, December 29, 1911. Parl. Pap. Cd. 6102, p. 8.

56 See reservation in Art. XLVIII.

57 "Although the separate States retain Ministers for Foreign Affairs (usually the Ministers-President), and the right to separate representation abroad—Bavaria, for instance, has Ministers at Vienna, St. Petersburgh,

Grand Duke of Mecklenburg-Schwerin concluded, subject to the approval of the German Empire, with the King of Sweden and Norway, a convention for the cession to the former of Wismar. The approval of the Empire was given in a treaty with Sweden and Norway concluded on even date.[58] A boundary agreement was concluded between Baden and Switzerland, December 21, 1906, the ratifications of which were exchanged, August 27, 1907, in which there was a mutual exchange of small tracts of territory. A convention expressly recognizing this agreement and giving it legal effect in Germany was concluded between Germany and Switzerland, October 29, 1907.[59] Extradition with foreign countries, so far as not covered by the imperial law or treaties, may be regulated by the States.[60]

§142. **Austria-Hungary.**—In Austria-Hungary treaties are negotiated by the Emperor through the joint minister for foreign affairs. The latter consults the premiers of the two states, and is subject to the interpellations of the dual delegations.[61] The Act

Paris, and Rome (Vatican and Quirinal), and Saxony at Vienna—foreign relations are now conducted almost entirely (a) in Germany, by the Imperial Foreign Office in Berlin, which was raised to federal status out of the Prussian Foreign Office in 1867, and (b) abroad, by the Ambassadors and Ministers appointed by the Emperor (see article 11)." Enclosure in despatch from Earl Granville to Sir Edward Grey, December 29, 1911. Parl. Pap. Cd. 6102, p. 10.

58 Brit. and For. State Papers, XCVI, 823, 824.

59 Id., C, 612, 614.

60 Moore, Extradition, I, 726.

61 "The Minister for Foreign Affairs being a 'joint' Minister, and as such forbidden to be a member of either the Austrian or the Hungarian Cabinet, only appears before the Delegations and not before either of the two Parliaments: and discussions on foreign affairs only take place in the latter bodies as the result of interpellations, which are addressed to the respective Prime Ministers. The joint Ministers cannot therefore lead the Parliaments, nor can the Parliaments control them. No direct influence can be exercised by either Parliament on the conduct of foreign affairs, nor is the Minister for Foreign Affairs in any way responsible to them. Thus, the occupation of Bosnia-Herzegovina was carried through by Count Andrássy against the wishes of both the Austrian and the Hungarian Parliaments. * * * These [delegations] consist of two bodies of sixty members each, of whom twenty are selected from the Upper House and forty from the Lower House of Austria and Hungary respectively. These members are elected annually, and meet simultaneously (though separately) in Vienna and Budapest alternately. The functions of the Delegations are, however, limited. In the sphere of foreign affairs, beyond passing the

of Union, in section 8 of Law XII as passed in 1867 by the Hungarian Parliament, and in section 1 of the Fundamental Law concerning joint affairs[62] of December 21, 1867, as passed by the Austrian Reichsrath, in declaring foreign affairs to be common to the two states, contains the provision that the approval of treaties in so far as the constitutions of the two states require is reserved to the respective legislatures, i. e. the Austrian Reichsrath and the Hungarian Parliament.[63] It is, therefore, necessary to look to the constitutions of the two countries in order to determine what treaties, if any, require legislative approval.

The five Fundamental Laws of December 21, 1867 form the body of the Austrian constitution. By article 6 of the Fundamental Law, concerning the exercise of executive power, the Emperor concludes treaties. For the validity of treaties of commerce and those that may burden the state or a portion of it, or impose obligations on individual subjects, the consent of the Reichsrath is necessary.[64] Section 11 of the law, concerning imperial representation, also enumerates among the duties of the Reichsrath the examination and approval of treaties of commerce, and all treaties that may burden the kingdom or a part of it, or impose obligations on individual subjects, or have as a result a territorial change in the kingdoms and lands represented in the Reichsrath.[65] Governmental power is to be exercised through responsible ministers.[66]

The constitution of Hungary is not contained in any single document, but is made up of laws and charters, some of which

---

estimates, their only duty is to receive information from the joint Minister for Foreign Affairs—in fact, to give him an opportunity of making statements." Enclosure in despatch from Mr. Russell to Sir Edward Grey, January 6, 1912. Parl. Pap. Cd. 6102, p. 2.

62 R. G. B. 146.

63 Oesterreich, Gesetze, XIX, 101, supplement, 83.

64 "Der Kaiser schliesst die Staatsverträge ab. Zur Gültigkeit der Handelsverträge und jener Staatsverträge, die das Reich oder Theile desselben belasten oder einzelne Bürger verpflichten, ist die Zustimmung des Reichsrathes erforderlich." R. G. B. 145. Id., 100.

65 "Es gehören daher zum Wirkungskreise des Reichsrathes: (a) die Prüfung und Genehmigung der Handelsverträge und jener Staatsverträge, die das Reich oder Theile desselben belasten, oder einzelne Bürger verpflichten, oder eine Gebietsänderung der im Reichsrathe vertretenen Königreiche und Länder zur Folge haben." R. G. B. 141. Id., 42.

66 Art. II.

are of early date. According to Hungarian writers, all treaties that may change the internal organization of the state, or touch upon the rights of the legislature to concur in levying taxes, in making expenditures, or in furnishing recruits, or that may cause a change of territory, require the approval of Parliament before they can be given effect.[67]

The commercial relations between the two countries are regulated by agreement, entered into in accordance with section 2 of the Fundamental Law and Act of Union of Austria, and section 61 of the Hungarian Law XII. As entered into in 1867, it was subject to termination at the end of every ten years; but it was with modifications successively renewed until 1897. On the failure of the Austrian Reichsrath to provide for its renewal in that year, it was provisionally extended by decrees of the Emperor until 1907, when it was renewed by legislative acts of the two states. This agreement provides that while it continues in force the two countries shall form a customs and commercial union. Treaties that have for their object the regulation of commercial relations abroad, especially those relating to commerce, tariffs, navigation, consuls, posts and telegraphs, are equally binding on the territories of the two states. The negotiation and conclusion of such treaties, subject to the constitutional consent of both legislatures, takes place through the common minister of foreign affairs on the basis to be agreed upon between the Governments of the two states.[68]

§143. Sweden.[69]—By Article XII of the constitution of

67 Ulbrich, Marquardsen's Handbuch des öffentlichen Rechts, IV, pt. I, div. I, p. 150.

68 Art. III. Gesetze, XIX, 325, 326; Osterreich Reichsgesetzblatt (1907), No. 129. See, also, Id., (1908), No. 124.

69 Prior to the dissolution in 1905 of the union of Sweden and Norway, the King by virtue of Article IV of the Act of Union of 1815 had the power to make peace, to conclude or dissolve treaties, and to send and receive diplomatic representatives. Martens, Nouveau Recueil des Traités, II, 612. Negotiations not only for Sweden alone, but also for the united kingdoms, were conducted on the advice of the Swedish minister. In those that touched upon matters relating to both kingdoms or to Norway alone, the Norwegian minister, who with two councillors represented Norway in the common council at Stockholm, was admitted into the ministerial council, in which all diplomatic affairs were discussed. Treaties were often concluded separately for the two countries. Numerous postal, telegraphic, and extradition conventions were so concluded. The postal union convention concluded at Washington, June 15, 1897, and the international telegraphic agreement concluded at Budapest, July 22, 1896, were

Sweden (1809), the King has the power to conclude treaties and alliances with foreign powers, after consultation with the minister of state and two other members of the council of state, including the minister for foreign affairs.[70]   All diplomatic correspondence with foreign powers or with Swedish diplomatic representatives abroad is to take place, without regard to its character, through the minister for foreign affairs.[71]   It is expressly provided in the constitution that no new taxes can be imposed,[72] or loans or new debts contracted, without the consent of the Rigsdag.[73]   No part of the kingdom can be disposed of by sale, gift or otherwise.[74]

§144. Norway.—By Article XXVI of the constitution of Norway (1814), the King has the power to commence war and conclude peace, to enter into and break off alliances, and to send and receive ambassadors.[75]   In the enumeration of the powers of the

signed by different representatives on the part of the two kingdoms. Treaties for the modification of customs duties were frequently concluded for the two countries separately. For instance, on June 11, 1895, two distinct commercial treaties were concluded with Belgium, the one for Sweden, and the other for Norway. 87 Brit. and For. State Papers 493, 834. Commercial treaties, which applied to Norway alone, were concluded March 22, 1894, with Switzerland, and December 31, 1895, with Portugal. 86 Id. 1024; 87 Id. 534.

70 "Konungen eger att i afhandlingar och förbund med främmande magter inga, sedan han, i den ordning föregaende paragraf stadgar, deröfver hört statsministern, ministern för utrikes ärendena och nagon annan tillkallad statsradets ledamot eller, der ministern för utrikes ärendena tillika är statsminister, tva andra tillkallade statsradets ledamöter." Text as printed by Oscar Alin at Stockholm 1891. For English translation, see Dodd, Modern Constitutions, II, 219; Larned, History for Ready Reference, I, 581.

71 Art. XI. This section likewise describes in detail the manner in which all questions of foreign affairs shall be considered by the King and the minister of state and the two other members of the council of state, including the minister for foreign affairs.

72 Art. LXXIII.

73 Art. LXXVI.

74 Art. LXXVIII. "The treaty-making power is vested in the King in Council, but any treaty affecting taxation or finance, or entailing a loan or a cession of territory, must be submitted to the Parliament." Parl. Pap. Cd. 6102, p. 24.

75 "Kongen har Ret til at sammenkalde Tropper, begynde Krig og slutte Fred, indgaa og ophæve Forbund, sende og modtage Gesandter." Grundloven. Printed at Christiania, 1893. See also French text of constitution with changes to May 25, 1905, enclosure in despatch from Norway, October 5, 1906; English translation by H. L. Braekstad (London, 1905); Dodd, Modern Constitutions, II, 123.

Storthing in Article LXXV (g), there is expressly included the power to have communicated to it the alliances and treaties which the King has entered into with foreign powers, with the exception of secret articles, which, however, shall not conflict with the public ones.[76] All orders issued by the King, with the exception of matters of military command, are to be countersigned by the minister of state.[77] The kingdom of Norway is declared to be a free, independent, indivisible and inalienable state.[78] The military and naval forces cannot be employed in an offensive war without the consent of the Storthing.[79] To the Storthing belongs the power to enact and repeal laws, to impose taxes, imposts, duties and other public burdens.[80] In treaties stipulating for special reductions in customs duties a clause is often inserted expressly providing for their approval by the Storthing. Such clauses are found in the commercial treaties concluded with Switzerland, March 22, 1894, with Belgium, June 11, 1895, and with Portugal, December 31, 1895.[81]

§145. **Denmark.**—By Article XVIII of the constitution of Denmark (1849, revised in 1866), the King declares war and concludes peace; he also enters into and breaks off alliances and commercial treaties; but he cannot, without the consent of the Rigsdag, cede any part of the country or enter into any engagement for a change in the existing constitutional organization.[82] The original article (XXIII) in the constitution of 1849 was

76 "Det tilkommer Storthinget: * * * (g) at lade sig meddele de Forbund og Traktater, Kongen, paa Statens Vegne, har indgaaet med fremmede Magter, med Undtagelse af hemmelige Artikler, som dog ei maa stride mod de offentlige."

77 Art. XXXI.

78 Art. I.

79 Art. XXV.

80 Art. LXXV, (a).

81 See as to the practice of submitting such treaties for the approval of the Storthing, Professor Aschehoug, Marquardsen's Handbuch des öffentlichen Rechts, IV, pt. 2, div. 2, pp. 18, 19; A. Færden, Political Constitution and Administration in Norway, 178.

82 "Kongen erkloerer Krig og flutter Fred, samt indgaaer og ophœver Forbund og Handelstractater; dog kan han ikke uden Rigsdagens Samtykke afstaae nogen Del af Landet, eller indgaae nogen Forpligtelse, som forandrer de bestaaende statsretlige Forhold." Samling af Love og Anordninger (1865-1869), 146. See for English translation, Brit. and For. State Papers, LVIII, 1235; for German translation, Marquardsen's Handbuch des öffentlichen Rechts, IV, pt. 2, div. 3, p. 74.

specific in requiring the consent of the Rigsdag to treaties for the cession of any portion of territory, for the disposition of any of the revenues of the state, or by which charges on the state should be incurred. It is expressly provided in Article XLVII of the present constitution that no tax can be imposed, altered or abolished, no loan be assumed, nor any domains belonging to the state be alienated, except in virtue of a law. The ministers are responsible for the conduct of the government.[83] The treaty signed January 24, 1902, for the cession to the United States of the Danish West Indies, failed because of the refusal of the Rigsdag to give its consent. It appears to be the practice not to ratify treaties that require legislation to render them effective and binding on individual subjects, or that involve an expenditure, until the necessary measures have been adopted by the Rigsdag.[84]

§146. **Spain.**—By the constitution of Spain (1876), Article LIV, sections 4 and 5, the King has the power to declare war, make peace, and to conduct diplomatic and commercial relations with other powers.[85] He must, according to Article LV, be authorized by a special law: (1) to alienate, cede or exchange any part of Spanish territory; (2) to incorporate any other territory into Spanish territory; (3) to admit foreign troops into the kingdom; (4) to ratify treaties of offensive alliance, special treaties of commerce, those that stipulate to give subsidies to any foreign power, and all those that may be binding individually on Spaniards. In no case can secret articles of a treaty annul public ones.[86] The terms of this constitutional provision clearly in-

83 Art. XII.

84 Marquardsen's Handbuch des öffentlichen Rechts, IV, pt. 2, div. 3, p. 75; Parl. Papers Cd. 6102, p. 6. See for the law of 1904, relating to copyright and its application to foreigners, 97 Brit. and For. State Papers 877, 888; the law of 1894, relating to patents, S. Doc. No. 20, 56th Cong., 2d Sess., 17. For the approval by the Rigsdag of arbitration treaties, see U. S. For. Rel., 1905, p. 292.

85 "Corresponde además al Rey: * * * 4°. Declarar la guerra y hacer y ratificar la paz, dando después cuenta documentada á las Cortes. 5°. Dirigir las relaciones diplomáticas y comerciales con las demás Potencias."

86 "El Rey necesita estar autorizado por una ley especial: 1°. Para enajenar, ceder ò permutar cualquiera parte del territorio español. 2°. Para incorporar cualquiera otro territorio al territorio español. 3°. Para admitir tropas extranjeras en el Reino. 4°. Para ratificar los tratados de alianza ofensiva, los especiales de comercio, los que estipulen dar subsidios á alguna Potencia extranjera, y todos aquellos que puedan obligar indi-

dicate that the special law, when required, is a condition precedent to the validity of the treaty as an international compact. Before entering upon the final peace negotiations with the United States at Paris for the relinquishment and cession of territorial rights in accordance with the terms of the provisional protocol of August 12, 1898, the Spanish ministry obtained the authorization of the Cortes in secret session.[87]

§147. **Portugal.**—By Article LXXV of the original constitution of Portugal of 1826, the King retained the treaty-making power with the sole express limitation that treaties concluded in time of peace for a cession or exchange of territory should be approved by the Cortes. The article was completely changed by Article X of the act of amendment of July 5, 1852, which provided that every treaty, concordat and convention should, before ratification, be submitted for the approval of the Cortes in secret session.[88] By Article XLVII, section 7, of the constitution of the republic (1911), the President is to negotiate treaties of commerce, peace, arbitration and other international conventions, submitting them to Congress for ratification. Treaties of alliance are to be submitted for the examination of Congress in secret session if two-thirds of the members so request. The duty of deciding definitively on treaties and conventions is specifically given to Congress.[89]

§148. **Switzerland.**—Under the constitution of Switzerland (1874), the power to make alliances and treaties for the Confederation is given to the Federal Assembly,[90] the national legislative body, composed of the National Council and the Council of States. The negotiations are conducted by the Federal Council,[91] the national executive body, consisting of seven members elected by the Assembly.[92] The right to make peace and to conclude

vidualmente á los españoles. En ningún caso los artículos secretos de un tratado podrán derogar los públicos." Manual para uso de los Señores Diputados (Madrid, 1907), 42. See for English translation, Brit. and For. State Papers, LXVII, 125.

87 Annual Register, 1898, (Chronicle of Events), p. 54.

88 Brit. and For. State Papers, L, 1276; XIII, 968.

89 Art. XXVI, Sec. 15. Revue du Droit Public, XXVIII, No. 4, p. 775; Hertslet's Commercial Treaties, XXVI, 840.

90 Art. LXXXV, sec. 5.

91 Art. CII, sec. 8.

92 The business of the Federal Council is distributed among seven departments, one of which is that of foreign affairs. Each of these is pre-

treaties with foreign powers, particularly treaties relating to tariffs and commerce, is expressly delegated to the Confederation;[93] but the Cantons retain the power to make among themselves conventions upon legislative, administrative or judicial subjects,[94] and to conclude with foreign powers treaties respecting the administration of public property, and border and police intercourse.[95] The Cantons are expressly prohibited from entering into treaties of a political character;[96] and every agreement entered into by a Canton is subject, on the protest of the Federal Council, or of another Canton, to the approval of the Federal Assembly.[97] It is the duty of the Federal Court in cases within its jurisdiction to apply the laws and resolutions of the Federal Assembly, and to "conform to treaties which shall have been ratified by the Federal Assembly."[98] The general extradition law of January 22, 1892, places extradition in the hands of the Federal Council.[99]

Some doubt has been entertained as to the power of the central government to give effect to a naturalization convention which would prescribe the conditions under which Swiss citizenship should be considered as having been forfeited.[100] As to the general question of the treaty-making power of the Confederation, the conclusion has been reached, says Professor Moses, "that the limitation of powers drawn between the Union and the Cantons with respect to internal affairs does not define the power of the Union with respect to foreign relations."[101] By the original constitution the powers of the central government extend to the pro-

sided over by one of the Councillors. All decisions, however, emanate from the Council, four of the members of which must concur in order to render a valid decision. Winchester, The Swiss Republic, 97.

93 Art. VIII.

94 Art. VII.

95 Art. IX.

96 Art. VII.

97 Art. LXXXV, sec. 5. Text, Larned, History for Ready Reference, I, 588. See for instances of Cantonal agreements, Vincent, Government in Switzerland, 201; Deploige, Referendum in Switzerland (translation by Trevelyan), 172.

98 Art. CXIII.

99 Brit. and For. State Papers, LXXXIV, 671.

100 U. S. For. Rel., 1897, p. 557.

101 Federal Government of Switzerland, 171. See also to the same effect Blumer, Handbuch des schweizerischen Bundesstaatsrechtes, I, 204.

tection of literary and artistic property, and, by an amendment of 1887, to the protection of patents.[102] The posts and telegraphs are controlled by the Confederation.[103] Switzerland is subject to the limitations of a permanently neutralized state.

§149. **Greece.**—Under the constitution of Greece (1864), treaties of peace, alliance and commerce are made by the King; but treaties of commerce and all others that include concessions that require, according to other provisions of the constitution, the sanction of a law, or that may burden the Greeks individually, are not effective until the assent of the legislature has been given.[104] A cession or exchange of territory can be made only by virtue of a law.[105]

§150. **Balkan States.**—In Servia, according to the constitution of 1889, (restored in 1903), the King makes treaties with foreign powers; but treaties of commerce, all treaties, the execution of which involves either a charge on the treasury or a modification of existing laws, as also all treaties that affect the public or private rights of Servian citizens, are not valid without the assent of the legislature.[106] A similar provision is found in the constitution of 1869.[107] The King of Roumania concludes with foreign states conventions of commerce and others of the same nature, but that these may have obligatory force they must be submitted to and approved by the legislature.[108] In Servia as well as in Roumania the territory of the state is declared to be inalienable.[109] The boundaries can be changed or rectified in Roumania only by virtue of a law,[110] and in Servia, if the modification is of little importance, only with the consent of the national assembly, and if it is of real importance, only with the consent of the grand national assembly, the sovereign power of the state.[111] In Montenegro, by the constitution of 1905, the King represents the state

102 Art. LXIV.
103 Art. XXXVI.
104 Art. XXXII.
105 Art. XXXIII. Brit. and For. State Papers, LVI, 575.
106 Art. LII.
107 Art. VIII.
108 Art. XCIII of the constitution of 1866, as amended in 1879 and 1884. Brit. and For. State Papers, LXXXI, 508; LXI, 1071; LVII, 273; LXXV, 1106.
109 Arts. IV and II, respectively.
110 Art. II.
111 Art. IV.

in all its relations with foreign states, declares war, makes treaties of peace and alliance, communicating them to the national assembly as soon as the interests and safety of the country permit; but the assent of the national assembly is necessary in case of treaties of commerce, and of all other treaties that may entail either a charge upon the finances of the state, or a modification of the laws of the land, or restrictions on the public or private rights of Montenegrin citizens.[112] The territory of the state is declared to be inalienable.[113] In Bulgaria, treaties are concluded in the name of the King. Treaties of peace, those that engage the finances of the state, conflict with existing laws, or relate to the civil or public rights of Bulgarian subjects, are definitive only after they have been voted by the national assembly.[113a] The territory of the kingdom cannot be enlarged or diminished without the consent of the grand national assembly. Rectifications of boundaries in uninhabited regions may be made with the consent of the ordinary national assembly.

§151. **Russia and Japan.**—In Russia[114] as also in Japan[115] the

112 Art. VII.

113 Art. XXXVI. Brit. and For. State Papers, XCVIII, 419.

113a Art. XVII of the constitution of 1879 as modified in 1911.

114 Art. XIII of the Fundamental Law of May 9, 1906. Dodd, Modern Constitutions, II, 184. "By the fundamental laws of the Empire, sections 12 and 13, the Emperor is supreme arbiter of all relations of the Empire with foreign Powers, and to him is reserved the management of the international policy of Russia; he declares war and peace, and also concludes treaties with foreign Powers. This prerogative is jealously guarded, and all questions thus specifically assigned to the Emperor alone are understood to be excluded from the competence of the Legislature. Consequently foreign affairs can only be discussed in the Duma when the budget of the Ministry of Foreign Affairs is presented, after previous consideration by the Budget Commission. The functions of this commission are, however, purely financial, and no special commission exists to deal with foreign affairs such as exist for questions of defense, finance, legislative proposals, &c. The Minister for Foreign Affairs can make a statement on foreign policy only by special command of the Emperor. The Duma has, however, the same powers of refusing credits in the case of the budget of the Ministry of Foreign Affairs as in the case of the budgets of other Ministries." Sir George Buchanan to Sir Edward Grey, February 5, 1912. Parl. Pap. Cd. 6102, p. 21.

115 Art. XIII of the constitution of 1889. Dodd, Modern Constitutions, II, 25. The imposition of a new tax or the modification of existing rates shall be made by law. Loans, or other charges on the treasury, require the consent of the imperial Diet. Art. LXII.

Emperor retains without express limitation the power to make peace and to conclude treaties.

§152. **Turkey.**—By Article VII of the constitution of 1876, as revised in 1909, the declaration of war, the making of peace, and the conclusion of treaties in general are classed among the prerogatives of the Sultan; but the consent of Parliament is required for the conclusion of treaties that concern peace, commerce, the abandonment or annexation of territory, the fundamental and personal rights of Ottoman subjects, or that involve an expenditure on the part of the state.[116]

§153. **Mexico and the Other American Republics.**—By Article LXXXV, section 10, of the original constitution of Mexico, as adopted in 1857, the President of the republic directs negotiations and concludes treaties. submitting them to the Federal Congress for ratification.[117] By the amendments of 1874, the Federal Congress was divided into two branches, and to the upper branch, or Senate, was given, by amendment to Article LXXII, as an exclusive power, the approval of all treaties and diplomatic conventions concluded by the Executive with foreign countries.[118] The States comprising the republic are prohibited from entering into alliances or treaties with other States or foreign powers. The frontier States may, however, unite with each other for offensive or defensive war against the Indians.[119]

In each of the remaining American republics, treaties are ne-

---

116 Brit. and For. State Papers, CII, 819, 820; For. Rel., 1909, p. 585.

By Article XXIV of the constitutional law of Persia of 1906, treaties and conventions are to be approved by the National Assembly, excepting such as it may be for the interests of the government or nation to keep secret. By Article LII of the supplementary constitutional law of October 8, 1907, it is provided that treaties, which, in accordance with Article XXIV of the constitutional law of 1906, are to be kept secret, must on the removal of the necessity be communicated to the National Assembly and Senate with necessary explanations, provided the interests and security of the country permit. Secret clauses cannot annul public ones. (Art. LIII.) It is specifically declared that the power to declare war and conclude peace rests with the sovereign. (Art. LI.) Changes of the frontier can only be made with the approval of the National Assembly (Art. XXII. Law of 1906). Martens, Recueil de Traités (3d series) IV, 6, 15, 16; 101 British and Foreign State Papers 527).

117 Rodriguez, American Constitutions (1905), I, 61.

118 Brit. and For. State Papers, LXXVIII, 994; Rodriguez, American Constitutions, I, 79.

119 Art. CXI, sec. 1.

gotiated by the President, but, with the exception of Cuba, require for their ratification the approval of the national legislature.[120] In Cuba the approval of the Senate alone is required, except in case of treaties of peace, which require the approval of Congress.[121] A permanent limitation on the treaty-making power of Cuba is recognized in the appendix to the constitution, and incorporated in the treaty with the United States of May 22, 1903, wherein it is provided that "the government of Cuba shall never enter into any treaty or other compact with any foreign power or powers which will impair or tend to impair the independence of Cuba, nor in any manner authorize or permit any foreign power or powers to obtain by colonization or for military or naval purposes, or otherwise, lodgment in or control over any portion of said island."[122] Article XXXI of the constitution of the Argentine Republic expressly provides that the constitution, the laws of Congress, and treaties with foreign powers are the supreme law of the nation binding on the provincial authorities, anything in their own provincial constitution, or laws to the contrary notwithstanding.[123]

---

120 Brazil (1891), Arts. XLVIII, sec. 16, and XXXIV, sec. 12 (Rodriguez, American Constitutions, I, 143, 151); Argentine Republic (1860), Arts. LXXXVI, sec. 14, and LXVII, sec. 19 (Id., I, 115, 124); Chile (1833), Art. LXXIII, sec. 19 (Id., II, 228); Bolivia (1880), Arts. LII, sec. 14, LIV, sec. 5, LXXXIX, sec. 1 (Id., II, 425, 426, 435); Peru (1860), Arts. XCIV, sec. 11, LIX, sec. 16, and LXII (Id., II, 263, 270); Colombia (1886), Arts. LXXVI, sec. 20, and CXX, sec. 10 (Id., II, 334, 347); Uruguay (1829), Arts. XVII, sec. 7, and LXXXI (Id., II, 162, 175); Paraguay (1870), Arts. CII, sec. 12, and LXXII, sec. 18 (Id., II, 396, 405); Panama (1904), Arts. LXV, secs. 6 and 7, and LXXIII, sec. 3 (Id., I, 404, 408); Costa Rica (1871), Arts. CI, sec. 9, and LXXII, sec. 4 (Id., I, 338, 347); Salvador (1886), Art. XCI, secs. 6 and 7 (Id., I, 282); Guatemala (1879, amended in 1887), Art. LXXVII, sec. 19 (Id., I, 253); Haiti (1889), Art. CI (Id., II, 70); Dominican Republic (1908), Arts. XXXV, sec. 17, and LIII, sec. 8 (For Rel., 1908, pp. 265, 267); Ecuador (1906), Arts. LIV, sec. 12, and LXXX, secs. 6 and 7 (Registro Oficial of December 24, 1906); Honduras (1894, re-enacted in 1907), Arts. XC, sec. 22, and CVIII, secs. 12 and 14; Nicaragua (1911, proclaimed in 1913), Arts. LXXXV, sec. 7, and CXI, sec. 10; Venezuela (1909), Arts. LVII, sec. 13, and LXXXI, sec. 5. See Art. XXXIV of the provisional constitution of Venezuela of 1914. Gaceta Oficial of April 20, 1914.

121 (1901). Arts. XLVII, sec. 6, LXVIII, sec. 7, and LIX, sec. 12, Rodriguez, American Constitutions, II, 123, 128, 132.

122 Id., II, 147.

123 Id., I, 106. See, also, Art. C.

§154. **Dependencies.**—Although the full power to enter into treaties is an attribute of soverign states, dependent states, or communities, may be entrusted in a limited degree with its exercise. Egypt, although nominally a province of the Ottoman Empire, exercised this power on the authority of firmans granted by the Sublime Porte. The firman granted to the Khedive, June 8, 1873, and renewed with unimportant changes, August 2, 1879, and March 27, 1892, to his successors, authorized the conclusion or renewal, without prejudice to the political treaties and sovereign rights of the imperial government, of conventions for tariff rates and commerce, and for regulating the protection of foreigners and their relations with the government and people of Egypt.[124] Besides numerous special postal and telegraphic conventions, Egypt was a signatory of the postal union conventions signed at Vienna, July 4, 1891, and at Washington, June 15, 1897, and of the international telegraphic convention signed at Budapest, July 22, 1896. Several treaties concerning judicial reform have been entered into by Egypt. On March 3, 1884, there was signed at Cairo a commercial treaty with Greece, which, after providing for reciprocal most-favored-nation treatment, regulated in some detail the tariff rates to be levied on Greek imports into Egypt. This treaty formed the basis of treaties subsequently concluded with Great Britain, the United States, Italy, Portugal, the Netherlands, Sweden and Norway, and Belgium. Since the Khedive had no diplomatic representatives at foreign courts, these treaties were concluded in Egypt by the foreign government through a consul or commercial agent, and by the Khedive through his minister for foreign affairs. The powers of the latter were expressly restricted "within the limits of the powers conferred by the imperial firmans."

By the treaty of Berlin, Bulgaria was nominally constituted a principality under the suzerainty of the Sultan. Prior to the recognition of her independence in 1908, Bulgaria, however, concluded, on her own responsibility, numerous non-political conventions, such as commercial, postal, telegraphic, railway and monetary conventions.[125] The only treaty of a strictly political nature to which Bulgaria was a party during this period, recorded in Ribier's Répertoire des Traités (1879-1897), is the treaty of

124 Brit. and For. State Papers, LXIII, 33; LXX, 297; LXXXIV, 638.
125 Id., LXXXVIII, 371; LXXXIX, 5, 1144.

peace with Servia of March 3, 1886; and it is the only one in which specific reference appears to have been made to the suzerainty of the Sultan. It was concluded and signed on the one hand by Bulgaria and the Sultan, jointly, and on the other by Servia.[126]

126 Id., LXXVII, 634. See, for treaties for the establishment of protectorates in Africa, in which a control of the treaty-making power has been taken over by the suzerain, Id., LXXII, 247; LXXV, 10.

PART III. THE OPERATION OF TREATIES AS BE-
TWEEN STATES.

CHAPTER XXI.

DATE OF TAKING EFFECT.

§155. **As a Compact Between States.**—A treaty is not definitively binding until the exchange of ratifications has taken place, and is accordingly not finally operative before that date. This results from the right of ratification, now generally recognized even though not expressly reserved in the treaty or full powers of the negotiators, and from that principle of mutuality by which neither party is bound by a contract until the other is also. The exchange of ratifications is more than a mere form. It is the mutual communication of the ratification and final acceptance of the treaty by the contracting parties, and the acknowledgment by each that the ratification of the other is in due form.[1] Even if it is expressly provided in the treaty that it shall go into effect immediately upon its signature, its operation is provisional, and subject to the final ratification of the parties; and, in case of rejection, acts by either party done in anticipation of a ratification are without validity.[2] Although a treaty is inchoate and not defin-

---

1 "The treaty did not take effect, till its ratification by both parties operated like the delivery of a deed, to make it the binding act of both. That it may and does relate to its date as between the two governments, so far as respects the rights of either under it, may be undoubted; but as it respects individual rights, in any way affected by it, a very different rule ought to prevail." Baldwin, J., United States v. Arredondo (1832), 6 Pet. 691, 748; United States v. Sibbald (1836), 10 Pet. 313, 323. "The exchange of the ratifications was like the delivery of a deed, and until that was done the transaction was not complete, and Porto Rico did not cease to be a foreign country within the meaning of the tariff laws. Until the ratifications were exchanged, it was competent for either power, or both, to recede and rescind its action." Ray, J., Armstrong v. Bidwell (1903), 124 Fed. 690, 692. That the ratification not the signature only gives to a treaty its definitive value, see protocol of the Berlin Conference of July 12, 1878. Hertslet's Map of Europe by Treaty, IV, 2757. The American government treated the exchange of ratifications at Constantinople, of the proposed naturalization convention of 1874, as invalid in view of the proviso attached by the Turkish government to its ratification. See supra, §§ 45, 55.

2 By Article XVIII of the convention, signed at Madrid, July 3, 1880, concerning the exercise of protection in Morocco, to which the United States was a signatory party, it was agreed that by the exceptional con-

itively binding until the exchange of ratifications, it is in good faith provisionally binding from the date of signing in the sense that neither party may, without repudiating the proposed treaty, voluntarily place itself in a position where it cannot comply with the conditions as they existed at the time the treaty was signed.[3] The conditions as they then existed are, in the absence of a clearly expressed intention otherwise, to be considered the conditions contemplated by the parties. Otherwise there would not be a perfect agreement, since the ratifications of the parties are, except by a mere coincidence, on different dates. To this extent the exchange of ratifications has a retroactive effect as to the rights of the contracting parties, confirming them as of the date on which the treaty was signed.[4]

sent of the contracting parties the stipulations of the convention should take effect on the day on which it was signed. Mr. Evarts, Secretary of State, in a communication of August 11, 1880, to the American negotiator, Mr. Fairchild, acknowledging the receipt of the convention, observed as to this stipulation that while this government could not accord validity to such an international compact in advance of the consent of the Senate, yet, in view of the exceptional circumstances under which the convention had been framed and of its limited operation within the territory of Morocco involving apparently no domestic legislation of this country, he deemed it entirely unlikely that any issue would arise, pending formal ratification, which would call for diplomatic intervention on the part of the Executive in a sense opposed to the convention. For. Rel., 1880, p. 922. Upon signing the convention for the pacification of the Levant, at London, July 15, 1840, the plenipotentiaries of Austria, Great Britain, Prussia, Russia, and Turkey, in virtue of their full powers, executed a protocol in which it was agreed that, in view of the fact that the interests of humanity imperiously required the avoidance of all possible delay in the pacification intended to be accomplished by the convention, the preliminary measures mentioned in Article II of the convention should be carried into effect at once without waiting for the exchange of ratifications. It was further stated that the respective plenipotentiaries recorded formally, by that instrument, the consent of their Courts to the immediate enforcement of these measures. Hertslet's Map of Europe by Treaty, II, 1022. See Hall, Int. Law (6 ed.), 325; Wheaton, §264.

3 See message of President Tyler to the Senate, May 15, 1844, in reference to a treaty then pending in the Senate for the annexation of Texas (Richardson, Messages and Papers of the Presidents, IV, 316); and note of Mr. Hay, Secretary of State, to Gen. Reyes, special commissioner of Colombia, January 5, 1904, in reference to a treaty to facilitate the construction of an interoceanic canal. (For. Rel., 1903, p. 299).

4 Hall (6 ed.), 326; Heffter, §87; Bluntschli, §421; Westlake, (2 ed.), I, 291; Twiss, Law of Nations (Peace, 2 ed.), 439; United States v. Arre-

The parties may, and usually do, by express provision, fix the date on which the treaty is to take effect. They may likewise give to the treaty a retrospective operation as to matters anterior to its date; and whether they have done so is solely a question of intent, to be determined by the accepted principles of construction. "It is true that in mere private cases between individuals, a court will and ought to struggle hard against a construction which will, by a retrospective operation, affect the rights of parties, but in great national concerns, where individual rights, acquired by war, are sacrificed for national purposes, the contract making the sacrifice ought always to receive a construction conforming to its manifest import; and if the nation has given up the vested rights of its citizens, it is not for the court, but for the government, to consider whether it be a case proper for compensation."[5] In the Chamizal arbitration under the convention between the United States and Mexico of June 24, 1910, the majority of the commission held that the treaty of November 12, 1884 was intended by the parties to have a retrospective operation.[6]

§156. As Affecting Rights of Individuals.—The operation of a treaty, as affecting the rights of the individual, depends upon the municipal law of the contracting parties. Before the treaty becomes effective as to such rights, legislation or other acts for its promulgation may be necessary. In the United States, where a treaty has the force of a legislative enactment, it becomes a law of the land affecting the rights of the individual only upon the exchange of ratifications and proclamation by the President. The principle of relation back to the date of signature has no application to rights of this character.[7] In Haver v. Yaker it was held

dondo, 6 Pet. 691, 748; United States v. Sibbald, 10 Pet. 313, 323; United States v. Reynes, 9 How. 127, 148; Davis v. Police Jury of Concordia, 9 How. 280, 289; United States v. D'Auterive, 10 How. 609; Montault v. United States, 12 How. 47, 51; Haver v. Yaker, 9 Wall. 32, 34; United States v. Lynde, 11 Wall. 632; In re Metzger, Fed. Cases, No. 9511; United States v. Grand Rapids & R. R. Co., 165 Fed. 297, 301; Notes to Treaties and Conventions (1889 ed.), 1228; Moore, Int. Law Digest, V, 244; Moore, Int. Arb., II, 2086, 2091.

5 Marshall, C. J., United States v. Schooner Peggy (1801), 1 Cranch 103, 110.

6 Am. Journal of Int. Law, V, 785, 805.

7 United States v. Arredondo, 6 Pet. 691, 748; Haver v. Yaker, 9 Wall. 32; Yeaker's Heirs v. Yeaker's Heirs, 4 Metc. (Ky.) 33; Ex parte Ortiz, 100 Fed. 955, 962; Bush v. United States, 29 C. Cls. 144; Beam v. United

by the Supreme Court that a stipulation in the treaty with Switzer-land, signed November 25, 1850, in reference to the right of Swiss subjects to inherit property located in the United States, became effective as to such right only upon the exchange of ratifications, and had no retroactive operation. Speaking for the court, Mr. Jus-tice Davis said: "It is undoubtedly true, as a principle of interna-tional law, that, as respects the rights of either government under it, a treaty is considered as concluded and binding from the date of its signature. In this regard the exchange of ratifications has a retroactive effect, confirming the treaty from its date. But a different rule prevails where the treaty operates on individual rights. The principle of relation does not apply to rights of this character, which were vested before the treaty was ratified. In so far as it affects them, it is not considered as concluded until there is an exchange of ratifications, and this we understand to have been decided by this court, in Arredondo's case, reported in 6th Peters. The reason of the rule is apparent. In this country, a treaty is something more than a contract, for the Federal Con-stitution declares it to be the law of the land. If so, before it can become a law, the Senate, in whom rests the authority to ratify it, must agree to it. But the Senate are not required to adopt or reject it as a whole, but may modify or amend it, as was done with the treaty under consideration. As the individual citizen, on whose rights of property it operates, has no means of knowing anything of it while before the Senate, it would be wrong in principle to hold him bound by it, as the law of the land, until it was ratified and proclaimed. And to construe the law, so as to make the ratification of the treaty relate back to its signing, there-by divesting a title already vested, would be manifestly unjust, and cannot be sanctioned."[8] Upon the proclamation of the treaty by the President, the individual first becomes apprised of the fact of the due ratification by both parties and the definitive conclusion of the treaty.[9]

States, 43 C. Cls. 61; United States v. Grand Rapids, &c., R. R. Co., 165 Fed. 297, 301.

8   9 Wall. 32.

9   Howell v. Bidwell, 124 Fed. 688; Shepard v. Northwestern Insurance Co., 40 Fed. 341, 347; United States v. Grand Rapids, &c., R. R. Co., 165 Fed. 297, 301. See also United States v. Sugar Refining Co., 202 U. S. 563; 6 Op. Atty. Gen. 750. It has been held that a proclamation covers the entire day on which it was made. Howell v. Bidwell, 124 Fed. 688, citing

§157. Treaties for Transfer of Territory.—It was a principle of the civil law in the transfer of corporeal property, adopted as a rule of international law in the transfer of territory, that the right to the property and possession must be united in order to give *plenum dominium*.[10] "All concur," said Sir William Scott, in the case of the Fama, "in holding it to be a necessary principle of jurisprudence, that to complete the right of property, the right to the thing, and the possession of the thing itself, should be united; or, according to the technical expression, borrowed either from the civil law, or as Barbeyrac explains it, from the commentators on the canon law, that there should be both the *jus in rem,* and the *jus in re.*—This is the general law of property, and applies, I conceive, no less to the right of territory than to other rights."[11] The Fama, the property of an inhabitant of Louisiana, had sailed from New Orleans, April 5, 1803, and had been captured by a British cruiser in May, 1803, and held as enemy (French) property on the ground that Louisiana had been ceded by Spain to France by the secret treaty of San Ildefonso. Actual possession of the territory had not been taken. Restitution of the prize was ordered on the ground that full sovereignty could not be held to have passed by the mere words of the treaty without actual delivery, and that until possession was actually taken the inhabitants were not impressed with the enemy character of the state to which by the treaty they were to be transferred. In Davis v. Police Jury of Concordia, it was held by the Supreme Court that, the ratification of a treaty of cession having a retroactive effect, an attempted grant in the ceded territory of a perpetual ferry franchise by the Spanish governor of Louisiana on February 19, 1801, was invalid, the treaty of San Ildefonso by which Spain retroceded Louisiana to France having been signed October 1, 1800, prior to the date of the grant. Mr. Justice Wayne, speaking for the court, said: "All treaties, as well those for cessions of territory as for other purposes, are binding upon the contracting parties, unless when otherwise provided in them, from the day they are signed. The ratification of them relates back to the time of

United States v. Norton, 97 U. S. 164; Lapeyre v. United States, 17 Wall. 191. See also Ashbaugh v. United States, 35 C. Cls. 554, 555.

10 Blackstone, Commentaries (Sharswood ed.), II, 310; The Fama (1804), 5 C. Rob. 106; Davis v. Police Jury of Concordia, 9 How. 280, 289; De Lima v. Bidwell, 182 U. S. 1, 194.

11 5 C. Rob. 106, 115.

signing. Vattel, B. 4, c. 2, sec. 22; Mart. Summary, B. 8, c. 7, sec. 5. It is true, that, in a treaty for the cession of territory, its national character continues, for all commercial purposes; but full sovereignty, for the exercise of it, does not pass to the nation to which it is transferred until actual delivery. But it is also true, that the exercise of sovereignty by the ceding country ceases, except for strictly municipal purposes, especially for granting lands. And for the same reason in both cases;—because, after the treaty is made, there is not in either the union of possession and the right to the territory which must concur to give *plenum dominium et utile*. To give that, there must be the *jus in rem* and the *jus in re*, or what is called in the common law of England the *juris et seisinae conjunctio*. * * * In this case, after the treaty was made, and until Louisiana was delivered to France, its possession continued in Spain. The right to the territory, though in France, was imperfect until ratified, but absolute by ratification from the date of the treaty."[12] In United States v. Reynes, Mr. Justice Daniel, for the court, said: "The dates of the treaties of St. Ildefonso and of Paris have already been mentioned—that of the former being the 1st of October, 1800, that of the latter the 30th of April, 1803. In the construction of treaties, the same rules which govern other compacts properly apply. They must be considered as binding from the period of their execution; their operation must be understood to take effect from that period, unless it shall, by some condition or stipulation in the compact itself, be postponed. * * * The treaty between the United States and the republic of France contains no article or condition by which its operation could be suspended. * * * This treaty therefore operated from its date; its subsequent ratification by the American government, and the formal transfer of the country to the American commissioners on the 20th of December, 1803, have relation to the date of the instrument. The rights and powers of sovereignty, on the part of Spain, over the territory, ceased with her transfer of that sovereignty to another government; it could not exist in different governments or nations at the same time. The power to preserve the peace and order of the community may be admitted to have been in the officers previously appointed by Spain, until the actual presence of the agents of the succeeding government; but this would not imply sovereign power still remaining in Spain,—for

12 9 How. 280, 289.

if she continued to be sovereign after expressly conceding her sovereignty to another government, she might still rightfully resist and control that government; for sovereignty from its nature is never subordinate."[13] In the later case of Montault v. United States, Chief Justice Taney said: "The definitive treaty of peace between Great Britain, France, and Spain, by which the territory in which this land is situated was ceded to Great Britain, was signed on the 10th of February, 1763, and consequently the French authorities could not, after that day, grant a title to lands lying in the ceded territory. This point was decided in the cases of the United States v. Reynes, 9 How. 127; The Police Jury of Concordia v. Davis, 9 How. 280; and the United States v. D'Auterive, 10 How. 609. And as the grant in question was not made until the 11th of March next following the date of the treaty, it was at that time the exercise of a power by the French authorities which they no longer possessed, and could convey no title."[14] Again in Doe v. Braden, in referring to the treaty with Spain of 1819, Chief Justice Taney said: "It was ratified, accordingly, by the President, and the ratifications exchanged on the 22d of February, 1821. And Florida, on that day, became a part of the territory of the United States, under and according to the stipulations of the treaty—the rights of the United States relating back to the day on which it was signed."[15] In an instruction to the military governor of Cuba, June 21, 1901, in respect of concessions made by the Spanish government in Cuba after the signing of the protocol of August 12, 1898, Mr. Root, Secretary of War, said: "The United States, on August 12, 1898, by reason of successful military operations, had induced Spain to sue for peace and was in a position to require Spain to comply with its demands. But the United States had not effected a complete conquest of all Cuba, because all parts of the island were not in the possession of our military forces. Under the laws of war, as long as Spain continued in possession of territory in Cuba, so long Spanish sovereignty continued over that particular territory, and the proprietary title in and to public property therein situate belonging to the Crown under Spanish law would remain with the Crown of Spain. While this condition continued, the govern-

13 9 How. 127, 148, 149.
14 12 How. 47, 51.
15 16 How. 635, 656.

25

ment of Spain would be justified in exercising sovereign powers in said territory, and the Crown of Spain would be justified in exercising the ordinary privileges appurtenant to the proprietary title of public property under the laws of Spain, provided such action as was taken was in good faith, i. e., with due regard to the rights of its adversary. This condition was terminated by the treaty of Paris. By that instrument sovereignty and title in Cuba (article 1) and proprietary title to the public property in the island (article 8) were relinquished by Spain, and provision made that 'upon its evacuation by Spain' the island was to be 'occupied by the United States,' and that the United States should 'so long as such occupation shall last assume and discharge the obligations that may under international law result from the fact of its occupation.' * * * (Article 1). The right of the United States to administer sovereign powers in Cuba, and its right to the proprietary title of public property theretofore possessed by the Crown of Spain, were completed by and date from the treaty of Paris, December 10, 1898."[16] Attorney General Knox, in an opinion dated October 17, 1901, likewise advised: "Nevertheless, the principle of binding obligation is so far in force as to justify the statement that a treaty is a valid agreement from the conclusion of negotiations, although subject to rejection, and is inchoate only because of this latter fact. The Supreme Court has decided that, as respects performance of the conditions of a grant by a private grantee, the date of a treaty is the date of its final ratification, but that so far as affects the relations of the sovereigns concerned, it operates when ratified from the date of its signature, and that, unless otherwise provided, treaties in their public relations take effect from signature, to which period the ratification relates back. * * * While certain provisions [in the treaty of peace with Spain] became operative from the date of exchange of ratifications, and others upon signature (e. g. Articles IV, VI) the relinquishment of sovereignty and cession of domain, which were the main purposes of the treaty, and were formulated in several articles, are unqualified and must be regarded as immediate and absolute from the date of signature, subject only to the possibility of a failure of ratification."[17]

It has been held that, although Porto Rico was ceded to the

16 Magoon's Reports, 602.
17 23 Op. 551, 558. See Griggs, Atty. Gen., 23 Op. 181, 182.

United States by a treaty signed December 10, 1898, and the authority of Spain had been superseded prior thereto by the military occupation of the United States, Porto Rico and the United States were, as regards the tariff laws, foreign countries until the exchange of ratifications on April 11, 1899.[19]

§158. Extradition Conventions.—Since a fugitive from justice has no vested right of asylum, the "principle that a treaty is not to be held to operate retroactively in respect to vested rights does not apply to conventions of extradition."[20] Extradition is a matter of procedure rather than of substantive law.[21] It has accordingly been held that an extradition convention may apply to offenses committed prior to its conclusion.[22] "The general principle of opposition to an ex post facto act is not regarded as applicable in this instance, since the criminal character of the act for which extradition is sought does not flow from the treaty of extradition, but from the antecedent criminal law."[23] Article XVII of the resolutions adopted by the Institute of International Law at its meeting at Oxford in 1880 provides that a law or convention of extradition may be applied to acts committed before it came into force.[24] In the convention with Belgium, signed March 19, 1874, it was expressly stipulated that its provisions should not, except in cases of murder and arson, apply to any crime committed prior to the date of the convention; and that the convention should take effect twenty days after the exchange of ratifications. The exchange took place on April 30, 1874. It was held that the convention covered a crime committed May 1, 1874, since it was

19 Dooley v. United States, 182 U. S. 222; Armstrong v. United States, 182 U. S. 243. See also Armstrong v. Bidwell, 124 Fed. 690, 692; American Sugar Refining Co. v. Bidwell, 124 Fed. 677, 683; Howell v. Bidwell, 124 Fed. 688; Santiago v. Nogueras, 214 U. S. 260, 265; Lincoln v. United States, 197 U. S. 419; 202 U. S. 484; MacLeod v. United States, 229 U. S. 416; Lascelles v. United States, 49 C. Cls. 382. See Twiss, Law of Nations (Rights and Duties in Time of Peace, 2 ed.), 439; Wayne, J., Davis v. Police Jury of Concordia, 9 How. 280, 289.

20 Moore, Extradition, I, 99; Twiss, Law of Nations (Peace), §240.

21 Westlake, Int. Law (2 ed.), I, 259.

22 In re Angelo de Giacomo (1874), 12 Blatchf. 391; In re Cannon, 14 Can. Cr. Cas. 186; case of Charles Kratz, For. Rel., 1903, pp. 674-685; Moore, Int. Law Digest, V, 248, and cases cited.

23 Mr. Evarts, Secretary of State, to Mr. Dichman, minister to Colombia, November 12, 1878, For. Rel., 1878, pp. 151, 153.

24 5 Annuaire 127.

committed after the date of the convention, although before it had taken effect.[25]

§159. **Treaties of Peace.**—The status existing at the time the treaty of peace was signed is, unless a contrary intention is clearly expressed, contemplated by the parties. Accordingly, in good faith, active military operations should be suspended upon the signing of the treaty. By continuing belligerent operations a party might make the restoration of the status quo at the time of the signing impossible. As in the case of other treaties, a treaty of peace is not, however, definitively binding until the exchange of ratifications; and a state of war in the technical sense continues until the date of the exchange.[26]   Three American merchant ships were seized in Swedish waters, August 11, 1812, by a British ship of war in consequence of an order of detention of American property in anticipation of war with the United States. Claim was made by the Swedish government for the ships so seized, on the ground that they were taken within the territorial waters of Sweden, and in violation of her rights as a neutral. The right to make the claim depended upon the question whether Sweden was at the time of the seizure at peace with Great Britain, and therefore a neutral. A treaty of peace had been signed on July 18, 1812, by plenipotentiaries; and had been ratified by the Prince Regent of Great Britain, August 4, 1812, seven days before the capture took place. It was not ratified by the King of Sweden until August 17, 1812, or six days after the capture. In holding that peace did not at the time of the capture exist between Sweden and Great Britain, and that Sweden was not therefore entitled to the benefit of a neutral character, Sir William Scott said: "The question, therefore, comes to this, whether a ratification is or is not necessary to give effect and validity to a treaty signed by plenipotentiaries. Upon abstract principles we know that, either in public or private transactions, the acts of those who are vested with a plenary power are binding upon the principal. But, as this rule was in many cases found to be attended with inconvenience, the later usage of states has been to require a ratifica-

25 In re Vandervelpen, 14 Blatchf. 137.

26 Ogden v. Blackledge (1804), 2 Cranch 272; Eliza Ann (1813), 1 Dod. 244; Torres v. United States, No. 565, under convention with Mexico of July 4, 1868, Moore, Int. Arb., IV, 3798; Hijo v. United States, 194 U. S. 315; Ex parte Ortiz, 100 Fed. 955; MacLeod v. United States, 229 U. S. 416.

tion, although the treaty may have been signed by plenipotentiaries. According to the practice now prevailing, a subsequent ratification is essentially necessary; and a strong confirmation of the truth of this position is, that there is hardly a modern treaty in which it is not expressly so stipulated; and therefore it is now to be presumed, that the powers of plenipotentiaries are limited by the condition of a subsequent ratification. The ratification may be a form, but it is an essential form; for the instrument, in point of legal efficacy, is imperfect without it. I need not add, that a ratification by one power alone is insufficient; that, if necessary at all, it must be mutual; and that the treaty is incomplete till it has been reciprocally ratified. * * * I am of opinion, therefore, that the ratification is the point from which the treaty must take effect."[27] Certain claims were presented to the United States and Mexican claims commission, constituted under the convention of July 4, 1868, for private property destroyed by the American forces as the result of the burning of the village of Zacualtipan, Mexico, February 25, 1848. The treaty of peace had been signed February 2, but it had not been ratified by either party on the date of the destruction of the property. In dismissing these claims, Dr. Francis Lieber, umpire, said: "Many of the best authorities hold that peace begins de jure when it is signed, and not from the day when it is ratified by the two supreme belligerent powers or the authorities which by the law of the land have alone the right to ratify. This, however, is far from being unconditional. If a peace were signed with a moral certainty of its ratification and one of the belligerents were, after this, making grants of land in a province which is to be ceded, before the final ratification, it would certainly be considered by every honest jurist a fraudulent and invalid transaction. But it is well understood that a peace is not a complete peace until ratified; that, as a matter of course, the ratifying authority has the power of refusing unless, for that time, it has given up this power beforehand, but there can be no doubt that so soon as peace has been preliminarily signed active hostilities ought to cease, according to the spirit of civilization and consistent with the very idea and object of the whole transaction, which is to stop the war and establish peace. It would be an unjustifiable act to continue vehement hostilities under such circumstances as if nothing had

27 Eliza Ann (1813), 1 Dod. 244, 248.

happened, wherever it is possible, and when the contrary is not plainly understood or actually expressed."[28] Upon the capture of the port of Ponce, Porto Rico, by the American forces, July 28, 1898, a vessel, the property of a Spanish subject, was taken and was thereafter used by the military authorities until April, 1899. The vessel was never in the custody of the navy, nor was it condemned as prize. Suit was brought by the owner of the vessel on contract for its use after the suspension of hostilities by the protocol signed August 12, 1898. The Supreme Court in dismissing the suit held that, the seizure having been made while the war was flagrant as an act of war within the limits of military operations, the transaction was not converted into one of implied contract because of the retention and use of the vessel pending negotiations for a treaty of peace. Speaking for the court, Mr. Justice Harlan said: "According to the established principles of public law, the owners of the vessel, being Spanish subjects, were to be deemed enemies, although not directly connected with military operations. The vessel was, therefore, to be deemed enemy's property. It was seized as property of that kind, for purposes of war, and not for any purposes of gain. * * * A state of war did not in law cease until the ratification in April, 1899, of the treaty of peace."[29]

The treaty of peace is usually preceded by an armistice, for the suspension of hostilities, and by preliminary articles, which may serve as the basis for the definitive treaty. The treaty of Zurich was preceded by the preliminaries signed at Villafranca, July 11, 1859; of Prague, by articles signed at Nickolsburg, July 26, 1866; of Frankfort, by articles signed at Versailles, February 26, 1871; of San Stefano, by articles signed at Adrianople, January 31, 1878; of Paris, by the protocol signed at Washington, August 12, 1898. No such preliminary articles preceded the treaty of Portsmouth of September 5, 1905. A provision is often inserted in the armistice or treaty specifying a future date for the suspension of hostilities in remote places. In the treaty of peace between Spain and the Low Countries, signed at Münster, January 30, 1648, a period of a year was allowed for the receipt of the news of peace

28 Torres v. United States, No. 565. Moore, Int. Arb., IV, 3798, 3800.
29 Hijo v. United States, 194 U. S. 315, 322. See also Herrera Nephews v. United States, 43 C. Cls. 430; 222 U. S. 558; MacLeod v. United States, 229 U. S. 416, 432, 433.

in the possessions of the East India Company, and a period of six months, in those of the West India Company. Hostilities were, however, to cease in these places if notice of peace was earlier received.[30] With modern facilities of communication, a much shorter period is required. By the armistice signed January 28, 1871, during the Franco-Prussian war, military operations were to cease in Paris on the day of signing, and in the departments within three days thereafter.[31] Provision was also made for the restitution of captures. In the treaty of peace between China and Japan, signed April 17, 1895, it was agreed that offensive military operations should cease upon the exchange of ratifications, which did not take place until May 8, 1895.[32] The protocol between the United States and Spain of August 12, 1898, provided that, upon the signing of the protocol, hostilities should be suspended, and that notice to this effect should be given as soon as possible by each government to the commanders of its forces. Thereafter, on August 14, but before notice of the suspension of hostilities had been received, occurred the capitulation of Manila to the American forces. It was expressly provided in Article III of the protocol of August 12, that, pending the conclusion of a treaty of peace, the United States should occupy and hold the city of Manila, together with the bay and harbor. In the subsequent negotiations, the Spanish government sought to maintain that the United States continued in occupation solely by virtue of this article, and that the capitulation of August 14 was "absolutely null by reason of its having been concluded after the belligerents had signed an agreement declaring the hostilities to be suspended." The government of the United States was unable to concur in this view and took the ground that, since it had been expressly provided in the protocol that notice should be given of the suspension of hostilities, the suspension was to be considered as having taken effect at the date of the receipt of the notice, which notice had been immediately given.[33] This seems to be a natural construction of the terms of the article, for otherwise the clause providing for the immediate notification would

30 Art. VII. Collection of Treatys (1732 ed.), II, 340.
31 Art. I. Brit. and For. State Papers, LXII, 49.
32 Art. X. Id., LXXXVII, 803. See for an armistice for the temporary suspension of hostilities, Takahashi, Cases on International Law during the Chino-Japanese War, 205.
33 For. Rel., 1898, pp. 813, 814, 830.

be redundant.[34]   In the treaty of peace between Italy and Turkey concluded at Lausanne, October 18, 1912, the two governments pledged themselves to take, immediately after the signature of the treaty, the necessary measures to bring about the immediate and simultaneous cessation of hostilities.[35]   It was agreed that the treaty should enter into force on the day of its signature.[36]

If a future date for the suspension of hostilities in remote places is specified in the treaty or armistice, active operations are, it is generally agreed, to cease upon the receipt of official notice, although the time allowed has not expired.[37]   The notification in such a case in order to be binding on the officer must be duly communicated by his own government.[38]   A capture made after the treaty of peace, or armistice, has been signed, but in ignorance of it and within the time specified for the cessation of hostilities, is good unless provision is made for its restitution.[39]   But a capture made after the date fixed for the cessation of hostilities, even in ignorance of that fact, must be restored.   An American schooner, the John, was captured by a British cruiser on March 5, 1815, after the date fixed in the treaty of peace for the cessation of hostilities, but in ignorance of the restoration of peace.   The captured vessel was lost at sea.   Sir William Scott held that, since the capture had been made in good faith, and the vessel had been lost through no negligence on the part of the captor, the captor was not personally answerable in the way of compensation for the damage which this misfortune had produced, although, if the vessel had not been lost, he could have been compelled to restore it to the owner.[40]   Subsequently, a claim for the loss of the vessel was presented against the government of Great Britain, and was allowed by the mixed commission under the convention of February 8, 1853.   Mr. Upham, the American commissioner, said: "They [the British government] acknowledge themselves bound by a constructive notice of the peace, and it was their own fault that

---

34 S. Doc. No. 148, 56th Cong., 2d Sess., 6; S. Doc. No. 62, 55th Cong., 3d Sess., 13, 15, 21.

35 Art. I.

36 Art. XI. Am. Journal of Int. Law, Supp., VII, 58; Martens (3d series), VII, 7.

37 Wheaton, §548; Halleck, I, 319.

38 See case of the Swineherd, Hall (6 ed.), 556.

39 The Somerset (1815), 2 Dod. 56.

40 2 Dod. (1818), 336, 341.

they did not take time enough, or did not use diligence enough to give *actual notice* of the peace. * * * No one can plead the destruction of property as the act of God, who is wrongfully in the use and control of such property. He is a wrongdoer from the outset; he has converted the property from the instant of possession, and the subsequent calamity which may happen, however inevitable it may be, is no excuse for its loss."[41] In the case of the Mentor, an American vessel destroyed by vessels of the British squadron off Delaware in 1783, after cessation of hostilities but before that fact had come to the knowledge of any of the parties, Sir William Scott said: "If by articles, a place or district was put under the king's peace, and an act of hostility was afterwards committed therein, the injured party might have a right to resort to a court of prize, to show that he had been injured by this breach of the peace, and was entitled to compensation; and if the officer acted through ignorance, his own government must protect him. For it is the duty of government, if they put a certain district within the king's peace, to take care that due notice shall be given to those persons by whose conduct that peace is to be maintained; and if no such notice has been given, nor due diligence used to give it, and a breach of the peace is committed through the ignorance of those persons, they are to be borne harmless, at the expense of that government whose duty it was to have given that notice."[42]

41 Moore, Int. Arb., IV, 3793.

42 1 C. Rob. (1799), 179, 183. The admiral in charge of the squadron, to which the vessels making the capture belonged, was neither present nor cognizant of the transaction; and the suit against him was dismissed.

CHAPTER XXII.

DETERMINATION OF DISPUTED INTERPRETATIONS OF TREATIES.

§160. **Difference Between the Enforcement of Treaties and of Private Contracts.**—In the case of contracts between individuals either party may of right compel the submission of a disputed interpretation to an independent tribunal for adjudication. No such legal right exists as between independent states except by agreement between the parties. In the absence of such an agreement either party to the treaty determines for itself in last resort the meaning of the terms of its own obligation, and the only recourse open to the aggrieved party is a resort to force or to a denunciation of the treaty. This results from the fact that the contracting parties are sovereign states over which no tribunal, except by their own consent, exercises a jurisdiction to determine issues between them. The contracting parties determining for themselves the terms of their own contract, it is peculiarly the duty of each to act in the utmost good faith.

§161. **Obligatory Arbitration. (a) General International Conventions.**—Although sovereign states are not legally bound, except by their own consent, to submit to arbitration controversies arising in the interpretation of treaties, all the principal powers of the world have formally declared arbitration to be the most effective, and, at the same time, the most equitable means of settling disputes of this character; and numerous conventions have been concluded between different states by which they have bound themselves to submit, subject to certain limitations, such differences to arbitration. Article XVI of the convention for the pacific settlement of international disputes, concluded at The Hague, July 29, 1899, and to which the principal powers of the world are parties,[1] reads: "In questions of a legal nature, and

1 Germany, Austria-Hungary, Belgium, Bulgaria, China, Denmark, Spain, the United States, Mexico, France, Great Britain, Greece, Italy, Japan, Luxemburg, Montenegro, Norway, the Netherlands, Persia, Portugal, Roumania, Russia, Servia, Siam, Sweden, Switzerland, and Turkey are signatory parties. Argentine Republic, Bolivia, Brazil, Chile, Colombia, Cuba, Dominican Republic, Ecuador, Guatemala, Haiti, Nicaragua, Panama, Paraguay, Peru, Salvador, Uruguay, and Venezuela are parties by adhesion.

especially in the interpretation or application of international conventions, arbitration is recognized by the signatory powers as the most effective, and at the same time the most equitable, means of settling disputes which diplomacy has failed to settle." This article is textually incorporated in Article XXXVIII of the convention concluded at the Second Hague Conference, October 18, 1907, except for the substitution of the word "contracting" for "signatory," and with the following additional clause: "Consequently, it would be desirable that, in disputes about the above mentioned questions, the contracting powers should, if the case arose, have recourse to arbitration, in so far as circumstances permit." In the original project presented by the Russian delegation to the Conference of 1899, arbitration was to be made obligatory in cases (not affecting the national honor or vital interests of the contracting states) of disagreement in the interpretation or application of treaties concerning postal and telegraphic service, international railways, protection of submarine telegraphic cables, rules for the prevention of collisions on the high seas, protection of literary, artistic and industrial property, monetary affairs, weights and measures, sanitary affairs, veterinary precautions, protection against the phylloxera, inheritances, extradition, mutual judicial assistance, and the navigation of international rivers and interoceanic canals, as also boundary conventions so far as they involved purely technical and not political questions.[2] Obligatory arbitration of any dispute that might arise out of treaties concerning monetary affairs and the navigation of international rivers and interoceanic canals, was objected to, in the Comité d' Examen, by the American member; and, on the motion of the German member, who opposed the general principle of obligatory arbitration, the article was stricken out in the committee.[3] During the proceedings of the Conference of 1907, various projects for obligatory arbitration of differences arising in the interpretation and application of treaties, subject to certain qualifications, were considered.[4] A project providing that differences of a legal nature, and, "primarily, those relating to the interpretation of treaties," that might arise in the future and that could not be settled by negotiation, should, provided they did not involve the

---

2 Conférence internationale de la Paix, pt. 4, p. 202.
3 Holls, Peace Conference at The Hague, 227.
4 Scott, The Hague Peace Conferences, I, 334-385.

vital interests, independence, or honor of the parties, or affect
interests of other nations not concerned in the dispute, be submitted to arbitration, was supported by the votes of thirty-two
delegations. Nine voted against it and three abstained from voting.[5] In this project it was specifically provided that differences
concerning the application and interpretation of conventional
stipulations relative to reciprocal gratuitous aid to indigent sick,
international protection of workingmen, means of preventing collisions at sea, weights and measures, measurements of vessels,
wages and estates of deceased sailors, and the protection of literary and artistic works, were of a nature to be and were to be submitted to arbitration without reservation.[6] Although this project
met with the approval of a majority of the delegations, it was not
adopted by the Conference as a part of the conventional agreement because of the prevailing wish for unanimity. The Final
Act as signed by the delegations, October 18, 1907, contained,
however, a recital that the Conference was unanimous in "declaring that certain disputes, in particular those relating to the interpretation and application of the provisions of international agreements, may be submitted to compulsory arbitration without any
restriction."[7]

In the project of an arbitration convention recommended by the
first international conference of American states in 1890, arbitration in controversies in regard to displomatic and consular privileges, boundaries, territories, navigation, indemnities, and the validity, construction and enforcement of treaties, was made obligatory, provided that such questions as, in the judgment of either
party to the controversy, might imperil its independence should
at the option of that nation be excepted.[8] Likewise in the convention for obligatory arbitration signed, January 29, 1902, by

5 The delegations of the United States, Argentine Republic, Bolivia,
Brazil, Chile, China, Colombia, Denmark, Dominican Republic, Ecuador,
Spain, France, Great Britain, Guatemala, Haiti, Mexico, Nicaragua, Nor-
way, Panama, Paraguay, the Netherlands, Peru, Persia, Portugal, Russia,
Salvador, Servia, Siam, Sweden, Uruguay, and Venezuela voted in the
affirmative; those of Germany, Austria-Hungary, Belgium, Bulgaria,
Greece, Montenegro, Roumania, Switzerland and Turkey voted in the
negative; and those of Italy, Japan, and Luxemburg did not vote. Id.,
I, 373.

6 Id., I, 370.

7 Id., II, 287.

8 S. Doc. No. 224, 51st Cong., 1st Sess.

the delegates of nine of the nineteen states represented at the second international conference of American states, it was provided that all controversies that did not in the exclusive judgment of either of the interested parties affect its national honor or independence should be submitted to arbitration; and it was expressly declared that independence and national honor should not be considered as being involved in controversies in regard to diplomatic privileges, rights of navigation, and the validity, construction and enforcement of treaties.[9]

§162. (b) Special Clauses and Treaties for Arbitration.—A clause may be inserted in the treaty itself by which the contracting parties agree to submit to arbitration, as therein provided for, any controversy that may arise in the construction and application of its terms. For instance, in Article XXIII of the universal postal-union convention signed at Vienna, July 4, 1891, which article is renewed in the convention signed at Washington, June 15, 1897, it is provided that disagreements between two or more parties to the union as to the interpretation of the terms of the convention shall be decided by arbitration in the manner prescribed in the article.[10] By a resolution introduced in the Chamber of Deputies of the Italian Parliament in November, 1875, and unanimously agreed to, the Government was requested to incorporate, if possible, in all treaties thereafter concluded, a clause to provide that any controversy that might arise in the execution or interpretation of the terms of the treaty should be referred to arbitration. A large number of the treaties entered into by Italy since that date have contained such provisions.[11] Many of the treaties concluded by Norway contain similar clauses. The Institute of International Law at Zurich in 1877 recommended the incorporation into treaties of provisions of this character.[12]

Many special conventions have been concluded in which the two contracting parties have agreed to submit to arbitration con-

9 S. Doc. No. 330, 57th Cong., 1st Sess., 41.

10 28 Stats. at L. 1093; 30 Stats. at L. 1645.

11 See for list, Report of M. le Chevalier Descamps to the First Hague Conference, Annex E.

12 In the unratified treaty between the United States and Denmark of January 24, 1902, for the cession to the United States of the Danish West Indies, provision was made that any differences arising in the execution or interpretation of the treaty should be submitted to the Permanent Court of Arbitration at The Hague. Art. VI.

troversies that may arise in the future between them in the interpretation of treaties, subject to certain qualifications, as for instance, that they do not involve third parties or affect the vital interests, national honor or independence of the contracting parties.[13]

13 A compilation by the International Bureau of the Permanent Court at The Hague of conventions of arbitration communicated to it prior to July 1, 1911, pursuant to the requirements of Article XLIII of the convention of 1907, for the pacific settlement of international disputes, shows ninety separate conventions of arbitration to have been concluded since June 8, 1899. Classified by countries they are as follows: Germany with Great Britain, July 12, 1904, renewed, November 23, December 7, 1909. The United States with Austria-Hungary, January 15, 1909; Bolivia, January 7, 1909; China, October 8, 1908; Costa Rica, January 13, 1909; Denmark, May 18, 1908; Ecuador, January 7, 1909; Spain, April 20, 1908; France, February 10, 1908; Great Britain, April 4, 1908; Haiti, January 7, 1909; Italy, March 28, 1908; Japan, May 5, 1908; Mexico, March 24, 1908; Norway, April 4, 1908; Paraguay, March 13, 1909; the Netherlands, May 2, 1908; Peru, December 5, 1908; Portugal, April 6, 1908; Salvador, December 21, 1908; Sweden, May 2, 1908; Switzerland, February 29, 1908. [It should be noted that the convention with Bolivia has not been ratified. There may be added the conventions with Brazil of January 23, 1909, and Uruguay of January 9, 1909.] Argentine Republic with Portugal, August 9, 1909; Uruguay, June 8, 1899. Austria-Hungary with the United States, January 15, 1909; Great Britain, July 16, 1910; Portugal, February 13, 1906.   Belgium with Denmark, April 26, 1905; Spain, January 23, 1905; Greece, (April 19) May 2, 1905; Nicaragua, March 6, 1906; Roumania, May (14) 27, 1905; Russia, October (17) 30, 1904; Sweden and Norway, November 30, 1904; Switzerland, November 15, 1904.   Bolivia with Brazil, June 25, 1909; Spain, February 17, 1902.   Brazil with Bolivia, June 25, 1909; China, August 3, 1909; Great Britain, June 18, 1909; Portugal, March 25, 1909; [the United States, January 23, 1909.]   China with the United States, October 8, 1908; Brazil, August 3, 1909.   Colombia with Spain, February 17, 1902; France, December 16, 1908; Great Britain, December 30, 1908.   Costa Rica with the United States, January 13, 1909.   Denmark with the United States, May 18, 1908; Belgium, April 26, 1905; Spain, December 1, 1905; France, September 15, 1905; Great Britain, October 25, 1905, renewed, March 3, 1911; Italy, December 16, 1905; Norway, October 8, 1908; the Netherlands, February 12, 1904; Portugal, March 20, 1907; Russia, (February 16) March 1, 1905; Sweden, July 17, 1908. Dominican Republic with Spain, January 28, 1902. Ecuador with the United States, January 7, 1909.   Spain with the United States, April 20, 1908; Belgium, January 23, 1905; Bolivia, February 17, 1902; Colombia, February 17, 1902; Denmark, December 1, 1905; Dominican Republic, January 28, 1902; France, February 26, 1904, renewed, February 3, 1909; Great Britain, February 27, 1904, renewed, January 11, 1909; Greece, December 16 (3), 1909; Guatemala, February 28, 1902; Honduras, May 13, 1905; Mexico, January 11, 1902;

Portugal, May 31, 1904; Russia, August 15 (2), 1910; Salvador, January 28, 1902; Sweden and Norway, January 23, 1905; Switzerland, May 14, 1907; Uruguay, January 28, 1902. France with the United States, February 10, 1908; Colombia, December 16, 1908; Denmark, September 15, 1905; Spain, February 26, 1904, renewed, February 3, 1909; Great Britain, October 14, 1903, renewed, October 14, 1908; Italy, December 25, 1903, renewed, December 24, 1908; Norway, July 9, 1904, renewed, November 5, 1909; the Netherlands, April 6, 1904, renewed, December 29, 1909; Portugal, June 29, 1906; Sweden, July 9, 1904, renewed, October 27, 1909; Switzerland, December 14, 1904, renewed, July 13, 1910. Great Britain with Germany, July 12, 1904, renewed, November 23, December 7, 1909; the United States, April 4, 1908; Austria-Hungary, July 16, 1910; Brazil, June 18, 1909; Colombia, December 30, 1908; Denmark, October 25, 1905, renewed, March 3, 1911; Spain, February 27, 1904, renewed, January 11, 1909; France, October 14, 1903, renewed, October 14, 1908; Italy, February 1, 1904, renewed, January 4, 1909; Norway, August 11, 1904, renewed, November 9, 1909; the Netherlands, February 15, 1905, renewed, December 16, 1909; Portugal, November 16, 1904, renewed, November 16, 1909; Sweden, August 11, 1904, renewed, November 9, 1909; Switzerland, November 16, 1904, renewed, November 3, 12, 1909. Greece with Belgium, (April 19) May 2, 1905; Spain, December (3) 16, 1909. Guatemala with Spain, February 28, 1902. Haiti with the United States, January 7, 1909. Honduras with Spain, May 13, 1905. Italy with the United States, March 28, 1908; Denmark, December 16, 1905; France, December 25, 1903, renewed, December 24, 1908; Great Britain, February 1, 1904, renewed, January 4, 1909; Norway, December 4, 1910; the Netherlands, November 20, 1909; Portugal, May 11, 1905, renewed April 21, May 30, 1910; Switzerland, November 23, 1904, renewed, November 16, 1909. Japan with the United States, May 5, 1908. Mexico with the United States, March 24, 1908; Spain, January 11, 1902. Nicaragua with Belgium, March 6, 1906; Portugal, July 17, 1909. Norway with the United States, April 4, 1908; Belgium, November 30, 1904; Denmark, October 8, 1908; Spain, January 23, 1905; France, July 9, 1904, renewed, November 5, 1909; Great Britain, August 11, 1904, renewed, November 9, 1909; Italy, December 4, 1910; Portugal, December 8, 1908; Russia, December 9 (November 26), 1904; Sweden, October 26, 1905; Switzerland, December 17, 1904. Paraguay with the United States, March 13, 1909. The Netherlands with the United States, May 2, 1908; Denmark, February 12, 1904; France, April 6, 1904, renewed, December 29, 1909; Great Britain, February 15, 1905, renewed, December 16, 1909; Italy, November 20, 1909; Portugal, October 1, 1904. Peru with the United States, December 5, 1908. Portugal with the United States, April 6, 1908; Argentine Republic, August 9, 1909; Austria-Hungary, February 13, 1906; Brazil, March 25, 1909; Denmark, March 20, 1907; Spain, May 31, 1904; France, June 29, 1906; Great Britain, November 16, 1904, renewed, November 16, 1909; Italy, May 11, 1905, renewed, April 21, May 30, 1910; Nicaragua, July 17, 1909; Norway, December 8, 1908; the Netherlands, October 1, 1904; Sweden, May 6, 1905; Switzerland, August 18, 1905. Roumania with Belgium, May (14) 27, 1905.

§163. **Questions for the Courts and for the Political Departments in the United States.**—Where the treaty operates infraterritorially, as in the United States, or becomes by subsequent enactment a part of the law of the land, questions respecting its meaning in cases involving rights between individuals under it as a municipal law are determined by the courts.[14]   In those states where the act to carry the treaty into effect, and not the treaty itself, comes before the courts, the construction of the treaty is a function of the legislative or the executive branch, as the case may be, not of the judicial.   And in the United States, although a

Russia with Belgium, October (17) 30, 1904; Denmark, (February 16) March 1, 1905; Spain, (August 2) 15, 1910; Sweden and Norway, (November 26) December 9, 1904. Salvador with the United States, December 21, 1908; Spain, January 28, 1902.   Sweden with the United States, May 2, 1908; Belgium, November 30, 1904; Denmark, July 17, 1908; Spain, January 23, 1905; France, July 9, 1904, renewed, October 27, 1909; Great Britain, August 11, 1904, renewed, November 9, 1909; Norway, October 26, 1905; Portugal, May 6, 1905; Russia, (November 26) December 9, 1904; Switzerland, December 17, 1904.   Switzerland with the United States, February 29, 1908; Belgium, November 15, 1904; Spain, May 14, 1907; France, December 14, 1904, renewed, July 13, 1910; Great Britain, November 16, 1904, renewed, November 3, 12, 1909; Italy, November 23, 1904, renewed, November 16, 1909; Portugal, August 18, 1905; Sweden and Norway, December 17, 1904.   Uruguay with Argentine Republic, June 8, 1899; Spain, January 28, 1902; [the United States, January 9, 1909.] The convention signed at the Second International American Conference, January 29, 1902, is credited in the list to each country whose delegates signed it, namely, Argentine Republic, Bolivia, Dominican Republic, Guatemala, Salvador, Mexico, Paraguay, Peru and Uruguay.

A supplemental compilation shows twenty-four additional conventions, which have been communicated to the Bureau since the first compilation and prior to September, 1914, concluded as follows: April 18, 1905, Italy and Peru; September 18, 1907, Argentine Republic and Italy; October 16, 1907, Italy and Mexico; April 7, 1909, Brazil and France; April 30, 1909, Brazil and Venezuela; July 13, 1909, Brazil and Norway; January 8, 1910, Costa Rica and Italy; August 5, 1910, Colombia and France; August (13) 26, 1910, Brazil and Russia; September 2, 1910, Spain and Italy; October 19, 1910, Austria-Hungary and Brazil; October (14) 27, 1910, Italy and Russia; November 18, 1910, Belgium and Italy; February 25, 1911, Ecuador and Italy; April 13, 1911, Italy and Sweden; May 11, 1911, Italy and Paraguay; May 17, 1911, Bolivia and Italy; August 9, 1911, Denmark and France; September 22, 1911, Brazil and Italy; November 27, 1911, Brazil and Denmark; May 31, 1913, Spain and Panama; June 19, 1913, Spain and Switzerland; August 8, 1913, Chile and Italy; September 2, 1913, Austria-Hungary and Switzerland.

14 Wilson v. Wall (1867), 6 Wall. 83, 89.

treaty operates by its own force as municipal law binding on the courts equally with an act of the legislature, the courts will follow the determinations of the political departments of the government, the executive and legislative, in questions involving primarily the external operation of the treaty as an international compact. In controversies with a foreign nation respecting boundaries and territorial jurisdiction, as defined by treaty, the courts have, for instance, frequently declared that they will not review a determination in this respect of the executive and legislative branches, clearly expressed, to ascertain whether it is right or wrong, but will follow it.[15] Chief Justice Marshall in Foster v. Neilson said: "In a controversy between two nations concerning national boundary, it is scarcely possible that the courts of either should refuse to abide by the measures adopted by its own government. There being no common tribunal to decide between them, each determines for itself on its own rights, and if they cannot adjust their differences peaceably, the right remains with the strongest. The judiciary is not that department of the government, to which the assertion of its interests against foreign powers is confided; and its duty commonly is to decide upon individual rights, according to those principles which the political departments of the nation have established. If the course of the nation has been a plain one, its courts would hesitate to pronounce it erroneous. We think then, however individual judges might construe the treaty of St. Ildefonso, it is the province of the court to conform its decisions to the will of the legislature, if that will has been clearly expressed. * * * After these acts of sovereign power over the territory in dispute, asserting the American construction of the treaty by which the government claims it, to maintain the opposite construction in its own courts would certainly be an anomaly in the history and practice of nations. If those departments which are entrusted with the foreign intercourse of the nation, which assert and maintain its interests against foreign powers, have unequivocally asserted its rights of dominion over a

15 De la Croix v. Chamberlain, 12 Wheat. 599, 602; Foster v. Neilson, 2 Pet. 253, 309; Cherokee Nation v. Georgia, 5 Pet. 1, 21; United States v. Arredondo, 6 Pet. 691, 711; Garcia v. Lee, 12 Pet. 511, 517; Lattimer v. Poteet, 14 Pet. 4; Pollard's Heirs v. Kibbe, 14 Pet. 353; Pollard's Lessee v. Files, 2 How. 591, 602; United States v. Reynes, 9 How. 127, 154; United States v. Lynde, 11 Wall. 632; In re Cooper, 143 U. S. 472, 502; United States v. Texas, 143 U. S. 621, 638.

26

country of which it is in possession, and which it claims under a treaty; if the legislature has acted on the construction thus asserted, it is not in its own courts that this construction is to be denied. A question like this respecting the boundaries of nations, is, as has been truly said, more a political than a legal question; and in its discussion, the courts of every country must respect the pronounced will of the legislature."[16]   Again, Mr. Justice Daniel, speaking for the court in United States v. Reynes, said: "Whether, by the treaties of St. Ildefonso and of Paris, the territory south of the thirty-first degree of north latitude, and lying between the Mississippi and Perdido, was ceded to the United States, is a question into which this court will not now inquire. The legislative and executive departments of the government have determined that the entire territory was so ceded. This court have solemnly and repeatedly declared, that this was a matter peculiarly belonging to the cognizance of those departments, and that the propriety of their determination it was not within the province of the judiciary to contravene or question."[17]   It is likewise well settled that the determination by the legislative and executive branches of the government as to the de facto or de jure sovereign of a territory is conclusive and binding on the courts.[18]   In reply to the argument, that the King of Spain did not have the right under the laws of Spain to annul grants of land made to individuals, as stipulated for in the treaty of 1819 for the cession of Florida to the United States, Chief Justice Taney, in Doe v. Braden, said: "But these are political questions and not judicial.

---

16   2 Pet. 253, 307, 309.

17   9 How. 127, 153.

18   Gelston v. Hoyt, 3 Wheat. 246, 324; United States v. Palmer, 3 Wheat. 610; The Divina Pastora, 4 Wheat. 52; Foster v. Neilson, 2 Pet. 253, 307, 309; Keene v. McDonough, 8 Pet. 308; Garcia v. Lee, 12 Pet. 511, 520; Williams v. Suffolk Ins. Co., 13 Pet. 415; United States v. Pico, 23 How. 321, 326; United States v. Yorba, 1 Wall. 412, 423; Stearns v. United States, 6 Wall. 589; Hornsby v. United States, 10 Wall. 224, 239; United States v. Lynde, 11 Wall. 632, 638; More v. Steinbach, 127 U. S. 70, 80; Jones v. United States, 137 U. S. 202, 212; Pearcy v. Stranahan, 205 U. S. 257, 265. "It is equally well settled in England. The Pelican, Edw. Adm. Appx. D; Taylor v. Barclay, 2 Sim. 213; Emperor of Austria v. Day, 3 De G., F. & J. 217, 221, 233; Republic of Peru v. Peruvian Guano Co., 36 Ch. D. 489, 497; Republic of Peru v. Dreyfus, 38 Ch. D. 348, 356, 359." Gray, J., Jones v. United States, 137 U. S. 202, 212. See, however, Tartar Chemical Co. v. United States, 116 Fed. 726.

They belong exclusively to the political department of the government. * * * The treaty is therefore a law made by the proper authority, and the courts of justice have no right to annul or disregard any of its provisions, unless they violate the Constitution of the United States. It is their duty to interpret it and administer it according to its terms. And it would be impossible for the executive department of the government to conduct our foreign relations with any advantage to the country, and fulfill the duties which the Constitution has imposed upon it, if every court in the country was authorized to inquire and decide whether the person who ratified the treaty on behalf of a foreign nation had the power, by its constitution and laws, to make the engagements into which he entered. In this case the King of Spain has by treaty stipulated that the grant to the Duke of Alagon, previously made by him, had been and remained annulled, and that neither the Duke of Alagon nor any person claiming under him could avail himself of this grant. It was for the President and Senate to determine whether the King by the constitution and laws of Spain, was authorized to make this stipulation and to ratify a treaty containing it. They have recognized his power by accepting this stipulation as a part of the compact, and ratifying the treaty which contains it. * * * Nor can the plaintiff's claim be supported unless he can maintain that a court of justice may enquire whether the President and Senate were not mistaken as to the authority of the Spanish monarch in this respect; or knowingly sanctioned an act of injustice committed by him upon an individual in violation of the laws of Spain. But it is evident that such a proposition can find no support in the Constitution of the United States; nor in the jurisprudence of any country where the judicial and political powers are separated and placed in different hands. Certainly no judicial tribunal in the United States ever claimed it, or supposed it possessed it."[19] So also, whether power remains in a foreign state to carry out its treaty obligations is a political question, the determination of which by the executive department of the government binds the courts. For instance, the fact, that the convention for the extradition of criminals, concluded between the United States and Prussia and other States of the Germanic Confederation, June 16, 1852, had been repeatedly recognized both by the government of Germany and by

19 16 How. 635, 657, 658.

the executive branch of the government of the United States as surviving the formation of the German Empire, of which Prussia and the other Germanic States form a part, has been considered conclusive on the courts as to its continuing obligation.[20] The courts have likewise declared that they will not go back of a treaty, duly executed, ratified, and proclaimed on the part of the United States, to determine whether it was executed by the proper officers on the part of the other contracting party;[21] or whether it was procured by duress or fraud;[22] or whether it is voidable as the result of infractions.[23] It was said by Chancellor Wythe in an early case: "That the treaty [of peace with Great Britain] admitted to have been once valid, hath been rendered invalid, by the failure of the British King to perform the articles thereof this court hath no more power to declare than it hath to declare the British King and the United States of America to be in a state of war."[24] These questions relate primarily to the operation of the treaty as in international compact. The courts know the treaty only as a municipal law, and have no jurisdiction over the parties to it.

20 Terlinden v. Ames, 184 U. S. 270, 285, 288. See also Disconto Gesellschaft v. Umbreit, 208 U. S. 570, 581, as to the treaty of commerce with Prussia of 1828. "I need not state the various revolutions and changes, which that government [that of the United Netherlands] has undergone, and its present form; nor attempt to support by reasoning, why treaties are, or ought to be binding upon the people of the same countries, although both or one of the governments have undergone revolutions or changes. This does not belong to this department of the government. We can know our exterior relations only through that branch or organ of the government, appointed by the form of it, to represent and act for us with foreign powers. The case states, that that organ or department of the government still considers the treaty as binding on us; and of course on the people of the other contracting party." Henderson, C. J., University v. Miller (1831), 14 N. C. 188, 193.

21 Fellows v. Blacksmith, 19 How. 366, 372; Leighton v. United States, 29 C. Cls. 288, 321; Maiden v. Ingersoll, 6 Mich. 373, 376. The same principle was applied by the High Court of the East Africa Protectorate in the case brought by the Masai tribe against the Attorney General and others. (1913), Cd. 6939. Am. Journal of Int. Law, VIII, 380, 388.

22 United States v. Old Settlers, 148 U. S. 427; The Fama, 5 C. Rob. 106, 113.

23 Jones v. Walker, 2 Paine 688; Ware v. Hylton, 3 Dall. 199, 259; Taylor v. Morton, 2 Curtis 454, 461; Ex parte Charlton, 185 Fed. 880; Charlton v. Kelly (1913), 229 U. S. 447.

24 Page v. Pendleton (1793), 1 Wythe's Repts. (Va. ed. 1852), 211, 217.

The consideration in the first instance of questions of a judicial nature, which may later come before the courts, naturally devolves at times upon the department of government entrusted with the conduct of negotiations with foreign nations; and in such case "a construction of a treaty by the political department of the government, while not conclusive upon a court called upon to construe such a treaty in a matter involving personal rights, is nevertheless of much weight."[25] Under the Articles of Confederation, the Secretary for Foreign Affairs found it advisable to submit questions arising in the construction of treaties to the Congress.[26] Under the Constitution, the Senate, a co-ordinate branch of the treaty-making power, has been consulted by the President upon such questions only in exceptional instances. On representations by the French government that certain acts of Congress, which imposed extra tonnage dues on foreign vessels and made no exception in favor of French vessels, contravened the fifth article of the treaty of 1778, President Washington submitted the question to the Senate for its consideration. The Senate advised as to the meaning of the article in a resolution adopted February 26, 1791.[27] The Executive likewise submitted for the consideration of the Senate the question that arose in 1868 between this government and the Ottoman Porte as to the correct version of Article IV of the treaty of May 7, 1830, concerning the territorial exemption to be enjoyed by American citizens in Turkey.[28] Instances are also to be found of the submission by the President to the Senate of awards of international commissions for its advice as to whether the commissioners have acted within their powers, i, e, interpreted correctly the convention under which they were appointed. The award of the commissioners, under the claims convention with Paraguay of February 4, 1859, was, for instance, communicated to the Senate for this purpose by President Bu-

---

25 Lurton, J., Charlton v. Kelly (1913), 229 U. S. 447, 468. At the request of President Washington, Jefferson, Secretary of State, addressed on July 18, 1793, a communication to the justices of the Supreme Court, making enquiries as to the propriety of asking their advice, among other things, on the construction of treaties. MSS. Jefferson Papers, series 1, Vol. VI, p. 186.

26 Dip. Cor. 1783-9, I, 245.

27 Ex. Journal, I, 77.

28 Notes to Treaties and Conventions (1889 ed.), 1371.

chanan, February 12, 1861.[29]   In the case of the recommendatory award of the King of the Netherlands, as arbitrator under the convention with Great Britain of September 29, 1827, for the determination of the northeastern boundary, the Senate, to which the question was submitted by President Jackson, advised that the award was not obligatory; and it was not so considered.[30]

29 Richardson, Messages, V, 664. See also message of President Lincoln of March 5, 1862. Id., VI, 67.

30 As to the nature of the award, see Moore, Int. Arb., I, 138.

CHAPTER XXIII.

AIDS IN THE INTERPRETATION OF TREATIES.

§164. **Intention of the Parties.**—"The intention, sufficiently known, furnishes the true matter of the convention."[1] The sole purpose of a resort to construction is to determine and give effect to the intention of the parties otherwise obscure.[2] Since the agency through which a state enters into treaties often consists of distinct bodies, which act independently of each other, as for instance in the United States the President and the Senate, it is peculiarly essential that the clear language of the written instrument should be considered as accurately expressing the intention of the parties. "Treaties are the subject of careful consideration before they are entered into, and are drawn by persons competent to express their meaning and to choose apt words in which to embody the purposes of the high contracting parties."[3]

§165. **General Purpose of the Treaty.**—The intention of the parties as there expressed is, however, to be determined by a consideration of the whole instrument, not by viewing the stipulations separately. From this it follows that a literal and narrow meaning of a clause may not be made to defeat the manifest purpose of the parties as gathered from the entire instrument. "We are not at liberty to ascribe a meaning to the terms of a treaty which would frustrate the known and proved purpose of the instrument, unless the words used in the instrument are such as to permit of no other construction. Whoever asserts a construction which would produce such a result must show not merely that it is a possible construction, but that it is a necessary construction, and that any other is impossible."[4]

---

1 Vattel, Bk. II, c. XVII, §274.

2 "It is not allowable to interpret what has no need of interpretation." Id., Bk. II, c. XVII, §263.

3 Day, J., Rocca v. Thompson, 223 U. S. 317, 332. See also the Nereide, 9 Cranch 388, 419; and the Neck, 138 Fed. 144.

4 Opinion of Elihu Root, Henry Cabot Lodge and George Turner, U. S. members of the Alaskan Boundary Tribunal of 1903. S. Doc. No. 162, 58th Cong., 2d Sess., I, 53. "The whole document will be taken together, and will be considered in connection with the attendant circumstances, the situation of the parties, and the object in view, and thus the literal mean-

Many cases are cited in the early books of the avoidance of the plain purpose of the treaty by the adoption of a restricted literal meaning of the terms.[5] By the ninth article of the peace of Utrecht between France and Great Britain, it was agreed that the French fortifications at Dunkirk should be destroyed. While destroying those at Dunkirk, the King of France proceeded to erect new ones a short distance away. The clear purpose of the stipulation had been to ensure Great Britain against the existence of French fortifications on the English Channel, not the mere destruction of the particular fortifications then standing. The British government objected to the narrow meaning given to the terms of the treaty, and ultimately the work was discontinued.[6]

Article I of the treaty of June 15, 1846, between the United States and Great Britain, for the establishment of a boundary line

ing of an isolated clause is often shown not to be the meaning really understood or intended." Mr. Phelps, Am. minister, to Lord Rosebery, June 2, 1886. S. Doc. No. 870, 61st Cong., 3d Sess., III, 778. See also Vattel, Bk. II, c. XVII, §287.

5 "Grotius quotes several instances of evidently false interpretations put upon treaties [De Jure Belli et Pacis, lib. II, cap. XVI, §5] :—the Plateans having promised the Thebans to restore their prisoners, restored them after they had put them to death. Pericles having promised to spare the lives of such of the enemy as laid down their arms [literally 'laid down their iron or steel'], ordered all those to be killed who had iron clasps to their cloaks. A Roman general having agreed with Antiochus to restore him half of his fleet, caused each of the ships to be sawed in two. All these interpretations are as fraudulent as that of Rhadamistus, who, according to Tacitus's account, having sworn to Mithridates that he would not employ either poison or the steel against him, caused him to be smothered under a heap of clothes." Vattel, Bk. II, c. XV, §233. "Mahomet, emperor of the Turks, at the taking of Negropont, having promised a man to spare his head, caused him to be cut in two through the middle of the body. Tamerlane, after having engaged the city of Sebastia to capitulate, under his promise of shedding no blood, caused all the soldiers of the garrison to be buried alive. [See Pufendorf, Law of Nature and Nations, Bk. V, c. XII, §3]; gross subterfuges which, as Cicero remarks, [De Offic. lib. III, c. XXXII] only serve to aggravate the guilt of the perfidious wretch who has recourse to them. To spare the head of any one, and to shed no blood, are expressions which, according to common custom, and especially on such an occasion, manifestly imply to spare the lives of the parties." Vattel, Bk. II, c. XVII, §273. See for other early instances, Phillipson, Int. Law and Custom of Ancient Greece and Rome, I, 407.

6 Wildman, Institutes of Int. Law, I, 178; Phillimore, Int. Law (2 ed.), II, 97.

between their respective territories west of the Rocky Mountains, provided for the continuation of the line along the 49th parallel westward to the middle of the channel which separated the continent from Vancouver Island, and "thence southerly through the middle of the said channel, and of Fuca's Straits, to the Pacific Ocean." As a matter of fact there proved to be two principal navigable channels—the Canal de Haro and Rosario Strait —leading from the middle of the channel through the archipelago to the Strait of Juan de Fuca. In support of the British contention for the Rosario Strait, the one nearer the continent, was the fact that a line through the Canal de Haro must proceed for some distance in a westerly direction, instead of southerly in accordance with the letter of the treaty. On the other hand the general purpose of the treaty, as disclosed by the treaty itself, had been to adopt the 49th parallel as the line for the division of the disputed territory, and to allow a deflection from that line only in order to avoid dividing Vancouver Island. This view as to the purpose of the agreement had been expressed in the Senate at the time of the ratification of the treaty.[7] The German Emperor, as arbitrator under the treaty of May 8, 1871, decided that the claim of the United States was "most in accordance with the true interpretations of the treaty."[8]

7 Mr. Bancroft, the American agent in the arbitration of the question before the German Emperor, said: "The language of the treaty taken as a whole, admits no interpretation but the American. The radical principle of the boundary is the forty-ninth parallel of north latitude, and the only reason for departing from that parallel was to yield the whole of Vancouver Island, and no more, to the power which would already possess the greater part of that island." (Memorial, 24). In instructions of June 19, 1826, Mr. Clay, Secretary of State, authorized Mr. Gallatin to offer as a final proposition the "extension of the line on the parallel of 49° from the Stony Mountains to the Pacific Ocean." (Id., 10). The British government in reply to this proposition, November 22, 1826, noted that the "cutting off the lower part of Vancouver Island" was quite inadmissible. To this Mr. Gallatin replied that since it seemed to cut Vancouver Island in an inconvenient manner, an exchange of that southern extremity might be made for an equivalent north of the 49th parallel on the mainland. In the later negotiations of 1845-6, the 49th parallel was taken as the basis of a compromise settlement, subject to the modification that Vancouver Island should go to Great Britain. (Id., 10-19).

8 Moore, Int. Arb., I, 214, 219, 220, 224, 229. See also arguments in the arbitration of the northeastern boundary question before the King of the Netherlands, as to the meaning of the terms "Highlands," "Atlantic Ocean," and "St. Lawrence," as used in Article II of the treaty of peace of 1783. Id., I, 107, 114.

By articles annexed to the general treaty of Vienna of 1815, it was provided that the navigation of the river Rhine should be free and open to the sea (jusqu'à la mer).[9] The stream which bears the name of the Rhine is in its lower course, after the separation from it of the Waal and the Leck, insignificant; and passage by it to the sea is intercepted. The government of the Netherlands admitted the application of the provision for free navigation to the channel bearing the name Leck only, and insisted that the right of free navigation ended at the point of tide water, since the stipulation read "to the sea," and that her rights of sovereignty extended without any restriction whatever over the sea even where it mixed with the waters of the Rhine. The riverain states (Prussia, Bavaria, and Hesse, with whose views France and Baden concurred) protested against this narrow meaning given to the terms of the treaty, and asserted that the purpose of the stipulation had been to insure free passage of vessels down the Rhine "into the sea," and vice versa; and that under the denomination of the Rhine were included all the real outlets of that river through the Netherlands. By the convention concluded at Mayence March 31, 1831, the Netherlands agreed that both the Leck and the Waal should be considered as continuations of the Rhine; and that their navigation should be open and free to the high sea as contended for by the riverain states.[10]

Another instance of the recognition of this principle is afforded by the action of Great Britain in continuing payments on the Russian-Dutch loan after the separation of the Belgic Provinces from the Netherlands. The convention concluded between Great Britain, Russia, and the Netherlands, May 19, 1815, contained the qualification that the payments to Russia on the Russian-Dutch loan, which were undertaken by Great Britain and the Netherlands, should cease in case the Belgic Provinces should at any time, prior to the complete liquidation of the loan, be severed from the dominions of the King of the Netherlands. On November 16, 1831, the day following the signature of the treaty by the powers of Europe for the separation of the Belgic Provinces, a convention was concluded between Great Britain and Russia,

---

9 Hertslet's Map of Europe by Treaty, I, 78, 273; Brit. and For. State Papers, II, 163.

10 Hertslet's Map of Europe by Treaty, II, 848; III, 1847; Brit. and For. State Papers, XVIII, 1076, 1078; Westlake, Int. Law, I, 153.

by which the former, recognizing the "spirit" rather than following the "letter" of the convention of May 19, 1815, agreed to continue to discharge the obligation assumed under that convention, regardless of the fact of separation. The contracting parties, after an examination of the considerations which entered into the convention of May 19, 1815, came to the conclusion that complete agreement did not exist "between the letter and spirit of that convention," when regarded in connection with the circumstances which attended the separation of the Belgic Provinces. The object of the convention of May 19, 1815, had been to afford to Great Britain a guarantee that Russia would, in all questions concerning Belgium, identify her policy with that which Great Britain had deemed the best adapted for the maintenance of a just balance of power in Europe, and on the other hand to secure to Russia the payment of a portion of her old Dutch debt in consideration of the general arrangements of the Congress of Vienna to which she had given her adhesion.[11]

The same principle has frequently been applied by the Supreme Court of the United States in construing treaties as municipal laws. It has, for instance, held that an English subject, who was an enlisted seaman on board an American vessel flying the American flag and accordingly under the protection of and owing a temporary allegiance to the United States, came within the meaning of the provision of Article IV of the treaty with Japan of June 17, 1857, that "Americans" who should commit offenses in Japan should be tried by the American consul. Mr. Justice Field, for the court, said: "It is a canon of interpretation to so construe a law or a treaty as to give effect to the object designed, and for that purpose all of its provisions must be examined in the light of attendant and surrounding circumstances. To some terms and expressions a literal meaning will be given, and to others a larger and more extended one. * * * The enquiry in all such cases is as to what was intended in the law by the legislature, and in the treaty by the contracting parties. * * * And in the present case, to carry out the intention of the treaty and statute in question, they will be construed to apply to all parties who are by public law, or the law of the country, entitled to be treated for the time, from their employment and service, as citizens."[12] It

---

11 Hertslet's Map of Europe by Treaty, I, 152; Brit. and For. State Papers, XVIII, 928. See also Phillimore, Int. Law (2 ed.), II, 111.

12 In re Ross, 140 U. S. 453, 475.

has also been held that the District of Columbia, as a political community, was included in the expression "States of the Union" as used in Article VII of the consular convention with France of February 23, 1853, such construction being necessary to give consistency to the provisions of the convention, and not to defeat the consideration given to France for her concession of certain rights to be enjoyed by citizens of the United States.[13]   Again, it has been held that, although there was no express limitation in Article X of the treaty with Great Britain of August 9, 1842, for the extradition of fugitives from justice, that the demanding country should try the fugitive for the crime only for which he was extradited, such a limitation was to be found in the "manifest scope and object of the treaty itself."[14]   In Article III of the treaty with Spain of February 22, 1819, after the description of the boundary line between the United States and Spain in its entirety from the Gulf of Mexico to the "South Sea," appears the clause "the whole being as laid down in Melish's map of the United States, published at Philadelphia, improved to the first of January, 1818." In the description immediately preceding this clause, it is provided, in reference to a particular portion, that the boundary line shall follow the course of the Red River westward to the "degree of longitude 100 west from London and 23 from Washington," thence due north to the Arkansas River.   The 100th meridian, astronomically located, proved to be more than one hundred miles further west than was indicated by the Melish map.   In 1896, when the territory on both sides of the line formed part of the United States, the Supreme Court was called upon, in determining the boundary of the State of Texas, to construe this provision of the treaty.   "Undoubtedly," said the court, "the intention of the two governments, as gathered from the words of the treaty, must control; and the entire instrument must be examined in order that the real intention of the contracting parties may be ascertained."   And it was held that, although the Melish map to which the contracting parties referred was to be given the same effect as if expressly made a part of the treaty, and, although this map was taken as a basis for the final settlement of the question of boundary, it was clear by viewing the entire instru-

13 Geofroy v. Riggs, 133 U. S. 258, 271.
14 United States v. Rauscher, 119 U. S. 407, 422, 423; Johnson v. Browne, 205 U. S. 309, 317, 318.

ment that the parties contemplated, as shown by Article IV of the treaty, a line subsequently to be fixed with more precision by commissioners and surveyors representing the respective countries; and that the reference in the treaty to the 100th meridian was to that meridian astronomically located, rather than to the 100th meridian as located on the Melish map.[15]

§166. **Contemporaneous Declarations and Prior Negotiations.**—It is a general rule of interpretation of written contracts, applicable to treaties, that prior negotiations are merged in the written instrument, and cannot be resorted to for the purpose of contradicting or explaining its plain provisions. The reason of the rule is obvious. The object of the written instrument is to record the final and common intention of the parties, which may have undergone a change during the progress of the negotiations. Moreover, in the case of treaties, the contracting parties are the states, not the individuals through whom the negotiations are conducted, whose acts are binding on the state only so far as they are duly authorized. However, in case of ambiguity or doubt in the application of the terms of a treaty, reference is frequently made to the contemporaneous declarations of the negotiators who framed the treaty, and to prior negotiations, not to make a treaty where the parties have failed to do so, nor to change the terms of the treaty actually made, but to determine the general object of the negotiations, the particular sense in which the terms, otherwise uncertain of application, were used at the time, or the conditions as they existed at the time of the conclusion of the treaty.[16] The records of international tribunals of arbitration contain many instances of the use of contemporaneous declarations and prior correspondence for this purpose. Thus, in the North Atlantic coast fisheries arbitration of 1910 between the United States and Great Britain, the tribunal, in determining whether the inhabitants of the United States, while exercising the liberties referred to in Article I of the convention of 1818, had a right to employ as members of the fishing crews of their vessels persons not inhabitants of the United States, took into consideration the correspondence between Mr. Adams and Lord Bathurst of 1815.

15 United States v. Texas, 162 U. S. 1, 36-38.
16 See Brawley v. United States, 96 U. S. 168, 173; Simpson v. United States, 199 U. S. 397, 399; United States v. Bethlehem Steel Co., 205 U. S. 105, 118.

Again, in denying the contention of the United States that the words in the treaty, "in common with British subjects," should be held not as importing a common subjection to regulation, but as intended to negative a possible pretension on the part of the United States to the liberties of fishery to the exclusion of British subjects, the tribunal observed that such an interpretation was "inconsistent with the historical basis of the American fishing liberty," and referred to the proposal submitted by John Adams in the negotiations of 1782 leading up to the first treaty of peace.[17]   In United States v. Texas, the Supreme Court of the United States referred to the diplomatic correspondence that led up to the treaty with Spain of February 22, 1819, "to show the circumstances under which the treaty of 1819 was made, and to bring out distinctly two facts,"—(1) that the negotiators had access to the map of Melish, improved to 1818, and published at Philadelphia (expressly referred to in the treaty); and (2) that the river referred to in the correspondence as Red River was believed by the negotiators to have had its source near Santa Fé and the Snow Mountains.[18]   Lord Chief Justice Alverstone, in a written opinion filed in support of the decision of the majority of the members of the Alaskan Boundary Tribunal, under the convention between the United States and Great Britain of January 24, 1903, as to the meaning of the word "coast" (la côte) as used in Article III, paragraph 2, of the treaty between Great Britain and Russia of 1825 in the description of the boundary line between their possessions, said: "It is in my opinion correctly pointed out, on behalf of the United States, that the word 'coast' is an ambiguous term, and may be used in two, possibly in more than two, senses. I think, therefore, we are not only entitled, but bound to ascertain as far as we can from the facts which were before the negotiators the sense in which they used the word 'coast' in the treaty. Before considering this latter view of the case, it is desirable to ascertain, as far as possible from the treaty itself, what it means, and what can be gathered from the language of the treaty alone." A consideration of the different passages

17 S. Doc. No. 870, 61st Cong., 3d Sess., I, 78; Am. Journal of Int. Law, IV, 948, 960, 962, 974. See case of Kinkead v. United States, 150 U. S. 483, in which correspondence between the Secretary of State and the Russian minister was considered in determining the meaning of Article VI of the treaty for the cession of Alaska.

18 162 U. S. 1, 23-27.

in the treaty, in which the word coast was used, led the learned
arbitrator to conclude that they did not, without reference to the
previous negotiations, enable one to answer whether the line
should follow the sinuosities of the shore line or should cross the
inlets. Before turning from the consideration of the language
of the treaty alone to a consideration of the negotiations, the
Lord Chief Justice observed: "There is, as far as I know, no
recognized rule of international law which would by implication
give a recognized meaning to the word 'coast' as applied to such
sinuosities and such waters different from the coast itself."[19]
The three American members of the tribunal, Elihu Root, Henry
Cabot Lodge, and George Turner, with whose decision Lord
Chief Justice Alverstone concurred, in the opinion filed by them
said: "We are of the opinion that the true construction of the
treaty is that which carries the line around the heads of the inlets,
and that the following considerations all require the adoption of
this construction:—1. The purpose of the treaty, well understood
by the negotiators, would be accomplished by this construction,
and would be defeated by the other construction. 2. The natural
and ordinary meaning of the terms used in the treaty, when applied to the natural features of the country known to the negotiators, or supposed by them to exist, require this construction. 3.
The meaning expressly given to the words used in the treaty by
the negotiators, in their written communications during the course
of the negotiations, requires this construction. 4. The official
maps published by Russia, Great Britain, Canada, British Columbia, and the United States—many in number—for a period of
more than sixty years after the treaty, known to the public officers of the different governments, and accepted as the basis of
official action, without a single exception carried the line around
the heads of all the inlets, and were wholly irreconcilable with the
other construction * * *. 5. For more than sixty years after
the treaty, Russia, and in succession to her the United States, oc-

19 S. Doc. No. 162, 58th Cong., 2d Sess., I, 37, 39. It may be noted
that the treaty by which the Alaskan Tribunal was constituted expressly
provides that the "tribunal shall also take into consideration any action
of the several governments or of their respective representatives preliminary or subsequent to the conclusion of said treaties so far as the
same tends to show the original and effective understanding of the parties
in respect to the limits of their several territorial jurisdictions under and
by virtue of the provisions of said treaties."

cupied, possessed, and governed the territory around the heads of the inlets without any protest or objection, while Great Britain never exercised the rights or performed the duties of sovereignty there, or attempted to do so, or suggested that she considered herself entitled to do so. This was a practical interpretation of the treaty by all parties concerned."[20] This same tribunal was called upon to determine the Portland Channel along which the line of demarcation was, by the treaty of 1825, to run. The treaty provided that the line should ascend along the channel "called" Portland Channel.[21] "The answer to this question," said Lord Alverstone, "as indicated by the learned counsel on both sides, depends upon the simple question: What did the contracting parties mean by the words 'the channel called the Portland Channel' in Article III of the treaty of 1825? This is a pure question of identity. In order to answer it one must endeavour to put oneself in the position of the contracting parties, and ascertain as accurately as possible what was known to them of the geography of the district so far as relates to the channel called the Portland Channel * * *. It was perfectly well known before, and at the date of the treaty, that there were two channels or inlets, the one called Portland Channel, the other Observatory Inlet, both of them coming out into the Pacific Ocean * * *. For the purpose of identifying the channel, commonly known as Portland Channel, the maps which were before the negotiators may be useful. This is one of the points upon which the evidence of contemporary maps as to general reputation is undoubtedly admissible."[22]

An unusual use of negotiators' testimony is found in the proceedings of the mixed commission constituted under Article V of the treaty of November 19, 1794, between the United States and Great Britain, to determine the St. Croix River and its source as described in Article II of the treaty of peace. The boundaries of the United States were defined as starting at an angle which

---

20 Id., 48-49.

21 "la dite ligne remontera au Nord le long de passe dite Portland Channel."

22 Id., 33-35. See also opinion of the U. S. members, Id., 43. See also opinion of Henry M. Duffield, umpire of the German-Venezuelan Claims Commission of 1903, in the case of Van Dissel & Co., Ralston's Report, 568; and opinion of Frank Plumley, umpire of the British-Venezuelan Claims Commission of 1903, in the case of Aroa Mines, Id., 358. See also Moore, Int. Arb., V, 4873, 4876.

was formed "by a line drawn due north from the source of Saint Croix River to the Highlands." There proved to be no river in that region then known by that name. Under these circumstances, President Adams and John Jay, the surviving American negotiators, made depositions to establish the map used by the negotiators. Likewise a letter written by Franklin was considered for the same purpose.[23]

Before proceeding to the exchange of ratifications of the treaty of April 19, 1850, between the United States and Great Britain, but after the adoption by the United States Senate of the resolution advising ratification, memoranda were filed by the negotiators in which it was stated that the language of Article I,—that neither party would ever "occupy, or fortify, or colonize, or assume or exercise any dominion over Nicaragua, Costa Rica, the Mosquito coast, or any part of Central America,"—was not understood by the contracting states, nor by themselves, to include the British settlement at Honduras and adjacent islands. Although the declaration of the American negotiator was given with the approval of the chairman of the Senate Committee on Foreign Relations, who professed to speak as to the understanding of the Senate—an assumption denied and much criticised later by different members—[24] it formed no part of the treaty, not having been mutally agreed to by the treaty-making authorities of the two states. A main purpose of the treaty had been to do away with British pretensions in Central America, not to confirm them, and any exception to this general purpose and to the wording of the treaty should have been expressly stated. Whether Belize was or was not excepted from the operation of the treaty, depended solely upon the geographical fact of its location without or within the boundaries of Central America as then known. But, if this fact was not clearly ascertainable, the memoranda, as expressions of those intimately connected with the formation of the article, could not be overlooked.[25]

23 Moore, Int. Arb., I, 18, et seq.

24 Brit. and For. State Papers, XLII, 200; Compilation of Reports of Sen. Com. on For. Rel., VIII, 47-61.

25 Mr. Marcy, Secretary of State, in a communication to Mr. Borland, U. S. minister to Central America, December 30, 1853, said: "It is believed that Great Britain has a qualified right over a tract of country called the Belize, from which she is not ousted by this treaty, because no part of that tract, when restricted to its proper limits, is within the boundaries of Central America." S. Doc. No. 194, 47th Cong., 1st Sess., 99.

27

It has been the consistent and frequently asserted view of the government of the United States that the general most-favored-nation clause in a treaty does not entitle the other contracting party to receive gratuitously special concessions in import duties made to a third party for valuable considerations. In the negotiations leading up to the treaty of commerce with Switzerland of November 25, 1850, the American negotiator proposed the insertion of a restrictive clause expressly declaring that the favor or concession should be extended freely if freely granted, or on allowing the same compensation or its equivalent if the concession were conditional. To this clause the Swiss negotiator objected, and it was abandoned by the American negotiator "out of friendly consideration for Switzerland." The treaty as submitted to the federal assembly of Switzerland for approval was accompanied with a message representing that the American negotiator had waived the usual American construction of the clause by withdrawing the proposed restrictive words. The treaty was ratified by the federal assembly under this representation. Likewise, the American negotiator in his despatch, transmitting the treaty, advised the Secretary of State of this alleged understanding. This dispatch was communicated by the President to the Senate in connection with the treaty, and the treaty was ratified without amendment of the clause in question. Under these circumstances the construction placed upon the clause by the Swiss government, although at variance with the long established American rule of construction of such clauses, was accepted by the government of the United States as correct, fifty years later when the question was raised. "Both justice and honor require that the common understanding of the high contracting parties at the time of the executing of the treaty should be carried into effect."[26] An explanatory note filed by the Russian minister as to the interpretation placed by his government on the treaty of 1824, between the United States and Russia, was at a later period used by the United States, who had succeeded Russia in all her rights to Alaska, in support of its contention in the Bering Sea controversy with Great Britain.[27]

26 Mr. Hay, Secretary of State, to Mr. Pioda, Swiss minister, November 21, 1898. For. Rel., 1899, pp. 746-748. See also United States v. Yorba, 1 Wall. 412; More v. Steinbach, 127 U. S. 70; Fourteen Diamond Rings v. United States, 183 U. S. 176, 180.

27 Foster, Practice of Diplomacy, 285, citing Fur Seal Arbitration, II, App. 276.

§167. **Practical Construction by Parties.**—A practical and common construction of the terms of a treaty by the parties through proper representatives shortly after its conclusion is quite conclusive as to their meaning.[28] Article VII of the treaty between the United States and Spain of 1795 provided that subjects or citizens of either of the contracting parties, "their vessels or effects," should not be liable to any embargo or detention on the part of the other, for any military expedition or other public or private purpose whatsoever. Numerous claims were presented to the Spanish Treaty Claims Commission, constituted to carry into effect Article VII of the treaty of peace between Spain and the United States of 1898, on account of the detention by the Spanish government of property in Cuba during the insurrection of 1895-8. Several of these arose out of an order prohibiting the exportation of leaf tobacco grown in certain provinces of Cuba. Against these claims it was urged that the prohibition in Article VII of the treaty of 1795 against embargoes related only to property on the sea; that the terms "vessels or effects" were synonymous with "vessels or cargoes"; and that the terms "embargo" and "detention" related only to vessels and their cargoes. In support of these contentions, reference was made to the conditions existing at the time of the conclusion of the treaty, to the main purpose of the treaty to insure American vessels against illegal detentions at that time so common, to contemporary written statements of Pinckney, the negotiator of the treaty, and to contemporaneous treaties. No question as to the meaning of the stipulation appears to have been raised (at least no instance was brought to the attention of the commission) until the outbreak of the Ten Years War, more than seventy years after the treaty was concluded. It was then asserted by the American Secretary of State, and thereafter consistently maintained by the government of the United States for a period of nearly thirty years, whenever the question was raised, that the prohibitions of the article applied to embargoes and detentions of property on land as well as to vessels and their cargoes on the sea. The Spanish government at first expressly denied the correctness of this construction, but later acquiesced in it. The commission, whose duties were those of an international rather than a domestic tri-

28 See Opinion of U. S. members of the Alaskan Boundary Tribunal of 1903, supra, §166. See also United States v. Texas, 162 U. S. 1.

bunal, held that the meaning of the treaty was determined by this practical construction by the parties. "Whether or not the clause was originally intended to embrace real estate and personal property on land as well as vessels and their cargoes, the same has been so construed by the United States, and this construction has been concurred in by Spain; and therefore the commission will adhere to such construction in making its decisions."[29]

By the treaties of 1848 and 1853 between the United States and Mexico, the Rio Grande from its mouth to a point a little higher than the present city of El Paso was constituted the boundary between the two countries. During the course of fifty years, accretions by the action of the river were formed on its northern bank in the vicinity of El Paso, with a corresponding loss of territory on the southern bank in the vicinity of the Mexican city of Juarez. It was the view of the Mexican government that the dividing line as established under the treaties was a fixed and invariable line which was not affected by the action of the river. The government of the United States on the other hand maintained that, according to the intent and meaning of the treaties, the boundary followed the channel of the river even though it had changed by a gradual accretion and erosion, and that only in case of a sudden change would the channel of the river cease to be the boundary. Article V of the treaty of February 2, 1848, provided as regards the line of boundary in dispute that it should proceed from a point in the Gulf of Mexico up the middle of the Rio Grande, following the deepest channel in case of more than one, to the point where it met the southern boundary of New Mexico. This provision was renewed in the treaty of 1853. Article V of the treaty of 1848 further provided that in order to designate the line with due precision upon authoritative maps, and to establish upon the ground landmarks which should show the limits of both republics as described in the article, each of the two governments would appoint a commissioner and surveyor to run and mark the boundary in its whole course to the mouth of the Rio Grande. The article further provided that the boundary line established by the article should be religiously respected by both parties, and that no change should ever be made therein except by the express and free consent of both nations. It is to be

29 No. 10 of the Governing Principles. Opinions of December 5, 1903, p. 7. See opinion of Commissioner Diekema, Id., 58.

noted that the article defined the boundary line from the Gulf of Mexico to the Pacific Ocean including the overland as well as the water sections. The majority of the commission, constituted under the convention of June 24, 1910, in deciding in favor of the contention of the United States on this point, said: "However strongly one might be disposed to think that the treaty of 1848, taken by itself, or the treaty of 1853, taken by itself, indicated an intention to establish a fixed line boundary, it would be difficult to say that the question is free from doubt. * * * It is in consequence of this legitimate doubt as to the true construction of the boundary treaties of 1848 and 1853 that the subsequent course of conduct of the parties, and their formal conventions, may be resorted to as aids to construction." After reviewing the subsequent practice of the two countries, the majority of the commission concluded that the two nations had, "by their subsequent treaties and their consistent course of conduct in connection with all cases arising thereunder, put such an authoritative interpretation upon the language of the treaties of 1848 and 1853 as to preclude them from now contending that the fluvial portion of the boundary created by those treaties is a fixed line boundary."[30]

By the General Act of Berlin of June 14, 1889, between the United States, Great Britain and Germany, for the neutrality and autonomous government of the Samoan Islands, it was agreed that neither of the contracting powers should exercise any "separate control over the islands or the government thereof."[31] It was further agreed that in case any question should arise in respect of the rightful election or appointment of a King, such question should not lead to war but should be presented for decision to the Chief Justice of Samoa, who should decide it conformably with the provisions of the Act and the laws and customs of Samoa not in conflict therewith; and that the signatory governments would abide by such decision. Such a question was submitted to and decided by the Chief Justice in 1898. The decision was objected to by the German consular representative on the ground that the proceedings had not been carried out in accordance with the provisions of the General Act of Berlin. The consular representatives of Great Britain and the United States accepted the decision as final; and the naval authorities of the two powers united

---

30 Am. Journal of Int. Law, V, 782, 797, 805.
31 Art. I.

in enforcing the decision, thereby causing some destruction of private property. In defense of this military action on the part of two only of the three signatory powers, it was contended that there was no limitation on the right of any one signatory power to enforce the provisions, and that, a fortiori, two, a majority of those powers, were entitled to take military action for that purpose.[32] The arbitrator, the King of Sweden and Norway, to whom the controversy was referred by the convention of November 7, 1899, decided otherwise. In reaching this conclusion the arbitrator took into consideration, not only the protocols of the proceedings of the Berlin Conference leading up to the treaty, from which it appeared that the plenipotentiaries had wished to establish the principle that in their dealings with Samoa the powers could only proceed by "common accord," but also the subsequent practice of the contracting parties, from which it appeared that in various instances the parties had accepted the principle of unanimous consent.[33]

Article IV of the treaty of June 17, 1857, between the United States and Japan, provided that Americans committing offenses "in Japan" should be tried by the American consular officers. In Article VI of the treaty concluded one year later, July 29, 1858, the clause read "Americans committing offenses against Japanese" should be tried in American consular courts. It is apparent that the clauses in the two treaties defining the consular jurisdiction are not identical. Under the first treaty the jurisdiction extended to offenses committed "in Japan," whereas in the second treaty it extended only to offenses committed "against Japanese." It was expressly declared in the treaty of 1858 (Article XII) that since "all the provisions" of the treaty of 1857 had been incorporated therein, the earlier treaty was revoked. "It will thus be perceived that the revocation of the treaty of 1857 was made upon the assumption and declaration that all its provisions were incorporated into the treaty of 1858. The revocation must, therefore, be held to be limited to those provisions and those only which are thus incorporated, that treaty still remaining in force as to the unincorporated provisions. This has been the practical construction given to the alleged revocation by the authorities of both countries—a construction which, in view of the erroneous state-

32 American Counter-Case, 31; British Counter-Case, 6.
33 Treaties, Conventions, &c. (1910 ed.), 1593.

ment as to the incorporation into the new treaty of all the provisions of the former one, is reasonable and just."[34]

§168. **Casus Omissus.**—Articles XVII and XVIII of the treaty between the United States and Spain of 1795 provided that, in case either party should be engaged in war, the vessels belonging to the subjects of the other party should be furnished with sea-letters or passports to be made out according to the "form annexed" to the treaty; and that upon the exhibition of this passport, "made out according to the form inserted" in the treaty, the vessel would be allowed to pursue her voyage. No such form of passport was annexed to the treaty. The reason for the omission did not appear. The Supreme Court of the United States refused to supply this omission and held the provision to be inoperative. Mr. Justice Story for the court said: "In the first place, this court does not possess any treaty-making power. That power belongs by the Constitution to another department of the government; and to alter, amend, or add to any treaty, by inserting any clause, whether small or great, important or trivial, would be on our part an usurpation of power, and not an exercise of judicial functions. Neither can this court supply a casus omissus in a treaty, any more than in a law. * * * The parties who formed this treaty, and they alone, have a right to annex the form of a passport. It is a high act of sovereignty, as high as the formation of any other stipulation of the treaty. It is a matter of negotiation between the governments. The treaty does not leave it to the discretion of either party to annex the form of the passport; it requires it to be the joint act of both. * * * The same powers which have contracted, are alone competent to change or dispense with any formality. The doctrine of a performance cy pres, so just and appropriate in the civil concerns of private persons, belongs not to the solemn compacts of nations, so far as judicial tribunals are called upon to interpret them. We can as little dispense with forms as with substance."[35]

The boundary line between the United States and Canada in its course through the Great Lakes was described in Article II of the treaty of peace of 1783 as passing through the middle of Lake Ontario to the water communication between that lake and Lake Erie; thence along the middle of said communication into

---

34 Field, J., In re Ross, 140 U. S. 453, 466.
35 The Amiable Isabella, (1821), 6 Wheat. 1, 71-73.

Lake Erie, through the middle of said lake until it arrived at the water communication between that lake and Lake Huron; thence along the middle of said water communication into Lake Huron; "thence through the middle of said lake to the water communication between that lake and Lake Superior; thence through Lake Superior." It will be noted that it was expressly provided that the line should pass through the middle of the water communications between Lake Ontario and Lake Erie, and between Lake Erie and Lake Huron, and that there was no reference to the line through the water communication between Lake Huron and Lake Superior. The joint commissioners, appointed under Article VII of the treaty of Ghent, to determine the boundary, treated this "omission as a mere inadvertance," and interpreted the provision as if the line had been expressly continued on through this water communication in the same phraseology as uniformly used with reference to every other water communication in the treaty, namely,— "through the middle."[36]

By the convention concluded between Great Britain and Portugal, June 11, 1891, for the settlement of boundaries between their respective possessions and spheres of influence in eastern and central Africa, it was agreed that the line of boundary, in one section, should follow the upper part of the eastern slope of the "Manica plateau" southward to the centre of the main channel of the Sabi. Upon an attempt to survey the line so described, it was found that the elevation of land called the "Manica plateau" became much depressed before reaching the Sabi, and ceased to have the elevation usually ascribed to a plateau. It was urged by Portugal that there was an omission in the treaty as a result of the supposition that the plateau extended southward to the Sabi. The arbitrator, to whom this, with other disputed questions as to the boundary line, was referred, held otherwise. "In our case," said the arbitrator, "the rule of legal interpretation, according to which the expressions made use of in a contract must be taken in the sense most in accordance with the intentions of the parties who have arranged it and the most favorable to the aim of the contract, obliges us to give to the word 'plateau' the

36 Moore, Int. Arb., I, 179. It may be noted that these commissioners ultimately failed to agree as to various parts of the boundary and no final decision was reached; and that the differences were not settled until the conclusion of the Webster-Ashburton treaty.

broadest possible signification—that is to say, to require only the minimum normal altitude—so as to be able to affirm its existence as far as the Sabi, as the high contracting parties had supposed, and so as thus to render possible the application of the text of Article II of the treaty. Following thus, from the legal point of view, an universal rule of interpretation, and from the technical point of view, the opinion of the most illustrious geographers to whom the two parties have made reference, we come to the conclusion that the plateau of Manica, though it falls gradually towards the south and becomes reduced to the smallest proportions, preserves, nevertheless, a sufficient elevation (as was supposed by the authors of the treaty) for it to be admitted that it exists right to the Sabi."[37]

§169. **Discrepancies Between the Two Texts.**—If the treaty is drawn up in the language of each of the contracting parties, and each is an original,[38] the texts are to be construed collectively. They are intended by the parties to be identical. Neither is to be preferred to the other. If the two can, without violence to the language, be made to agree, that construction which establishes this conformity is to prevail.[39] In case they cannot be made to harmonize, other rules of construction must be resorted to for the purpose of determining, if possible, the common intention of the parties. In last resort, the text in the language of the party which by the stipulation incurs the obligation will, it seems, prevail in determining what obligation has been incurred.[40] The rule of construction in the English law of grants as between private

37 Paul-Honoré Vigliani, arbitrator under the declaration concluded between Great Britain and Portugal, January 7, 1895. Moore, Int. Arb., V, 4985, 5011.

38 The parties may expressly agree in the treaty which text, in case of conflict, shall be taken as the standard. See, for instance, Article XVII of the treaty of October 8, 1903, between the United States and China.

39 Marshall, C. J., United States v. Percheman, 7 Pet. 51, 88; Edmonds, J., In re Metzger, 1 Barb. 248; Moore, Int. Arb., V, 4985, 4990, 4992.

40 "An incorrected discrepancy might prove embarrassing, in view of the rule of international law that when a treaty is executed in duplicate in two languages, each party has the right to appeal to its own text, in the interpretation of its provisions, unless it be exceptionally stipulated that the one or the other shall be the standard; but this expedient is rarely resorted to, and is, besides, in its nature offensive to the one or the other contractant." Mr. Hay, Secretary of State, to Mr. Storer, minister to Spain, December 20, 1901.

individuals,—that the terms are to be construed against, rather than in favor of, the grantor,[41]—has no application in determining which of the two conflicting texts of a treaty is to be accepted as defining the concession made or obligation incurred. The reason of the rule is wanting. The words of the treaty are the words of both parties. The doubt as to the intention of the parties results not from the use by the grantor of ambiguous terms in defining the grant, but from the failure of the parties to use terms of identical meaning in the two languages. For this failure the grantee, as such, is not less responsible than the grantor.[42]

The Spanish and English texts, both declared to be originals, of Article VIII of the treaty of February 22, 1819, by which Spain ceded Florida to the United States, were not identical in meaning as to the confirmation of the grants to land in Florida

41 A different rule prevails as to grants by the state to private individuals. "By a familiar rule, every public grant of property, or of privileges or franchises, if ambiguous, is to be construed against the grantee and in favor of the public." Gray, J., Central Transportation Co. v. Pullman's Car Co., 139 U. S. 24, 49, citing Charles River Bridge v. Warren Bridge, 11 Pet. 420, 544-548; Dubuque & Pacific R. R. Co. v. Litchfield, 23 How. 66, 88, 89; Slidell v. Grandjean, 111 U. S. 412, 437, 438; Oregon Railway v. Oregonian Railway, 130 U. S. 1, 26, 27.

42 "But here a distinction must be taken between an indenture and a deed-poll; for the words of an indenture, executed by both parties, are to be considered as the words of them both; for, though delivered as the words of one party, yet they are not his words only, because the other party hath given his consent to every one of them. But in a deed-poll, executed only by the grantor, they are the words of the grantor only, and shall be taken most strongly against him." Blackstone, Commentaries (Sharswood ed.), II, 379. Pothier gives the following as a rule (No. 7) of interpretation: "In case of doubt, a clause ought to be interpreted against the person who stipulates any thing, and in discharge of the person who contracts the obligation. In stipulationibus cum quaeritur qui actum sit, verba contra stipulatorem interpretanda sunt." Evans in his notes says: "The rule of the English law is directly the reverse, and the words of an engagement are to be construed most strongly against the person engaging. These two opposite rules have probably both resulted from the same maxim, that verba ambigua fortius accipiuntur contra proferentum. By the Roman law, the words of the stipulation were necessarily those of the person to whom the promise was made; the person promising, only assented to the question proposed by the person stipulating. There is nothing similar to this in the covenants and engagements used in England; but an indenture is the deed of both parties and the words it contains are taken as the words of both, except as to those parts which are in their nature only applicable to one of them." Pothier on Obligations (Evans), I, 58.

made by the King of Spain prior to January 24, 1818. In the Spanish text it was provided that the grants "quedarán ratificadas y reconocidas" (shall remain ratified and confirmed), whereas the clause in the English text read "shall be ratified and confirmed." In construing these clauses, the Supreme Court of the United States, by Mr. Justice Baldwin, said: "The King of Spain was the grantor, the treaty was his deed, the exception was made by him, and its nature and effect depended on his intention, expressed by his words, in reference to the thing granted and the thing reserved and excepted in and by the grant. The Spanish version was in his words and expressed his intention, and though the American version showed the intention of this government to be different, we cannot adopt it as the rule by which to decide what was granted, what excepted and what reserved; the rules of law are too clear to be mistaken, and too imperative to be disregarded by this court. We must be governed by the clearly expressed and manifest intention of the grantor, and not the grantee in private a fortiori in public grants."[43]

The convention of January 15, 1880, between the United States and France, for the adjudication by a mixed commission of claims of the citizens of the one against the other, was signed in duplicate, each in the English and French languages. The English text provided for the submission of all claims of citizens of France against the United States arising out of acts committed by the civil or military authorities of the government of the United States, "upon the high seas or within the territorial jurisdiction of the United States," during the period from April 13,

---

43 United States v. Arredondo, (1832), 6 Pet. 691, 741. The umpire, Jackson H. Ralston, of the Italian-Venezuelan Commission, constituted under the protocol of February 13, 1903, laid down the following rules of construction: "(a) If two meanings are admissible, that is to be preferred which is least for the advantage of the party for whose benefit a clause is inserted; (b) the sense which the acceptor of conditions attaches to them ought rather to be followed than that of the offerer; (c) two meanings being admissible, preference is given to that which the party proposing the clause knew at the time was held by the party accepting it; (d) doubtful stipulations should be interpreted in the least onerous sense for the party obligated; (e) conditions not expressed cannot be invoked by the party who should have clearly expressed them." Case of Sambiaggio, Ralston's Report, 666. See also opinion as to the acceptance of the English as the "basic" language in preference to the Italian text in case of conflict, case of Guastini, Id., 749.

1861 to August 20, 1866. In the proceedings before the commission, counsel for the United States urged that the word "territorial," in the clause just quoted, was a word of limitation and was used in contradistinction to the word "legal"; that while the legal jurisdiction of the United States during the period in question extended over all the territory within its recognized boundaries, territorial jurisdiction was limited to that territory over which it actually exercised jurisdiction; and that this territorial jurisdiction ended with the line of bayonets.[44] The majority of the commission adopted this construction. The clause in the French text (which does not appear to have been taken into consideration by the commission) reads: "sur le territoire des États-Unis." The question was, upon the request of the agent of France, referred to the two governments. Mr. Frelinghuysen, American Secretary of State, in a note of May 9, 1882, to Mr. Outrey, French minister, in acknowledging the correctness of the French contention, said: "The examination which I have made of the negotiations preliminary to the treaty, and of each text, convinces me that the words 'territorial jurisdiction,' when used in the first article of the treaty, were intended to have the force of the word 'territory,' which is in fact used in the French text. So far as the decision in the Chourreau case was in conflict with this definition of the words territorial jurisdiction as being synonymous with the word territoire in the French text, it failed to carry out the purposes of the two governments and should be corrected."[45] It may also be noted that, as to the reciprocal obligation on the part of France, the treaty provided, according to the English text, for the submission of claims of American citizens arising out of acts committed by the French civil or military authorities upon the high seas or within the "territory" of France, its colonies, and dependencies.

By Article II of the treaty of December 30, 1853, Mexico released the United States, according to the English text, "from all liability on account of the obligations" contained in Article XI of the treaty of Guadalupe Hidalgo. The Spanish text of the clause merely provided for a release "de las obligaciones del Ar-

44 See Prize Cases, 2 Black 635, 674; United States v. Rice, 4 Wheat. 246.

45 Case of Chourreau v. United States, No. 43. Boutwell's Report, 134-146; Moore, Int. Arb., II, 1145.

ticulo XI." Mexico, in view of the Spanish text, considered this article as releasing the United States only from the "obligation" to execute Article XI of the treaty of Guadalupe Hidalgo, and not from the "liability" to make indemnity for any violations of that article in the past. It was held by the umpire of the United States and Mexican Claims Commission of 1868, Sir Edward Thornton, that if there were any conflict between the two texts the English must prevail, since the clause in question was ingrafted as an amendment by the Senate of the United States in the English language, and it was the fault of the Mexican government if the Spanish text prepared by it did not correspond with the English; and that moreover the Spanish text of the amendment had never been acted upon by the Senate of the United States.[46]

A protracted controversy between the government of the United States and the Ottoman Porte has resulted from a conflict between the English and Turkish versions of Article IV of the treaty of May 7, 1830. The draft of the treaty presented by the American commissioner, in strict conformity with which the Turkish text was said to have been drawn up and signed, was, it appears, in the French language. The Senate and President in ratifying the treaty acted on an English translation. On the return of the instrument to Constantinople for exchange the Ottoman Government observed that there had been returned "the translation made in Washington, instead of the one signed at Constantinople." To remove this objection the American chargé

46 Moore, Int. Arb., III, 2432, 2436, 2446. As to the controversy between the American and Spanish commissioners in the peace negotiations at Paris in 1898, respecting the meaning to be given to the English word "disposition" and the French word "disposition" as used respectively in the English and French texts of the protocol of August 12, 1898, in reference to the Philippines, see Sen. Doc. No. 62, 55th Cong., 3d Sess., pt. I, pp. 119, 129, 174. See also the decision of the arbitrator under the declaration of January 7, 1895, between Great Britain and Portugal, as to the meaning of the English words "upper part" and the Portuguese word "crista" as used in the treaty between two countries of June 11, 1891, in defining the boundary line between their possessions in Africa along the Manica plateau, Moore, Int. Arb., V, 4985, 4990, 4992. The arbitrator in this case, in referring to the meaning given by him to the terms of the treaty, said: "This interpretation, which is certainly in conformity with the spirit of the convention, renders the two texts identical, and causes to disappear all differences between the expressions 'upper part' and 'crista' of the slope."

d'affaires, who was empowered only to exchange the ratifications and to make explanations respecting the rejection by the Senate of a separate article to the treaty, signed a memorandum in which the Turkish text was virtually recognized as the original—an act not expressly disavowed by his government. The President in communicating the treaty to the Senate, and later in proclaiming it, alluded to the original in the Turkish language, which was said to be accompanied with an English translation believed to be correct. The English version remained unchallenged for a period of more than thirty-five years. Moreover, language similar to the English version has been used in treaties subsequently concluded by Turkey with Belgium and Portugal. Conceding the authority of the Turkish text and the correctness of the translation presented by the Ottoman government—that American citizens "shall be punished through the agency of their ministers and consuls, according to the practice observed in regard to other Franks," and not, as the English text, would have it, that they shall be "tried" and "punished"—nevertheless the right to try is incident to and involved in the right to punish. Moreover, the rights in question belong to the United States in virtue of the most-favored-nation clause of the treaty. Such are the contentions of the government of the United States.[47]

§170. **Construed in the Light of Accepted Principles of International Law.**—Stipulations are to be construed in a sense which best corresponds with the accepted principles of international law, rather than in derogation of them. "It ought to be presumed (if the words of the article will bear us out in it) that they intended to provide for and effectuate that more extended and rational responsibility which the law of nations indicates."[48] In referring to Article VIII of the treaty of 1819 with Spain, Chief Justice Marshall in the case of the United States v. Percheman said: "This article is apparently introduced on the part of Spain, and must be intended to stipulate expressly for that security to private property which the laws and usages of nations would, without express stipulation, have conferred. No construction which

---

47 For. Rel., 1900, p. 914.

48 William Pinkney, commissioner, under Article VII of the treaty of November 19, 1794, between the United States and Great Britain, in the case of the Betsey. Moore, Int. Arb., III, 3196. See also Story, J., in United States v. the Amistad, 15 Pet. 518, 595-596.

would impair that security further than its positive words require, would seem to be admissible.   Without it, the titles of individuals would remain as valid under the new government as they were under the old."[49]   The tribunal of arbitration constituted, pursuant to The Hague convention for the pacific settlement of disputes, under an agreement between Great Britain and France of October 13, 1904, to determine the right of certain dhows of Muscat to fly the French flag, said, in its award rendered August 8, 1905: "In default of a definition of the term 'protégé' in the General Act of the Brussels Conference [of July 2, 1890] this term must be understood in the sense which corresponds best as well to the elevated aims of the Conference and its Final Act, as to the principles of the law of nations, as they have been expressed in treaties existing at that time, in internationally recognized legislation and in international practice."[50]   So also the tribunal of arbitration in the matter of the North Atlantic coast fisheries, in deciding against the contention of the United States that the liberties of fishery enjoyed by the inhabitants of the United States constituted an international servitude in favor of the United States, said: "This doctrine being but little suited to the principle of sovereignty which prevails in states under a system of constitutional government such as Great Britain and the United States, and to the present international relations of sovereign states, has found little, if any, support from modern publicists.   It could therefore in the general interest of the community of nations, and of the parties to this treaty, be affirmed by this tribunal only on the express evidence of an international contract."[51]   The umpire of the mixed claims commission, constituted under the protocol of February 13, 1903, between Italy and Venezuela, in overruling the contention that Venezuela had by the terms of the protocol admitted liability for damages committed by insurgents, said: "If it had been the contract between Italy and Venezuela, understood and consented to by both, that the latter should be held for the acts of revolutionists—something in derogation of the general

49   7 Pet. 51, 88.   See also Vilas v. Manila, 220 U. S. 345.

50   Melville W. Fuller, Chief Justice of the United States, Jonkheer A. F. de Savornin Lohman, member of the lower branch of the States-General of the Netherlands, and H. Lammasch, member of the upper house of the Austrian Parliament, arbitrators.   Recueil des Actes et Protocoles, etc., 71.

51   S. Doc. No. 870, 61st Cong., 3d Sess., I, 76; Am. Journal of Int. Law, IV, 958.

principles of international law—this agreement would naturally have found direct expression in the protocol itself and would not have been left to doubtful interpretation."[52] The umpire of the British-Venezuelan Commission in holding to like effect said: "International law is not in terms invoked in these protocols, neither is it renounced. But in the judgment of the umpire, since it is a part of the law of the land of both governments, and since it is the only definitive rule between nations, it is the law of this tribunal interwoven in every line, word, and syllable of the protocols, defining their meaning and illuminating their text; restraining, impelling, and directing every act thereunder."[53] The majority of the members of the commission in the Chamizal arbitration under the convention between the United States and Mexico of June 24, 1910, in reaching the conclusion that the boundary line between the two countries along the Rio Grande as established by the treaties of 1848 and 1853 was not a fixed and invariable line, as the words of the treaties taken alone might seem to indicate, but an arcifinious boundary, took into consideration the accepted principle of international law that a fluvial boundary continues notwithstanding gradual modifications of the course of the river caused by accretion on the one bank and erosion of the other.[54]

§171. **General Rules.**—It is generally stated that the words of a treaty are to be taken as used with their plain and natural meaning. The tribunal of arbitration in the matter of the North Atlantic coast fisheries, in sustaining the right of Great Britain to make reasonable regulations as to the exercise of the liberties of fishery enjoyed by inhabitants of the United States under Article I of the treaty of 1818 "in common with British subjects," said: "These words are such as would naturally suggest themselves to the negotiators of 1818 if their intention had been to express a common subjection to regulations as well as a common right."[55] This rule is subject to the qualification that words with a customary meaning in international usage or in the public law of

---

52 Ralston, case of Sambiaggio, Ralston's Report, 666, 689.

53 Plumley, case of Aroa Mines, Id., 344, 386.

54 Eugene Lafleur, third commissioner, Anson Mills, American commissioner. Fernando Beltram y Puga, Mexican commissioner, dissented. Am. Journal of Int. Law, V, 782, 794. See also Moore, Int. Arb., V, 4876.

55 S. Doc. No. 870, 61st Cong., 3d Sess., I, 79. Am. Journal of Int. Law, IV, 961. See also Collins v. O'Neil, 214 U. S. 113.

each of the contracting parties are to be understood as used in this customary or technical sense, unless a contrary intention clearly appears from the context. Treaties are viewed as having been prepared with care and deliberation by those versed in international law and familiar with the legal signification of words.[55a] By the protocol of February 13, 1903, with Great Britain, Venezuela admitted liability for "injury" to, or wrongful seizure of, property. It was held by the umpire of the commission under the protocol that the word "injury" was not used in its colloquial sense but with its legal signification as importing a wrong.[56] If terms used in a treaty have definite but different legal meanings in the contracting states, and there is no common and generally received meaning in the public law of nations, that meaning which obtains within the state to which the provision specifically applies at the time of the conclusion of the treaty is, it seems, to prevail. By Article XIV of the treaty of October 3, 1866, between Austria and Italy, it was stipulated that the in-

---

55a See, however, Maltass v. Maltass (1844), 1 Rob. Ecc. Cases, 67, 76, in which Dr. Lushington said: "It has never been the habit of those engaged in diplomacy to use legal accuracy, but rather to adopt more liberal terms."

56 Plumley, umpire, case of De Lemos, Ralston's Report, 302, 309. As to the meaning given by the same umpire to the words "claim," "injury," "seizure," "justice," and "equity," as used in the protocol, see case of Aroa Mines, Id., 344, 350-387. See also for discussion before the other commissions of 1903 at Caracas of the principle involved in the decision in the De Lemos Case, cases of Kummerow, Id., 526; Sambiaggio, Id., 666; Guastini, Id., 730; Padrón, Id., 923; and Mena, Id., 931. See as to the legal intendment of the word "settlers" as used in Article II of the treaty of November 19, 1794, between the United States and Great Britain, Jackson v. Porter, 1 Paine 457, 482; of "possessory" rights as used in the treaty of June 15, 1846, between the United States and Great Britain, Town v. De Haven, 5 Sawy. 146; of rights of pueblos under the treaty of February 2, 1848, between the United States and Mexico, Tripp v. Spring, 5 Sawy. 209. See also opinion of C. A. Logan, arbitrator under the Chilean-Peruvian protocol of March 2, 1874, Moore, Int. Arb., II, 2085, 2101; opinion of John Little, U. S. commissioner of the United States and Venezuelan Claims Commission under the convention of December 5, 1885, Id., IV, 3623; opinion of Paul Honoré-Vigliani, arbitrator under the convention of January 7, 1895, between Great Britain and Portugal, as to the customary meaning of "plateau" in Africa, Id., V, 4985, 5010. See, in general, Marshall, C. J., the Nereide, 9 Cranch 388, 419; Baldwin, J., United States v. Arredondo, 6 Pet. 691, 743; Day, J., Rocca v. Thompson, 223 U. S. 317, 332.

28

habitants of the territory ceded by the former should, for a specified time, enjoy the privilege of withdrawing with their property. In Austria the term inhabitant was applicable to such persons as were domiciled according to Austrian law, while in Italy it applied to one who lived in a commune and was registered as a resident. The term was ultimately given its meaning in the Austrian law, which was on the date of the treaty applicable to the territory.[57] The umpire, John Hamilton Gray, of the commission to determine the fisheries reserved under Article I of the reciprocity convention of June 5, 1854, between the United States and Great Britain, construed the term "river" (in which all fisheries were reserved to British fishermen), as distinguished from the words "bays," "harbors" and "creeks" (in which American fishermen were to enjoy fishery liberties), in the light of the local legislation of the country in which the stream of water was located, regardless of the volume of water.[57a] The majority of the tribunal of arbitration on the North Atlantic coast fisheries held that, in the clause of Article I of the treaty of 1818, by which the United States renounced, except within certain specified limits, any liberty of fishery theretofore enjoyed "within three marine miles of any of the coasts, bays, creeks, or harbours of His Britannic Majesty's dominions in America," the word "bays" was used in a geographical sense and not in the sense of political control, "because to express the political concept of dominion as equivalent to sovereignty, the word 'dominion' in the singular would have been an adequate term and not 'dominions' in the plural; this latter term having a recognized and well settled meaning as descriptive of those portions of the earth which owe political allegiance to His Majesty; e. g., 'His Britannic Majesty's Dominions beyond the Seas.' "[58] But if the words of a treaty have a common and accepted meaning in international usage, they are to be taken as used with this meaning and not in any artificial or special sense impressed by local law, unless it clearly appears that this special and restricted meaning was intended by the parties. "Should there appear to be a meaning in the word

---

57 Hall (6 ed.), 329; Rivier, II, 125; Brit. and For. State Papers, LVI, 700.

57a Moore, Int. Arb., I, 457.

58 S. Doc. No. 870, 61st Cong., 3d Sess., I, 93; Am. Journal of Int. Law, IV, 979. Luis M. Drago dissented. See Id., 989.

of one language not found in that of the other, of course it should be disregarded, and only that meaning taken which is common to both."[59] And the plain purpose of the treaty is not to be defeated through the failure of the parties to express themselves in the usual technical terms of the local law of one of the parties.[60]

59 Little, U. S. commissioner, in construing the words "claim" and "reclamacion" as used respectively in the English and Spanish texts of the convention between the United States and Venezuela of December 5, 1885. Case No. 18, Moore, Int. Arb., III, 3623.

60 See Geofroy v. Riggs, 133 U. S. 258, 271, in which the District of Columbia as a political division was held to fall within the terms "States of the Union" as used in the treaty of 1853 with France. See also Benson v. McMahon, 127 U. S. 457, construing the term "forgery" as used in Article III of the extradition convention with Mexico of December 11, 1861. In Wilson v. Shaw, 204 U. S. 24, 33, it was held that the title of the United States to the Canal Zone in Panama was not imperfect either because the treaty with Panama did not contain the technical terms used in ordinary conveyances of real estate or because the boundaries were not minutely described in the treaty, the description being sufficient for identification, and the Zone having been practically identified by the concurrent action of the two nations interested in the matter. See also Grin v. Shine, 187 U. S. 181, 184, and Wright v. Henkel, 190 U. S. 40, 57, in which it is declared that in construing and carrying out extradition conventions the ordinary technicalities of criminal proceedings are applicable only to a limited extent, since foreign powers are not expected to be versed in the niceties of our criminal laws, and that where the proceeding is manifestly taken in good faith a technical non-compliance with some formality of criminal procedure should not be allowed to stand in the way of a faithful discharge of our obligations. "In construing any treaty between the United States and an Indian tribe, it must always (as was pointed out by the counsel for the appellees) be borne in mind that the negotiations for the treaty are conducted, on the part of the United States, an enlightened and powerful nation, by representatives skilled in diplomacy, masters of a written language, understanding the modes and forms of creating the various technical estates known to their law, and assisted by an interpreter employed by themselves; that the treaty is drawn up by them and in their own language; that the Indians, on the other hand, are a weak and dependent people, who have no written language and are wholly unfamiliar with all the forms of legal expression, and whose only knowledge of the terms in which the treaty is framed is that imparted to them by the interpreter employed by the United States; and that the treaty must therefore be construed, not according to the technical meaning of its words to learned lawyers, but in the sense in which they would naturally be understood by the Indians." Gray, J., Jones v. Meehan, 175 U. S. 1, 10-11, citing Worcester v. Georgia, 6 Pet. 515; Kansas Indians, 5 Wall. 737, 760; Choctaw Nation v. United States, 119 U. S. 1, 27, 28. See also, to like effect, United States v. Winans, 198 U. S. 371, 380.

In general, words should be given the meaning which will tend
to give efficacy to the treaty and to secure equality and reciprocity
in the benefits to be received by the parties.[61] "An interpretation
of such an instrument, which precisely quadrates with the reciprocal rights and obligations of the parties to it, is such an one as
must be received and will be received by the common sense of
mankind, if it can be sustained without violence to the letter of
the contract."[62] It is never to be presumed that either party intended to perpetrate a fraud on the other.[63] A limitation on the
exercise of the sovereignty of a state within its own territorial
limits cannot be implied, but must be founded upon an express
stipulation.[64] A treaty is not to be construed so as to impair the
right of self-preservation and self-defense unless the terms will
admit of no other construction.[65] It is not to be presumed that
states will lightly bargain away such rights. The specific enumeration of certain rights with respect to a particular subject
matter is a negation of all other analagous rights with respect to
the same subject matter. The presumption is that the parties
having expressed some, have expressed all, or as stated in the
Latin phrase, expressio unius est exclusio alterius.[66] "If he who
could and ought to have explained himself clearly and fully has
not done it, it is the worse for him; he cannot be allowed to in-
troduce subsequent restrictions which he has not expressed."[67]
If the ambiguous words are those of one party only, as might be
the case in an agreement recorded by an exchange of notes or
counter-declarations, or in the counterpart in its own language,

61 Jones v. Walker, 2 Paine 688, 720.

62 William Pinkney, commissioner, under Article VII of the treaty
between the United States and Great Britain of November 19, 1794, in the
case of the Betsey. Moore, Int. Arb., III, 3196.

63 Story, J., United States v. Amistad, 15 Pet. 518, 595. See also
Brig Betsey, 39 C. Cls. 452.

64 Decision of the tribunal of arbitration in the matter of the North
Atlantic coast fisheries, 1910, S. Doc. No. 870, 61st Cong., 3d Sess., I,
74, 84; Am. Journal of Int. Law, IV, 956, 966.

65 Frazer, American commissioner, in the Calcutta Saltpetre Cases,
British and American Claims Commission. Papers Relating to the Treaty
of Washington, VI, 234.

66 Brewer, J., Tucker v. Alexandroff, 183 U. S. 424, 436. See also
decision of the tribunal of arbitration in the matter of the North Atlantic
coast fisheries, Am. Journal of Int. Law, IV, 963.

67 Vattel, Bk. II, c. XVII, §264; Phillimore, Int. Law (2 ed.), II, 104.

they are to be construed against rather than in favor of the party using them. It was a maxim of early Roman law that an agreement obscurely expressed or of doubtful meaning was to be interpreted against the person who had it in his power to set down the terms more clearly.[68] So far as a treaty comes before a domestic court of one of the contracting parties as a municipal law, it should be construed with the utmost good faith and with a view to carry out the apparent intention of the parties. It is primarily a compact between the two nations.[69] "This court would not readily lean to favor a restricted construction of language, as applied to the provisions of a treaty, which always combines the characteristics of a contract, as well as a law."[70] "Where a treaty admits of two constructions, one restrictive as to the rights, that may be claimed under it, and the other liberal, the latter is to be preferred. Shanks v. Dupont, 3 Pet. 242. Such is the settled rule in this court."[71] No word, clause, or provision is presumably redundant; and effect is, if possible, to be given to each of them. "Treaties are formed upon deliberate reflection. Diplomatic men read the public treaties made by other nations and cannot be supposed either to omit or insert an article, common in public treaties, without being aware of the effect of such omis-

---

68 "Veteribus placet pactionem obscuram vel ambiguam venditori et qui locavit nocere, in quorum fuit potestate legem apertius conscribere." Digest of Justinian, Bk. II, Tit. XIV, 39. See Pothier, Obligations (Evans), 58. Supra, §169, foot-note 42.

69 Geofroy v. Riggs, 133 U. S. 258, 271; Tucker v. Alexandroff, 183 U. S. 424, 437; Johnson v. Browne, 205 U. S. 309, 317.

70 Johnson, J., the Bello Corrunes, 6 Wheat. 152, 171.

71 Swayne, J., Hauenstein v. Lynham, 100 U. S. 483, 487. "Whether the trade should have been conceded under any qualifications [Article XIII of the treaty of 1794 with the United States] or restrictions is one thing; it having been conceded now, to attempt to cramp it by a narrow, rigorous, forced construction of the words of the treaty is another and a very different consideration. We cannot suppose, that an indirect advantage was intended to be reserved to the East India Company by so framing the treaty that the American trade might by construction be put under disadvantage; because this would be a chicanery unworthy of the British government, and contrary to the character of its negotiations, which have been at all times distinguished for their good faith to a degree of candour which has been supposed sometimes to have exposed it to the hazard of being made the dupe of more refined politicians." Eyre, Ch. J., Marryat v. Wilson (1799), 1 Bos. & Pull. 429, 435. See also Moore, Int. Arb., II, 1837, 1839, 1840; Id., III, 3624; Ralston's Report, 557.

sion or insertion."[72] It was the contention of the government of the United States in the North Atlantic coast fisheries arbitration that the words "coasts, bays, creeks, or harbours," in Article I of the treaty of 1818 were used only to express different parts of the coast and were intended to be equivalent to the word "coast," whereby the three marine miles should be measured from the sinuosities of the coast line, and the renunciation would apply to the waters of bays only within the three miles. The majority of the tribunal decided otherwise, giving as one of the reasons: "Because it is a principle of interpretation that words in a document ought not to be considered as being without any meaning if there is not specific evidence to that purpose and the interpretation referred to would lead to the consequence, practically, of reading the words 'bays, creeks, and harbours' out of the treaty; so that it would read 'within three miles of any of the coasts' including therein the coasts of the bays and harbours." The tribunal added that the word "coasts" was used in the plural form, whereas the contention of the United States would require its use in the singular.[73]

A treaty supersedes all previous inconsistent stipulations between the same parties; but treaties with a third party are unaffected by a subsequent treaty to which it has not given its assent. In case of conflict between provisions of the same treaty, a special provision prevails over a general; a prohibitory or imperative, over a permissive.[74] It is generally stated that words qualifying general terms are to be construed strictly.[75] Article I of the treaty of Ghent of December 24, 1814, between the United States and Great Britain, provided for the mutual restitution of all territory taken by either party during the war, without causing any destruction or carrying away any of the artillery or other public property "originally captured in the said forts or places, and which shall remain therein upon the exchange of the ratifications of this treaty, or any slaves or other private property." The United States contended that the clause, "originally captured in said forts or places, and which shall remain therein upon the exchange of ratifications," was a qualification as to the artillery and other

72 Marshall, C. J., the Nereide, 9 Cranch 388, 419.

73 S. Doc. No. 870, 61st Cong., 3d Sess., I, 96; Am. Journal of Int. Law, IV, 982.

74 Grotius, Bk. II, c. XVI, §XXIX.

75 See Moore, Int. Arb., IV, 3625.

public property, and not a limitation as to slaves and other private property thereafter referred to. The Emperor of Russia, to whom the question was referred under Article V of the treaty of 1818, upon a construction of the text of the article as it stood, decided in favor of the contention of the United States.[76] No priority is attached to the numerical order of the provisions in the same treaty. Each provision is supposed to be drawn with due regard to all of the provisions pari materia in the same instrument.[77] It has been held that the treaties of alliance and commerce of 1778, between the United States and France, having been concluded on the same day, and as the result of the same negotiation, and signed by the same plenipotentiaries, are in "diplomatic effect, one instrument";[78] that the declaration attached to the convention of 1800, between the United States and France, having been made ten months after the signature of the convention and with a purpose entirely foreign to the intent of the parties when they framed that convention, can not be resorted to to explain the preceding articles;[79] that the recitals in the preamble to a treaty, as to the object of the treaty, may be referred to for the purpose of resolving an ambiguity, but not for the purpose of contradicting the clear terms used in the express stipulations of the treaty;[80] and that the averment in the preamble to the treaty between the United States and Great Britain of August 9, 1842,— that portions of the line of boundary between the United States and the British dominions in North America had not theretofore been ascertained and determined,—is to be regarded as a truth admitted, and, accordingly, that the line of boundary theretofore undetermined was co-extensive with the conventional line expressly agreed upon in the treaty.[81] An editorial caption forms no part of the treaty.[82]

76 Moore, Int. Arb., I, 350, 360.
77 "Incivile est nisi tota lege perspecta una aliqua particula ejus proposita judicare vel respondere." Digest of Justinian, Bk. I, Tit. III, 24.
78 Gray v. United States, 21 C. Cls. 340, 350.
79 The Ship Tom, 29 C. Cls. 68, 80; 39 C. Cls. 290, 292.
80 Garrison v. United States, 30 C. Cls. 272, 282.
81 Little v. Watson (1850), 32 Me. 214, 222.
82 Cushing v. United States, 22 C. Cls. 1, 33.

CHAPTER XXIV.

THE AMERICAN CONSTRUCTION OF THE MOST-FAVORED-NATION CLAUSE.[1]

§172. Concessions in Matters of Commerce.—In a communication to the Congress of the Confederation, February 20, 1787, the Netherlands minister protested against an act of the legislature of the State of Virginia, which exempted French brandies imported in French and American vessels from certain duties to which like commodities imported in vessels of the Netherlands were left liable, as in contravention of the most-favored-nation clause in Article II of the treaty of 1782. This article provided that the subjects of the Netherlands should pay in the ports of the United States no other or greater duties or imposts of whatever nature or denomination than those which the nations the most favored were or should be obliged to pay; and that they should enjoy all the rights, liberties, privileges, immunities and exemptions in trade, navigation and commerce which the most favored nations did or should enjoy. The article contained no express qualification that the favor or privilege should be extended freely if freely given or for an equivalent if conditional. John Jay, the Secretary for the Department of Foreign Affairs, to whom the protest had been referred, in his report to Congress in October, 1787, said: "It is observable that this article takes no notice of cases where compensation is granted for privileges. Reason and equity, however, in the opinion of your Secretary, will supply this deficiency. * * * Where a privilege is gratuitously granted, the nation to whom it is granted becomes in respect to that privilege a favoured nation * * * but where the privilege is not gratuitous, but rests on compact, in such case the favour, if any there be, does not consist in the privilege yielded, but in the consent to make the contract by which it is yielded. * * * The favour, therefore, of being admitted to make a similar bargain, is all that in such cases can reasonably be demanded under the article. Besides, it would certainly be inconsistent with the most obvious principles of justice and fair construction, that

---

[1] Reprinted with additions from Am. Journal of Int. Law of October, 1913, VII, 708.

because France purchases, at a great price, a privilege of the United States, that therefore the Dutch shall immediately insist, not on having the like privileges at the like price, but without any price at all."[2]   It may give additional weight to the view as here expressed to note that in the opinion of the Secretary, the reduction in question of the duty on French brandies by the State of Virginia having been gratuitous, the subjects of the Netherlands were entitled to the same reduction.   This rule of construction as announced by Jay—that a special concession made for a valuable consideration does not pass automatically and without equivalent under the general most-favored-nation clause—has since been regularly maintained, at least in respect of special concessions in import duties, by subsequent Secretaries of State—by Secretaries Adams, Clay, and Van Buren, in respect of Article VIII of the treaty of April 30, 1803, with France; by Secretary Livingston in respect of Articles V and IX of the treaty of August 27, 1829, with Austria; by Secretary Frelinghuysen in respect of Article II of the treaty of July 3, 1815, with Great Britain; by Secretaries Bayard, Gresham, and Sherman in respect of various treaties.[3]   The reason of the rule was stated by Mr. Sherman, Secretary of State, as follows: "It is clearly evident that the object sought in all the varying forms of expression is equality of international treatment, protection against the wilful preference of the commercial interests of one nation over another.   But the allowance of the same privileges and the same sacrifice of revenue duties, to a nation which makes no compensation, that had been conceded to another nation for an adequate

2 Secret Journals, IV, 409. The same view was taken by Jefferson as to a most-favored-nation clause, when conditionally expressed, in a letter to Monroe, December 10, 1784. Writings (Ford ed.), IV, 19. See also Writings of Monroe, I, 36.

3 See Moore, Int. Law Digest, V, 257-319. See also Memorandum by John Ball Osborne, Sen. Doc. No. 29, 62d Cong., 1st Sess. The position taken by the government in 1898, in reference to the most-favored-nation clause in the treaty of 1850 with Switzerland, is not an exception to the rule. There existed a clear agreement between the parties in respect of the interpretation to be placed upon the clause. See supra, §166; For. Rel., 1899, pp. 746-748. As to the rule of construction in foreign countries, see M. L. E. Visser, Revue de Droit International et de Législation Comparée, 1902 (2d series), IV, 66, 159, 270; S. K. Hornbeck, American Journal of International Law, III, 395, 619, 797; C. C. Hyde, Id., III, 57; J. R. Herod, Favored Nation Treatment; and N. D. Harris, Proceedings of American Society of International Law, Fifth Annual Meeting (1911), 228.

compensation, instead of maintaining, destroys that equality of
market privileges which the 'most-favored-nation' clause was
intended to secure. It concedes for nothing to one friendly nation
what the other gets only for a price. It would thus become the
source of international inequality and provoke international hostility."[4]

The same rule has, as regards special concessions in import
duties based upon valuable considerations, been applied by the
Supreme Court. In the case of Whitney v. Robertson, the court,
by Mr. Justice Field, said: "In Bartram v. Robertson, decided at
the last term (122 U. S. 116), we held that brown and unrefined
sugars, the produce and manufacture of the island of St. Croix,
which is part of the dominions of the king of Denmark, were not
exempt from duty by force of the treaty with that country, because similar goods from the Hawaiian Islands were thus exempt.
The first article of the treaty with Denmark provided that the
contracting parties should not grant 'any particular favor' to other
nations in respect to commerce and navigation, which should not
immediately become common to the other party, who should
'enjoy the same freely if the concession were freely made, and
upon allowing the same compensation if the concession were conditional.' 11 Stat. 719. The fourth article provided that no 'higher
or other duties' should be imposed by either party on the importation of any article which is its produce or manufacture, into the
country of the other party, than is payable on like articles, being
the produce or manufacture of any other foreign country. And
we held in the case mentioned that 'those stipulations, even if
conceded to be self-executing by the way of a proviso or exception
to the general law imposing the duties, do not cover concessions
like those made to the Hawaiian Islands for a valuable consideration. They were pledges of the two contracting parties, the United States and the king of Denmark, to each other, that in the imposition of duties on goods imported into one of the countries
which were the produce or manufacture of the other, there should
be no discrimination against them in favor of goods of like character imported from any other country. They imposed an obligation upon both countries to avoid hostile legislation in that respect. But they were not intended to interfere with special ar-

4 Mr. Sherman to Mr. Buchanan, January 11, 1898. Moore, Int. Law
Digest, V, 278.

rangements with other countries founded upon a concession of special privileges.' The counsel for the plaintiffs meet this position by pointing to the omission in the treaty with the Republic of San Domingo of the provision as to free concessions, and concessions upon compensation, contending that the omission precludes any concession in respect of commerce and navigation by our government to another country, without that concession being at once extended to San Domingo. We do not think that the absence of this provision changes the obligations of the United States. The 9th article of the treaty with that republic, in the clause quoted, is substantially like the 4th article in the treaty with the king of Denmark. And as we said of the latter, we may say of the former, that it is a pledge of the contracting parties that there shall be no discriminating legislation against the importation of articles which are the growth, produce, or manufacture of their respective countries, in favor of articles of like character, imported from any other country. It has no greater extent. It was never designed to prevent special concessions, upon sufficient considerations, touching the importation of specific articles into the country of the other. It would require the clearest language to justify a conclusion that our government intended to preclude itself from such engagements with other countries, which might in the future be of the highest importance to its interests."[5]

Accordingly, to entitle the claimant under the most-favored-nation clause, even if not conditionally expressed, to the privilege or concession, it must appear either that the particular privilege claimed has been extended gratuitously to the third power; or that the claimant nation has extended to the United States the exact equivalent for which the particular privilege was extended to the third power; or that the act depriving the claimant of the particular privilege claimed is discriminatory. If the privileges claimed have been specifically extended by treaty stipulations, they are presumed to have been based upon a consideration and not to have been gratuitous, for the usual purpose of a treaty is to secure benefits for concessions, not to record the exchange of free gifts. This presumption does not arise if the privileges have been extended unconditionally by acts of legislation, not in exe-

---

5 124 U. S. 190, 192. See also Shaw & Co. v. United States, 20 Treasury Decisions, 718; 1 Ct. Cust. Appls. 426; Taylor v. Morton, 2 Curtis, 454; Ropes v. Clinch, 8 Blatchf. 304.

cution of treaty stipulations, for such acts are not presumably the result of negotiation with foreign nations. It has been held by the Court of Customs Appeals that the right of free entry into the United States of untaxed pulp made from untaxed wood, provided for in section 2 of the act of July 26, 1911, "to promote reciprocal trade relations with the Dominion of Canada and for other purposes," was granted by the United States to Canada without consideration, and that the same right of free entry therefore passed automatically to other powers enjoying most-favored-nation treatment.[6] In treaties of commerce the equivalent for which a particular concession is made may be such that the exact equivalent can be offered by no other nation, such, for instance, as considerations based upon extent of territory, population, variety of products, and propinquity. So also the treaty may comprise various articles, of which a particular article may be consented to by one of the parties in consideration of benefits received in other articles.

Attorney General Williams, however, advised that the provisions of Article IV of the treaty with Belgium of July 17, 1858, which exempted steam vessels of the United States and of Belgium engaged in regular navigation between the two countries from the payment of tonnage, anchorage, and light-house dues, became immediately applicable, *mutatis mutandis,* to Sweden and Norway, by virtue of Article II of the treaty of April 3, 1783, and Articles VIII and XVII of the treaty of July 4, 1827 with those countries, and to Bremen, by virtue of Article IX of the treaty of December 20, 1827 with the Hanseatic Republics.[7] This view was accepted by the government of the United States, and resulted in the termination of the treaty with Belgium, pursuant to notice.[8] In case of Sweden and Norway, it appeared that no line of steam vessels of the United States was, at the time, engaged in regular navigation between the United States and Sweden and Norway. Accordingly, it could not with certainty be stated, observed the Attorney General, whether tonnage duties would or would not be levied on American vessels in the ports of those countries. "It is," he concluded, "to be presumed that they will, when the occa-

---

6 Importations from Norway, Russia, Austria-Hungary, and Germany were involved in the decision. American Express Co. et al. v. United States, and Bertuch & Co. et al. v. United States, 4 Ct. Cust. Appls. 146.

7 14 Op. 468, 530. See also 16 Op. 276, 626.

8 Notes to Treaties and Conventions, 1776-1887, p. 1248.

sion shall arise, faithfully perform their duty under the treaties; for the obligations imposed by them are reciprocal." In case of Bremen, it appeared that no tonnage tax was imposed on American vessels entering from ports of the United States.

With respect to discriminatory legislation, it has been held that an act of Congress of June 26, 1884, section 14, which imposed a duty of three cents per ton on all vessels entering from any foreign port in "North America, Central America, the West India Islands, the Bahama Islands, the Bermuda Islands, or the Sandwich Islands, or Newfoundland," and a duty of six cents per ton on vessels from all other foreign ports, did not entitle German vessels entering the United States from European ports to the three cent rate, under the treaties of December 20, 1827, and May 1, 1828, since the classification was merely geographical, the three cent rate applying to vessels of all nations coming from the privileged ports.[9] So also it has been held that a State pilotage law, which subjected all vessels, domestic and foreign, engaged in foreign trade to pilotage regulations, but exempted pursuant to law coast-wise steam vessels of the United States, was not in conflict with the stipulation in the treaty with Great Britain, that British vessels should not be subject to any higher or other charges than vessels of the United States, since such exemption did not "operate to produce a discrimination against British vessels engaged in foreign trade and in favor of vessels of the United States in such trade."[10]

It was the view of the government of the United States that an act of the British Parliament of 1836, by which rough rice imported from the coast of Africa was admitted on the payment of a duty of one penny a quarter, while the same article imported from all other countries, including the United States, was subjected to the payment of a duty of twenty shillings a quarter, was discriminatory and in contravention of the provision in the treaty of 1815 that no higher duties should be levied in either country on articles the growth or manufacture of the other than those paid on the

9 North German Lloyd S. S. Co. v. Hedden, 43 Fed. 17. See, to like effect, 18 Op. Atty. Gen. 260.

10 Olsen v. Smith, 195 U. S. 332, 344. See also Compagnie Francaise &c. v. Louisiana State Board of Health, 186 U. S. 380, 394, dissenting opinion of Mr. Justice Brown, 397, 400; Powers v. Comly, 101 U. S. 789; Head Money Cases, 112 U. S. 580; Thingvalla Line et al. v. United States, 24 C. Cls. 255.

same articles the growth or manufacture of any other foreign country. The British government ultimately conceded the correctness of this view, and directed the repayment of the excess duties so exacted.[11] By the tariff act of the United States of August 30, 1842, it was provided that the increased import duties, imposed by the act, should not apply to goods shipped in vessels which had actually left their last port of lading eastward of the Cape of Good Hope or beyond Cape Horn prior to September 1, 1842.[12] It was held by the mixed claims commission, under the convention of February 8, 1853, that goods imported from Great Britain during the period in which vessels from the eastward of the Cape of Good Hope continued to arrive at ports of the United States were entitled under the terms of the treaty of 1815 to exemption from the payment of the increased rates.[13] A similar ruling was made by the commission as to a provision in the tariff act of May 22, 1824, which exempted from the operation of the increased rates imposed by the act goods imported from ports or places eastward of the Cape of Good Hope or beyond Cape Horn, prior to January 1, 1825.[14] The contention of the government of the United States, that the imposition by Great Britain of export duties on woolen goods shipped to the United States after the duty on similar articles exported to various other countries had been repealed was in violation of the provision in the treaty of 1815, that no higher or other duties should be imposed on the exportation of any article from the one country to the territory of the other than such as were payable on the exportation of the like articles to any other foreign country, was likewise sustained in principle by this same commission.[15] Attorney General Olney, in an opinion dated November 13, 1894, advised that Germany was not, by virtue of the most-favored-nation clause in the treaty of May 1, 1828, entitled to the free entry of salt into the United States under paragraph 608 of the tariff act of August 27, 1894. This paragraph placed salt on the free list, but provided that the rate of duty existing prior to the passage of the act should be collected on salt imported from any country which imposed a duty on salt exported from the United States. Ameri-

---

11 Richardson, Messages, IV, 259; Moore, Int. Arb., IV, 3362.
12 Sec. 25. 5 Stats. at L. 566.
13 Moore, Int. Arb., IV, 3361.
14 Id., 3363.
15 Id., 3363; Richardson, Messages, IV, 259.

can salt was dutiable on importation into Germany. In the course of the opinion, the Attorney General said: "The form which the provisions of our recent tariff act relating to salt may have assumed is quite immaterial. It enacts, in substance and effect, that any country admitting American salt free shall have its own salt admitted free here, while any country putting a duty upon American salt shall have its salt dutiable here under the pre-existing statute. In other words, the United States concedes 'free salt' to any nation which concedes 'free salt' to the United States. Germany, of course, is entitled to that concession upon returning the same equivalent. But otherwise she is not so entitled, and there is nothing in the 'most-favored-nation clause' which compels the United States to discriminate against other nations and in favor of Germany by granting gratuitously to the latter privileges which it grants to the former only upon the payment of a stipulated price."[16] The same conclusion was reached by the Court of Customs Appeals as to concessions for reciprocal considerations made under section 3 of the tariff act of 1897.[17] The court said: "Section 3 of the tariff act of 1897 was a general law; its attitude toward every nation was uniform. It offered no special favor to France, or Germany, or Italy, or any other country. Every foreign nation was treated alike by the terms of the law. It was equally within the opportunity of England to negotiate a reciprocity treaty as it was within the opportunity of France."

§173. **Administration on Estates of Deceased Aliens.**—State courts have in various cases coming before them held that the consuls of a nation enjoying most-favored-nation treatment were entitled to privileges and rights in administration on the estates of deceased countrymen extended by treaty to consuls of a third nation. The Supreme Court of Louisiana has, for instance, held that French consuls, by virtue of the most-favored-nation clause in Article XII of the treaty with France of 1853, have the same right as enjoyed by Belgian consuls under Article XV of the treaty with Belgium of 1880, to appear in all proceedings on behalf of absent or minor heirs.[18] The surrogates of Westchester[19]

16 21 Op. 80.

17 Shaw & Co. v. United States, 20 Treasury Decisions (31500) 718, 725; 1 Ct. Cust. Appls. 426, 433.

18 Succession of Rabasse, 47 La. Ann. 1452; 49 Id. 1405. See also Succession of Amat, 18 Id. 405; In re Peterson's Will, 101 N. Y. S. 285.

and Albany[20] counties of New York, the Appellate Division of the Supreme Court of New York,[21] and the Supreme Court of Alabama[22] have held that Italian consuls, by virtue of the most-favored-nation clause in Article XVII of the consular convention between the United States and Italy of May 8, 1878, were entitled to all the rights and privileges in the administration on the estates of deceased countrymen enjoyed by consuls of the Argentine Republic under Article IX of the treaty of July 27, 1853.[23] Article IX of the Argentine treaty was construed in each of these cases as conferring on the consul the right of administration in preference to one otherwise having a prior right under the local laws. The same view was taken by the Supreme Judicial Court of Massachusetts[24] as to the rights of a Russian consul under the most-favored-nation clause in Article VIII of the treaty of 1832 between the United States and Russia. The surrogate of New York county[25] placed a different construction on the Argentine treaty.

In each of the above cases the court merely considered the question whether the right claimed was embraced in the terms of the Argentine treaty. It does not appear that the right of the consular officer to invoke, under the most-favored-nation clause, any privilege extended by treaty to consuls of a third power was questioned. In a case coming before the District Court of Appeal of California, this right was questioned;[26] but neither that court nor the Supreme Court of California, affirming the decision, found it necessary to decide this question. The claim was denied on the ground that Article IX of the Argentine treaty was not intended to commit to the consular officers the administration in preference to those entitled by the local law.[27] This decision was affirmed by the Supreme Court of the United States.[28] The ques-

19 In re Fattosini's Estate, 67 N. Y. S. 1119, and In re Lobrasciano's Estate, 77 N. Y. S. 1040.

20 In re Silvetti's Estate, 122 N. Y. S. 400.

21 In re Scutella's Estate, 129 N. Y. S. 20.

22 Carpigiani v. Hall, 172 Ala. 287.

23 See, also, In re Davenport, 89 N. Y. S. 537; In re Bristow, 118 N. Y. S. 686.

24 McEvoy v. Wyman, 191 Mass. 276.

25 In re Logiorato's Estate, 69 N. Y. S. 507.

26 In re Ghio's Estate, Am. Journal of Int. Law, IV, 726.

27 157 Cal. 552.

28 Rocca v. Thompson, 223 U. S. 317.

tion whether the most-favored-nation clause in the Italian treaty automatically carried the privileges of the Argentine treaty in this respect was expressly excepted by the Supreme Court from its decision. It was held that by the terms of Article IX of the Argentine treaty, (that in case a citizen of either of the contracting parties shall die intestate in the territories of the other the proper consular officer of the country to which the deceased belonged "shall have the right to intervene in the possession, administration and judicial liquidation of the estate of the deceased, conformably with the laws of the country,") it was not intended to give to the consul the right of original administration to the exclusion of one entitled by local law to administer the estate. In the argument before the court it was urged that the rights and privileges enjoyed by Argentine consuls were granted for and in consideration of valuable rights and privileges granted by the Argentine Republic under the treaty to American consuls; and that, under the rule applied in the case of Whitney v. Robertson, in respect of valuable concessions in import duties, these rights and privileges granted to Argentine consuls for valuable equivalents did not pass automatically and without equivalents to third powers. It has subsequently been held by the Supreme Court of Minnesota that Article XIV of the treaty with Sweden of June 1, 1910,—the provisions of which had been invoked by an Austrian consul under the most-favored-nation clause in Article XV of the treaty with Austria of July 11, 1870,—gave to the consul the right to administration only so far as the local laws permitted.[29] The surrogate of New York county has held that Article X of the treaty with Paraguay of February 4, 1859, and Article XIV of the treaty with Sweden of June 1, 1910, gave to consuls of those countries the right to administration; and that the same right was, by virtue of the most-favored-nation clause, enjoyed by consuls of Italy,[30] and of Austria-Hungary.[31] Likewise, the surrogates of Schenectady,[32] Herkimer,[33] Erie,[34] and

---

29 Austro-Hungarian Consul v. Westphal, 120 Minn. 122. A similar construction has been given to the terms of the treaty by the Supreme Court of California in Fontana v. Hynes (1915), 146 Pac. 651.

30 In re Baglieri's Estate, 137 N. Y. S. 175.

31 In re Jarema's Estate, 137 N. Y. S. 176.

32 In re Lombardi, 138 N. Y. S. 1007.

33 In re Riccardo, 140 N. Y. S. 606.

34 In re Madaloni's Estate, 141 N. Y. S. 323.

29

Jefferson,[35] counties, New York, have ruled that an Italian consul, invoking under the most-favored-nation clause the provisions of Article XIV of the treaty between the United States and Sweden of June 1, 1910, has the right to administration on the estate of an Italian subject dying intestate in the United States. In the first named case the right of the consul was upheld in preference to a distant resident relative not entitled to succeed to the personalty; in the second, in preference to resident creditors; in the third, in preference to a brother residing in this country, the father of the decedent being a subject and resident of Italy; and in the fourth, in preference to a resident brother without pecuniary interest in the estate, the widow and children of the intestate residing in Italy. The Court of Appeals, in reversing the surrogate in the last named case, did not question the right of the Italian consul to claim the privileges conferred on Swedish consuls by the treaty, but construed Article XIV of this treaty as merely adding such foreign consuls to the list of those eligible as administrators so as to enable them to administer on the estates of their fellow countrymen when no one having a prior right under the local law was competent or willing to act[35a]

§174. **Consular Jurisdiction Over Seamen.**—Mr. Buchanan, Secretary of State, denied the right of the Austrian government, under the most-favored-nation clause, to the benefit of stipulations in the treaties between the United States and certain other powers conferring upon their respective consuls jurisdiction over disputes between the masters and crews of vessels. In a note to the Austrian chargé d'affaires, May 18, 1846, Mr. Buchanan said: "Seeing that the right now under consideration, where it can be

---

35 In re D'Adamo's Estate, 141 N. Y. S. 1103; 144 N. Y. S. 429.

35a. In re D'Adamo's Estate (1914), 212 N. Y. 214. This ruling has been followed in In re D'Agostino (1914), 151 N. Y. S. 957, and In re Comparetto (1914), 151 N. Y. S. 961. As to the right of foreign consuls to exemption from attendance in court as witnesses in virtue of most-favored-nation privileges, see Baiz v. Malo, 58 N. Y. S. 806; United States v. Trumbull, 48 Fed. 94; In re Dillon, 7 Sawy. 561. The Supreme Court of Montana has likewise conceded to the Italian consul, in virtue of the most-favored-nation clause of the Italian treaty, the same privileges as are enjoyed by Swedish consuls under Article XIV of the treaty with Sweden; and has held that the consul is entitled, as against the nominee of a non-resident heir, to administer the estate of a deceased countryman dying intestate in the State. In re Infelise's Estate (1915), 149 Pac. 365.

claimed under a treaty wherein it is expressly conferred is, in every such instance, given in exchange for the very same right conferred in terms equally express upon the consuls of the United States, it can not be expected that it will be considered as established by the operation of a general provision which, if it were allowed so to operate, would destroy all reciprocity in this regard, leaving the United States without that equivalent in favor of their consuls, which is the consideration received by them for the grant of this right wherever expressly granted."[36]

In 1866, Attorney General Speed, on the other hand, advised that the American consul at Honolulu had, by virtue of the most-favored-nation clause in Article X of the treaty between the United States and the Hawaiian Islands, the same jurisdiction of disputes on American merchant vessels between American citizens as was conferred upon French consuls by treaty between the Hawaiian Islands and France.[37] The opinion of the Attorney General was adopted by Mr. Seward in his instructions of July 3, 1866, to the American minister-resident at Honolulu.[38] It was stated by Mr. Justice Bradley in Dainese v. Hale[39] that citizens of the United States, by virtue of the treaty of 1862 with the Ottoman Porte, seemed to be guaranteed the same right to have their civil controversies decided by their own minister and consuls as enjoyed by subjects of other Christian nations. The treaty in question provided, in Article I, that all rights, privileges or immunities, which the Sublime Porte then granted or might thereafter grant to or suffer to be enjoyed by the subjects of any other foreign power, should be equally granted to and exercised and enjoyed by the citizens of the United States. The rights of exterritoriality enjoyed by the subjects of other powers and sought in this case were, however, based, not upon reciprocal concessions, but upon long usage and custom and the early Capitulations.

36 Moore, Int. Law Digest, V, 261.

37 11 Op. Atty. Gen. 508.

38 Mr. Seward to Mr. McCook, July 3, 1866. Dip. Cor., 1866, II, 488. See opinion of Attorney General Cushing, in 1853, holding that the stipulation for the restitution of deserting seamen, in our treaty with Norway and Sweden of July 4, 1827, did not extend to Denmark in virtue of the most-favored-nation clause in respect of navigation and commerce, 6 Op. Atty. Gen. 148. See, however, Consular Regulations of the United States (1896), §78.

39 91 U. S. 13, 18.

§175. **Patents and Trade-marks.**—Of the right of American citizens, under the most-favored-nation clause in our treaty with Japan, to the same protection in trade-marks and patents in Japan, as secured to German subjects by treaty stipulation, Mr. Olney, Secretary of State, in instructions to the American minister to Japan, November 12, 1896, said: "In the Department's judgment, the provision of the treaty of 1854, to which you refer, does not mean if Japan shall grant privileges to Germany in consideration of similar privileges granted by the latter to the former, the same privileges shall be granted gratuitously to the United States. The clause 'that these same privileges and advantages shall be granted likewise to the United States and to the citizens thereof, without any consultation or delay,' only refers, in my opinion, to privileges granted gratuitously to a third power and not to privileges granted in consideration of concessions made by another government."[40]

§176. **Right to Hold and Dispose of Real Estate.**—With respect to the extension to aliens of the right to hold real property, Mr. Bayard, Secretary of State, applying the same rule as in favors or concessions in matters of commerce, said: "This quality of reciprocity, which takes a case out of the category of gratuitousness, belongs, I apprehend, to all our concessions to foreign states giving their citizens rights to hold real estate in the United States. Such concessions are based on reciprocity. We give the rights to them because they give the right to us. Hence such privileges can not be claimed under 'the most-favored-nation' clause by foreign governments to which they are not specially conceded."[41] The Supreme Court of Louisiana has held that the clause in Article XXII of the treaty of 1871 with Italy, providing that in "the case of real estate, the citizens and subjects of the two contracting parties shall be treated on the footing of the most-favored-nation," entitles Italian subjects to the same exemptions from the payment of the tax imposed on real estate inherited by alien non-resident heirs as enjoyed by subjects and citizens of France under Article VII of the treaty of 1853. The court said: "The heir [a citizen and resident of the kingdom of Italy] of the deceased is quite as much entitled to the protection of the French

---

40 Moore, Int. Law Digest, V, 315.

41 Mr. Bayard, Secretary of State, to Mr. Miller, June 15, 1886. Moore, Int. Law Digest, V, 272.

treaty, as were the subjects and citizens of France—he having invoked the benefit of the 'most-favored-nation' clause in the Italian treaty with the United States."[42]

§177. **Rights of Residence.**—Article VI of the treaty with China of 1868 has been on numerous occasions before the Federal courts for construction. This article reads: "Citizens of the United States visiting or residing in China shall enjoy the same privileges, immunities or exemptions in respect to travel or residence as may there be enjoyed by the citizens or subjects of the most-favored-nation; and, reciprocally, Chinese subjects visiting or residing in the United States shall enjoy the same privileges, immunities and exemptions in respect to travel or residence as may there be enjoyed by the citizens or subjects of the most-favored-nation." It was held by the circuit court, district of California, that a provision in the constitution of the State of California, which prohibited the employment by a corporation formed under the laws of the State, in any capacity, of any Chinese or Mongolian, and an act of the legislature of that State, which provided for the punishment of violations of this provision, were in conflict with the treaty with China and were therefore void. Mr. Justice Sawyer said: "Any legislation or constitutional provision of the State of California which limits or restricts that right to labor to any extent, or in any manner not applicable to citizens of other foreign nations visiting or residing in California, is in conflict with this provision of the treaty; and such are the express provisions of the constitution and statute in question."[43] An act of the legislature of Oregon which prohibited the employment of Chinese laborers on street improvements or public works, and at the same time permitted all other aliens so to be employed, was declared by Mr. Justice Deady in the circuit court, district of Oregon,[44] to be in conflict with the treaty between the United States and China, which, by its most-favored-nation clause, secured to the Chinese residents the same right to be employed and to labor for a living as the subjects of any other nation.[45] In an earlier

---

42 Succession of Rixner, 48 La. Ann. 552, 565. See Frederickson v. State of Louisiana, 23 How. 445; Prevost v. Greneaux, 19 How. 1; Duck Lee v. Boise Development Co., 21 Idaho 461.

43 Parrott's Case, 6 Sawy. 349, 375.

44 Baker v. City of Portland, 5 Sawy. 566.

45 See also I. M. Ludington's Sons, 131 N. Y. S. 550; People v. Warren, 34 N. Y. S. 942.

case[46] the same judge said: "Article VI of the treaty with China of July 28, 1868, provides that citizens and subjects of the two nations shall respectively enjoy the same privileges, immunities or exemptions, in respect to travel or residence 'within the country of the other,' as may there be enjoyed by the citizens or subjects of the most-favored-nation. The right to reside in the country with the same privileges as the subjects of Great Britain or France, implies the right to follow any lawful calling or pursuit which is open to the subjects of these powers. Therefore the provisions in the mining regulations of Poorman creek, which, in effect, forbid Chinamen from working in a mining claim for themselves or others, as well as the clause of the State constitution to the same effect, seem to be in direct conflict with this article of the treaty; and if so, are therefore void." In declaring a statute of the State of California, which prohibited all aliens incapable of becoming electors of the State from fishing in the waters of the State, to be in contravention of Articles V and VI of the treaty with China, Mr. Justice Sawyer said: "Citizens of other States having no property right which entitles them to fish against the will of the State, a fortiori the alien, from whatever country he may come, has none whatever in the waters or the fisheries of the State. Like other privileges he enjoys as an alien by permission of the State, he can only enjoy so much as the State vouchsafes to yield to him as a special privilege. To him it is not a property right, but, in the strictest sense, a privilege or favor. To exclude the Chinaman from fishing in the waters of the State, therefore, while the Germans, Italians, Englishmen and Irishmen, who otherwise stand upon the same footing, are permitted to fish ad libitum, without price, charge, let, or hindrance, is to prevent him from enjoying the same privileges as are 'enjoyed by the citizens or subjects of the most-favored-nation'; and to punish him criminally for fishing in the waters of the State, while all aliens of the Caucasian race are permitted to fish freely in the same waters with immunity and without restraint, and exempt from all punishments, is to exclude him from enjoying the same immunities and exemptions 'as are enjoyed by the citizens or subjects of the most-favored-nation'; and such discriminations are in violation of Articles V and VI of the treaty with China, cited in full in Parrott's case. The same privileges which are granted to other

46 Chapman v. Toy Long, 4 Sawy. 28, 36.

aliens, by treaty or otherwise, are secured to the Chinaman by the stipulations of the treaty. Conceding that the State may exclude all aliens from fishing in its waters, yet if it permits one class to enjoy the privilege, it must permit all others to enjoy, upon like terms, the same privileges whose governments have treaties securing to them the enjoyment of all privileges granted to the most-favored-nation."[47] The circuit court, northern district of California (Sawyer, C. J.), held an ordinance of the city of San Francisco, which made it unlawful for any Chinese to locate, reside, or carry on business within the limits of the city and county of San Francisco, except in a certain prescribed district, and which required all Chinese inhabitants theretofore located outside the prescribed district to remove within a specified time, to be in contravention of our treaty pledge with China.[48] Likewise, the circuit court, southern district of California (Ross, D. J.), held that a covenant in a deed not to convey or to lease to a Chinaman, being at variance with our treaty with China, was not enforceable in a court of equity of the United States.[49] Mr. Justice Field, in circuit, in declaring an ordinance of the city of San Francisco, which arbitrarily prohibited the conduct of the laundry business within certain sections of the city, to be in conflict with the treaty provisions with China, said: "The petitioner [a subject of the Emperor of China] is an alien, and under the treaty with China is entitled to all the rights, privileges, and immunities of subjects of the most-favored-nation with which this country has treaty relations. Being a resident here before the passage of the recent act of Congress, restricting the immigration of subjects of his country, he has, under the pledge of the nation, the right to remain, and follow any of the lawful ordinary trades and pursuits of life, without let or hindrance from the State, or any of its subordinate municipal bodies, except such as may arise from the enforcement of equal and impartial laws."[50]

In a report to the President, January 7, 1893, on a bill then pending in the Senate to prohibit for a period of one year, on account of the prevalence of cholera, the admission into the United States

47 In re Ah Chong, 6 Sawy. 451, 455. See Leong Mow v. Board of Commissioners, 185 Fed. 223.

48 In re Lee Sing (1890), 43 Fed. 359.

49 Gandolfo v. Hartman (1892), 49 Fed. 181. See also Duck Lee v. Boise Development Co. (1912), 21 Idaho 461.

50 In re Quong Woo (1882), 13 Fed. 229, 233.

of any alien coming, for settlement or permanent residence, from any except American countries, Mr. Foster, Secretary of State, said: "The only pertinence of the 'favored-nation' clauses included under the second class, hereinbefore referred to [those securing generally to the citizens or subjects of another country the same privileges of residence and trade as enjoyed by the citizens or subjects of the most-favored-nation], is that the bill puts no restriction upon immigration from American countries. If immigration from those countries were to be allowed on account of some treaty obligation, or as a favor, it might give occasion for other countries to invoke a favored-nation clause in their treaty. Such absence of restriction, however, with reference to American countries is not in fact based upon either, but depends simply upon the fact that the threatened danger which it is the purpose of the legislation to avert does not exist in this hemisphere. I see no opportunity for invoking a favored-nation clause unless the danger in question equally existed in American countries, and the immigration therefrom in magnitude and other respects should make the case exactly the same with respect to both American and European countries, so that a restriction with respect to one and not the other would have in it no element of reasonable discretion, but plainly be an act of discrimination."[51]   A case quite different arose in 1900 at the time of the threatened epidemic of bubonic plague. The board of health of the city of San Francisco adopted regulations which prohibited any Asiatic person from leaving the city without first submitting to inoculation with a serum supposed to be preventive, but the administration of which to a person who had been exposed to the disease was dangerous to life. The government of Japan remonstrated against these regulations as in derogation of the rights of travel and residence guaranteed to subjects of Japan in the most-favored-nation clause of Article I of the treaty of 1894.[52]   The circuit court, northern district of California,[53] held the regulations to be discriminatory and in violation of the constitutional guarantee of the equal protection of the law, without entering into the question of treaty rights. These regulations, said the court, "are directed against the Asiatic race

51 Moore, Int. Law Digest, IV, 153, 157. See, to same effect, North German Lloyd S. S. Co. v. Hedden, 43 Fed. 17.
52 For. Rel., 1900, pp. 737-757; Id., 1901, p. 375.
53 Wong Wai v. Williamson, 103 Fed. 1, 9.

exclusively, and by name. There is no pretense that previous residence, habits, exposure to disease, method of living, or physical condition has anything to do with their classification as subject to the regulations. They are denied the privilege of traveling from one place to another, except upon conditions not enforced against any other class of people."[54]

The decision in each of the cases above noted was based upon the fact of discrimination (the inhibitions of the Constitution being therefore sufficient to cover the case), and did not involve the question whether the favor or concession enjoyed by the subjects of other powers, but denied to the claimant, was extended to those other powers gratuitously or in consideration of equivalents. As to what constitutes discrimination against a race, the decisions of the Supreme Court in cases which have arisen under the Fourteenth Amendment to the Constitution afford liberal and not uncertain standards. "The equal protection of the laws is a pledge of the protection of equal laws."[55]

54 See, for discussion evoked in 1906 by the passage of a resolution by the board of education of San Francisco for the segregation of children of Orientals, Cong. Record, 59th Cong., 2d Sess., 297, 301, 303, 674, 1231, 1234, 1235, 1236, 1237, 1515, 1522, 1579, 3132; Proceedings of the American Society of International Law (April 19-20, 1907), 44, 150, 173, 194, 201, 211, 213.

55 Matthews, J., Yick Wo v. Hopkins, 118 U. S. 356, 369. In the recent case of Truax et al. v. Raich (decided November 1, 1915), the Supreme Court by Mr. Justice Hughes said: "The act [of Arizona of December 14, 1914], it will be observed, provides that every employer (whether corporation, partnership, or individual) who employs more than five workers at any one time 'regardless of kind or class of work, or sex of workers' shall employ 'not less than eighty per cent. qualified electors or native-born citizens of the United States or some sub-division thereof.' It thus covers the entire field of industry with the exception of enterprises that are relatively very small. * * * It is an act aimed at the employment of aliens, as such, in the businesses described. * * * It is sought to justify this act as an exercise of the power of the State to make reasonable classifications in legislating to promote the health, safety, morals and welfare of those within its jurisdiction. But this admitted authority, with the broad range of legislative discretion that it implies, does not go so far as to make it possible for the State to deny to lawful inhabitants, because of their race or nationality, the ordinary means of earning a livelihood. It requires no argument to show that the right to work for a living in the common occupations of the community is of the very essence of the personal freedom and opportunity that it was the purpose of the Amendment to secure. Butchers' Union Co. v. Crescent City Co., 111 U.

S. 746, 762; Barbier v. Connolly, 113 U. S. 27, 31; Yick Wo v. Hopkins, supra; Allgeyer v. Louisiana, 165 U. S. 578, 589, 590; Coppage v. Kansas, 236 U. S. 1, 14. If this could be refused solely upon the ground of race or nationality, the prohibition of the denial to any person of the equal protection of the laws would be a barren form of words. It is no answer to say, as it is argued, that the act proceeds upon the assumption that 'the employment of aliens unless restrained was a peril to the public welfare.' The discrimination against aliens in the wide range of employments to which the act relates is made an end in itself and thus the authority to deny to aliens, upon the mere fact of their alienage, the right to obtain support in the ordinary fields of labor is necessarily involved. It must also be said that reasonable classification implies action consistent with the legitimate interests of the State, and it will not be disputed that these cannot be so broadly conceived as to bring them into hostility to exclusive Federal power. The authority to control immigration—to admit or exclude aliens—is vested solely in the Federal government. Fong Yue Ting v. United States, 149 U. S. 698, 713. The assertion of an authority to deny to aliens the opportunity of earning a livelihood when lawfully admitted to the State would be tantamount to the assertion of the right to deny them entrance and abode, for in ordinary cases they cannot live where they cannot work. And, if such a policy were permissible, the practical result would be that those lawfully admitted to the country under the authority of the acts of Congress, instead of enjoying in a substantial sense and in their full scope the privileges conferred by the admission, would be segregated in such of the States as chose to offer hospitality. * * * No special public interest with respect to any particular business is shown that could possibly be deemed to support the enactment, for as we have said it relates to every sort. The discrimination is against aliens as such in competition with citizens in the described range of enterprises and in our opinion it clearly falls under the condemnation of the fundamental law. The question of rights under treaties was not expressly presented by the bill, and, although mentioned in the argument, does not require attention in view of the invalidity of the act under the Fourteenth Amendment." A provision in the law of New York, which prohibited the employment on public works of all others than citizens of the United States, was held by the Supreme Court in Heim v. McCall, and Crane v. People, decided November 29, 1915, not to be in contravention of the guaranties of the Fourteenth Amendment or of treaties with foreign nations.

CHAPTER XXV.

TERMINATION OF TREATIES.

§178. Effect of Change in Form of Government.—A treaty is a compact between states, not organs of government. Consequently its obligation is not, in general, dependent upon the continuance of the particular form of government under which it happened to be concluded.[1] Treaties, the purposes of which are peculiar to the existing form,[2] as also agreements of a personal nature between crowned heads, which are not properly termed international treaties,[3] are to be expected. Thus the Family Compact of August 15, 1761, between the Kings of France and Spain, the aim of which was to render permanent the duties which were a "natural consequent of relationship and friendship," came to an end when the Bourbons ceased to reign in France.[4] Of this character was also the alliance entered into September 26, 1815, by the Emperors of Austria and Russia, and the King of Prussia.[5] So also it is possible that, by the new order of things and the changed condition of one of the parties, the considerations entering into the treaty might be so materially changed as to give to the other contracting party the option of declaring the treaty to be

---

1 "Hence it follows, that as after the change of a democracy into a monarchy, the treaty is still in force, in regard to the new sovereign; so if the government, from a monarchy, becomes a republic, the treaty made with the king does not expire, unless it was manifestly personal." Burlamaqui, Principles of Natural and Politic Law (Translation by Nugent, 2 ed.), II, 321. See also Vattel, Bk. II, c. XII, §§185, 186.

2 Grotius, Bk. II, c. XVI, §16; Vattel, Bk. II, c. XII, §185.

3 Hall, Int. Law (6 ed.), 317.

4 De Clercq, I, 81. In August, 1790, Spain requested France to make common cause against Great Britain in the Nookta Sound controversy; but the National Assembly of France declared the compact not to be binding on the nation. In Article II, possessions in any part of the world had been mutually guaranteed. Twiss, Law of Nations (Peace 2 ed.) §233; Rivier, Principes du Droit des Gens, II, 36, 121.

5 See for view of the Italian government that the convention of September 15, 1864, for the protection of Pontifical territory and for the withdrawal of French troops, ceased to be obligatory with the fall of Napoleon III, King, History of Italian Unity, II, 374. For text of the convention, see De Clercq, IX, 129. See for other instances, Rivier, Principes du Droit des Gens, II, 120, et seq.

at an end. This would however result not from the mere fact of a change in the form of the government, but from a change in the essential conditions upon which the treaty was based.

An interesting discussion took place in April, 1793, between President Washington's advisors, on the proposition of receiving the new minister from the republic of France with an express reservation of the question whether the treaties of commerce and alliance of 1778 ought not to be deemed temporarily and provisionally suspended. Hamilton, the Secretary of the Treasury, in support of such a reservation, urged that, if a nation thought fit to make changes in its form of government which rendered treaties theretofore concluded between it and another nation useless, or dangerous, or hurtful to that other nation, the latter had a right to renounce those treaties; that a contracting state had a right to take care of its own happiness and could not be obliged to suffer this to be impaired by the means which its ally had adopted for its own advantage contrary to the ancient state of things; that the treaties continued absolutely binding on the party making the change and would bind the other unless in due time it declared its election to renounce them, which in good faith it ought to do only if the change had rendered them "useless or materially less advantageous, or more dangerous than before"; that an alliance might be formed because each had confided in the strength and efficacy of the government of the other, while the newly-formed government might be feeble, fluctuating, and liable to provoke wars; that, as to the French treaties, since France was in an unsettled condition, it was his opinion that the United States had an option to consider the operation of these treaties as suspended, and would eventually have a right to renounce them, if such changes should take place as could "bona fide be pronounced to render a continuance of the connections which result from them disadvantageous or dangerous." Jefferson, the Secretary of State, with whom Randolph, the Attorney General, concurred, in taking a different view declared that all acts by the proper agents under the authority of the nation were the acts of the nation, were obligatory on it, and enured to its use, and could in no wise be annulled or affected by any change in the form of the government or of the persons administering it; that consequently "the treaties between the United States and France were not treaties between the United States and Louis Capét, but between the two nations of America and France," and, the nations remaining in existence, though both of them had since changed their forms of government, the treaties were not annulled by these changes. He however admitted that conditions might arise which would release one of the parties from treaty obligations. "When performance, for instance, becomes impossible, non-performance is not immoral. So if performance becomes self-destructive to the party, the law of self-preservation overrules the laws of obligation to others"; but the danger which absolves "must be great, inevitable and imminent." As to the French treaties, no part of them, he declared, except the clause of guarantee, held up "danger even at a distance."[6] The minister was received without the proposed reservation; and the treaties were recognized by the United States as continuing in force until abrogated by the joint resolution of Congress passed in 1798.[7]

§179. **Effect of Change in State Entity.**—The obligation of a treaty, as distinguished from rights already conveyed or transferred under it, comes to an end upon the extinguishment of one of the contracting parties with the consequent loss of power to perform.[8] "It is also an implied condition of the continuing obligation of a treaty that the parties to it shall keep their freedom of will with respect to its subject-matter except in so far as the treaty is itself a restraint upon liberty, and the condition is one which holds good even when such freedom of will is voluntarily given up."[9] The principle that a treaty between two parties is

6 Works of Hamilton (Lodge ed.), IV, 74; Writings of Jefferson (Ford ed.), VI, 219.

7 See Hooper v. United States (1887), 22 C. Cls. 408; The Brig William (1888), 23 C. Cls. 201.

8 See West Rand Central Gold Mining Co. v. Rex (1905), L. R., 2 K. B. 391, 400. See as to the use of the term obligation in the law of private contracts as giving rise to rights in personam, as distinguished from rights in rem, Savigny, Obligations, c. 1, §3 (Brown's epitome, 3); Pothier, Obligations (Evans' translation), I, 2; Holland, Jurisprudence (11 ed.), 239, 253-255; Pollock, Contracts (7 ed.), 1; Anson, Contracts (12 ed.), 3, 4, 6. "Obligatio est juris vinculum, quo necessitate adstringimur alicuius solvendae rei secundum nostrae civitatis jura." Justinian, Institutes, Bk. III, Tit. 13. "In the language of the Roman law, and of all the modern systems which are offsets from the Roman law, the term 'obligation' is restricted to the duties which answer to rights in personam." Austin, Jurisprudence (5 ed. by Campbell), I, 370. See, however, Marshall, C. J., Fletcher v. Peck, 6 Cranch 87, 136.

9 Hall, Int. Law (6 ed.), 350.

not annulled by an inconsistent subsequent treaty between one of them and a third party does not have full application in such cases. "It cannot be supposed that a state will subordinate its will to that of another state, or to a common will of which its own is only a factor, except under the pressure of necessity or of vital needs."[10]

The treaty of commerce and navigation concluded June 10, 1846, and the convention of extradition concluded January 18, 1855, between the United States and Hanover, and the convention abolishing droit d' aubaine and emigration taxes concluded May 27, 1846, between the United States and Nassau, have been considered as at an end upon the final and complete incorporation of these two kingdoms into Prussia in 1866.[11] The Italian government considered the treaties between foreign powers and Tuscany, the Two Sicilies and the several other Italian states to have been extinguished, at least for most purposes, upon the consolidation of these states with Sardinia in 1860. Treaties theretofore concluded by Sardinia, the nucleus of the consolidated kingdom of Italy, were regarded as still binding and applicable to the whole kingdom.[12] Shortly after the consolidation, new treaties were however concluded with many of the treaty powers. It has been held by the tribunals of both France and Italy that Article XXII of the treaty between France and Sardinia concluded March 24, 1760, providing for the execution of judgments of the courts of the one in the territory of the other, was applicable to the kingdom of Italy after the consolidation, and binding upon the two countries.[13] Upon the permanent occupation of

10 Id., 351. See, also, Vattel, Bk. II, c. XII, §176.

11 U. S. For. Rel., 1875, p. 479. See for decree of the King of Prussia, dated September 20, 1866, uniting "forever with the Prussian monarchy," Hanover, Hesse-Cassel, Nassau and Frankfort, Hertslet's Map of Europe by Treaty, III, 1741. As to treaties between Hanover and the Netherlands likewise terminated, see Archives diplomatiques, 1868, p. 745; Kiatibian, Conséquences juridiques des Transformations Territoriales, 30-31.

12 Dip. Cor. 1864, IV, 328, 334. See also Kiatibian, Conséquences juridiques des Transformations Territoriales, 81-82, 89. It may be noted that in the treaty concluded with Great Britain August 6, 1863, it was expressly provided that the treaties "in force," among which those with the Two Sicilies were enumerated, were to be superseded by the new treaty. Art. XX. Brit. and For. State Papers, LIII, 45.

13 Kiatibian, 101, citing decisions of the Court of Paris, December 1, 1879, and the tribunal of St. Quentin, October 30, 1885; Larivière, Trans-

Madagascar in 1895, the French government, in response to an enquiry on the part of the United States, declared that the maintenance of the treaty of friendship and commerce, concluded between the United States and Madagascar, May 13, 1881, under which American consuls enjoyed certain rights of civil and criminal jurisdiction, would be inconsistent with the new order of things created by the occupation. At the same time assurance was given that the conventions applicable to the government and citizens of the United States in France or French possessions would be extended to the Island. After the passage of the law for the formal annexation of the Island as a French colony, the treaties previously existing between Madagascar and foreign countries were declared to be at an end, and the system of conventions in force in French colonies to be substituted therefor.[14]   A

formations Territoriales des Etats, 103, citing decree of the Court of Paris of December 1, 1879, (Sirey 1881, pt. 2, p. 145). See also Hall, Int. Law (6 ed.), 99. For a discussion of the question whether the kingdom of Italy was formed by the territorial aggrandizement of the kingdom of Sardinia, whose King became the King of Italy, or by the consolidation and extinguishment as well of the kingdom of Sardinia as of all the other Italian states, see Kiatibian, 81-103, citing Esperson (Journal du droit international privé, 1884, p. 366), Fiore (Id., 1878, p. 245), and Holtzendorff (Handbuch, II, 33).

14 For. Rel., 1896, pp. 123, 125. See also in this connection Influence de l' établissement d'un protectorat sur les traités by Paul Pic in Revue générale de droit international public (1896), III, 613. "It was in these circumstances, for instance, that no sooner had the law of the 6th August last been voted than the United States government, as I informed Mr. Howard in the interview I have already referred to, recognized, without making any objection, that the treaties concluded between them and the Queen of Madagascar were thereupon abrogated, and that the only conventional system which could be applied to their nationals as well as to their commerce in the Island was that which regulated their relations with France. This situation has furthermore been admitted by every other European country." Mr. Hanotaux to Sir E. Monson, April 23, 1897. Parl. Pap., Africa No. 8, (1897), (C. 8700), 60, 62. The British government recognized the right of French courts to exercise jurisdiction over British subjects in the Island (see Id., 60), but contended that under the arrangement between France and Great Britain of 1890, by which the protectorate of France was recognized by Great Britain, the former was bound to recognize the commercial rights of British subjects already established by treaty with Madagascar. See the Marquess of Salisbury to Sir E. Monson, July 9, 1898. Parl. Pap., France No. 1 (1899), (C. 9091), 19. As to the effect of the annexation of Algiers to France on the treaties between the United States and Algiers, see Mahoney v. United States (1869), 10 Wall. 62.

convention, for the renunciation of extraterritorial rights enjoyed by the United States in Zanzibar and the mainland dominions of the Sultan of Zanzibar within the British protectorate of East Africa, under the treaties of September 21, 1833 with the Sultan of Muscat and July 3, 1886 with Zanzibar, was concluded with Great Britain, as suzerain, February 25, 1905, and became effective in 1907, upon the renunication by other powers of similar rights.[15] Under the treaty of May 12, 1881, by which a French protectorate over Tunis was established, France undertook to guarantee the execution of the treaties then existing between Tunis and the different European powers. New treaties were subsequently concluded. By a convention concluded March 15, 1904, the United States expressly renounced the right to invoke in Tunis the stipulations of the treaties previously concluded with that country; and France expressly agreed to extend to the consuls and citizens of the United States in Tunis the advantages of all treaties and conventions existing between the United States and France.[15a] In the joint resolution of July 7, 1898, by which the Hawaiian Islands were annexed to the United States, it was declared that all treaties then existing between those Islands and foreign powers should forthwith cease, being replaced by the treaties then existing or thereafter to be concluded between the United States and such foreign powers.[16] In the agreement concluded between Japan and Korea, November 17, 1905, by which the former assumed full control of the foreign relations of the latter, it was expressly provided that the government of Japan undertook to see to the execution of treaties then existing between Korea and other powers.[17] By the treaty of August 29,

15 101 Brit. and For. State Papers 231-239, 648.

15a "There has as yet been no change in the old treaties, but * * * negotiations tending to extend French treaties to the protectorate of Tunis, in lieu of the old United States treaties with the Bey, have been proposed by the French government and are now under consideration." Mr. Day, Assist. Secretary of State, to Mr. Gorham, November 16, 1897, Moore, Int. Law Digest, V, 402.

16 30 States at L. 750. See Mr. Sherman, Secretary of State, to Mr. Toru Hoshi, Japanese minister, June 25, 1897, Moore, Int. Law Digest, V, 349; Mr. Bacon, Secretary of State, to the Belgian minister, February 13, 1909, For. Rel., 1909, p. 38. As to the effect of annexation on private debts, see 22 Op. Atty. Gen. 583; Hall, 99; Rivier, I, 70, 213. That this abrogation of the treaties did not extinguish any vested rights, see Moore, Int. Law Digest, I, 504.

17 Art. II. 98 Brit. and For. State Papers 1140.

1910, the Emperor of Korea made complete and permanent cession to Japan of all rights of sovereignty over the whole of Korea. In announcing this complete annexation, the Japanese government declared that, the treaties theretofore concluded by Korea with foreign powers having ceased to be operative, the treaties of Japan would so far as practicable be applied to that territory.[18]

During the course of the Napoleonic wars the United Netherlands was, after various changes both in territory and in form of government, finally incorporated into the French Empire, and entirely disappeared as a separate nation. In the reconstruction of Europe at the Congress of Vienna in 1815, the Belgic and certain other provinces were joined to the United Netherlands and the whole designated as the kingdom of the Netherlands. The state thus formed, although in general considered the successor to, differed in name, territory, and form of government from, the state which had entered into the treaty of October 8, 1782 with the United States. In the negotiations immediately following the restoration of 1815, the government of the Netherlands took the view that the treaty was no longer in force. This was not at the time questioned by the United States. Later, in 1818 and 1819, during the negotiations for a settlement of spoliation claims, the government of the United States, however, contended that the treaty was not annulled; but the contention was not pressed. On subsequent occasions both governments have considered the treaty as at an end.[19]

It may be stated as a general principle that the territory of the annexed or incorporated state becomes impressed with the treaties of the acquiring state so far as locally applicable, to be determined in each instance by the character of the particular treaty and the nature of the union. The former republic of Texas, upon its admission as a State into the Union on terms of equality with the other States, undoubtedly became bound and privileged by all the treaties of the United States, of which it had become an integral part. On the other hand, it is conceivable that not all treaties of

18 For. Rel., 1910, pp. 681, 682. As to the termination of the treaties with the Lew Chew Islands, see For. Rel., 1873, I, pp. 553, 554, 555, 564.

19 For. Rel., 1873, II, p. 720. In University v. Miller, decided in 1831, the Supreme Court of North Carolina held that the question, whether the treaty continued in force after these changes, was one for the political, not the judicial, department to determine, and enforced the treaty as a law of the land. 14 N. C. 188, 193.

30

the United States became immediately applicable to the territory acquired from Spain in 1898, so long as held merely as "appurtenant" to the United States and not within the full operation of the Constitution and laws of the United States. The German government has denied the applicability of the naturalization convention, concluded between the United States and the North German Confederation, February 22, 1868, to the territory of Alsace-Lorraine, acquired from France in 1871, because of the peculiar relation which this territory bears to the Empire.[20]

Rights in or over the territory, or real rights,[21] which have been created or transferred by treaty, do not expire with the extinguishment of the state conveying such rights, but survive as against the succeeding territorial sovereign. The instruments under which such rights have passed out of the one state into the other remain unchanged as documents of title. Vattel states the rule as follows: "But it is here to be observed, that treaties or alliances which impose a mutual obligation to perform certain acts, and whose existence consequently depends on that of the contracting powers, are not to be confounded with those contracts by which a perfect right is once for all acquired, independent of any mutual performance of subsequent acts. If, for instance, a nation has forever ceded to a neighboring prince the right of fishing in a certain river, or that of keeping a garrison in a particular fortress, that prince does not lose his rights, even though the nation from whom he has received them happens to be subdued, or in any other manner subjected to a foreign dominion. His rights do not depend on the preservation of that nation; she

20 See Moore, Int. Law Digest, III, 364, et seq. It has also been maintained by the German government that "extradition between Alsace-Lorraine and the United States is not regulated by treaty." For. Rel., 1900, p. 520. See Article XVIII of the additional convention concluded at Frankfort, December 11, 1871, between France and Germany, as to the provisional application of certain treaties to Alsace-Lorraine. Hertslet's Map of Europe by Treaty, III, 1971. By Article XVII of the treaty of Zurich concluded November 10, 1859, between Austria, France and Sardinia, treaties were expressly extended to the territory acquired by Sardinia from Austria. Id., II, 1409. See also Article III of the treaty of March 29, 1864, for the union of the Ionian Islands to Greece, by which the treaty rights of the powers were continued. Id., III, 1592.

21 The distinction between jus in rem and jus in personam is indicated by early writers on the Roman law in the use of the words dominium and obligatio. Austin, Jurisprudence (5 ed. by Campbell), I, 383.

had alienated them; and the conqueror by whom she has been subjected can only take what belonged to her."[22] The annexing state, for instance, accepts the territory with the boundaries as established in the treaties between the annexed state and other nations. Although it is usually stated that all the treaties between the United States and Hanover fell with the incorporation of that kingdom into Prussia in 1866, the United States, under the convention of November 6, 1861, in consideration of a valuable money equivalent paid in lump sum, acquired a right to a complete and permanent exemption from the payment of the Stade and Brunshausen dues, and tolls of any kind, on American vessels ascending or descending the Elbe, which survived as against the new territorial sovereign. Likewise, by the convention concluded between the United States and Panama, November 18, 1903, to facilitate the construction of an interoceanic canal, permanent rights in the territory of Panama were acquired by the United States, for valuable considerations, which would survive any change of sovereignty over the Isthmus.

If a state, after incorporation into another, while losing its international personality still retains a territorial identity with full power of action over the subject-matter of a treaty previously concluded, the other contracting party may reasonably insist upon a recognition by the new or acquiring state of the continuing obligation of the treaty, so far as consistent with the new order of things. The continuance of the obligation under such circumstances would however result from the subsequent recognition or mutual agreements of the parties, rather than through state succession. A convention of extradition was concluded June 16, 1852, between the United States and Prussia and certain other States of the Germanic Confederation. By Article III of the naturalization convention concluded February 22, 1868, between the United States and the North German Confederation, of which these German States then formed a part, the extradition convention was extended to all of the States of the North German Confederation. In 1871, Prussia as well as all of the other States became merged in the German Empire. The several States of the Empire still retain the power of regulating, by agreement with foreign powers or by laws enacted for their own territories, the subject of extradition so far as not restricted by imperial law or trea-

22 Bk. II, c. XIII, §203.

ties. The King of Prussia, the former chief executive of the North German Confederation, also still retains as Emperor the power to carry out international obligations in this respect. Both governments have, by repeatedly requesting and granting the surrender of fugitives thereunder, recognized the convention as continuing in force; and the courts of the United States have continued to enforce it as the law of the land.[23] Likewise, the general treaty of amity and commerce concluded May 1, 1828, between the United States and Prussia, has been recognized by both governments as surviving the formation of the Empire.[24] The most-favored-nation clause of Article IX of this treaty has been invoked by the German government in favor of German products without regard to whether these products were the produce or manufacture of Prussia or of the other States of the Empire. "The treaty of 1828 with Prussia has always been considered by the German government as applicable to the whole of the Empire, although it was made with but a single State."[25] In the German note of

23 Terlinden v. Ames (1902), 184 U. S. 270. See, In re Stupp (1873), 11 Blatchf. 124; In re Wiegand, 14 Blatchf. 370; In re Behrendt (1884), 22 Fed. 699; In re Risch (1888), 36 Fed. 546; In re Krojanker (1890), 44 Fed. 482; In re Reiner (1903), 122 Fed. 109; Ex parte Glaser (1910), 176 Fed. 702, in which the convention has been recognized as continuing in force. The extradition convention of September 12, 1853, between the United States and Bavaria, has likewise been recognized as in force since the formation of the Empire. In re Hermann Thomas (1874), 12 Blatchf. 370, 379; Ex parte Zentner (1910), 188 Fed. 344.

24 Disconto Gesellschaft v. Umbreit, 208 U. S. 570, 581; 12 Op. Atty. Gen. 463; For. Rel., 1883, p. 369; For. Rel., 1885, pp. 404, 443, 444; For. Rel., 1887, p. 370; For. Rel., 1895, p. 539. See also United States v. Diekelman (1875), 92 U. S. 520; The Elwine Kreplin (1872), 9 Blatchf. 438; Ex parte Newman, 14 Wall. 152.

25 Mr. Jackson, Am. chargé d'affaires at Berlin, to Mr. Olney, Secretary of State, March 21, 1896. For. Rel., 1896, p. 192. Mr. Olney, as Attorney General, advised that, while the treaty was to be taken as operative as respects so much of the German Empire as constituted the kingdom of Prussia, no facts or considerations with which he had been made acquainted justified the assumption that it was to be taken as effective as regards other portions of the Empire. 21 Op. Atty. Gen. 80, 81. See also Mr. Olney, Secretary of State, to Baron von Thielmann, November 25, 1896, For. Rel., 1896, pp. 208, 209. In the case of the North German Lloyd S. S. Co. v. Hedden, the court observed that the treaty with the Hanseatic Republics of December 20, 1827, and the treaty with Prussia of May 1, 1828, had been "held by both the American and German governments to be valid for all Germany." 43 Fed. 17, 19.

April 5, 1915, and in the American reply thereto, respecting liability for the sinking of the American vessel Frye with its
cargo, both governments recognized the continuing validity of the
provisions in Article XIII of the treaty of July 11, 1799, renewed
in Article XII of the treaty of May 1, 1828, against the confiscation and condemnation of contraband.[25a]   The provisions respecting the rights of succession and inheritance in Article XIV of the
treaty of May 1, 1828 with Prussia,[26] in Articles I to III of the
treaty of January 21, 1845 with Bavaria,[27] in Articles II and III
of the treaty of May 14, 1845 with Saxony,[28] in Article VII of
the treaty of December 20, 1827 with the Hanseatic Republic of
Bremen,[29] and in Article II of the treaty of April 10, 1844 with
Württemberg[30] have been enforced as the law of the land over-
riding inconsistent State legislation by the courts of various of
the States of the United States in cases coming before them since
the formation of the Empire.   But the question as to the continuing obligation of a treaty is a political one, and, in the absence
of a determination by the proper department of the government,
the courts continue to recognize it as the law of the land.

In a note addressed to Texas, upon its incorporation into
the United States as a State of the Union by a joint resolution of Congress, it was asserted by the government of Great
Britain that the voluntary surrender of independence could not
annul existing treaties.[31]   The view of the United States in this
instance, which involved treaties of commerce, was, as expressed
by Mr. Fish, Secretary of State, September 18, 1876, that, the
union between the United States and Texas having been effected
by the legislation of the parties, treaties between the latter and

25a   Diplomatic Correspondence with Belligerent Governments (Printed
by the Department of State, May 27, 1915), 87-88.

26   In re Beck (1890), 11 N. Y. S. 199; Doehrel v. Hillmer (1897), 102
Io. 169; Wilcke v. Wilcke (1897), 102 Io. 173; Butschkowski v. Brecks
(1913), 94 Neb. 532.

27   Opel v. Shoup (1896), 100 Io. 407.

28   Ehrlich v. Weber (1905), 114 Tenn. 711.

29   Schultze v. Schultze (1893), 144 Ill. 290.

30   Wieland v. Renner (1883), 65 How. Pr. Repts. 245; Kull v. Kull
(1885), 37 Hun 476; Scharpf v. Schmidt (1898), 172 Ill. 255. See, contra,
In re Strobel's estate (1896), 39 N. Y. S. 169.

31   S. Doc. No. 375, 29th Cong., 1st Sess., 3, 5.   Treaties of commerce
had been concluded by Texas with France, September 25, 1839, and with
Great Britain, November 13, 1840.

foreign powers were necessarily cancelled, "so far at least as those treaties were inconsistent with the Constitution of this country, which requires customs duties to be uniform throughout the United States."[32] The British contention does not appear to have been pressed after the union with the United States was accomplished, and the character of the union became known. On June 20, 1895, the republics of Honduras, Nicaragua, and Salvador entered into a compact, by which they were to form a single political entity, called the Greater Republic of Central America, as regards intercourse with foreign powers, but were to retain their autonomy and independence as regards their internal affairs. In receiving, December 24, 1896, a minister from this union, the President of the United States expressly stated that the recognition was accorded with the understanding that the responsibility of each of the republics to the United States should remain wholly unaffected.[33] No change appears to have been made in the diplomatic representation of the United States in Central America.[34]

A state formed by separation from another, whether the personality of the original state still exists or is completely lost by disintegration, succeeds to such treaty burdens of the parent state as are permanent and attached to the territory embraced in the new state.[35] The treaty of limits concluded January 12, 1828, between the United States and Mexico, "having been entered into at a time when Texas formed a part of the United Mexican States," was formally recognized as binding by Texas after separation from Mexico.[36] The right of way or transit across the Isthmus of Panama upon any modes of communication then existing, or which might thereafter be constructed, guaranteed to the government and citizens of the United States in Article XXXV of the treaty of 1846 with New Granada, in return for

32 Wharton, Int. Law Digest, I, 23.

33 For. Rel., 1896, pp. 370, 390.

34 President McKinley, annual message, December 5, 1898, For. Rel., 1898, p. LXX. See for dissolution of the union, Id., 172-178. See as to the proposed union of the five states of Central America in 1885, For. Rel., 1885, pp. 81, 94, 95.

35 See Hall (6 ed.), 92; Rivier, I, 72-73, II, 228; Fiore, §§346-356; Bluntschli, §47; Westlake, I, 59, et seq.; President Roosevelt, message to Congress, January 4, 1904, For. Rel., 1903, p. 278.

36 Treaties and Conventions (1889 ed.), 1079. See also United States v. Texas, 143 U. S. 621.

obligations assumed on the part of the United States, was declared by the government of the United States, upon the separation of the State of Panama from Colombia in 1903, to be a burden on the territory in the nature of a covenant running with the land, to the duties and benefits of which the new state of Panama succeeded. "The treaty vested in the United States a substantial property right carved out of the rights of sovereignty and property which New Granada then had and possessed over the said territory. The name of New Granada has passed away and its territory has been divided. Its successor, the government of Colombia, has ceased to own any property in the Isthmus. A new republic, that of Panama, which was at one time a sovereign state, and at another time a mere department of the successive confederations known as New Granada and Colombia, has now succeeded to the rights which first one and then the other formerly exercised over the Isthmus. But as long as the Isthmus endures, the mere geographical fact of its existence, and the peculiar interest therein which is required by our position, perpetuate the solemn contract which binds the holders of the territory to respect our right to freedom of transit across it, and binds us in return to safeguard for the Isthmus and the world the exercise of that inestimable privilege."[37] By Article XCII of the general treaty of Vienna of June 9, 1815, a portion of the territory of Savoy belonging to Sardinia was made a part of the neutrality of Switzerland as recognized and guaranteed by the signatory powers.[38] These provisions as to the neutrality of Savoy were expressly adopted by Sardinia and Switzerland in Article VII of the treaty concluded by them at Turin, March 16, 1816.[39] In the treaty concluded at Turin, March 24, 1860, between France and Sardinia, for the transfer of Savoy and Nice by the latter to the former, the contracting parties expressly recognized that Sardinia could transfer the neutralized parts of Savoy only on the conditions under which she possessed them, and that it would be incumbent on France to come to an understanding on this subject both with the powers represented at the Congress of Vienna, and with the Swiss

37 President Roosevelt, annual message, December 7, 1903, For. Rel., 1903, p. XXXIII. See also special message of January 4, 1904, and note of Mr. Hay, Secretary of State, to General Reyes, special minister from Colombia, January 5, 1904. Id., 277, 305.

38 Hertslet's May of Europe by Treaty, I, 262.

39 Id., I, 427.

Confederation, and to give them the guarantees required by the stipulations in the treaty of Vienna.[40] After the cession of the Sulu Islands by Spain to the United States under the treaty of peace of 1898, it was diplomatically urged by the German government that certain protocols concluded between Spain, Germany, and Great Britain, March 11, 1877, and March 7, 1885, to define the rights of trade and commerce to be enjoyed by those powers in the Islands, were of merely local application and were accordingly not affected by a change of sovereignty over the territory to which they applied.[41] The reply of the United States was that the agreements, being of a commercial character, did not attach to the soil or become a lien upon the territory which the new sovereign was bound to assume, but were at an end.[42]

The doctrine of the liability of the seceding portion to treaty obligations of the parent state has in some instances been asserted in latitude sufficient to include those of a purely national character. Upon what principle of law the doctrine is based is not clear. There can be no doubt that the parties may by mutual agreement provide for the continued application of the treaties. In 1823, during the war by which Colombia established her independence of Spain, John Quincy Adams, Secretary of State of the United States, declared the provision, that free ships should make free goods in Article XV of the treaty between the United States and Spain concluded in 1795, when Colombia was a part of the Spanish nation, to be binding on Colombia after her declaration of independence. "To all the engagements of Spain with other nations affecting their rights and interests, Colombia, so far as she was affected by them, remains bound in honor and in justice. The stipulation now referred to is of that character."[43] This view was reasserted by Mr. Forsyth, Secretary of State, in 1839, and adopted by the United States and Ecuadorian mixed claims com-

---

40 Id., II, 1429, 1430. See for proposals of the French government to this end, and reply of the British government, Id., 1448, 1450. No conference for this purpose appears to have been held. See for protest of Switzerland against the transfer as a violation of the pledge of neutrality, Id., 1415, 1435.

41 The German ambassador to the Secretary of State, July 31, 1900.

42 Magoon's Reports, 302, 303, 316, 317.

43 J. Q. Adams, Secretary of State, to Mr. Anderson, minister to Colombia, May 27, 1823. MSS. Inst., IX, 307; Moore, Int. Arb., II, 1574; Moore, Int. Law Digest, V, 341.

mission under the convention of November 25, 1862. Mr. Has-
saurek, the American commissioner, in the opinion for the commission, said: "That a state never loses any of its rights, nor is
discharged from any of its obligations, by a change in the form
of its civil government, is one of the fundamental principles of
international law. It applies, by analogy, to cases such as the
one before us, where one part of a nation separates itself from
the other. It is evident that on the creation of a new state, by a
division of territory, that new state has a sovereign right to enter
into new treaties and engagements with other nations; but until
it actually does, the treaties by which it was bound as a part of
the whole state will remain binding on the new state and its subjects."[44] The government of the United States, upon recognizing
Texas as an independent state, gave notice that it considered the
treaty of amity, commerce and navigation concluded between the
United States and Mexico, April 5, 1831, as mutually binding
upon the United States and Texas. The treaty was subsequently
recognized by Texas.[45]   In the Berlin Congress of 1878, when

44 Moore, Int. Arb., III, 3221, 3223.
45 H. Doc. No. 12, 27th Cong., 2d Sess. Mr. Forsyth, Secretary of
State, in a communication to Messrs. Wharton and Hunt, Texan commissioners, March 13, 1837, said: "The President considers the Texan flag
as entitled to all the privileges stipulated for the Mexican flag in the treaty
between the United States and Mexico, and the United States will claim
for their flag all the benefits of that treaty in the Texan ports until some
other arrangement shall be made between the two governments." Notes
to Texan Legation, VI, 1. In a note dated June 23, 1838, Mr. Irion, Secretary of State of Texas, advised Mr. La Branche, Am. chargé d'affaires
in Texas: "With regard to your note of the 23 of March transmitting
a copy of the Treasury circular of the United States, dated 2d February,
by which the fifth and sixth articles of the treaty of amity, navigation and
commerce existing between the United States and Mexico are declared to
be binding on Texas, I have the honor to state that the President having
considered the subject directs me to inform you that the stipulations indicated by the circular will be observed by this government. The application
on the part of the United States relative to the treaty aforesaid, calling
on this government for a declaration whether or not it considers the whole
treaty obligatory, has also been submitted to his Excellency for consideration, respecting which I am likewise directed to state that it will be observed by this government till a new treaty shall be formed." Enclosure
in despatch No. 11 of June 24, 1838. See also note from Mr. Irion, December 8, 1838, enclosed in despatch No. 14, of December 12, 1838. "The
treaty between the United States and Mexico of the 5th of April, 1831,
being considered and acknowledged as mutually binding upon the United

the subject of the future status of Servia and Bulgaria was under consideration, Bismarck declared that he regarded it as a principle of the law of nations, which could only be confirmed by a declaration of the congress, that a province might not by separation from a state enfranchise itself from the treaties to which it had up to that time been subjected.[46]   It was expressly stipulated in the general treaty, signed at the close of the congress, with respect to Servia,—which was constituted an independent state— that the conditions of commercial intercourse with foreign countries, the immunities and privileges of foreign subjects, as well as the rights of consular jurisdiction and protection, should remain in full force until replaced by new arrangements.[47]   With respect to Bulgaria, which was constituted an autonomous principality, nominally under the suzerainty of the Sultan, it was provided that all treaties existing between the Porte and foreign powers should be maintained.[48]

Upon the dissolution of the union between Norway and Sweden in 1905, each of these states gave notice that it considered the treaties theretofore concluded in common and applicable to both kingdoms, as continuing in force and binding on each of them separately.   Many treaties had been concluded separately for the two kingdoms, and no question could arise as to the survival of such treaties.[49]   It was the expressed view of the government of the United States that the treaties then existing between the United States and Sweden and Norway were severally binding on each of the two kingdoms and unaffected by the separation.[50]   The British government in acknowledging the receipt of the notices observed that the dissolution of the union undoubtedly afforded Great Britain the right to examine de

States and the republic of Texas, you will make yourself familiar with its provisions." Mr. Forsyth, Secretary of State, to Mr. Flood, chargé d'affaires in Texas, April 25, 1840. MSS. Inst. I, 22. See, for termination of the commercial articles of the treaty pursuant to notive given by the Texan government, May 19, 1841, Id., 32.

46   69 Brit. and For. State Papers 934, 961.

47   Art. XXXVII.   Hertslet's Map of Europe by Treaty, IV, 2787.

48   Art. VIII.   See also Arts. X and XXXVIII.

49   Mr. Grip, Swedish minister, to Mr. Root, Secretary of State, November 20, 1905. For. Rel., 1905, p. 872.   Mr. Hauge, Norwegian chargé d'affaires, to Mr. Root, Secretary of State, December 7, 1905, Id., p. 873.

50   Mr. Root, Secretary of State, to the Japanese minister, November 10, 1905. Id., pp. 867, 868.

novo the treaty engagements by which it was bound to the "dual monarchy."[51] If the union, which had existed since 1815, be considered merely personal, in which both states had a common head or representative, a common agent, in the conduct of foreign relations, no doubt could exist as to the continuing force of the treaties, since a mere dissolution of the union would effect no change in the identity of the two states, the real parties to the treaties. Upon the division in 1831 of the republic of Colombia into the three republics of Ecuador, New Granada and Venezuela, each of the republics so formed assumed a pro rata share of the existing financial obligations, and asserted the right to the benefits of the treaties previously concluded by Colombia.[52] A general treaty of commerce and navigation concluded with the United States, November 30, 1836, by Santa Cruz as "Protector of the North and South Peruvian States, President of the Republic of Bolivia, charged with the direction of the foreign relations of the Peru-Bolivia Confederation," was repudiated by Peru after the dissolution of the Confederation on the ground that it had been concluded by an invader and not in accordance with the constitutional requirements. Mr. Buchanan, Secretary of State, maintained that Peru was not released from the treaty by the mere fact of dissolution. The question was disposed of by the conclusion of a new treaty.[53]

51 Marquess of Lansdowne to Baron de Bildt, Swedish minister, November 16, 1905; and Marquess of Lansdowne to M. Irgens, November 23, 1905. 98 Brit. and For. State Papers 833-837.

52 Moore, Int. Arb., III, 3225. Mr. Forsyth, Secretary of State, to Mr. Semple, chargé d'affaires at Bogata, February 12, 1839. MSS. Inst. to Colombia, XV, 67; same to same, October 20, 1839, Id., 69; Mr. Forsyth to Mr. McAfee, July 18, 1836, Id., 30. A convention of commerce and navigation concluded April 18, 1829, between Great Britain and Colombia, was expressly adopted and confirmed as to Venezuela by a convention concluded October 29, 1834. Handbook of Commercial Treaties between Great Britain and Foreign Powers (1912), 1037.

53 In 1835, Santa Cruz, the President of Bolivia, invaded Peru, assumed control of the government, and in 1836 issued a proclamation dividing Peru into two States—North Peru and South Peru, which together with Bolivia he designated the Peru-Bolivia Confederation. In this capacity he concluded treaties with the United States and Great Britain. In 1839, he was driven from Peru. See Señor Osma, Peruvian minister, to Mr. Buchanan, Secretary of State, April 22, 1847. MSS. Notes from Peruvian Legation; Mr. Buchanan to Sr. Osma, June 9, 1847. MSS. Notes to Peruvian Legation, I, 2. See also declaration signed February 9, 1848, by Mr. Buchanan and Sr. Osma.

§180. Rebus Sic Stantibus.—It appears to have been a maxim of the early writers on the civil law that *conventio omnis intelligitur rebus sic stantibus.*[54] Grotius limits the application of the maxim, as a condition to the continuing validity of treaties, to cases in which it is clear that the existing state of things was the sole cause of the agreement.[55] And Vattel says: "But we ought to be very cautious and moderate in the application of the present rule: it would be a shameful perversion of it, to take advantage of every change that happens in the state of affairs, in order to disengage ourselves from our promises: were such conduct adopted, there could be no dependence placed on any promise whatever. That state of things alone, in consideration of which the promise was made, is essential to the promise: and it is only by a change in that state, that the effect of the promise can be lawfully prevented or suspended."[56] G. F. von Martens also says that a "total change of circumstances which, at the time of making the treaty, had the force of conditions, renders the contract no longer obligatory, and when the object of the treaty ceases to exist, the treaty ceases also."[57] Phillimore states the rule as follows: "When that state of things which was essential to, and the moving cause of, the promise or engagement, has undergone a material change, or has ceased, the foundation of the promise or engagement is gone, and their obligation has ceased. This proposition rests upon the principle that the condition of rebus sic stantibus is tacitly annexed to every covenant."[58] The rule has been adopted by most modern writers. Oppenheim says: "The vast majority of publicists, as well as the governments of the members of the family of nations, defend the principle *conventio omnis intelligitur rebus sic stantibus,* and they agree, therefore, that all treaties are concluded under the tacit condition rebus sic

54 An early invocation of the principle is found in the argument of Lyciscus, the Acarnarian envoy at Sparta, recorded at Polybius as follows: "If the circumstances are the same now as at the time when you made alliance with the Aetolians then your policy ought to remain on the same lines. * * * But if they have been entirely changed, then it is fair that you should now deliberate on the demands made to you as on a matter entirely new and unprejudiced." Bk. IX, 37. Cited in Phillipson, Int. Law and Custom in Ancient Greece and Rome, I, 409.

55 Bk. II, c. XVI, §25.

56 Bk. II, c. XVII, §296.

57 Law of Nations (Cobbett's translation, 4 ed.), 352.

58 Int. Law (2 ed.), II, 109.

stantibus."[59] It has been held by the Court of Claims of the United States, in applying the principles of international law governing the relations between the United States and France during the period which gave rise to the so-called French spoliation claims, that the United States was justified in annulling in 1798 the treaties concluded with France in 1778, because of the infractions on the part of France and of the change in essential conditions; and that the treaties thereupon ceased to operate as international compacts.[60] The court, by Davis, J., said: "A treaty which on its face is of indefinite duration and which contains no clause providing for its termination may be annulled by one of the parties under certain circumstances. As between the nations it is in its nature a contract, and if the consideration fail, for example, or if its important provisions be broken by one party, the other may, at its option, declare it terminated. * * * We are of opinion that the circumstances justified the United States in annulling the treaties of 1778; that the act was a valid one, not only as a municipal statute but as between the nations; and that thereafter the compacts were ended."[61]

The danger in the application of a rule of such uncertain standard is pointed out by Vattel. It may easily serve as a pretext for release from onerous treaty obligations. Such a change as would justify the invocation of the rule would seldom not be recognized by the other party as ground for new negotiations in respect of the subject matter based upon other considerations. Such was the case when Russia sought in 1870 release from the obligation imposed by the treaty of Paris of 1856 with respect to the neutralization of the Black Sea.[62] Likewise, the abrogation of the treaty of 1850 between the United States and Great Britain, concerning an interoceanic canal, was accomplished by the substitution of a new convention in 1901, wherein the change of conditions was

59 Int. Law (2 ed.), I, 572. See Hall (6 ed.), 342; F. de Martens (translation by Léo, 1883), 510-515; Klüber (2 ed.), §165; Bluntschli (translation by Lardy), Afts. 415, 460; Heffter (translation by Bergson, 1883), §81; Bonfils (7 ed.), §857; Taylor, §394; S. Doc. No. 31, 63d Cong., 1st Sess.; and Nys (1912 ed.), II, 532.

60 Hooper v. United States (1887), 22 C. Cls. 408; The Brig William (1888), 23 C. Cls. 201.

61 22 C. Cls. 408, 416, 425.

62 See Earl Granville's reply to the Russian note of denunciation, Hertslet's Map of Europe by Treaty, III, 1898, 1900.

recognized. "Evidently the right of denouncing a treaty is an imperfect one, demanding for its perfection in any case better definition than in the present state of international law is attainable, but not therefore to be condemned in toto, only to be exercised with a grave sense of moral responsibility."[63]   States in invoking the rule have usually sought to place the right of denunciation also upon other grounds, such as a previous breach of the treaty by the other party.   This was the case in the instances above noted with reference to the French treaties of 1778, the treaty between the United States and Great Britain of 1850, and the treaty of Paris of 1856.   So also Servia in asserting in 1913 a right either to a revision or to a denunciation of the treaty with Bulgaria of (February 29) March 13, 1912, as to the line of delimitation in Macedonia, claimed the right on the ground of a previous breach of the treaty by Bulgaria as well as on the ground that the war against Turkey had been changed by the aggressive action of Bulgaria in Thrace from one of liberation, as contemplated by the parties at the time of the conclusion of the treaty, to one of conquest, and that Servia had lost the Adriatic littoral while Bulgaria had acquired Thrace, a condition not contemplated by the parties when the treaty was concluded.   The issue was determined only by force of arms.[64]

§181. **Effect of War.**—It is the usual but not uniform practice for the parties expressly to agree in the treaty of peace as to the renewal of treaties existing between them at the outbreak of the war.[65]   But without such express stipulation as to renewal, it is

---

63 Westlake, Int. Law (2 ed.), I, 296.

64 Report of International Commission of Inquiry into the Balkan Wars, 43, 60, 61, 208-210.

65 Prior to the French Revolution, this express renewal regularly embraced in its terms all treaties between the parties of an executed as well as of an executory character, not inconsistent with the new treaty of peace, concluded since the Peace of Westphalia. For instance, by Article II of the treaty of peace signed at Paris, February 10, 1763, "the treaties of Westphalia of 1648; those of Madrid, between the crowns of Great Britain and Spain, of 1667 and 1670; the treaties of peace of Nimeguen of 1678 and 1679; of Ryswyck of 1697; those of peace and of commerce of Utrecht of 1713; that of Baden of 1714; the treaty of the triple alliance of The Hague of 1717; that of the quadruple alliance of London of 1718; the treaty of peace of Vienna of 1738; the definitive treaty of Aix-la-Chapelle of 1748; and that of Madrid, between the crowns of Great Britain and Spain, of 1750; as well as the treaties between the crowns of

now generally agreed that there are treaty obligations of such character as will survive a state of war. The tribunal of arbitration on the North Atlantic coast fisheries in its decision rendered, September 7, 1910, said: "International law in its modern development recognizes that a great number of treaty obligations are not annulled by war, but at most suspended by it."[66] That acts previously done or rights already transferred under the sanction of a treaty are not nullified by a mere state of war is not open to doubt. Treaties that are intended to establish a permanent status between the parties by an act done once for all, designated by earlier writers as transitory conventions,[67] and by an eminent recent authority as depositive,[68] are essentially documents of title, and as such are not affected by a subsequent war. Treaties by which territory has been ceded or boundaries established or permanent rights in territory acknowledged are of this character. Like other rights they are however subject to the law of conquest. In the controversy between the United States and Great Britain, as to the effect of the war of 1812 on the "liberties" to be enjoyed by American fishermen in British dominions in North America, as defined in the treaty of 1783, of which liberties the treaty of Ghent made no mention, it was contended by John Quincy Adams, minister of the United States at London, that the treaty of 1783 was not in its general provisions one of those, which, by common understanding and usages of civilized nations, could be considered as annulled by a subsequent war between the parties. The treaty was considered by Adams, as it had also been by the other American commissioners who negotiated the treaty of Ghent, as one of partition, in which the rights thereafter to be enjoyed by each party were defined, and in which nothing was received by

Spain and Portugal, of the 13th of February, 1668; of the 6th of February, 1715; and of the 12th of February, 1761; and that of the 11th of April, 1713, between France and Portugal, with the guaranties of Great Britain; * * * as well as all the treaties in general, which subsisted between the high contracting parties before the war" were renewed and confirmed in all points not inconsistent with the new treaty as if inserted word for word. Chalmers, Collection of Treaties, I, 470.

66 S. Doc. No. 870, 61st Cong., 3d Sess., I, 75.

67 Vattel, Bk. II, c. XII, §192; G. F. von Martens, Law of Nations (Cobbett's translation, 4 ed.), 53, 56; Wheaton, Elements of Int. Law, §268.

68 Westlake, Int. Law (2 ed.), I, 60.

the United States as a grant.[69]   To this contention, Lord Bathurst, on October 30, 1815, replied: "To a position of this novel
nature Great Britain can not accede.   She knows of no exception

---

69 See McIlvaine v. Coxe's Lessee, 4 Cranch 209, 212; Harcourt v.
Gaillard, 12 Wheat. 523, 527. In the first conference, August 8, 1814, in the
negotiations at Ghent, the British commissioners stated that Great Britain
did not intend "to grant to the United States gratuitously the privileges
formerly granted by treaty to them of fishing within the limits of British
sovereignty, and of using the shores of British territories for purposes connected with the fisheries." (Appendix to Case of the United States, North
Atlantic Coast Fisheries Arbitration. S. Doc. No. 870, 61st Cong., 3d
Sess., II, 242). To this suggestion the American commissioners replied
that they were not authorized to bring into discussion any of the rights
or liberties which the United States had theretofore enjoyed in relation
to the fisheries; that "from their nature and from the peculiar character
of the treaty of 1783, by which they were recognized, no further stipulation" had been deemed necessary to entitle the United States to continue in
their full enjoyment. (Id., 250). At a later conference, December 1, 1814,
the American commissioners, however, proposed, as a result of an attempt of
the British commissioners to secure an express stipulation as to the right of
British subjects to navigate the Mississippi, to insert in the treaty a provision declaring that the inhabitants of the United States should "continue to
enjoy the liberty to take, dry and cure fish in places within the exclusive
jurisdiction of Great Britain, as secured by the former treaty of peace,"
together with a provision continuing the freedom of navigation of the
Mississippi to British subjects. (Id., 253). This proposal was met by the
British commissioners with a counter-proposal by which the two countries should agree to enter into future negotiations respecting the terms,
conditions and regulations under which the inhabitants of the United
States should have the liberty of taking and curing fish in certain parts
of British dominions in North America. (Id., 254). To this the American
commissioners refused to agree, as implying an abandonment by the United
States of a right in the fisheries; but at the same time they declared their
willingness to leave the treaty silent on the subject. (Id., 255). The
British commissioners, although reiterating their original view as expressed in the conference of August 8, agreed to omit any reference to
the subject in the treaty. (Id., 256). The American commissioners—
John Quincy Adams, James A. Bayard, Henry Clay, Jonathan Russell,
and Albert Gallatin—in their final report dated December 25, 1814, transmitting the treaty to the Secretary of State, said: "We contended that the
whole treaty of 1783 must be considered as one entire and permanent compact, not liable, like ordinary treaties, to be abrogated by a subsequent war
between the parties to it; as an instrument recognizing the rights and
liberties enjoyed by the people of the United States as an independent
nation, and containing the terms and conditions on which the two parts
of one empire had mutually agreed, thenceforth, to constitute two dis-
tince and separate nations. In consenting, by that treaty, that a part of

to the rule, that all treaties are put an end to by a subsequent war between the same parties." His lordship doubtless used the term treaty in the restricted sense of executory contracts, designated by earlier writers "treaties properly so-called," in contradistinction to "transitory conventions," for he admitted that the treaty contained irrevocable provisions, and that it was by no means unusual for treaties to contain recognitions and acknowledgments of title in the nature of perpetual obligation; and he further added that the "right" to take fish as recognized in Article III of the treaty was of this permanent character, but that the "liberty" to take fish as therein provided was a concession "strictly dependent on the treaty itself"; that the claim of an independent state to occupy and use at its discretion any portion of the territory of another, without compensation or corresponding indulgence, could not rest on any other foundation than conventional stipulation.[70] A new treaty was concluded October 20, 1818, which defined the fishery liberties forever thereafter to be enjoyed by inhabitants of the United States within British dominions in North America, and which contained an express renunciation on the part of the United States of any liberty theretofore enjoyed or

the North American continent should remain subject to the British jurisdiction, the people of the United States had reserved to themselves the liberty, which they had ever before enjoyed, of fishing upon that part of its coasts, and of drying and curing fish upon the shores, and this reservation had been agreed to by the other contracting party. We saw not why this liberty, then no new grant, but the mere recognition of a prior right always enjoyed, should be forfeited by war, any more than any other of the rights of our national independence; or why we should need a new stipulation for its enjoyment more than we needed a new article to declare that the King of Great Britain treated with us as free, sovereign, and independent States." (Id., 258). Mr. Monroe, Secretary of State, in his instructions to Mr. Adams, July 21, 1815, said: "Every right appertaining to the fisheries, which was secured by the treaty of 1783, stands now as unshaken and perfect as it then did, constituting a vital part of our political existence, and resting on the same solid foundation as our independence itself. In the act of dismemberment and partition, the rights of each party were distinctly defined. So much of territory and incidental rights were allotted to one, so much to the other; and as well might it be said, because our boundary had not been retraced in the late treaty, in every part, that certain portions of our territory had reverted to England, as that our right to fish, by whatever name secured, had experienced that fate." (Id., 263).

70 Am. State Papers, For. Rel., IV, 352, 354; Moore, Columbia Law Review, I, 217.

claimed within three marine miles of any of the coasts, bays, creeks or harbours of British dominions, not included in the limits as therein defined.[71] The tribunal in the North Atlantic coast fisheries arbitration held "that the treaty of 1818 was in different terms, and very different in extent, from that of 1783, and was made for different considerations. It was, in other words, a new grant."[72]

In 1823, the Supreme Court of the United States was called upon to decide as to the effect of the war of 1812 upon private rights vested under Article VI of the treaty of 1783, and Article IX of the treaty of 1794, with Great Britain. It was held that even the termination of a treaty could not divest rights of property already vested under it. Mr. Justice Washington, in the opinion of the court, said: "But we are not inclined to admit the doctrine urged at the bar, that treaties become extinguished, ipso facto, by war between the two governments, unless they should be revived by an express or implied renewal on the return of peace. * * * There may be treaties of such a nature, as to their object and import, as that war will put an end to them; but where treaties contemplate a permanent arrangement of territorial, and other national rights, or which, in their terms, are meant to provide for the event of an intervening war, it would be against every principle of just interpretation to hold them extinguished by the event of war. If such were the law, even the treaty of 1783, so far as it fixed our limits, and acknowledged our independence, would be gone, and we should have had again to struggle for both upon original revolutionary principles. Such a construction was never asserted, and would be so monstrous as to supersede all reasoning. We think, therefore, that treaties stipulating for permanent rights, and general arrangements, and professing to aim at perpetuity, and to deal with case of war as well as of peace, do not cease on the occurrence of war, but are, at most, only suspended while it lasts; and unless they are waived by the parties, or new and repugnant stipulations are made, they revive in their

71 This express renunciation was considered important by the American negotiators. See Messrs. Gallatin and Rush to Mr. Adams, October 20, 1818, S. Doc. No. 870, 61st Cong., 3d Sess., II, 307. The law officers of the Crown, in an opinion dated August 30, 1841, advised "that the treaty of 1783 was annulled by the war of 1812." Id., III, 1047.

72 Id., I, 80.

operation at the return of peace."[73] Article IX of the treaty of 1794 provided that the citizens of the one country then holding lands in the territory of the other should continue to hold them, and might sell or devise the same in like manner as natives, and that neither they nor their heirs or assigns should, as regards these lands and the legal remedies incident thereto, be regarded as aliens. This stipulation was likewise held by the High Court of Chancery of Great Britain to be permanent in its operation as to rights vested on the date of the exchange of ratifications of the treaty. Sir John Leach, Master of the Rolls, in pronouncing the decision said: "The relations, which had subsisted between Great Britain and America, when they formed one empire, led to the introduction of the ninth section of the treaty of 1794, and made it highly reasonable that the subjects of the two parts of the divided empire should, notwithstanding the separation, be protected in the mutual enjoyment of their landed property; and, the privileges of natives being reciprocally given, not only to the actual possessors of lands, but to their heirs and assigns, it is a reasonable construction that it was the intention of the treaty that the operation of the treaty should be permanent, and not depend upon the continuance of a state of peace."[74]

By Article I of a convention signed February 17, 1834, Spain

73 Society for Propagation of Gospel, &c. v. New Haven, et al., 8 Wheat. 464, 494-495. See also Society for Propagation of Gospel, &c. v. Wheeler, et al. (1814), 2 Gal. 105, 136.

74 Sutton v. Sutton, 1 Russell & Mylne 663, 675. "As affecting and securing the rights of individuals, the provisions in the ninth article [of the treaty of 1794] for titles in lands, may be considered as executed by the acceptance and ratification of the treaty; but the remedies incident to those titles, as well as the remedies incident to the personal rights of the individuals, are necessarily suspended during the state of war. * * * It is the case therefore of lands holden in 1794, by a British subject, if that is the national character of the demandant. It is a right not forfeited by the declaration of war, but the remedy is suspended. He is not to be answered upon this demand, until the restoration of peace." Sewall, C. J., Hutchinson v. Brock (1814), 11 Mass. 119, 122, 124. "There seems, however, to be no doubt that this article is one of those stipulations which are distinguished by some of the writers on the law of nations as *real* in their own nature; and which are accomplished by the act of ratification, so that they cannot be dissolved by any subsequent event." Jackson, J., Fox v. Southack, et al. (1815), 12 Mass. 143, 148. The war of 1812 did not affect the rights of British creditors under the treaty of 1783 otherwise than to suspend the right of suing. McNair v. Ragland (1830), 16 N. C. 516.

agreed to pay to the United States as the balance due on account of claims of American citizens for seizures and confiscations during the war between Spain and her revolting American colonies, and in final settlement thereof, the sum of twelve millions of rials vellon, in one or several inscriptions, as preferred by the government of the United States, of "perpetual rents, on the great book of the consolidated debt of Spain," bearing interest at five per cent. per annum. Interest on the inscription or inscriptions was to be paid every six months. Certain certificates of "renta perpetua de España" were duly issued by Spain to carry out the treaty, and distributed by the government of the United States to the claimants in settlement of their claims against Spain released by the convention. In discharge of the interest due the holders of these certificates, there was paid annually, since 1847, to the government of the United States by the Spanish government the sum of $28,500.[75] The convention of 1834 was not referred to in the treaty of peace of December 10, 1898; and no provision for its renewal was made. On the usual date of payment in 1898, a state of war existed between the two countries, and the annual payment was not made. When this fact was first brought to the attention of the Spanish government in 1899, after the restoration of peace, reply was made that, since the debt arose "out of a treaty which was suspended in virtue of the late war," action on it should be deferred until the important question of the "renovation of the agreements celebrated between the two countries" had been decided by the two governments.[76] To this, the government of the United States replied that it considered the payment of the debt and the making of commercial, consular and extradition treaties as distinct matters, since the obligation to pay the debt was made perpetual by the provisions of the convention.[77] Subsequently, the Spanish government admitted a distinction in this respect by making, in December, 1899, independently of the question of the renewal of other treaties, the payment for the year 1899, as also for the year 1898.[78] Great Britain likewise continued after the Crimean War

75 Moore, Columbia Law Review, I, 213; For. Rel., 1899, pp. 708-714.
76 For. Rel., 1899, p. 709.
77 Id., 710.
78 By Article XXIX of the treaty of amity and commerce concluded between the two countries, July 3, 1902, the treaties antedating the treaty of peace were expressly abrogated, except the convention of 1834, which was continued in force.

the annual payments to Russia on the moiety of the Russian-Dutch loan (five per cent. in interest and one per cent. in reduction) assumed by Great Britain under the treaty of May 19, 1815, and renewed in the convention of November 16, 1831. It was however expressly provided in Article V of the treaty of 1815 that the payments should not be interrupted in the event of war between the parties, the Emperor of Russia "being actually bound to his creditors by a similar agreement." The purpose of the treaty was to afford to Great Britain "a guarantee that Russia would, on all questions concerning Belgium, identify her policy with that which the Court of London had deemed the best adapted for the maintenance of a just balance of power in Europe; and, on the other hand to secure to Russia the payment of a portion of her old Dutch debt, in consideration of the general arrangements of the Congress of Vienna, to which she had given her adhesion."[79]

Treaties entered into in contemplation of war and for the purpose of regulating belligerent operations and in derogation of belligerent rights are binding on the parties during war. Vattel, in discussing the general proposition that war annuls treaties, says: "Yet here we must except those treaties by which certain things are stipulated in case of a rupture,—as, for instance, the length of time to be allowed on each side for the subjects of the other nation to quit the country,—the neutrality of a town or province, insured by mutual consent, etc. Since, by treaties of this nature, we mean to provide for what shall be observed in case of a rupture, we renounce the right of cancelling them by a declaration of war."[80] States have from an early day entered into treaty stipulations of this character; and they are indeed worthless if not binding when the very state of affairs exists which was contemplated by the parties. In a decree of the Spanish government, April 23, 1898, on the outbreak of hostilities with the United States, it was declared that the state of war terminated all agreements, compacts and conventions which had been in force up to that time between the two countries.[81] In Ar-

79 18 Brit. and For. State Papers 928; Hertslet's Map of Europe by Treaty, I, 152; Twiss (War 2 ed.), 112.

80 Bk. III, c. X, §175. See also Rutherforth, Institutes of Natural Law (3 ed.), II, 590.

81 For. Rel., 1898, p. 774.

ticle XIII of the treaty of 1795, which treaty was specifically mentioned in the decree, it was stipulated that, in case of war between the parties, merchants in the cities and towns where they resided should be allowed one year for collecting and transporting their goods and merchandise. When the attention of the Spanish government was called to this article, it expressed an unwillingness to make any exception to the decree already issued, but offered to enter into a special agreement for the provisional application of the provisions of the article. The United States declined the proposal on the ground that the provisions being expressly applicable to a state of war between the contracting parties were not abrogated by it.[82] It is difficult to perceive how any greater obligation would be imposed on the belligerents to observe a special stipulation entered into after the outbreak of hostilities, than would result from engagements entered into, previously, solely with a view to a state of war. No decree of expulsion was issued.

Treaties between three or more parties are unaffected by a war between two of them so far as regards the obligations of either of them to the remaining party or parties. There exist many international conventions, which are intended to have general application and to establish uniformity of action among modern states in respect of their subject matter, and which are the result of the recognition by the parties of reciprocal and like duties of each toward all others. Such conventions differ in nature from special treaties which are the result of bargain; and, in the absence of any express provisions for renewal, they have been recognized as continuing in force upon the restoration of peace. The Spanish government, although it asserted at the outbreak of the war with the United States the general principle that a state of war puts an end to all treaties between the parties, admitted, in the negotiations for the renewal of treaties following the conclusion of peace, "as settled international law that all the general international conventions between civilized nations which existed before the war to which Spain and the United States were parties, such as the international postal union, the convention for submarine cables, the conventions on the subject of industrial property and Geneva Red Cross conventions were at most only temporarily suspended between the countries by the war and revived

82 Id., 972.

proprio vigore on the conclusion of peace."[83] The privileges of reciprocal registration of copyrights under the agreement between the two countries reached in 1895, and given effect in the United States by the proclamation of the President of July 10, 1895, were suspended during the period of the war, but upon the proclamation of the treaty of peace, April 11, 1899, the privileges were immediately accorded by the United States to subjects of Spain without any express renewal. No new proclamation was considered necessary. By exchange of notes in November, 1902, the agreement was expressly re-established as regards its operation in Spain.[84]

Treaties of alliance are necssarily dissolved by the outbreak of war between the contracting parties. The operation of agreements regulating commercial intercourse is, except by special agreement, suspended during hostilities between the parties. This is a necessary result of a state of war. Moreover, a belligerent in order to cripple an adversary may withhold any privilege of this character conferred by treaty.[85] Whether such treaties are merely suspended in their operation during the period of the war and revive on the restoration of peace, or are definitively terminated if not expressly renewed, is a question on which writers on international law are not agreed.[86] The practice of nations may, by implication at least, be considered as in derogation of the doctrine of the revival of such treaties proprio vigore. Moreover, it is the undoubted right of a belligerent to make the renewal of former treaty relations a condition of peace,—ultimately to be determined by the victor,—and the failure to do so might, in view of the usual practice of making express provision as to renewal, be considered as a waiver or an abandonment of that right.

The treaty of peace between the United States and Mexico of

83 Mr. Storer, Am. minister at Madrid, to Mr. Hay, Secretary of State, August 21, 1900.

84 Treaties, Conventions, &c. (1910 ed.), 1710.

85 Vattel, Bk. III, c. X, §175.

86 G. F. von Martens (Cobbett's translation, 4 ed.), 56; Calvo, IV, §1931, V, §3152; T. A. Walker, Science of Int. Law, 327; T. J. Lawrence, §§144-6; Heffter, §§181, 182; Bonfils, §860; Hall (6 ed.), 378; Halleck (Baker ed.), I, 346; Westlake (2 ed.), II, 32-35. See for summary of views of the various authorities, Moore, Columbia Law Review (1901), I, 209-223; Moore, Int. Law Digest, V, 382-385. See also project adopted by the Institute of International Law at its session in Christiania in August, 1912, Am. Journal of Int. Law, VII, 149, 153.

February 2, 1848 expressly provided that the treaty of commerce and navigation between the two countries of April 5, 1831, with the exception of the additional article thereto, was thereby "revived."[87]   By the treaty of peace between Austria and Sardinia signed at Milan, August 6, 1849, all treaties between the parties in force at the outbreak of the war were fully renewed and confirmed so far as not altered by that treaty.[88]   By the treaty of peace between Prussia and Denmark, signed at Berlin, July 2, 1850, all treaties were "re-established."[89]   In the treaty of Paris of March 30, 1856, at the close of the Crimean war, it was expressly stipulated that, until the treaties or conventions which existed before the war between the belligerent powers had been either renewed or replaced by new agreements, trade should be carried on in accordance with the regulations in force before the war; and that the subjects of the respective parties should in all other matters be treated upon the footing of the most-favored-nation.[90]   The treaty of Zurich of November 10, 1859, between Austria, France and Sardinia, confirmed as between Austria and Sardinia the treaties in force at the outbreak of the war so far as compatible with the new treaty.[91]   No such renewal was provided for as between Austria and France.   In the treaty of peace between Austria, Prussia and Denmark signed at Vienna, October 30, 1864, all treaties concluded before the war not abrogated or modified by the treaty were "re-established in their vigor."[92]   The treaty of peace between Austria and Prussia, signed at Prague, August 23, 1866, provided that all the conventions concluded between the contracting parties before the war were thereby again brought into force so far as by their nature they had not lost their effect by the dissolution of the relations of the Germanic Confedera-

87 Article XVII. See Richardson, Messages and Papers of the Presidents, IV, 537.
88 Art. II.
89 Art. II.
90 Art. XXXII. In the conference on March 25, 1856, Count Walewski had observed that, the state of war having invalidated the treaties which had existed between Russia and the belligerents, it was proper to insert a provisional stipulation as to the commercial relations of the parties. 46 Brit. and For. State Papers 17, 99.
91 Art. XVII.
92 Art. II.

tion.[93] The treaty of peace between Austria and Italy signed at
Vienna, October 3, 1866, likewise made provision for the temporary renewal of treaties.[94] In the treaty of Frankfort of May 10,
1871, at the close of the Franco-Prussian war, it was agreed that,
the treaties of commerce with the different Germanic States having been annulled by the war, the governments of the two countries would adopt as the basis of their commercial relations reciprocal most-favored-nation treatment. The article provided
further that the conventions of navigation, and those relative to
service of international railroads, and for the reciprocal protection of works of art should be renewed.[95] An additional convention signed December 11, 1871, revived, with reservations, treaties
existing before the war.[96] In the preliminary treaty of peace of
San Stefano between Russia and Turkey, signed March 3, 1878,
it was provided that all treaties of commerce and navigation, and
those relative to the status of Russian subjects within Turkish
dominions, and which had been abrogated by the state of war,
should come into force again so far as compatible with the new
treaty.[97] By the treaty of peace between Chile and Peru signed
at Lima, October 20, 1883, it was agreed that, until a special
treaty should be concluded, the mercantile relations between the
two countries should be the same as had existed before the war.[98]
The agreement of truce between Chile and Bolivia signed April
4, 1884, which served as a treaty of peace, provided for most-
favored-nation treatment in commercial privileges.[99] In the

---

93 Art. XIII. In the treaties of peace concluded by Prussia with the
other German States—with Württemburg, August 13, 1866 (Art. VII),
with Baden, August 17, 1866, (Art. VII), with Bavaria, August 22, 1866
(Arts. VII and VIII), with Hesse-Darmstadt, September 3, 1866 (Arts.
VII and VIII), with Saxe-Meiningen, October 8, 1866 (Art. II), and with
Saxony, October 21, 1866 (Arts. XI and XII),—provisions were inserted
for the renewal of treaties. Hertslet's Map of Europe by Treaty, III,
1703, 1708, 1713, 1731, 1769, 1774.

94 Arts. XX and XXI.

95 Art. XI.

96 Art. XVIII.

97 Art. XXIII.

98 Art. XI. The treaty of peace between Chile and Spain of June 12,
1883 provided that, until new treaties should be concluded, the state of
affairs which preceded the interruption of their relations was revived.
Art. III.

99 Art. V.

treaty of peace between China and Japan signed April 17, 1895, it was recognized that all treaties between the two countries had, "in consequence of the war," come to an end. The contracting parties engaged to appoint immediately upon the exchange of ratifications plenipotentiaries to conclude new treaties of commerce and navigation.[100] During the peace negotiations between the United States and Spain at Paris, the American commissioners, under instructions, proposed to insert in the treaty a clause expressly to provide that certain named treaties (comprising those which had not already been executed or become obsolete) should "be held to continue in force."[101] The Spanish commissioners rejected the proposal on the ground that the determination of what treaties were obsolete would involve a more extended examination than the commission was in a position to give; but they added that this did not imply that the two governments might not later take up the subject. The American commissioners further urged the express renewal of the articles on extradition, trade-marks and copyrights, and proposed to revive them temporarily by a modus vivendi, but this proposition was also rejected. Accordingly, no provision was inserted in the treaty of peace for the renewal of treaties. A new general treaty of amity and commerce was concluded, July 3, 1902. In Article XXIX of this treaty it is declared that all treaties and agreements between the United States and Spain "prior to the treaty of Paris shall be expressly abrogated and annulled" with the exception of the claims convention of February 17, 1834, "which is continued in force by the present convention." A new extradition convention was concluded, June 15, 1904.[102] In the treaty of peace between Japan and Russia concluded at Portsmouth, September 5, 1905, it was expressly provided that, the treaty of commerce and navigation between the two countries having been annulled by the war, the two governments engaged to adopt as the basis of their commercial relations, pending the conclusion of a new treaty for that purpose, the system of reciprocal most-favored-nation treat-

---

100 Art. VI.

101 S. Doc. No. 148, 56th Cong., 2d Sess., 7; S. Doc. No. 62, 55th Cong., 3d Sess., 249, 254.

102 The extradition conventions of 1877 and 1882 had been considered as at an end. See Mr. Hay, Secretary of State, to the governor of Porto Rico, June 19, 1900. Moore, Int. Law Digest, IV, 257. For the restoration of privileges of copyright registration, see supra, 451.

ment in respect of import and export duties, transit and tonnage dues, and the admission and treatment of agents, subjects, and vessels of the one in the territory of the other.[103]   The treaty of peace between Italy and Turkey signed at Lausanne, October 18, 1912, provided that all the treaties, conventions and engagements of any kind and nature, in force between the parties before the declaration of war, should again enter into immediate effect, and that the two governments, as also their respective subjects, should be placed toward one another in the identical situation in which they were before the outbreak of hostilities.[104]   No provision for the renewal of treaties appears to have been made in the treaty of peace between Turkey and the Balkan Allies signed at London, May (17) 30, 1913,[105] or in the treaty of peace between Bulgaria and Roumania, Greece, Montenegro and Servia signed at Bucharest, (July 28) August 10, 1913.[106]   The treaty of peace between Bulgaria and Turkey signed at Constantinople, September (16) 29, 1913, contained a provision that the two contracting parties bound themselves to "put back into force," immediately after the signing of the treaty, for a period of one year, the convention of commerce and navigation of February (6) 19, 1911, and the consular declaration of (November 18) December 2, 1909.   It was further agreed that a mixed commission should be appointed to negotiate new treaties in reference to these subjects.[107]   The treaty of peace between Greece and Turkey signed at Athens, November (1) 14, 1913, provided that all treaties, conventions and acts, concluded or in force at the time diplomatic relations between the parties were broken off, should be "restored in full force" upon the signature of the treaty.[108]   Similar provision was made in the treaty of peace between Servia and Turkey signed at Constantinople, March (1) 14, 1914.[108a]

In the British-Venezuelan protocol signed February 13, 1903, for the adjudication of claims of British subjects against Venezuela, it was expressly agreed that inasmuch as it might be con-

103 Art. XII.

104 Art. V. Am. Journal of Int. Law, Sup., VII, 59; Martens, Recueil de Traités (3 series), VII, 8.

105 Am. Journal of Int. Law, Sup., VIII, 12.

106 Id., 13.

107 Art. IV. Id., 31.

108 Art. II. Id., 46.

108a Art. I. Martens (3 series), VIII, 643.

tended that the establishment of a blockade of Venezuelan ports by the British naval forces had ipso facto created a state of war between Great Britain and Venezuela, and that any treaty between the two countries had thereby been abrogated, it should be recorded in an exchange of notes that the convention between the two countries of October 29, 1834 should be deemed to be renewed and confirmed pending the conclusion of a new treaty of amity and commerce.[109]   By exchange of notes on even date the treaty of 1834 was expressly renewed and confirmed.[110]   The protocol between Venezuela and Italy signed on the same date, February 13, 1903, likewise contained a provision in which it was expressly declared that the treaty of amity, commerce and navigation between the two countries of June 19, 1861 was renewed and confirmed.[111]   In the protocol concluded between Venezuela and Germany, no such provision is found.[112]

§182. Effect of Infractions.—The difficulty of compelling specific performance, or of obtaining compensation in mitigation of damages, by means other than those which do not assure full reparation to the innocent party, renders it even more necessary and equitable, than in the case of private contracts, that upon a breach of a treaty the continuance of the obligation should be made dependent upon the will of the party faithfully performing. But what constitutes a breach of this character? In defense of the denunciation in 1870 of the provisions of the treaty of Paris of 1856 for the neutralization of the Black Sea, it was urged on the part of the Russian government that the treaty with

109 Art. VII.

110 Handbook of Commercial Treaties, &c., between Great Britain and Foreign Powers (1912), 1039.

111 Art. VIII.

112 The tribunal of arbitration constituted under the protocols of May 7, 1903, to determine the question of preferential treatment, in its decision rendered, February 22, 1904, declared that a state of war between Germany, Great Britain and Italy, on the one hand, and Venezuela, on the other, had existed as the result of the blockade of the Venezuelan ports instituted by these three powers. It may also be noted that in the treaty of commerce concluded between the United States and China, October 8, 1903, after the Boxer uprising of 1900, it was expressly agreed that all of the provisions of the several treaties between the two countries which were in force on January 1, 1900 were continued in force and effect, except so far as modified by the new treaty or other treaties to which the United States was a party. Art. XVII.

respect to these provisions had been violated through the repeated entrance under various pretexts of vessels of war of other powers into the Straits, and of whole squadrons into the Black Sea. An investigation showed that, in the course of the fifteen years since the conclusion of the treaty, vessels of war had been allowed to pass through the Straits not in strict conformity with the terms of the treaty as follows: in 1862, one British; in 1866, one American; in 1868, two American, two Austrian, one French and one Russian; and in 1869, one Prussian.[113] It may be doubted that the Russian government would have asserted a right of denunciation on this ground alone. "The admission of a few isolated ships at different times was not an act in itself calculated," says Hall, "to endanger the objects of the treaty, viz, the settlement of Eastern affairs and the security of Turkey, or to impair the efficacy of the safe-guards given to Russia by way of compensation for the loss of naval power."[114] Prior to signing the treaty of London of March 13, 1871, by which the onerous obligations were, independently of the question raised as to the right of denunciation, modified, the plenipotentiaries of Austria-Hungary, Germany, Great Britain, Italy, Russia and Turkey, in conference, January 17, 1871, formally declared "that it is an essential principle of the law of nations that no power can free itself from the engagements of a treaty, nor modify the stipulations thereof, except with the assent of the contracting parties, by means of an amicable arrangement."[115] The principle was laid down by Grotius that "every article of the agreement has the force of a condition,"[116] and by Vattel that the several articles of the same treaty cannot be considered "as so many distinct and independent treaties."[117] Without doubt, every promise made by one party "may go to make up the consideration in return for which essential parts of the agreement are conceded or undertaken,"[118] and it is not for the party committing the breach to determine what is, or is not, essential in the eyes of the other. Nevertheless, it is conceivable that the several stipulations

113 Hertslet's Map of Europe by Treaty, III, 1895.

114 Int. Law (6 ed.), 346.

115 61 Brit. and For. State Papers 1198. The French plenipotentiary signed the declaration on March 13, 1871.

116 Bk. II, c. XV, §15.

117 Bk. II, c. XIII, §202; Bk. IV, c. IV, §47.

118 Hall (6 ed.), 344.

may be so independent and reciprocal in themselves that even the aggrieved party can show no relation between the stipulation violated and the others embodied in the same general treaty. A standard is to be sought which, in requiring strict observance, will not at the same time encourage pretexts for release from onerous treaty obligations. "There can be no question that the breach of a stipulation which is material to the main object, or if there are several, to one of the main objects, liberates the party other than that committing the breach from the obligations of the contract; but it would be seldom that the infraction of an article which is either disconnected from the main object, or is unimportant, whether originally or by change of circumstances, with respect to it, could in fairness absolve the other party from performance of his share of the rest of the agreement, though if he had suffered any appreciable harm through the breach he would have a right to exact reparation and an end might be put to the treaty as respects the subject-matter of the broken stipulation."[119]

§183. **Termination by Agreement.**—A treaty supersedes all pre-existing treaties between the same parties inconsistent with its provisions.[120] As nations may by mutual agreement annul treaties binding on them, so a provision may be, and often is, inserted in the treaty itself, by which the contracting parties agree that it may be terminated by a notice given by the one to the other.

§184. **Termination by Notice in the United States.**—In the United States some doubt has existed as to what body is authorized to give such notice. On the recommendation of President Polk,[121] Congress passed a joint resolution, approved April 27, 1846, to authorize the President, at his discretion, to give the required notice for the termination of the treaty with Great Britain of August 6, 1827, relative to the joint occupation of the northwest territory.[122] The controversy between the two governments as to the western boundary had reached an acute stage, and the question of the termination of the treaty under conditions as they then existed might well be considered a matter for Congress to decide.

---

119 Id., 344.

120 See La Republique Francaise v. Schultz, 57 Fed. 37, 40; In re Ross, 140 U. S. 453, 466; In re Strobel's estate, 39 N. Y. S. 169; S. Rept. No. 776, pt. 2, 57th Cong., 1st Sess., 32, et seq.

121 Annual message, December 2, 1845, Richardson, Messages and Papers of the Presidents, IV, 395.

122 9 Stats. at L. 109.

Although notice was duly given, the treaty was as a matter of fact superseded, before the expiration of the time required by the treaty as sufficient notice, by a new treaty signed, June 15, 1846. Ten years later the question was discussed at some length in the Senate with reference to the proposed termination of the treaty of commerce and navigation with Denmark of April 26, 1826. President Pierce, in his annual message to Congress, December 4, 1854, declared it expedient that the required notice for its termination should be given.[123]   The Senate in executive session, March 3, 1855, unanimously passed such a resolution.[124]   Acting under the authority of this resolution, the Executive caused the notice to be given to the government of Denmark, April 14, 1855.[125]   Subsequently, the authority of the resolution was questioned by Mr. Sumner in the Senate, avowedly on the ground that it would be equivalent to a repeal of a law of the land by the action of the Senate alone.[126]   The Senate Committee on Foreign Relations, to which the matter was referred, made a full report, April 7, 1856, in which the right of the Senate to authorize notice to be given was maintained.[127]   The treaty was considered by the Executive as terminated on April 15, 1856, pursuant to the notice; but by Article V of the treaty of April 11, 1857, it was, with the exception of the fifth article, renewed.[128]   The following treaties have subsequently been terminated pursuant to notice given by the government of the United States in each instance on the authority of a joint resolution of Congress: convention with Great Britain of June 5, 1854; treaty with Belgium of July 17, 1858;

123 Richardson, Messages and Papers of the Presidents, V, 279. "It is probable that two years might elapse before the existing convention [April 26, 1826, with Denmark] could be terminated, as an act must first pass Congress to enable the President to give the required notice, after which a year must expire before it could be rendered effectual." Mr. Buchanan, Secretary of State, to Mr. Flenniken, minister to Denmark, October 14, 1848, Moore, Int. Law Digest, I, 661.

124 Ex. Journal, IX, 430.

125 Richardson, Messages and Papers of the Presidents, V, 334.

126 Cong. Globe, 34th Cong., 1st Sess., 599, 601, 1147.

127 The committee observed, however, that no legislation had been necessary to carry the treaty under consideration into effect. Compilation of Reports of Sen. Com. on For. Rel., VIII, 108.

128 "It [the treaty of April 26, 1826] was afterwards abrogated, but subsequently renewed, with the exception of one article, on the 12th of January, 1858." Field, J., Bartram v. Robertson, 122 U. S. 116, 118.

and Articles XVIII-XXV, inclusive, and Article XXX of the treaty with Great Britain of May 8, 1871.[129] It should, however, be noted that in case of the convention of 1854 and the articles of the treaty of 1871, treaty provisions were terminated, which had, in accordance with an express reservation in the treaty itself, been carried into effect by Congressional legislation. In the act approved March 4, 1915, to promote safety at sea and the welfare of American seamen, and to abolish arrest and imprisonment as a penalty for desertion, the President was requested and directed, within ninety days after the passage of the act, to give notice to foreign governments that so much of any treaties as might be in conflict with the provisions of the act would terminate on the expiration of the periods of notice provided for in such treaties.[130] Such notices were duly given.

129 13 Stats. at L. 566; 18 Id. 287; 22 Id. 641. See, as to the termination of Article XXIX of the treaty of May 8, 1871, by virtue of the notice, message of President Harrison, February 2, 1893. S. Ex. Doc. No. 40, 52nd Cong., 2d Sess. Although Article XXXII, for the application of Articles XVIII-XXV to Newfoundland, was not expressly referred to in the act of Congress directing notice to be given, it was included in the notice as given by the Executive, and was considered as having coming to an end with the other articles. See proclamation of the President of January 31, 1885. Richardson, Messages, VIII, 280.

130 Sec. 16. 38 Stats. at L. 1164, 1184. See for other instances of the denunciation of certain articles only of a treaty, For. Rel., 1899, pp. 754-757; Moore, Int. Law Digest, V, 324-335. The right to denounce a treaty in part will hardly be questioned especially if the particular articles denounced are such as can be considered reciprocal obligations based upon mutual and equivalent concessions. If the other contracting party prefers a total to a partial denunciation it has but to give the required notice.

President Hayes in his message to the House of Representatives, March 1, 1879, setting forth the reasons for the veto of a bill which directed the abrogation of Articles V and VI of the treaty with China of July 28, 1868, said: "The authority of Congress to terminate a treaty with a foreign power by expressing the will of the nation no longer to adhere to it is as free from controversy under our Constitution as is the further proposition that the power of making new treaties or modifying existing treaties is not lodged by the Constitution in Congress, but in the President, by and with the advice and consent of the Senate, as shown by the concurrence of two-thirds of that body. A denunciation of a treaty by any government is confessedly justifiable only upon some reason both of the highest justice and of the highest necessity. The action of Congress in the matter of the French treaties in 1798, if it be regarded as an abrogation by this nation of a subsisting treaty, strongly illustrates the character and degree of justification which was then thought suitable to such a proceeding. * * * The his-

So far as a treaty is a mere compact between nations, or so far as it operates ipso facto as a law of the land, it would seem that the President should have the power, with the concurrence of two-thirds of the Senate, to give notice for its termination. There is no doubt that he may in the same way replace it with a new treaty.

A notice of the intention of the United States to terminate the agreement with Great Britain of 1817, relative to vessels of war on the Great Lakes, was given, pursuant to the reservation of that right, by the Executive on November 23, 1864. A resolution with a view to such termination had during the preceding session of Congress passed the House, but had failed of consideration in the Senate. After the notice had been communicated to the British government, a joint resolution was passed by Congress, approved February 9, 1865, which "adopted and ratified" the notice "as if the same had been authorized by Congress." Notwithstanding this legislative sanction, the notice was, before the expiration of the required six months, withdrawn by the Executive;

---

tory of the government shows no other instance of an abrogation of a treaty by Congress. Instances have sometimes occurred where the ordinary legislation of Congress has, by its conflict with some treaty obligation of the government toward a foreign power, taken effect as an *infraction* of the treaty, and been judicially declared to be operative to that result; but neither such legislation nor such judicial sanction of the same has been regarded as an *abrogation*, even for the moment, of the treaty. On the contrary, the treaty in such case still subsists between the governments, and the casual infraction is repaired by appropriate satisfaction in maintenance of the treaty. The bill before me does not enjoin upon the President the abrogation of the entire Burlingame treaty, much less of the principal treaty of which it is made the supplement. As the power of modifying an existing treaty, whether by adding or striking out provisions, is a part of the treaty-making power under the Constitution, its exercise is not competent for Congress, nor would the assent of China to this partial abrogation of the treaty make the action of Congress in thus procuring an amendment of a treaty a competent exercise of authority under the Constitution. The importance, however, of this special consideration seems superseded by the principle that a denunciation of a part of a treaty not made by the terms of the treaty itself separable from the rest is a denunciation of the whole treaty. As the other high contracting party has entered into no treaty obligations except such as include the part denounced, the denunciation by one party of the part necessarily liberates the other party from the whole treaty." (Richardson, Messages and Papers of the Presidents, VII, 518-519.) The treaty in question contained no **express** provision for termination by notice.

32

and the arrangement has subsequently been recognized by both governments as subsisting.[131] Notice of the intention of the United States to terminate the treaty with Russia of December 18, 1832 was communicated, by direction of the President, to the Russian government on December 17, 1911. A joint resolution for the abrogation of the treaty, but in terms unacceptable to the President, had already been passed by the House of Representatives. In a message of December 18, 1911, the President advised the Senate, "as a part of the treaty-making power," of his action in giving the notice "with a view to its ratification and approval" by that body.[132] A joint resolution was thereafter passed by both houses, and approved December 21, 1911, which adopted and ratified the notice thus given.[133] The notice given, March 23, 1899, to the Swiss government by the Secretary of State of the intention of this government to terminate Articles VIII-XII of the treaty of November 25, 1850 does not appear to have had any other than Executive authority.[134]

The period of time specified in the treaty, which is to elapse between the date the notice is given and the final termination of the treaty, has in the various notices given by the United States been reckoned from the date on which the notice was presented at the foreign office of the other contracting party.[135]

§185. **Termination in the United States in Case of Adverse Breach.**—James Madison in a private letter to Edmund Pendleton dated January 2, 1791, in discussing the operation of treaties in the United States as the supreme law of the land, raised the question whether, in case it should be advisable to take advantage of an adverse breach, Congress, or the President and Senate,

131 H. Doc. No. 471, 56th Cong., 1st Sess., 28-34. See report of Mr. Seward, in Executive session, from the Senate Committee on Foreign Relations, May 18, 1858, to which had been referred, in legislative session on May 15, a *joint* resolution to authorize the President to give notice of intention to terminate the treaty with Hanover of June 10, 1846. In the report it was recommended that the word *joint* be stricken out. Ex. Journal, X, 417, 418.

132 Cong. Record, 62d Cong. 2d Sess., 453.

133 37 Stats. at L. 627.

134 For. Rel., 1899, pp. 754-7. See for circular of the Treasury Department giving notice that the articles would cease to have operation on March 23, 1900, T. D. 22092. See also T. D. 22494.

135 See, also, For. Rel., 1865, I, p. 259; Id., 1874, p. 65; Id., 1899, p. 757; Id., 1883, p. 435.

would be the competent judges.[136]   It was Congress that acted in
the case of the treaties of 1778 with France. By the act, approved
July 7, 1798, it was declared that, since the treaties had been repeatedly violated on the part of the French government, and since
attempts to negotiate an amicable adjustment had been repelled
with indignity, the Untied States was freed and exonerated from
them, and that thenceforth they should not be regarded as legally
obligatory on the government or citizens of the United States.[137]
Such an act is to be distinguished from the termination of a treaty
by mutual agreement. An abrogation by Congress approved by
the President, while necessarily binding on the courts of this
country, and sufficient to terminate the operation of the treaty as
municipal law, will seldom be accepted by the other contracting
party as conclusive. Thus, in the negotiations at Paris in 1800, the
French government refused to admit that the treaties had been
annulled by the single act of abrogation on the part of the United
States, and could see no reason to distinguish in the settlement of
claims between the periods prior and subsequent to July 7,
1798.[138]

In the controversy that arose with Great Britain over the construction of Article X of the treaty of August 9, 1842, for the
mutual surrender of fugitives from justice, the termination of the
article was contemplated. Although the treaty contained an ex-

---

136 Letters and other Writings, I, 524.

137 1 Stats. at L. 578.

138 Moore, Int. Arb., V, 4430. See for final disposition of the question,
Treaties and Conventions (1889 ed.), 330. "We are of opinion that
the circumstances justified the United States in annulling the treaties of
1778; that the act was a valid one, not only as a municipal statute but as
between the nations; and that thereafter the compacts were ended."
Davis, J., Hooper, Admr. v. United States (1887), 22 C. Cls. 408,
425. "The decree of the French Government abrogating so much of the
treaty of 1778 as related to contraband goods on neutral vessels justified
its own cruisers in seizing vessels and its own prize courts in condemning
them, but without notice to and acquiescence on the part of the United
States the decree could not ex proprio vigore extend to the treaty rights
of the United States. In July, 1798 (Act 7th July, 1798, 1 Stat. L. 578),
the United States abrogated the treaty in toto, and thereby relieved France
from all obligations under it. This court in these spoliation cases has
always recognized that release from treaty obligation, and has given to
France the full benefits, whatever they may have been, of such exemption."
Nott, C. J., The Ship James & William v. United States (1902), 37 C. Cls.
303, 306.

press provision for the termination of the article by notice, the immediate question was whether the refusal of Great Britain to grant extradition under the article had released the United States from the obligation.[139] President Grant, in referring the matter to Congress in a special message of June 20, 1876, observed that it was for the wisdom of Congress to determine whether the article was to be longer regarded as "obligatory on the government of the United States or as forming part of the supreme law of the land." He added that, should the attitude of the British government remain unchanged, he would not, without an expression of the wish of Congress, take any action either in making or granting requisitions for the surrender of fugitive criminals under the treaty. The operation of the article was, as a matter of fact, suspended for a period of six months, but upon the adjustment of the controversy it was again regarded by both countries as in full force.[140] To the argument, in the case of Ex parte Charlton,[141] that the refusal of Italy to surrender Italian subjects under the extradition convention of 1868 was such a breach of a reciprocal duty as to release the United States from the obligation to surrender its own citizens, Rellstab, D. J., replied that the option of considering the convention as at an end must be exercised by the "political departments—Congress or the treaty-making power—possibly the executive power within certain limitations; assuredly not the judiciary." In affirming the decision of the lower court, the Supreme Court, by Lurton, J., said: "If the attitude of Italy was, as contended, a violation of the obligation of the treaty, which, in international law, would have justified the United States in denouncing the treaty as no longer obligatory, it did not automatically have that effect. If the United States elected not to declare its abrogation, or come to a rupture, the treaty would remain in force. It was only voidable, not void; and if the United States should prefer, it might waive any breach which in its judgment had occurred and conform to its own obligation as if there had been no such breach. * * * That

139 Art. XI.
140 Moore, Extradition, I, 211; Richardson, Messages and Papers of the Presidents, VII, 373, 414. See as to proposed action by Congress for alleged infraction of treaty rights by the summary action against American fishermen in Fortune Bay, Newfoundland, the President's messages to the two houses of Congress, May 17, 1880. Richardson, VII, 590.
141 185 Fed. 880, 887.

the political branch of the government recognizes the treaty obligation as still existing is evidenced by its action in this case. * * * The executive department having thus elected to waive any right to free itself from the obligation to deliver up its own citizens, it is the plain duty of this court to recognize the obligation to surrender the appellant as one imposed by the treaty as the supreme law of the land and as affording authority for the warrant of extradition."[142]

§186. Repeal of Treaty as Municipal Law in the United States.—It is well established in our jurisprudence that an act of Congress approved by the President may terminate the operation of a prior treaty as a law binding on the courts.[143] "When the two relate to the same subject, the courts will always endeavor to construe them so as to give effect to both, if that can be done without violating the language of either; but if the two are inconsistent, the one last in date will control the other, provided always the stipulation of the treaty on the subject is self-executing."[144] The operation of the treaty as a municipal law is not, however, to be confused with the obligation of the international compact, which cannot be thus terminated by an act of one only of the parties.[145]

---

142 Charlton v. Kelly (1913), 229 U. S. 447, 473, 474, 476. See supra, 368.

143 Taylor v. Morton, 2 Curtis 454; The Cherokee Tobacco Cases, 11 Wall. 616; United States v. Forty-three Gallons of Whiskey, 108 U. S. 491, 496; Head Money Cases, 112 U. S. 580, 598; Botiller v. Dominguez, 130 U. S. 238, 247; The Chinese Exclusion Case, 130 U. S. 581, 600.

144 Whitney v. Robertson (1888), 124 U. S. 190, 194.

145 See Mr. Blaine, Secretary of State, to Baron Fava, Italian minister, June 23, 1890, For. Rel., 1890, pp. 559, 563; message of President Arthur to the Senate, April 4, 1882, S. Ex. Doc. No. 148, 47th Cong. 1st Sess. "The law which they were attempting to enforce was a law of the republic of Haiti in violation of the treaty between the two nations. It need hardly be stated that the obligations of a treaty are as binding upon nations, as are private contracts upon individuals. This principle has been too often cited by publicists and enforced by international decisions to need amplification here." William R. Day, arbitrator under the protocol between the United States and Haiti of October 18, 1899.

APPENDIX I.

A DIGEST OF DECISIONS OF AMERICAN COURTS CONSTRUING TREATIES, ARRANGED BY COUNTRIES AND TREATIES.
ALGIERS.

Treaty of Peace and Amity Concluded December 22-23, 1816.

Arts. XIX-XXII. The right to exercise the powers conferred on American consuls in Algiers by the treaty concluded in 1816 ceased when that country passed under the jurisdiction of a Christian nation, and the treaty thus came to an end. The provision of the act of Congress of May 1, 1810, fixing the salary of the consul at Algiers and assigning to him certain duties, treating that place as belonging to a Mohammedan power, ceased to be operative when that country became a province of France. Mahoney v. United States (1869), 10 Wall. 62.

ARGENTINE REPUBLIC.
Treaty of Friendship, Commerce and Navigation Concluded July 27, 1853.

Art. IX. The provision, that if any citizen of either of the contracting parties shall die without will or testament, in the territory of the other, the consul-general or consul of the nation to which the deceased belonged, or the representative of such consul-general or consul, in his absence, "shall have the right to intervene in the possession, administration and judicial liquidation of the estate of the deceased, conformably with the laws of the country, for the benefit of the creditors and legal heirs," was not intended to take from the States the right of local administration provided by their laws, upon the estates of deceased citizens of a foreign country, and to commit the same to the consuls of such foreign nation, to the exclusion of those entitled to administer as provided by the local laws of the State within which such foreigner resided and left property at the time of decease. Rocca v. Thompson (1912), 223 U S. 317, affirming 157 Cal. 552. See also In re Logiorato's Estate (1901), 69 N. Y.

S. 507. See, contra, In re Fattosini's Estate (1900), 67 N. Y. S. 1119; In re Lobrasciano's Estate (1902), 77 N. Y. S. 1040; McEvoy v. Wyman (1906), 191 Mass. 276; In re Silvetti's Estate (1907), 122 N. Y. S. 400; Carpigiani v. Hall (1911), 172 Ala. 287; In re Scutella's Estate (1911), 129 N. Y. S. 20. See also under Denmark, In re Peterson's Will (1906), 101 N. Y. S. 285; under Italy, In re Davenport (1904), 89 N. Y. S. 537, and In re Bristow (1909), 118 N. Y. S. 686.

AUSTRIA-HUNGARY.

Treaty of Commerce and Navigation Concluded August 27, 1829.

Art. V. See Art. II of the treaty with Sweden and Norway of April 3, 1783.

Extradition Convention Concluded July 3, 1856.

Under a warrant issued by a commissioner of the United States circuit court, southern district of New York, the prisoner was brought before that court from the State of New Jersey, for examination in a proceeding to extradite him to Austria, upon a charge of embezzlement of public funds. The charge not being sustained, the prisoner was discharged, but, upon leaving the commissioner's room, was arrested by the sheriff under an order of arrest in a civil suit in the State court to recover the same funds. Both proceedings were promoted and prosecuted by the same agents and attorneys. *Held,* that the case fell within the general principles announced in United States v. Rauscher, 119 U. S. 407, and In re Reinitz, 39 Fed. 204, and that the prisoner was entitled to immunity from arrest until the lapse of a reasonable time to return to New Jersey whence he had been brought. One day was allowed for that purpose. In re Baruch (1890), 41 Fed. 472.

Art. I. The term "forgery" as used in the convention should have, so far as this government is concerned, its common-law definition, which includes forgery of commercial paper, though the crime of forgery, as known to the law of Austria-Hungary, may comprehend only the falsification of public obligations, and though the crime of forging commercial paper, charged against the prisoner, may there be classified as "fraud by means of forgery." In re Adutt (1893), 55 Fed. 376.

Consular Convention Concluded July 11, 1870.

Art. VIII. Under the provision, that consuls-general, consuls, vice-consuls and consular agents of the two countries, in the exercise of their duties, may apply to the authorities within their district for the protection of the rights of their countrymen, the imperial and royal consul of Austria-Hungary is entitled to maintain a suit in the Federal courts to restrain a local beneficial association from using the name of the Austro-Hungarian Emperor as a part of its corporate name and his portrait as a part of its advertising literature for the false and fraudulent purpose of inducing subjects of the Emperor, resident in the United States, to believe that the association is conducted under the customs of their home country and that their Emperor is identified with and a patron of it. Von Thodorovich v. Franz Josef Beneficial Ass'n. (1907), 154 Fed. 911.

Art. XV. Quære: Whether the most-favored-nation clause carries the benefit of a provision of a consular convention between the United States and another country, conferring upon the consular representatives of the parties thereto the right to administer upon the estates of their deceased nationals. Austro-Hungarian Consul v. Westphal (1912), 120 Minn. 122. See Sweden, Art. XIV of the treaty of June 1, 1910.

The most-favored-nation clause of the treaty gives to a consul of Austria-Hungary the right to administer on the estate of a countryman dying intestate in the United States, that right having been granted by treaty to consuls of Paraguay and Sweden. In re Jarema's Estate (1912), 137 N. Y. S. 176. See, however, In re Estate of D'Adamo (1914), 212 N. Y. 214, under Art. XIV of the treaty with Sweden of June 1, 1910.

Trade-mark Convention Concluded November 25, 1871.

Art. I. A word having become public property in Hungary, it also became, under the treaty, public property in the United States. Having once become public property in the United States, a subsequent change in the law of Hungary, in this particular, does not affect the case. The right to individual appropriation once lost is gone forever. Saxlehner v. Eisner & Mendelson Co. (1900), 179 U. S. 19.

The provision in the convention with Austria, that if a trade-mark has become public property in the country of origin it shall be equally free in the territory of the other contracting party, does not prevent the appropriation in this country, by prior use here, of a word which is not the subject of appropriation under the laws of Austria. J. & P. Baltz Brewing Co. v. Kaiserbrauerei, Beck & Co. (1896), 74 Fed. 222.

BELGIUM.
Extradition Convention Concluded March 19, 1874.

Art. III. It is expressly provided that the provisions of the convention shall not apply to any crimes, except those of murder and arson, committed prior to the date of the convention. The convention was signed March 19, 1874, and the ratifications were exchanged April 30, 1874. It was not to take effect until twenty days after the exchange of ratifications. *Held,* that a crime committed in Belgium on May 1, 1874, was covered by the convention. In re Vandervelpen (1877), 14 Blatchf. 137.

Art. VI. This article expressly provides for requisition on the part of the government applying, and consent of the government applied to. It is not necessary that the warrant on such requisition be issued by the President. It is sufficient if it issues from the Department of State under its official seal. In foreign relations, and executive acts imposed by treaty stipulations, the President acts through that Department. Where the complaint charges the crime of forgery as having been committed on a certain day, in that "one wilfully &c., uttered and put in circulation forged or counterfeit papers, or obligations, or other titles, or instruments of credits," without specifying the kind of obligations forged, or the character of the papers, or the nature of titles, &c., it is defective at common law, does not fairly inform accused of the charge, and does not show probable cause for arrest. Ex parte Van Hoven (1876), 4 Dill. 411.

See as to the construction of the statutes for the extradition of criminals and their application under this convention, In re Stupp (1875), 12 Blatchf. 501.

Consular Convention Concluded March 9, 1880.

Art. XI. The provision conferring power on Belgian consuls in the United States to take cognizance of differences between the captains, officers and crews of Belgian merchant vessels, and providing that the local authorities shall not interfere except when a disorder arises of such a nature as to disturb the tranquility and public order on shore or in the port, or when a person of this country or not belonging to the crew shall be concerned therein, does not deprive the local authorities of jurisdiction over a case of felonious homicide committed on board a Belgian merchant vessel in a port of the United States, by one Belgian upon the person of another Belgian, both belonging to the crew of the vessel. Wildenhus's Case (1887), 120 U. S. 1.

Art. XV. The provision in the treaty with Belgium, conferring on the delegate appointed by the Belgium consul authority to represent absent or minor heirs, is within the treaty-making power and must prevail if in conflict with a State statute. Succession of Rabasse (1895), 47 La. Ann. 1452.

BRAZIL.

Claims Convention Concluded January 27, 1849.

Assignment of claim held to be valid. Lewis v. Bell (1854), 17 How. 616.

CHILE.

Treaty of Peace, Amity, Commerce, and Navigation Concluded May 16, 1832.

Art. XXV. Under the most-favored-nation clause of this article, the same immunity from compulsory attendance in court as witnesses as enjoyed by French consuls under the treaty with France of February 23, 1853, was claimed in United States v. Trumbull (1891), 48 Fed. 94; but the court found other grounds on which to base its decision.

CHINA.

Treaty of Peace, Amity, and Commerce Concluded July 3, 1844.

Art. XXI. Under this treaty, and the act of Congress carrying it into effect, the United States commissioner and consuls constitute a judiciary for the government of the citizens of the United States in China, and are governed by the law of nations, the laws of the United States, the common law, and the decrees and regulations of the commissioner. An alien friend may sue an American in the consular courts in China established under this treaty. Forbes v. Scannell (1859), 13 Cal. 242.

Claims Convention Concluded November 8, 1858.

Where a demand was made by the government of the United States upon China for redress of certain specific injuries to American citizens, and the Chinese government paid a gross sum in satisfaction of all claims of American citizens, it must be held in a suit to recover a portion of that fund that China recognized her liability for the acts complained of. Where it appears that the government of the United States formerly asserted with knowledge of the facts certain claims to be valid, and demanded reparation for them, it will be held that, as between the claimants and the government of the United States, the question was settled that such claims constituted legitimate claims against China. Hubbell et al. v. United States (1879), 15 C. Cls. 546.

Treaty of Trade, Consuls, and Emigration Concluded July 28, 1868.

Art. IV. An act of the legislature of California making it an offense to disinter or remove from the place of burial the remains of any deceased person, without a permit, for which a fee of ten dollars must be paid, does not violate the provision in the treaty with China, that Chinese subjects in the United States shall enjoy entire liberty of conscience, and shall be exempt from all disability or persecution on account of their religious faith or worship. In re Wong Yung Quy (1880), 6 Sawy. 442. See as to office of writ of habeas corpus, s. c. Id. 237.

Arts. V and VI. (See also treaty of November 17, 1880). A mining regulation, authorized by a State, which in effect forbids Chinese from working in a mining claim for themselves or for others, seems to be in direct conflict with the provision in Article VI of the treaty with China, that the citizens or subjects of China visiting or residing in the United States shall enjoy the same privileges, immunities, and exemptions in respect of travel or residence as may there be enjoyed by citizens or subjects of the most favored nation. If in conflict therewith it is void. Chapman v. Toy Long (1876), 4 Sawy. 28.

A legislative act of the State of Oregon, which prohibits the employment by contractors of Chinese on street improvements or public works, but which permits all other aliens so to be employed, is in conflict with the provisions in the treaty with China pledging to the Chinese, resident here, the same right to be employed and labor for a living as enjoyed by the subjects of any other nation, and is therefore void. Baker v. City of Portland (1879), 5 Sawy. 566.

The privileges and immunities, which, under the treaty, the Chinese are entitled to enjoy to the same extent as enjoyed by the subjects of the most favored nation, are all those which are fundamental, among which is the right to labor and to pursue any lawful employment in a lawful manner. A provision of the constitution of the State of California, as likewise legislation for its enforcement, providing that no corporation formed under the laws of the State shall, directly or indirectly, in any capacity, employ any Chinese or Mongolian, is in conflict with the provisions in the treaty and therefore void. In re Tiburcio Parrott (1880), 6 Sawy. 349.

A statute of the State of California, which prohibits all aliens incapable of becoming electors of the State from fishing in the waters of the State (construed in connection with other contemporaneous statutes expressly directed against the Chinese), violates the provisions of the treaty with China granting Chinese subjects residing in the United States the same privileges in respect of residence and travel as may be enjoyed by citizens of the most favored nation, and is therefore void. In re Ah Chong (1880), 6 Sawy. 451. See also Ex parte Ah Fook (1874), 49 Cal. 402; reversed in Chy Lung v. Freeman et al. (1875), 92 U. S. 275.

Immigration Treaty Concluded November 17, 1880.

Art. I. The act of October 1, 1888 (25 Stats. at L. 504), which prohibited the entry into the United States of laborers, who had departed before its passage with certificates of permission to return issued under the act of May 6, 1882 (22 Stats. at L. 58), as amended by the act of July 5, 1884 (23

Stats. at L. 115), was a constitutional exercise of legislative power, and, so far as it conflicted with treaties between the United States and China, operated to that extent to supersede them as part of the municipal law of the United States. A certificate so issued to a Chinese laborer conferred no right to return to the United States of which he could not be deprived by a subsequent act of Congress. Chae Chan Ping v. United States (The Chinese Exclusion Case, 1889), 130 U. S. 581.

The result of the legislation respecting the Chinese (acts of May 6, 1882, July 5, 1884, and October 1, 1888), would seem to be this: that no laborers of that race shall hereafter be permitted to enter the United States, or even to return after having departed from the country, though they may have previously resided therein and have left with a view of returning; and that all other persons of that race, except those connected with the diplomatic service, must produce a certificate from the authorities of the Chinese government, or of such other foreign government as they may at the time be subjects of, showing that they are not laborers, and have the permission of that government to enter the United States, which certificate is to be viséd by a representative of the government of the United States. Wan Shing v. United States (1891), 140 U. S. 424.

The term "laborers" as used in this treaty, as also in the treaty of March 17, 1894, and the acts of Congress in restriction of Chinese immigration, has been before the courts for construction in numerous cases. Among such determinations are the following: A Chinese laborer, who has acquired the right of residence in the United States under the treaty, does not lose such right by shipping on board of an American vessel, in an American port, as one of its crew for a voyage to a foreign port and back, and making such voyage under his shipping articles, though he may have landed at different times at such foreign port by permission of the captain, his connection with the vessel as part of the crew not being severed. In re Ah Tie et al. (Case of the Chinese Laborers, 1882), 7 Sawy. 542. An American vessel is deemed to be a part of the territory of the United States, and the crew of a vessel, whilst on board, are within the jurisdiction of the United States, and, if foreigners, do not lose any right of residence in the United States previously acquired under a treaty. In re Ah Sing (Case of the Chinese Cabin Waiter, 1882), 7 Sawy. 536; In re Moncon (1882), 8 Sawy. 350. The terms "Chinese laborers" as used in the act of May 6, 1882, to execute the treaty with China, must have the same signification as when used in the treaty, and must mean the subjects of the Emperor of China to which the provisions of the treaty relate; and the inhibitions of the act cannot be construed to exclude from our shores laborers who are Chinese by race and language, but who are not, and never were, subjects of the Emperor of China, or resident within his dominions. United States v. Douglas (1883), 17 Fed. 634. The term "laborer" is used in the treaty with China of November 17, 1880, and the act in aid thereof, of May 6, 1882, in its popular sense and includes only those whose occupation involves physical toil and who work for wages. A Chinese actor or theatrical performer is not a "laborer" within the purview of the treaty or law; and such person is, therefore, entitled to come to and reside in the United States at pleasure. In re Ho King (1883), 8 Sawy. 438. A Chinese laborer, born in the island of Hong-Kong after its cession to Great Britain, is within the provisions of the act of May 6, 1882. The purpose of the act was to exclude laborers coming from China, subject to the stipulations of the treaty of 1880, and also to exclude laborers of the Chinese race coming from any other part of the world. In re Ah Lung (1883), 9 Sawy. 306. The words "Chinese laborers" as used in section 6 of the act of May 6, 1882, as amended by the act of July 5, 1884, have no reference to seamen in the ordinary pursuit of their vocation on the high seas, who may touch upon our shores, and may land temporarily for the purpose only of obtaining a chance to ship for some other foreign voyage as soon as possible and who do not intend to make any stay here, or enter upon any of the occupations on land within this country. In re Ah Kee (1884), 22 Blatchf. 520; In re Moncon, 8 Sawy. 350; In re Ho King, 8 Sawy. 438. The words "Chinese laborers" as used in section 6 of the act of May 5, 1882, have the same meaning as in the treaty with China of 1880, in which they are broad enough in their true meaning and intent to include Chinese gamblers and highbinders, since Article II of the treaty by exclusion provides that no Chinese should be entitled to the benefit of the general provisions of the Burlingame treaty, except those who come to the United States for purposes of teaching, study, mercantile transactions, travel or curiosity. United States v. Ah Fawn (1893), 57 Fed. 591. A restaurant proprietor, who keeps a place for serving meals, and provides, prepares, and cooks raw materials to suit the tastes of his patrons, is a laborer, and is not privileged to enter the United States as a merchant. In re Ah Yow (1894), 59 Fed. 561. To be a merchant within the definition of section 2 of the act of November 3, 1893, his interest must be real, and appear in the business and partnership articles in his own name. It is not necessary that his name appear in the firm designation. Lee Kan v. United States (1894), 62 Fed. 914. See United States v. Pin Kwan (1900), 100 Fed. 609. A Chinaman serving a term of imprisonment at hard labor is a "laborer" within section 6 of the act of May 5, 1892, requiring Chinese to register, and not a "merchant" within the exception of section 2 of the act of November 3, 1893, though prior to his imprisonment he owned an interest, in the name of another, in a mercantile firm, and retains it during his imprisonment. United States v. Wong Ah Hung (1894), 62 Fed. 1005. A Chinese person, who during his residence in the United States was engaged in business as a member of a firm of dealers in fancy goods, but who, occasionally, during a year previous to his departure for a temporary visit worked for short periods as a house servant in order to accommodate an old employer at times when he was without a servant, was engaged in manual labor within the meaning of section 2 of the act of November 3, 1893. Lew Jim v. United States (1895), 66 Fed. 953. A Chinese person, who during half his time is engaged in cutting and sewing garments for sale by a firm of which he is a member, is not a merchant within the meaning of section 2 of the act of November 3, 1893. Lai Moy v. United States (1895), 66 Fed. 955. A Chinese person, who was a merchant at the time of the passage of the act of May 5, 1892, and during the period for registration, was not liable to deportation by subsequently becoming a laborer. United States v. Sing Lee (1896), 71 Fed. 680. The words "Chinese laborers" in section 1 of the act of November 3, 1893, amending section 6 of the act of May 5, 1892, and relating to certificates of residence, include a Chinaman engaged in the business of keeping a restaurant and lodging house, and all Chinese persons dependent upon their labor for self-support, whether actually employed as laborers or not. United States v. Chung Ki Foon (1897), 83 Fed. 143. Respondent, a Chinaman, came to this country for the first time in June, 1897. From that date until his arrest, September 9, 1897, under the statute relating to Chinese immigration, he worked in a laundry in Hannibal, Missouri. He testified that he had an interest of $1,000 in a Chinese grocery business conducted under the name of One Lung, at 43 Mott Street, New York City. *Held,* that this did not constitute him a "merchant" under the act of November 3, 1893; but that he was a "laborer" within the meaning of section 2, and liable to deportation. United States v. Yong Yew (1897), 83 Fed. 832. A Chinese person, whose chief occupation is that of a laundryman, is a laborer within the meaning of the law. In re Leung (1898), 86 Fed. 303. Where a Chinaman is admitted into this country upon presentation of a certificate in conformity with section 6 of the act of May 6, 1882, as amended by the act of July 5, 1884, identifying him as a merchant, proof, that ever since he was permitted to land he has continuously engaged in manual labor, will overcome the effect of such certificate as prima facie evidence of his right to remain in the United States. United States v. Ng Park Tan (1898), 86 Fed. 605. The status of minor children of a laborer is that of their father. United States v. Chu Chee et al. (1899), 93 Fed. 797. A mercantile business conducted in the name of the partnership is conducted in the name of a partner in the firm, within the meaning of section 2 of the Chinese deportation act of 1893, although his name does not appear in the firm name. United States v. Wong Ah Gah (1899), 94 Fed. 831. See also Wong Fong v. United States (1896), 77 Fed. 168. A Chinese subject, who owns an interest in a mercantile firm but is not actively engaged in the conduct of its business, and who works as head cook in a restaurant of which he is a part proprietor, is a laborer, and not a merchant, within the meaning of the act of November 3, 1893. Mar Bing Guey v. United States (1899), 97 Fed. 576. Chinese persons, who were in this country prior to May 5, 1892, and who from 1891 to 1894 carried on a mercantile business under a corporate title, although the business was not conducted in their individual names, and who had books of account and articles of partnership, were merchants within the meaning of section 6 of the act of May 5, 1892, as amended by the act of November 3, 1892, and were not required to register under the terms of that act, and cannot be deported for failing so to do. Tom Hong v. United States (1904), 193 U. S. 517. See, also, as to definition of merchant, United States v. Sun (1896), 76 Fed. 450; In re Chu Poy (1897), 81 Fed. 826; United States v. Yee Gee You (1907), 152 Fed. 157. A Chinese minor lawfully entering the United States as the son of a Chinese merchant domiciled in this country lost such status on the return of his father to China to remain permanently, leaving the son, who was still a minor, in this country. The status of the son thereafter was determined by his own occupation. The fact that a Chinese laborer was a minor of 19 or 20 years at the time of the passage of the registration acts did not exempt him from the duty of registering thereunder. United States v. Joe Dick (1905), 134 Fed. 988. Neither the treaty of 1880, nor subsequent legislation relating to Chinese exclusion, has any relation to Chinese persons, not of the laboring class, who were at the time of the adoption of that treaty domiciled in the United States, and who have since continued to reside therein; and such a person, who temporarily leaves the country, with the intention of returning, cannot be excluded on his return because he is not included in one of the classes expressly excepted from the operation of the exclusion acts, and who alone are permitted to enter the United States by rules 1 and 2 of the regulations adopted by the Department of Commerce and Labor; such rules are applicable only to persons seeking to enter for the first time. Ex parte Ng Quong Ming (1905), 135 Fed. 378. A Chinese person, who was lawfully in the United States in business as a merchant and continued in such business until after the time for registration of all

Chinese laborers then within the United States, could not thereafter be deported on subsequently becoming a laborer, since he was not able to procure a certificate within the time specified in the act of 1892, not being at the time a laborer and entitled to a laborer's certificate. In re Chin Ark Wing (1902), 115 Fed. 412. See also United States v. Moy Yim (1902), 115 Fed. 652; United States v. Louie Juen (1904), 128 Fed. 522; In re Yew Bing Hi (1904), 128 Fed. 319; United States v. Leo Won Tong (1904), 132 Fed. 190; Ow Yang Dean v. United States (1906), 145 Fed. 801. Section 4 of the act of Congress of May 6, 1882, as amended by the act of July 5, 1884, which prescribes that the certificate to be produced by a Chinese laborer as the "only evidence permissible to establish his right of re-entry" into the United States, is not applicable to Chinese laborers who, residents in this country at the date of the treaty of November 17, 1880, departed by sea before May 6, 1882, and remained out of the United States until after July 5, 1884, and then returned by sea. Chew Heong v. United States (1884), 112 U. S. 536. See also United States v. Jung Ah Lung (1888), 124 U. S. 621, as to identification of a Chinese laborer returning to the United States in case the certificate duly issued has been stolen. See also In re Chin Ah On (1883), 9 Sawy. 343; In re Tong Ah Chee (1883), 9 Sawy. 346; In re Tung Yeong (1884), 9 Sawy. 620; In re Leong Yick Dew (1884), 10 Sawy. 38; In re Ah Quan (1884), 21 Fed. 182 (wife and children of Chinese, other than laborers) ; In re Shong Toon (1884), 10 Sawy. 268; In re Ah Moy (1884), 21 Fed. 785; In re Chew Heong (1884), 10 Sawy. 361; In re Ah Ping (1885), 23 Fed. 329. Under section 6 of the act of July 5, 1884, construed in connection with the treaty of November 17, 1880, the wives and minor children of Chinese merchants domiciled in this country may enter the United States without such certificates. United States v. Mrs. Gue Lim (1900), 176 U. S. 459, 464; In re Chung Toy Ho (1890), 42 Fed. 398; In re Lee Sing (1898), 85 Fed. 635; United States v. Gue Lim (1897), 83 Fed. 136. See, contra, In re Ah Quan (1884), 21 Fed. 182; In re Ah Moy (1884), 21 Fed. 785; In re Wo Tai Li (1888), 48 Fed. 668; In re Lum Lin Ying (1894), 59 Fed. 682; In re Li Foon (1897), 80 Fed.

881. As to the wife of an American citizen, see Tsoi Sim v. United States (1902), 116 Fed. 920.

Arts. II and III. (See also treaty of July 28, 1868, Arts. V and VI).

Those subjects of the Emperor of China, who have the right temporarily or permanently to reside within the United States, are entitled to enjoy the protection guaranteed by the Constitution and afforded by the laws. An administration of a municipal ordinance for the carrying on of a lawful business within the corporate limits violates the provisions of the Constitution if it makes arbitrary and unjust discriminations founded on differences of race between persons otherwise in similar circumstances. Yick Wo v. Hopkins (1886), 118 U. S. 356. See also Barbier v. Connolly (1885), 113 U. S. 27; Soon Hing v. Crowley (1885), 113 U. S. 703.

Congress has the power under the Constitution to provide for the punishment of persons guilty of depriving Chinese subjects of any of the rights, privileges, immunities, or exemptions guaranteed to them by the treaty of November 17, 1880; but Congress has not made such provision, either in §5519, §5508, or §5336, Rev. Stats. §5519 is unconstitutional, and ineffective as a provision for the punishment of a conspiracy, within a State, to deprive an alien of rights guaranteed to him therein by a treaty. In describing the offense against a citizen of the United States for which punishment is provided for in §5508, the word "citizen" is used in its political sense, with the same meaning which it has in the Fourteenth Amendment to the Constitution, and not as being synonymous with "resident," "inhabitant," or "person." To constitute the offense described in the first clause of §5336, it is not enough that a law of the United States is violated; but there must be a forcible resistance to a positive assertion of its authority as a government. To constitute an offense under the second clause of §5336, there must be a forcible resistance to the authority of the United States while endeavoring to carry its laws into execution. Baldwin v. Franks (1887), 120 U. S. 678.

Section 6 of the act of May 6, 1882, as amended by the act of July 5, 1884, does not apply to Chinese merchants already domiciled in the United States, who, having left the country for temporary purposes, *animo revertendi*, seek to re-enter it on their return to their business and their homes. Lau Ow Bew v. United States (1892), 144 U. S. 47.

Section 6 of the act of May 5, 1892, requiring all Chinese laborers within the United States at the time of its passage, and who are entitled to remain in the United States, to apply within a year to a collector of internal revenue for a certificate of residence, and providing that any one who does not so do, or is afterwards found in the United States without such a certificate, shall be deemed and adjudged to be unlawfully in the United States, and shall be deported from the United States to his own country, unless he shall clearly establish, to the satisfaction of the judge, that by reason of accident, sickness or other unavoidable cause, he was unable to procure his certificate, and, by at least one credible white witness, that he was a resident of the United States at the time of the passage of the act, is constitutional and must be upheld by the courts as a municipal law, even if in conflict with treaty provisions of earlier date. Fong Yue Ting v. United States (1893), 149 U. S. 698.

Under the treaty with China, a Chinese resident of this country is entitled to all the rights, privileges and immunities of subjects of the most favored nation with which this country has treaty relations; and, if a resident here before the passage of the act of Congress restricting immigration of Chinese, he has a right to remain and follow any of the lawful ordinary trades and pursuits of life. In re Quong Woo (1882), 13 Fed. 229.

A city ordinance which arbitrarily requires all Chinese inhabitants to remove from the portion of the city theretofore occupied by them to another designated part of the city, or outside the city, is in direct conflict with the Constitution, treaties, and statutes of the United States, particularly in the sense that it is discriminatory and unequal in its operation, and involves an arbitrary confiscation of property without due process of law. In re Lee Sing (1890), 43 Fed. 359.

A covenant in a deed not to convey or lease land to a Chinaman is contrary to the public policy of the government, in contravention of its treaty with China, and in violation of the Fourteenth Amendment to the Constitution, and is accordingly not enforceable in a court of equity. Gandolfo v. Hartman (1892), 49 Fed. 181.

Under the most-favored-nation clause of the Chinese treaties, and the provisions of treaties with foreign powers that the citizens or subjects of such foreign powers shall be accorded the same privileges and rights as native citizens and shall not be charged any higher imposts or duties than paid by native citizens, a State is not restrained from imposing such conditions on the right to take fish from the tide waters of the State as it sees fit, notwithstanding the license fee exacted from aliens is higher than that exacted from its own citizens. The right to take fish from the tide waters of the State is a property right, not a mere privilege of citizenship, held in trust by the State for its citizens. Leong Mow v. Board of Commissioners (1911), 185 Fed. 223.

Under the treaty with China, citizens of the Chinese Empire residing either permanently or temporarily in the United States are granted the same rights, privileges, immunities, and exempions as are enjoyed by citizens and subjects of the most favored nation. Accordingly they can hold a lease interest in real estate in Idaho. Duck Lee v. Boise Development Co. (1912), 21 Idaho 461.

Art. IV. The provision in this article, that if the legislation adopted by the United States in accordance with the treaty shall be "found to work hardship upon the subjects of China, the Chinese minister at Washington may bring the matter to the notice of the Secretary of State of the United States, who will consider the subject with him," does not exclude judicial cognizance, or confine the remedy of the Chinese subject, in a given case of hardship, to diplomatic action. United States v. Jung Ah Lung (1888), 124 U. S. 621.

Convention Regulating Chinese Immigration Concluded March 17, 1894.

Section 12 of the act of May 6, 1882, as amended by the act of July 5, 1884, and as continued in force by the act of May 5, 1892, prescribing the procedure for deportation, is in absolute harmony with the treaty of 1894, and is accordingly not superseded by that treaty. United States v. Lee Yen Tai (1902), 185 U. S. 213. See also Lee Lung v. Patterson (1902), 186 U. S. 168; Chin Bak Kan v. United States (1902), 186 U. S. 193.

Section 3 of the act of May 5, 1892, putting the burden of proving the right to remain in this country on Chinese arrested under the act, and section 6 of the same act requiring Chinese laborers, who are entitled to remain in the United States, to obtain certificates of residence, are brought forward by the act of April 29, 1902 (32 Stats. at L. 176), continuing all laws then in force "so far as the same are not inconsistent with treaty obligations." Ah How v. United States (1904), 193 U. S. 65.

The purpose and effect of the act of April 29, 1902 (32 Stats. at L. 176), as amended by the act of April 27, 1904 (33 Stats. at L. 428), which provides that all laws in force on April 29, 1902, regulating, suspending, or prohibiting the coming of Chinese persons into the United States, or their residence therein, "are hereby re-enacted, extended and continued without modification, limitation, or condition," was to continue all such laws in force after the expiration of the treaty with China on December 8, 1904. Hong Wing v. United States (1906), 142 Fed. 128.

Art. II.   The provision, that the general prohibition of the entry of Chinese laborers into this country contained in Article 1 "shall not apply to the return to the United States of any registered Chinese laborer who has a lawful wife, child or parent in the United States, or property therein of the value of one thousand dollars, or debts of like amount due him and pending settlement," has reference to the condition of the laborer at the time of his return.   In re Ong Lung (1903), 125 Fed. 814.

Art. III.   By the treaty of 1894, the privilege of transit across the territory of the United States could only be enjoyed subject to such regulations of the government of the United States as might be necessary to prevent the privilege from being abused.   The treaty, in recognizing the privilege and providing that it should continue, proceeded on the ground of its existence and continuance under governmental regulations, and no act of Congress was required to carry it into effect.   Under existing regulations the action of the collectors of customs in refusing transit cannot be interfered with by the courts.   Fok Yung Yo v. United States (1902), 185 U. S. 296.

A Chinaman, admitted to residence in this country upon a certificate duly issued and viséd as provided for in Article

III of the treaty, cannot be deported for having wrongfully entered the United States upon a fraudulent certificate, unless there is some competent evidence to overcome the legal effect of the certificate. Liu Hop Fong v. United States (1908), 209 U. S. 453.

COLOMBIA.

Treaty of Peace, Amity, and Commerce Concluded December 12, 1846.

Art. XXX. A vice consul of Colombia, being entitled under the most-favored-nation clause to all the rights, prerogatives, and immunities given in this respect to vice consuls of France under Article II of the treaty of 1853, cannot be compelled to attend as a witness. This provision is not annulled by the clause in Article V of the consular convention of May 4, 1850, providing that, when the presence of consuls may be required in courts of justice, they shall be summoned in writing. Baiz v. Malo (1899), 58 N. Y. S. 806, citing United States v. Trumbull, 48 Fed. 96.

CUBA.

Commercial Convention Concluded December 11, 1902.

Art. VIII. Within the meaning of the convention, the Philippine Islands are not a foreign or another country; and the tariff reductions on articles imported from Cuba are not to be based on tariff rates on the same articles brought from the Philippine Islands. The provisions of Article VIII of the convention are not to be construed so as to give to Cuba advantages over shipments coming into the United States from a part of its own territory. Faber v. United States (1911), 221 U. S. 649.

Art. IX. Under the convention, and the act of Congress of December 17, 1903, to give it effect, imports from Cuba were not entitled to the reduction of duties until December 27, 1903, the date proclaimed by the President of the United States and the President of Cuba for the commencement of the operation of the convention. After the amendment of the convention by the Senate and the acceptance thereof by Cuba, the date on which it should go into effect was to be determined by the act of Congress rather than by the original provision of the convention fixing as the date the tenth day after the exchange of ratifications. United States v. American Sugar Refining Company (1906), 202 U. S. 563; Franklin Sugar Refining Co. v. United States (1906), 202 U. S. 580; United States v. M. J. Dalton Co. (1907), 151 Fed. 144.

DENMARK.

Treaty of Friendship, Commerce, and Navigation Concluded April 26, 1826.

Art. I. The act of August 3, 1882 (22 Stats. at L. 214), requiring owners of vessels to pay a tax for every passenger, not a citizen of the United States, brought from a foreign port to the United States, applies to those brought by Danish ships, notwithstanding the treaty with Denmark. Head Money Cases (1884), 112 U. S. 580. The act of June 26, 1884 (23 Stats. at L. 58, §22) excepts from the passenger tax vessels plying between the ports of the United States and those of Canada and Mexico. Danish vessels, arriving from a port in Denmark, are not exempt under the most-favored-nation clause in the treaty from the payment of the tax. In case of a conflict with a prior treaty the statute must prevail in the courts of this country. Thingvalla Line et al. v. United States (1889), 24 C. Cls. 255.

Art. IV. This article contains a pledge of the contracting parties that there shall be no discriminating legislation against the importation of articles, the growth, produce or manufacture of the respective countries, in favor of articles of like character imported from any other country. It is not designed to prevent special concessions, upon sufficient considerations, touching the importation of specific articles into the country of the other, and does not carry with it automatically such concessions. Bartram v. Robertson (1887), 122 U. S. 116.

Art. VII. A statute of Iowa, which imposes a collateral inheritance tax of 20 per cent. in case the beneficiaries are non-resident aliens, while it is only 5 per cent. otherwise, does not conflict with the provision in the treaty with Denmark of 1826, renewed in 1857,—"that no higher or other duties, charges or taxes of any kind shall be levied in the territories or dominions of either party, upon any personal property, money or effects of their respective citizens or subjects, on the removal of the same from their territories or dominions reciprocally, either upon the inheritance of such property, money or effects, or otherwise, than are or shall be payable in each state upon the same, when removed by a citizen or subject of such state, respectively,"—since the tax is not a tax upon property, but merely a tax upon the succession or transmission of the property occasioned by the death of the owner. That portion of the property deducted by the executor or administrator and paid to the State Treasurer pursuant to the statute never reaches the beneficiary. In re Anderson's Estate (1914), 147 N. W. (Iowa) 1098. See later case of McKeown v. Brown (1914), 149 N. W. (Iowa) 593, under Article I of the convention with Great Britain of March 2, 1899.

Art. VIII.   Under the most-favored-nation clause, a consul of Denmark, invoking the rights and privileges enjoyed by the consuls of Italy under Article XXII of the treaty of 1871, and by the consuls of the Argentine Republic under Article IX of the treaty of 1853, cannot appear for an infant party in a proceeding for the probate of a will, so as to give the Surrogate's Court jurisdiction of such party, without the issuance of a citation. In re Peterson's Will (1906), 101 N. Y. S. 285.

DOMINICAN REPUBLIC.

Treaty of Amity and Commerce Concluded February 8, 1867.

Art. IX.   This article is a pledge of the contracting parties that there shall be no discriminating legislation against the importation of articles, the growth, produce, or manufacture of their respective countries, in favor of articles of like character imported from any other country. It was never intended to prevent special concessions to other countries, upon sufficient considerations, and does not carry with it automatically such concessions. Whitney v. Robertson (1888), 124 U. S. 190.

FRANCE.

Treaties of Amity and Commerce, and Alliance Concluded February 6, 1778.

The treaties of alliance and commerce with France of 1778, having been concluded on the same day and as the result of the same negotiation, and signed by the same plenipotentiaries, are in diplomatic effect one instrument. Gray, Admr. v. United States (1886), 21 C. Cls. 340.

The abrogation of a treaty may be justified as the result of a breach by the other party or as a result of a change of circumstances. The United States was justified in annulling the treaties of 1778; and the act of July 7, 1798, was effective as between the nations. The compact ended, July 7, 1798. Thereafter, the relations between the two nations were governed by international law and not by the treaties of 1778. Hooper, Admr. v. United States (1887), 22 C. Cls. 408; The Brig William (1888), 23 C. Cls. 201.

The United States abrogated the treaties of 1778 by the act of July 7, 1798, and thereby relieved France from all obligations under them. The Ship James and William (1902), 37 C. Cls. 303; The Schooner Endeavor (1909), 44 C. Cls. 242.

The treaty of 1794 between the United States and Great Britain did not release France from any obligation of the treaties of 1778. The Ship James and William (1902), 37 C. Cls. 303.

Treaty of Amity and Commerce Concluded February 6, 1778.

Art. II. The most-favored-nation clause in the treaty related to duties and rights and benefits in the ports of the parties. Provisions which declare what shall be regarded as contraband or non-contraband of war relate to the procedure of the two nations in time of war and are not affected by a treaty of either with another power. Ship James and William (1902), 37 C. Cls. 303.

Art. XI. "Upon every principle of fair construction, this article gave to the subjects of France a right to purchase and hold lands in the United States." Chirac v. Chirac (1817), 2 Wheat. 259, 271.

The treaty of 1778 allowed citizens of either country to hold lands in the other; and the title, once vested in a French subject, was not divested by the abrogation of that treaty, and the expiration of the subsequent convention of 1800. Carneal v. Banks (1825), 10 Wheat. 181.

Art. XIV. Neutral property in an enemy's ship was subject to forfeiture under Article XIV of the treaty. Bolchos v. Darrel (1795), Bee's Admr. Repts. 74.

Art. XVII. No foreign power can of right institute, or erect, any court of judicature of any kind within the jurisdiction of the United States, except such only as may be warranted by, and in pursuance of, treaties. The admiralty jurisdiction, which has been exercised in the United States by the consuls of France, not being so warranted, is not of right. Glass v. The Sloop Betsey (1794), 3 Dall. 6, 16.

"It is true, both by the law of nations, and the treaty with France, if a French privateer brings an enemy's ship into our ports, which she has taken as prize on the high seas, the United States, as a nation, have no right to detain her, or make any enquiry into the circumstances of the capture. But this exemption from enquiry, by our courts of justice, in this respect, only belongs to a French privateer, lawfully commissioned, and, therefore, if a vessel claims that exemption, but does not appear to be duly entitled to it, it is the express duty of the court, upon application, to make enquiry, whether she is the vessel she pretends to be, since her title to such exemption depends on that very fact." Iredell, J., Talbot v. Janson (1795), 3 Dall. 133, 159.

This article was pleaded in bar to the jurisdiction of the district court of the United States in cases of captures by French privateers on the high seas and brought into our ports, and the plea sustained in British Consul v. Schooner Favourite (1794); Stannick v. Ship Friendship (1794); Salderondo v. Ship Nostra Signora del Camino et al. (1794); Reid v. Ship Vere (1795); British Consul v. Ship Mermaid (1795); and Moodie v. Ship Amity (1796). Bee's Admr. Repts. 39, 40, 43, 66, 69, 89.

Article XXV of the treaty between the United States and Great Britain of 1794, in which similar privileges and exemptions as to prizes in ports were granted to Great Britain, was in conflict with the provision in Article XVII of the treaty with France, that "no shelter or refuge shall be given in their ports to such as shall have made prize of the subjects, people or property of either of the parties." Gray, Admr. (1886), 21 C. Cls. 340.

Art. XIX. By this article French vessels, whether public and of war, or private and of merchants, may, on any urgent necessity, enter our ports and be supplied with all things needful for repairs. "In the present case, the privateer only underwent a repair; and the mere replacement of her force cannot be a material augmentation; even if an augmentation of force could be deemed (which we do not decide) a sufficient cause for restitution." Moodie v. Ship Phoebe Anne (1796), 3 Dall. 319. See also Geyer v. Michel, (1796), 3 Dall. 285.

Arts. XXIII and XXV. Where an American vessel carried the passport or sea-letter prescribed by Article XXV of the treaty, it was a case where free ships made free goods under Article XXIII; and the cargo could not be condemned for want of evidence of its neutrality. The Ship James and William v. United States (1902), 37 C. Cls. 303.

Art. XXIV. By the treaty of 1778 with France, it was declared that tar and turpentine should not be reputed contraband, and, until the abrogation of the treaty by the act of Congress approved July 7, 1798, French condemnations on the ground that tar and turpentine were contraband were illegal. The Ship James and William v. United States (1902), 37 C. Cls. 303.

Art. XXV. A sea-letter is not the only document by which the neutral character of a vessel belonging to citizens of the United States may be established. Tunno v. Preary (1794), Bee's Admr. Repts. 6.

Arts. XXV and XXVII. A ship with the passport or sea-letter, and certificate or manifest, as provided for in Article XXV of the treaty, was free under Article XXVII from search upon the high seas. The absence of these two papers did not render the merchant vessel liable to condemnation, but simply left her without the benefits of the article and subject to the rules of international law. The Brig Venus (1892), 27 C. Cls. 116.

Consular Convention Concluded November 14, 1788.

Art. IX. As to the evidence required for the issuance of a warrant for the apprehension under this article of a deserter from a French vessel, see United States v. Lawrence (1795), 3 Dall. 42.

Art. XII. A French subject who has taken the oath of allegiance to the United States is not within the twelfth article of the convention. Portier v. Le Roy (1794), 1 Yeates (Pa.) 371.

Treaty of Peace, Commerce, and Navigation Concluded September 30, 1800.

The treaty was not a treaty of peace; nor did it conclude or recognize a state of war or a condition of hostility. Cushing, Admr. v. United States (1886), 22 C. Cls. 1. See also Gray, Admr. v. United States (1886), 21 C. Cls. 340.

Art. II. (Retrenchment).

By the bargain with France, the United States obtained the renunciation of the French claims against it and a relinquishment from its obligations under the treaties of 1778, and, in consideration therefor, released France from all claims of American citizens. The use, to which the claims of citizens thus released were put, was a public use, since the bargain solved the strained relations between the two countries and forever put an end to the treaties of 1778. Gray, Admr. v. United States (1886), 21 C. Cls. 340; Cushing, Admr. v. United States (1886), 22 C. Cls. 1; Hooper, Admr. v. United States (1887), 22 C. Cls. 408. See also Blagge v. Balch (1896), 162 U. S. 439.

A claim arising after the conclusion of the treaty, though prior to its final ratification, was not relinquished under Article II. The Schooner Jane (1888), 23 C. Cls. 226.

The supplemental article to the treaty of 1800, not having been appended to the treaty until several months after that instrument was signed, cannot be referred to for the purpose of explaining the preceding articles. The Ship Tom (1904), 39 C. Cls. 290.

Art. IV. A final condemnation in an inferior court of admiralty, where a right of appeal exists and has been claimed, is not a definitive condemnation within the meaning of the treaty. The court is as much bound as the executive to take notice of a treaty, and will reverse the original decree of condemnation (although it was correct when made) and order restitution of the property under the treaty, although the treaty was concluded after the original condemnation. United States v. Schooner Peggy (1801), 1 Cr. 103.

Art. VII. The provision, that the citizens of one country holding lands in the other may dispose of the same by testament, or otherwise, and inherit lands in the respective countries, without being obliged to obtain letters of naturalization, applies equally to those who took by descent as to those who acquired by purchase. The stipulation, "that in case the laws of either of the two states should restrain strangers from the exercise of the rights of property with respect to real estate, such real estate may be sold, or otherwise disposed of, to citizens or inhabitants of the country where it may be," does not affect the rights of a French subject, who takes or holds by the treaty, so as to deprive him of the power of selling to citizens of this country. It gives to a French subject, who has acquired lands by descent or devise, the right, during life, to sell or otherwise dispose thereof, if lying in a State where lands purchased by an alien, generally, would be immediately escheatable. The instant the descent was cast on a French subject, his rights became complete and could not be affected by the subsequent expiration of the treaty. Chirac v. Chirac (1817), 2 Wheat. 259.

"This article, by its terms, suspended, during the existence of the treaty, the provisions of the common law of Maryland and of the statutes of that State of 1780 and of 1791, so far as they prevented citizens of France from taking by inheritance from citizens of the United States, property, real or personal, situated therein." Geofroy v. Riggs (1890), 133 U. S. 258, 266.

Treaty for the Cession of Louisiana Concluded April 30, 1803.

Art. I. By the treaty of St. Ildefonso of October 1, 1800, Spain ceded Louisiana to France; and, by the treaty of Paris of April 30, 1803, France transferred her rights to the territory to the United States. The political departments of the government asserted title under the treaty to the territory between the Iberville and the Perdido rivers, and the courts have followed the determination in this respect of the legislative and executive branches. Grants of land in this disputed territory by the crown of Spain after the treaty of St. Ildefonso were void. Foster v. Neilson (1829), 2 Pet. 253; United States v. Arredondo (1832), 6 Pet. 691; Garcia v. Lee (1838), 12 Pet. 511; Keene v. Whitaker (1840), 14 Pet. 170; United States v. Reynes (1850), 9 How. 127; United States v. Lynde (1870), 11 Wall. 632.

Art. II. As to public property as distinguished from private property, see New Orleans v. United States (1836), 10 Pet. 662; Pollard's Lessee v. Hagan (1845), 3 How. 212; United States v. King (1849), 7 How. 833, 847; Slidell v. Grandjean (1883), 111 U. S. 412.

By the cession of Louisiana, the government of the United States succeeded to all the property and interests formerly possessed by the governments of France and Spain in that province. A right reserved by the terms of a grant to use the land for any fortification is more than the right of eminent domain. It is a right to use the land for that purpose without compensation; and this reserved right passed to the United States under the treaty of cession. Josephs v. United States (1865), 1 C. Cls. 197. See dissenting opinion, 2 C. Cls. 586.

Art. III. An adjudication made by a Spanish tribunal in Louisiana is not void because it was made after the cession of the country to the United States, for it is historically known that the actual possession of the country was not surrendered until some time after the proceedings and adjudication in the case took place. It was the judgment, therefore, of a competent Spanish tribunal, having jurisdiction of the case, and rendered while the country, though ceded, was, de facto, in the possession of Spain, and subject to Spanish laws. Such judgments, so far as they affect the private rights of the parties thereto, must be deemed valid. Keene v. McDonough (1834), 8 Pet. 308, 310.

A grant by the Spanish governor, dated January 2, 1804, for lands included within the limits of Louisiana was void, Spain having parted with her title to that province by the treaty of St. Ildefonso of October 1, 1800, and France having ceded the same province to the United States by the treaty of Paris of April 30, 1803. Such a grant could not be protected by the provision in the treaty for the protection of the people of Louisiana in the free enjoyment of their liberty and property, the term property being applicable only to possessions or rights founded in justice and good faith, and based upon authority competent to their creation. The treaty of St. Ildefonso between Spain and France and of Paris between France and the United States should be construed as binding on the parties thereto from the respective dates of those treaties. United States v. Reynes (1850), 9 How. 127.

After the treaty of St. Ildefonso was signed, and until Louisiana was delivered to France, its possession continued in Spain. The right to the territory, though in France, was imperfect until ratified, but absolute by ratification from the date of the treaty. Accordingly, the Spanish governor had no right, after October 1, 1800, to grant a perpetual ferry franchise; and such an attempted grant is not property protected by the treaty between the United States and France. Davis v. Police Jury of Concordia (1850), 9 How. 280. See also United States v. D'Auterive (1850), 10 How. 609.

The United States regards the stipulation, that the inhabitants of the ceded territory shall be protected in the free enjoyment of their property, as the avowal of a principle which would have been held equally sacred though it had not been inserted in the contract. The term "property," as applied to lands, comprehends every species of title, inchoate or complete, legal or equitable, and embraces those rights which lie in contract, executory as well as executed. Soulard v. United States (1830), 4 Pet. 511; Delassus v. United States (1835), 9 Pet. 117; Smith v. United States (1836), 10 Pet. 326; Strother v. Lucas (1838), 12 Pet. 410; Hornsby v. United States (1869), 10 Wall. 224; Carpenter v. Rannels (1873), 19 Wall. 138; Morton v. Nebraska (1874), 21 Wall. 660; Bryan v. Kennett (1885), 113 U. S. 179.

"This court has defined property to be any right, legal or equitable, inceptive, inchoate, or perfect, which before the treaty with France in 1803, or with Spain in 1819, had so attached to any piece or tract of land, great or small, as to affect the conscience of the former sovereign, 'with a trust,' and make him a trustee for an individual, according to the law of nations, of the sovereign himself, the local usage or custom of the colony or district; according to the principles of justice, and rules of equity. 6 Peters 709, 714; 8 Peters 450; 9 Peters 133, 144, 737; 10 Peters 105, 324, 331, 35, 36. The same principle has been applied by this court, to the right of a Spanish town, as a municipal corporation. 10 Peters 718 to 736; passim, 144, 734, 736; 10 Peters 105, 324, 331, 335, 336 * * *. This court has also uniformly held that the term grant, in a treaty, comprehends not only those which are made in form, but also any concession, warrant, order or permission to survey, possess or settle, whether evidenced by writing or parol, or presumed from possession; (vide the cases last cited,) 8 Peters 466-7; 9 Peters 152, 170; 10 Peters 331-340; S. P. 10 Peters 718 &c.; and that in the term laws, is included custom and usage, when once settled." Baldwin, J., Strother v. Lucas (1838), 12 Pet. 410, 436.

The obligation of perfecting titles under Spanish concessions, which was assumed by the United States in the Louisiana treaty, was of an executory character to be carried out by the legislative department of the government. United States v. Wiggins (1840), 14 Pet. 334; Chouteau v. Eckhart (1844), 2 How. 344. See also United States v. Reynes (1850), 9 How. 127; United States v. Philadelphia and New Orleans (1850), 11 How. 609; Dent v. Emmeger (1871), 14 Wall. 308. See also New Orleans v. United States (1836), 10 Pet. 662.

This article contemplates two objects: First, that Louisiana shall be admitted into the Union as soon as possible upon an equal footing with the other States; and second, that until such admission the inhabitants of the ceded territory shall be protected in the free enjoyment of their liberty, property, and religion. Had any of these rights been violated while this stipulation continued in force the individual supposing himself to be injured might have brought his case into the Supreme Court under section 25 of the judiciary act. But this stipulation ceased to operate when Louisiana became a member of the Union. The inhabitants of Louisiana enjoy all the advantages of American citizens, in common with their brethren in sister States, when their titles are decided by the tribunals of the State. New Orleans v. Armas (1835), 9

Pet. 224. A decision of a State court against the validity of a title set up under a complete grant issued prior to the cession would be subject to revisal by the Supreme Court under section 25 of the judiciary act. McDonogh v. Millaudon (1845), 3 How. 693.

The stipulation, that the inhabitants of the ceded territory shall be incorporated into the Union of the United States and admitted as soon as possible, according to the principles of the Constitution, to the enjoyment of all the rights, advantages and immunities of citizens of the United States, has no bearing upon the question of title of the State of Iowa to the land beneath its lakes. Iowa v. Rood (1902), 187 U. S. 87.

This article was consummated as regards the State of Louisiana upon its admission as a State into the Union, April 30, 1812. Church of St. Francis &c. v. Martin (1843), 4 Rob. (La.) 62.

A native of Saxony, who resided in the territory of Louisiana at the time of the cession to the United States, and who continued there to reside until 1811, when he removed to the State of Pennsylvania, became a citizen of the United States and as such entitled to vote. In re Harrold (1840), 1 Pa. L. J. 119. See also United States v. Laverty (1812), 3 Mart. 733; State v. Primrose (1842), 3 Ala. 546.

Art. VI. "When the United States acquired and took possession of the Floridas under the Louisiana treaty, the treaties which had been made with the Indian tribes remained in force over all the ceded territories, as the laws which regulate the relations with all the Indians who were parties to them. They were binding on the United States as the fundamental laws of Indian right, acknowledged by royal orders and municipal regulations." Grier, J., Wilson v. Wall (1867), 6 Wall. 83, 87.

Convention as to Claims, and Duties on Wines and Cotton Concluded July 4, 1831.

The powers and duties of the commissioners under this convention were the same as those which were exercised by the commissioners under the treaty of 1819 with Spain, as determined in the cases of Comegys v. Vasse, 1 Pet. 212, and Sheppard v. Taylor, 5 Pet. 710. Frevall v. Bache (1840), 14 Pet. 95.

The commissioners under this convention had no power to decide ultimately between two or more conflicting American claimants. The decision of the commissioners was conclusive as to the question whether the claim was valid against the French government under the convention, but not as to the question whether it was good against the indemnity awarded. If the property seized belonged to a firm, one member of which was not a citizen of the United States, his share of the loss could not be allowed as a claim under the convention; but he would be entitled to receive out of the sum awarded to the other members what he had paid for freight, and for moneys advanced. The commissions of the consignee are not chargeable to the French government under the convention; they are a charge against the indemnity only, since they would have been a charge against the proceeds, if the property had not been seized by the French government, and had been sold by the consignee. The consignees were entitled to a reasonable compensation for their trouble and expense in making reclamation against the French government. Ridgway v. Hays (1836), 5 Cr. C. C. 23. See also New York Ins. Co. v. Roulet (1840), 24 Wend. 505; Radcliff v. Coster (1839), 1 Hoff. Ch. 99; Lestapies v. Ingraham (1846), 5 Barr (Pa.) 71; Roberts v. United States, Dev. C. Cls. §§ 702, 703.

The convention of 1831 does not extend to the claims renounced and, from an international point of view, extinguished by the treaty of 1800. Gray, Admr. v. United States (1886), 21 C. Cls. 340.

The commissioners under this convention were authorized to make their award in favor of the person who was the legal and ostensible owner of the property seized, at the time of the seizure, and were not bound to ascertain the rights, and decide litigations between conflicting claimants, citizens of the United States. They might select that one whom they deemed best entitled, and award to him the portion of the indemnity applicable to the claim, and leave the others to settle their disputes before the ordinary tribunals of the country according to the municipal laws of the land. No citizen could, by any judgment of the commissioners, be deprived of his right to resort to the ordinary tribunals of the country to establish his claim to participate in the sum awarded for the whole loss. The party who receives the sum awarded for the whole claim is a trustee for such as may be entitled to participate therein. Dutilh's Admr. v. Coursault (1837), 5 Cr. C. C. 349. See Dev. C. Cls. §§ 702, 703.

The awards of the commissioners under the convention were conclusive as to the validity and amount of claims upon France for damages and injuries, but were not conclusive as to the conflicting rights of different persons to the funds awarded. Lee, Admx. v. Thorndike, Admr. (1841), 2 Metc. 313.

Claims arising after the conclusion of the treaty of 1800, though prior to its ratification, were not relinquished by Article II of that treaty; but they were relinquished to France by the convention of 1831. The decisions of the commissioners under the convention of 1831 adverse to the jurisdiction of such claims are not conclusive upon the Court of Claims; neither can they be reviewed and corrected. The Schooner Jane (1888), 23 C. Cls. 226.

Extradition Convention Concluded November 9, 1843.

The provisions of the convention operate as a rule of law without the aid of legislation and are as binding on the courts as acts of Congress. A treaty takes effect from its date irrespective of its ratification, unless a different period is fixed by the contracting parties or must be adopted in order to fulfill their manifest intention. The questions,—whether the United States government is bound by a convention to deliver up an alleged fugitive from justice apprehended and detained by a Federal court for trial for offenses committed by him in the foreign country, not crimes by our laws; whether he is within the description of persons named in the convention as subject to extradition when the convention went into operation; and whether the obligations assumed by the convention will be fulfilled,—are addressed to the political, not the judicial, department. The laws of France, and not those of the United States, form the basis for the enquiry as to whether an extraditable offense has been committed. The convention provides that the laws of the place of refuge are to be applied to the investigation as if the crime had been committed where the arrest was made. A person against whom a complaint has been made and accepted before a judge of instruction in France is a person accused within the meaning of the convention, although no indictment has been found against him. In re Metzger (1847), Fed. Cases No. 9511. Where a district judge, at his chambers, decides that there is sufficient cause for the surrender of a person claimed by the French government, and commits him to custody to await the order of the President of the United States, the Supreme Court has no jurisdiction to issue a writ of habeas corpus for the purpose of reviewing that decision. s. c. 5 How. 176.

The convention of 1843 cannot in any sense be held to execute itself. It was not intended to act in præsenti. It was a contract between the two nations to be executed only in futuro by legislation. Without such legislation the courts have no power to act in executing the convention. Although it may be regarded as executing itself so far as to establish the right of the French government to the surrender of a criminal, legislation is required to enforce the delivery and to secure the subsequent possession of the fugitive. A prisoner who has been merely charged, or accused, before a magistrate in France authorized to arrest, is not a party accused—mis en accusation—within the meaning of the convention; and he cannot be demanded by the French government, nor surrendered by the American, by the terms of the convention. Where a treaty is drawn up in the French, as well as in the English, language, and both are originals and are intended by the parties to be identical, that construction ought to prevail which establishes a conformity between the two. In re Metzger (1847), 1 Barb. 248.

Consular Convention Concluded February 23, 1853.

Art. II. The provision of the Constitution, which secures to the accused in criminal prosecutions the right to have compulsory process for obtaining witnesses in his favor, does not authorize the issuing of such process to ambassadors, who by public law, or consuls, who by express treaty, are not amenable to the process of the courts. In re Dillon (1854), 7 Sawy. 561. See Baiz v. Malo (1899), 58 N. Y. S. 806, under Colombia, treaty of 1846; In re Peterson's Will (1906), 101 N. Y. S. 285, under Denmark, treaty of 1826.

Art. III. By this article, it is stipulated that the authorities shall in no case examine or seize papers deposited in consular offices. Where a subpœna duces tecum, directed to a consul of France, is prayed for, it is the duty of the court to require the party praying for it to show that the document is not an official paper protected by the treaty. In re Dillon (1854), 7 Sawy. 561.

Art. VII. This convention has no effect upon the succession of a person who died in 1848. Prevost v. Greneaux (1856), 19 How. 1.

The District of Columbia, as a political community, is one of "the States of the Union" within the meaning of these terms as used in this article; and a citizen of France can take land in the District of Columbia by descent from a citizen of the United States. "In all the States of the Union by whose laws aliens are permitted to hold real estate, so long as such laws remain in force, Frenchmen shall enjoy the right of possessing personal and real property by the same title and in the same manner as citizens of the United States. They shall be free to dispose of it as they may please—by donation, testament, or otherwise—just as those citizens themselves. But as to the States by whose existing laws aliens are not permitted to hold real estate, the treaty engages that the President shall recommend to them the passage of such laws as may be necessary for the purpose of conferring that right." "In all political communities in the United States where legislation permits aliens to hold real estate, the disability of Frenchmen from alienage in disposing and inheriting property, real and personal, is removed." Geofroy v. Riggs (1890), 133 U. S. 258, 270, 272.

By the terms of this article citizens and subjects of France are entitled to acquire by inheritance and otherwise real estate in all respects the same as citizens of the United States in those States by whose laws an alien is permitted to hold real estate. Since the constitution and statutes of Nebraska permit aliens to hold and acquire real estate in the same manner as citizens, the provision of a statute prohibiting nonresident aliens from acquiring real estate by inheritance or otherwise is inoperative so far as it relates to citizens or subjects of France. Bahuaud v. Bize (1901), 105 Fed. 485.

Under the provisions of this convention, the subjects of France cannot in Louisiana, where they enjoy the right of possessing and owning real and personal property, be subjected to taxes on transfer, inheritance, or any others different from those paid by our own citizens, or to taxes which shall not be equally imposed. Succession of Dufour (1855), 10 La. Ann. 391; Succession of Amat (1866), 18 La. Ann.

403; Succession of Rixner (1896), 48 La. Ann. 552; Succession of Rabasse (1897), 49 La. Ann. 1405.

By the convention of 1853 a subject of France can hold and convey lands free from the right of escheat in the State of Tennessee. Baker v. Shy (1871), 9 Heisk. 85.

Art. VIII. After a seaman has been properly arrested on the request of the French consul under the convention of 1853, he can be held in prison at the disposal of the consul for sixty days as provided for in § 4081, Rev. Stats., and the courts cannot discharge him within that period against the protest of the consul, because of the fact that the vessel to which he belonged has left the port at which he was arrested. The departure of the vessel from the port need have no effect upon the imprisonment of the persons arrested. By the terms of the treaty, the persons arrested, and not the vessel, are held "during the whole of their stay, at the disposal of the consuls." The only method of enforcing treaty provisions for the arrest of seamen on requisition of foreign consuls is pursuant to the act of June 11, 1864, now §§ 4079, 4080, 4081, Rev. Stats.; and thereunder the requisition must be made to the district court or judge, and the arrest must be made by the marshal, and an arrest by a local chief of police is not authorized; but if after a seaman so arrested has been produced before the district court on habeas corpus and the court finds that his case comes under the treaty and that he should be held, the mere fact that he was arrested by a person not authorized to do so does not entitle him to his discharge. Dallemagne v. Moisan (1905), 197 U. S. 169.

Art. XII. Under Article XV of the treaty with Belgium of 1880, French consuls, in virtue of the most-favored-nation clause, have the right to represent absent heirs, French subjects, of a succession opened here. Such provision is within the treaty-making power and must prevail if in conflict with a State statute. Succession of Rabasse (1895), 47 La. Ann. 1452.

Additional Article to Extradition Convention Concluded February 10, 1858.

Where the defendant subscribed for one share of the stock of a French corporation, and agreed with the other subscribers to devote his entire time to the management of the corporation's affairs, and, in consideration of his services, to receive 40% of the profits, he was a person "hired or salaried" by the corporation within the meaning of the provision in the convention authorizing extradition for embezzlement by any person, hired or salaried, to the detriment of his employer. In re Balensi (1903), 120 Fed. 864.

Trade-mark Convention Concluded April 16, 1869.

Since the international industrial property convention of 1883, to which both the United States and France are parties, covers the whole subject matter of the convention of 1869, the earlier one may be considered as impliedly repealed. La Republique Francaise v. Schultz (1893), 57 Fed. 37.

Claims Convention Concluded January 15, 1880.

See Bodemüller v. United States (1889), 39 Fed. 437; Burthe v. Denis (1890), 133 U. S. 514.

Reciprocal Commercial Agreement Signed May 28, 1898.

"While it may be true that this commercial agreement, made under authority of the tariff act of 1897, § 3, was not a treaty possessing the dignity of one requiring ratification by the Senate of the United States, it was an international compact, negotiated between the representatives of two sovereign nations and made in the name and on behalf of the contracting countries, and dealing with important commercial relations between the two countries, and was proclaimed by the President. If not technically a treaty requiring ratification, nevertheless it was a compact authorized by the Congress of the United States, negotiated and proclaimed under the authority of its President. We think such a compact is a treaty under the Circuit Court of Appeals Act, and, where its construction is directly involved, as it is here, there is a right of review by direct appeal to this court." The word "statuary" in the agreement is to be construed as having the same meaning as when used in the act of Congress under which the agreement was made. It includes only such statuary as is cut, carved, or otherwise wrought by hand as the work of a sculptor. Altman & Co. v. United States (1912), 224 U. S. 583, 601.

The reciprocal commercial agreement with France proclaimed May 30, 1898, providing for a reduction in the duty on "brandies, or other spirits," being the result of negotiations and representations had with reference, among other things, to liquers and cordials, and the French text of the agreement containing the word "liquers," merchandise known as "liquers" is included in the agreement. Nicholas v. United States (1900), 122 Fed. 892; United States v. Luyties (1904), 130 Fed. 333; United States v. Julius Wile Bro. & Co. (1904), 130 Fed. 331.

The provision for the reduction of duty on "brandies or other spirits" supersedes the provision for a different rate in schedule G, § 1, par. 263, of the tariff act of July 24, 1897, on the alcohol in excess of 10% found in fruit preserved in spirits. La Manna, Azema & Farnam v. United States (1906), 144 Fed. 683; Mihalovitch, Fletcher & Co. v. United States (1908), 160 Fed. 988.

Merchandise from Algeria, imported into the United States, is not subject to the reduced rates of duty provided for on merchandise imported from France proper. The amendatory and additional agreement, proclaimed August 22, 1902, which provides that the agreement of 1898 shall "apply also to Algeria," was intended to have prospective operation only. United States v. Tartar Chemical Co. (1903), 127 Fed. 944. See also United States v. Julius Wile Bro. & Co. (1904), 130 Fed. 331.

In order to be entitled to the benefits of the reciprocal commercial agreements concluded under section 3 of the tariff act of July 24, 1897, importers must furnish satisfactory evidence that their importations were produced in as well as exported from the country with which the agreement was made. Migliavacca Wine Co. v. United States (1905), 148 Fed. 142.

GERMAN EMPIRE AND THE GERMAN STATES.

(1) GERMAN EMPIRE.

Consular Convention Concluded December 11, 1871.

Arts. VIII and X. The provision, which authorizes German consuls to act as legal representatives of the German Emperor's subjects, does not constitute such consuls administrators of the estates of deceased persons nor authorize a consul to recover wages due a deceased seaman, who was a German subject, unless the consul represents heirs who are entitled to the money and who are German subjects. The General McPherson (1900), 100 Fed. 860.

Art. X. Neither this article nor any other article of the convention of 1871 provides that subjects of the Empire shall be permitted to take or hold real estate in the United States, except so far as the right to do so was guaranteed by treaties then existing. Wunderle v. Wunderle (1893), 144 Ill. 40, 55.

Art. XIII. Under this article, which gives to the consular officers of each country exclusive power to take cognizance of and determine differences between the captains and crews of vessels of their own nation, and prohibits the courts of the other country from interfering therein, the courts of the United States cannot, so long as the relation of seaman to a German vessel is not terminated, entertain a libel for wages and construe the contract of shipment; but must remit the whole matter to the German consul for adjudication. The Burchard (1890), 42 Fed. 608.

The article does not expressly or by implication grant privileges or confer powers which exempt a German vessel employing seamen in a port of this country from the obligation to observe the restrictive provisions of section 24 of the act of December 21, 1898, (30 Stats. 763); nor does it deprive the admiralty courts of the United States of jurisdiction to determine the rights of an American seaman who enters and leaves the service of a German vessel within this country, where the original contract of service was void under the statutes of the United States. The Neck (1905), 138 Fed. 144.

Under this article a court of admiralty of the United States is without jurisdiction of a suit against a German vessel to recover wages, brought by seamen, who are not citizens of the United States, but who signed before a German consul in a port thereof and were discharged in another port after completing their term of service; and such jurisdiction is not conferred merely by the fact that they were paid wages in advance in violation of section 24 of the act of December 21, 1898, (30 Stats. 763). The Bound Brook (1906), 146 Fed. 160.

The provision, that consular representatives of either country "shall have exclusive charge of the internal order of the merchant-vessels of their nation, and shall have the exclusive power to take cognizance of and to determine differences of every kind which may arise, either at sea or in port, between the captains, officers, and crews, and especially in reference to wages and the execution of mutual contracts," does not include a claim by a seaman against a vessel or owner for a tort, so as to exclude the jurisdiction of a United States court of admiralty of a suit on such a claim against a German vessel. The Baker (1907), 157 Fed. 485.

Under this article a court of admiralty of the United States is without jurisdiction of a suit between an alien seaman and a German vessel arising out of his contract of employment. The Koenigin Luise (1910), 184 Fed. 170. See also Meyer v. Basson (1875), 10 Phila. 414.

Art. XVII. The provision, that citizens of Germany shall enjoy in the United States "the same protection as native citizens" in respect of trade-marks, does not prevent a citizen of Germany from acquiring by prior use in this country a trade-mark in a particular word, although by the laws of Germany, words alone, and apart from some symbol or design, are not the subject of appropriation. J. & P. Baltz Brewing Co. v. Kaiserbrauerei, Beck & Co. (1896), 74 Fed. 222.

The provision, that, with regard to marks or labels of goods, or of their packages, the citizens of Germany shall enjoy in the United States the same protection as native citizens, does not give to a citizen of Germany, who has acquired the right to a trade-mark in that country, a similar right to the trade-mark in the United States. Richter v. Reynolds (1893), 59 Fed. 577.

Reciprocal Commercial Agreement Concluded July 10, 1900.

The reciprocal commercial agreement with Germany negotiated under section 3 of the tariff act of July 24, 1897, which allows a reduction of duty on "spirits," supersedes the provision for a different rate in schedule G, section 1, par. 263, of said act, on the alcohol in excess of 10% found in fruit preserved in spirits. Mihalovitch, Fletcher & Co. v. United States (1908), 160 Fed. 988.

(2) GERMAN STATES.

BADEN.

The disability imposed upon non-resident aliens by section 1 of the alien act of Illinois of 1887, is not removed by any existing treaty between the United States and the Grand Duchy of Baden or between the United States and the German Empire. Wunderle v. Wunderle (1893), 144 Ill. 40, 55.

BAVARIA.

Convention Abolishing Droit d' Aubaine and Taxes on Emigration Concluded January 21, 1845.

Arts. I.-III. The provisions of the convention conferring on subjects of Bavaria a right, notwithstanding their alienage, to take by inheritance lands in the United States, according to the laws here controlling descent, remove from them the disability imposed by a State statute on non-resident aliens of inheriting lands within its limits. Opel v. Shoup (1896), 100 Iowa 407.

Subjects of Bavaria are by virtue of this convention exempt from the tax of 10% imposed by statute in Louisiana on successions going to non-resident aliens. Succession of Crusius (1867), 19 La. Ann. 369.

Extradition Convention Concluded September 12, 1853.

This convention was not abrogated by the operation of the constitution of the German Empire adopted in 1871. In re Hermann Thomas (1874), 12 Blatchf. 370.

Art. I. The provision, for the extradition of persons charged with forgery or utterance of forged papers, is applicable where it appears that written instruments have been falsely uttered by the accused for the purpose of fraud and deceit, and that the instruments are of such a description that they may defraud or deceive if issued with such intent. The convention is now in force notwithstanding Bavaria has become a part of the German Empire. Ex parte Zentner (1910), 188 Fed. 344.

HANOVER.

Treaty of Commerce and Navigation Concluded June 10, 1846.

Art. X. The provision, that the subjects of the King of Hanover shall have free access to the tribunals, in their litigious affairs, on the same terms which are granted by the law and usages of the country to native citizens and subjects, refers only to ordinary litigation, and does not extend to a right of litigation against the government afterwards created in favor of its own citizens, to the exclusion of aliens; and it does not entitle such subjects to maintain an action in the Court of Claims under the act of March 3, 1891, giving that court jurisdiction of certain claims "for property of citizens of the United States" taken or destroyed by Indians belonging to any band or tribe in amity with the United States. Valk v. United States (1894), 29 C. Cls. 62; affirmed, 168 U. S. 703.

Under the treaty, which allows non-resident alien heirs the right to sell the real estate of their ancestor, within a reasonable time, the right to sell carries with it the ownership as a necessary incident to the power of sale; but such ownership is less than a fee simple absolute, the resident heirs being vested with the remainder of the title, and such remainder draws the full fee simple title into the resident heirs upon failure of the condition upon which the non-resident alien heirs took their title. Where a treaty allows a non-resident alien heir the right to sell the real estate of an ancestor within a reasonable time, but does not specify what is to be a reasonable time, and there are no statutes providing what shall be a reasonable time for the sale of such property, the question as to what is a reasonable time is necessarily left to judicial construction. It was held that, under all of the circumstances presented, a delay from 1862 to 1868 was unreasonable, and that as a consequence the resident heirs had become vested with a fee simple title. Ahrens v. Ahrens (1909), 144 Iowa 486.

HANSEATIC REPUBLICS.

(BREMEN, HAMBURG AND LUBECK.)

Treaty of Friendship, Commerce and Navigation Concluded December 20, 1827.

Art. VII. The word "representatives" in the second clause of Article VII refers to all who take by will or descent, including devisees and heirs, as well as to executors and administrators. The heirs of an American citizen, who are citizens of Bremen, have the prescribed term of three years for the disposal of real estate, which they would have inherited but for their alienage. They take a fee in such lands determinable by the non-exercise of the power of sale within three years. The treaty suspends, during the period of three years, the operation of the alien law of the State, which makes non-resident aliens incapable of taking lands by descent. Schultze v. Schultze (1893), 144 Ill. 290.

Art. IX. See under Art. IX of the treaty of May 1, 1828, with Prussia. See 14 Op. Atty. Gen. 530.

Consular Convention Concluded April 30, 1852.

Art. I. Under the terms of this convention the Federal courts have no jurisdiction of a suit for wages brought by a seaman against the captain of a vessel belonging to Bremen, where the parties are citizens of Bremen. Kendept v. Korner (1854), Fed. Cases No. 7693.

The convention of April 30, 1852, between the United States and the Hanseatic League, does not preclude a citizen of the United States, who has served as a seaman on board a vessel belonging to one of the Hanse Towns, and has returned home, from bringing his action for wages for such services in the admiralty courts of the United States. Leavit v. The Shakespeare (1871), Fed. Cases No. 8167.

HESSE.

Convention Abolishing Droit d' Aubaine and Taxes on Emigration Concluded March 26, 1844.

"Hesse Cassel having become a part of Prussia in 1866, its citizens thereby became Prussian subjects. The above treaty became merged in the one existing at that time between Prussia and the United States, which was concluded in 1828, and which is still in force and effect." In re Beck (1890), 11 N. Y. S. 199, 200.

See Bollermann v. Blake (1883), 94 N. Y. 624.

PRUSSIA.

Treaty of Amity and Commerce Concluded July 11, 1799.

Art. X. Since the treaty with Prussia allows citizens and subjects of the one to sell real estate which descends to them in the territory of the other, Poles, who are subjects of Prussia, are allowed to take under the residuary clause of a will. Hart v. Executors of Hart (1801), 2 Desaus. Eq. (S. C.) 57.

Art. XIII. This article, which was revived by the treaty of 1828, has reference to captures and detentions after a voyage has been commenced and not to detentions in port to enforce port regulations. United States v. Diekelman (1875), 92 U. S. 520.

Treaty of Commerce and Navigation Concluded May 1, 1828.

Art. I. This treaty has been recognized by both governments as continuing in force after the formation of the German Empire in 1871; but there is nothing therein that undertakes to change the well recognized rule between states and nations by which a country is permitted first to protect the rights of its own citizens in local property before it may be taken out of its jurisdiction for administration in favor of those residing beyond its borders. Disconto Gesellschaft v. Umbreit (1908), 208 U. S. 570.

Art. IX. The act of Congress of June 26, 1884, sec. 14 (23 Stats. at L. 57), levies a duty of three cents per ton on all vessels "from any foreign port or place in North America, Central America, the West India Islands, the Bahama Islands, the Bermuda Islands, or the Sandwich Islands, or Newfoundland," and a duty of six cents per ton on vessels from any other foreign port. German vessels arriving from European ports are not entitled, under the provisions in the treaties of December 20, 1827, and May 1, 1828,—that the United States shall not grant any particular favor regarding commerce or navigation to any other foreign nation which shall not immediately become common to Germany,—to enter on the payment of the duty of three cents per ton. The classification in said act is merely geographical, the three cent rate applying to vessels of all nations coming from the privileged ports. If an act of Congress is in conflict with a prior treaty the act must control the judiciary. North German Lloyd S. S. Co. v. Hedden (1890), 43 Fed. 17. See Art. XVII of the treaty with Sweden and Norway of July 4, 1827. See 21 Op. Atty. Gen. 80.

Art. X. Under this article the district courts of the United States have no jurisdiction of a suit in rem for wages by the crew of a Prussian vessel. The Elwine Kreplin (1872), 9 Blatchf. 438. A petition for a writ of mandamus to the circuit judge to compel him to entertain jurisdiction of the case on appeal, and to hear and decide on the merits, was dismissed by the Supreme Court. Ex parte Newman, 14 Wall. 152.

Art. XIII. This article contemplates the establishment of blockades, and makes special provision for the government of the parties in case they exist. The vessels of one nation are bound to respect the blockades of the other. United States v. Diekelman (1875), 92 U. S. 520.

Art. XIV. The provision for the removal of the disability of aliens to inherit is valid and within the treaty-making power of the President and the Senate. People v. Gerke (1855), 5 Cal. 381.

A statute of the State of New York, which makes the right of adult alien males to inherit lands dependent upon the filing of a deposition of their intention to become citizens before the consummation of proceedings by the State to defeat their title, is superseded, as to citizens of Prussia, by the treaty with Prussia of 1828, providing that subjects of that country, disqualified by alienage from inheriting land in the United States, shall be allowed a "reasonable" time to sell the same and to withdraw the proceeds. A sale of decedent's lands on foreclosure proceedings within two years and four months after death is a sale within a "reasonable" time. In re Beck (1890), 11 N. Y. S. 199.

Under the provisions of this treaty, a non-resident alien can inherit land in Iowa from a citizen; and in case of his death, his children though non-resident aliens will take what would have descended to the father. A treaty providing that aliens may inherit lands is controlling, though in conflict with statutes of the State. Doehrel v. Hillmer (1897), 102 Iowa 169; Wilcke v. Wilcke (1897), 102 Iowa 173.

In so far as the local statutes are in conflict with the treaty, the provisions of the treaty must govern. A treaty giving citizens of a foreign country the right to take lands by descent in this country is superior to and controls any State legislation against the holding of lands by aliens. Butschkowski v. Brecks (1913), 94 Neb. 532, 534.

Extradition Convention Concluded June 16, 1852.

The German government having officially recognized and continued to recognize the convention between the United States and the kingdom of Prussia of June 16, 1852 as still in force and not terminated because of impossibility of performance, and the Executive Department of the government of the United States having accepted this view and proceeded accordingly, it is not for the courts to question the correctness of these conclusions. The offenses were charged as having been committed "contrary to the laws of Prussia." Although the violated laws were prescribed by imperial authority, they were nevertheless the laws of Prussia administered as such by the Prussian court before which the charges were pending. Terlinden v. Ames (1902), 184 U. S. 270.
Art. I. The convention provides that the contracting parties shall, on requisition, deliver up to justice all persons who, being charged with the crimes therein specified "committed within the jurisdiction of either party, shall seek an asylum, or shall be found within the territories of the other." A fugitive, alleged to be a native and subject of Prussia, was arrested in the United States for extradition to Prussia charged with having committed at Brussels in Belgium "and within the legal jurisdiction of Prussia" crimes specified in the convention. It was contended that, inasmuch as such crimes were, at the time they were committed, punishable by the laws of Belgium, the accused being a subject of Prussia was, by the law of Prussia, subject to be punished for said crimes in Prussia. There was no extradition convention between the United States and Belgium. It was held by Blatchford, J., that the case was covered by the convention. In re Joseph

Stupp (1873), 11 Blatchf. 124. See, however, opinion of the Attorney General, 14 Op. 281.

The embezzlement of funds of a savings bank, established, maintained and owned by a city in Germany, by a cashier, who is a public official appointed by the city, is an embezzlement of public moneys within the meaning of the convention. In re Reiner (1903), 122 Fed. 109.

Under the provision in the convention for the delivery of persons charged with crime upon such evidence of criminality as, according to the laws of the place where the fugitive is found, would justify his apprehension and commitment for trial, if the crime had there been committed, it is sufficient that a prima facie case be made, such as, in the absence of explanation, would justify conviction, or such evidence produced as, in case of trial and conviction thereon, would sustain the verdict. In re Risch (1888), 36 Fed. 546.

It is not necessary, to justify extradition, to present evidence sufficient to sustain a conviction, evidence justifying a commiting magistrate in holding the accused by imprisonment or by bail to await subsequent proceedings being sufficient. Ex parte Glaser (1910), 176 Fed. 702.

The certificate of the royal judge of Prussia, that depositions, taken in a criminal court upon a charge of forgery, are valid evidence according to the laws existing in Prussia, is equivalent to a statement that such documents are valid evidence there of the crime of forgery charged. The certificate of the principal diplomatic officer of the United States, in the language of the statute, is sufficient. In re Behrendt (1884), 22 Fed. 699. See also In re Krojanker (1890), 44 Fed. 482.

SAXONY.

Convention Abolishing Droit d' Aubaine and Emigration Taxes Concluded May 14, 1845.

Arts. II and III. The clear meaning of Article II of the convention is, as regards the right of inheritance, that the aliens protected thereby shall have the same right as citizens in the same situation,—that is, shall inherit just as they would if they were citizens—with the qualification that this right shall be subject to the exercise of a power to sell the land and withdraw the proceeds within a time limited. In case of conflict between the statutes of a State and the terms of a treaty the latter must prevail. Ehrlich v. Weber (1905), 114 Tenn. 711.

WURTTEMBERG.

Convention Abolishing Droit d' Aubaine and Emigration Taxes Concluded April 10, 1844.

Art. II. The provision, that, where on the death of any person holding real property within the territory of one party such real property would by the laws of the land descend on such citizen or subject were he not disqualified by alienage "such citizen or subject shall be allowed two years to sell the same, which term may be reasonably prolonged according to the circumstances," is in effect a statute of limitation. Seven years having elapsed between the death of the ancestor and the commencement of the action, and there being nothing to show that a prolongation of the term of two years had been applied for or obtained, it was held that the time prescribed by the treaty must apply. Wieland v. Renner (1883), 65 How. Pr. Repts. 245.

The convention intends to confer on the alien heir, for the period of two years, precisely the same rights that he would enjoy if he were a citizen, subject simply to the obligation to sell and convey, within that period or such other period as the State or country shall see fit to confer upon him by prolonging the time, the fee to some one capable of holding it, or to become, or declare his intention of becoming, a citizen of this country. In the meantime he may possess and take care of the property, improve it, and exercise all the authority of ownership, for the purpose of making it more productive and valuable, and may himself enjoy such rents and profits as he can obtain therefrom. The convention is a part of the supreme law of the land and supersedes all local statutes that contravene its provisions. Kull v. Kull (1885), 37 Hun 476.

The provision, that where land owned by a citizen or subject of the one country would descend to a citizen or subject of the other, were he not disqualified by alienage, such citizen or subject may sell the same, and withdraw the proceeds, exempt from all duties of detraction, was abrogated by the treaty of December 11, 1871, between the United States and the Emperor of Germany, who, under the constitution of the empire, of which the kingdom of Württemberg has become a part, represents the empire among nations, enters into alliances and treaties with foreign countries. It was however held that the tax, in question, imposed by the laws of the State on all property, which should pass by will or the intestate laws, was not a "duty of detraction" within the meaning of the convention, but a succession tax to which all persons including citizens were subjected. In re Strobel's Estate (1896), 39 N. Y. S. 169.

The operation of the alien act of the State of Illinois of 1887 (laws of 1887 p. 5) is suspended by the convention between the United States and Württemberg, which convention was not abrogated by the absorption of the State of Württemberg into the German Empire. Under Article II of the convention, whereby aliens may take the fee to real estate and be allowed a term of two years to sell the same, "which term may be reasonably prolonged, according to circumstances," the alien need take no formal step to prolong the term. The courts may allow the alien heirs such time, in addition to the two years' limitation, as is reasonable, under the circumstances, to enable them to sell. Scharpf v. Schmidt (1898), 172 Ill. 255.

Art. III. This article does not include the case of a citizen or subject of the respective countries residing at home, and disposing of property there in favor of a citizen or subject of the other. Consequently a statute of the State of Louisiana which imposes a tax of 10% on the amount of certain legacies left by a citizen of that State to subjects of the King of Württemberg is not in conflict with the provisions of the convention. Frederickson v. State of Louisiana (1859), 23 How. 445.

GREAT BRITAIN.

Provisional Articles of Peace Concluded November 30, 1782.

The treaty was in force from January 20, 1783, the date on which terms of peace were concluded between France and Great Britain. Hylton's Lessee v. Brown (1806), 1 Wash. C. C. 343; s. c. Id. 298.

A vessel captured after the operation of the preliminary articles of peace cannot be condemned. Bain v. Schooner Speedwell (1784), 2 Dall. 40.

Definitive Treaty of Peace Concluded September 3, 1783.

"The treaty of peace contains a recognition of their independence, not a grant of it." Cushing, J., M'Ilvaine v. Coxe's Lessee (1808), 4 Cranch 209, 212.

"It has never been admitted by the United States, that they acquired anything by way of cession from Great Britain, by that treaty. It has been viewed only as a recognition of pre-existing rights, and on that principle, the soil and sovereignty within their acknowledged limits, were as much theirs at the declaration of independence as at this hour. By reference to the treaty, it will be found, that it amounts to a simple recognition of the independence and the limits of the United States, without any language purporting a cession, or relinquishment of right, on the part of Great Britain." Johnson, J., Harcourt v. Gaillard (1827), 12 Wheat. 523, 527. It was held that a grant made by the British governor of Florida, after the Declaration of Independence, within the territory between the Mississippi and Chatahoochee rivers, and between the 31st degree of north latitude, and a line drawn from the mouth of the Yazoo river due east to the Chatahoochee, was invalid as the foundation of title in the courts of the United States. See also Henderson v. Poindexter's Lessee (1827), 12 Wheat. 530.

The question, who were citizens of the United States, is not alluded to in the treaty of peace. It left all such persons in the situation in which it found them, neither making those citizens who had by the laws of any of the States been declared aliens, nor releasing from their allegiance any who had become, and were claimed, as citizens. The subject was left to the laws of the respective States. M'Ilvaine v. Coxe's Lessee (1808), 4 Cranch 209.

The treaty of peace acted upon the state of things as it existed at that period. All those, whether natives or otherwise, who then adhered to the American States, were virtually absolved from all allegiance to the British crown. All those, who then adhered to the British crown, were deemed and held to be subjects of that crown. The treaty was a treaty operating between the states on each side, and the inhabitants thereof. In the language of the seventh article it was a firm and perpetual peace between His Britannic Majesty and the States, and "between the subjects of the one and the citizens of the other." Those who were originally subjects of Great Britain and then adhered to her, and were claimed by her as subjects, the treaty deemed them such. If they were originally British subjects, but then adhering to the States, the treaty deemed them citizens. Shanks v. Dupont (1830), 3 Pet. 242. See also Inglis v. Trustees of the Sailor's Snug Harbour (1830), 3 Pet. 99.

Under the treaty of peace with Great Britain, the United States succeeded to all the rights in that part of old Canada, which now forms the State of Michigan, that existed in the King of France prior to its conquest from the French by the British in 1760. Among these rights was that of dealing with the seigniorial estate of lands granted out as seigniories by the King, after a forfeiture had occurred for non-fulfillment of the conditions of the fief. United States v. Repentigny (1866), 5 Wall. 211.

Art. II. The line of territorial boundary between the United
    States and the British provinces on the bay and waters of
    Passamaquoddy is in the middle of the stream or channel be-
    tween the territories of the two nations, the line being run at
    low-water mark. The Fame (1822), Fed. Cas. No. 4634.

Art. IV. The right of action to recover debts due to a British
    subject, sequestered by a statute of the State of Georgia dur-
    ing the war, was revived by the restoration of peace, as well
    as by the very terms of the treaty of peace. State of Georgia
    v. Brailsford (1794), 3 Dall. 1.

    The provisions of Article IV, of their own force, nullified
    State laws for the sequestration of debts due to British
    subjects, and any payment made thereunder, and revived the
    right of recovery as against the principal debtor, notwith-
    standing payment to the State under the said acts. Ware v.
    Hylton (1796), 3 Dall. 199; Page v. Pendleton (1793), 1
    Wythe's Repts. (Va.) 211, 217; Jones v. Walker (Opinion
    by Jay, C. J., not dated), 2 Paine 688; Hamilton & Co. v.
    Eaton (1796), 1 Hughes 249; Hylton's Lessee v. Brown
    (1806), 1 Wash. C. C. 298; s. c. Id. 343.

    The treaty prevented the operation of the act of limitations
    of Virginia upon British debts contracted before that treaty,

it being an impediment to the recovery of debts. Hopkirk v. Bell (1806), 3 Cranch 454, 4 Cranch 164. See to the same effect, Dunlop & Wilson v. Alexander's Admr. (1808), 1 Cranch C. C. 498. See also Ogden v. Blackledge (1804), 2 Cranch 272.

The constitution of a State must yield to the treaty of peace which is supreme. Gordon's Lessee v. Kerr et al. (1806), 1 Wash. C. C. 322.

Where the copartnership owed the alien partners for advances, the resident partner's share of those advances constituted, in equity, a debt, which he owed his copartners, and which is within the treaty. "The treaty revived the rights of the British creditors, and gave them as full force as if the confiscation acts had never passed. It abrogated those acts altogether, and left those rights as those of other friendly aliens. Upon the breaking out of a new war, they depended upon the general doctrine respecting debts to alien enemies. They were not forfeited. There was a temporary disability to sue, which ceased with the war." Ruffin, J., McNair v. Ragland, et al. (1830), 16 N. C. 516, 526.

Art. V. This article applies to those cases where an actual confiscation has taken place, and stipulates expressly that in such cases the interest of all persons having a lien upon such lands shall be preserved. Neither the confiscation, nor any act in consequence of the confiscation, can constitute a legal impediment to the prosecution of their just rights. If the act of confiscation, independently of the treaty, would be construed to destroy the claim of the mortgagee, a British merchant, the treaty reinstates the lien in full force, and the subsequent sale of the property could only pass it with the burden imposed upon it. Higginson v. Mein (1808), 4 Cranch 415, 419.

"The interest by debt intended to be protected by the treaty, must be an interest holden as a security for money at the time of the treaty; and the debt must still remain due." Marshall, C. J., Owings v. Norwood's Lessee (1809), 5 Cranch 344, 347. See Smith v. State of Maryland (1810), 6 Cranch 286.

The effect of the provisions of this article was to guarantee to the party all the rights and interests which he then had in confiscated and other lands, in the full force and vigor which they then possessed. He was to meet with no impediment to the assertion of his just rights; and no future confiscations were to be made of his interest in any land. His just rights were at that time to have the estate, whenever it should fall into possession, free of all incumbrances or liens for improvements created by the tenants for life, or by purchasers under the State. To deny him possession, until he should pay for all such improvements, would be an impediment to his just rights, and a confiscation, pro tanto, of his estate in the lands. Carver v. Jackson (1830), 4 Pet. 1, 100. See also Fisher v. Harnd{en (1812), 1 Paine C. C. 55; 1 Wheat. 300.

Art. VI. (See also Art. IX of treaty of November 19, 1794.)

Proceedings to show that one who was seeking a restoration of his estate was attainted with treason for adhering to the King of Great Britain would contravene an express article of the treaty of peace and could not be sustained. Respublica v. Gordon (1788), 1 Dall. 233.

The sixth article of the treaty of peace of 1783 completely protected the titles of British subjects to lands in the United States from forfeiture by way of escheat for the defect of alienage, and was not intended to be confined to confiscations jure belli. Orr v. Hodgson (1819), 4 Wheat. 453.

The treaty of peace provides only for titles existing at the time and not as to those subsequently acquired. Blight's Lessee v. Rochester (1822), 7 Wheat. 535.

The property of British corporations in this country was protected by Article VI of the treaty of peace in the same manner as that of natural persons; and the title thus protected was confirmed by Article IX of the treaty of 1794, so that it could not be forfeited by any intermediate legislative act, or other proceeding, for the defect of alienage. Even the termination of a treaty by war does not divest rights of property already vested under it. Society for Propagation of Gospel, &c., v. Town of New Haven (1823), 8 Wheat. 464.

Article VI of the treaty of 1783 not only barred the escheat of lands held by British subjects in New York, but gave them capacity to transmit them by descent; but the descent must be to a citizen. Where a British subject holding lands here died prior to the treaty of 1794, leaving no citizen heirs, his lands escheated, and the provisions of the treaty did not pass the lands to alien heirs. Brown v. Sprague (1848), 5 Denio 545.

See also Morris v. United States (1899), 174 U. S. 196, 231.

Treaty of Amity, Commerce and Navigation Concluded November 19, 1794.

Art. II. The "precincts and jurisdiction" of a post, referred to in Article II, are not to be considered as extending three miles in every direction by analogy to the jurisdiction of a country over that distance of the sea; but they must be established by proof. The clauses in Article II and Article IX, providing that settlers within such precincts shall be protected in the enjoyment of their property, were intended to protect legal and equitable interests in land, and not trespassers and intruders without right. Jackson ex dem. Sparkman v. Porter (1825), 1 Paine 457. See also Forsyth v. Reynolds (1853), 15 How. 358; United States v. Repentigny, 5 Wall. 211; Crane v. Reeder, 21 Mich. 24.

Art. VII. Money paid pursuant to the award of the commissioners under the treaty of 1794 was to be paid over according to the interests of those concerned; and where a sum was awarded nominally to one, the interest of which was in another, that other is entitled to the benefit intended, and may recover the money in an action for money had and received. Heard v. Bradford (1808), 4 Mass. 326.

Art. IX. (See also Arts. V and VI of the treaty of September 3, 1783).

"Now, we cannot yield to the argument that Denny Fairfax had no title, but a mere naked possession or trust estate. In our judgment, by virtue of the devise to him, he held a fee simple in his own right. At the time of the commencement of this suit (in 1791) he was in complete possession and seizin of the land. That possession and seizin continued up to and after the treaty of 1794, which being the supreme law of the land, confirmed the title to him, his heirs and assigns, and protected him from any forfeiture by reason of alienage. It was once in the power of the commonwealth of Virginia, by an inquest of office or its equivalent, to have vested the estate completely in itself or its grantee. But it has not so done, and its own inchoate title (and of course the derivative title, if any, of its grantee) has by the operation of the treaty become ineffectual and void. It becomes unnecessary to consider the argument as to the effect of the death of Denny Fairfax pending the suit, because admitting it to be correctly applied in general, the treaty of 1794 completely avoids it. The heirs of Denny Fairfax were made capable in law to take from him by descent, and the freehold was not, therefore, on his death, cast upon the commonwealth." Story, J., Fairfax's Devisee v. Hunter's Lessee (1813), 7 Cranch 603, 627. See also Jackson v. Clarke (1818), 3 Wheat. 1; Owings v. Norwood's Lessee (1809), 5 Cranch 344; Smith v. State of Maryland (1810), 6 Cranch 286; Society for Propagation of Gospel, &c., v. Town of Pawlet (1830), 4 Pet. 480.

Under Article IX, by which it is provided that British subjects then holding lands in the United States, and their heirs or assigns, so far as respects those lands, and the remedies incident thereto, shall not be considered as aliens, the parties must show that the title to the land was in them, or their ancestors, at the time the treaty was made. Harden v. Fisher (1816), 1 Wheat. 300.

An alien may take, by purchase, a freehold estate which can be divested on the ground of alienage only by inquest of office or some legislative act equivalent thereto. A defeasible title thus vested during the War of the Revolution in a British born subject, who has never become a citizen, is completely protected and confirmed by the ninth article of the treaty of 1794. Craig v. Radford (1818), 3 Wheat. 594.

The ninth article applies to the title of the parties, whatever it is, and gives it the same legal validity as if the parties were citizens. It is not necessary that they should show an actual possession or seizin, but only that the title was in them at the time the treaty was made. Under the description of heirs it was not intended to include any other persons than such as were British subjects or citizens of the United States at the time of the descent cast. Orr v. Hodgson (1819), 4 Wheat. 453.

Where a British subject came to the United States after the treaty of peace of 1783, and died before the signature of the treaty of 1794, the heirs were not protected by Article IX of that treaty. "The treaty of 1794, like that of 1783, provides only for existing rights. It does not give title. Had James conveyed or devised the property to John, the title would have vested in him, subject to the right of the government to seize the land; and the treaty would have confirmed that title, so if the law would have vested the estate in him by descent. But as the fact is, he had no title, nothing on which the treaty could operate." Marshall, C. J., Blight's Lessee v. Rochester (1822), 7 Wheat. 535, 544.

Title to property held by British corporations, in this country, protected by Article VI of the treaty of peace, was confirmed by Article IX of the treaty of 1794, so that it could not be forfeited by any intermediate legislative act, or other proceeding, for the defect of alienage. Even the termination of a treaty by war does not divest rights of property already vested under it. Society for Propagation of the Gospel, &c. v. Town of New Haven (1823), 8 Wheat. 464.

Under Article IX it is not necessary for the alien to show that he was in the actual possession or seizin of the land at the date of the treaty. The treaty applies to the title, whatever that may be, and gives it the same legal validity as if the parties were citizens. The title of an alien mortgagee is protected by the treaty. Hughes v. Edwards (1824), 9 Wheat. 489.

All British born subjects, whose allegiance Great Britain has never renounced, ought, upon general principles of interpretation, to be held within the intent, as they certainly are within the words, of the treaty of 1794. This stipulation being for the benefit of British subjects who became aliens by the events of the war, there is no reason why all persons should not be embraced in it who sustained the character of British subjects, although they might also have been treated as American citizens. Shanks v. Dupont (1830), 3 Pet. 242.

Corporations as well as individuals are within its purview. "It was obviously the design of the contracting parties, to remove the disability of alienage, as to persons within the purview of the article, and to procure to them a perfect enjoyment and disposal of their estates and titles. If, during war, their right to grant, sell or devise, such estates and titles were suspended, it would materially impair their value. If the remedies incident to such estates for trespasses, disseisins, and other tortious acts, were during war suspended, not only would the security of the property be endangered, but if the war should last for many years, the statute of limitations of the various States would, by lapse of time, bar the party of his remedy, and in some cases of his estate. This seems against the spirit and intent of the article, and puts the party upon the footing of an alien enemy, while the language concedes to him all the benefits of a native." Story, J., Society for Propagation of the Gospel, &c. v. Wheeler et al. (1814), 2 Gall. 105, 136.

Rights vested under Article IX of the treaty of 1794 were not divested by the war of 1812 between the United States and Great Britain. Fox v. Southack (1815), 12 Mass. 143; Fiott v. Commonwealth (1855), 12 Grat. (Va.) 564. See also Hutchinson v. Brock (1814), 11 Mass. 119.

"Complainant [a British subject] is entitled as mother of Ann Robertson [intestate] to the whole of her personal estate, and to the real if the British treaty now pending, be ratified by our government." Decree for complainant. Megrath v. Admrs. of John and Ann Robertson (August, 1795), 1 Desaus. Eq. (S. C.) 445, 449.

"These words ought to have a very liberal interpretation, in advancement of their beneficial end. They ought to apply, in furtherance of the amicable intention of the two nations, to every British subject who, at the time of the treaty, was in the enjoyment of lands within the United States, and whose title thereto would be valid, independent of the plea of alienism. In all such cases the treaty may be considered as doing away the plea." Kent, J., Jackson v. Lunn (1802), 3 Johns. Cases 109, 123.

"Nelson, therefore, must be deemed to have been a British subject in 1794; and it appearing that he had purchased the lands in question previously to that period the treaty settled his right thereto, and, upon his death, it descended to his heirs, notwithstanding they were aliens. * * * The treaty is the paramount law; and the act of 1804, being contrary to it, * * * is inoperative." Van Ness, J., Jackson v. Wright (1809), 4 Johns. 75, 79.

A British subject held the premises in fee within the meaning of the article, at the time of the conclusion and ratification of the treaty. He thereafter sold the same to defendant. Title cannot now be questioned by the commonwealth. Commonwealth v. Sheafe (1810), 6 Mass. 441.

"But if they were obliged to take by descent, their rights are protected by the 9th article of the treaty of 1794, which declares, that British subjects shall hold as before the war." Duncan v. Beard (1820), 2 Nott & McC. (S. C.) 400, 408.

Under Article IX of the treaty of 1794 the title of British subjects to land in the United States is valid and alienable, the same as if the holder had been a citizen of the United States. Watson v. Donnelly (1859), 28 Barb. 653; People v. Snyder (1868), 51 Barb. 589; Munro v. Merchant (1858), 26 Barb. 383; 28 N. Y. 9; Foxwell v. Craddock (1855), 1 Pat. & H. (Va.) 250.

The treaty of 1794 does not take away the plea of alienage in actions relating to lands acquired after that treaty, but merely extends to lands then held by British subjects. Jackson v. Decker (1814), 11 Johns. 418; Orser v. Hoag (1845), 3 Hill 79.

The treaty was only intended to secure to actual owners the lands belonging to them at its date, without any retrospective operation as to those which had been antecedently lost. Read v. Read (1804), 5 Call 160.

The treaty of 1794 secured the rights of British subjects to the real estate which they held at that time. Marshall v. Conrad (1805), 5 Call 364.

A British subject to whom a devise of land was made in 1781 could by the treaty of 1794 hold and alien the lands so devised to him. Stephen's Heirs v. Swann (1838), 9 Leigh 404.

The stipulations for the protection of the rights of property imposed upon the government of the United States no new obligation, but were merely in affirmance of the law of nations. May v. Specht et al. (1849), 1 Manning (Mich.) 187.

The provisions of Article IX, which secured to British

subjects the right to grant, sell or devise the estates they held at the date of the treaty, applied only to valid titles. The provisions against the effect of alienage of the heirs or assignees of such grantors would not apply to mere possessory rights without any title in fact, which by a subsequent act of Congress were enlarged into freeholds where there had been continuous occupancy and improvement. Crane v. Reeder (1870), 21 Mich. 24. See also, supra, under Art. II.

Art. X. See Brown v. United States (1814), 8 Cranch 110.

Art. XVIII, Par. 3. "This treaty is conceived to be a correct exposition of the law of nations. * * * Neither the law of nations nor the treaty admits of the condemnation of the neutral vessel for the intention to enter a blockaded port, unconnected with any fact. * * * By the language of the treaty it would appear that a second attempt, after receiving notice, must be made, in order to constitute the offense which will justify a confiscation. 'It is agreed,' says that instrument, 'that every vessel so circumstanced (that is, every vessel sailing for a blockaded port, without knowledge of the blockade) may be turned away from such port or place, but she shall not be detained, nor her cargo, if not contraband, be confiscated, unless, after notice, she shall again attempt to enter.' These words strongly import a stipulation that there shall be a free agency on the part of the commander of the vessel, after receiving notice of the blockade, and that there shall be no detention nor condemnation, unless, in the exercise of that free agency, a second attempt to enter the invested place shall be made." Marshall, C. J., Fitzsimmons v. Newport Ins. Co. (1808), 4 Cranch 185, 199, 200.

"Waiving the question whether this clause of Jay's treaty was abrogated by the war of 1812, and accepting it as a correct exposition of the law of nations, it applies only to vessels which have sailed for a hostile port or place without knowing that the same is either besieged, blockaded or invested." Brown, J., The Adula (1900), 176 U. S. 361, 371.

Art. XXV. The provisions of this article were in conflict with those of Article XVII of the treaty of commerce with France of 1778, in which it was agreed that no shelter or refuge should be given to vessels which had made prize of French ships. Gray, Admr., v. United States (1886), 21 C. Cls. 340.

Art. XXVII. A murder committed on board a British vessel of war on the high seas is committed within the jurisdiction of Great Britain, within the meaning of the treaty; and if the murderer is found in this country, the courts are bound to deliver him up (even in the absence of any legislation), there being sufficient evidence of criminality to justify the apprehension and commitment of the prisoner for trial, and the requisition having been made by the British consul, the officer authorized to make the same. United States v. Robbins (1799), Fed. Cases No. 16175; Bee's Admr. Repts. 266; United States v. Cooper (1800), Fed. Cases No. 14865. See also In re Washburn (1819), 3 Wheeler's Criminal Cases 473. See In re Kaine (1852), 14 How. 103, 111; Fong Yue Ting v. United States (1893), 149 U. S. 698, 714.

Treaty of Peace and Amity Concluded December 24, 1814.

Art. I. Under the treaty of Ghent and the subsequent conventions of London of 1818 and St. Petersburg of 1822, the owners of slaves carried off by British forces at the close of the war of 1812 were entitled to indemnity therefor, but not to the slaves. Foushee v. Blackwell (1843), 1 Rob. (Va.) 488.

Art. VI. "We do not accept the doctrine that, because by the treaty between the United States and Great Britain the boundary line between the two countries is run through the centre of the lakes, their character as seas is changed, or that the jurisdiction of the United States to regulate vessels belonging to their citizens navigating those waters and to punish offenses committed upon such vessels, is in any respect impaired. Whatever effect may be given to the boundary line between the two countries, the jurisdiction of the United States over the vessels of their citizens navigating those waters and the persons on board remains unaffected." Field, J., United States v. Rodgers (1893), 150 U. S. 249, 265.

Under Article IV of the treaty of Ghent, the small island called "Pope's Folly" in the bay of Passamaquoddy is within the jurisdiction of the United States. Open Boat (1823), Fed. Cas. No. 10548.

A bay six miles in length and breadth, known as Munoskong Bay, connected with Mud Lake, from the head of which to Lake Huron is a distance of 24 miles, navigable and practically level with Lake Huron, and having a similar current, is a part of it and not of St. Mary's river; and the riparian owners have title to the meander line of the bay. Ainsworth v. Munoskong Hunting & Fishing Club (1909), 159 Mich. 61.

Treaty of Commerce and Navigation Concluded July 3, 1815.

Art. I. The permission mutually given to citizens of the one to reside and to trade in the territories of the other, is in express terms made subject to the laws of the two countries, respectively. The reference to the laws of this country necessarily applies to laws of the States in respect of the privileges within the several States. Norris v. City of Boston, and Smith v. Turner (Passenger Cases, 1849), 7 How. 283, 472.

No treaty gives to subjects of Great Britain any different measure of justice than that secured to citizens of this country. Barrington v. Missouri (1907), 205 U. S. 483, 487; Spies v. Illinois (1887), 123 U. S. 131, 182.

A corporation organized in Great Britain, having its principal place of business in that country, is not a subject of that country within the meaning of a treaty giving subjects of that country the right to do business in any of the States of the United States on the same terms as natives. Scottish Union, &c., v. Herriott (1899), 109 Iowa 606. See 187 U. S. 651.

Art. II. A State pilotage law, which subjects all vessels, domestic and foreign, engaged in foreign trade, to pilotage regulations, but which exempts pursuant to law coastwise steam vessels of the United States, is not in conflict with the provision in the treaty with Great Britain, that "no higher or other duties or charges shall be imposed in any ports of the United States on British vessels than those payable in the same ports by vessels of the United States." The regulations, in question, apply without discrimination to all vessels, domestic or foreign, engaged in foreign trade. Olsen v. Smith (1904), 195 U. S. 332. See also Compagnie Francaise, &c. v. Louisiana

State Board of Health (1902), 186 U. S. 380. See Passenger Cases (1849), 7 How. 283.

A treaty cannot be invoked by an individual to defeat liability for a tax imposed by a subsequent act of Congress. The tonnage tax imposed on the use of foreign-built yachts by §37 of the tariff act of August 5, 1909 (36 Stats. at L. 112), may be collected by an action in the nature of debt against the yacht owner. United States v. Billings (1911), 190 Fed. 359; s. c. 232 U. S. 261. See also Rainey v. United States (1914), 232 U. S. 310.

Convention Respecting Fisheries, Boundary and the Restoration of Slaves Concluded October 20, 1818.

Art. III. Under this article the Oregon territory was free and open to the citizens and subjects of both the United States and Great Britain. During the period of joint occupation, the territory being, as to British subjects therein, British soil, and, as to citizens of the United States, American soil, a child born in the territory was born in the allegiance of the parents. McKay v. Campbell (1871), 2 Sawy. 118; see Opinions of the Justices (1878), 68 Me. 589.

Treaty Concerning Boundaries, Suppression of Slave Trade and Extradition Concluded August 9, 1842.

Act II. A substantial diversion of the waters forming a part of the international boundary between the United States and Canada would constitute a violation of Article II of the treaty of 1842, declaring that all water communication from Lake Superior to the Lake of the Woods shall be free and open to citizens of both countries. The act of Congress of March 3, 1899, c. 425, reserves to the United States control over navigable waters within the States, subject to the conditions expressed in the statute. The act does not affect or in any respect modify the treaty. It merely authorizes the Secretary of War to determine whether any contemplated enterprise will divert the waters or otherwise improperly affect navigation. If Congress in the manner provided by this act approves an enterprise, the question of the violation of the treaty thereby is no longer for the consideration of the courts, as a subsequent act of Congress, if inconsistent with the terms of an existing treaty, abrogates the treaty, so far as

36

the courts and citizens of this country are concerned. Minnesota Canal & Power Co. v. Pratt (1907), 101 Minn. 197.

Art. IV. The treaty established, between the monument at the source of the St. Croix river and the St. John river, a new conventional line of boundary between the State of Maine and the Province of New Brunswick, irrespective of the line provided for by the treaty of 1783. One who, at the time of the ratification of the treaty of 1842, was, and had for several years been, in possession of land under a grant from said Province, had a title which by Article IV was "held valid, ratified and confirmed" to him, although the lands lay, in fact, within the limits of the United States as established conventionally by the treaty. The provision of the treaty is binding on the court without the interposition of any legislative action. Grants of land made by authority of the British government, and coming within the scope of this provision, cannot be vacated even in a suit for the same land brought by a grantee of the State. Little v. Watson (1850), 32 Me. 214.

Art. VII. The United States and Great Britain having by the treaty of 1783 divided and appropriated the lakes and their connecting waters, the courts of neither, while this treaty remains in force, can for jurisdictional purposes, and especially for criminal jurisdiction, consider that portion of these waters within the limits of the other as differing in any respect from the lands. The treaty of 1842, conceding to the vessels, &c., of both nations a right of passage through the channels and passages thus appropriated, does not deprive either of that complete and exclusive jurisdiction over that part of the lakes and rivers on its side of the line which any nation may exercise over land within its acknowledged limits. People v. Tyler (1859), 7 Mich. 161.

The courts of the United States have jurisdiction, under section 5346, Rev. Stats., to try a person for an assault with a dangerous weapon committed on a vessel belonging to a citizen of the United States, when such vessel is in the Detroit river, out of the jurisdiction of any particular State, and within the territorial limits of the Dominion of Canada. United States v. Rodgers (1893), 150 U. S. 249.

Art. X. (See also extradition convention concluded July 12, 1889).

The treaty, the acts of Congress, Rev. Stats., §§5272, 5275, and the proceedings by which the defendant was extradited, clothe him with the right to exemption from trial for any other offense than that for which he was extradited, until he has had an opportunity to return to the country from which he was taken for the purpose alone of trial for the offense specified in the demand for his surrender. United States v. Rauscher (1886), 119 U. S. 407. Although the treaty of 1842 has no express limitation, that the demanding country shall try the person for that crime only for which he was extradited, such a limitation is to be found in the manifest scope and object of the treaty itself. Johnson v. Browne (1907), 205 U. S. 309, 317. See to same effect United States v. Watts (1882), 14 Fed. 130; Commonwealth v. Hawes (1878), 13 Bush 697; State v. Vanderpool (1883), 39 Ohio St. 273; Ex parte Hibbs (1886), 26 Fed. 421. See, contra, United States v. Caldwell (1871), 8 Blatchf. 131; United States v. Lawrence (1876), 13 Blatchf. 295; In re Miller (1885), 23 Fed. 32.

Under the treaty of 1842 and the convention of 1889, a surrendered person can be tried for an offense committed in this country after his arrival; and the trial for such offense does not have to await the conclusion of the trial of the offense for which he was surrendered. Accordingly one, who, on the trial of the offense for which he was surrendered and which resulted in a disagreement, committed perjury, can be indicted and tried for that offense without being allowed an opportunity to leave this country and without waiting for the final conclusion of the trial for the crime for which he was surrendered. Collins v. O'Neil (1909), 214 U. S. 113. See also Collins v. Johnston (1915), 237 U. S. 502, 511.

Under §5270, Rev. Stats., if the committing magistrate has jurisdiction of the subject-matter and of the accused, and the offense charged is within the terms of the treaty, and the magistrate, in arriving at a decision to hold the accused, has before him competent legal evidence on which to exercise his judgment as to whether the facts are sufficient to establish the criminality of the accused for the purposes of extradition, such decision cannot be reviewed on habeas corpus. Bryant v. United States (1897), 167 U. S. 104, 105; McNamara v.

Henkel (1913), 226 U. S. 520, 523. See to like effect In re Oteiza y Cortes, 136 U. S. 330, 334; Benson v. McMahon, 127 U. S. 457, 463; In re Stupp, 12 Blatchf. 501; Ornelas v. Ruiz, 161 U. S. 502, 508; Terlinden v. Ames, 184 U. S. 270, 278; Grin v. Shine, 187 U. S. 181, 192; Yordi v. Nolte, 215 U. S. 227, 232; Elias v. Ramirez, 215 U. S. 398, 407; Glucksman v. Henkel, 221 U. S. 508, 512.

A complaint before a commissioner, if made solely upon information and belief, is bad; but it need not be made upon the personal knowledge of the complainant if he annex to such complaint a certified copy of the indictment, or equivalent proceeding, which may have been found in the foreign country, or the depositions of witnesses having personal knowledge of the facts, taken under the statute. Rice v. Ames (1901), 180 U. S. 371.

Where an extradition convention provides that the surrender shall only be made "upon such evidence of criminality as, according to the laws of the place where the fugitive or person so charged shall be found, would justify his apprehension and commitment for trial if the crime or offense had there been committed," one who is arrested in one of the States cannot be delivered up except upon such evidence of criminality as under the laws of that State would justify his apprehension and commitment for trial if the crime had there been committed. Pettit v. Walshe (1904), 194 U. S. 205.

Under the treaty with Great Britain, prisoners charged with piracy committed contrary to acts of Parliament, and on board a British vessel, may be arrested here and surrendered without any special act of Congress to carry that treaty into effect. The British Prisoners (1845), 1 Woodb. & M. 66.

In proceedings for the extradition of a fugitive from justice, a preliminary mandate from the executive department of the government is not necessary under the treaty of extradition of 1842 with Great Britain. No extradition can be consummated without action by the executive in the last instance. Ex parte Ross (1869), 2 Bond 252; In re Herres (1887), 33 Fed. 165.

The lowest grade of inexcusable homicide is within the generic term murder as used in the extradition treaty of 1842. In re Palmer (1873), Fed. Cases No. 10679.

A judge of the United States has authority to issue his warrant for the arrest of a supposed criminal under the extradition treaty with Great Britain, and the statutes passed to aid in carrying that and similar treaties into effect, when due complaint is made to him, without a previous application having been made to the President. Manslaughter is not one of the crimes enumerated in the treaty, and is not included in murder which is therein mentioned. In re Kelley (1874), 2 Lowell 339.

Checks or drafts drawn by an agent and signed with the name of the principal, and by the agent, "per procuration," are not forgeries, whether the agent had or had not authority to draw them, since in either case they are nothing different from what they purport to be. False entries made in the usual books of account, or memoranda directing such entries by others, made by an officer or employee of a bank for the purpose of concealing his embezzlements, do not constitute forgery, as defined and recognized by the courts of England; and where a person is held for extradition to England for forgery, on such proofs only of acts committed in England, he should be discharged on habeas corpus. In re Tully (1884), 20 Fed. 812.

An extradited person arrested in a civil action before he has had time, after his acquital of the offense for which he was extradited, to return to the place from which he was brought, is "in custody in violation of the Constitution or of a law or treaty of the United States" within the meaning of Rev. Stats., §§752, 753, relating to writs of habeas corpus in the Federal courts, though the prisoner is held under process from a State court. In re Reinitz (1889), 39 Fed. 204.

The treaty of 1842 with Great Britain, which provides for the extradition of persons charged with forgery, allows the extradition from Canada of a fugitive who is charged with an act which was forgery by the laws of Great Britain in 1842. Where an indicted person, who has escaped to Canada, and against whom an extradition warrant has been issued, returns to this country voluntarily, under an agreement that he shall only be tried for the offense for which he has been indicted, and he is thereupon tried and convicted, the objection that the crime for which he was tried was not an extraditable offense must be raised at the trial in order to be available. An application for the release of such person on habeas corpus because not tried for an extraditable offense does not raise any question under the Constitution, treaties or laws of the United States. In re Cross (1890), 43 Fed. 517.

Upon an application for extradition made on behalf of the British government the arrest of a British subject who is seeking an asylum within the United States may be made upon a British vessel within our territory. In re Newman (1897), 79 Fed. 622.

One accused of poisoning resulting in death in Canada may be extradited though it appears that the poison, if administered at all, was given in this country. Sternaman v. Peck (1897), 83 Fed. 690.

Under the provisions of this article that a person can be surrendered only "upon such evidence of criminality as, according to the laws of the place where the fugitive or person so charged shall be found, would justify his apprehension and commitment for trial if the crime or offense had there been committed," it is the duty of the authorities of the country upon which demand for extradition is made to determine in the final instance whether the facts set forth in the information or other papers charge the commission of an offense within the provisions of the treaty, and, in the absence of fraud practiced upon them, their decision cannot be questioned. Where an extradition treaty uses general names such as "murder" or "arson" in defining extraditable crimes, such names are not necessarily confined to their meaning at common law, but the question whether a given offense comes within the treaty must be determined by the law as it exists in the two countries at the time extradition is requested. Cohn v. Jones (1900), 100 Fed. 639.

It being provided by the treaty, under which extradition of a person on the charge of embezzlement is sought, that the evidence of criminality must be shown according to the laws of the place where he is found, and the laws of Oregon not allowing one to be held for embezzlement where ownership of the property was in part in him, or he was a partner in the business from which the fund was derived, extradition will be denied on testimony that the accused and others went "in together" in the business from which the money was derived, with an agreement to divide the profits, although defendant put no money into the enterprise. In re Frank (1901), 107 Fed. 272.

The provision in the treaty with Great Britain for the extradition of persons charged with offenses "committed within the jurisdiction" of either party does not authorize the extradition of a person charged with the commission of an offense in a place or country which was not at the time within the jurisdiction of the country seeking the extradition, although it has since been brought within such jurisdiction. The territory of the South African Republic was not a part of the dominions of Great Britain, in an ordinary or unqualified sense, prior to the proclamation of Lord Roberts of 1900, making it a British colony, nor in such sense as to bring it within the purview of the treaty. In re Taylor (1902), 118 Fed. 196.

An information in extradition proceedings, which charges the accused with "assault with intent to kill and murder," sufficiently brings the offense within the provision of Article X for the extradition of persons charged with "assault with intent to commit murder." United States v. Piaza (1904), 133 Fed. 998.

A complaint for the arrest and examination of an alleged offender need not set out the offense with the particularity of an indictment, but it is sufficient if it conforms to the requirements of a preliminary complaint under the local law where the accused is found. In re Herskovitz (1901), 136 Fed. 713.

Numerous cases have arisen in extradition proceedings under this article, involving questions of evidence, rights of the accused, procedure, bail, warrant of arrest, the sufficiency of the complaint, office of writ of habeas corpus, &c., which seem to relate to the general subject of extradition rather than to the particular treaty provisions. Among these, not otherwise noted, are the following: In re Kaine (1852), 14 How. 103; Ex parte Kaine (1853), 3 Blatchf. 1; Ex parte Van Aernam (1854), 3 Blatchf. 160; In re Heilbronn (1854), Fed. Cases No. 6323; Muller's Case (1863), Fed. Cases No. 9913; In re Macdonnell (1873), 11 Blatchf. 79, 170; People v. Fiske (1873), 45 How. Prac. 294; In re Dugau (1874), 2 Lowell 367; In re Fowler (1880), 4 Fed. 303; Ex parte Lane (1881), 6 Fed. 34; In re Wadge (1883), 15 Fed. 864, affirmed 16 Fed. 332; In re Kelley (1885), 25 Fed. 268, 26 Fed. 852; Ex parte Hibbs (1886), 26 Fed. 421; In re Ferrelle (1886), 28 Fed. 878; In re McPhun (1887), 30 Fed. 57; In re Fergus (1887), 30 Fed. 607; In re Charleston (1888), 34 Fed. 531; In re Herres (1887), 33 Fed. 165; People v. Board of Supervisors (1890), 8 N. Y. S. 752; In re Mineau (1891), 45 Fed. 188; Hall v. Patterson (1891), 45 Fed. 352; In re Carrier (1893), 57 Fed. 578; Ex parte Sternaman (1896), 77 Fed. 595; 80 Fed. 883; 83 Fed. 690; In re Newman (1897), 79 Fed. 622; In re Orpen (1898), 86 Fed. 760; In re Herskovitz (1901), 136 Fed. 713; In re Mitchell (1909), 171 Fed. 289.

Treaty Establishing Boundary West of the Rocky Mountains Concluded June 15, 1846.

Art. I. "The title of the United States to Oregon was founded upon original discovery and actual settlement by citizens of the United States, authorized or approved by the government of the United States; as well as upon the cession of the Louisiana Territory by France in the treaty of 1803, and the renunciation of the claims of Spain in the treaty of 1819. * * * While the right to Oregon was in contest between the United States and Great Britain, the citizens of the one and the subjects of the other were permitted to occupy it under the conventions of 1818 and 1827 * * * . Its boundary on the north was defined by the treaty with Great Britain of June 15, 1846." Gray, J., Shively v. Bowlby (1894), 152 U. S. 1, 50.

Art. III. The stipulation, that the United States would respect "the possessory rights" of British subjects then in the occupation of land or other property lawfully acquired in the territory south of the 49th parallel, was a mere promise which of itself conferred no right to or in the soil, and for the violation of which the British subject would only have a claim against the United States for compensation in money or kind. Town v. De Haven (1878), 5 Sawy. 146. See Bishop of Nesqually v. Gibbon (1895), 158 U. S. 155; Stark v. Starr (1876), 94 U. S. 477; Barney v. Dolph (1878), 97 U. S. 652; Lownsdale et al. v. Parrish (1858), 21 How. 290.

Art. IV. Article IV of the treaty—compromising and adjusting the respective rights of the United States and Great Britain over the northwestern coast of North America—confirming title to the Puget's Sound Agricultural Co.—is but declaratory of the law of nations, which in case of change of sovereignty leaves private rights and relationships undisturbed. The clause "shall be confirmed" had the effect of vesting title in the Puget's Sound Agricultural Co. to its property at once upon the ratification of the treaty, and is to be considered as equivalent to a legislative act to that effect. Puget Sound Agricultural Co. v. Pierce County (1861), 1 Wash. T. 159.

Reciprocity Convention Concluded June 5, 1854.

The convention of 1854 for commercial reciprocity, and the act of Congress of August 5, 1854 (10 Stats. at L. 587), for carrying it into effect, did not operate to repeal the previous laws with reference to penalties and forfeitures that had already been incurred. Their effect was to suspend the previous statutes after a given time, so far only as they affected certain enumerated articles, and to admit them thereafter free of duty. 134, 901 Feet of Pine Lumber (1858), 4 Blatchf. 182.

Art. III. Staves for pipes, hogsheads, and other casks, and split white ash timber chiefly designed to be used in the manufacture of long shovel handles, the growth and product of Canada, were not free from duty under the provision in the convention, that "timber and lumber of all kinds, round, hewed, and sawed, unmanufactured in whole or in part" should be admitted free of duty. United States v. Hathaway (1866), 4 Wall. 404; United States v. Quimby, Id. 408.

Naturalization Convention Concluded May 13, 1870.

Art. I. Former citizens of the United States, who have by naturalization become British subjects, are, while domiciled in the United States, entitled by treaty to all the rights of native-born British subjects. Newcomb v. Newcomb (1900), 108 Ky. 582.

Treaty of Washington Concluded May 8, 1871.

Arts. I-XVII. The government cannot be held liable as a trustee for money received from a foreign government in pursuance of a treaty for the satisfaction of claims of American citizens, unless the trust be declared by treaty or statute. The Court of Claims has no jurisdiction of an action to recover a part of the Alabama fund covered into in the Treasury. There is no contract express or implied to pay it. Great Western Ins. Co. v. United States (1884), 19 C. Cls. 206; affirmed in 112 U. S. 193, on the ground that the claim grew out of a treaty, and accordingly expressly excluded from the jurisdiction of the Court of Claims. See United States v. Weld (1888), 127 U. S. 51.

The sum awarded by the tribunal of arbitration at Geneva constituted a national fund, in which no individual claimant had any rights, legal or equitable, and which Congress could distribute as it pleased. The decisions and awards of the Court of Commissioners of Alabama Claims, under the statutes of the United States, were conclusive as to the amount to be paid upon each claim adjudged to be valid, but not as to the party entitled to receive it. A claim decided by that court to be a valid claim against the United States is property which passes to the assignee of a bankrupt under an assignment made prior to the decision. Williams v. Heard (1891), 140 U. S. 529.

A claim of a British subject, resident of this country, against the United States, of which the commission organized under the treaty took cognizance and made an award for its payment, passed to the assignee in bankruptcy, the assignment being made prior to the award. Phelps v. McDonald (1878), 99 U. S. 298.

Extradition Convention Concluded July 12, 1889.

(See also Art. X of the treaty of August 9, 1842, supra).

Art. I. The offense charged (fraud by a corporate director) must, according to the terms of Article I, section 4, be "made criminal by the laws of both countries." If the offense charged is criminal by the laws of the demanding country and by the laws of the State of the United States in which the alleged fugitive is found, it comes within the convention and is extraditable. Absolute identity of statutes is not necessary, provided the essential character of the transaction is the same, and made criminal by both statutes. While bail should not ordinarily be granted in cases of extradition, it is not held that the circuit courts may not in any case extend that relief. Wright v. Henkel (1903), 190 U. S. 40.

Persons, surrendered by Canada to the United States under sections 4 and 10 of Article I of the extradition convention of 1889, to be tried for the crime of "participation in fraud by an agent or trustee," were tried for such crime where the indictment charged them with conspiracy with a disbursing officer of the government to defraud the United States by presenting false and fraudulent claims to such officer and by his allowance and payment of the same from public money in his hands, the acts and transactions charged and proved before the extradition commissioner and under the indictment being the same. The question whether or not a fugitive shall be surrendered by a country in which he has sought asylum must of necessity be decided by the government of such country, and its decision, approved by its courts, that the offense charged is within the terms of an extradition convention between that country and the one making the demand, is final, and the question cannot again be raised in the courts of the latter country after extradition. While the extradition of a person from a foreign country for trial in the United States and the indictment on which he is tried must be for the same criminal acts, it does not follow that the crime must have the same name in both countries. It is sufficient if the acts in question are criminal in both countries and are within the terms of the convention under which the extradition is granted. Greene v. United States (1907), 154 Fed. 401. See also 146 Fed. 766, 776, 778, 781, 784, 787, 789, 793, 796, 801, 803. Writ of certiorari denied, 207 U. S. 596.

Art. III. A person charged with larceny was extradited from Canada under the extradition convention with Great Britain, gave bail for appearance at the trial, and returned to Canada. Upon his return voluntarily, before the time fixed for the trial, he was arrested on a capias issued before his extradition, charging him with an offense for which he was not extraditable. It was held that under the circumstances the accused had the right to have the offense for which he was extradited disposed of, and then to depart in peace, and that the arrest was in abuse of the high process under which he had originally been brought into the United States, and could not be sustained. Cosgrove v. Winney (1899), 174 U. S. 64.

A person extradited under the convention of 1889 cannot be "punished" for an offense other than that for which his extradition has been demanded, even though prior to his extradition he had been convicted and sentenced therefor. Johnson v. Browne (1907), 205 U. S. 309.

Art. VI. The provision, that "the extradition of fugitives under the provisions of this convention and of the said tenth article [of the treaty of August 9, 1842] shall be carried out in the United States and in Her Majesty's dominions, respectively, in conformity with the laws regulating extradition for the time being in force in the surrendering state," contemplates the laws of the United States regulating extradition, and has no reference whatever to the laws of the particular State of the Union within which the procedings are taken. Rice v. Ames (1901), 180 U. S. 371, 377.

Modus Vivendi Respecting the Fur-Seal Fisheries in Bering Sea Signed June 15, 1891.

See North American Commercial Co. v. United States (1898), 171 U. S. 110.

Convention Relating to Fur-Seals in Bering Sea Concluded February 29, 1892.

Art. XIV. The award of the arbitrators under this convention, by which the contracting parties agreed that the decision of the tribunal of arbitration should be a final settlement of all questions submitted, became the supreme law of the land and as binding on the courts as an act of Congress. By the award it was settled that the United States has no exclusive jurisdiction in the waters of the Bering Sea outside the ordinary three mile limit, and no right of property in or protection over the fur-seals frequenting the islands of the United States when found outside of such three-mile limit. Therefore the act of March 2, 1889, declaring that Rev. Stats., §1956, which forbids the killing of fur-bearing animals in Alaska and the waters thereof, shall apply to "all the do-

minion of the United States in the waters of Behring Sea,"
must be construed to mean the waters within three miles of
the shores of Alaska. La Ninfa (1896), 75 Fed. 513.

Convention as to Tenure and Disposition of Real and Personal Property Concluded March 2, 1899.

Art. I. This article contemplates the elimination of the disqualification of alienage, under the statute of the State of Delaware, in the next of kin, and puts non-resident aliens next of
kin on the same footing as if they were residents of the
State at the time of the death of the intestate. A statute of
the State, which provides that any such kindred, being aliens
and not residing within the limits of the United States at the
time of intestate's death, shall be passed by, and the effect
shall be the same as if they were dead, must give way to
the convention. Dockstader v. Kershaw (1903), 4 Pennewill
398.

A provision in the code of Iowa, which, while imposing an
inheritance tax of 5 per cent. of the value of property passing to collateral relatives, subjects property passing to persons, who are alien non-residents of the United States, to a
tax of 20 per cent. of its value, violates the provision in the
convention with Great Britain entitling a citizen or subject
of that country to sell real property, which would by the
laws of the land pass to him were he not disqualified on account of alienage, and to remove the proceeds therefrom
without restraint or interference, and "exempt from any succession, probate or administrative duties or charges" other
than those which may be imposed in like cases upon the
citizens or subjects of this country. Accordingly, a tax of
only 5 per cent. may be collected on property passing to a
non-resident subject of Great Britain. The treaty is paramount to State legislation in this respect. Where the personal property of the decedent was insufficient to discharge
his debts, and the administrator, under order of the court,
sold land for the payment of debts, the property inherited
by a non-resident alien heir was real property within the
meaning of the treaty. McKeown v. Brown (1914), 149 N.
W. (Iowa) 593.

Art. II. Under the provisions of this article, subjects of Great
Britain are liable to no other taxes upon successions to per-

sonal property than are payable by citizens of the United
States. "It will be noted therefore that this article covers
succession, possession, and disposal of personal property all
to be subject to such duties only as the citizens of the country
where the property lies will be liable to pay in like cases.
No reason appears therefore why any different effect should
be given to the terms of the treaty as applied to personal
property than was given in the McKeown case, supra, as applied to real property." In re Moynihan's Estate (1915),
151 N. W. (Iowa) 504.

Convention Concerning the Boundary Waters Between the United States and Canada Concluded January 11, 1909.

Art. I. In view of the provision in this treaty—that the navigation
of navigable boundary waters shall be free and open for the
purpose of commerce to the inhabitants and ships of both
countries, equally, subject to any laws and regulations of
either country, within its own territory, not inconsistent with
such privilege of free navigation, and applying equally without discrimination to the inhabitants and vessels of both
countries,—the city of Sault Ste. Marie has no power to
prescribe and fix rates of fare to be charged by the Canadian owner and operator of ferry-boats across St. Mary's
river between Ontario and Michigan as a municipal regulation. International Transit Co. v. City of Sault Ste. Marie
(1912), 194 Fed. 522.

"Assuming that, by reason of the local considerations
pertinent to the operation of ferries, there exists in the absence of Federal action a local protective power to prevent
extortion in the rates charged for ferriage from the shore of
the State, and to prescribe reasonable regulations necessary
to secure good order and convenience, we think that the action of the city in the present case in requiring the appellee
to take out a license, and to pay a license fee, for the privilege of transacting the business conducted at its wharf, was
beyond the power which the State could exercise either directly or by delegation. In this view, it is unnecessary to
consider the question raised with respect to the treaty with
Breat Britain." City of Sault Ste. Marie v. International
Transit Co. (1914), 234 U. S. 333, 342, affirming decree in
194 Fed. 522.

GREECE.

Treaty of Commerce and Navigation Concluded December 22, 1837.

Art. XV. The provision, that a vessel arriving directly from Greece and provided with a prescribed bill of health shall be subjected to no other quarantine than such as may be necessary for the visit of the health officer of the port, has reference to the particular form of document which shall be taken by a ship for the purpose of establishing that infectious or contagious diseases did not exist at its point of departure. It was not intended to nullify the quarantine power, since the concluding section of the article expressly subjects the vessel holding such certificate to quarantine detention, if on its arrival a general quarantine has been established against all ships coming from the port whence the ship holding the certificate had sailed. It was not intended to deal with the exercise by the government of its power to legislate for the safety and health of its people, or to render the exertion of such a power nugatory, by exempting the vessels of Greece when coming to the United States from the operation of such laws. Especially is this true where the restriction imposed upon the vessel is based, not upon the conditions existing at the port of departure, but upon the presence of an infectious or contagious malady at the port of arrival, which, in the nature of things, could not be covered by the certificate relating to the state of health at the port whence the ship had sailed. Compagnie Francaise de Navigation a Vapeur v. Louisiana State Board of Health (1902), 186 U. S. 380.

Consular Convention Concluded December 2, 1902.

Art. XI. The privileges enjoyed by consuls of Sweden under the convention of June 1, 1910, in the administration of estates of deceased countrymen, were claimed by the consul of Greece, under the most-favored-nation clause of this article, in Fontana v. Hynes (1915), 146 Pac. 651.

ITALY.

Extradition Convention Concluded March 23, 1868.

A person may be surrendered under the convention for the crime of murder committed in Italy before the conclusion of the convention. In re Angelo de Giacomo (1874), 12 Blatchf. 391.

Art. I. The stipulation for the extradition from one country to the other of persons charged with crime in the demanding country, "provided, that this shall only be done upon such evidence of criminality as, according to the laws of the place where the fugitive or person so charged shall be found, would justify his or her apprehension and commitment for trial, if the crime had been there committed," does not warrant the return to Italy of a person there charged with murder, where the only proof presented of his connection with the offense is hearsay. Ex parte Fudera (1908), 162 Fed. 591.

Arts. I and II. The word "persons" in the extradition convention with Italy of 1868 as amended in 1884, providing for the surrender of persons charged with certain enumerated crimes, is sufficiently broad to embrace citizens and subjects of the contracting parties. A citizen of the United States, who, while in Italy, commits an offense and then flees to the United States, is within the convention, and may be extradited thereunder, though Italy has construed the word so as not to include its citizens and subjects. Whether the United States is released from the obligations of the convention as the result of the violation of its provisions by Italy, is a political, not a judicial, question; and the executive department having elected to waive any right to free itself from the obligation to deliver up its own citizens, it is the duty of the court to recognize the obligation. Ex parte Charlton (1911), 185 Fed. 880; affirmed in Charlton v. Kelly (1913), 229 U. S. 447.

In the extradition of a person to Italy under section 7, Article II of the convention of 1868, which provides for the extradition of persons charged with "the embezzlement of public moneys, committed within the jurisdiction of either party, by public officers or depositors," if the accused is charged with having as treasurer of a hospital embezzled its funds, the proof must show that the hospital was a public institution, that the accused, as its treasurer, was a public officer or depositor, and that the money taken was public money. Ex parte Ronchi (1908), 164 Fed. 288.

Treaty of Commerce and Navigation Concluded February 26, 1871.

Arts. II, III and XXIII. The treaty only requires equality of treatment, and that the same rights and privileges be accorded to a citizen of Italy that are accorded to a citizen of the United States under like circumstances. Storti v. Massachusetts (1901), 183 U. S. 138.

If an Italian subject, sojourning in this country, is himself given all the direct protection and security afforded by the laws to our own people, including all rights of action for himself or his personal representatives to safeguard the protection and security, the provision in the treaty,—that citizens of each country shall receive, in the States and Territories of the other, the most constant protection and security, "and shall enjoy in this respect the same rights and privileges as are or shall be granted to the natives, on their submitting themselves to the conditions imposed upon the natives,"—is not violated by a statute which gives a right of action for damages for death to native resident relatives but not to nonresident alien relatives, although the existence of such a right might indirectly and remotely promote his safety. Maiorano v. Baltimore & Ohio R. R. Co. (1909), 213 U. S. 268, affirming 216 Pa. 402.

The provisions in these articles do not create in Italian subjects, not resident in the United States, any new or substantial rights of person or property to be enforced in the United States; their purpose, so far as they concern rights of person or property of non-resident Italians, is limited to the prevention of invidious discriminations in favor of citizens of the United States and against subjects of Italy, with respect to the enjoyment or enforcement in the United States of privileges and rights of person and property, arising and existing wholly independently of such provisions. Whether a non-resident alien may recover for wrongful death of an alien resident in Pennsylvania depends upon the statutes of that State, aside from the Italian treaty, as to which the Federal courts sitting in Pennsylvania are bound by the deci-

37

sions of the Pennsylvania Supreme Court. A non-resident alien is not entitled to the benefit of the act of Pennsylvania of April 15, 1851 (P. L. 674), §§18, 19, or the act of April 26, 1855 (P. L. 309), §1, giving a right of action to members of the family of a person whose death has been caused by the wrongful act of another. Fulco v. Schuylkill Stone Co. (1909), 169 Fed. 98, citing Deni v. Penna. R. R. Co., 181 Pa. 525; Maiorano v. Baltimore & Ohio R. R. Co., 216 Pa. 402; Zeiger v. Penna. R. R. Co., 158 Fed. 809; and Zeiger v. Penna. R. R. Co., 151 Fed. 348. See also Debitulia v. Lehigh & Wilkes-Barre Coal Co. (1909), 174 Fed. 886; Di Paolo v. Laquin Lumber Co. (1910), 178 Fed. 877.

Residence and citizenship do not qualify the right of recovery under the Railroad Employers' Liability Act of Congress of April 22, 1908, as amended April 5, 1910. "In ruling upon the statute the district court considered that the reasoning in Deni v. Penna. R. R., 181 Pa. St. 525, and in Maiorano v. Baltimore & Ohio R. R., 213 U. S. 268, applied. In the Deni case the Supreme Court of Pennsylvania, passing upon a statute of the State which permitted certain named relatives to recover damages for death occurring through negligence, held that the statute had no extra-territorial force and that plaintiff in the action was not within its purview, though its language possibly admitted of the inclusion of non-resident aliens. The Maiorano case came to this court on writ of error to the Supreme Court of Pennsylvania, where the doctrine of the Deni case was repeated and applied. This ruling was simply accepted by this court as the construction of the State statute by the highest court of the State." McGovern v. Philadelphia & Reading Ry. Co. (1914), 235 U. S. 389, reversing 209 Fed. 975.

The treaty gives to subjects of Italy no greater rights in suits against a municipality for loss of life through mob violence than those enjoyed by citizens of the United States. City of New Orleans v. Abbagnato (1894), 62 Fed. 240.

Under these articles Italian subjects have no greater rights to carry on trade and traffic in liquors within a State than enjoyed by citizens of the United States. Cantini v. Tillman (1893), 54 Fed. 969.

An act of the State of Pennsylvania of May 8, 1909 (P. L.

466), prohibiting the hunting or killing of wild animals or game, and to that end the ownership or possession of a shot gun or rifle, by an unnaturalized foreign-born resident within the State, is not in contravention of the treaty with Italy. Commonwealth v. Patsone (1911), 231 Pa. 46, affirmed, 232 U. S. 138.

"The equality of rights that it [Article III] assures is equality only in respect of protection and security for persons and property. The prohibition of a particular kind of destruction and of acquiring property in instruments intended for that purpose establishes no inequality in either respect. It is to be remembered that the subject of this whole discussion is wild game, which the State may preserve for its own citizens if it pleases. Geer v. Connecticut, 161 U. S. 519, 529. We see nothing in the treaty that purports or attempts to cut off the exercise of their powers over the matter by the States to the full extent. Compagnie Francaise de Navigation a Vapeur v. State Board of Health, 186 U. S. 380, 394, 395." "It will be time enough to consider whether the statute can be constrained or upheld as precluding Italians from possessing a stock of guns for purposes of trade when such a case is presented." Holmes, J., Patsone v. Commonwealth of Pennsylvania (1914), 232 U. S. 138, 145.

An act of the State of Vermont, providing for the payment by all citizens, residents of the State, of a fee of seventy-five cents for a hunter's license, and by all others of a fee of ten dollars for such license, does not violate the provisions in the treaty with Italy, that the citizens or subjects of each country shall receive in the States and Territories of the other the most constant security and protection for their person and property and shall enjoy in this respect the same rights and privileges which are granted to natives, provided that they submit themselves to the conditions imposed on natives. The petitioner, an Italian subject, a resident of the State for fourteen years, and a taxpayer, was held not entitled to the benefit of the lower fee. The treaty does not entitle Italian subjects "to share equally with the natives in such privileges as the legislature may grant in the wild game of the State." Bondi v. MacKay (1913), 87 Vt. 271.

A provision in a statute of New York (sec. 14 of the

Labor Law, L. 1909, c. 36; Cons. Laws, c. 31), that in the construction of public works by the State or a municipality, or by persons contracting with the State or such municipality, only citizens of the United States shall be employed, does not violate any constitutional right of the alien, or conflict with the treaty between the United States and Italy. People v. Crane (1915), 214 N. Y. 154; affirmed by the Supreme Court, in Heim et al. v. McCall et al. and Crane v. People, 239 U. S. 175, 195. See also People v. I. M. Ludington's Sons (1911), 131 N. Y. S. 550; People v. Warren (1895), 34 N. Y. S. 942.

Art. XXII. See In re Peterson's Will (1906), 101 N. Y. S. 285, under Article VIII of the treaty of 1826 with Denmark.

Under the most-favored-nation clause of this treaty, citizens and subjects of Italy are entitled to the same tax exemptions and to the same right to acquire and dispose of real and personal property, by donation, testament, or otherwise, as enjoyed by the citizens and subjects of France. Accordingly, by virtue of Article VII of the treaty of 1853 with France, a subject and resident of Italy is exempt from the payment of the tax of 10 % levied against foreign heirs by a statute of Louisiana on property situated in that State, the title to which is derived by testamentary disposition from his mother, a subject of Italy at the time of her death. Succession of Rixner (1896), 48 La. Ann. 552. See under Article VII of treaty of 1853 with France.

Art. XXIII. The provision in the treaty with Italy, giving the citizens of either party free access to the courts of justice of the other, with the right to employ counsel in all trials at law, has no application to the examination by the board of immigration inspectors of incoming Italian aliens with respect to their qualifications. United States ex rel. Buccino v. Williams (1911), 190 Fed. 897; United States ex rel. Falco v. Williams (1911), 191 Fed. 1001.

Art. XXIV. The most-favored-nation clause of this article refers only to favors in respect of commerce and navigation. Patsone v. Commonwealth of Pennsylvania (1914), 232 U. S. 138.

Consular Convention Concluded May 8, 1878.

Art. XI. In view of the provisions of this article, a justice of the peace has no power to compel the clerk to issue admiralty process against an Italian ship for the wages of a seaman. Where the master of an Italian vessel, in one of the ports of the United States, is guilty of a barbarous and malicious assault upon a seaman on such vessel, he is not protected by the terms of this article, and the district court may, in its discretion, take jurisdiction of the case, for the protection of the seaman and the redress of his wrongs. The Salomoni (1886), 29 Fed. 534.

Art. XVII. "If it should be conceded for this purpose that the most-favored-nation clause in the Italian treaty carries the provisions of the Argentine treaty to the consuls of the Italian Government in the respect contended for, (a question unnecessary to decide in this case), yet there was no purpose in the Argentine treaty to take away from the States the right of local administration provided by their laws, upon the estates of deceased citizens of a foreign country, and to commit the same to the consuls of such foreign nation, to the exclusion of those entitled to administer as provided by the local laws of the State within which such foreigner resides and leaves property at the time of decease." Rocca v. Thompson (1912), 223 U. S. 317, 334. See to like effect In re Logiorato's Estate (1901), 69 N. Y. S. 507. The same powers as enjoyed by consuls of the Argentine Republic under Article IX of the treaty of 1853 were conceded to Italian consuls, under the most-favored-nation clause of this article, in In re Fattosini's Estate (1900), 67 N. Y. S. 1119; In re Lobrasciano's Estate (1902), 77 N. Y. S. 1040; In re Silvetti's Estate (1907), 122 N. Y. S. 400; In re Scutella's Estate (1911), 129 N. Y. S. 20; and Carpigiani v. Hall (1911), 172 Ala. 287.

Where the public administrator is appointed to administer upon the estate of an Italian subject, who died a resident of New York, and the sole next of kin resides in Italy, the administrator may turn over the balance of the estate to the consul general of Italy; and it is not necessary that the next of kin be cited and paid directly. In re Davenport (1904), 89 N. Y. S. 537.

The Italian consul has the right to represent alien minor next of kin of a deceased Italian subject in the judicial settlement of the accounts of the administrator of the deceased;

and the appointment of a special guardian for such minors after the consul has appeared is improvident and should be vacated. In re Bristow (1909), 118 N. Y. S. 686.

Under the most-favored-nation clause of this article the consuls of Italy enjoy the same rights to administer on the estates of Italian citizens dying intestate in the United States as are conferred on consuls of Sweden in Article XIV of the convention with that country of June 1, 1910. In re Baglieri's Estate (1912), 137 N. Y. S. 175; In re Lombardi (1912), 138 N. Y. S. 1007; In re Riccardo (1913), 140 N. Y. S. 606; In re Madaloni's Estate (1913), 141 N. Y. S. 323; In re Infelise's Estate (1915), 149 Pac. (Mont.) 365. See also In re Estate of D'Adamo, 141 N. Y. S. 1103; 144 N. Y. S. 429; 212 N. Y. S. 214.

Additional Extradition Convention Concluded June 11, 1884.

Art. II. "Construed in the light of the original and supplementary conventions with Italy and of §5270, Rev. Stats., we do not find that it was obligatory that the 'formal demand' referred to in the 1884 clause should be proven in the preliminary proceeding within forty days after the arrest. That is a demand made upon the executive authority of the United States by the executive authority of Italy. Its presentation was not necessary to give the examining magistrate jurisdiction. Such a formal demand was in fact made on July 28, 1910, less than forty days after the arrest. That, together with the certificate of the magistrate and the evidence submitted to him, was the authority of law under which the Secretary of State issued his warrant of extradition." Lurton, J., Charlton v. Kelly (1913), 229 U. S. 447, 464.

Convention of Commerce and Navigation Concluded February 25, 1913.

Art. I. (Amending first paragraph of Art. III of treaty of February 26, 1871.) The provision—that the citizens of the respective countries "shall receive in the States and Territories of the other the most constant security and protection for their persons and property and for their rights, including that form of protection granted by any State or national law which establishes a civil responsibility for injuries or for death caused by negligence or fault and gives to relatives or heirs of the injured party a right of action, which right shall not be restricted on account of the nationality of said relatives or heirs; and shall enjoy in this respect the same rights and privileges as are or shall be granted to nationals, provided that they submit themselves to the conditions imposed on the latter"—does not confer on an alien Italian plaintiff, when bringing an action in New York, greater or different rights of procedure and form of remedy than those accorded to residents and citizens of that State. Teti v. Consolidated Coal Co. (1914), 217 Fed. 443.

JAPAN.

Treaty Concerning Commerce and Consuls Concluded June 17, 1857.

Art. IV. The provision of this article, that "Americans committing offenses in Japan" should be tried by the American consul general or consul, and should be punished according to American laws, was not fully incorporated into the provision of Article VI of the subsequent treaty concluded July 29, 1858, that "Americans committing offenses against Japanese" should be tried in American consular courts and punished according to American law. Not being so incorporated, it remained in force, although in Article XII of the second treaty it was expressly declared that "as all the provisions" of the treaty of 1857 had been incorporated therein that treaty was revoked. In view of the legislation of Congress, to give effect to the treaty, the term "Americans" included all persons who, as the result of their employment and service, were, by public law or the law of this country, entitled at the time to be treated as citizens, namely, a British born subject serving as a member of the crew of an American vessel. In re Ross (1891), 140 U. S. 453.

Treaty of Commerce and Navigation Concluded November 22, 1894.

Arts. I-II. Paupers or persons likely to become a public charge have not been given by the treaty with Japan full liberty to enter or reside in the United States. That instrument expressly excepts from its operation any ordinance or regulation in respect of "police and public security." A statute excluding paupers or persons likely to become a public charge, of whatever country, is manifestly one of police and public security. The Japanese Immigrant Case (1903), 189 U. S. 86.

These articles contain no allusion to fishing privileges, and do not purport to grant any right to sea rovers to resort to American fishing grounds for the purpose of taking fish for their own consumption or otherwise. The act of Congress of June 14, 1906, (34 Stats. 263), making it unlawful for any non-resident alien to catch or kill fish in the waters of Alaska, except with rod, spear, or gaff, overrides the provisions in the treaty if in conflict therewith. The Tokai Maru (1911), 190 Fed. 450. Petition for writ of certiorari denied, 225 U. S. 703.

MEXICO.

Treaty of Amity, Commerce and Navigation Concluded April 5, 1831.

Art. XIV. Since the constitution of Mexico provided that a Mexican citizen should not be expelled without a legal trial, and the treaty with the United States of 1831 extended the judicial rights of the citizens of the one country to those of the other residing therein, it was unjustifiable for Mexico to expel, summarily, without trial, an American citizen for alleged complicity with Santa Anna in the revolution of 1844, the revolution at the time of the expulsion having come to an end, and civil authority having been restored. Atocha v. United States (1872), 8 C. Cls. 427. Findings of the Court of Claims held to be final in Ex parte Atocha, 17 Wall. 439.

Claims Convention Concluded April 11, 1839.

In 1816 an association called the Baltimore Company was organized in Baltimore, Maryland, for the purpose of furnishing advances and supplies in fitting out a military expedition against Mexico, then a part of the dominions of the King of Spain. An assignment of a share of this company, made in 1829 to a bona fide purchaser for a valuable consideration, was valid. Although the transaction was illegal in 1816, and had not changed its character in 1829, yet the assignment was not tainted with any illegality. The claim against Mexico, having its origin in an effort to establish the independence of Mexico, rested entirely upon her sense of honor in acknowledging the obligation after her independence was achieved; but after the debt was admitted, the bona fide assignee became substituted to all the rights of the original shareholder. McBlair v. Gibbes (1854), 17 How. 232. See also Baldwin v. Ely (1850), 9 How. 580; Gill v. Oliver's Executors (1850), 11 How. 529; Deacon v. Oliver (1852), 14 How. 610; Williams v. Gibbes (1854), 17 How. 239; Williams v. Gibbes (1857), 20 How. 535; Mayer v. White (1860), 24 How. 317.

Treaty of Peace, Friendship, Limits and Settlement Concluded February 2, 1848.

Art. V. The United States obtained military possession of California in 1846. The civil government, thereupon established by the President as commander-in-chief in the exercise of a belligerent right over a conquered territory, was the existing government when the territory was ceded to the United States as a conquest and did not cease as a matter of course upon the restoration of peace; and it was rightfully continued after peace was made with Mexico until Congress legislated otherwise under its constitutional power to dispose of and make all needful rules and regulations respecting the territory or other property belonging to the United States. Import duties were collected in the territory, prior to the receipt of notice of the exchange of ratifications, at rates fixed by the President as commander-in-chief, and, after the receipt of the notice and until the arrival of the collector, November 13, 1849, appointed under the act of Congress of March 3, 1849, in conformity with the rates imposed by acts of Congress on imports into the other ports of the United States. Such duties on goods arriving from foreign countries were legally exacted. Cross v. Harrison (1853), 16 How. 164.

Art. VII. See United States v. Rio Grande Irrigation Co. (1899), 174 U. S. 690; 184 U. S. 416.

Arts. VIII and IX. These various stipulations are wholly inapplicable to the persons, who, before the revolution in Texas, had been citizens of Mexico, and who, by that revolution, had been separated from Mexico. They have no reference to territory within the acknowledged limits of Texas. McKinney v. Saviego (1855), 18 How. 235; Basse v. Brownsville (1875), 154 U. S. 610.

The cession of the country to the United States did not impair the rights of private property. They were consecrated by the law of nations and protected by the treaty. The treaty was but a formal recognition of the pre-existing sanction in the law of nations. The act of March 3, 1851, to ascertain and settle private land claims in the State of California, was passed to assure to the inhabitants of the ceded territory the benefit of the rights thus secured to them. It recognizes both legal and equitable rights, and should be administered in a liberal spirit. A right of any validity before the cession was equally valid afterwards. United States v. Moreno (1863), 1 Wall. 400.

The declaration of the Mexican commissioners, who negotiated the treaty, that no grants of land were made by the Mexican governors of California after May 13, 1846, does not affect the right of parties who, subsequently to that date, obtained grants from the governors whilst their authority and jurisdiction continued. The authority and jurisdiction of Mexican officers in California are regarded as having ended on July 7, 1846. The political department has designated that date as the period when the conquest of California was completed and the Mexican officers displaced, and in this respect the judiciary will follow the conclusion of the political department. United States v. Yorba (1863), 1 Wall. 412, 423. See also United States v. Pico, 23 How. 321, 326; Stearns v. United States, 6 Wall. 589; Hornsby v. United States, 10 Wall. 224, 239; More v. Steinbach, 127 U. S. 70, 80.

The treaty did not divest the pueblo, which existed at the site of the present city of San Francisco, of any rights of property, or alter the character of the interests, it may have held in any lands under the former government. It made no distinction in the protection to be given between the property of individuals and the property held by towns under the Mexican government. Townsend v. Greeley (1866), 5 Wall. 326.

In order that a perfect title to land might vest under a grant from the Mexican government a delivery of possession by its officers was necessary. United States v. Fossat, 20 How. 413; Van Reynegan v. Bolton, 95 U. S. 33; More v. Steinbach, 127 U. S. 70; Pinkerton v. Ledoux, 129 U. S. 346.

No title to lands in California, dependent upon Spanish or Mexican grants, can be of any validity, which has not been submitted to and confirmed by the board provided for that purpose under the act of March 3, 1851, (9 Stats. 631), or, if rejected by that board, confirmed by the district court or by the Supreme Court of the United States. Botiller v. Dominguez (1889), 130 U. S. 238.

By the term property, as applied to lands, all titles are embraced, legal or equitable, perfect or imperfect. By the stipulations of the treaty the United States is bound to protect such property rights. Hornsby v. United States, 10 Wall. 224, 242; United States v. Rose, 23 How. 262. See United States v. Sutter, 21 How. 170. The United States is bound to protect all rights of property emanating from the Mexican government prior to the treaty. Knight v. United States Land Assoc., 142 U. S. 161; Astiazaran v. Santa Rita & Mining Co., 148 U. S. 80; United States v. Chaves, 159 U. S. 452.

A grant not complete and perfect, which can be confirmed by the court of private land claims, must be one which the claimant could, by right and not by grace, have demanded should be made perfect by the former government, had not the territory been transferred to the United States; and by the treaty no grant could be considered obligatory which had not been thertofore located. Ainsa v. United States, 161 U. S. 208, 223; United States v. Santa Fe, 165 U. S. 675, 714; United States v. Sandoval, 167 U. S. 278, 293; Bergere v. United States, 168 U. S. 66, 85; Hays v. United States, 175 U. S. 248.

The act of Congress of June 21, 1860, (12 Stats. 71), confirming Mexican grants, was intended to be a discharge of the obligations of the treaty. It is a confirmation of rights which existed and as they existed. If there be two claims under two patents, each of which reserves the rights of the other parties, the enquiry must extend to the character of the original concession. The controversy can only be settled by determining which of these two gives the better right to the demanded premises. Jones v. St. Louis Land Co. (1914), 232 U. S. 355.

The obligation, which the United States assumed by the treaty with Mexico, was to protect all rights of property acquired under the laws of that country. The property rights of pueblos, equally with those of individuals, were entitled to protection, and in the legislation of Congress provision was made for their investigation and confirmation. The right and power of the government in the execution of its treaty obligations to protect the claim of the city of San Francisco, as successor of the pueblo, were superior to any subsequently acquired rights or claims of the State, or of individuals. Tripp v. Spring (1878), 5 Sawy. 209. See Knight v. United States Land Assoc. (1891), 142 U. S. 161.

The act of February 8, 1850, relating to Spanish land grants and declaring void any sales of lands pending official investigation thereunder of the titles, was not violative of the provision in the treaty of Guadalupe Hidalgo, that Mexicans in the disputed territory should be granted their property rights, since the object of the act was to protect these rights by suitable methods for their proof. Baldwin v. Goldfrank (1894), 9 Tex. Civ. App. 269; 88 Tex. 249.

In the clause granting to all Mexicans residing in the ceded territory the privilege to elect within a year to retain Mexican citizenship, and providing that those who did not so elect should be considered as having elected to become citizens of the United States, the word "Mexicans" did not include naturalized citizens of Mexico; and a native born British subject, but a naturalized Mexican citizen, remaining in the ceded territory, having failed to make the election, did not become an American citizen, but was remitted to his original status of a British subject. Tobin v. Walkinshaw et al. (1856), 1 McAll. 186.

The language of the treaty cannot be construed as having changed the character of Mexican citizenship during the year prescribed in the treaty within which to make the declaration of intention to retain Mexican citizenship. A Mexican became an American citizen at the end of the year by reason of remaining in the territory and taking no action looking to his retention of Mexican citizenship, but not till then. Vallejos,

Admr. v. United States et al. (1900), 35 C. Cls. 489. See also De Baca et al. v. United States (1901), 37 C. Cls. 482; 189 U. S. 505.

Under the treaty all Mexicans established in California on May 30, 1848, who did not on or before May 30, 1849 declare their intention to continue their Mexican citizenship, are to be deemed American citizens. People v. Naglee (1850), 1 Cal. 232.

The treaty of Guadalupe Hidalgo operated directly to fix the status of the residents of the ceded territory in their relation as citizens of the respective countries of Mexico and the United States. People v. De la Guerra (1870), 40 Cal. 311.

It was not required that the right of election secured under the treaty to Mexican citizens in the territory of New Mexico should be exercised in any particular mode; and a declaration of intention by a Mexican citizen to retain his citizenship, made by signing his name in a list authoirzed to be kept by the clerks of the prefects' courts by a proclamation of the military governor of New Mexico, was a sufficient exercise of such right of election, and was not affected by a subsequently declared intention to withdraw such declaration not shown to have been acted upon. Quintana v. Tomkins (1853), 1 N. M. 29. See, generally, Carter v. Territory (1859), 1 N. M. 317; United States v. Lucero (1869), 1 N. M. 422.

See also Sena v. United States (1903), 189 U. S. 233; In re Rodriguez (1897), 81 Fed. 337.

Art. XV. Where a prior assignee of a claim against Mexico gave no information of the assignment until a subsequent assignee had prosecuted the claim before the commissioners, and obtained an award in his favor, the equities of these parties were equal, and the possessor of the legal title ought to retain the fund. The award was not conclusive as between the claimants. Judson v. Corcoran (1854), 17 How. 612. See also Atocha v. United States (1872), 8 C. Cls. 427; 17 Wall. 439.

Protocol. "By the rejection of this article [tenth] this government distinctly declared that it did not propose to recognize any grants which were not at the time of the treaty of cession recognized by the Mexican government as valid or any whose conditions, either precedent or subsequent, had not been fully performed." Brewer, J., Cessna v. United States (1898), 169 U. S. 165, 186.

The protocol to the treaty of Guadalupe Hidalgo announced that the American government by suppressing the tenth article did not intend to annul grants of lands made by Mexico in the ceded territories, but that those grants should preserve their legal value, and the grantees might cause their titles to be acknowledged before American tribunals, and that, conformably to the law of the United States, legitimate titles existing in the ceded territories were those which were legitimate titles under the Mexican law in Texas up to March 2, 1836. State v. Gallardo (1911), 135 S. W. (Tex.) 664.

Extradition Convention Concluded December 11, 1861.

(See also extradition convention concluded February 22, 1899.)

Art. I. "The proceeding before the commissioner is not to be regarded as in the nature of a final trial by which the prisoner could be convicted or acquitted of the crime charged against him, but rather of the character of those preliminary examinations which take place every day in this country before an examining or committing magistrate for the purpose of determining whether a case is made out which will justify the holding of the accused, either by imprisonment or under bail, to ultimately answer to an indictment, or other proceeding, in which he shall be finally tried upon the charge made against him. The language of the treaty * * * explicitly provides that 'the commission of the crime shall be so established as that the laws of the country in which the fugitive or the person so accused shall be found would justify his or her apprehension and commitment for trial if the crime had been there committed.' This describes the proceedings in these preliminary examinations as accurately as language can well do it." Miller, J., Benson v. McMahon (1888), 127 U. S. 457, 463, affirming 34 Fed. 649.

A writ of habeas corpus cannot perform the office of a writ of error; and, in extradition proceedings, if the committing magistrate has jurisdiction of the subject-matter and of the accused, and the offense charged is within the terms of the convention of extradition, and the magistrate, in arriving at a decision to hold the accused, has before him competent legal evidence on which to exercise his judgment as to whether the facts are sufficient to establish the criminality of the accused for the purposes of extradition, such decision cannot be reviewed on habeas corpus. Whether an extraditable crime has been committed is a question of mixed law and fact, but chiefly of fact; and the judgment of the magistrate rendered in good faith on legal evidence that the accused is guilty of the act charged, and that it constitutes an extraditable crime, cannot be reviewed on the weight of evidence, and is final for the purposes of the preliminary examination unless palpably erroneous in law. It is enough if it appear that there was legal evidence on which the commissioner might properly conclude that the accused had committed offenses within the treaty as charged, and so be justified in exercising his power to commit him to await the action of the executive department. Ornelas v. Ruiz (1896), 161 U. S. 502.

"The complaint should set forth clearly and briefly the offense charged. It need not be drawn with the formal precision of an indictment. If it be sufficiently explicit to inform the accused person of the precise nature of the charge against him it is sufficient. The extreme technicality with which these proceedings were formerly conducted has given place to a more liberal practice, the object being to reach a correct decision upon the main question—is there reasonable cause to believe that a crime has been committed? The complaint may, in some instances, be upon information and belief. The exigencies may be such that the criminal may escape punishment unless he is promptly apprehended by the representatives of the country whose law he has violated. From the very nature of the case it may often happen that such representative can have no personal knowledge of the crime. If the offense be one of the treaty crimes and if it be stated clearly and explicitly so that the accused knows exactly what the charge is, the complaint is sufficient to authorize the commissioner to act. The foregoing propositions are, it is thought, sustained by the following authorities: In re Farez, 7 Blatchf. 345, Fed. Cases No. 4645; In re Roth, 15 Fed. 506; In re Henrich, 5 Blatchf. 414, Fed. Cases No. 6369; Ex parte Van Hoven, 4 Dill. 415, Fed. Cases No. 16859; In re Breen, 73 Fed. 458; Ex parte Lane, 6 Fed. 34; In re Herres, 33 Fed. 165; Castro v. De Uriarte, 16 Fed. 93; In re Macdonnell, 11 Blatchf. 79, Fed. Cases No. 8771." Coxe, J., Ex parte Sternaman (1896), 77 Fed. 595, 596, quoted with approval in Yordi v. Nolte (1909), 215 U. S. 227, 230, affirming 166 Fed. 921. As to the sufficiency of evidence, see Elias v. Ramirez (1910), 215 U. S. 398; In re Urzua (1911), 188 Fed. 540.

The provision of the convention with Mexico, for the surrender of persons "accused of the crimes enumerated," means that the fugitive is to be accused in due form of law. Accordingly, one who is charged upon information, as well as one charged by indictment, is accused within the meaning of the convention, since an information is one of the forms of accusation prescribed by statute. State of Iowa v. Rowe (1898), 104 Iowa 323.

Art. III. The crime of "forgery" as embraced in Article III is not confined to the English common law offense of forgery, but includes the making, forging, uttering, and selling to the public, fraudulent printed tickets of admission to an operatic performance, bearing on their face in print the name of the manager of the operatic company, and also stamped with his name and seal. It seems that such an offense is also included in the crime of forgery as defined by the English common law. Benson v. McMahon (1888), 127 U. S. 457.

A person extradited from Mexico under the convention has the right to claim exemption from trial upon any other charge than that mentioned in the extradition proceedings, a right which he cannot waive under the provisions of the convention. Ex parte Coy (1887), 32 Fed. 911. See also People v. Gray (1884), 66 Cal. 271; Blandford v. State (1881), 10 Tex. App. 627.

A person was extradited from Mexico upon an information charging that he had counseled and advised another to commit the crime of embezzlement of public moneys, and upon affidavits tending to prove the facts alleged, which were found by the Mexican authorities to show the commission of the crime, and that there were suspicions that the accused was an accomplice in its commission sufficient to justify his arrest and trial. After his return to Iowa from which State he had fled, he was indicted for embezzlement, as a principal, a statute of that State having abrogated the distinction between principals and accessories, and making all concerned in the commission of a crime principals. *Held,* that he was not detained for trial for an offense different from that for which he was extradited. In re Rowe (1896), 77 Fed. 161.

Art. IV. Where, upon the extradition of a person charged to be a fugitive from justice, a warrant for his arrest is issued by the "county judge and extradition agent," the function so performed is judicial, and not administrative, and is for the purpose of preliminary examination; and the warrant is not invalid because it fails to show his authority as an extradition agent under the provision in the convention to the effect that, within the frontier States and Territories of each country, the surrender may be made by the chief civil authority thereof, or by such chief civil or judicial authority of the districts or counties bordering on the frontier as may for this purpose be authorized by said chief civil authority of the frontier State or Territory. Ex part McCabe (1891), 46 Fed. 363.

Art. VI. In view of the express provision that "neither of the contracting parties shall be bound to deliver up its own citizens under the stipulations of this treaty," and of the recognized principle of international law that, in the absence of a treaty stipulation, a nation is under no obligation to surrender fugitives from justice, the United States will not surrender one of its citizens charged with a murder committed in Mexico. Ex parte McCabe (1891), 46 Fed. 363.

Claims Convention Concluded July 4, 1868.

Although the awards made by the commissioners under the authority of this convention, in which it is specifically provided that the parties will "consider the result of the proceedings of this commission as a full, perfect and final settlement," are on their face final and conclusive as between the United States and Mexico, they are only so until set aside by agreement between the two governments or otherwise; and the United States may treat with Mexico for a retrial of any case decided by the commission, and the President may withhold from any claimant his distributive share of any sums paid by Mexico under the convention, while negotiating for a retrial of his case. Frelinghuysen v. Key (1884), 110 U. S. 63; La Abra Silver Mining Co. v. Frelinghuysen, Id. See also Alling v. United States (1885), 114 U. S. 562; Bayard v. United States (1888), 127 U. S. 246; Boynton v. Blaine (1891), 139 U. S. 306; La Abra Silver Mining Co. v. United States (1899), 175 U. S. 423.

So long as the government retains money received from a foreign power in payment of an award, it should in the discharge of its moral and international obligations enquire and ascertain its duty with respect to the fund, not only toward the citizen for whom it was received, but the government from which it was received. United States v. L⌐Abra Silver Mining Co. (1894), 29 C. Cls. 432. See also 32 C. Cls. 521.

Extradition Convention Concluded February 22, 1899.

(See extradition convention concluded December 11, 1861.)

Art. X. Where a complaint in extradition proceedings was based on the information and belief of the vice-consul general of the demanding country, and it appeared that the sources of his information and the grounds of his belief, that petitioner had committed the crime of murder and that a warrant had been issued in Mexico for his arrest and that a requsition accompanied by the warrant and duly authenticated depositions in support thereof were about to be or had been made, were official correspondence between deponent and the Department of Foreign Affairs of Mexico and official communications between the deponent and the Mexican government, the complaint was not defective on the ground of not sufficiently alleging the sources of deponent's information and the grounds of belief. Ex parte Dinehart (1911), 188 Fed. 858.

NETHERLANDS.

Treaty of Peace and Commerce Concluded October 8, 1782.

Art. VI. The provision, that subjects of either party may dispose of their "effects" by testament, donation or otherwise, and their heirs although unnaturalized shall receive such succession ab intestato, includes real as well as personal estate. In virtue of this article, an alien heir can inherit real estate located in the State. It is for the department of the government appointed to represent and act for us with foreign powers, not the judicial, to determine whether a treaty has ceased to be binding because of changes in the organization of the other contracting party since the concluson of the treaty.   University v. Miller (1831), 14 N. C. 188.

NORWAY.

(See Sweden and Norway.)

OTTOMAN EMPIRE.

Treaty of Commerce and Navigation Concluded May 7, 1830.

Art. II.   See Oscanyan v. Arms Co. (1880), 103 U. S. 261, 272.

Treaty of Commerce and Navigation Concluded February 25, 1862.

Art. I.   The treaty of 1862 (if not that of 1830) has the effect of conceding to the United States the same privileges, in respect of consular courts and the civil and criminal jurisdiction thereof, as are enjoyed by other Christian nations.   Dainese v. Hale (1875), 91 U. S. 13.   See also Dainese v. United States (1879), 15 C. Cls. 64.

PANAMA.

Convention for the Construction of a Ship Canal Concluded November 18, 1903.

Art. II.   The title of the United States to the Canal Zone in Panama is not imperfect either because the treaty with Panama does not contain technical terms used in ordinary conveyances of real estate or because the boundaries are not sufficiently defined for identification, the territory in question having been practically identified by the concurrent action of the two interested nations.   Wilson v. Shaw (1907), 204 U. S. 24.

PARAGUAY.

Treaty of Commerce and Navigation Concluded February 4, 1859.

Art. X.   This article gives to consuls of Paraguay the right to name an administrator of the estate of a deceased countryman who has died in this country intestate.   In re Baglieri's

Estate (1912), 137 N. Y. S. 175. See, however, In re Estate of D'Adamo (1914), 212 N. Y. 214.

PERSIA.

Treaty of Friendship and Commerce Concluded December 13, 1856.

Art. IV. The act of Congress of June 6, 1872, (17 Stats. 232), imposing an additional ad valorem duty of ten per centum on goods, the growth and produce of countries east of the Cape of Good Hope, when imported from places west of the Cape of Good Hope, is not in violation of the treaty with Persia, since the subjects of Persia exporting their products directly to the United States are required to pay no higher duties than are paid by the "merchants and subjects of the most favored nation." Powers v. Comly (1879), 101 U. S. 789.

PERU.

Extradition Convention Concluded September 12, 1870.

Where the prisoner has been kidnapped in the foreign country and brought by force against his will within the jurisidction of the State whose law he has violated, with no reference to an extradition convention, though one existed, and with no attempt to proceed under the convention, the Supreme Court can give no relief, since these facts do not establish any right under the Constitution, or laws, or treaties of the United States. The conventions of extradition do not guarantee a fugitive from the justice of one of the countries an asylum in the other. They only make provision that for certain crimes he shall be deprived of that asylum and surrendered to justice, and prescribe the mode in which this shall be done. Ker v. Illinois (1886), 119 U. S. 436.

PORTUGAL.

Treaty of Commerce and Navigation Concluded August 26, 1840.

Art. II. This article is confined exclusively to vessels, and does not include cargoes or make any provision for indirect trade. Oldfield v. Marriott (1850), 10 How. 146.

RUSSIA.

Treaty of Commerce and Navigation Concluded December 18, 1832.

Art. VI. The stipulation in the treaty, that the products of Russia shall not be subjected to a higher rate of duty than like products imported into the United States from other countries, addresses itself to the political and not the judicial department of the government, and the courts cannot try the question whether it has or has not been observed. An act of Congress approved by the President repeals a prior treaty with which it conflicts, so far as the treaty is a municipal law, provided the subject matter is within the legislative power of Congress. Taylor v. Morton (1855), 2 Curtis 454. See 2. Black 481; also Curtis's Admx. v. Fiedler, Id. 461.

It being provided by Article VI that no higher duties shall be imposed on the importation into the United States of any article, the produce or manufacture of Russia, than are or shall be payable on the like articles, the produce or manufacture of any other foreign country, and Congress having by section 1 of the act of August 5, 1861 (12 Stats. 292) imposed a duty on unmanufactured Russia hemp of forty dollars per ton, and on Manila and other hemps of India of twenty-five dollars per ton, such legislation is a declaration by Congress that such provision of the treaty shall no longer operate as the law of the land in respect of the duty on unmanufactured Russia hemp. Ropes v. Clinch (1871), 8 Blatchf. 304. See Art. XVII of the treaty with Sweden and Norway of July 4, 1827.

Art. VIII. The most-favored-nation clause carries with it the privileges and powers conferred on consuls of the Argentine Republic under Article IX of the treaty of 1853. McEvoy v. Wyman (1906), 191 Mass. 276.

Art. IX. A member of the Russian naval service, sent to the United States to become one of the crew of a cruiser, then in course of construction in the United States, who deserts before the vessel has received her crew on board, or has been commissioned for active service and is still in process of construction, but after the vessel has been launched, is a deserter from a Russian ship of war within the meaning of the treaty of 1832. Tucker v. Alexandroff (1902), 183 U. S. 424.

On demand of a Russian vice-consul, process was issued by a United States commissioner, upon which a deserter from a Russian naval vessel was arrested and detained in prison for surrender to the vice-consul or master of the vessel, in accordance with the requirement of Article IX of the treaty of 1832, that such assistance shall be rendered by either country to the other in such cases on proper demand and at the cost of the party making the demand. The person so held was discharged on a writ of habeas corpus by the district court, on the ground that he was not a deserter within the meaning of the treaty; but, on an appeal being taken, such court required him to enter into a recognizance with a surety to appear and abide the judgment of the higher court. The judgment of the district court was finally reversed by the Supreme Court, and, the defendant failing to appear, suit was brought by the United States on the recognizance and the amount of the penalty was paid into court by the surety. *Held,* that the recognizance was not taken for the benefit of the vice-consul or the Russian government, and that the court had no power under the treaty or any rule of comity to award the amount recovered thereon to him in reimbursement for costs expended in the proceedings. Tucker v. United States (1907), 157 Fed. 386.

Treaty for the Acquisition of Alaska Concluded March 30, 1867.

Art. I. The district court for the district of Alaska has jurisdiction in admiralty to forfeit vessels for violating the provisions of Rev. Stats., §1956, on any of the navigable waters of the United States which were acquired by the treaty with Russia. It is a well settled principle that an application to a court to review the action of the political department of the government, upon a question then pending between it and a foreign power, and to determine whether the government is right or wrong, should be denied. In re Cooper (1892), 143 U. S. 472.

Arts. II, III, IV and VI. The commissioners appointed by the governments of the United States and Russia for the transfer of Alaska had no power to vary the language of the treaty or to determine questions of title or ownership. The building constructed by the Russian-American Company in 1845 on land belonging to Russia became thereby, so far as disclosed by the facts in the case, the property of the Russian government, and, being transferred to the United States by the treaty, no property or ownership in it remained in the Russian-American Company, which it could transfer to a private person adversely to the United States. Kinkead v. United States (1893), 150 U. S. 483.

Lands granted in fee simple by Russia prior to the treaty did not pass to the United States. The courts will protect the possession of the owners of such fee, such protection being among the obligations assumed by the United States under the treaty. Callsen v. Hope (1896), 75 Fed. 758.

Art. III. Under the treaty and subsequent legislation by Congress, Alaska is to be considered as incorporated into the United States; and in legislating therefor Congress is under the prohibitions of the Fifth and Sixth Amendments to the Constitution, giving to one accused of a misdemeanor the right of a trial by a common law jury. Rassmussen v. United States (1905), 197 U. S. 516. See also Binns v. United States, 194 U. S. 486; In re Minook (1904), 2 Alaska 200; McFarland v. Alaska Perseverance Mining Co. (1907), 3 Alaska 308.

Such Russian subjects as remained in Alaska after three years became citizens of the United States by virtue of the treaty and subsequent laws of Congress incorporating Alaska into the United States. In re Minook (1904), 2 Alaska 200.

The Athapascan stock, including the native bands of the Tanana, belong to the uncivilized tribes in Alaska, which, according to the terms of Article III of the treaty, by which Alaska was ceded to the United States, are subject to such laws and regulations as the United States may from time to time adopt in regard to the aboriginal tribes of that country. All the vacant and unappropriated lands in Alaska at the date of cession became a part of the public domain and public lands of the United States. United States v. Berrigan (1905), 2 Alaska 442.

Extradition Convention Concluded March 28, 1887.

Art. VI. An order made by an officer in Russia, who purports to act as an examining magistrate, in which the fact of defendant's flight is recited, and in which he is ordered to be brought before an examining magistrate, and which is evidently designed to secure the apprehension of the accused and his production before an examining magistrate, although not in the form of a warrant of arrest as used in this country, is a sufficient compliance with the provision of the convention requiring an authenticated copy of the warrant of arrest or of some other equivalent judicial document issued by a judge or magistrate of the demanding government. Furthermore, Congress not having required, by section 5270, Rev. Stats., the production of a warrant of arrest by the foreign magistrate has waived that requirement of the convention. Grin v. Shine (1902), 187 U. S. 181.

Where the complaint refers to the instruments, alleged to have been forged, as bills of exchange, and the evidence discloses them to be promissory notes, the variance will not defeat surrender, where the instruments are identified and there is a plain case of forgery. If an extraditable crime under the law of the State where the accused is found is sufficiently charged, the effect of variance between complaint and proof is a matter to be decided on general principles irrespective of the law of that State. Even though the complaint be sworn to on information and belief, if it is supported by testimony of witnesses stated to have deposed, the court will presume that they were sworn; and the complaint is sufficient. Glucksman v. Henkel (1911), 221 U. S. 508.

Art. VII. While this article undoubtedly contemplates a prior certificate of the Secretary of State, the language is merely permissive, and does not compel the production of such certificate before the warrant can issue. Grin v. Shine (1902), 187 U. S. 181.

Under section 5270, Rev. Stats., which provides generally for the issuance of a warrant in extradition proceedings on a complaint under oath, a certificate of the Secretary of State that the application for the extradition of the person named has been made by the foreign government is not necessary to the issuance of such warrant, even where, as in the case of Russia, the convention provides for such certificate. In re Schlippenbach (1908), 164 Fed. 783.

SALVADOR.

Extradition Convention Concluded May 23, 1870.

Art. I. In the examination of persons found in California, charged with being fugitives from the justice of Salvador, the evidence of criminality must conform to, and be weighed and judged by, the laws of this country, particularly the laws of California; and the evidence of criminality which will justify holding the accused need be such only as ordinarily obtains at a preliminary examination and shows probable cause, or such as would justify a cautious man in believing the accused guilty. In re Ezeta (1894), 62 Fed. 972.

Art. II. Sec. 1. Homicide as defined in section 361 of the penal code of Salvador constitutes murder as defined in the convention. Id.

Art. II. Sec. 4. Under the definition of robbery as "the action of feloniously and forcibly taking from the person of another goods or money, by violence, or putting him in fear," is included the taking of money or goods from the presence or view of the party robbed, by violence, or by putting him in fear. Id.

Art. III. The testimony showed that the alleged hanging of four persons, May 29, 1894, by officers under President Ezeta,—the killing of C. H., June 3, 1894, by President Ezeta and the other defendants, his officers,—the robbery of a bank, June 5, 1894, by President Ezeta,—and the killing of C., June 6, 1894, by President Ezeta and one of his officers,—all took place during the existence of a state of siege in Salvador, proclaimed April 29, 1894, and during the progress of actual hostilties between the contending forces, wherein Ezeta and his companions were seeking to maintain the authority of the then existing government against a revolutionary uprising; that such acts were associated with the actual conflict of such armed forces; that the four persons were hung because they did not assist in defending the government; that C. H. was killed because he was considered a spy; that the robbery of the bank was for the purpose of paying Ezeta's soldiers and was what is known in the Central and South American states as a "forced loan," recognized in Article XXIX of the treaty of December 6, 1870, between the United States and Salvador; and that the killing of C. was the result of a report that he had gone over to the enemy. *Held,* that such offenses were of a political character and not extraditable under the convention. Id.

SPAIN.

Treaty of Friendship, Boundaries, Commerce and Navigation Concluded October 27, 1795.

Art. II. By the treaty of 1795, the boundary line between the United States and Spain ran through the middle of the St. Mary's River in its whole course to the Atlantic Ocean. The only access from the ocean to the Spanish waters running into the St. Mary's as well as to the adjacent Spanish territories was through this river. By the general principles of the law of nations, the waters of the whole river must be considered as common to both nations for all purposes of navigation, as a common highway necessary for the advantageous use by each of its own territorial rights and possessions. The Apollon (1824), 9 Wheat. 362.

The provisions of this article do not import to be a cession of territory, but the adjustment of a boundary controversy between the two nations. It is understood as an admission that the right was originally in the United States to the territory north of the boundary therein defined. Accordingly, Spanish grants made, after the treaty of peace between the United States and Great Britain, within the territory east of the river Mississippi, and north of a line drawn from that river at the 31st degree of north latitude east to the middle of the river Apalachicola, have no intrinsic validity; and the holders must depend for their titles exclusively on the laws of the United States. Henderson v. Poindexter's Lessee (1827), 12 Wheat. 530; Pollard's Lessee v. Hagan (1845), 3 How. 212; Lessee of Hickey v. Stewart (1845), 3 How. 750; La Roche v. Jones, 9 How. 155; Robinson v. Minor (1850), 10 How. 627.

Art. VI. The treaty with Spain enjoins restitution of captures only in case they are made by pirates or within our jurisdictional limits. The Neustra Señora de la Caridad (1819), 4 Wheat. 497.

The provisions of this article apply exclusively to the protection and defense of Spanish ships within our territorial jurisdiction and provide for their restitution only when captured therein. The Santissima Trinidad (1822), 7 Wheat. 283.

This article seems to have principally in view cases in which the property of the subjects of either party has been taken possession of during war, within the territorial jurisdiction of the other. United States v. The Amistad (1841), 15 Pet. 518, 592.

Art. VIII. This article provides for cases where the shipping of the inhabitants of either party is forced through stress of weather, pursuit of pirates, or enemies, or any other urgent necessity, to seek shelter in the ports of the other. United States v. The Amistad (1841), 15 Pet. 518, 592.

Art. IX. The Carthagenians are not to be considered as pirates, a state of war having been recognized by the government of the United States as existing between Spain and her colonies. A capture made by them on the high seas is not to be restored, not having been made by pirates and not made within the jurisdictional limits of the United States, the only two cases in which the treaty enjoins restitution. The Neustra Señora de la Caridad (1819), 4 Wheat. 497. See, generally, United States v. The Amistad (1841), 15 Pet. 518, 592; Case of Le Tigre (1820), 3 Wash. C. C. 567, 575.

Art. XI. The words "personal goods" in the first clause of Article XI refer to and cover movable property only. Real estate, or immovable property, is referred to and dealt with only in the third clause. Succession of Sala (1898), 50 La. Ann. 1009.

Art. XIV. If citizens of the United States take from a state at war with Spain a commission to cruise against that power contrary to Article XIV of the treaty, such acts are to be considered as piratical acts, at least for all civil purposes, and the offending parties cannot appear and claim in the courts of the United States the property thus taken. It seems that the terms, "a state with which the said King shall be at war," in the article, include the South American provinces which have revolted against Spain. The Bello Corrunes (1821), 6 Wheat. 152.

The provision, prohibiting citizens or subjects of the respective contracting parties from taking commissions to cruise against the other under the penalty of being considered as pirates, is confined to private armed vessels and does not extend to public ships. The Santissima Trinidad (1822), 7 Wheat. 283.

Art. XV. The stipulation "that free ships shall also give freedom to goods" does not imply the converse proposition that "enemy ships shall make enemy goods." The Nereide (1815), 9 Cranch 388.

The term "subjects" in the treaty when applied to persons owing allegiance to Spain must be construed in the same sense as the term "citizens" or "inhabitants" when applied to persons owing allegiance to the United States, and as extending to all persons domiciled in the Spanish dominions. The Pizarro (1817), 2 Wheat. 227.

Art. XVII. The want of a sea-letter, or passport, or certificate as to ownership, port of departure, &c., as described in Article XVII of the treaty, is not a substantive ground for condemnation. It only justifies the capture, and authorizes the captor to send the ship into a proper port for adjudication; and the ownership of the vessel may be proved by other evidence. The Pizarro (1817), 2 Wheat 227.

This article so far as it purports to give any effect to passports as to ownership of vessels is imperfect and inoperative in consequence of the failure to annex to the treaty the form of passport. By the treaty free ships make free goods, but the form of passport, by which the freedom of the ship was to have been conclusively established, never having been annexed to the treaty, the proprietary interest of the ship is to be proved according to the ordinary rules of prize courts, and, if thus shown to be Spanish, will protect the cargo on board, to whomsoever it may belong. The Amiable Isabella (1821), 6 Wheat. 1.

The provision for certain passports and certificates, as evidence of property on board of the ships of both countries, is in its terms applicable only to cases where either of the parties is engaged in a war. United States v. The Amistad (1841), 15 Pet. 518, 595.

Treaty of Friendship, Cession of the Floridas, and Boundaries Concluded February 22, 1819.

"The treaty did not take effect till its ratification by both parties operated like the delivery of a deed to make it the binding act of both. That it may and does relate to its date as between the two governments, so far as respects the rights of either under it, may be undoubted; but as respects individual rights, in any way affected by it, a very different rule ought to prevail." Baldwin, J., United States v. Arredondo (1832), 6 Pet. 691, 748. United States v. Sibbald (1836), 10 Pet. 313, 323.

The written declaration of the King of Spain, annexed to the treaty at the time of ratification, admitting that certain grants of land in Florida were annulled and declared void, having been submitted to the Senate with the treaty and acted upon by it and ratified by the President, is a part of the treaty and is as obligatory as if the provision had been inserted in the body of the treaty itself. With the exchange of the ratifications of the treaty, Florida became a part of the United States, under and according to the stipulations of the treaty—the rights of the United States relating back to the day on which it was signed. Doe v. Braden (1853), 16 How. 635.

Art. II. A cession of territory is never understood to be a cession of the property belonging to its inhabitants. The King ceded that only which belonged to him. United States v. Percheman (1833), 7 Pet. 51. This article undoubtedly transferred to the United States all the political power which our government could acquire, and all the royal domain held by the crown of Spain; but it did not operate on the property of individuals. United States v. Clarke (1834), 8 Pet. 436, 449; Mitchel v. United States (1835), 9 Pet. 711. The King of Spain could not by treaty or otherwise impart to the United States any of his royal prerogatives; nor does the United States have capacity to receive or exercise them. Every nation acquiring territory, by treaty or otherwise, holds it subject to the constitution and laws of its own government, and not according to those of the government ceding it. Pollard's Lessee v. Hagan (1845), 3 How. 212.

See Trustees of Internal Improvement Fund v. Root (1912), 63 Fla. 666.

Art. III.   Although the parties took the Melish map, improved
to 1818 (to which the same effect is to be given as if it had
been expressly made a part of the treaty), as a basis for the
final settlement of the question of boundary, they contemplated, as shown by the fourth article of the treaty, that the
line was subsequently to be fixed with more precision by
commissioners and surveyors representing the respective
countries.   The reference in the treaty to the 100th meridian
was to that meridian astronomically located, and not necessarily to the 100th meridian as located on the Melish map,
where as a matter of fact it was located far east of the true
100th meridian.   United States v. Texas (1896), 162 U. S.
1.   See also Spears v. State (1880), 8 Tex. App. 467.

Art. VI.   This treaty is the law of the land and admits the inhabitants of the ceded territory to the enjoyment of the
privileges, rights, and immunities of citizens of the United
States.   They do not however participate in political power;
they do not share in the government until Florida shall become a State.   In the meantime, Florida continues to be a
territory of the United States, governed by virtue of that
clause of the Constitution which empowers Congress to
"make all needful rules and regulations respecting the territory or other property belonging to the United States."
Marshall, C. J., American Insurance Co. v. Canter (1828),
1 Pet. 511, 542.

A free negro, who was an inhabitant of Florida at the date
of the treaty by which Spain ceded that territory to the
United States, lost the status of an alien by the operation of
that treaty.   Tannis v. St. Cyre (1852), 21 Ala. 449.

Art. VIII.   The clause in the English text, that all grants of land
made by His Catholic Majesty, or by his lawful authorities,
prior to January 24, 1818, "shall be ratified and confirmed"
to the persons in possession of the lands, imports a contract addressed to the political department, not the judicial; and the legislative department must execute the
contract before it can become a rule of the court.   Marshall,
C. J., Foster v. Neilson (1829), 2 Pet. 253.   This article was
intended expressly to stipulate for the security to private
property which the laws and usages of nations would without
express stipulation have conferred.   The words of the Eng-

lish text, "grants shall be ratified and confirmed," and those of
the Spanish text, the English translation of which is "shall
remain ratified and confirmed," were, since both are originals,
intended by the parties to be identical. In order that the two
texts may conform with each other they are to be construed
as importing that the grants are ratified and confirmed by
force of the instrument itself without the aid of legislation.
United States v. Percheman (1833), 7 Pet. 51; United
States v. Arredondo (1832), 6 Pet. 691. See also United
States v. Clarke (1834), 8 Pet. 436. But the provision applies only to grants made in territory which at the time of
the grant belonged to Spain. A boundary line determined
as the true one by the political departments of the government must be recognized as the true one by the judicial department. Foster v. Neilson (1829), 2 Pet. 253; Garcia v.
Lee (1838), 12 Pet. 511; Pollard's Heirs v. Kibbe (1840),
14 Pet. 353. "It is the settled doctrine of the judicial department of this government, that the treaty of 1819 ceded
no territory west of the river Perdido, but only that east of
it; and therefore all grants made by Spain after the United
States acquired the country from France, in 1803, are void, if
the lands granted lay west of that river * * *. It was thus
held in Foster and Elam v. Neilson, 2 Peters 254, and again in
Garcia v. Lee, 12 Peters 515, and is not now open to controversy in this court." Catron, J., Pollard's Lessee v. Files
(1844), 2 How. 591, 602. Spain in ceding the Floridas to
the United States only ceded so much thereof as belonged to
her, and accordingly did not cede the territory lying between
the Perdido and the Mississippi rivers. The stipulation in
Article VIII of the treaty of 1819, to confirm Spanish grants
of land in the ceded territory, did not embrace grants made
in the territory west of the Perdido after Spain ceded Louisiana to France by the treaty of St. Ildefonso in 1800, since
after that date the territory did not belong to Spain. United
States v. Lynde (1870), 11 Wall. 632, citing United States
v. D'Auterive, 10 How. 609; United States v. Philadelphia
& New Orleans, 11 How. 609; Montault v. United States,
12 How. 47; United States v. Castant, 12 How. 437. The
words "lawful authorities" in Article VIII and "competent
authorities" in the ratification must be taken to refer to those

persons who exercised the granting power by the authority of the crown. United States v. Clarke (1834), 8 Pet. 436. A claim to lands in East Florida, the title to which was derived from grants by the Creek and Seminole Indians ratified by the local authorities of Spain before the cession, was confirmed. Mitchel v. United States (1835), 9 Pet. 711. See also Smith v. United States (1836), 10 Pet. 326. The clause in the English text, "owners in possession of such lands,"—in the Spanish version, "proprietarios,"—was for the benefit of those who were purchasers under the faith of a public grant. The law deems every man to be in the legal seizin and possession of land to which he has a perfect and complete title. This gives to the words "in possession of such lands" their well settled and fixed meaning. Possession does not imply occupation or residence. United States v. Arredondo (1832), 6 Pet. 691, 743; Mitchel v. United States (1835), 9 Pet. 711; United States v. Sibbald (1836), 10 Pet. 313, 323. Owners of lands are allowed by this article the same time for fulfilling the conditions of their grants from the date of the treaty as is allowed in the grant from the date of the instrument. United States v. Clarke (1835), 9 Pet. 168; United States v. Sibbald (1836), 10 Pet. 313. In case of failure to perform or to attempt to perform the conditions within the time limited, the grant lapsed. United States v. Mills' Heirs (1838), 12 Pet. 215. The perfect titles made by Spain before January 24, 1818, within the ceded territory, are intrinsically valid and exempt from the provisions of the eighth article; and they need no sanction from the legislative or judicial departments of this government. The eighth article was intended to apply to claims the validity of which at the date of the treaty depended upon the performance of conditions in consideration of which the concessions had been made and which must have been performed before Spain would have been bound to perfect the titles. The United States was bound by the article after the cession, to the same extent that Spain was bound before the ratification of the treaty, to perfect this class of cases by legislation and adjudication. United States v. Wiggins (1840), 14 Pet. 334.

A grantee of land in Florida, who had never caused the same to be severed from the public domain by survey, or identified, was without actual seizin or seizin in law, and not within the protection of the treaty of 1819. United States v. Miranda, 16 Pet. 153. The power to survey lands in conformity to concessions made prior to January 24, 1818 existed up to the change of flags. United States v. Huertas, 9 Pet. 171; United States v. Heirs of Clarke, 16 Pet. 228; United States v. Acosta, 1 How. 24. See especially as to various grants attempted to be brought under the protection of this article, and for reviews of decisions of the court, Lessee of Pollard's Heirs v. Kibbe (1840), 14 Pet. 353; O'Hara v. United States (1841), 15 Pet. 275; United States v. Delespine (1841), 15 Pet. 319; United States v. Breward (1842), 16 Pet. 143; United States v. Miranda (1842), 16 Pet. 153; United States v. Hanson (1842), 16 Pet. 196; United States v. Heirs of Clarke et al. (1842), 16 Pet. 228; United States v. Acosta (1843), 1 How. 24.

Arts. IX and XI. The object of the treaty was to invest the commissioners with full power and authority to receive, examine and decide upon the amount and validity of asserted claims upon Spain for damages and injuries. Their decision within the scope of this authority is conclusive and final. But it does not follow that this authority extends to the adjustment of all conflicting rights of different citizens to the fund awarded. The commissioners are to look to the original claim for damages and injuries against Spain, and it is wholly immaterial who the legal or equitable owner of the claim may be, provided he is an American citizen. The right to compensation for damages and injuries, to which citizens of the United States were entitled, and which, under the treaty, were to be the subject of compensation, passed by abandonment to the underwriters of property which had been seized or captured. The right to compensation from Spain, held under abandonment made to underwriters and accepted by them, for damages and injuries, which were to be satisfied under the treaty, passed to the assignees of the bankrupt, who held such rights by the provisions of the bankruptcy law of the United States. It is not universally, though it may be ordinarily, the test of a right, that it may be enforced in a court of justice. Claims and debts due by a sovereign are not capable of being so enforced. It does not follow that because an unjust sentence cannot be reversed, that the party injured has lost all right to justice or all claim, upon principles of public law, to remuneration. The treaty recognized an existing right in the aggrieved parties to compensation, and did not turn upon the notion of donation or gratuity. Compensation was demanded by our government as matter of right, and as such was granted by Spain. Comegys et al. v. Vasse (1828), 1 Pet. 193. See also Delafield v. Colden (1828), 1 Paige (N. Y.) 139; Yard v. Cramond (1835), 5 Rawle (Pa.) 18; Humphrey's Admx. v. United States, Dev. Ct. Cls. 204, §§ 678-693; and Thomas v. United States, Id., §§ 694, 695. See, also, United States v. Ferreira, 13 How. 40; Meade v. United States, 9 Wall. 691; Gray, Admr. v. United States, 21 C. Cls. 340.

Agreement for Settlement of Certain Claims of Citizens of the United States Against Spain of February 11-12, 1871.

The Secretary of State was not liable to pay interest or income derived from the investment of a sum of money received as part of an award made by the Spanish-American claims commission, which sum of money was eventually paid to the petitioner. The award was to be paid by the Spanish government to the government of the United States. It was paid to the Secretary of State, representing the government of the United States. The money withheld was withheld by the United States, and the petitioner's claim based on the withholding was a claim against the United States, and fell within the well settled principle that interest is not allowed on claims against the United States, unless the government has stipulated to pay interest, or it is given by express statutory provision. Angarica v. Bayard (1888), 127 U. S. 251, affirming 4 Mackey 310.

Extradition Convention Concluded January 5, 1877, as Amended by the Supplementary Convention Concluded August 7, 1882.

Art. II. Sec. 12. Under the penal code of Cuba, Art. 401, which makes it a crime for a public employee to take public funds of which he has charge by virtue of his office, a public officer who, by falsely certifying the invoices in which certain coupons are enclosed, obtains possession of money paid out by the Spanish bank, which could not pass from the bank's possession to his own except as a consequence of his official act, is guilty of an extraditable offense. In re Cortes (1890), 42 Fed. 47; affirmed in 136 U. S. 330.

If the commissioner has jurisdiction of the subject matter and of the person of the accused, and the offense charged is within the terms of an extradition convention, and the commissioner, in arriving at a decision to hold the accused, has before him competent legal evidence on which to exercise his judgment as to whether the facts are sufficient to establish the criminality of the accused for the purposes of extradition, such decision of the commissioner cannot be reviewed by a circuit court or by the Supreme Court, on habeas corpus. In re Oteiza y Cortes (1890), 136 U. S. 330.

Art. XI. The provision, that it shall be "competent" for the demanding government to obtain a mandate or preliminary warrant, is permissive only, and not obligatory. The demanding government may, at its option, proceed under section 5270, Rev. Stats., without a preliminary mandate, or may demand it under the provisions of the convention. Castro v. De Uriarte (1883), 16 Fed. 93.

Treaty of Peace Concluded December 10, 1898.

Art. I. As between the United States and Cuba, that island is territory held in trust for its inhabitants to whom it rightfully belongs, and to whose exclusive control it will be surrendered when a stable government shall have been established; and within the meaning of the act of June 6, 1900 (31 Stats. 656), providing for the surrender of fugitives, Cuba is foreign territory which cannot be regarded in any constitutional, legal or international sense as a part of the territory of the United States, notwithstanding the fact that it is under a military governor, appointed by and representing the President, in the work of assisting the inhabitants of the island in establishing a government of their own. Neely v. Henkel (1901), 180 U. S. 109.

The Isle of Pines is de facto under the jurisdiction of the republic of Cuba, and, as regards the United States, foreign country within the meaning of the tariff act of 1897. Pearcy v. Stranahan (1907), 205 U. S. 257.

Art. II. Upon the exchange of ratifications of the treaty of peace between the United States and Spain, April 11, 1899, Porto Rico ceased to be a "foreign country" within the meaning of the tariff laws. De Lima v. Bidwell (1901), 182 U. S. 1.

Duties on imports from the United States into Porto Rico collected by the military commander and by the President as commander-in-chief, from the time possession was taken of the island until the exchange of the ratifications of the treaty, were legally exacted under the war power. The authority of the President as commander-in-chief to exact duties on goods arriving at Porto Rico from New York ceased with the exchange of the ratifications of the treaty of peace. Dooley v. United States (1901), 182 U. S. 222.

The island of Porto Rico was not by operation of the treaty of peace incorporated into the "United States" in the sense in which these words are used in the provision of the Constitution requiring all duties, imposts and excises to be uniform "throughout the United States." Downes v. Bidwell (1901), 182 U. S. 244.

The provision in the Constitution, declaring that no tax or duty shall be laid on articles exported from any State, has reference to articles exported to a foreign country, and does not prohibit the imposition of a tax on articles arriving in Porto Rico from the States. Dooley v. United States (1901), 183 U. S. 151.

Vessels engaged in trade between Porto Rican ports and the port of New York are engaged in the coasting trade in the sense in which these words are used in the New York pilotage statutes; and steam vessels engaged in such trade are coastwise steam vessels under §4444, Rev. Stats. Huus v. New York & Porto Rico Steamship Co. (1901), 182 U. S. 392.

The treaty, although signed December 10, 1898, and ratified by Spain (which was the last to ratify) on March 19, 1899, did not become effective for the purposes of the tariff laws until the exchange of ratifications, April 11, 1899, and all importations of merchandise arriving from Porto Rico prior to that date were subject to duty. Armstrong v. Bidwell (1903), 124 Fed. 690. See also American Sugar

Refining Co. v. Bidwell, 124 Fed. 677; American Sugar Refining Co. v. Bidwell, 124 Fed. 683; Howell v. Bidwell, 124 Fed. 688; Ex parte Ortiz, 100 Fed. 955; Lascelles v. United States, 49 C. Cls. 382.

By the ratifications of the treaty of peace, Porto Rico ceased to be subject to Spain, and became subject to the legislative power of Congress; but, pending the action of Congress and the necessary delay in establishing civil government, there was no interregnum, and the authority to govern the territory ceded by the treaty was, by the law applicable to conquest and cession, under the military control of the President as commander-in-chief. The authority of the military government during the period between the cession and action by Congress is of large, though it may not be of unlimited, extent. But whatever may be the limits, it includes the power to establish courts of justice. Santiago v. Nogueras (1909), 214 U. S. 260.

Art. III. No distinction, so far as the question determined in the case of De Lima v. Bidwell (supra) is concerned, can be made between the Philippines and Porto Rico, after the ratification of the treaty of peace, April 11, 1899, either because of the passage by the Senate, alone, and without the concurrence of two-thirds of the members present, of a joint resolution in respect of the intention of the Senate in advising ratification of the treaty, or because of the armed resistance to the dominion of the United States by the natives in the Philippines. Fourteen Diamond Rings v. United States (1901), 183 U. S. 176.

After the title to the Philippine Islands passed to the United States upon the exchange of ratifications of the treaty of peace, there was nothing in the Philippine insurrection of sufficient gravity to give to the islands the character of a foreign country within the meaning of the tariff laws. Lincoln v. United States (1905), 197 U. S. 419; 202 U. S. 484.

Technically, a state of war as to third persons existed between the United States and Spain until the exchange of the ratifications of the treaty, notwithstanding the suspension of active hostilities by the protocol of August 12, 1898. MacLeod v. United States (1913), 229 U. S. 416. See also 45 C. Cls. 339.

Art. IV. The provision, that the United States will for a term of ten years admit Spanish ships and merchandise to the ports of the Philippine Islands on the same terms as enjoyed by ships and merchandise of the United States, does not give to merchandise imported into the Philippines from Spain a different status from that imported from the United States. Neither does it give to citizens of Spain a preference over citizens of the United States in this respect. They are entitled to the same terms. Struckmann v. United States (1909), 44 C. Cls. 202; affirmed, 223 U. S. 712.

Art. VI. In the light of all the surrounding circumstances it will not be assumed that the United States in carrying out its stipulations for the capitulation of Manila would commit an act of inhumanity such as separating the surrendered officers from their wives and children by furnishing the former with cabin, and the latter with steerage, accommodations on the voyage to Spain under the repatriation provision of the treaty of peace. Ceballos & Co. v. United States (1909), 214 U. S. 47.

Art. VII. Claims of Spanish subjects against the United States for indemnity for illegal seizures and detentions of property during the war of 1898 were relinquished by the treaty of peace. A state of war did not cease until the ratification of the treaty in April, 1899. Hijo v. United States (1904), 194 U. S. 315; Herrera v. United States (1912), 222 U. S. 558.

Art. VIII. The privilege of practicing law was not a property right protected by Article VIII of the treaty. Bosque v. United States (1908), 209 U. S. 91.

The Roman Catholic Church has been recognized as possessing legal personality, and its property rights have been solemnly safeguarded by the treaty of Paris. In so doing the treaty has merely followed the recognized rule of international law, which would have protected the property of the Church in Porto Rico, after the cession. This juristic personality and the ownership of property by the Church had been recognized in the most formal manner by the concordats between Spain and the papacy and by the Spanish laws from the beginning of settlements in the Indies. Ponce v. Roman Catholic Church (1908), 210 U. S. 296, 323. See also O'Reilly de Camara v. Brooke (1908), 209 U. S. 45.

The property rights of private individuals recognized and protected by the treaty did not include the right to hold in perpetuity offices of a quasi-public nature, such as that of procurador; and the United States did not so restrict its sovereign authority that it could not, consistently with the treaty, abolish a system so entirely foreign to the conceptions of the American people, and inconsistent with the spirit of our institutions. Sanchez v. United States (1910), 216 U. S. 167.

The legal entity of the city of Manila survived both its military occupation by, and cession to, the United States; and, as in law the present city as the successor of the former city is entitled to the property rights of its predecessor, it is also subject to its liabilities. The relinquishment to the United States of all the public property belonging to the crown of Spain in the Philippine Islands did not include property belonging to municipalities, and the property and property rights of municipalities were safeguarded precisely as were those of individuals. Vilas v. City of Manila (1911), 220 U. S. 345.

See also Eastern Extension, Australasia and China Telegraph Co. v. United States, 46 C. Cls. 646; 48 C. Cls. 33; 231 U. S. 326.

Art. IX. The immigration act of March 3, 1891 (26 Stats. 1084), relates to foreigners, as respects this country—to persons owing allegiance to a foreign government. Citizens of Porto Rico are not "aliens," and upon arrival by water at the ports of our mainland are not "alien immigrants" within the intent and meaning of the act. Gonzales v. Williams (1904), 192 U. S. 1.

It is clear from the language of this article that it was the intention of the framers of the treaty to reserve to Congress, so far as it could be constitutionally done, a free hand in dealing with these newly-acquired possessions. The legislation on the subject shows that Congress has hitherto refrained from incorporating the Philippine Islands into the United States to such extent as would require the enactment therefor by Congress of a system of laws which should include the right of trial by jury. Dorr v. United States (1904), 195 U. S. 138.

Under the treaty, a Spanish resident of the Philippine Islands, who left there in May, 1899, without making any declaration of intention to preserve his allegiance to Spain, and who remained away until after the expiration of eighteen months after the ratification of the treaty, continued to be a Spaniard, and did not, even though he intended to return, become a citizen of the islands under the new sovereignty, and therefore is not eligible to admission to practice at the bar under the rules established by the military and civil authorities of the Philippine Islands. The laws applicable to other foreigners, referred to in the article, have reference not to Spanish laws, but to the laws to be enacted by the new sovereignty. Bosque v. United States (1908), 209 U. S. 91.

Provision is made in Article IX of the treaty by which Spanish subjects, natives of the Peninsula, may preserve their allegiance to Spain; but that provision has no reference to corporations; nor is there any other provision in the treaty providing therefor. Martinez v. Asociacion de Señoras (1909), 213 U. S. 20.

A citizen of Porto Rico is not an alien to the United States, and is not prohibited by §1068, Rev. Stats., from maintaining an action in the Court of Claims. Narciso Basso v. United States (1905), 40 C. Cls. 202.

Art. XIII. The provision, for the protection of industrial property in the ceded territory, will not be construed as contravening principles of morality and fairness and as protecting a trade-mark fraudulently registered prior to the treaty. Ubeda v. Zialcita (1913), 226 U. S. 452.

SWEDEN AND NORWAY.

Treaty of Amity and Commerce Concluded April 3, 1783.

Art. II. The right of free entry into the United States of untaxed pulp made from untaxed wood provided for in section 2 of the act of July 26, 1911, "to promote reciprocal trade relations with the Dominion of Canada and for other purposes," having been granted by the United States to Canada without consideration, passed automatically to other powers enjoying most-favored-nation treatment. American Express Co. et al. v. United States; and Bertuch & Co. et al. v. United States (1913), 4 Ct. Cust. Appls. 146. See also 14 Op. Atty. Gen. 468.

Art. VI. The provision in Article VI of the treaty of 1783, continued in force by Article XVII of the treaty of 1827,—that the subjects of the two nations may dispose of their "fonds et biens" (translated "goods and effects") by testament, donation, or otherwise, and that their "heirs," in whatever place they may reside, shall receive the succession "even ab intestato,"—covers real estate as well as personal property. Non-resident alien subjects of the kingdom of Sweden, by virtue of this provision, take and hold real estate in Illinois by descent or otherwise, the provisions of the alien act of the State of 1887 (Laws of 1887, p. 5) to the contrary notwithstanding. Adams v. Akerlund (1897), 168 Ill. 632.

The words "goods and effects" do not include real estate. A non-resident alien is not empowered to inherit an interest in lands in Iowa by virtue of the provision in the treaty of 1783 with Sweden, that the subjects of the contracting parties in the respective states, although unnaturalized, may dispose of and inherit "goods and effects." Meier v. Lee (1898), 106 Iowa 303.

The terms "goods and effects" as used in the treaty cover real estate passing by will or descent. The provision, that inheritances shall be exempt from all duty called "droit de détraction," does not cover a tax upon the succession to or transfer of property. The words "freely dispose of" do not relate to property passing by descent. There is nothing in the treaty which requires uniformity of taxes upon property passing to citizens of the United States and to citizens and subjects of Sweden; and the State may accordingly impose and collect a collateral inheritance tax of 20 per cent. on property passing to such alien heirs, though the tax on property passing to native resident heirs is only 5 per cent. An inheritance tax is not fundamentally a tax upon property, but a tax upon the right of succession, or the right to receive the property by will or descent. In re Peterson's Estate (1915), 151 N. W. (Iowa) 66.

In so far as the rights to succession of property of deceased persons are concerned, the citizens of each country stand on an equal footing. Accordingly, a statute of the

State which imposes an inheritance tax of 25 per cent. on all sums passing to or for the benefit of collateral relatives or strangers of the blood, who are aliens not residing in the United States, and a tax of only 3 per cent. on property passing to citizens of this country, is in conflict with the treaty and must give way to it. The words "goods and effects" in the treaty include real, as well as personal, property. Although the word "heirs" in its technical common-law meaning is restricted to those who take by inheritance only, it applies in the civil law to all persons who are called to the succession whether by the act of the party or by operation of law; and the phrase "their heirs shall receive the succession" as used in the treaty refers to the right of succession of those who receive by testament, as well as those who receive by operation of law. In re Stixrud's Estate (1910), 58 Wash. 339.

This treaty enables non-resident aliens to inherit land in the State of Nebraska, notwithstanding conflicting statutory provisions. The terms "goods and effects" as used in the treaty include real estate. Erickson v. Carlson et al. (1914), 95 Neb. 182.

The words "goods and effects" as used in this article do not embrace real estate. The intestate, who was the owner of land in Kansas, died without wife or issue, his father and mother having previously died. Among his surviving brothers and sisters some were aliens and some citizens. One of his surviving sisters, an alien, had two children who were citizens. *Held,* that the sister, being an alien, could not inherit a share of the estate, and that after her death her children, although citizens, were incapable of inheriting through her. Johnson v. Olson (1914), 92 Kan. 819.

Treaty of Commerce and Navigation Concluded July 4, 1827.

Art. XIII. A district court of the United States is not, by the provisions of this article—conferring on Swedish consuls the right to sit as judges and arbitrators in such differences as may arise between the captain and crews of a Swedish vessel, unless the order or tranquility of the country shall be disturbed,—prohibited from exercising its authority in a case within the terms of the treaty, where there is no consul, or other officer of Sweden, within the territorial jurisdiction of the court. The Amalia (1880), 3 Fed. 652.

Any person, who, in pursuance of any arrangement or contract, for a long or a short period or voyage, is on board of a Norwegian vessel aiding in her navigation, is a member of her crew within the meaning of this article; and the consul of the kingdom of Norway and Sweden has exclusive jurisdiction of any difference arising between him and the master of such vessel, whether such person is or is not an American citizen and shipped at an American port. The Marie (1892), 49 Fed. 286.

The Norwegian consul has exclusive jurisdiction to hear and determine complaints of ill-treatment of seamen shipping from an American port for a voyage on a Norwegian vessel. The Welhaven (1892), 55 Fed. 80.

An action for seamen's wages (a Swede by birth, but shipping from an American port) earned on board of a Swedish vessel is, under the treaty, cognizable only before the Swedish consul; and the State courts have no jurisdiction thereof. Norberg v. Hillgreu (1846), 5 N. Y. Leg. Obs. 177.

Under this article the courts of this country have no jurisdiction of an action for wages brought by a seaman, a Norwegian subject, against the master of a Norwegian vessel. Tellefsen v. Fee (1897), 168 Mass. 188.

Giving this article the liberal construction required in case of treaties, it governs in all matters of difference between the captain of a Norwegian vessel lying in a port of the United States, or the officer then in command of the vessel, and members of the crew, relating to a matter of ship discipline, whether the occurrences complained of took place on the vessel or on the wharf at which the vessel lay; and where all parties concerned are citizens of Norway, and the affair is not of such seriousness as to disturb the public peace, the local courts are without jurisdiction to arrest and detain officers of the ship, on warrants issued at the instance of a seaman, whether before or after his discharge from the vessel. Ex parte Anderson (1910), 184 Fed. 114.

In view of the provisions of the treaty of July 4, 1827, with Sweden and Norway, and of that with Sweden of June 1, 1910, both of which vest in the consular officers of each country exclusive jurisdiction to hear and determine "differences" which may arise between the officers and crews of merchant vessels of such country either at sea or in port, without interference by the local authorities unless in case of breach of the peace, &c., a court of admiralty is without jurisdiction of a suit by a foreign seaman on a Swedish vessel against such vessel based on the alleged negligence of the master by which libelant was injured in an American port and compelled to leave the vessel. The Ester (1911), 190 Fed. 216.

The Swedish consul is not entitled under any law or treaty to take from an administrator, duly appointed under the laws of the State, succession opened in the State as of a foreigner, a Swede by birth, not domiciled in the State, but leaving property therein. Such a right would be incompatible with the sovereignty of the State whose jurisdiction extends over the property of foreigners as well as of citizens found within its limits. Succession of Thompson (1854), 9 La. Ann. 96.

Art. XIV. Where a Swedish seaman deserted in a port of the United States, and later voluntarily returned to his country,—thus placing himself under the control of his own government,—that government, having by a subsequent official act authorized him to emigrate to the United States, is precluded from demanding his surrender as a deserter, under the provisions of the treaty. In re Pederson (1851), Fed. Cases No. 10,899a.

SWEDEN.

Consular Convention Concluded June 1, 1910.

Art. XI. See Sweden and Norway, treaty of July 4, 1827, Art. XIII.

Art. XIV. Where a seaman of an American merchant vessel, a subject of the King of Sweden, died without will or known relatives or next of kin in the United States, and his effects were turned into the registry of the circuit court, the Swedish consul, being eligible under the treaty to take out letters of administration on the estate, was competent to receive the effects under § 4544, Rev. Stats. In re Holmberg's Estate (1912), 193 Fed. 260.

This article purports to give to the consuls of the parties thereto the right to administer upon the estates of their deceased nationals only "so far as the laws of each country will permit." Austro-Hungarian Consul v. Westphal (1912), 120 Minn. 122.

This provision is to be construed as adding such foreign consuls to the list of those eligible as administrators so as to enable them to administer upon the estates of their fellow citizens when no one having a prior right under the local law is competent or willing to act. It is not intended by this provision to supersede the local law and confer a right of administration upon the foreign consul that is exclusive and permanent to all others; and, under the code of New York, where a subject of the King of Italy died, intestate, in the State, leaving a wife, a child, a father and a mother residing in Italy, and a brother residing in the State, the latter, although he has no interest in decedent's estate, is entitled to letters of administration thereon in preference to the Italian consul. In re Estate of D'Adamo (1914), 212 N. Y. 214, reversing 144 N. Y. S. 429. Prior to this decision by the Court of Appeals, the following rulings had been made by various surrogates: This article gives to a consular officer of Sweden the right to be appointed administrator of the estate of a citizen of his country dying intestate in this country, in preference to a brother and one of the next of kin. In re Baglieri's Estate (1912), 137 N. Y. S. 175. The consul has the right of administration on the estate of a countryman dying in this country intestate and without resident heirs or next of kin, in preference to a distant resident relative not entitled to succeed to the personalty. In re Lombardi (1912), 138 N. Y. S. 1007. A consul has the right, in preference to resident creditors, to administration on the estate of a deceased countryman, dying intestate in this country, leaving as his heirs at law and next of kin non-resident aliens. In re Riccardo (1913), 140 N. Y. S. 606. Under the treaty with Sweden, giving consuls authority to take charge of the property left by decedents for the benefit of the lawful heirs and creditors, and giving them the right to be appointed administrators, the consul is entitled to letters of administration on the estate of a decedent, whose father is not a citizen or resident of this country, as against a brother residing in the country. In re Madaloni's Estate (1913), 141 N. Y. S. 323.

The provisions of this article do not give to the consul the right to administer, in preference to one so entitled under the local laws of the State in which the deceased lived and left property. His right either to temporary possession or to be appointed administrator is subject to the laws of the State, i. e., in California to the provision in the local law that, in the absence of the next of kin entitled to inherit, the public administrator is entitled to letters of administration. Fontana v. Hynes (1915), 146 Pac. 651.

Under this article, the consular agent, in the absence and under the authority of the consul general, is entitled, as against the nominee of a non-resident heir, to administer the estate of a deceased countryman dying intestate in Montana. In re Infelise's Estate (1915), 149 Pac. 365.

SWITZERLAND.

Treaty of Friendship, Commerce, and Extradition Concluded November 25, 1850.

Art. V. Yaker, a naturalized American citizen, died in 1853, intestate, seized of real estate in Kentucky. He left a widow, a resident and citizen of that State, and certain heirs and next of kin, aliens and residents in Switzerland. By the laws of Kentucky in 1853, the date of the death, the alien heirs were not allowed to inherit, and the widow was entitled to the estate. As to private rights thus vested the exchange of ratifications of the treaty, November 8, 1855, had no retroactive effect. Yeaker's Heirs v. Yeaker's Heirs (1862), 4 Metc. 33; Haver v. Yaker (1869), 9 Wall. 32.

The provision of the treaty—that in case real estate situated within the territories of one of the contracting parties shall fall to a citizen of the other party, who on account of his being an alien is not permitted to hold such property in the State or Canton in which it may be situated, there shall be accorded to the said heir, or other successor, such term, as the laws of the State or Canton will permit, to sell such property,—is the supreme law of the land, and by its terms the incapacity of a citizen of Switzerland, next of kin of the intestate, is so far removed as to entitle him to recover and sell the land whereof the intestate died seized in fee, and to withdraw and export the proceeds thereof. His rights thus secured are not barred by the lapse of time, if no statute of the State where the land is situated prescribes the term within which they are to be asserted. Hauenstein v. Lynham (1879), 100 U. S. 483. See also Jost v. Jost (1882), 1 Mackey 487.

The article provides that citizens of each country, and their heirs, having personal property in the jurisdiction of the other, shall have absolute power of disposition, and that this provision shall be applicable in case of real estate in the States and Cantons which permit foreigners to "hold or inherit" real estate. In case any State or Canton does not permit foreigners to "hold" real estate, there shall be accorded such term, as the State or Canton may fix, within which to sell it and withdraw the proceeds. A statute of the State of Indiana providing that aliens may "take and hold" land by devise and descent only, and may convey the same within five years, and that all property left at that time shall escheat, does not permit aliens to "hold" real property within the meaning of the treaty, but merely recognizes the terms of the treaty by giving five years in which to dispose of the property; and accordingly it is not in contravention of the treaty. Lehman v. State (1909), 45 Ind. App. 330; 88 N. E. 365.

Art. XIII. The place where a crime was committed is the proper place in which to try the person charged with having committed it; and nothing is required to warrant extradition under the treaty, except that evidence of the fact of the commission of the crime shall be produced, sufficient to justify a commitment for trial for the crime. The word "country" in the treaty necessarily means, under our form of government, the special political jurisdiction within which the fugitive is found. In re Farez (1870), 7 Blatchf. 345. See generally as to the requirements of the warrant for the apprehension of the fugitive, and of the complaint, In re Farez, 7 Blatchf. 34, 345; In re Roth (1883), 15 Fed. 506.

It is immaterial what prior charges have been made in Switzerland against the accused if the complaint here presented charge a treaty offense; and if the commission of the offense be duly established before the commissioner, the accused cannot be discharged on habeas corpus, though it should appear that a proceeding for a different and less offense, not included in the treaty, had been previously taken against him in Switzerland. Documentary proofs being in German and describing the proceedings in Switzerland as for "unterschlagung," which may mean embezzlement ("soustraction") or only abuse of trust ("d'abus de confiance"), the latter not being a treaty offense, and the certificate to the authentication of the documents stating, in French, that they were for a proceeding "d'abus de confiance," the error in the certificate, if it was such, is immaterial, and it is to be presumed that the requisition for the accused is for a trial for the treaty offense. In re Roth (1883), 15 Fed. 506.

Art. XIV. Under the provision for the delivery of persons charged with certain crimes "when these crimes are subject to infamous punishment," it is sufficient if the crime is subject to infamous punishment in the country where committed, without its being also subject to infamous punishment in the country from which the extradition is demanded. Showing that forgery is punishable by imprisonment in the state prison by the laws of the Canton of Berne, in Switzerland, in which Canton the crime was committed, is showing that it is subject to infamous punishment in the country where it was committed, within the meaning of the convention. In re Farez (1870), 7 Blatchf. 345.

Art. XV. A mandate for the apprehension of the fugitive, purporting to be issued by the government of the United States, and issued under the hand of the Secretary of State and the seal of the Department of State, is a sufficient mandate. In re Farez (1869), 7 Blatchf. 34.

TWO SICILIES.

Claims Convention Concluded October 14, 1832.

Since the commissions of the supercargo would have been a charge upon the proceeds of the sales of the cargo, if it had arrived at the place of its destination, they are to be considered as a charge upon the fund, which stands in the place of those proceeds of sales, and were not a proper charge against the King of the Two Sicilies, under the treaty of indemnity. Stewart's Admx. v. Callaghan (1835), 4 Cranch C. C. 594.

INTERNATIONAL CONVENTIONS.

Postal Union Convention Signed at Berne October 9, 1874.

Art. XXV of the Regulations. This convention is the law of the land; and, under it, dutiable goods cannot lawfully be imported in the foreign mail. Goods so imported are liable to seizure. Cotzhausen v. Nazro (1882), 107 U. S. 215.

Convention for International Protection of Industrial Property Concluded at Paris March 20, 1883.

"The various stipulations of the convention of 1883 are of the character that require legislation to give them full effect, and such legislation has not been had, and consequently the convention remains without effect or operation." Rousseau v. Brown (1903), 21 App. Cases (D. C.) 73, 77.

Citizens of Canada, who are engaged in the manufacture of trade-marked articles, and who have a place of business in the State of New York, where they make and ship such articles for sale in the United States, may sue in the United States courts for the infringement of their trade-marks by its citizens. Kerry et al. v. Toupin (1894), 60 Fed. 272.

The word "Vichy" used in connection with mineral waters and derived from the locality in France where the waters are obtained is a trade name, or "nom commercial," within the meaning of the industrial property convention, and as such entitled to protection in the United States, though it has not been deposited as required by the convention in the case of trade-marks. La Republique Francaise et al. v. Schultz (1893), 57 Fed. 37.

It was not intended by Article VIII of the industrial property convention to put citizens of a foreign country on a more favorable footing than our own citizens, or to exempt them from ordinary defenses which might be made by the party prosecuting. This article was designed merely to protect citizens of other countries in their right to sue in the courts of the United States as if they were citizens thereof. Under Article II the rights of the French Republic are the same and no greater than those of the United States would be. French Republic v. Saratoga Vichy Co. (1903), 191 U. S. 427.

Under Article VI of the convention for the protection of industrial property of March 20, 1883, to which both France and the United States are parties, providing that every trade-mark regu-

40

larly deposited in the country of origin shall be admitted to deposit and so protected in all other countries of the union, the owner of a trade-mark registered in France is entitled to protection in this country, whether or not such mark would have been allowed under the statutes of this country. Rossmann v. Garnier (1914), 211 Fed. 401.

Additional Act for the Protection of Industrial Property Concluded at Brussels December 14, 1900.

Art. I.   Article 4 *bis,* inserted in the international convention for the protection of industrial property of March 20, 1883 by the additional act signed at Brussels, December 14, 1900, proclaimed by the President, August 25, 1902, as controlled and construed by the act of March 3, 1903, (32 Stats. 1225), "to effectuate the provisions" of such additional convention, did not have the effect of changing the term of an existing United States patent as fixed by statute at the time of its issuance. United Shoe Machinery Co. v. Duplessis Shoe Machinery Co. (1907), 155 Fed. 842; Malignani v. Hill-Wright Electric Co. (1910), 177 Fed. 430; Malignani v. Jasper Marsh Consolidated Co. (1910), 180 Fed. 442; Commercial Acet. Co. v. Searchlight Gas Co. (1912), 197 Fed. 908; Cameron Septic Tank Co. v. City of Knoxville (1913), 227 U. S. 39; Commercial Acetylene Co. v. Schroeder (1913), 203 Fed. 276. See, contra, Hennebique Construction Co. v. Myers (1909), 172 Fed. 869.

Convention Respecting the Rights and Duties of Neutral Powers and Persons in War on Land Concluded at The Hague October 18, 1907.

Art. XI.   The provision that a "neutral power which receives on its territory troops belonging to the belligerent armies shall intern them, as far as possible, at a distance from the theatre of war," which act of internment consists in disarming such troops and keeping them in honorable confinement, does not violate any provision of the Constitution of the United States, nor require legislation to render it effective, and is therefore a part of the law of the land which the President has full power to execute. The two parties engaged in civil war in Mexico are belligerent parties according to the law of nations; and the fact that the United States has not accorded official recognition to either does not affect its right and duty to execute such treaty provision with respect to troops of either party who seek asylum in its territory. Ex parte Toscano et al. (1913), 208 Fed. 938.

(General Subjects.)
ALIEN DISABILITY.
Convention with Bavaria Abolishing Droit d' Aubaine and Taxes on Emigration Concluded January 21, 1845.

Arts. I-III. The provision of the convention, conferring on subjects of Bavaria a right, notwithstanding their alienage, to take by inheritance lands in the United States, according to the laws here controlling descent, removes from them the disability imposed by a State statute on non-resident aliens of inheriting lands within its limits. Opel v. Shoup (1896), 100 Iowa 407.

Treaty of Amity and Commerce with France Concluded February 6, 1778.

Art. XI. "Upon every principle of fair construction, this article gave to the subjects of France a right to purchase and hold lands in the United States." Chirac v. Chirac (1817), 2 Wheat. 259, 271.

The treaty of 1778 allowed citizens of either country to hold lands in the other; and the title, once vested in a French subject, was not divested by the abrogation of that treaty, and the expiration of the subsequent convention of 1800. Carneal v. Banks (1825), 10 Wheat. 181.

Treaty of Peace, Commerce and Navigation with France Concluded September 30, 1800.

Art. VII. The provision, that the citizens of one country, holding lands in the other, may dispose of the same by testament, or otherwise, and inherit lands in the respective countries, without being obliged to obtain letters of naturalization, applies equally in the case of those who took by descent as of those who acquired by purchase. The stipulation, "that in case the laws of either of the two states should restrain strangers from the exercise of the rights of property with respect to real estate, such real estate may be sold, or otherwise disposed of, to citizens or inhabitants of the country

where it may be," does not affect the rights of a French subject, who takes or holds by the treaty, so as to deprive
him of the power of selling to citizens of this country. It
gives to a French subject, who has acquired lands by descent
or devise, the right, during life, to sell or otherwise dispose
thereof, if lying in a State where lands purchased by an
alien, generally, would be immediately escheatable. The instant the descent was cast on a French subject, his rights
became complete and could not be affected by the subsequent
expiration of the treaty. Chirac v. Chirac (1817), 2 Wheat.
259.

"This article, by its terms, suspended, during the existence of the treaty, the provisions of the common law of
Maryland and of the statutes of that State of 1780 and of
1791, so far as they prevented citizens of France from taking by inheritance from citizens of the United States, property, real or personal, situated therein." Geofroy v. Riggs
(1890), 133 U. S. 258, 266.

Consular Convention with France Concluded February 23, 1853.

Art. VII. This convention has no effect upon the succession of
a person who died in 1848. Prevost v. Greneaux (1856),
19 How. 1.

The District of Columbia, as a political community, is one
of "the States of the Union" within the meaning of these
terms as used in this article; and a citizen of France can
take land in the District of Columbia by descent from a citizen of the United States. "In all the States of the Union
by whose laws aliens are permitted to hold real estate, so
long as such laws remain in force, Frenchmen shall enjoy
the right of possessing personal and real property by the
same title and in the same manner as citizens of the United
States. They shall be free to dispose of it as they may
please—by donation, testament, or otherwise—just as those
citizens themselves. But as to the States by whose existing
laws aliens are not permitted to hold real estate, the treaty
engages that the President shall recommend to them the
passage of such laws as may be necessary for the purpose
of conferring that right." "In all political communities in
the United States where legislation permits aliens to hold

real estate, the disability of Frenchmen from alienage in disposing and inheriting property, real and personal, is removed." Geofroy v. Riggs (1890), 133 U. S. 258, 270, 272.

By the terms of this article citizens and subjects of France are entitled to acquire by inheritance and otherwise real estate in all respects the same as citizens of the United States in those States by whose laws an alien is permitted to hold real estate. Since the constitution and statutes of Nebraska permit aliens to hold and acquire real estate in the same manner as citizens, the provision of a statute prohibiting non-resident aliens from acquiring real estate by inheritance or otherwise is inoperative so far as it relates to citizens or subjects of France. Bahuaud v. Bize (1901), 105 Fed. 485.

By the convention of 1853 a subject of France can hold and convey lands free from the right of escheat in the State of Tennessee. Baker v. Shy (1871), 9 Heisk. 85.

Consular Convention with Germany Concluded December 11, 1871.

Art. X. Neither this article nor any other article of the convention of 1871 provides that subjects of the Empire shall be permitted to take or hold real estate in the United States, except so far as the right to do so was guaranteed by treaties then existing. Wunderle v. Wunderle (1893), 144 Ill. 40, 55.

Definitive Treaty of Peace with Great Britain of September 3, 1783.

Art. VI. (See also Art. IX of treaty of November 19, 1794.)
Proceedings to show that one who was seeking a restoration of his estate was attainted with treason for adhering to the King of Great Britain would contravene an express article of the treaty of peace and could not be sustained. Respublica v. Gordon (1788), 1 Dall. 233.

The sixth article of the treaty of peace of 1783 completely protected the titles of British subjects to lands in the United States from forfeiture by way of escheat for the defect of alienage, and was not intended to be confined to confiscations jure belli. Orr v. Hodgson (1819), 4 Wheat. 453.

The treaty of peace provides only for titles existing at the time and not as to those subsequently acquired. Blight's Lessee v. Rochester (1822), 7 Wheat. 535.

The property of British corporations in this country was protected by Article VI of the treaty of peace in the same manner as that of natural persons; and the title thus protected was confirmed by Article IX of the treaty of 1794, so that it could not be forfeited by any intermediate legislative act, or other proceeding, for the defect of alienage. Even the termination of a treaty by war does not divest rights of property already vested under it. Society for Propagation of Gospel, &c., v. Town of New Haven (1823), 8 Wheat. 464.

Article VI of the treaty of 1783 not only barred the escheat of lands held by British subjects in this State, but gave them capacity to transmit them by descent; but the descent must be to a citizen. Where a British subject holding lands here died prior to the treaty of 1794, leaving no citizen heirs, his lands escheated, and the provisions of the treaty did not pass the lands to alien heirs. Brown v. Sprague (1848), 5 Denio 545.

Treaty of Amity, Commerce and Navigation with Great Britain of November 19, 1794.

Art. IX.   (See also Arts. V and VI of the treaty of September 3, 1783.)

"Now, we cannot yield to the argument that Denny Fairfax had no title, but a mere naked possession or trust estate. In our judgment, by virtue of the devise to him, he held a fee simple in his own right. At the time of the commencement of this suit (in 1791) he was in complete possession and seizin of the land. That possession and seizin continued up to and after the treaty of 1794, which being the supreme law of the land, confirmed the title to him, his heirs and assigns, and protected him from any forfeiture by reason of alienage. It was once in the power of the commonwealth of Viriginia, by an inquest of office or its equivalent, to have vested the estate completely in itself or its grantee. But it has not so done, and its own inchoate title (and of course the derivative title, if any, of its grantee) has by the operation of the treaty become ineffectual and void. It becomes unnecessary to consider the argument as to the effect of the death of Denny Fairfax pending the suit, because admitting it to be correctly applied in general, the treaty of 1794 completely avoids it. The heirs of Denny Fairfax were made capable in law to take from him by descent, and the freehold was not, therefore, on his death, cast upon the commonwealth." Story, J., Fairfax's Devisee v. Hunter's Lessee (1813), 7 Cranch 603, 627. See also Jackson v. Clarke (1818), 3 Wheat. 1; Owings v. Norwood's Lessee (1809), 5 Cranch 344; Smith v. State of Maryland (1810), 6 Cranch 286; Society for Propagation of Gospel, &c., v. Town of Pawlet (1830), 4 Pet. 480.

Under Article IX, by which it is provided that British subjects then holding lands in the United States, and their heirs or assigns, so far as respects those lands, and the remedies incident thereto, shall not be considered as aliens, the parties must show that the title to the land was in them, or their ancestors, at the time the treaty was made. Harden v. Fisher (1816), 1 Wheat. 300.

An alien may take, by purchase, a freehold estate which can be divested on the ground of alienage only by inquest of office or some legislative act equivalent thereto. A defeasible title thus vested during the War of the Revolution in a British born subject, who has never become a citizen, is completely protected and confirmed by the ninth article of the treaty of 1794. Craig v. Radford (1818), 3 Wheat. 594.

The ninth article applies to the title of the parties, whatever it is, and gives it the same legal validity as if the parties were citizens. It is not necessary that they should show an actual possession or seizin, but only that the title was in them at the time the treaty was made. It was not intended by the article to include any other persons than such as were British subjects or citizens of the United States at the time of the descent cast. Orr v. Hodgson (1819), 4 Wheat. 453.

Where a British subject came to the United States after the treaty of peace of 1783, and died before the signature of the treaty of 1794, the heirs were not protected by Article IX of that treaty. "The treaty of 1794, like that of 1783, provides only for existing rights. It does not give title. Had James conveyed or devised the property to John, the title would have vested in him, subject to the right of the government to seize the land; and the treaty would have confirmed that title, so if the law would have vested the estate in him by descent. But as the fact is, he had no title, nothing on which the treaty could operate." Marshall, C. J., Blight's Lessee v. Rochester (1822), 7 Wheat. 535, 544.

Title to property held by British corporations, in this country, protected by Article VI of the treaty of peace, was confirmed by Article IX of the treaty of 1794, so that it could not be forfeited by any intermediate legislative act, or other proceeding, for the defect of alienage. Even the termination of a treaty by war does not divest rights of property already vested under it. Society for Propagation of the Gospel, &c., v. Town of New Haven (1823), 8 Wheat. 464.

Under Article IX it is not necessary for the alien to show that he was in the actual possession or seizin of the land at the date of the treaty. The treaty applies to the title, whatever that may be, and gives it the same legal validity as if the parties were citizens. The title of an alien mortgagee is protected by the treaty. Hughes v. Edwards (1824), 9 Wheat. 489.

All British born subjects, whose allegiance Great Britain has never renounced, ought, upon general principles of interpretation, to be held within the intent, as they certainly are within the words, of the treaty of 1794. This stipulation being for the benefit of British subjects who became aliens by the events of the war, there is no reason why all persons should not be embraced in it who sustained the character of British subjects, although they might also have been treated as American citizens. Shanks v. Dupont (1830), 3 Pet. 242.

Corporations as well as individuals are within its purview. "It was obviously the design of the contracting parties, to remove the disability of alienage, as to persons within the purview of the article, and to procure to them a perfect enjoyment and disposal of their estates and titles. If, during war, their right to grant, sell or devise, such estates and titles were suspended, it would materially impair their value. If the remedies incident to such estates for trespasses, disseisins, and other tortious acts, were during war suspended, not only would the security of the property be endangered, but if the war should last for many years, the statute of limitations of the various States would, by lapse of time, bar the party of his remedy, and in some cases of his estate. This seems against the spirit and intent of the article, and puts the party upon the footing of an alien enemy, while the language concedes to him all the benefits of a native." Story, J., Society for Propagation of the Gospel, &c., v. Wheeler et al. (1814), 2 Gall. 105, 136.

Rights vested under Article IX of the treaty of 1794 were not divested by the war of 1812 between the United States and Great Britain. Fox v. Southack (1815), 12 Mass. 143; Fiott v. Commonwealth (1855), 12 Grat. (Va.) 564. See also Hutchinson v. Brock (1814), 11 Mass. 119.

"Complainant [a British subject] is entitled as mother of Ann Robertson [intestate] to the whole of her personal estate, and to the real if the British treaty now pending, be ratified by our government." Decree for complainant. Megrath v. Administrators of John and Ann Robertson (August, 1795), 1 Desaus. Eq. (S. C.) 445, 449.

"These words ought to have a very liberal interpretation, in advancement of their beneficial end. They ought to apply, in furtherance of the amicable intention of the two nations, to every British subject who, at the time of the treaty, was in the enjoyment of lands within the United States, and whose title thereto would be valid, independent of the plea of alienism. In all such cases the treaty may be considered as doing away the plea." Kent, J., Jackson v. Lunn (1802), 3 Johns. Cases 109, 123.

The treaty was only intended to secure to actual owners the lands belonging to them at its date, and had no retrospective operation as to those which had been antecedently lost. Read v. Read (1804), 5 Call 160.

The treaty secured the rights of British subjects to real estate which they held at that time. Marshall v. Conrad (1805), 5 Call 364.

"Nelson, therefore, must be deemed to have been a British subject in 1794; and it appearing that he had purchased the lands in question previously to that period, the treaty settled his right thereto, and, upon his death, it descended to his heirs, notwithstanding they were aliens. * * * The treaty is the paramount law; and the act of 1804, being contrary to it, * * * is inoperative." Van Ness, J., Jackson v. Wright (1809), 4 Johns. 75, 79.

A British subject held the premises in fee at the time of the conclusion and ratification of the treaty. He thereafter sold the same. The title cannot now be questioned by the commonwealth. Commonwealth v. Sheafe (1810), 6 Mass. 441.

"But if they were obliged to take by descent, their rights are protected by the 9th article of the treaty of 1794, which declares, that British subjects shall hold as before the war." Duncan v. Beard (1820), 2 Nott and McC. 400, 408.

Under Article IX of the treaty of 1794 the title of British subjects to land in the United States is valid and alienable, the same as if the holder had been a citizen of the United States. Watson v. Donnelly (1859), 28 Barb. 653; People v. Snyder (1868), 51 Barb. 589; Munro v. Merchant (1858), 26 Barb. 383; 28 N. Y. 9; Foxwell v. Craddock (1855), 1 Pat. & H. (Va.) 250.

The treaty of 1794 does not take away the plea of alienage in actions relating to lands acquired after that treaty, but merely extends to lands then held by British subjects. Jackson v. Decker (1814), 11 Johns. 418; Orser v. Hoag (1845), 3 Hill 79.

A British subject to whom a devise of land was made in 1781 could by the treaty of 1794 hold and alien the lands so devised to him. Stephen's Heirs v. Swann (1838), 9 Leigh 404.

The stipulations for the protection of the rights of property imposed upon the government of the United States no new obligation, but were merely in affirmance of the law of nations. May v. Specht et al. (1849), 1 Manning (Mich.) 187.

The provisions of Article IX, which secured to British subjects the right to grant, sell or devise the estates they held at the date of the treaty, applied only to valid titles. The provisions against the effect of alienage of the heirs or assignees of such grantors would not apply to mere possessory rights without any title in fact, which by a subsequent act of Congress were enlarged into freeholds where there had been continuous occupation and improvement. Crane v. Reeder (1870), 21 Mich. 24. See also, supra, under Art. II.

Convention as to Tenure and Disposition of Real and Personal Property with Great Britain of March 2, 1899.

Art. I. This article contemplates the elimination of the disqualification of alienage, under the statute of the State of Delaware, in the next of kin, and puts non-resident aliens next of kin on the same footing as if they were residents of the State at the time of the death of the intestate. The treaty is paramount to the statute of the State. Dockstader v. Kershaw (1903), 4 Pennewill 398.

Treaty of Commerce and Navigation with Hanover Concluded June 10, 1846.

Art. X. Under the treaty, which allows non-resident alien heirs the right to sell the real estate of their ancestor, within a reasonable time, the right to sell carries with it the ownership as a necessary incident to the power of sale; but such ownership is less than a fee simple absolute, the resident heirs being vested with the remainder of the title, and such remainder draws the full fee simple title into the resident heirs upon failure of the condition upon which the non-resident alien heirs took their title. Where a treaty allows a non-resident alien heir the right to sell the real estate of an ancestor within a reasonable time, but does not specify what is to be a reasonable time, and there are no statutes providing what shall be a reasonable time for the sale of such property, the question as to what is a reasonable time is necessarily left to judicial construction. It was held that, under all of the circumstances presented, a delay from 1862 to 1868 was unreasonable, and that as a consequence the resident heirs had become vested with a fee simple title. Ahrens v. Ahrens (1909), 144 Iowa 486.

Convention of Friendship, Commerce and Navigation with the Hanseatic Republics Concluded December 20, 1827.

Art. VII. The word "representatives" in the second clause of Article VII refers to all who take by will or descent, including devisees and heirs, as well as to executors and administrators. The heirs of an American citizen, who are citizens of Bremen, have the prescribed term of three years to dispose of real estate, which they would have inherited but for their alienage. They take a fee in such lands determinable by the non-exercise of the power of sale within three years. The treaty suspends, during the period of three years, the operation of the alien law of the State, which makes non-resident aliens incapable of taking lands by descent. Schultze v. Schultze (1893), 144 Ill. 290.

Convention with Hesse Abolishing Droit d' Aubaine and Taxes on Emigration Concluded March 26, 1844.

See Bollermann v. Blake (1883), 94 N. Y. 624.

Treaty of Peace and Commerce with the Netherlands Concluded October 8, 1782.

Art. VI. The provision, that subjects of either party may dispose of their "effects" by testament, donation or otherwise, and their heirs although unnaturalized shall receive such succession ab intestato, includes real as well as personal estate; and, in virtue of the treaty, an alien heir can inherit lands situated in North Carolina. University v. Miller (1831), 14 N. C. 188.

Treaty of Amity and Commerce with Prussia Concluded July 11, 1799.

Art. X. Since the treaty with Prussia allows citizens and subjects of the one to sell real estate which descends to them in the territory of the other, Poles, who are subjects of Prussia, are allowed to take under the residuary clause of a will. Hart v. Executors of Hart (1801), 2 Desaus. Eq. (S. C.) 57.

Treaty of Commerce and Navigation with Prussia Concluded May 1, 1828.

Art. XIV. The provision for the removal of the disability of aliens to inherit is valid and within the treaty-making power of the President and the Senate. People v. Gerke (1855), 5 Cal. 381.

A statute of the State of New York, which makes the right of adult alien males to inherit lands dependent upon the filing of a deposition of their intention to become citizens be-

fore the consummation of proceedings by the State to defeat
their title, is superseded, as to citizens of Prussia, by the
treaty with Prussia of 1828, providing that subjects of that
country, disqualified by alienage from inheriting land in the
United States, shall be allowed a "reasonable" time to sell
the same and to withdraw the proceeds. A sale of decedent's
lands on foreclosure proceedings within two years and four
months after death is a sale within a "reasonable" time. In
re Beck (1890), 11 N. Y. S. 199.

Under the provisions of this treaty, a non-resident alien can
inherit land in Iowa from a citizen; and in case of his death,
his children though non-resident aliens will take what would
have descended to the father. A treaty providing that
aliens may inherit lands is controlling, though in conflict
with statutes of the State. Doehrel v. Hillmer (1897), 102
Iowa 169; Wilcke v. Wilcke (1897), 102 Iowa 173.

In so far as the local statutes are in conflict with the
treaty, the provisions of the treaty must govern. A treaty
giving citizens of a foreign country the right to take lands
by descent in this country is superior to and controls any
State legislation against the holding of lands by aliens.
Butschkowski v. Brecks (1913), 94 Neb. 532.

Convention with Saxony Abolishing Droit d' Aubaine and Emigration Taxes Concluded May 14, 1845.

Arts. II and III. The clear meaning of Article II of the convention is, as regards the right of inheritance, that the aliens protected thereby shall have the same right as citizens in the
same situation,—that is, shall inherit just as they would if
they were citizens—with the qualification that this right shall
be subject to the exercise of a power to sell the land and
withdraw the proceeds within a time limited. Ehrlich v.
Weber (1905), 114 Tenn. 711.

Treaty of Friendship, Boundaries, Commerce and Navigation with Spain Concluded October 27, 1795.

Art. XI. The words "personal goods" in the first clause of Article XI refer to and cover movable property only. Real
estate, or immovable property, is referred to and dealt with
only in the third clause. Succession of Sala (1898), 50 La.
Ann. 1009.

Treaty of Amity and Commerce with Sweden Concluded April 3, 1783.

Art. VI. The provision in Article VI of the treaty of 1783, continued in force by Article XVII of the treaty of 1827,—that the subjects of the two nations may dispose of their "fonds et biens" (translated "goods and effects") by testament, donation, or otherwise, and that their "heirs," in whatever place they may reside, shall receive the succession "even ab intestato,"—covers real estate as well as personal property. Non-resident alien subjects of the kingdom of Sweden, by virtue of this provision, take and hold real estate in Illinois by descent or otherwise, the provisions of the alien act of the State of 1887 (Laws of 1887, p. 5) to the contrary notwithstanding. Adams v. Akerlund (1897), 168 Ill. 632.

The words "goods and effects" do not include real estate. A non-resident alien is not empowered to inherit an interest in lands in Iowa by virtue of the provision in the treaty of 1783 with Sweden, that the subjects of the contracting parties in the respective states, although unnaturalized, may dispose of and inherit "goods and effects." Meier v. Lee (1898), 106 Iowa 303.

The terms "goods and effects" as used in the treaty cover real estate passing by will or descent. In re Peterson's Estate (1915), 151 N. W. (Iowa) 66; In re Anderson's Estate, 147 N. W. 1098.

In so far as the rights to succession of property of deceased persons are concerned, the citizens of each country stand on an equal footing. The words "goods and effects" in the treaty include real, as well as personal, property. Although the word "heirs" in its technical common-law meaning is restricted to those who take by inheritance only, it applies in the civil law to all persons who are called to the succession whether by the act of the party or by operation of law; and the phrase "their heirs shall receive the succession" as used in the treaty refers to the right of succession of those who receive by testament, as well as those who receive by operation of law. In re Stixrud's Estate (1910), 58 Wash. 339.

This treaty enables non-resident aliens to inherit land in the State of Nebraska, notwithstanding conflicting statutory provisions. The terms "goods and effects" as used in the treaty include real estate. Erickson v. Carlson et al. (1914), 95 Neb. 182.

The provision relating to the disposition of "goods and effects" does not embrace real estate. The intestate, who was the owner of land in Kansas, died without wife or issue, his father and mother having previously died. Among his surviving brothers and sisters some were aliens and some citizens. One of his surviving sisters, an alien, had two children who were citizens. *Held,* that the sister, being an alien, could not inherit a share of the estate, and that after her death her children, although citizens, were incapable of inheriting through her. Johnson v. Olson (1914), 92 Kan. 819.

Treaty of Friendship, Commerce and Extradition with Switzerland Concluded November 25, 1850.

Art. V. The provision of the treaty—that in case real estate situated within the territories of one of the contracting parties shall fall to a citizen of the other party, who on account of his being an alien is not permitted to hold such property in the State or Canton in which it may be situated, there shall be accorded to the said heir, or other successor, such term, as the laws of the State or Canton will permit, to sell such property,—is the supreme law of the land, and by its terms the incapacity of a citizen of Switzerland, next of kin of the intestate, is so far removed as to entitle him to recover and sell the land whereof the intestate died seized in fee, and to withdraw and export the proceeds thereof. His rights thus secured are not barred by the lapse of time, if no statute of the State where the land is situated prescribes the term within which they are to be asserted. Hauenstein v. Lynham (1879), 100 U. S. 483. See also Jost v. Jost (1882), 1 Mackey 487.

The article provides that citizens of each country, and their heirs, having personal property in the jurisdiction of the other, shall have absolute power of disposition, and that this provision shall be applicable in case of real estate in the States and Cantons which permit foreigners to "hold or inherit" real estate. In case any State or Canton does not permit foreigners to "hold" real estate, there shall be accorded such term, as the State or Canton may fix, within which to sell it and withdraw the proceeds. A statute of the State of Indiana, providing that aliens may "take and hold" land by devise and descent only, and may convey the same within five years, and that all property left at that time shall escheat, does not permit aliens to "hold" real property within the meaning of the treaty, but merely recognizes the terms of the treaty by giving five years in which to dispose of the property; and accordingly it is not in contravention of the treaty. Lehman v. State (1909), 45 Ind. App. 330, 88 N. E. 365.

Convention with Württemberg Abolishing Droit d' Aubaine and Emigration Taxes Concluded April 10, 1844.

Art. II. The provision, that "such citizen or subject shall be allowed two years to sell the same, which term may be reasonably prolonged according to the circumstances," is in effect a statute of limitation. Seven years having elapsed between the death of the ancestor and the commencement of the action, and there being nothing to show that a prolongation of the term of two years had been applied for or obtained, it was held that the time prescribed by the treaty must apply. Wieland v. Renner (1883), 65 How. Pr. Repts. 245.

The convention intends to confer on the alien heir, for the period of two years, precisely the same rights that he would enjoy if he were a citizen, imposing upon him simply the obligation to sell and convey, within that period or such other period as the State or country shall see fit to confer upon him by prolonging the time, the fee to some one capable of holding it, or to become, or declare his intention of becoming, a citizen of this country. In the meantime he may possess and take care of the property, improve it, and exercise all the authority of ownership, for the purpose of making it more productive and valuable, and may himself enjoy such rents and profits as he can obtain therefrom. The convention is a part of the supreme law of the land and supersedes all local statutes that contravene its provisions. Kull v. Kull (1885), 37 Hun 476.

The provision, that where land owned by a citizen or subject of the one country would descend to a citizen or subject of the other, were he not disqualified by alienage, such citizen or subject may sell the same, and withdraw the proceeds, exempt from all duties of detraction, was abrogated by the treaty of December 11, 1871, between the United States and the Emperor of Germany, who, under the constitution of the empire, of which the kingdom of Württemberg has become a part, represents the empire among nations, enters into alliances with foreign countries, &c. It was however held that the tax, in question, imposed by the laws of the State on all property which should pass by will or the intestate laws, was not a "duty of detraction" within the meaning of the treaty, but a succession tax to which all persons including citizens were subjected. In re Strobel's Estate (1896), 39 N. Y. S. 169.

The operation of the alien act of the State of Illinois of 1887 (laws of 1887, p. 5) is suspended by the convention between the United States and Württemberg, which convention was not abrogated by the absorption of the State of Württemberg into the German Empire. Under Article II of the convention, whereby aliens may take the fee to real estate and be allowed a term of two years to sell the same, "which term may be reasonably prolonged, according to circumstances," the alien need take no formal step to prolong the term. The courts may allow the alien heirs such time, in addition to the two years' limitation, as is reasonable, under the circumstances, to enable them to sell. Scharpf v. Schmidt (1898), 172 Ill. 255.

Art. III. This article does not include the case of a citizen or subject of the respective countries residing at home, and disposing of property there in favor of a citizen or subject of the other. Consequently a statute of the State of Louisiana which imposes a tax of 10% on the amount of certain legacies left by a citizen of that State to subjects of the King of Württemberg is not in conflict with the convention. Frederickson v. State of Louisiana (1859), 23 How. 445.

DISCRIMINATORY LEGISLATION.

Convention with Bavaria Abolishing Droit d' Aubaine and Emigration Taxes Concluded January 21, 1845.

Arts. I-III. Subjects of Bavaria are by virtue of this convention exempt from the payment of the tax of 10% imposed by the State on property passing to non-resident aliens. Succession of Crusius (1867), 19 La. Ann. 369.

Treaty of Trade, Consuls, and Emigration with China Concluded July 28, 1868.

Arts. V. and VI. (See also treaty of November 17, 1880.) A mining regulation, authorized by a State, in effect forbidding Chinese from working in a mining claim for themselves or for others, seems to be in direct conflict with Article VI of the treaty with China, under which the citizens or subjects of China visiting or residing in the United States are guaranteed the same privileges, immunities and exemptions in respect of travel or residence as may there be enjoyed by citizens or subjects of the most favored nation. If in conflict therewith it is void. Chapman v. Toy Long (1876), 4 Sawy. 28.

A legislative act of the State of Oregon which prohibits the employment by contractors of Chinese on street improvements or public works, but which permits all other aliens so to be employed, is in conflict with the provisions in the treaty with China, pledging to the Chinese, resident here, the same right to be employed and labor for a living as enjoyed by the subjects of any other nation, and is therefore void. Baker v. City of Portland (1879), 5 Sawy. 566.

The privileges and immunities, which, under the treaty, the Chinese are entitled to enjoy to the same extent as enjoyed by the subjects of the most favored nation, are all those which are fundamental, among which is the right to labor and to pursue any lawful employment in a lawful manner. A provision of the constitution of the State of California, as likewise legislation for its enforcement, providing that no corporation formed under the laws of the State shall, directly or indirectly, in any capacity, employ any Chinese or Mongolian, is in conflict with the provisions in the treaty and therefore void.   In re Tiburcio Parrott (1880), 6 Sawy. 349.

A statute of the State of California, prohibiting all aliens incapable of becoming electors of the State from fishing in the waters of the State (construed in connection with various other contemporaneous statutes expressly aimed against the Chinese), violates the provisions of the treaty with China recognizing the rights of the citizens of China to immigrate to the United States for the purposes of trade, and providing that Chinese subjects residing in the United States shall enjoy the same privileges in respect of residence and travel as may be enjoyed by citizens of the most favored nation, and is therefore void.   In re Ah Chong (1880), 6 Sawy. 451.   See also Ex parte Ah Fook (1874), 49 Cal. 402; reversed in Chy Lung v. Freeman et al. (1875), 92 U. S. 275.

Immigration Treaty with China Concluded November 17, 1880.

Arts. II and III.   (See also treaty of July 28, 1868, Arts. V and VI.)

Those subjects of the Emperor of China, who have the right temporarily or permanently to reside within the United States, are entitled to enjoy the protection guaranteed by the Constitution and afforded by the laws.   An administration of a municipal ordinance for the carrying on of a lawful business within the corporate limits violates the provisions of the Constitution if it makes arbitrary and unjust discriminations founded on differences of race between persons otherwise in similar circumstances.   Yick Wo v. Hopkins (1886), 118 U. S. 356.   See also Barbier v. Connolly (1885), 113 U. S. 27; Soon Hing v. Crowley (1885), 113 U. S. 703.

Congress has the power under the Constitution to provide for the punishment of persons guilty of depriving Chinese subjects of any of the rights, privileges, immunities, or exemptions guaranteed to them by the treaty of November 17, 1880; but Congress has not made such provision, either in §5519, §5508, or §5336, Rev. Stats. §5519 is unconstitutional, and ineffective as a provision for the punishment of a conspiracy, within a State, to deprive an alien of rights guaranteed to him therein by a treaty.   In describing the offense against a citizen of the United States for which punishment is provided for in §5508, the word "citizen" is used in its political sense, with the same meaning which it has in the Fourteenth Amendment to the Constitution, and not as being synomymous with "resident," "inhabitant," or "person." To constitute the offense described in the first clause of §5336, it is not enough that a law of the United States is violated; but there must be a forcible resistance to a positive assertion of its authority as a government. To constitute an offense under the second clause of §5336, there must be a forcible resistance to the authority of the United States while endeavoring to carry its laws into execution. Baldwin v. Franks (1887), 120 U. S. 678.

Under the treaty with China, a Chinese resident of this country is entitled to all the rights, privileges and immunities of subjects of the most favored nation with which this country has treaty relations; and, if a resident here before the passage of the act of Congress restricting immigration of Chinese, he has a right to remain and follow any of the lawful ordinary trades and pursuits of life. In re Quong Woo (1882), 13 Fed. 229.

A city ordinance which arbitrarily requires all Chinese inhabitants to remove from the portion of the city theretofore occupied by them to another designated part of the city, or outside the city, is in direct conflict with the Constitution, treaties, and statutes of the United States, particularly in the sense that it is discriminatory and unequal in its operation, and involves an arbitrary confiscation of property without due process of law. In re Lee Sing (1890), 43 Fed. 359.

A covenant in a deed not to convey or lease land to a Chinaman is contrary to the public policy of the government, in contravention of its treaty with China, and in violation of the Fourteenth Amendment to the Constitution, and is accordingly not enforceable in a court of equity. Gandolfo v. Hartman (1892), 49 Fed. 181.

Under the most-favored-nation clause of the Chinese treaties, and the provisions of treaties with foreign powers that the citizens or subjects of such foreign powers shall be accorded the same privileges and rights as native citizens and shall not be charged any higher imposts or duties than paid by native citizens, a State is not restrained from imposing such conditions on the right to take fish from the tide waters of the State as it sees fit, notwithstanding the license fee exacted from aliens is higher than that exacted from its own citizens. The right to take fish from the tide waters of the State is a property right, not a mere privilege of citizenship, held in trust by the State for its citizens. Leong Mow v. Board of Commissioners (1911), 185 Fed. 223.

Under the treaty with China, citizens of the Chinese Empire residing either permanently or temporarily in the United States are granted the same rights, privileges, immunities, and exemptions as are enjoyed by citizens and subjects of the most favored nation. Accordingly they can hold a lease interest in real estate in Idaho. Duck Lee v. Boise Development Co. (1912), 21 Idaho 461.

Commercial Convention with Cuba Concluded December 11, 1902.

Art. VIII. Within the meaning of the convention, the Philippine Islands are not a foreign or another country; and the tariff reductions on articles imported from Cuba are not to be based on tariff rates on the same articles brought from the Philippine Islands. The provisions of Article VIII of the convention are not to be construed so as to give to Cuba advantages over shipments coming into the United States from a part of its own territory. Faber v. United States (1911), 221 U. S. 649.

Treaty of Friendship, Commerce and Navigation with Denmark Concluded April 26, 1826.

Art. I. The act of August 3, 1882, (22 Stats. 214), which requires owners of vessels to pay a tax for every passenger, not a citizen of the United States, brought from a foreign port to the United States, applies to those brought by Danish ships, notwithstanding the treaty with Denmark. Head Money cases (1884), 112 U. S. 580. The act of June 26, 1884, (23 Stats. 58, §22) excepts from the passenger tax vessels plying between the ports of the United States and those of Canada and Mexico. Danish vessels, arriving from a port in Denmark, are not exempt under the most-favored-nation clause in the treaty from the payment of the tax. In case of a conflict with a prior treaty the statute must prevail in the courts of this country. Thingvalla Line et al. v. United States (1889), 24 C. Cls. 255.

Art. IV.   This article contains a pledge of the contracting parties that there shall be no discriminating legislation against the importation of articles, the growth, produce or manufacture of the respective countries, in favor of articles of like character imported from any other country. It is not designed to prevent special concessions, upon sufficient considerations, touching the importation of specific articles into the country of the other, and does not carry with it automatically such concessions. Bartram v. Robertson (1887), 122 U. S. 116.

Art. VII.   A provision in a statute of Iowa, which imposes a collateral inheritance tax of 20% in case the beneficiaries are non-resident aliens, while it is only 5% otherwise, does not conflict with the provision in Article VII of the treaty with Denmark of 1826, renewed in 1857, that no higher taxes shall be levied by either party "upon any personal property, money or effects" of the citizens or subjects of the other party on the removal of the same from the country, "either upon the inheritance * * * or otherwise" than in case of its own citizens or subjects, since the tax is not a tax upon property, but merely a tax upon the succession or transmission of property occasioned by the death of the owner. That portion of the property deducted by the executor or administrator and paid to the State Treasurer pursuant to the statute never reaches the beneficiary. In re Anderson's Estate (1914), 147 N. W. (Iowa) 1098. See later case of McKeown v. Brown (1914), 149 N. W. 593, under the convention with Great Britain of March 2, 1899.

Treaty of Amity and Commerce with the Dominican Republic Concluded February 8, 1867.

Art. IX.   This article is a pledge of the contracting parties that there shall be no discriminating legislation against the importation of articles, the growth, produce, or manufacture of their respective countries, in favor of articles of like character imported from any other country. It was never intended to prevent special concessions, upon sufficient considerations, and does not carry with it automatically such concessions. Whitney v. Robertson (1888), 124 U. S. 190.

Consular Convention with France Concluded February 23, 1853.

Art. VII. Subjects of France cannot be subjected to taxes on transfer, inheritance, or any others different from those paid by our own citizens, or to taxes which shall not be equally imposed. Succession of Dufour (1855), 10 La. Ann. 391; Succession of Amat (1866), 18 La. Ann. 403; Succession of Rixner (1896), 48 La. Ann. 552; Succession of Rabasse (1897), 49 La. Ann. 1405.

Convention of Commerce and Navigation with Great Britain Concluded July 3, 1815.

Art. I. The permission mutually given to citizens of the one to reside and to trade in the territories of the other is in express terms made subject to the laws of the two countries respectively. The reference to the laws of this country necessarily applies to laws of the States in respect of the privileges within the several States. Norris v. City of Boston, and Smith v. Turner (Passenger Cases), 7 How. 283, 472.

No treaty gives to subjects of Great Britain any different measure of justice than that secured to citizens of this country. Barrington v. Missouri (1907), 205 U. S. 483, 487; Spies v. Illinois (1887), 123 U. S. 131, 182.

A corporation organized in Great Britain, having its principal place of business in that country, is not a subject of that country within the meaning of a treaty giving subjects of that country the right to do business in any of the States of the United States on the same terms as natives. Scottish Union &c. v. Herriott (1899), 109 Iowa 606. See 187 U. S. 651.

Art. II. A State pilotage law, which subjects all vessels, domestic and foreign, engaged in foreign trade, to pilotage regulations, but which exempts pursuant to law coastwise steam vessels of the United States, is not in conflict with the provision in the treaty with Great Britain, that "no higher or other duties or charges shall be imposed in any ports of the United States on British vessels than those payable in the same ports by vessels of the United States." The regulations, in question, apply without discrimination to all vessels, domestic or foreign, engaged in foreign trade. Olsen v. Smith (1904), 195 U. S. 332. See also Compagnie Francaise &c v. Louisiana State Board of Health (1902), 186 U. S. 380. See Passenger Cases (1849), 7 How. 283.

A treaty cannot be invoked by an individual to defeat liability for a tax imposed by a subsequent act of Congress. The tonnage tax imposed on the use of foreign-built yachts by §37 of the tariff act of August 5, 1909 (36 Stats. at L. 112) may be collected by an action in the nature of debt against the yacht owner. United States v. Billings (1911), 190 Fed. 359. Decree affirmed and modified in 232 U. S. 261.

A classification for taxation of foreign-built yachts is not so repugnant to justice as to amount to a denial of due process of law because domestic-built yachts are not subject to the same tax; nor is §37 of the tariff act of 1909, which imposes a tax on the use of foreign-built yachts owned or chartered by citizens, unconstitutional for lack of uniformity. Billings v. United States (1914), 232 U. S. 261; Rainey v. United States (1914), 232 U. S. 310.

Convention with Great Britain as to Tenure and Disposition of Real and Personal Property Concluded March 2, 1899.

Art. I. A provision in the code of Iowa, which, while imposing an inheritance tax of 5% of the value of property passing to collateral relatives, subjects property passing to persons, who are alien non-residents of the United States, to a tax of 20% of its value, violates the provision in the convention with Great Britain entitling a citizen or subject of that country to sell real property, which would by the laws of the land pass to him were he not disqualified on account of alienage, and to remove the proceeds therefrom without restraint or interference, and "exempt from any succession, probate or administrative duties or charges" other than those which may be imposed in like cases upon the citizens or subjects of this country. McKeown v. Brown (1914), 149 N. W. (Iowa) 593.

Art. II. Under the provisions of this article, subjects of Great Britain are liable to no other taxes upon successions to personal property than are payable by citizens of the United

States. "It will be noted therefore that this article covers succession, possession, and disposal of personal property all to be subject to such duties only as the citizens of the country where the property lies will be liable to pay in like cases. No reason appears therefore why any different effect should be given to the terms of the treaty as applied to personal property than was given in the McKeown case, supra, as applied to real property." In re Moynihan's Estate (1915), 151 N. W. (Iowa) 504.

Treaty of Commerce and Navigation with Greece Concluded December 22, 1837.

Art. XV. The provision, that a vessel arriving directly from Greece and provided with a prescribed bill of health shall be subjected to no other quarantine than such as may be necessary for the visit of the health officer of the port, has reference to the particular form of document which shall be taken by a ship for the purpose of establishing that infectious or contagious diseases did not exist at its point of departure. It was not intended to nullify the quarantine power, since the concluding section of the article expressly subjects the vessel holding such certificate to quarantine detention, if on its arrival a general quarantine has been established against all ships coming from the port whence the ship holding the certificate had sailed. It was not intended to deal with the exercise by the government of its power to legislate for the safety and health of its people, or to render the exertion of such a power nugatory, by exempting the vessels of Greece when coming to the United States from the operation of such laws. Especially is this true where the restriction imposed upon the vessel is based, not upon the conditions existing at the port of departure, but upon the presence of an infectious or contagious malady at the port of arrival, which, in the nature of things, could not be covered by the certificate relating to the state of public health at the port of departure. Compagnie Francaise &c. v. Louisiana State Board of Health (1902), 186 U. S. 380.

Treaty of Commerce and Navigation with Hanover Concluded June 10, 1846.

Art. X. The provision, that the subjects of the King of Hanover shall have free access to the tribunals, in their litigious affairs, on the same terms as granted by the law and usages of the country to native citizens and subjects, refers only to ordinary litigation and does not include a right of litigation against the government afterwards created in favor of its own citizens, to the exclusion of aliens; and it does not entitle such subjects to maintain an action in the Court of Claims under the act of March 3, 1891, giving that court jurisdiction of certain claims "for property of citizens of the United States" taken or destroyed by Indians belonging to any band or tribe in amity with the United States. Valk v. United States (1894), 29 C. Cls. 62; affirmed, 168 U. S. 703.

Treaty of Commerce and Navigation with Italy Concluded February 26, 1871.

Arts. II, III and XXIII. The treaty only requires equality of treatment, and that the same rights and privileges be accorded to a citizen of Italy that are accorded to a citizen of the United States under like circumstances. Storti v. Massachusetts (1901), 183 U. S. 138.

If an Italian subject, sojourning in this country, is himself given all the direct protection and security afforded by the laws to our own people, including all rights of action for himself or his personal representatives to safe-guard the protection and security, the provision in the treaty—that citizens of each country shall receive, in the States and Territories of the other, the most constant protection and security "and shall enjoy in this respect the same rights and privileges as are or shall be granted to the natives, on their submitting themselves to the conditions imposed upon the natives,"—is not violated by a statute which gives a right of action for damages for death to native resident relatives but not to non-resident alien relatives, although the existence of such a right might indirectly and remotely promote his safety. Maiorano v. Baltimore & Ohio R. R. Co. (1909), 213 U. S. 268, affirming 216 Pa. 402.

The provisions in these articles do not create in Italian subjects, not resident in the United States, any new or substantial rights of person or property to be enforced in the United States; their purpose, so far as they concern rights of person or property of non-resident Italians, is limited to the prevention of invidious discriminations in favor of citizens of the United States and against subjects of Italy, with respect to the enjoyment or enforcement in the United States of privileges and rights of person and property, arising and existing wholly independently of such provisions. Whether a non-resident alien may recover for wrongful death of an alien resident in Pennsylvania depends upon the statutes of that State, aside from the Italian treaty, as to which the Federal courts sitting in Pennsylvania are bound by the decisions of the Pennsylvania Supreme Court. A non-resident alien is not entitled to the benefit of the act of Pennsylvania of April 15, 1851, (P. L. 674) §§18, 19, or the act of April 26, 1855, (P. L. 309) §1, giving a right of action to members of the family of a person whose death has been caused by the wrongful act of another. Fulco v. Schuylkill Stone Co. (1909), 169 Fed. 98, citing Deni v. Penna. R. R. Co., 181 Pa. 525; Maiorana v. Baltimore & Ohio R. R. Co., 216 Pa. 402; Zeiger v. Penna. R. R. Co., 158 Fed. 809; and Zeiger v. Penna. R. R. Co., 151 Fed. 348. See also Debitulia v. Lehigh & Wilkes-Barre Coal Co. (1909), 174 Fed. 886; Di Paolo v. Laquin Lumber Co. (1910), 178 Fed. 877.

Residence and citizenship do not qualify the right of recovery under the Railroad Employers' Liability Act of Congress of April 22, 1908, as amended April 5, 1910. "In ruling upon the statute the district court considered that the reasoning in Deni v. Penna. R. R., 181 Pa. St. 525, and in Maiorano v. Baltimore & Ohio R. R., 213 U. S. 268, applied. In the Deni case the Supreme Court of Pennsylvania, passing upon a statute of the State which permitted certain named relatives to recover damages for death occurring through negligence, held that the statute had no extra-territorial force and that plaintiff in the action was not within its purview, though its language possibly admitted of the inclusion of non-resident aliens. The Maiorano case came to this court on writ of error to the Supreme Court of Pennsylvania, where the doctrine of the Deni case was repeated and applied. This ruling was simply accepted by this court as the construction of the State statute by the highest court of the State." McGovern v. Philadelphia & Reading Ry. Co. (1914), 235 U. S. 389, reversing 209 Fed. 975.

The treaty gives to subjects of Italy no other rights, in suits against a municipality for loss of life through mob violence, than those enjoyed by citizens of the United States. City of New Orleans v. Abbagnato (1894), 62 Fed. 240.

Under these articles Italian subjects have no greater rights to carry on trade and traffic in liquors within a State than enjoyed by citizens of the United States. Cantini v. Tillman (1893), 54 Fed. 969.

An act of the State of Pennsylvania of May 8, 1909, (P. L. 466), which prohibits the hunting or killing of wild animals or game, and to that end the ownership or possession of a shot gun or rifle, by an unnaturalized foreign-born resident within the State, is not in contravention of the treaty with Italy. Commonwealth v. Patsone (1911), 231 Pa. 46, affirmed, 232 U. S. 138.

"The equality of rights that it [Article III] assures is equality only in respect of protection and security for persons and property. The prohibition of a particular kind of destruction and of acquiring property in instruments intended for that purpose establishes no inequality in either respect. It is to be remembered that the subject of this whole discussion is wild game, which the State may preserve for its own citizens if it pleases. Geer v. Connecticut, 161 U. S. 519, 529. We see nothing in the treaty that purports or attempts to cut off the exercise of their powers over the matter by the States to the full extent. Compagnie Francaise de Navigation a Vapeur v. State Board of Health, 186 U. S. 380, 394, 395." "It will be time enough to consider whether the statute can be construed or upheld as precluding Italians from possessing a stock of guns for purposes of trade when such a case is presented." Holmes, J., Patsone v. Commonwealth of Pennsylvania (1914), 232 U. S. 138, 145.

An act of the State of Vermont, providing for the payment by all citizens, residents of the State, of a fee of seventy-five cents for a hunter's license, and by all others of a fee of ten dollars for such license, does not violate the provisions in the treaty with Italy, that the citizens or subjects of each country shall receive in the States and Territories of the other the most constant security and protection for their person and property and shall enjoy in this respect the same rights and privileges which are granted to natives, provided that they submit themselves to the conditions imposed on natives. An Italian subject, a resident and taxpayer of the State, is not entitled to the lower fee. The treaty does not entitle Italian subjects to share equally with natives in such privileges as the legislature of the State may grant in the wild game of the State. Bondi v. MacKay (1913), 87 Vt. 271.

A provision in a statute of New York (Sec. 14 of the Labor Law. L. 1909, c. 36; Cons. Laws, c. 31.), that in the construction of public works by the State or a municipality, or by persons contracting with the State or such municipality, only citizens of the United States shall be employed, does not violate any constitutional right of the alien, or conflict with the treaty between the United States and Italy. People v. Crane (1915), 214 N. Y. 154; affirmed by the Supreme Court, November 29, 1915, in Heim et al. v. McCall et al., and Crane v. People, 239 U. S. 175, 195. See also People v. I. M. Ludington's Sons (1911), 131 N. Y. 550; People v. Warren (1895), 34 N. Y. S. 942.

Treaty of Commerce and Navigation with Italy Concluded February 25, 1913.

Art. 1. (Amending first paragraph of Art. III of treaty of February 26, 1871.) The provision—that the citizens of the respective countries shall receive in the States and Territories of the other the most constant security and protection for their person and property and for their rights, including that form of protection granted by any State or national law which establishes a civil responsibility for injuries or for death caused by negligence or fault and gives to relatives or heirs of the injured party a right of action, which shall not be restricted on account of the nationality of the relatives or heirs, and shall enjoy in this respect the same rights and privileges as granted to nationals provided that they submit themselves to the conditions imposed on the latter—does not confer on an alien Italian plaintiff, when bringing an action in New York, greater or different rights of procedure and form of remedy than those accorded to residents and citizens of that State. Teti v. Consolidated Coal Co. (1914), 217 Fed. 443.

Treaty of Commerce and Navigation with Japan Concluded November 22, 1894.

Arts. I and II. Paupers or persons likely to become a public charge have not been given by the treaty with Japan full liberty to enter or reside in the United States. That instrument expressly excepts from its operation any ordinance or regulation in respect of "police and public security." A statute excluding paupers or persons likely to become a public charge, of whatever nationality, is manifestly one of police and public security. The Japanese Immigrant Case (1903), 189 U. S. 86.

These articles contain no allusion to fishing privileges, and do not purport to grant any right to sea rovers to resort to American fishing grounds for the purpose of taking fish for their own consumption or otherwise. The act of Congress of June 14, 1906 (34 Stats. 263), making it unlawful for any non-resident alien to catch or kill fish in the waters of Alaska, except with rod, spear or gaff, overrides the provisions in the treaty if in conflict with them. The Tokai Maru (1911), 190 Fed. 450. Petition for writ of certiorari denied, 225 U. S. 703.

Treaty of Friendship and Commerce with Persia Concluded December 13, 1856.

Art. IV. The act of Congress of June 6, 1872, (17 Stats. 232), imposing an additional ad valorem duty of ten per centum on goods, the growth and produce of countries east of the Cape of Good Hope, when imported from places west of the Cape of Good Hope, is not in violation of the treaty with Persia, since the subjects of Persia exporting their products directly to the United States are required to pay no higher duties than are paid by the "merchants and subjects of the most favored nation." Powers v. Comly (1879), 101 U. S. 789.

Treaty of Commerce and Navigation with Portugal Concluded August 26, 1840.

Art. II. This article is confined exclusively to vessels, and does not include cargoes or make any provision for indirect trade. Oldfield v. Marriott (1850), 10 How. 146.

Treaty of Commerce and Navigation with Prussia Concluded May 1, 1828.

Art. I.   While the treaty of 1828 with Prussia has been recognized as being still in force by both the United States and the German Empire, there is nothing therein undertaking to change the well recognized rule between states and nations permitting a country first to protect the rights of its own citizens in local property before it may be taken out of the jurisdiction for administration in favor of those residing beyond its borders.   Disconto Gesellschaft v. Umbreit (1908), 208 U. S. 570.

Art. IX.   The act of Congress of June 26, 1884, sec. 14 (23 Stats. at L. 57), levies a duty of three cents per ton on all vessels "from any foreign port or place in North America, Central America, the West India Islands, the Bahama Islands, the Bermuda Islands, or the Sandwich Islands, or Newfoundland," and a duty of six cents per ton on vessels from any other foreign port.   German vessels sailing from European ports are not entitled, under the stipulation in the treaties of December 20, 1827, and May 1, 1828, that the United States shall not grant any particular favor regarding commerce or navigation to any other foreign nation which shall not immediately become common to Germany, to enter on the payment of the three cents per ton, since the classification in said act is merely geographical, the three cent rate applying to vessels of all nations coming from the privileged ports.   If an act of Congress is in conflict with a prior treaty, the act must control the judiciary.   North German Lloyd S. S. Co. v. Hedden (1890), 43 Fed. 17.   See Art. XVII of the treaty with Sweden and Norway of July 4, 1827.   See 21 Op. Atty. Gen. 80.

Treaty of Commerce and Navigation with Russia Concluded December 18, 1832.

Art. VI.   The stipulation in the treaty, that the products of Russia shall not be subjected to a higher rate of duty than like products imported into the United States from other conutries, addresses itself to the political and not the judicial department of the government, and the courts cannot try the question whether it has or has not been observed.   An act of

Congress approved by the President repeals a prior treaty with which it conflicts, so far as the treaty is a municipal law, provided the subject matter is within the legislative power of Congress. Taylor v. Morton (1855), 2 Curtis 454. See 2 Black 481; also Curtis's Admx. v. Fiedler, Id. 461.

It being provided by Article VI that no higher duties shall be imposed on the importation into the United States of any article, the produce or manufacture of Russia, than are or shall be payable on the like articles, the produce or manufacture of any other foreign country, and Congress having by section 1 of the act of August 5, 1861 (12 Stats. 292) imposed a duty on unmanufactured Russia hemp of forty dollars per ton, and on Manila and other hemps of India of twenty-five dollars per ton, such legislation is a declaration by Congress that such provision of the treaty shall no longer operate as the law of the land in respect of the duty on unmanufactured Russia hemp. Ropes v. Clinch (1871), 8 Blatchf. 304. See Art. XVII of the treaty with Sweden and Norway of July 4, 1827.

Treaty of Peace with Spain Concluded December 10, 1898.

Art. IV. The provision, that the United States will for a term of ten years admit Spanish ships and merchandise to the ports of the Philippine Islands on the same terms as enjoyed by ships and merchandise of the United States, does not give to merchandise imported into the Philippines from Spain a different status from that imported from the United States. Neither does it give to citizens of Spain a preference over citizens of the United States in this respect. They are entitled to the same terms. Struckmann v. United States (1909), 44 C. Cls. 202; affirmed, 223 U. S. 712.

Treaty of Amity and Commerce with Sweden Concluded April 3, 1783.

Art. II. The right of free entry into the United States of untaxed pulp made from untaxed wood provided for in section 2 of the act of July 26, 1911, "to promote reciprocal trade relations with the Dominion of Canada and for other puposes," having been granted by the United States to Canada without consideration, passed automatically to other powers enjoying most-favored-nation treatment. American Express

Co. et al. v. United States; and Bertuch & Co. et al. v. United States (1913), 4 Ct. Cust. Appls. 146. See also 14 Op. Atty. Gen. 468.

Art. VI. A statute of the State of Washington which imposes an inheritance tax of 25% on all property passing to collateral relatives or strangers of the blood, who are aliens not residing in the United States, and a tax of only 3 % on property passing to citizens, is in conflict with the provisions of the treaty and must give way to them. In re Stixrud's Estate (1910), 58 Wash. 339.

The provision that inheritances shall be exempt from all duty called "droit de détraction" does not cover a tax upon the succession to or transfer of property. The words "freely dispose of" do not relate to property passing by descent. There is nothing in the treaty which requires uniformity of taxes upon property passing to citizens of the United States and to citizens and subjects of Sweden; and the State may accordingly impose and collect a collateral inheritance tax of 20% on property passing to such alien heirs, though the tax on property passing to native resident heirs is only 5%. An inheritance tax is not fundamentally a tax upon property, but a tax upon the right of succession, or the right to receive the property by will or descent. In re Peterson's Estate (1915), 151 N. W. (Iowa) 66.

PROPERTY RIGHTS IN CEDED TERRITORY.

Treaty with France for the Cession of Louisiana Concluded April 30, 1803.

Art. II. As to public property as distinguished from private property, see New Orleans v. United States (1836), 10 Pet. 662; Pollard's Lessee v. Hagan (1845), 3 How. 212; United States v. King (1849), 7 How. 833, 847; Slidell v. Grandjean (1883), 111 U. S. 412.

By the cession of Louisiana, the government of the United States succeeded to all the property and interests formerly possessed by the governments of France and Spain in that province. A right reserved by the terms of a grant to use the land for any fortification is more than the right of eminent domain. It is a right to use the land for that purpose without compensation; and this reserved right passed to the

42

United States under the treaty of cession. Josephs v. United States (1865), 1 C. Cls. 197. See dissenting opinion, 2 C. Cls. 586.

Art. III. An adjudication made by a Spanish tribunal in Louisiana is not void because it was made after the cession of the country to the United States, for it is historically known that the actual possession of the country was not surrendered until some time after the proceedings and adjudication in the case took place. It was the judgment, therefore, of a competent Spanish tribunal, having jurisdiction of the case, and rendered while the country, though ceded, was, de facto, in the possession of Spain, and subject to Spanish laws. Such judgments, so far as they affect the private rights of the parties thereto, must be deemed valid. Keene v. McDonough (1834), 8 Pet. 308, 310.

A grant by the Spanish governor, dated January 2, 1804, for lands included within the limits of Louisiana was void, Spain having parted with her title to that province by the treaty of St. Ildefonso of October 1, 1800, and France having ceded the same province to the United States by the treaty of Paris of April 30, 1803. Such a grant could not be protected by the provision in the treaty for the protection of the people of Louisiana in the free enjoyment of their liberty and property, the term property being applicable only to possessions or rights founded in justice and good faith, and based upon authority competent to their creation. The treaty of St. Ildefonso between Spain and France and that of Paris between France and the United States should be construed as binding on the parties thereto from the respective dates of those treaties. United States v. Reynes (1850), 9 How. 127.

After the treaty of St. Ildefonso was signed, and until Louisiana was delivered to France, its possession continued in Spain. The right to the territory, though in France, was imperfect until ratified, but absolute by ratification from the date of the treaty. Accordingly, the Spanish governor had no right, after October 1, 1800, to grant a perpetual ferry franchise; and such an attempted grant is not property protected by the treaty between the United States and France. Davis v. Police Jury of Concordia (1850), 9 How. 280. See also United States v. D' Auterive (1850), 10 How. 609.

The United States regards the stipulation, that the inhabitants of the ceded territory shall be protected in the free enjoyment of their property, as the avowal of a principle which would have been held equally sacred though it had not been inserted in the contract. The term "property," as applied to lands, comprehends every species of title, inchoate or complete, legal or equitable, and embraces those rights which lie in contract, executory as well as executed. Soulard v. United States (1830), 4 Pet. 511; Delassus v. United States (1835), 9 Pet. 117; Smith v. United States (1836), 10 Pet. 326; Strother v. Lucas (1838), 12 Pet. 410; Hornsby v. United States (1869), 10 Wall. 224; Carpenter v. Rannels (1873), 19 Wall. 138; Morton v. Nebraska (1874), 21 Wall. 660; Bryan v. Kennett (1885), 113 U. S. 179.

"This court has defined property to be any right, legal or equitable, inceptive, inchoate, or perfect, which before the treaty with France in 1803, or with Spain in 1819, had so attached to any piece or tract of land, great or small, as to affect the conscience of the former sovereign, 'with a trust,' and make him a trustee for an individual, according to the law of nations, of the sovereign himself, the local usage or custom of the colony or district; according to the principles of justice, and rules of equity. 6 Peters 709, 714; 8 Peters 450; 9 Peters 133, 144, 737; 10 Peters 105, 324, 331, 35, 36. The same principle has been applied by this court, to the right of a Spanish town, as a municipal corporation. 10 Peters 718 to 736; passim, 144, 734, 736; 10 Peters 105, 324, 331, 335, 336 * * *. This court has also uniformly held that the term grant, in a treaty, comprehends not only those which are made in form, but also any concession, warrant, order or permission to survey, possess or settle, whether evidenced by writing or parol, or presumed from possession; (vide the cases last cited,) 8 Peters 466-7; 9 Peters 152, 170; 10 Peters 331-340; S. P. 10 Peters 718 &c.; and that in the term laws, is included custom and usage, when once settled." Baldwin, J., Strother v. Lucas (1838), 12 Pet. 410, 436.

The obligation of perfecting titles under Spanish concessions, which was assumed by the United States in the Louisiana treaty, was of an executory character, to be carried out by the legislative department of the government. United

States v. Wiggins (1840), 14 Pet. 334; Chouteau v. Eckhart (1844), 2 How. 344. See also United States v. Reynes (1850), 9 How. 127; United States v. Philadelphia and New Orleans (1850), 11 How. 609; Dent v. Emmeger (1871), 14 Wall. 308. See also New Orleans v. United States (1836), 10 Pet. 662.

This article contemplates two objects: First, that Louisiana shall be admitted into the Union as soon as possible upon an equal footing with the other States; and second, that until such admission the inhabitants of the ceded territory shall be protected in the free enjoyment of their liberty, property, and religion. Had any of these rights been violated while this stipulation continued in force the individual supposing himself to be injured might have brought his case into the Supreme Court under section 25 of the judiciary act. But this stipulation ceased to operate when Louisiana became a member of the Union. The inhabitants of Louisiana enjoy all the advantages of American citizens, in common with their brethren in sister States, when their titles are decided by the tribunals of the State. New Orleans v. Armas (1835), 9 Pet. 224. A decision of a State court against the validity of a title set up under a complete grant issued prior to the cession would be subject to revisal by the Supreme Court under section 25 of the judiciary act. McDonogh v. Millaudon (1845), 3 How. 693.

The stipulation, that the inhabitants of the ceded territory shall be incorporated into the Union of the United States and admitted as soon as possible, according to the principles of the Constitution, to the enjoyment of all the rights, advantages and immunities of citizens of the United States, has no bearing upon the question of title of the State of Iowa to the land beneath its lakes. Iowa v. Rood (1902), 187 U. S. 87.

This article ceased to have any effect as to the State of Louisiana upon its admission into the Union, April 30, 1812. Church of St. Francis &c. v. Martin (1843), 4 Rob. (La.) 62.

Art. VI. "When the United States acquired and took possession of the Floridas under the Louisiana treaty, the treaties which had been made with the Indian tribes remained in force over all the ceded territories, as the laws which regulate the relations with all the Indians who were parties to them. They were binding on the United States as the fundamental laws of Indian right acknowledged by royal orders and municipal regulations." Grier, J., Wilson v. Wall (1867), 6 Wall. 83, 87.

Definitive Treaty of Peace with Great Britain Concluded September 3, 1783.

Under the treaty of peace with Great Britian, the United States succeeded to all the rights in that part of old Canada, which now forms the State of Michigan, that existed in the King of France prior to its conquest from the French by the British in 1760. Among these rights was that of dealing with the seigniorial estate of lands granted out as seignories by the King, after a forfeiture had occurred for non-fulfillment of the conditions of the fief. United States v. Repentigny (1866), 5 Wall. 211.

Treaty of Amity, Commerce and Navigation with Great Britain of November 19, 1794.

Art. II. The "precincts and jurisdiction" of a post, referred to in Article II, are not to be considered as extending three miles in every direction by analogy to the jurisdiction of a country over that distance of the sea; but they must be established by proof. The clauses in Article II and Article IX, providing that settlers within such precincts shall be protected in the enjoyment of their property, were intended to protect legal and equitable interests in land, and not trespassers and intruders without right. Jackson ex dem. Sparkman v. Porter (1825), 1 Paine 457. See alsc Forsyth v. Reynolds (1853), 15 How. 358; United States v. Repentigny, 5 Wall. 211; Crane v. Reeder, 21 Mich. 24.

Treaty with Great Britain Establishing Boundary West of the Rocky Mountains Concluded June 15, 1846.

Art. III. The stipulation, that the United States would respect "the possessory rights" of British subjects then in the occupation of land or other property lawfully acquired in the territory south of the 49th parallel, was a mere promise which of itself conferred no right to or in the soil, and for the violation of which the British subject would only have a claim against the United States for compensation in money or kind.

Town v. De Haven (1878), 5 Sawy. 146. See Bishop ot Nesqually v. Gibbon (1895), 158 U. S. 155; Stark v. Starr (1876), 94 U. S. 477; Barney v. Dolph (1878), 97 U. S. 652; Lownsdale et al. v. Parrish (1858), 21 How. 290.

Art. IV. Article IV of the treaty—compromising and adjusting the respective rights of the United States and Great Britain over the northwestern coast of North America—confirming title in the Puget's Sound Agricultural Co.—is but declaratory of the law of nations, which in case of change of sovereignty leaves private rights and relationships undisturbed. The clause "shall be confirmed" had the effect of vesting title in the Puget's Sound Agricultural Co. to its property at once upon the ratification of the treaty, and is to be considered as equivalent to a legislative act to that effect. Puget Sound Agricultural Co. v. Pierce County (1861), 1 Wash. T. 159.

Treaty of Peace, Friendship, Limits, and Settlement with Mexico Concluded February 2, 1848.

Arts. VIII and IX. These various stipulations are wholly inapplicable to the persons, who, before the revolution in Texas, had been citizens of Mexico, and who, by that revolution, had been separated from Mexico. These stipulations had no reference to territory within the acknowledged limits of Texas. McKinney v. Saviego (1855), 18 How. 235; Basse v. Brownsville (1875), 154 U. S. 610.

The cession of the country to the United States did not impair the rights of private property. They were consecrated by the law of nations and protected by the treaty. The treaty was but a formal recognition of the pre-existing sanction in the law of nations. The act of March 3, 1851, to ascertain and settle private land claims in the State of California, was passed to assure to the inhabitants of the ceded territory the benefit of the rights thus secured to them. It recognizes both legal and equitable rights, and should be administered in a liberal spirit. A right of any validity before the cession was equally valid thereafter. United States v. Moreno (1863), 1 Wall. 400.

The declaration of the Mexican commissioners, who negotiated the treaty, that no grants of land were made by the Mexican governors of California after May 13, 1846, does not affect the rights of parties who, subsequently to that date, obtained grants from the governors whilst their authority and jurisdiction continued. The authority and jurisdiction of Mexican officers in California are regarded as having terminated on July 7, 1846. The political department has designated that date as the period when the conquest of California was completed and the Mexican officers displaced, and in this respect the judiciary will follow the conclusion of the political department. United States v. Yorba (1863), 1 Wall. 412, 423. See also United States v. Pico, 23 How. 321, 326; Stearns v. United States, 6 Wall. 589; Hornsby v. United States, 10 Wall. 224, 239; More v. Steinbach, 127 U. S. 70, 80.

The treaty did not divest the pueblo, which existed at the site of the present city of San Francisco, of any rights of property, or alter the character of the interests, it may have held in any lands under the former government. It makes no distinction in the protection it provides between the property of individuals and the property held by towns under the Mexican government. Townsend v. Greeley (1866), 5 Wall. 326.

In order that a perfect title to land might vest under a grant from the Mexican government, a delivery of possession by its officers was necessary. United States v. Fossat, 20 How. 413; Van Reynegan v. Bolton, 95 U. S. 33; More v. Steinbach, 127 U. S. 70; Pinkerton v. Ledoux, 129 U. S. 346.

No title to lands in California, dependent upon Spanish or Mexican grants, can be of any validity, which has not been submitted to and confirmed by the board provided for that purpose under the act of March 3, 1851 (9 Stats. 631), or, if rejected by that board, confirmed by the district court or by the Supreme Court of the United States. Botiller v. Dominguez (1889), 130 U. S. 238.

By the term property, as applied to lands, all titles are embraced, legal or equitable, perfect or imperfect. By the stipulations of the treaty the United States is bound to protect such property rights. Hornsby v. United States, 10 Wall. 224, 242; United States v. Rose, 23 How. 262. See United States v. Sutter, 21 How. 170. The United States is bound to protect all rights of property emanating from the Mexican government prior to the treaty. Knight v. United States

Land Assoc., 142 U. S. 161; Astiazaran v. Santa Rita & Mining Co., 148 U. S. 80; United States v. Chaves, 159 U. S. 452.

A grant not complete and perfect, which can be confirmed by the court of private land claims, must be one which the claimant could, by right and not by grace, have demanded should be made perfect by the former government, had not the territory been transferred to the United States; and by the treaty no grant could be considered obligatory which had not been theretofore located. Ainsa v. United States, 161 U. S. 208, 223; United States v. Santa Fe, 165 U. S. 675, 714; United States v. Sandoval, 167 U. S. 278, 293; Bergere v. United States, 168 U. S. 66, 85; Hays v. United States, 175 U. S. 248.

The act of Congress of June 21, 1860 (12 Stats. 71), confirming Mexican grants, was intended to be a discharge of the obligations of the treaty. It was a confirmation of rights which existed and as they existed. If there be two claims under two patents, each of which reserves the rights of the other parties, the enquiry must extend to the character of the original concession. The controversy can only be settled by determining which of these two gives the better right to the demanded premises. Jones v. St. Louis Land Co. (1914), 232 U. S. 355.

The obligation, which the United States assumed by the treaty with Mexico, was to protect all rights of property acquired under the laws of that country. The property rights of pueblos, equally with those of individuals, were entitled to protection, and in the legislation of Congress provision was made for their investigation and confirmation. The right and power of the government in the execution of its treaty obligations to protect the claim of the city of San Francisco, as successor of the pueblo, were superior to any subsequently acquired rights or claims of the State, or of individuals. Tripp v. Spring (1878), 5 Sawy. 209. See Knight v. United States Land Assoc. (1891), 142 U. S. 161.

The act of February 8, 1850, relating to Spanish land grants and declaring void any sales of lands pending official investigation thereunder of the titles, was not violative of the provision in the treaty of Guadalupe Hidalgo, that Mexicans in the disputed territory should be granted their property rights, since the object of the act was to protect these rights by suitable methods for their proof. Baldwin v. Goldfrank (1894), 9 Tex. Civ. App. 269; 88 Tex. 249.

Protocol. "By the rejection of this article [tenth], this government distinctly declared that it did not propose to recognize any grants which were not at the time of the treaty of cession recognized by the Mexican government as valid or any whose conditions, either precedent or subsequent, had not been fully performed." Brewer, J., Cessna v. United States (1898), 169 U. S. 165, 186.

The protocol to the treaty of Guadalupe Hidalgo announced that the American government by suppressing the tenth article did not intend to annul grants of lands made by Mexico in the ceded territories, but that those grants should preserve their legal value, and the grantees might cause their titles to be acknowledged before American tribunals, and that, conformably to the law of the United States, legitimate titles existing in the ceded territories were those which were legitimate titles under the Mexican law in Texas up to March 2, 1836. State v. Gallardo (1911), 135 S. W. (Tex.) 664.

Treaty with Russia for the Acquisition of Alaska Concluded March 30, 1867.

Arts. II, III, IV and VI. The commissioners appointed by the governments of the United States and Russia for the transfer of Alaska had no power to vary the language of the treaty or to determine questions of title or ownership. The building constructed by the Russian-American Company in 1845 on land belonging to Russia became thereby, so far as disclosed by the facts in the case, the property of the Russian government, and, being transferred to the United States by the treaty, no property or ownership in it remained in the Russian-American Company, which it could transfer to a private person adversely to the United States. Kinkead v. United States (1893), 150 U. S. 483.

Lands granted in fee simple by Russia prior to the treaty did not pass to the United States. The courts will protect the possession of the owners of such fee, such protection being among the obligations assumed by the United States under the treaty. Callsen v. Hope (1896), 75 Fed. 758.

Treaty of Friendship, Cession of the Floridas, and Boundaries Concluded with Spain February 22, 1819.

Art. II. A cession of territory is never understood to be a cession of the property belonging to its inhabitants. The King ceded that only which belonged to him. United States v. Percheman (1833), 7 Pet. 51. This article undoubtedly transferred to the United States all the political power which our government could acquire, and all the royal domain held by the crown of Spain; but it did not operate on the property of individuals. United States v. Clarke (1834), 8 Pet. 436, 449; Mitchel v. United States (1835), 9 Pet. 711. The King of Spain could not by treaty or otherwise impart to the United States any of his royal prerogatives; nor does the United States have capacity to receive or exercise them. Every nation acquiring territory, by treaty or otherwise, holds it subject to the constitution and laws of its own government, and not according to those of the government ceding it. Pollard's Lessee v. Hagan (1845), 3 How. 212.

Art. VIII. The clause in the English text, that all grants of land made by His Catholic Majesty, or by his lawful authorities, prior to January 24, 1818, "shall be ratified and confirmed" to those in possession, imports a contract addressed to the political department, not the judicial; and the legislative department must execute the contract before it can become a rule of the court. Marshall, C. J., Foster v. Neilson (1829), 2 Pet. 253. This article was intended expressly to stipulate for the security to private property which the laws and usages of nations would without express stipulation have conferred. The words of the English text, "grants shall be ratified and confirmed," and those of the Spanish text, the English translation of which is "shall remain ratified and confirmed," were, since both are originals, intended by the parties to be identical. In order that the two texts may conform with each other they are to be construed as importing that the grants are ratified and confirmed by force of the instrument itself without the aid of legislation. United States v. Percheman (1833), 7 Pet. 51; United States v. Arredondo (1832), 6 Pet. 691. See also United States v. Clarke (1834), 8 Pet. 436. But the provision applies only to grants made in territory which at the time of the grant be-

longed to Spain. A boundary line determined as the true one
by the political departments of the government must be
recognized as the true one by the judicial department. Foster
v. Neilson (1829), 2 Pet. 253; Garcia v. Lee (1838), 12 Pet.
511; Pollard's Heirs v. Kibbe (1840), 14 Pet. 353. "It is
the settled doctrine of the judicial department of this government, that the treaty of 1819 ceded no territory west of the
river Perdido, but only that east of it; and therefore all
grants made by Spain after the United States acquired the
country from France, in 1803, are void, if the lands granted
lay west of that river * * *. It was thus held in Foster and
Elam v. Neilson, 2 Peters 254, and again in Garcia v. Lee, 12
Peters 515, and is not now open to controversy in this court."
Catron, J., Pollard's Lessee v. Files (1844), 2 How. 591,
602. Spain in ceding the Floridas to the United States only
ceded so much thereof as belonged to her, and accordingly did
not cede the territory lying between the Perdido and the Mississippi rivers. The stipulation in Article VIII of the treaty
of 1819, to confirm all Spanish grants of land in the ceded
territory, did not embrace grants made in the territory west of
the Perdido after Spain ceded Louisiana to France by the
treaty of St. Ildefonso in 1800, since after that date the territory did not belong to Spain. United States v. Lynde (1870),
11 Wall. 632, citing United States v. D'Auterive, 10 How. 609;
United States v. Philadelphia & New Orleans, 11 How. 609;
Montault v. United States, 12 How. 47; United States v. Castant, 12 How. 437. The words "lawful authorities" in Article
VIII, and "competent authorities" in the ratification, must
be taken to refer to those persons who exercised the granting
power by the authority of the crown. United States v. Clarke
(1834), 8 Pet. 436. A claim to lands in East Florida, the
title to which was derived from grants by the Creek and Seminole Indians ratified by the local authorities of Spain before
the cession, was confirmed. Mitchel v. United States (1835),
9 Pet. 711. See also Smith v. United States (1836), 10 Pet.
326. The clause in the English text, "owners in possession of
such lands,"—in the Spanish version, "proprietarios,"—was
for the benefit of those who were purchasers under the faith
of a public grant. The law deems every man to be in the
legal seizin and possession of land to which he has a perfect

and complete title. This gives to the words "in possession of such lands" their well settled and fixed meaning. Possession does not imply occupation or residence. United States v. Arredondo (1832), 6 Pet. 691, 743; Mitchel v. United States (1835), 9 Pet. 711; United States v. Sibbald (1836), 10 Pet. 313, 323. Owners of lands are allowed by this article the same time for fulfilling the conditions of their grants from the date of the treaty as is allowed in the grant from the date of the instrument. United States v. Clarke (1835), 9 Pet. 168; United States v. Sibbald (1836), 10 Pet. 313. In case of failure to perform or to attempt to perform the conditions within the time limited, the grant lapsed. United States v. Mills' Heirs (1838), 12 Pet. 215. The perfect titles made by Spain before January 24, 1818, within the ceded territory, are intrinsically valid and exempt from the provisions of the eighth article; and they need no sanction from the legislative or judicial departments of this government. The eighth article was intended to apply to claims the validity of which at the date of the treaty depended upon the performance of conditions in consideration of which the concessions had been made and which must have been performed before Spain would have been bound to perfect the title. The United States was bound by the article after the cession, to the same extent that Spain was bound before the ratification of the treaty, to perfect this class of cases by legislation and adjudication. United States v. Wiggins (1840), 14 Pet. 334.

A grantee of land in Florida, who had never caused the same to be severed from the public domain by survey, or identified, was without actual seizin or seizin in law, and not within the protection of the treaty of 1819. United States v. Miranda, 16 Pet. 153. The power to survey lands in conformity to concessions made prior to January 24, 1818 existed up to the change of flags. United States v. Huertas, 9 Pet. 171; United States v. Heirs of Clarke, 16 Pet. 228; United States v. Acosta, 1 How. 24. See especially as to various grants attempted to be brought under the protection of this article, and for reviews of decisions of the court, Lessee of Pollard's Heirs v. Kibbe (1840), 14 Pet. 353; O'Hara v. United States (1841), 15 Pet. 275; United States v. Delespine (1841), 15 Pet. 319; United States v. Breward (1842), 16 Pet. 143;

United States v. Miranda (1842), 16 Pet. 153; United States v. Hanson (1842), 16 Pet. 196; United States v. Heirs of Clarke et al. (1842), 16 Pet. 228; United States v. Acosta (1843), 1 How. 24.

Treaty of Peace with Spain Concluded December 10, 1898.

Art. VIII.   The privilege of practicing law was not a property right protected by Article VIII of the treaty.   Bosque v. United States (1908), 209 U. S. 91.

The Roman Catholic Church has been recognized as possessing legal personality, and its property rights have been solemnly safeguarded by the treaty of Paris.   In so doing the treaty has merely followed the recognized rule of international law, which would have protected the property of the Church in Porto Rico, subsequently to the cession.   This juristic personality of and the ownership of property by the Church have been recognized in the most formal manner by the concordats between Spain and the papacy and by the Spanish laws from the beginning of settlements in the Indies.   Ponce v. Roman Catholic Church (1908), 210 U. S. 296, 323.   See also O'Reilly de Camara v. Brooke (1908), 209 U. S. 45.

The property rights of private individuals recognized and protected by the treaty did not include the right to hold in perpetuity offices of a quasi-public nature, such as that of procurador; and the United States did not so restrict its sovereign authority that it could not, consistently with the treaty, abolish a system so entirely foreign to the conceptions of the American people, and inconsistent with the spirit of our institutions.   Sanchez v. United States (1910), 216 U. S. 167.

The legal entity of the city of Manila survived both its military occupation by, and cession to, the United States; and, as in law the present city as the successor of the former city is entitled to the property rights of its predecessor, it is also subject to its liabilities.   The relinquishment to the United States of all the public property belonging to the crown of Spain in the Philippine Islands did not include property belonging to municipalities, and the property and property rights of municipalities were safeguarded precisely as were those of individuals.   Vilas v. City of Manila (1911), 220 U. S. 345.

Art. XIII. The provision, for the protection of industrial property in the ceded territory, will not be construed as contravening principles of morality and fairness and as protecting a trademark fraudulently registered prior to the treaty. Ubeda v. Zialcita (1913), 226 U. S. 452.

APPENDIX II.

FORMS.

THE UNITED STATES.

Full Power to Sign a Treaty.

WILLIAM HOWARD TAFT,
President of the United States of America,

TO ALL TO WHOM THESE PRESENTS SHALL COME, GREETING:

KNOW YE, That reposing special trust and confidence in the integrity, prudence and ability of Chandler P. Anderson, counselor for the Department of State, I have invested him with full and all manner of power and authority for and in the name of the United States to meet and confer with any person or persons duly authorized by the Government of His Britannic Majesty, being invested with like power and authority, and with him or them to negotiate, conclude and sign an agreement modifying the rules and methods of procedure under the award of The Hague Tribunal of September 7, 1910, in the matter of the arbitration of the North Atlantic Coast Fisheries, the same to be transmitted to the President of the United States for his ratification, by and with the advice and consent of the Senate thereof.

IN TESTIMONY WHEREOF, I have caused the seal of the United States to be hereunto affixed.

[Seal.] Given under my hand at the City of Washington this fourteenth day of February in the year of our Lord one thousand nine hundred and twelve, and of the Independence of the United States of America the one hundred and thirty-sixth.

WM. H. TAFT.

By the President:
P. C. KNOX,
Secretary of State.

Resolution of the Senate Advising and Consenting to the Ratification of a Treaty.

IN EXECUTIVE SESSION, SENATE OF THE UNITED STATES.

May 20, 1914.

Resolved (Two-thirds of the Senators present concurring therein), That the Senate advise and consent to the ratification of the convention (Executive F, Sixty-third Congress, Second Session), signed May 9, 1914, by the plenipotentiaries of the United States and the Netherlands, extending the duration of the arbitration convention between the two countries concluded May 2, 1908.

Attest: JAMES M. BAKER,
Secretary.

Resolution of the Senate Advising and Consenting to the Ratification of a Treaty with Amendment.

IN EXECUTIVE SESSION, SENATE OF THE UNITED STATES.

July 26, 1909.

Resolved (Two-thirds of the Senators present concurring therein), That the Senate advise and consent to the ratification of an extradition treaty between the United States and the Dominican Republic, signed at Santo Domingo on June 19, 1909; with the following

AMENDMENT

In Article II, on page 2, line 22, strike out after the word "Nations" the comma and the words "or by statute."

Attest: CHARLES G. BENNETT,
Secretary.

Ratification by the President.

WOODROW WILSON,
President of the United States of America,

TO ALL TO WHOM THESE PRESENTS SHALL COME, GREETING:

KNOW YE, That whereas a treaty between the United States of America and the Republic of China looking to the advancement of the cause of general peace, was concluded and signed by their respective plenipotentiaries at Washington on the fifteenth day of September, one thousand nine hundred and fourteen, the original of which treaty is hereto annexed;

AND WHEREAS the Senate of the United States by their resolution of October 12, 1914, (two-thirds of the Senators present concurring therein) did advise and consent to the ratification of the said treaty;

Now, THEREFORE, be it known that I, Woodrow Wilson, President of the United States of America, having seen and considered the said treaty, do hereby, in pursuance of the aforesaid advice and consent of the Senate, ratify and confirm the same and every article and clause thereof.

IN TESTIMONY WHEREOF, I have caused the seal of the United States to be hereunto affixed.

[Seal.] Given under my hand at the City of Washington this seventeenth day of June in the year of our Lord one thousand nine hundred and fifteen, and of the Independence of the United States of America the one hundred and thirty-ninth.

WOODROW WILSON.

By the President:

ROBERT LANSING,
Secretary of State ad interim.

[Here follows the text of the treaty.]

Protocol of Exchange of Ratifications.

The undersigned plenipotentiaries having met for the purpose of exchanging the ratifications of the treaty signed at Washington on the fifteenth day of September, one thousand nine hundred and fourteen, between the United States of America and the French Republic to facilitate the settlement of disputes, and the ratifications of the treaty aforesaid having been carefully compared and found exactly conformable to each other, the exchange took place this day in the usual form.

IN WITNESS WHEREOF, they have signed the present protocol of exchange and have affixed their seals thereto.

DONE at Washington, this twenty-second day of January, one thousand nine hundred and fifteen.

[Seal.]   WILLIAM JENNINGS BRYAN.
[Seal.]   JUSSERAND.

43

Proclamation of the Treaty.

By the President of the United States of America.
A PROCLAMATION.

WHEREAS a convention between the United States of America and the Kingdom of Sweden defining the rights, privileges, and immunities of consular officers was concluded and signed by their respective plenipotentiaries at Washington on the first day of June, one thousand nine hundred and ten, the original of which convention, being in the English and Swedish languages, is word for word as follows: [Here follows the text of the convention.]

AND WHEREAS the said convention has been duly ratified on both parts, and the ratifications of the two governments were exchanged in the City of Washington on the eighteenth day of March, one thousand nine hundred and eleven;

Now, THEREFORE, be it known that I, WILLIAM HOWARD TAFT, President of the United States of America, have caused the said convention to be made public, to the end that the same and every article and clause thereof may be observed and fulfilled with good faith by the United States and the citizens thereof.

IN TESTIMONY WHEREOF, I have hereunto set my hand and caused the seal of the United States to be hereunto affixed.

[Seal.] Done at the City of Washington this twentieth day of March in the year of our Lord one thousand nine hundred and eleven, and of the Independence of the United States of America the one hundred and thirty-fifth.

WM. H. TAFT.

By the President:
HUNTINGTON WILSON,
Acting Secretary of State.

GREAT BRITAIN.

Ratification by the King.

GEORGE, by the Grace of God, of the United Kingdom of Great Britain and Ireland and of the British Dominions beyond the Seas King, Defender of the Faith, Emperor of India, &c., &c., &c. To all and singular to whom these Presents shall come, Greeting:

WHEREAS a Treaty between Us and Our Good Friends the United States of America with regard to the establishment of a Peace Commission was concluded and signed at Washington on the fifteenth day of September, in the year of Our Lord One Thousand Nine Hundred and Fourteen, by the Plenipotentiaries of Us and of Our said Good Friends, duly and respectively authorized for that purpose, which Treaty is, word for word, as follows: [Here follows the text of the treaty.]

WE, having seen and considered the Treaty aforesaid, have approved, accepted, and confirmed the same in all and every one of its Articles and Clauses, as We do by these Presents approve, accept, confirm, and ratify it for Ourselves, Our Heirs and Successors; engaging and promising upon Our Royal Word that We will sincerely and faithfully perform and observe all and singular the things which are contained and expressed in the Treaty aforesaid, and that We will never suffer the same to be violated by any one, or transgressed in any manner, as far as it lies in Our power. For the greater testimony and validity of all which, We have caused the Great Seal of Our United Kingdom of Great Britain and Ireland to be affixed to these Presents, which We have signed with Our Royal Hand.

GIVEN at Our Court of St. James, the eighth day of October, in the year of Our Lord One Thousand Nine Hundred and Fourteen, and in the Fifth year of Our Reign.

GEORGE R. I.

[Seal appended.]

FRANCE.

Ratification by the President.

LE PRÉSIDENT DE LA RÉPUBLIQUE FRANÇAISE

A tous ceux qui ces presentes Lettres verront,
SALUT

Une Convention ayant été conclue, le 15 Janvier 1880, entre la France et les Etats-Unis d' Amérique, pour régler certaines réclamations élevées par des citoyens de chacun des deux Pays contre l'autre;

Convention dont la teneur suit: [Here follows the text of the convention.]

AYANT vu et examiné la dite Convention, Nous l' avons approuvée et approuvons, en vertu des dispositions de la loi votée par le Sénat et par la Chambre des Députes; DECLARONS qu'elle est acceptée, ratifiée et confirmée, et PROMETTONS qu'elle sera inviolablement observée.

EN FOI DE QUOI, Nous avons donné le présentes revêtues du Sceau de la République,

A Paris, le 9 Juin 1880.

[Seal.]   JULES GRÉVY.

Par le Président de la République:

C. DE FREYCINET.

RAYMOND POINCARE
Président de la République Française

A TOUS CEUX QUI CES PRESENTES LETTRES VERRONT, SALUT:

Un Traité ayant été signé à Washington le 13 Septembre 1914, entre la France et les Etats-Unis d' Amérique pour faciliter le réglement des litiges, Traité dont la teneur suit: [Here follows the text of the treaty.]

AYANT vu et examiné le dit Traité, Nous l'avons approuvé et approuvons en toute et chacune des dispositions qui y sont contenues;

DECLARONS qu'il est accepté, ratifié, et confirmé, et PROMETTONS qu'il sera inviolablement observé.

EN FOI DE QUOI, Nous avons donné les présentes, revêtues du Sceau de la République.

A Bordeaux, le 3 Décembre 1914.

[Seal.]   POINCARE.

Par le Président de la République:
Le Ministre des Affaires Etrangéres,
DELCASSE.

INDEX.

Page.

Administration on estates of deceased aliens ....

... 34, 260-262, 266, 411-414, 466, 468, 470, 539, 545, 546, 559, 561, 584-586

African slave trade, legislation to enforce treaty provisions against.. 239

African tribes, agreements with 313

Agency in treaty making 1, 2, 5

Agreement, distinguished from treaty 7, 102, 143, 500

Agreements,

    By States of the United States 24, 48, 141-149

    By the President 102-140

Alabama claims 534

Alaska,

    Acquisition of 210, 562

    Appropriation to carry treaty into effect 175-177

    Boundaries of 378-380, 536

    Incorporation of, into the United States 210-212, 563

    Property rights in 629

    Status of inhabitants of 210, 212, 563

Algiers,

    Advice of Senate as to negotiations with 69

    Application of commercial agreement with France to 501

    Appropriations for conduct of negotiations with 164, 167, 171, 172

    Termination of treaties with 466

Aliens,

    Administration on estates of deceased ....

34, 260-262, 266, 411-414, 466, 468, 470, 485, 539, 545, 546, 559, 561, 584-586

    Deportation of 480, 481-483, 548

    Discriminatory legislation in respect of

        Access to courts of justice 544, 613, 617

        Action for wrongful death 259, 614, 615

        Fisheries 255, 260, 607, 609, 618

        Game 255, 260, 616

        Inheritance taxes 252, 416, 606, 610, 611, 612, 621

        Labor 253, 254, 255, 256, 417-419, 421-422, 606, 607, 608, 617

    Enforcement of treaty rights of ..37, 51, 54, 61, 62, 241, 256, 269-272, 479

    Exclusion of 471-479, 481-483

    Rights of, in Great Britain to take and hold real property 284

    Rights of, to religious freedom 34, 264, 471

    Rights of, under treaties to inherit and hold real property .....

    .... 33, 35, 59, 247-251, 591-605

    Time within which to dispose of 599, 603, 604, 605

Allegiance,

    Change of, in Great Britain 282

Page.

Effect of treaty for transfer of territory on 200
Alliance,
    Effect of war on treaties of 451
    Treaties of, in the United States 20, 47, 61, 171
Alsace-Lorraine, application of treaties to 430
Alternat, the 5, 32
Amendment of treaties,
    By the Congress of the Confederation 21, 29
    By the Senate 79–82, 95, 346
        Explanation of 85
    In France 305
Amendments of the treaty provisions of the Constitution proposed
    by State conventions 62–63
Appropriations, treaties involving,
    In American republics 337, 338
    Austria-Hungary 328, 329
    Belgium 315, 316
    Bulgaria 336
    Denmark 332
    France 174, 304, 308, 311
    Germany 325
    Great Britain 280
    Greece 335
    Italy 320, 323
    Luxemburg 317
    Montenegro 336
    Netherlands 318
    Norway 331
    Persia 337
    Portugal 333
    Roumania 335
    Servia 335
    Spain 332
    Sweden 330
    Switzerland 334
    Turkey 337
    United States 164–182
Arbitration conventions, ratification of,
    In foreign countries 300, 314, 317, 332, 333
    In the United States 73, 84, 98, 101, 119
Arbitration of controversies arising in the interpretation of treaties
    .... 15, 358–363
    Compulsory 359, 361–364
    General conventions for 358–361
    Special conventions for 361–364
Argentine Republic 338
    Treaties with, construed 466

Page.

Arica, treaty between Peru and Chile respecting 226
Armistice,
 Conclusion of, by officer 8
 Preliminary to conclusion of terms of peace 354–356
 Suspension of hostilities under 354–356
Arson, as an extraditable crime 530
Articles of Confederation,
 Adoption of 24
 Committee to prepare 19
 Defects of 32, 34, 36, 49, 51
 Delays in ratification of treaties under 30, 31
 Dickinson's draft of 24
 States prohibited from making treaties under 24, 48
 Treaty-making power under 24, 27, 28, 32–42, 60
Assault, as an extraditable offense 531
Athapascans of Alaska, status of 563
Austria-Hungary 327–329
 Treaties with, construed 467–469
Aves Island claims, convention for settlement of 83, 108
Baden, treaties with, construed 504
Baltimore Company, claims of 548
Bates agreement 119
Bavaria,
 Survival of treaties of 432, 433, 504
 Treaties with, construed 504
Bayonne, concessions extorted from Ferdinand VII at 4
Belgium 315–317
 Neutralization of 13, 317
 Treaties with, construed 469–470
 Treaty with the United States of 1857 198
Belize, British 381
Bering Sea, jurisdiction over 227, 536
Bills of rights and constitutions of States not to be altered by
 treaties 62, 63
Black Sea, Russian denunciation of provisions of treaty of Paris re-
 lating to neutralization of 441, 442, 456–457
Blockades 508, 522
Bolivia 338
Boundaries,
 Adjustment of, by treaty in foreign states 292, 313, 318, 325, 327, 335, 336
 Adjustment of, by treaty in the United States 225, 229
 Agreements between States of the Union concerning 145–149
 Judiciary to follow determinations of political branch of ques-
  tions concerning 365, 490, 562
 Legislation to give effect to conventions for determining and
  marking 240
 Modi vivendi concerning 106, 113, 114, 144
 Of the United States as defined in treaties ....
  .... 373, 376, 378–380, 384, 387, 490, 513, 514, 523, 526, 566, 570

Page.

Boundary waters,
    Diversion of 525
    Free navigation of 538, 566
    Jurisdiction over vessels in 523, 526
Brazil 338
    Treaties with 470
Bremen (See Hanseatic Republics),
    Survival of treaties of 433
British creditors, enforcement of treaty pledge concerning ....
    .... 34, 36–42, 154, 514–517
Bulgaria 336
    Status of, under the treaty of Berlin 438
Bundesrath,
    Committee of foreign affairs in 326
    Rights of, with respect to treaties 324, 325
Calls on the President for papers 93, 165, 173
Canada, commercial reciprocity with 72, 125, 190, 191–195
Cantons of Switzerland, treaty-making power of 334
Capitulations, conclusion of, incidental to the military power 8
Caption of treaty 403
Captures,
    After the signing of terms of peace 356–357
    Distinguished from detentions in port 507
    Restitution of, under the treaty with Spain 566–567
    Treaty-making power and rules concerning 28, 241
Cartels, conclusion of, incidental to military power 8
Casus omissus 387–389
Cession of territory. (See territory.)
Chamizal arbitration 345, 384, 396
Chile 338
    Treaties with, construed 470
China, treaties with, construed 470–483
Chinese,
    Deportation of 480, 481–483
    Discriminatory legislation respecting 253–257, 417–419, 471–483
    Exclusion of 471–479, 481–483
Citizens, extradition of 98, 540, 557
Citizenship,
    Admission to, by treaty ....
    ....200, 202–205, 206, 207, 209, 210, 212, 493, 494, 552, 553, 563, 570
    Election of, in ceded territory 207, 209, 210, 212, 552–553, 580
    Loss of, in Great Britain 282–283
    Under the first treaty with Great Britain 513
Civil suits, jurisdiction of Federal courts over 269
Claims,
    Adjustment and settlement of, by the President 108
    Assignment of 470, 534, 548, 553, 573
    Finality of decisions of commissioners respecting..495–496, 534, 557, 573

Page.

Legislation to give effect to conventions for adjudication of   240
Right of the United States in money received in payment of ..
.... 534, 557, 558, 574
Clayton-Bulwer treaty,
 Abrogation of 441, 442
 Declarations filed by negotiators of   381
Collisions at sea, international regulations concerning   127
Colombia   338
 Application of treaties of Spain to   436
 Effect on treaties of division of   439
 Treaties with, construed   483
Commerce, treaties of,
  In foreign states 280-282, 308, 309, 315, 316, 317, 319, 320, 321, 322,
  .... 325, 328, 329, 331, 332, 333, 334, 335, 336, 337-338
  In the United States 183-199
   Not to abrogate a law   63
   To require concurrence of two-thirds of the whole number
    of Senators   63
Committee of Foreign Affairs of the Continental Congress   23
Committee of Secret Correspondence of the Continental Congress..   23
Committee on Foreign Relations of the Senate   75
 Members of, as negotiators of treaties   78
Compacts between States of the Union 24, 48, 141-149
Concordats, nature of   8
Congress, (See laws.)
 Acquisition of territory by act of 135-140
 Advisory resolutions of, respecting negotiations 73-75
 Agreements in virtue of acts of 121-140
 Approval by, of treaties for cession of territory 59, 61, 63, 225
 Consent of, to State agreements 141, 145-149
 Excluded from treaty making 46, 58
 Legislation to give effect to treaties 164-245
 Power of, to provide for enforcement of treaty obligations ..
 .... 241, 256 269-272
Consent, freedom of   3
Constitution of the United States,
 Provisions of, relating to treaties 65, 151, 269
 Treaties in conflict with, invalid 63, 246, 267
Consuls,
 Administration on estates of deceased aliens ....
 .. 34, 260-262, 266, 411-415, 466, 468, 470, 501, 539, 545, 559, 561, 584-586
 Exemption from compulsory attendance as witnesses 470, 483, 497
 Inviolability of papers of   497
 Jurisdiction over disputes between crews and masters of vessels
 .... 34, 234-235, 470, 502-503, 506, 508, 544, 582, 584
 Jurisdiction over offenses committed on vessels in port ....
 .... 235, 470, 545, 583

Page.

Legislation to give effect to treaty provisions concerning .. 126, 234–235
Representatives of absent or minor heirs 261, 411, 485, 499, 545
Right of, to receive effects of a deceased seaman 584
Right of, to recover wages due a deceased seaman 501
Convention, as distinguished from treaty 7
Copyright,
    Effect of war on conventional agreements respecting 451
    In foreign states 286, 312, 332
    In the United States 127, 238, 242
Corporations,
    Not subjects within the meaning of the treaty with Great Britain
      of 1815 524
    Property rights of, protected under the treaty of 1794 .... 594, 596
    Protocol with Greece of 1890 concerning 116
    Status of, in territory ceded by Spain in 1898 580
Costa Rica 338
Court of Customs Appeals, review by Supreme Court of decree or
    judgment of, involving treaties 273
Courts of justice, right of access to 259, 505, 544
Creditors, (See British creditors.)
    Prior rights of local 507
Cree Indians, deportation of 105
Criminal actions to enforce treaty rights of aliens 269–272, 479
Cuba 338
    Agreements with the United States as to naval and coaling sta-
      tions 139
    Commercial reciprocity with 193–194, 483
    Status of, under treaty of 1898 575
    Treaties with, construed 483–484
Cushing-Calderon protocol of 1877 115
Danish West Indies, proposed cession of, to the United States....
    .... 82, 226, 332, 361
Date of treaties 343–357
    As between states 343–345, 347–351, 489
    As municipal law 345–347, 351, 569, 586
    For suspension of hostilities 354–357
    For transfer of territory 347–351, 491, 492, 569, 576
    Of extradition 351–352, 469, 540
    Of peace 352–354, 577, 578
Death, right of action for 259, 614, 615
Debts. (See British creditors.)
Declarations of negotiators, in the interpretation of treaties ... 377, 381–382
De facto sovereign of territory, a political question 366
Definitive treaty of peace with Great Britain of 1783,
    Boundaries under 513
    Citizenship under 513
    Debts protected by 514–517
    Effect of war on 443–446

Page.

Ratification of 31-32
Recognition, not a grant, of rights 513
Delegation of power 1, 8, 60, 120, 122, 265
Denmark 331-332
Treaties with, construed 484-485
Denunciation of treaties, (See termination) 458-462
Partial 460, 462
Russian, of 1870 ....441, 442, 456-457
Department of Foreign Affairs of the United States 23, 25, 93
Department of State of the United States 93
Dependencies, exercise of treaty powers by 339
Depositive treaties 443
Deserter, defined 561, 584
Detraction, duties of 34, 605, 621
Discrepancies between the two versions of a treaty 389-394, 497, 571
Discriminatory legislation in respect of
    Access to courts of justice 544, 613, 617
    Action for wrongful death 259, 614, 615
    Fisheries 255, 260, 607, 609, 618
    Game 255, 260, 616
    Inheritance taxes 252, 416, 606, 610, 611, 612, 621
    Labor 253, 254, 255, 256, 417-419, 421-422, 606, 607, 608, 617
    Ownership of real property 256, 416, 608, 609
    Pilotage regulations 409, 611
    Quarantine regulations 264, 265, 613
    Tariff rates 406-407, 409-411, 609, 610, 618, 619
    Tonnage duties 121, 198, 405, 406, 408-409, 609, 612, 619
    Suspension of 121, 185, 198
District of Columbia, as one of the States of the Union under the
    convention with France of 1853 498
Dominican Republic 338
Convention for commercial reciprocity with 99, 193
Modus vivendi as to collection of revenues of 114
Proposed annexation of 82, 84, 96, 137, 226
Treaties with, construed 485
Droit d'aubaine, exemption from, pledged by treaties under Ar-
    ticles of Confederation 33
Duma of Russia, duties of 336
Dunkirk, destruction of fortifications at 372
Duration of treaties 5
Duress,
    Effect of, on treaties 3
    Municipal courts not to set treaty aside for 368
Ecuador 338
Effects, meaning of,
    In the treaty with the Netherlands of 1782 ....600, 601
    In the treaty with Spain of 1795 383
    In the treaty with Sweden of 1783 ....602, 603

Page.

Egypt, treaties entered into by 339
Embargo on property in Cuba by Spanish government, 1895-1898 ... 383
Embezzlement, as an extraditable crime..500, 510, 529, 530, 540, 557, 574, 588
Enemy ships, goods in, subject to capture 487
Equality of states 5
Error, writ of, review of final judgments or decrees of State courts
    on 272
Essentials of the validity of treaties 3
Exchange of notes, as constituting a treaty 6
Exchange of ratifications,
    Constructive 92
    Effect and necessity of 6, 343
    Extension of time for 31, 87, 89–92
    In virtue of powers conferred by the President 93
    Retroactive effect of 344, 346, 347–350
Executive agreements 102–133
Executive power of United States 102
Exclusion of aliens 471–479, 481–483
Expressio unius est exclusio alterius 400
Expulsion of aliens 480, 481–483, 548
Extinguishment of a state,
    Effect on treaties 425–440
    Question of, a political question 367–368
Extradition of fugitives,
    Bail 531, 535
    By States of the United States 142–144
    Certificates in 510, 528, 546, 564, 588
    Citizens 98, 540, 557
    Complaint (see evidence) 469, 528, 531, 555, 558, 564
    Demand 546
    Evidence 489, 510, 523, 527, 528, 530, 531, 540, 554, 558, 565, 575, 587
    Exemption from punishment for offenses not included in requi-
      sition 536
    Exemption from trial for offenses not included in requisition ..
    .... 467, 527, 529, 556
    Operation of conventions of,
      In Great Britain 284–286
      In other foreign states 311, 316, 319, 322, 327, 334
      In the United States 230–233, 496, 523, 528, 529
        Liberal construction of 399
    Political offenses 565
    Retroactive operation of conventions of 351, 469, 540
    Trial for offense committed here after surrender 527
    Trial of person involuntarily in this country 560
    Trial of person voluntarily in this country 529, 535
    Variance between complaint and evidence 564
    Warrant of arrest 469, 529, 531, 557, 564, 575, 587
Extraterritorial rights in Turkey 393, 559

Page.

Family Compact, the 423
Fecials, college of 6
Federal Letter adopted by Congress, April 13, 1787 37
Federalist, the 54-56
Federal jurisdiction of cases arising under treaties..37, 51, 54, 61, 62, 269-276
Finances. (See appropriations.)
Fisheries,
    Effect of war on American liberties in 443-445
    Exclusion of aliens from 255, 260, 418-419, 607, 609, 618
    Legislation in Great Britain to give effect to conventions con-
        cerning 282, 288, 291
    Modi vivendi concerning 112-113
    Subject to treaty regulation 45, 63, 263
Florida,
    Acquisition of 227-229, 569-574
    Boundaries of 376, 490, 570
    Cession of territory under treaty for acquisition of 228-229
    Delay in ratification of treaty 90
    Incorporation into United States 205-207
    Property rights in 630-633
    Status of native inhabitants 205-207
Fluvial boundaries 384, 396
Force,
    Effect of, on treaties 4
    Rights acquired by 4
    Use of, to compel observance of treaties by States of United
        States 49, 51
Forgery, as an extraditable crime 467, 504, 529, 556, 588
Foreign Affairs,
    Committee of, in the Continental Congress 23
    Committee of, in the German Bundesrath 326
    Committee on, in the Senate 75
    Department of 23, 25, 93
    Secretary of, duties 25, 93
Foreign intercourse,
    President's control of 93
    Prohibited to the States 141, 143, 144
Form of treaties 5
Forms of ratification 635
Fortune Bay, settlement of claims for property destroyed at 109
France 301-314
    Appropriations to carry out the convention with the United
        States of 1831 ....174, 304
    Treaties of 1778,
        Abrogation of 424-425, 441, 442, 460, 462-463, 486, 489
        Conclusion of 19, 20
    Treaties with, construed 486-501

Page.

Fraud,

    As an extraditable offense 534, 535

    Effect of, on treaties   3

    Municipal courts not to set treaty aside for   368

    Presumption against   400

Free ships, free goods 488, 568

French spoliation claims   489

Game laws, discriminatory 255, 260, 616

Germany 323–327

    Effect of formation of Empire on treaties with States of .....

    .... 431–433, 504–512

    Treaties with, construed 501–512

Grants,

    In disputed territory 223–224

    Protected by treaty with France of 1803 621–624

    Protected by treaty with Mexico of 1848 626–629

    Protected by treaty with Spain of 1819 630–633

    Rules as to construction of 389, 390

Great Britain 279–300

    Treaties with, construed 512–538

Great Lakes,

    Agreement for limitation of naval forces on 102, 461

    Boundary in   523

    Jurisdiction over vessels in 523, 526

Greater Republic of Central America, effect on treaties of forma-

    tion of   434

Greece   335

    Protocol of 1890 concerning status of corporations   116

    Treaties with, construed   539

Guano islands   139

Guarantee, as sanction to treaties   12–14

Guatemala   338

Habeas corpus, writ of,

    Issued by Federal courts where person is in prison in violation

    of a treaty   272

    Office of, in extradition proceedings 527, 529, 531, 554

Haiti   338

Hamburg. (See Hanseatic Republics.)

Hamilton's sketch of government in the Federal Convention   43

Hanover,

    Extinguishment of treaties with 426, 431

    Treaties with, construed   506

Hanseatic Republics. (Bremen, Hamburg and Lubeck.)

    Survival of treaties of 432, 433

    Treaties with, construed   506

Hawaiian Islands,

    Annexation to the United States 84, 99, 138

    Conventions for commercial reciprocity with...72, 82, 189, 192, 193, 196

Page.

Effect on treaties of annexation to United States 428
"Heirs," as used in treaty with Sweden of 1783 602
Helgoland, cession of, to Germany 296
Hesse, termination of treaties with 506
Holy Alliance, personal league 1, 423
Homicide, as an extraditable crime 528, 529, 565
Honduras 338
Horse Shoe Reef, cession of, to United States 114
Hostages to ensure fulfillment of treaties 9, 11
House of Representatives,
    Appropriations to carry treaties into effect 164–182, 186
    Bills for raising revenue to originate in 46, 183, 194, 196
    Excluded from participation in treaty making 46–48, 53, 54, 55, 56, 57, 61
    Treaties involving modification of revenue laws 183–199
Hungary. (See Austria-Hungary.)
Impeachment, in Great Britain 279
Indian tribes,
    Agreements with 133
    Collective naturalization of 200
    Rules as to construction of treaties with 399
    Status of 134
    Title to lands in virtue of treaty with 245
Industrial property, enforcement of conventions for protection of,
    In foreign states 286–288, 312, 319, 323, 325, 332, 335
    In the United States 129–131, 236, 416, 589–590
Infamous punishment 588
Infraction of treaties,
    Effect of 456–458
    Function of Congress in case of 462–465
    Municipal courts not to set treaty aside for 368
Inheritance taxes, discriminatory 252, 416, 606, 610, 611, 612, 621
Internment, under The Hague convention of 1907 ....245, 590
Interpellations,
    In Austria-Hungary 327
    In German Reichstag 325
    In Italian Parliament 320
Interpretation of treaties 358–403
    Arbitration of controversies arising in 358–363
    Declarations of negotiators 377, 381–382
    General purpose 371–377
    General rules 396–403
    In light of accepted principles of international law 394–396
    Intent 371
    Maps 376, 378, 380, 381
    Omissions 387–389
    Political and judicial questions in the United States 364–370
    Practice of parties 383–387
    Prior negotiations 377–382

Page.

Variance between texts 389–394
Ionian Islands, union with Greece 430
Isle of Pines, status of 575
Italian States, extinguishment of treaties with 426
Italy 320–323
    Treaties with, construed 258–260, 540-547
Japan 336
    Treaties with, construed 547–548
Jay treaty,
    Appropriations to give effect to 165–171, 178, 183
    Qualified approval of, by the Senate 79
Juan de Fuca strait, boundary in 373
Jurisdiction of Federal courts, over cases arising under treaties....
    ....37, 51, 54, 61, 62, 269–276
Jury trial,
    In Alaska 212
    In the Philippines 219
Kasson conventions for commercial reciprocity 82, 193
Kid's band of Indians, agreement with Mexico concerning 105
Kongo,
    Annexation of, to Belgium 317
    Berlin Conference concerning 95
    Brussels Conference concerning 114
Korea,
    Alliance with Japan 4
    Effect on treaties of annexation to Japan 428
Laborer, as used in treaties with China 473–479, 480
Labor laws, discriminatory ....
    .... 253, 254, 255, 256, 417–419, 421–422, 606, 607, 608, 617
Language of treaties 6
    Standard in case of discrepancies 389–393, 497, 571
Laws,
    Operation of treaties as 36–42, 49–51, 53, 54, 57, 59, 60, 61, 62,
           151, 153–163, 170, 238–239, 286, 321, 338, 345–346
    Repeal of, by treaties 46, 61, 63, 160, 161, 536
    Termination of operation of treaties by ....
    .... 161, 463, 465, 525, 561, 609, 612, 618, 619, 620
Leeward Islands, annexation of, by France 313
Lew Chew Islands, termination of treaties with 429
Louisiana,
    Acquisition of 490
    Appropriations to carry treaty into effect 172
    Boundaries of 228, 490
    Incorporation of, into the United States 202–205
    Privileges granted to French vessels in 184
    Property rights in 491–494
    Status of native inhabitants of 202–205, 493, 494

Page.

Lubeck. (See Hanseatic Republics.)
Luxemburg 317
    Neutralization of 317
Madagascar,
    Effect on treaties of annexation to France 426-427
    French dominion over 313, 314
Maine,
    Agreement with New Brunswick as to boundaries 113, 114
    Agreement with United States as to boundaries 138
Manica plateau 388
Manslaughter, as an extraditable crime 529
Maps, use of, in interpretation of treaties 376, 378, 380, 381
Marque and reprisal, acceptance of letters of, by subjects of neu-
    trals 239, 242-243
Melish map, as basis of the treaty with Spain of 1819 ....376, 378, 570
Merchant, as used in the Chinese exclusion acts 475-479
Mexican grants, as confirmed in treaty of 1848 626-629
Mexico 337
    Convention of 1883 for commercial reciprocity with 192
    Incorporation into United States of territory acquired from ..207-209
    Treaties with, construed 548-559
Military forces, passage through territory of United States of for-
    eign 104
Mississippi River, free navigation of 27, 444
Mitchell's map 4
Modus vivendi,
    Definition of 7
    Executive agreements for 103, 112-114
Money order argeements 131
Montenegro 335
Mora claim, settlement of 108
Morocco, provisional operation of convention of 1880 relating to ... 343
Mosquito coast 381
Most favored nation 404-422
    Administration on estates of deceased aliens ....
    .... 411-414, 468, 485, 539, 545, 546, 561
    Consular jurisdiction over seamen 414-415
    Consular representation of absent or minor heirs 499
    Definitions of contraband of war 488
    Exemption of consuls from compulsory attendance as witnesses 470, 483
    Extraterritorial rights in Turkey 559
    Inheritance taxes 416, 544
    Ownership of real property 416, 480, 481, 608, 609
    Patents and trade-marks 416
    Tariff concessions 406-407, 409-411, 484, 485, 580, 618, 619, 620
    Tonnage duties 405-406, 407-409, 484, 619
    Treaty with Switzerland of 1850 ....198, 382
Munoskong Bay, part of Lake Huron 524

Page.

Murder, as an extraditable crime 529, 530, 565
Nassau, extinguishment of treaties with 426
Naturalization,
 By treaty ..200, 202–205, 206, 207, 209, 210, 212, 493, 494, 552, 553, 563, 570
 Convention with Turkey of 1874 ....87, 100
 Legislation in Great Britain to give effect to conventions on ..282–283
Navigation of rivers, treaties for cession of rights in, to be made
  only with concurrence of both houses of Congress 63
Netherlands, The 317–320
 Termination of treaty with the United States of 1782 429
 Treaties with, construed 558–559
Neutrality, power of President and Senate to conclude treaty of .. 241
New York, boundary agreements of 147
Nicaragua 338
Nice, annexation of, to France 226, 306, 322
Niemen, conference between Napoleon and Emperor Alexander on
  the 1
Norway 330–331
Norway and Sweden, union of 329
 Effect on treaties of dissolution of 438
 Treaties with, construed 580–586
Notice for termination of treaties 458–462
 Partial denunciation 460, 462
 Period of time 462
Oath, use of 9
Obligation of treaties,
 Defined 8, 425
 Distinguished from operation of treaty as municipal law 465
 Distinguished from rights in rem 425, 430
 Mutuality of 55, 62, 376
Office, right to quasi public, not a property right protected by treaty
  of 1898 633
Oral treaties 5
Oregon territory,
 Action of Senate on treaty respecting 70
 Citizenship in, during period of joint occupation 525
 Title of United States to 532
Ottoman Empire. (See Turkey.)
Panama 338
 Permanent right of transit across 434
 Treaties with, construed 559
Paraguay 338
 Treaties with, construed 559–560
Parlement of Paris, registration of treaties by 301
Passamaquoddy Bay, boundary in 514, 523
Patents. (See industrial property.)
Paterson's plan of revision, in the Federal Convention 50
Pavia, treaty after defeat of 301

Page.

Peace, treaties of,

    Date of 352–357

    Majority vote in case of 25, 44

    Ratification of, by Congress 46

    Suspension of military operations upon signing 352

    Termination of state of war upon final ratification of 352–354

Penal sanction to treaties in the United States 239, 269–272

Persia 337

    Treaties with, construed 560

Peru 338

    Treaties with, construed 560

Peru-Bolivia Confederation, effect on treaties of dissolution of 439

Pheasants, Isle of, conference on II

Philippine Islands,

    Acquisition of 212, 577

    Privileges accorded under the treaty to Spanish vessels in trade 620

    Status of 212, 216–219, 483, 577, 579

Pillau, oral treaty of 5

Pilotage regulations, discriminatory 409, 611

Pinckney's plan of a constitution, in the Federal Convention 49

Piracy, treaty provisions for definition of 28, 239, 242, 243, 567

Pirates, restitution of captures by 566, 567

Plateau, as used in the convention between Great Britain and Portu-

    gal of 1891 388

Plebiscite on transfer of territory 226

Poitiers, treaty after defeat at 301

Police power of the States as affected by treaties ....

    .... 263, 264, 265, 539, 547, 616, 618

Political offenses under extradition conventions 565

Political questions in the United States 364–370

    Boundaries 365, 490, 562

    Change in government and organization of other contracting

        party 368, 433

    De facto or de jure sovereign of a territory 366, 627

    Duress 368

    Extinction of state or loss of power 367–368

    Fraud 368

    Infractions 368, 464–465, 540

    Power of the other contracting party over the subject matter of

        the treaty 367, 368, 509

Pontifical territory, convention for protection of 423

Pope's Folly, title to island of 523

Portland Channel, as determined by the Alaskan boundary tribunal 380

Porto Rico,

    Acquisition of 212–216, 576

    Status of 212–216, 576–577, 579

Portugal 333

    Treaties with, construed 560

Page.

Possession, as essential to full sovereignty over territory 347, 348, 349
Possession, as used in the Florida treaty 631
Possessory rights, as used in the treaty with Great Britain of 1846 .. 625
Postal conventions,
    In foreign states 288, 310, 311, 323, 325, 326, 329, 335
    In the United States 29, 131, 589
Powers of negotiators 2–3, 93
    Form of 635
Practical construction of treaties 379, 383, 387
Practice of law, a privilege, not a property right protected under the
    treaty with Spain of 1898 633
Preamble as part of a treaty 403
Precedence 5, 32
Precincts and jurisdiction of a post, as used in treaty with Great
    Britain of 1794 625
Preliminary articles of peace 104, 354
President,
    Calls on, for papers relating to treaty negotiations 93, 165, 173
    In the Senate chamber 67
    Powers of 43, 93–133
    Ratification of treaties by 94, 97, 636
    Representative of nation in foreign relations 93, 97
Priority of stipulations 402, 403
Privateers, in ports of neutrals 487, 488
Prize court, appeals from a national court to an international 243
Prizes, exemption in port from local jurisdiction 236, 487, 522
Proclamation, application of laws dependent upon 121–129
Proclamation of treaties,
    By the President 94, 638
    Effect of 345, 346
Procès-verbal, definition of 6
Procurador, right to office of, not a property right protected by
    treaty of 1898 633
Property rights in ceded territory 621–634
Protectorates,
    Exercise of treaty-making power in case of 339
    In Africa 340
Protocol, definition of 6
Provisional articles of peace with Great Britain of 1782,
    Date of 512, 513
    Ratification of 30
Provisional operation of treaties 343
Prussia,
    Effect of formation of Empire on treaties of 431–433, 507, 509
    Treaties with, construed 507–510
Puget Sound Agricultural Co., rights of, under treaty with Great
    Britain of 1846 ....162, 626
Qualifications strictly construed 402
Quarantine regulations and treaty provisions 264, 265, 613

Page.

Randolph's resolutions, in the Federal Convention 49
Ratification of treaties,
    Essential 2, 343, 352
    Exchange or deposit of 6, 89-92, 93, 344, 346, 347-350
    Form of 6
    Forms of 636, 638-640
    In foreign states ....
       279, 308, 315, 318, 320, 321, 325, 328, 330, 331, 332, 333, 335, 336, 337, 338
    In the United States 81, 94
Real property,
    Most favored nation treatment respecting 416, 480, 481, 608, 609
    Rights of aliens in Great Britain to acquire and hold 284
    Rights of aliens in the United States to acquire and hold under
       treaty 33, 35, 59, 247-251, 480, 481, 591-605
    Time within which alien is to dispose of 599, 603, 604, 605
       Reasonable time 599, 605
Real rights, as affected by change of state entity 425, 430, 434
Rebus sic stantibus, as a condition of treaties 440-442
Reciprocity, commercial,
    Agreements under acts of Congress for..122-124, 193-195, 500-501, 503
    Legislation to give effect to conventions for 189-199
"Red line map," in the Webster-Ashburton negotiations 3
Redundancy, not to be presumed 401-402
Reichsrath of Austria, rights of, in respect of treaties 328
Reichstag of Germany, rights of, in respect of treaties 324, 325
Religious freedom, treaty provisions for 34, 471
Re-measurement of vessels, exemption from 126, 288
Repeal. (See termination.)
Representatives of deceased persons 545, 599
Retrospective operation of treaties 345, 346-350, 489
Revenue laws,
    Extension of, to newly-acquired territory ....
    .... 203, 205, 207-208, 211, 213-215, 217
    Treaties involving,
       In France 304, 306, 309
       In Great Britain 280-282
       In other foreign states 315, 316, 317, 319, 320, 321, 322, 325, 328,
             329, 331, 332, 333, 334, 335, 336, 337-338
       In the United States 47, 63, 183-199
Rhine, free navigation of, under treaty of Vienna 374
Rigsdag of Denmark, duties of 331
Rigsdag of Sweden, duties of 330
Rio Grande, boundary in 384
Robbery, as an extraditable crime 565
Robbins, extradition of Jonathan 230, 523
Roman Catholic Church, property rights of, protected by treaty with
    Spain of 1898 633

Page.

Roumania 335
Russia 336
   Denunciation of provisions of treaty of Paris of 1856 441, 442, 456–457
   Status of corporations in.................................... 117
   Treaties with, construed 561–564
Russian-American Company, property rights of, under treaty of 1867   629
Russian-Dutch loan, payments on, after the Crimean war 449
   After the separation of the Belgic Provinces from the Nether-
     lands 374
St. Bartholomew, retrocession of, to France 226, 312
St. Croix river, identification of 380
St. John. (See Danish West Indies.)
St. Mary's river,
   Boundary in 387
   Free navigation of 538
St. Mary's river (in Florida),
   Free navigation of 566
St. Thomas. (See Danish West Indies.)
Salvador 338
   Treaties with, construed 565–566
Salvage at sea, legislation to give effect to convention respecting 239
Samoan Islands, Berlin Act of 1889 respecting 106, 385
   Division of 227
Sanction of treaties 8–15
San Francisco school question of 1906 257
San Ildefonso, secret treaty of 347, 348, 365, 366, 490, 491, 492
San Jacinto, settlement of claims for damages by 111
San Jacinto, treaty signed by Santa Anna after capture at 4
San Juan island, agreement for joint occupation of 106
Sardinia, application of treaties of, to kingdom of Italy 426
Savoy,
   Annexation of, to France 226, 306, 322
   Effect of annexation to France on neutrality of 435
Saxony,
   Effect of formation of Empire on treaties of 433
   Treaties with the United States 510
Schools, rights of Japanese under treaty of 1894 respecting 257
Seamen,
   Apprehension of deserting,
     In foreign states 286, 316
     In the United States 34, 233–235, 499, 561, 584
   Jurisdiction of consuls over differences affecting ....
     ....34, 234–235, 470, 502–503, 506, 508, 544, 582–584
   Right of consul to receive effects of a deceased 584
   Right of consul to recover wages due a deceased 501
Secrecy,
   Necessity of, in the consideration of treaties ...48, 54, 55, 56, 57, 58, 62
   Removal of injunction of 84

Page.

Secret sessions of the Senate 84
Secret treaties in foreign states 303, 308, 315, 317, 326, 331, 332, 333, 338
Secretary for Foreign Affairs in the United States 23, 25, 26, 93
Secretary of State, creation of office of 93
Secretary of the United States for the Department of Foreign Affairs 25, 26
Self-preservation, treaties not to be construed as impairing right of 400
Senate,
 Advice and consent of 47, 55, 57, 67-92, 636
 Amendments of treaties by 79-82, 95
 Appointment of members of, as negotiators 78
 Construction of treaties by 369
 Power to make treaties exclusively vested in 43, 50, 56
 Quorum of, for consideration of treaties 44-46, 82
 Reconsideration of treaties by 82
 Rejection of treaties by 81, 82
 Secret sessions of 84
Servia 335
 Effect on treaties of establishment of independence of 438
 Denunciation of alliance with Bulgaria 442
Slaves, indemnity for, under treaty with Great Britain of 1814 523
Society Islands, acquisition of, by France 312
South African Republic, status of, prior to 1900 531
Sovereignty,
 Attributes of 1, 265
 Limitations on, strictly construed 400
Spain 332-333
 Boundaries with, under treaty of 1795 566
 Claims convention of 1834 with 119, 447-448
 Convention of 1884 for commercial reciprocity 193
 Treaties with, construed 566-580
Spanish grants in Florida 630-633
Special missions, authorized by President 77-78
States-General of France, repudiation of treaties by 301
States of the United States,
 Acts of, to give way to treaties ....
 .... 36-42, 49-51, 53, 59, 60, 61, 62, 63, 151, 153-160, 246-268, 591-605
 Agreements by 24, 48, 141-149
 Delivery of fugitives of justice by 142-144
 Force to compel observance of treaties 49
 Police power of 263, 264, 265, 539, 547, 616, 618
 Prohibited from entering into treaties 24, 48, 141, 265
Steamboat inspection, exemption from 126
Storthing of Norway, duties of 331
Submarine cables, legislation to give effect to convention for protection of 239
Subsidies, subject of treaty negotiation 48
Succession of states 425-465

Page.

Succession taxes. (See inheritance taxes.)
Sulu islands,
    Agreement of 1899 with Sultan of 119
    Effect of cession to the United States on treaties of 436
Supreme Court of the United States (see Federal jurisdiction;
    error, writ of; habeas corpus, writ of) 54
    Review of decisions of, by an international tribunal 243–244
Sureties for fulfillment of treaties 11
Sweden (see also Sweden and Norway) 329–330
    Treaties with, construed 580–586
Sweden and Norway,
    Effect on treaties of dissolution of union 438
    Treaties with, construed 580–586
    Union betweeen 329
Switzerland 333–335
    Most-favored nation clause in treaty of 1850 with 198, 382
    Neutralization of 13, 335
    Treaties with, construed 586–588
Tacna, plebiscite in, under treaty between Peru and Chile of 1883 .. 226
Tahiti, cession to France of islands to leeward of 313
Tariff concessions, discriminatory (see revenue laws) ....
    .... 406–407, 409–411, 609, 610, 618, 619, 620
Technical meaning of terms 397–399
Termination of treaties 423–465
    As municipal law in United States ....
    .... 161, 171, 465, 473, 480, 481, 525, 561, 609, 612, 618, 619, 620
    By agreement 458
    By notice 458–465
    By subsequent treaty 500
    Condition of rebus sic stantibus 440–442
    Effect of change in form of government 423–425, 466
    Effect of change in state entity 425–440, 506, 507, 509, 511, 512
    Effect of infractions 456–458
    Effect of war 442–456
Territoriality of crime,
    Death resulting from poisoning 530
Territory, acquisition or cession of,
    In France 308, 312–314
    In Great Britain 292–298
    In other foreign states ....
    315, 316, 317, 318, 320, 322, 325, 328, 329, 330, 331, 332, 335, 336, 337–338
    In the United States,
        Acquisition,
            By act of Congress 135–140
            By treaty 200–220, 490–494, 549, 562, 569–574, 576–580
            Status of native inhabitants ....
            200, 201, 202–205, 206, 207, 209, 210, 212, 493, 494
        Cession,

Page.

By treaty 44, 45, 46, 47, 59, 60, 61, 186, 220–229
Consent of Congress to 59, 61, 63, 225
Plebiscite of native inhabitants 226
Property rights 201, 202, 205, 207, 210, 212, 621–634
Retroactive effect of ratification of treaties for 347–351
Texas,
    Annexation to the United States 82, 135
    Effect on treaties of annexation 433, 434
    Effect on treaties of separation from Mexico 437
Tilsit, treaties concluded at I
Tonnage duties, discriminatory 198, 405, 407–409, 609, 612, 619
    Suspension of 121, 185, 198
Tort, jurisdiction of Federal courts over suits by aliens for 269
Trade-marks, (See industrial property.)
    In foreign states 130, 286, 312, 316, 335
    In the United States 129, 236–238, 240, 416, 468, 469, 503
Transitory conventions 425, 430, 434, 443
Treaty,
    Definition of 3, 423
    Essentials of the validity of 3
    Executed, as document of title 425, 430, 434, 443
    Form of 5
    Nature of 55, 57, 160
    Obligation of 8, 55, 425
    Operative in the United States as a law of the land ..36–42, 49–51, 53,
    ... 54, 57, 59, 60, 61, 62, 151, 153–163, 170, 238–239, 286, 321, 338, 345–346
        Of executory character..162–163, 232, 236, 238, 493, 497, 532, 570, 589
    Severable articles of 457–458
Treaty-making power,
    Defined by the constitution, or fundamental law of a state I
    Nature of 55, 57, 60, 61
    Of dependencies .... I, 339
    Unlimited in sovereign states .... I, 265
Treaty-making power of the United States under the Constitution,
    limitations on..58, 59, 60, 62–63, 168, 169, 170, 177, 218, 241–245, 246–268
Truce, conclusion of, as incidental to official station 8
Tunis,
    Effect on treaties of establishment of French protectorate over 428
    Suzerainty of France over 310, 313
Turkey 337
    Conflicting versions of the treaty of 1830 393
    Extraterritorial rights of United States in 393, 559
    Independence and integrity of, guaranteed 14
    Protocol of 1874 as to rights of American citizens to hold real es-
    tate in 115
    Ratification of naturalization convention of 1874 ....87, 100
    Treaties with, construed 559
Tuscany, extinguishment of treaties with 426

                                                                  Page.

Two Sicilies,
    Extinguishment of treaties with 426
    Treaties with, construed 588
Uruguay 338
Venezuela 338
Vessels, (See seamen.)
    Discriminatory tonnage duties ....
    .... 121, 185, 198, 405–406, 408–409, 609, 612, 619
    Exemption from inspection 126
    Exemption from remeasurement 126, 288
    Hospitality to disabled 127
    Sea-letter as evidence of ownership 488, 568
Villafranca, preliminary articles signed at 1, 354
Virginius, case of the 107
Visitation and search, treaty provisions concerning 28
Voidable, distinguished from void 464
Wales Island, under the Alaskan boundary decision 227
War,
    Effect of, on treaties 442–456
        Alliance 451
        Commerce and navigation 451
        Copyright 451, 454
        Documents of title 443
        Express renewal of treaties 442, 451–456
        Extradition 454
        International conventions, or law treaties 450–451
        Permanent obligations 447–448
        Rights conveyed under treaties 443–449, 520
        Rights of third parties 450–451
        Rules of war 449–450
    Effect on, of the signing of treaty of peace 352–354
    Power of President and Senate to restrict the exercise by Con-
      gress of the power to declare 241
    Rights acquired by 4
    State of, continues until final ratification of treaty 352–354, 577, 578
Ware v. Hylton, analyzed 154–159
Webster-Ashburton treaty,
    Agreement between United States and Maine and Massachusetts
      incorporated into 138
    Consent of Maine and Massachusetts 222
    Legislation to give effect to 239
    Suppression of map during negotiation of 3
White slave traffic, ratification of convention for suppression of 98
Witnesses, exemption of consuls from compulsory attendance as..
    .... 470, 483, 497
Worship, privileges of, granted by treaty 34, 264, 471
Württemberg,
    Effect of formation of Empire on treaties of 433, 511, 512

Page.

Treaties with, construed 511–512
Zanzibar, renunciation of extraterritorial rights in 227, 428
Zollverein of the German States, convention of 1844 for commercial
    reciprocity with 82
    Adverse report on 189
    Comments on, by Mr. Calhoun 241, 247